San Francisco in the 1930s

The publisher gratefully acknowledges the generous support
of the Valerie Barth and Peter Booth Wiley Endowment Fund
in History of the University of California Press Foundation.

CISCO

IN THE 1930s

The WPA Guide to the City by the Bay

Federal Writers Project of the
Works Progress Administration

INTRODUCTION BY DAVID KIPEN

University of California Press
Berkeley   Los Angeles   London

The publisher gratefully acknowledges the generous support of the
Valerie Barth and Peter Booth Wiley Endowment Fund in History
of the University of California Press Foundation.

University of California Press, one of the most distinguished
university presses in the United States, enriches lives around the
world by advancing scholarship in the humanities, social sciences,
and natural sciences. Its activities are supported by the UC Press
Foundation and by philanthropic contributions from individuals
and institutions. For more information, visit www.ucpress.edu.

University of California Press
Berkeley and Los Angeles, California

University of California Press, Ltd.
London, England

ISBN 978-0-520-26880-7 (paper : alk. paper)
Library of Congress Control Number: 2010940090

19   18   17   16   15   14   13   12   11
10   9   8   7   6   5   4   3   2   1

Manufactured in the United States of America

This book is printed on Cascades Enviro 100, a 100% post
consumer waste, recycled, de-inked fiber. FSC recycled
certified and processed chlorine free. It is acid free,
Ecologo certified, and manufactured by BioGas energy.

Contents

I. Gateway to the West

II. *"The City"*

III. *Around the World in San Francisco*

IV. Around the Bay

V. Appendices

Illustrations

ix

Maps

The San Francisco Seven

"San Francisco has no single landmark by which the world may identify it."
—FEDERAL WRITERS PROJECT GUIDE
TO SAN FRANCISCO, 1940 (p. 174)

Landmarks can take a while to announce themselves. First opened in 1937, the Golden Gate Bridge rates only a couple of artful paragraphs in the guidebook before you, compared to fully 25 pages for Golden Gate Park. Plainly, there'd be no getting away with that ratio today. Like the bridge itself at first, this Federal Writers Project guide has gone remarkably unappreciated since its publication in 1940—read to tatters by a dedicated cadre of writers, lefties, and urbanists, updated without glory once, yet never truly celebrated for the indispensable navigational beacon it is. To explore the Bay Area without a copy handy is tantamount to steaming through the Golden Gate without a depth chart. Far from having "no single landmark," San Francisco, between 1937 and 1940, got two.

A few years earlier, on July 27, 1935, President Roosevelt had signed legislation authorizing the Federal Writers Project. Part of the New Deal's Works Progress Administration, the Project recognized that scribblers, no less than stonemasons and bridge builders, needed work. For any reader, the crowning glory of the New Deal will always be the American Guides, a series of travel companions to 48 states, many cities, and any number of deserts, rivers, and other wonders—all created to "hold up a mirror to America." John Steinbeck navigated by the American Guides to write his perennially underestimated *Travels With Charley,* in which he called them "the most comprehensive account of the United States ever got together, and nothing since has even approached it."

Fun with classification: The San Francisco guide is just one product of the American Guide Series, which, in turn, were only one endeavor of the larger Federal Writers Project (FWP), which also turned out a raft of invaluable studies, including oral histories of freed slaves. The FWP, meanwhile, was but a single arm of Federal One, which also included the music, art, and theater projects that gave Orson Welles, among other artists, their biggest sandbox to date. And Federal One—stay with me here—was part of the Works Progress Administration (WPA), which belonged to a whole Scrabble rack of acronyms that came out of the New Deal. Finally, the New

Deal was shorthand for all the programs devised to fight the Depression under the leadership of the most effective monogram of them all: FDR. He wrote this guide or nobody did.

Reading the San Francisco guide is the second-best cure for homesickness, short of a ticket, that any shanghaied Northern Californian could ask for. (And if you're rusty on the etymology of *shanghai,* page 122 is there for you.) For locals and newcomers alike, transplants and tourists both, a copy of *San Francisco in the 1930s* belongs in every pannier of every rental bike the whole Bay round, and the glove box of every Zipcar besides.

1. POTRERO HILL, BARD THEREOF

Casual readers may at first question this guide's amiably eccentric structure. Soon enough, though, the WPA guide to San Francisco resolves into four very roughly equal parts: I. Gateway to the West; II. "The City"; III. Around the World in San Francisco; and IV. Around the Bay. The inner pair supplies essays and walking tours around San Francisco proper. Of the outer pair, the first furnishes background essays on the Greater Bay Area, and the fourth suggests driving tours around it. The overall effect starts to look like a close-up of a pair of hands warmed within a larger pair—as if a native in 1940 had met a chill-chapped Easterner's aeroplane at Mills Field, and they'd clasped hands before embarking on an adventure.

Not to sound like an auto mechanic reflexively running down the work of his predecessor ("What kind of ignoramus told you *that,* lady?"), but about the only thing wrong with the original WPA guide to San Francisco was its preface. In it Walter McElroy, project supervisor for California and unmistakably a gifted editor, says little about the book itself before unburdening himself of two solid pages of undifferentiated acknowledgments. I'm probably prouder than anybody alive to read that "Joseph Henry Jackson, Book Editor, *San Francisco Chronicle*" pitched in as an expert reader, but I'd be even happier to have some inkling as to who wrote or edited what here.

According to Jerre Mangione's invaluable *The Dream and the Deal: The Federal Writers' Project, 1935–1943,* the great San Francisco poet Kenneth Rexroth did plenty of both, but how much, and which parts exactly? Circumstantial evidence points at least to the subsections called "Wild Life," "Centers of Learning," "Argonauts of Letters," and "Metropolitan Scene" as Rexroth's, plus maybe a whole lot besides. When we read that "the inglorious past is slipping fast from Kearny Street . . . cocktail bars are marching northward against the tawdry remains of an era of architectural horror and moral obliquity"—one of Rexroth's pet words—it's hard not to hear the signature incantatory swing of the Bard of Potrero Hill.

You don't have to be a Rexroth buff to want to know just how much credit for the guide belongs to the author of "Requiem for the Spanish Dead"—whether drafted by him for others to water down, or by others for him to punch up. But until some scholar with the tenure to undertake it can locate the San Francisco FWP office's elusive manuscripts and tissue-type the actual prose, we'll just have to ascribe authorship to one of those shadowy literary composites, like Homer, or J, or the Pearl Poet.

2. EXCELSIOR HEIGHTS, OR THE CITY SPEAKS

Ironically for a region as cussedly individualistic as the Bay Area, the best prior history of the region relied on assembly-line methods and thankless contributions, too. Hubert Howe Bancroft's histories of California emerged from a system so communalist, it makes the MGM Writers Building look like Wordsworth's Lake Country. When the WPA guide says of Bancroft, "One of the pioneers of mass production methods in literature, he directed a large staff of anonymous collaborators," you can almost hear the commiseration from scrivener to scrivener across the decades.

But as someone whose professional life has dwelt suspiciously on the recovery and championship of lost voices—of West Coast writing at the *San Francisco Chronicle*, of screenwriters in my first book—I hope it's not out of line to note that there's a definite speaker audible here, no less distinctive for going unnamed. What you hear in these pages, loud and clear as a sonic boom during fleet week, is the voice of San Francisco. From Bret Harte's roaring '49ers to Allen Ginsberg's full-throated howl, from the buzzing of Ambrose Bierce's *Wasp* to the struck-porcelain clarity of Jade Snow Wong's stories to the singing wires of Thomas Pynchon's Telegraph Avenue syncopation, there's always been a headquarters-be-damned vitality to this voice, transcending the stylings of any one singer. Compounded of braggadocio, tomorrow-we-die swagger, underdog empathy, bumptious wit, arrant know-it-allery, polysyllabic excess, and gollywhomping beauty, the San Francisco voice is what's left in the prospector's pan after all the slurry of ego and era drains away.

Voice is hard to anatomize, never more so than when it belongs, not to a single speaker, but to an unruly office full of them. If we could run the WPA guide through the old voiceprint machine at the Exploratorium, what spikes and troughs would the spectrogram betray? Here are just a few signature crotchets of that *vox sanfranciscensis*, proof against all of Federal One's increasingly exasperated efforts to housebreak it:

Superlatives. In its entry for the Palace Hotel, the guide calls San Francisco "a town reared on superlatives," and it's a hard point to argue. Few pages pass without at least one, and three to a paragraph isn't unheard of. Mere lines apart, we learn that the Great Highway is, over one stretch, "the widest boulevard in the United States," and that the Fleishhacker Swimming Pool is said "to be the world's largest outdoor plunge" (p. 324). When hearing such claims in person, a good fact-checking reflex is always to ask what the second-widest boulevard, or the second-largest outdoor plunge, might be. Absent corroboration, though, let's take the original guide editors' word for it. They are, as a San Franciscan might say, the best.

Periodic sentences. These stately constructions wind heroically down the pages of the guidebook like a parade, with the main clause fetching up at last near the end, like a grand marshal. Just one relatively brief example: "Through narrow Carquinez Strait, six miles long, joining San Pablo Bay with shallow Suisun Bay to the east, pour the combined waters of California's two greatest rivers, the Sacramento and the San Joaquin, which drain the Central Valley and the Sierra Nevada's western slopes" (p. 7). They don't write 'em like that anymore. All that's missing is the fife-and-drum corps.

Sesquipedalianism. The WPA guide to San Francisco is inevitably, gloriously, a guide to English as it was spoke and wrote on these shores circa 1940, with all the verbal vividness that entails. *Fecundate. Bagnio. Obliquity. Amygdaloid.* If using a word readers may not know is a crime, call out the vocabulary constabulary. But if nobody ever used a six-bit word for fear of intimidating us, how would our vocabulary ever grow? And let's not forget the words everybody knows now, but didn't always. Would anyone write a San Francisco guidebook today in which the word *Victorian* appears just once—and *that* referring to a mansion, rather than an apartment building? Makes you wonder what future landmarks around us today we're ignoring, just as the FWP office ignored all those Victorians.

3. LOS PECHOS DE LA CHOLA, OR THE BREASTS OF THE INDIAN MAIDEN

There are other, less appealing voices here, too, underneath the first. It helps to listen for them, and even then pages can go by without so much as a whisper. But read through waterfront entries especially, like this one on the city of Alameda, and you can hear them ticking as patiently as a bomb: "Long used as a repair yard, [the Bethlehem Steel Company shipbuilding division] (*"no visitors"*) is being refitted to do its part in the Government's 1940 naval expansion program." Can you hear the voice now? It's the one that says, "Millions of GIs and war workers are about to turn your quaint little guidebook into a curio overnight."

But it gets worse. All too often we glimpse flashes of what an identity politician might defensibly call racism, what a tenured bluestocking might lazily call "a historical narrative"—and what a literary journalist just calls dated, dehumanizing, bad writing. That we read how "the Indians timorously kept their distance, prepared to make—if necessary—proper obeisance" (p. 13) to Sir Francis Drake, and how the Californios waxed "grateful for the luxuries brought to Yerba Buena Cove by foreign traders" (p. 22) (this in a chapter called "A Frontier to Conquer") would be bad enough. But we also learn that, "though the padres occasionally lost patience and punished petty crimes with rawhide when sweet words were of no avail, they did not generally ill treat their converts" (p. 20).

Still tempted to make excuses for the guide as "a product of its time"? Check out this endearing chestnut:

The mission founders knew privation, struggle, and opposition. To Christianize the Indians, who sometimes fought against preemption of their land, it was sometimes necessary to use the sword and the whip. The natives often rebelled against the hard, monotonous work forced upon them. During church services guards equipped with long goads moved among the congregation, prodding natives who assumed other than a kneeling position. For outstanding work, however, the Indians were rewarded with beads and gaudy trinkets. (pp. 432–33)

This passage is either oblivious to the point of schizophrenia, or ironic past the threshold of black comedy, or heavily rewritten by multiple hands. I still can't tell which.

4. GOLD MINE HILL,
OR ASSAYING THE BONANZA

The WPA guide to San Francisco can still tell you a great deal about how to get the most out of the Bay Area, but rather less about how to make the most of the guide itself. Readers have to figure out for themselves, for example, that the type size shrinks a few points whenever a driving tour shifts from the main drag into another of its wonderful shunpike side excursions. The way most people enjoy a book (i.e., reading it front to back) is plainly contraindicated. It's a guidebook, after all, and most readers will want to tackle it from the outside in, looking for a general topic in the table of contents, or maybe a particular one in the index, and then jumping to the appropriate page. This works well for readers who know what they want, but less so for browsers and grazers.

My advice for readers new to the American Guides, leisure permitting, might be to interleave the expository chapters up front with the open-air tours in back. Too much unrelieved swotting is bad for the circulation. Besides, for the true bibliotourist, visiting a landmark before reading about it is just as much fun as visiting it afterward. They're coequal joys. The only difference is, those who prepare for a journey as if studying for a test always have to do some mental work to forget their imaginary vistas when confronted with the real thing.

If only as a demonstration project—what gold miners might call a core sample, and data miners a search term—let's follow the arbitrary keyword *Chronicle* from the index to two distinct and, in their own ways, quite delightful places. First, in a historical chapter titled "Bonanza (1856–1875)," we learn that *San Francisco Chronicle* owner-editor Charles de Young once drew iron on the Scots-Irish minister and mayoral candidate Isaac Kalloch and "blazed away." Later the wounded Kalloch's son, only naturally, had to avert "further damage to his father's battered reputation by fatally shooting De Young." This bloodletting won't come as news to amateur students of Bay history, but even for those who've heard the story before, the antic, antique cheer of the language polishes it to a new sheen. The capper comes when, with "public sentiment in his favor, young Kalloch was acquitted" (p. 105). Everybody loves a journalist.

In these parlous times of newspaper buyouts and layoffs and fadeaways, it's oddly reassuring to happen across a second reference to the *Chronicle* 75 pages later, when the newspaper's offices claim their august place on a walking tour between the Emporium department store and "one-third of the Nation's entire gold reserve" over at the U.S. Mint. There in the guide, the *Chron*'s enduring three-story pile at 5th and Mission is accurately dismissed as "Industrial Gothic." Somewhere, the shades of Isaac Kalloch and his trigger-happy son are smiling.

5. LAUREL HILL, OR
THE ENCYCLOPAEDIA AND THE TRAPDOOR

A listing for Laurel Hill Cemetery clarifies just how bloody Bay Area politics used to be. Local history mavens may recall that State Supreme Court Justice David S. Terry killed Senator David Broderick in a pistol duel in 1859, but do they know that California's first-ever congressman, Edward Gilbert, fell to the pistol of General James W. Denver, for whom Colorado's capital was named? California politicians who bristle at term limits would do well to remember there have always been, from the very first, worse ways to go.

That the Chronicle Building and U.S. Mint still stand, albeit with less of their very different kinds of capital inside, is more than one can say for the Emporium. Such a .667 slugging percentage for architectural survival is about par for these tours. It's anybody's pigeon which is more fun to read about: all that bygone civic furniture, or some of the eyesores still out there hulking down at us. This gets at the nut of how best to enjoy the guide: Is it for visitors or habitués? Is it a portable *encyclopaedia norcaliforniensis* for today, or a trapdoor to 1940?

If you don't know by now that the answer to such rhetorical choices is always, always both, then reading modern American essayistic nonfiction must be a never-ending cavalcade of surprises for you. *Of course* the WPA guide to San Francisco is as indispensable today as the day it was published—both for the reliability of what hasn't changed (the Chronicle Building still looks like the top three stories of an undistinguished buried skyscraper) and the compulsively readable enormity of what has.

In one chapter, we learn that "Oakland's tempo of living varies with the time of day: by dawn commuters are on the move, feeder highways to

the San Francisco–Oakland Bay Bridge are alive with speeding cars . . ."
Speeding cars? Can any reader today look on those words and not weep? Is it·
any wonder California is broke, when no modern Bay Area patrolman could
write a speeding ticket between the weekday hours of 6 and 10 A.M. if his
life depended on it?

So maybe the WPA guide isn't the ideal tip sheet to your morning commute. That's what we have nextmuni.com for. But as a wormhole from your
seat on the N Judah into 1940, the guide is well nigh unimprovable. Like
any decent time capsule, it's really a time machine.

6. MCLAREN RIDGE,
OR THE MAN WHO PLANTED REDWOODS

But who wants a time machine stuck in reverse? Luckily, every page of this
guide doubles as an exhortation to study the Bay around us, and envision
the San Francisco of 70 years from now in its place. According to the fasci-
nating chronology of the Bay Area that follows the text, at least three noteworthy ribbon-cuttings took place in 1940: (1) the Funston Avenue approach
to the Golden Gate Bridge, (2) the Bay's first low-cost housing project, at
Holly Courts, and (3) the return of the Golden Gate International Exposition to Treasure Island. Is anything opening in 2010 that competes? We're
celebrating plenty of anniversaries these days, the San Francisco Museum
of Modern Art's for one, but of grand openings, not so many. And what
could imaginably open 70 years from now, in 2080—by which time even
high-speed rail will look like the mass-transit equivalent of a not-very-
cherry Hispano-Suiza? The WPA Guide to San Francisco represents,
among so much else, an open invitation to discuss these very questions of
bygone ambition and comparative modern modesty.

The life of "Uncle John" McLaren, who gets a loving page in the Golden
Gate Park chapter, is a reproach to dreamers of small dreams. Named park
superintendent as "a sandy-haired young Scottish landscape gardener" in 1887,
McLaren was eventually "exempted . . . from enforced retirement" (p. 331)
by an act of the Board of Supervisors in 1922. Still at his trowel when the guide
went to press 17 years later, Supt. McLaren was planting redwood seedlings
well into his 90s. Some of that same posterity-mindedness must have animated
the makers of this guide, so sturdy and shade-giving all these years later.

Yes, writers tend to get misty-eyed on the subject of the Federal Writers
Project, like grown men reminiscing about a daft uncle who used to give
them candy. This is natural, even forgivable, but not especially useful. A
government recently disinclined to guarantee its soldiers body armor seems
unlikely to promise its writers much anytime soon, except material. But if
we can't reconstitute the Writers Project in anything like its original form, at
least we can take inspiration from that gloriously collective voice.

The word *collective* fell a bit differently on 1930s ears than it does on ours, redolent of the leftism for which the FWP was eventually red-baited out of existence by a Congress that had never much liked it in the first place. Yet collective this guide's voice most assuredly is—the conjoined sound of an entire region, majestic as the hills and salty as the bay. It's as if the city itself is talking to us across the years, telling its story and daring us to believe it. Few stretchers got past the project's prodigious fact-checking apparatus, but San Francisco has always told its true story as if it were a lie, or at least a myth. The overall effect resembles that of an impeccable historian trying to fake a polygraph into recording a false positive.

7. DIAMOND HEIGHTS, OR STOCKTON HOUSE REBUILT

San Francisco in the 1930s reads, as it should, like the streaky autobiography of a seismic boomtown. Its historical chapters teem with juicy anecdotes from the depression of 1854, the panic of 1873, the crash of 1893, and so on, up to the Great Depression that midwifed the book in the first place. That's the dirty secret of this city: its topography and its history are different cars on the same rollercoaster. You can't get from beach to bay without using all your gears, any more than you can get from 1849 to 1940, and beyond, without overusing a few superlatives—and pejoratives. Any landing is, at best, only a breather from which to contemplate the next cliff, or chasm.

Fittingly, the guide ends with Stockton House, the last point of interest on the San Jose driving tour: "one of a number of houses cut to size and brought around the Horn by Commodore Robert F. Stockton. It has a wide veranda and, rising from the central gable, a square balustraded turret." As last lines go, not exactly "I been there before," but look closer. In the battles of Rio San Gabriel and La Mesa in 1847, Commodore Stockton all but captured California for the United States, and became its first governor. Prefabricated in the commodore's native New Jersey, Stockton House traveled thousands of miles in the belly of a ship—its brothers jettisoned overboard for ballast—to fetch up at the south end of San Francisco Bay. There it stood for just shy of a century until, a little extra research reveals, it finally fell to make way for San Jose Airport. Named for a conqueror, built with no feel for its eventual site, and demolished for a purpose its builder never foresaw, this California landmark has survived only as two anticlimactic sentences in a book that slept for 70 years.

Now the book has resurfaced and you've picked it up, like a tiny, shiny fleck in a millrace. Heft it in your hands. Assay it, even. It's heavier than it looks.

David Kipen
Los Angeles, 2010

Preface 1940

So many books have been written about San Francisco and its neighbor cities around San Francisco Bay that the writing of still another may seem to call for explanation. But for all those who have shared in the compilation and editing of this book—research workers, reporters, writers, editors, and supervisors of the Northern California Writers' Project in San Francisco and Oakland—it needs no apology. All throughout the long labor of preparing it they have realized only too keenly how much remains to be written about a city whose history has been the stuff of legend since its beginning—how much remained before it was written and still remains afterward. For this book, although we have crowded between its covers uncounted thousands of those facts which go to make up the story of a great metropolitan center—names and dates, descriptions of places and people, tales and anecdotes and even some myths—still leaves much of the story untold, as any book must. But the book will have accomplished its purpose if what it leaves unsaid the reader will want to know.

During the preparation of this volume, Margaret Wilkins acted as State Editorial Supervisor, Paul Johnson as State Research Supervisor, and Willis Foster as Oakland District Supervisor. Wallace Boyle, Charles Coppock, S. S. Greenleaf, and Dorothy Wagner served as editors; Juanita Turner and Gordon Williams as research editors. Although virtually the entire San Francisco, Oakland, and San Rafael staffs shared in the compilation of the book, the writing of the final manuscript was done largely by Jackson Barber, Dean Beshlich, Marc Bliss, Madeline Gleason, Gladys Pittman, Thomas Ray, Kenneth Rexroth, and Dorothy Van Ghent of the San Francisco staff and Porter Chaffee, Henry Darnell, Frances Garoutte, Howard Hoffman, Ethel Manning, and Thomas Patterson of the Oakland staff. Much of the section "North of the Bay" is the work of Cora Vernon Lee, Sacramento District Supervisor. We are indebted for the essay "Before the Footlights" to Lawrence Estavan, Supervisor of the History of the San Francisco Theater Project. The index was compiled by Max Loewenthal and the bibliography by W. Stanley. The maps were prepared by

George Hill and J. H. Marion and some of the photographs by Theodore Baron, James Hall, and Howard Hoffman of the project staff. For their generous cooperation in reading and criticizing various chapters, we are particularly indebted to Dr. Herbert E. Bolton, Chairman, Department of History, University of California; Alfred Frankenstein, Music and Art Editor, San Francisco *Chronicle;* Clyde Healy, Assistant City Engineer, San Francisco; Joseph Henry Jackson, Book Editor, San Francisco *Chronicle;* Dr. Alfred L. Kroeber, Department of Anthropology, University of California; Cornel Lengyel, Supervisor, History of Music Project, Work Projects Administration; Charles Lindstrom, Assistant Curator, San Francisco Museum of Art; George Mullaney, Director of Publications, San Francisco Board of Education; George Pettit, Assistant to the President, University of California; Dr. Frank Fenton, San Francisco State College; M. Sprague, Associate Meteorologist, United States Weather Bureau; Dr. George R. Stewart, Jr., Associate Professor of English, University of California; Dr. Theodore E. Treutlein, San Francisco State College; C. M. Wheeler, Vice-President, McCormick Steamship Company.

We are extremely grateful for the assistance provided by the following librarians: Robert Rae and his assistants, Mary A. Byrne, Jessica Fredericks, Edith Mau, Elinor Sturgis, of the San Francisco Public Library; Mary O. Carmody and Helen Bryant of the Mechanics'-Mercantile Library; Dr. Herbert Priestley and Edna Parratt of the Bancroft Library; Richard Taggert of the University of California Library; John B. Kaiser and Mabel W. Thomas of the Oakland Public Library; Susan T. Smith of the Berkeley Public Library; Jane I. Curtis and Theodora T. Larsen of the Alameda Public Library; Mary Barmby of the Alameda County Library; Edith Daley of the San Jose Public Library; Virginia Vail of the Marin County Library; and Jessie A. Lea of the Martinez Public Library. We also are grateful to the librarians of the San Francisco *Chronicle,* Marjorie D. Brown and Dorothy M. Frisch; of the San Francisco *Call-Bulletin,* Stuart Rasmussen; of the San Francisco *Examiner,* Dwight Newton, for their help.

Of the many organizations and public agencies which assisted us, we are especially indebted to the Alameda City Clerk's and City Auditor's offices; Alameda County Development Association; California Historical Society; California State Automobile Association; California State Board of Education, Board of Harbor Commissioners, Division of Mines, Fish and Game Commission, and Park Commission; Californians, Inc.; the Chambers of Commerce of Alameda, Berkeley, Oakland, San Francisco, San Jose, Santa Rosa, and Sonoma; Contra Costa County Development Association; Marvelous Marin, Inc.; National Automobile Club; Northern California Hotel Association; Oakland

Park Commission; Pacific Coast Labor Bureau; Redwood Empire Association; San Francisco City and County Board of Education, Board of Health, Assessor's Office, M. H. de Young Memorial Museum, Palace of the Legion of Honor, Park Commission, Police Department, and Recreation Commission; San Francisco Convention and Tourist Bureau; San Francisco Hotel Association; Shell Travel Bureau; Society of California Pioneers; Southern Pacific News Bureau; Standard Oil Company of California; United States Coast and Geodetic Survey, Department of Agriculture, National Park Service, and Travel Bureau; and the Wine Institute of California.

For special assistance we are indebted to Harris Allen of the Federal Housing Authority; Joseph Allen, State Supervisor, Northern California Art Project; W. N. Burkhardt, Editor-in-chief, San Francisco *News;* Joseph Cumming, President, Downtown Association; A. C. Dearborn, United States Travel Bureau; Ignatius Dwyer, Deputy Registrar of Voters, City and County of San Francisco; Luisa Vallejo Emparan; William A. Gaw, California School of Fine Arts; Wanda Hannah; G. Lansing Hurd, Secretary, Santa Rosa Chamber of Commerce; Chingwah Lee, editor, *Chinese Digest;* Major Truman Martin, Press Relations Officer, Ninth Corps Area, United States Army; E. P. Meadows, Supervisor, Project 10945, Work Projects Administration; Irving Morrow; Laura Bride Powers; Robert Sibley, Executive Manager, Associated Students of the University of California; Charles Stewart; John Swett, Jr.; Edward van Ribbink, editor, *Oakland Tribune Year Book;* James J. Walsh; Eric Walter, Assistant Superintendent, Golden Gate Park.

WALTER MCELROY, *State Supervisor*

PART I
Gateway to the West

The Bay and the Land

*". . . an immense arm of the sea, or an estuary, which pene-
trated into the land as far as the eye could reach . . ."*
                                        —Padre Juan Crespi

WHEN the first settlers, led by Lieutenant Jose Joaquin Moraga,
arrived June 27, 1776, on the site of San Francisco, the American people were yet to declare themselves a Nation—though
within seven days they would do so, 3,000 miles away on the Atlantic
seaboard.   Seven decades would pass before the heirs of '76 would raise
their flag on this site.   Two years more, and the name of San Francisco
would go round the world.

It "never was a village"—this had been its proud boast.   Where
barren sand dunes, marshes, and brackish lagoons had surrounded an
abandoned mission and a decaying fort with rusty cannon, San Francisco
sprang into life overnight—a lusty, brawling he-man town of tents and
deserted ships.   Business, mushroomlike, flourished in mud-deep streets.
Almost before it had achieved a corporate identity, San Francisco was a
metropolis—to be named in the same breath with Boston or Buenos
Aires, Stockholm or Shanghai.

When the other cities of the Coast were still hamlets in forest clearings or desert cow-towns, San Francisco was "The City."   It is "The
City" still.   Massed on the tip of its Peninsula, its skyscrapers tower
skyward from the peaks of the highest hills: great shafts of concrete
banked in swirling billows of white mist when the fogs move in from
the sea—glittering with pinpoints of reflected light from their countless
windows when the sun shines from a clear blue sky.   Crowding on each
other, the hills rear their endless terraces of buildings, descending to the
water's edge like steps, cleft by streets that strike up the steepest slopes
and plunge down the deepest valleys with reckless fidelity to their
straight and narrow paths.

Around the curving Peninsula's tip jut widespread fingers that are
piers harboring their great ships.   Soaring to heights greater than the
hilltop skyscrapers, the girders of the bridge towers lift their slim steel
spans high above the smokestacks of passing ships.   Over their suspended
roadbeds traffic streams across the racing tides of the Golden Gate to
the bluffs and thicket-choked gullies of the Marin shore and across the
Bay's wide sweep of gray-green water to the mainland.   There, on the

3

eastern shores of the Bay, rising like the tiers of a vast amphitheater to wooded crests, spread mile after mile of buildings—homes and schools, business blocks and factories.   And on every side the age-old hills—vivid with the green of fresh-growing grass after winter rains, sere and brown in summer—encircle the blue water: wilderness neighbor to the city.

THE OPENING OF THE GATE

If some titanic convulsion of the earth were to drain San Francisco Bay of all its waters, it would look merely like one of those shallow, hill-rimmed valleys which stretch away from its upper and lower reaches.   Through a gap in the chain of hills along its eastern edge, a great river would pour into its upper end and, winding southward, flood out to sea through a deep gorge hollowed in the coastal range.   Within the recent geologic past the Bay was just such a valley, the Golden Gate such a river canyon.   But as time went on, the valley sank until ocean waters came flooding through the Gate to submerge all but the peaks of its hills.   Last of all in the long series of the earth's transformations from which emerged that part of the planet known as California was the Bay's creation.   But the geologic upheavals destined to open the Golden Gate had begun long before.

West of today's Pacific shore, perhaps 500 million years ago, rose a land mass extending into what is now the Pacific Ocean.   Where the Sierra Nevada now rises is thought to have been a low land mass, lapped on the Nevada side by an inland sea.   As the eons passed, this great basin sea advanced westward into California, retreated and advanced again, until by 200 million years ago it may have reached as far as the site of Monterey—well over toward that westward-lying coast along the ocean.

Eventually the ocean itself found its way into the watery area that later was to become California.   The western land mass probably was cut off from the mainland, forming an elongated island of which the present Farallon Islands were a part.   Eastward lay a submerged trough, and into this trough sediment was continually draining from the island's slopes.   To the incredible depth of over three miles the sediment was laid down in the water, slowly solidifying.   From this trough was later elevated the San Francisco Peninsula, its foundations partly composed of the thick deposits which drained from the westward island.

And then began that long series of geologic events which finally resulted in the emergence of the coastline of California.   Between 120 and 150 million years ago the ridges of both the Coast Range and the Sierra Nevada were pushed up.   Unlike the Sierra Nevada, which was to maintain its general structure despite erosion, the Coast Range rose from the inland sea only to sink again.   At least three times the ocean engulfed the region between the Sierra Nevada and the westward island and advanced to the foothills of the Sierra Nevada.

At a point about 36 million years ago, the picture of California begins to emerge in clearer detail. On the eastern border is the wall of the Sierra, following about the same direction as in the twentieth century, but lower, less rugged, its slopes covered with luxuriant vegetation. Still under water, the center of the State is a great inland sound, extending far enough westward to submerge the site of San Francisco. A long island stretches northwest from the present vicinity of Salinas. Islands are scattered in the sound.

For many million years the geography of this California changed little; but great activity was brewing in the earth. Far offshore the bottom of the sea was sinking. As it sank, the land along the coast was thrust upwards, buckling under the pressure. All of California was rising, but the extra thrust upon its western edge caused a slip along which occurred a sidewise movement of at least 700 feet and possibly as much as 20 miles. Along this same fault, extending from Point Arena south to the Mojave Desert, there was to be a shift of about eight feet in the year A.D. 1906, which would cause a great disturbance in the city of San Francisco. (Because the rock mass is broken along the fault, any abnormal strain within the earth is apt to be taken up there; such movements occur frequently, but rarely displace the surface more than two-tenths of an inch.) The same thrusts that were to cause the San Francisco Peninsula's earthquake fault also helped to lift it above the sea. There was pronounced folding of the Coast Range at this time, not only on the Peninsula, but along the line of the Berkeley Hills.

About one million years ago the Great Valley was becoming filled with sediment. Brackish water still covered part of the valley; it drained, not through the Golden Gate, which did not yet exist, but through various other outlets; one at the Russian River and another at Monterey Bay. The San Francisco-Marin area probably was separated from the mainland by marshes, so shallow that they could be crossed by the primitive elephant (whose fossils have been found near Menlo Park). The last great uplift raised the Sierra Nevada Range to a height of 4,000 feet above its present elevation; the Coast Range shared in this uplift.

Most recent of California's important geological events have been those which formed San Francisco Bay and the Golden Gate. As the marshes along the coast and farther inland dried, continued folding in the Coast Range blocked off the drainage of the Great Valley through the Russian River and Monterey Bay, forcing the rivers to find another outlet. They converged in a new course through a canyon north of the Berkeley Hills at what is now Carquinez Strait, thence down through a valley, and finally through the mountains that extended up the San Francisco Peninsula and northward into Marin County.

However solid the earth may have seemed beneath the feet of the first human inhabitants when they came (probably between 30 and 40 centuries ago) to hunt game and pick wild fruit in the coastal valley behind the river's mouth, it was sinking imperceptibly. The sea cliffs to the west were tilting upward on their outer side; but every year the floor of the coastal valley was a little lower. As fast as the sea cliffs rose, the river scoured deeper its channel through them, thus gradually carving down the sides of the Golden Gate. Then finally came a time when the floor of the coastal valley sank beneath sea level. The ocean flooded through the mouth of the river over 400 square miles of the Indians' hunting ground. The land would go on sinking until the very shell mounds which the first settlers left behind them on dry land were lapped by the tides; and yet as it sank, the rivers would lay down their rich silt, torn from mountain sides and lowlands of the Central Valley basin, over the bottom of the Bay. So was made, for how long no one can tell, the harbor known today as San Francisco Bay.

EARTH AND WATER

Midway in the great chain of mountain ridges that stretches along the continent's edge down the southeast-tending California coast is a narrow gap. Between its steep headlands the long Pacific rollers, breaking in spray against the cliffs to north and south, pour in swift tides. As the headlands recede on either side, an expanse of water opens out, stretching eastward to low, gently sloping hills. To the north, wooded peaks rise steeply above bluffs close at hand; to the northeast, barren capes guard a distant strait. Southward a sheet of water extends farther than a man can see, between marsh-edged flat lands. Here, where ocean tides roll in over a valley long sunk below sea level, salt water mingles with fresh, is muddied with the yellow silt of rivers, pouring into the Bay's upper reaches. At either end, sloping valleys walled like the Bay between ranges of hills that parallel each other, east and west, spill their creeks into it. Among the encircling hills, sloughs and canyons twist to the water's edge.

So well hidden from the sea beyond its narrow gateway by mountainous coastal walls that exploring navigators passed it by for more than two centuries, San Francisco Bay is one of the world's largest landlocked harbors. Measured along a straight line from the mouth of Sonoma Creek in the north to the mouth of Coyote Creek in the south, it is approximately 60 miles long and measures 14 miles at its greatest width. Its outlet to the sea, the Golden Gate, is three miles long and, at its widest point, a mile wide. In all, the Bay covers an area of a little more than 400 square miles. Although more than 70 per cent of its area is less than 18 feet deep, it reaches a depth of from 100 to 140 feet in its central part and of 357 feet in the main channel of the Golden Gate. North of its narrowest point, the strait between Points San Pedro and San Pablo—where it is known as San Pablo Bay—the water is shallower.

Into San Pablo Bay empties the drainage of the valleys to the north and the hinterland to the east. Petaluma, Sonoma, and Napa Creeks pour in from the north. Through narrow Carquinez Strait, six miles long, joining San Pablo Bay with shallow Suisun Bay to the east, pour the combined waters of California's two great rivers, the Sacramento and the San Joaquin, which drain the Central Valley and the Sierra Nevada's western slopes. The gorge cut by the silt-laden river waters, winding out to sea through the succession of bays and straits, can be traced by the yellow stream that crosses the Bay's blue ripples. The river's ancient delta, built up through the ages before the ocean broke through the Golden Gate, has been traced as far out to sea as the Farallon Islands, 23 miles off Point Bonita.

The peaks of low hills once rising from the drowned valley's floor are islands now. Opposite the Golden Gate, rocky Alcatraz (130 alt.) rises abruptly from the swift tides. Northward, divided by narrow straits from the coves and inlets of the Marin shore, rise green-clad Angel (782 alt.) and Belvedere (350 alt.). A little to the southeast the rugged hump of Yerba Buena (343 alt.) appears almost midway across the Bay.

From opposite sides of the Golden Gate the sheer bluffs at land's end of the San Francisco and Marin Peninsulas face each other. The narrow hilly strip of the San Francisco Peninsula stretches 30 miles southward from the Golden Gate between Bay and ocean, tapering in width from 7 miles at its tip to approximately 21 where it merges with the mainland. On the Bay side it is bordered with mud flats and salt marshes; on the ocean, with rugged cliffs and sandy beaches. The tip of the Peninsula, walled off from the south by the steep narrow ridge of San Bruno Mountain (1,315 alt.), is a rough square with jagged outlines, scored haphazardly by rocky hills and winding valleys, once a rolling waste of sand dunes and marsh-girt lagoons. In the center of this area rises a dominant crescent-shaped range, culminating in Twin Peaks (904 alt.), Mount Davidson (916 alt.), and Mount Sutro (909 alt.). Southward spreads a zone of billowing hills, merging into San Bruno Mountain. Beyond troughlike Merced Valley, cutting from Bay to ocean parallel with San Bruno Mountain, the Peninsula is scored with parallel ridges running north and south—among them, Buriburi Ridge (700 alt.), the Sawyer Ridge (about 1,200 alt.), and Montara Mountain (1,952 alt.). Between the Buriburi and Sawyer

Ridges lies a 15-mile-long segment of the San Andreas Rift Valley, following the course of the San Andreas earthquake fault. Farther south the Santa Cruz Mountains, of which these Peninsula ridges are the northern offshoots, lift their wooded slopes to greater heights. Some 80 miles from the tip of the San Francisco Peninsula they taper off into low hills where Monterey Bay cuts its crescent line into the coast.

The Golden Gate is but a narrow break in the great mountain chain of the Coast Range, which continues northwest up the Marin Peninsula under the name of the Bolinas Ridge. An irregularly shaped, deeply and intricately dissected mountain mass, the Marin Peninsula is criss-crossed by ridges radiating from its highest point, at the southern end of the Bolinas Ridge—Mount Tamalpais (2,604 alt.). The deep canyons that scar the flanks of the ridges widen into gently sloping valleys merging with salt marshes on the Bay side; on the ocean side they twist tortuously to the sea, where the hillsides end abruptly in sheer cliffs. Paralleling the Bolinas Ridge on the west is the long narrow valley which follows the course of the San Andreas fault. Its northern reaches are filled with the waters of marsh-bordered Tomales Bay, extending southeastward like a thin finger, laid along a line as straight as if it had been sheared off with a knife. To the west, hilly, triangular Point Reyes Peninsula juts into the ocean like a plowshare, sheltering behind its long promontory curving Drake's Bay with its white-faced cliffs like the chalk cliffs at Dover. East of the Marin Peninsula's hilly mass the flat reaches of Sonoma and Napa Valleys merge into tule marshes at the Bay's edge, divided from each other by the gentle slopes of the mountains.

Along the Bay's eastern shore, beyond the narrow coastal plain, stretches the serrated skyline of the Berkeley Hills, culminating in Bald Peak (1,930 alt.); and behind, across a line of narrow, shallow valleys, rise the rugged crests of a parallel ridge culminating in Rocky Ridge (2,000 alt.). To the east, broad flat Ygnacio Valley extends north to the shores of Suisun Bay and south into the narrow, level San Ramon Valley. From the valley's edge steep slopes rise in long sweeping lines to the summit of Mount Diablo (3,849 alt.). To the south, San Ramon Valley meets narrow, 40-mile-long Livermore Valley. Beyond, the ridges of the Mount Diablo Range extend to meet the Mount Hamilton Range, paralleling the Peninsula ridges and the Santa Cruz Mountains across the Bay.

South of the Bay's southern tip, the fertile plains of the Santa Clara Valley extend for 70 miles between the walls of the Mount Hamilton (4,029 alt.) Range and the Santa Cruz Mountains, 15 miles apart—a long, narrow extension of that same valley whose upper reaches, now submerged, are the Bay itself. From the marshes of the Bay's southern end, the valley floor slopes upward gradually toward the south, where offshoots of the two mountain ranges curve inward and enclose it.

THE CLIMATE

The Bay of San Francisco and its shores share with the rest of the Coast the moderate climate which it owes chiefly to the prevailing winds off the Pacific. Because of the break in the coast line the region has a climate even milder than enjoyed elsewhere along the Coast, because it receives more than its share of ocean-cooled air currents, sucked in by forced draft through the Golden Gate. Their deflection in various directions by the hills gives contingent sections widely differing weather.

At the tip of the San Francisco Peninsula, the mean annual temperature is 56.4° F.; the mean temperature of the coldest month, January, is 50° F. and of the warmest month, September, 61.5° F. But just northward across the Gate, mean temperatures are approximately five degrees lower in winter and five degrees higher in summer. Cold months are likewise colder and warm ones warmer on the eastern side of the Bay and down the Peninsula. The average annual rainfall at Kentfield in Marin County, less than 15 miles north of the Gate, is more than twice that of San Francisco—45.33 inches as against 21.85 inches. South of the city, rainfall decreases progressively, reaching an average of 15 inches at San Jose.

Although the tip of the San Francisco Peninsula enjoys sunshine for an average of 66 per cent of all the daylight hours in the year, it has acquired a more celebrated reputation for its fogs. They are of two principal varieties. Tule fog, a winter phenomenon, consists of low-hanging clouds of condensed vapor which drift about the Bay in serpentine fashion, sometimes blanketing completely one section of city or Bay while another is bright with sunlight. Most prevalent is the white fog which forms off the headlands on either side of the Golden Gate and drifts inland as the temperature rises inland in the warm valley section of the State. This fog forms in huge blankets, averaging about 1,700 feet thick, sometimes shrouding the entire tip of the Peninsula and spreading across the Bay to its eastern shore.

The Bay region, like most of the California coast, knows two seasons —the wet and the dry—and throughout much of the area the difference in average temperatures between them is seldom more than ten degrees. Even this slight difference is usually nullified by cooling breezes off the ocean which take the sting out of summer heat. At the tip of the San Francisco Peninsula early autumn is actually warmer than summer— for summer is the season of fogs. Only the rains, which come between October and May, call more than momentary attention to the change in seasons.

The temperature, rainfall, and even the winds follow predictable cycles, permitting residents to fall into a pattern of adaptations, less pronounced than those required by four seasons, but quite as regular. The weather's summer schedule is particularly dependable. A San Franciscan knows, almost to a certainty, that he will waken on a July morning in a world of light, bright fog and little wind. By noon the sun will be shining, and still will shine at midafternoon, though presently it will be hidden by the billows of white vapor that tumble over the hills and through the Gate. Within an hour a stiff salt breeze will be driving this fog, like a band of frantic wraiths, through hills and valleys; but the wind will be dying and the fog dispersing by half past seven. With the lengthening of night will come a softness, lightness, and clarity in the air which makes sleep seem a dullard's habit.

WILD LIFE

Simple and clear was the pattern of vegetation around San Francisco Bay before the coming of the white man. Along the coast, in the region of greatest winter rain and heaviest summer fog, were the redwood forests, extending almost without interruption from southern Oregon to San Francisco Bay and continuing south in canyons and other fog traps to the coast below Carmel. The grass and oak savannah extended eastward to the Sacramento Valley and along the floors of the principal inter-mountain valleys of the Coast Range. A thicket of low-growing chaparral clothed the interior ranges and the dry southern slopes. Fringing the Bay were marshes choked with tule rushes.

Conspicuous changes have taken place in the outlines of the three major types of vegetation. Much of the forest has been replaced by grass, brush, or crops; the early grassland area is occupied by cultivated land. However, the region is fortunate to possess many game preserves, water districts, and other sections where natural conditions still prevail and many more that are being restored. The residents are making a start toward restriction of destructive lumbering, bad range management, poor fire control, and unregulated killing of game and fish.

Typical virgin areas of forest are preserved in Muir Woods National Monument and Santa Cruz Redwood Park. Here are trees, many from 1,000 to 2,000 years old, rising 300 feet or more with diameters of 12 to 16 feet. Their clean, gently tapering shafts, clothed with thick, purplish, massively fluted bark, rise uninterrupted by branches for approximately a third of their height. The foliage is delicate and feathery, but dense enough to keep perpetual twilight on the forest floor. Scattered among the great columns are smaller trees: broad-leaf maple, madrone, golden chinquapin, and California laurel. In separate stands, usually along the ridges at the inner margin of the fog belt, is found the somber, massive Douglas fir. Forming close thickets are huckleberries, azaleas, rhododendrons, California buckthorn (the dried bark of which is medicinal cascara sagrada), salal, wild currants and gooseberries, salmon- and thimble-berries, and elder. And in the damper shade, watered by the fog which the trees precipitate, Woodwardia and sword ferns give cover to mosses, dogtooth violets, true violets, wild ginger, redwood sorrel, trillium, fritillaria, clintonia, and the pungent yerba buena which gave San Francisco its first Spanish name.

The redwood forest and its associated meadows and streams are particularly rich in animal life; raccoons, skunks, wild cats, woodrats, and weasels are fairly common. As is natural in so deep a forest, birds are not conspicuous. Those most often seen are the varied and hermit thrushes, quail, flycatchers, California tanagers, robins, various sparrows and warblers.

The chaparral formation in California is remarkable, both for its high degree of development and for its numerous methods of adjustment to the long dry summers, wet winters, periodic fires, and intense sunshine. Its root systems are often extensive; its leaves protect themselves from excessive evaporation by turning their broad surfaces away from the sun, by growing in small, needle-like shapes, and by resorting to other devices such as thick skins, coatings of fuzz, exudations of resin, and restriction in the number of "pores." Many typical shrubs have the ability to sprout after fires from the root's crown. Others seed profusely and grow vigorously in burnt-over soil. The most widespread members of the chaparral are the various species of ceanothus, used by the Indians for soap; manzanita, with white bell-like blossoms, red or chocolate bark, neat oval leaves; California buckeye, which blooms in heavy clusters and bears fig-shaped fruits; chamise (*adenostoma*); chaparral pea; many dwarf oaks; and yerba santa, with pale lavender flowers and leaves spotted with resin.

The chaparral was the home of the extinct California grizzly and the now rarely seen California condor. Typical of both chaparral and grasslands are the brush rabbit, coyote, gray fox, various rats and mice, pocket gophers, and moles. Some of the more distinctive birds are the California jay, stellar jay, California thrasher, Anna hummingbird, house finch, mourning dove, and valley quail. Hawks, owls, and buzzards are very common.

Formerly the savannah was covered with a thick sod of perennial grasses; today it is dominated by the aggressive annual wild oat, a Spanish importation. However, the spring still brings a flourishing abundance of California poppies, lupines, nemophilas, cream cups, brodiaea, owl's clover, Indian paintbrushes, irises, shooting stars, and many composites.

One of the region's most interesting natural environments is the marshy border of the sloughs and estuaries where willows and cotton-woods grow. Wading birds are numerous; also the great blue heron, night heron, bittern, egret, and snowy egret. The estuaries, filled with tule rushes, are favorite nesting places for pelicans, coots and ducks, wrens, red-winged blackbirds, and many warblers.

Along the seacoast too, there is a distinct community of wild life. Gulls, terns, cormorants, and brown and white pelicans congregate in numbers. Hair seals and sea lions are still abundant, though the fur seal has disappeared.

Offshore, all along the Pacific Coast of North America, grow great beds of brown kelp, plants which in some cases are as large as redwood trees. This dense marine thicket provides shelter for a host of small fish, many of them valuable for food. Perch and rock and tom cod are typical species. Other ocean fishes found fresh in San Francisco markets are sea bass, various flatfish, halibut, and salmon. Crab, abalone, clams, shrimp, and oysters (both native and planted) are the principal shellfish. Bay and river fishes include shad, steelhead, striped bass, and several species of native and imported trout.

In 1940 the San Francisco Bay communities are as close as any urban area in the United States to primitive landscapes. At distances but little farther than city limits are forests, thickets of chaparral, and tule marshes, so wild that any explorer but the more experienced woodsman might easily imagine himself the region's first inhabitant.

A Frontier to Conquer

"The hills were wardens of the far-sought gold
And streams were glad in valleys unprofaned . . ."
—George Sterling, *The Homing of Drake*

ROM the chalk-white bluffs of the bay sheltered by Point Reyes, the coast-dwelling natives saw with amazement an immense object borne on billowing wings loom out of the mist at sea on June 17 (Julian Calendar), 1579. The man whom they sent the next day to reconnoiter paddled back excitedly to tell of living beings, white of skin and bearded, aboard this apparition. Concluding that these visitors were no less than spirits returned from the dead, the Indians timorously kept their distance, prepared to make—if necessary—proper obeisance. For three days longer the spirits remained in their abode, which rested on the water, its wings folded. On the third day it moved in toward the shore, and the spirits landed.

So came the first white men to set foot in the region of San Francisco Bay—men of Francis Drake's company in the *Golden Hinde*. They had left England a year and a half earlier in company with four other ships, bound round the world in the service of Queen Elizabeth to plunder the ships and cities of her enemy, Philip II of Spain. Now only the flagship remained.

After two days ashore, they were visited by the awed inhabitants of the country, who brought gifts of feathers and tobacco. "This country our Generall named *Albion*," the chaplain wrote, both because "of the white bancks and cliffes" and in order that "it might haue some affinity, euen in name also, with our own country . . ." And before Drake's five weeks' stay had ended, he recorded further, "our Generall caused to be set vp a monument of our being there, as also of her maiesties and successors right and title to that kingdom; namely, a plate of brasse, fast nailed to a great and firme post; whereon is engrauen her graces name, and the day and yeare of our arriuall there, and of the free giuing vp of the prouince and kingdom, both by the king and people, into her maiesties hands . . ." Thus having established his Queen's title to a new kingdom on the other side of the world, Francis Drake lifted anchor on July 23 and sailed away. The Indians were grief-stricken. As night fell, they lighted beacon fires on the hills.

NATIVES OF THE COUNTRY

In the Indians' geography the only land that lay beyond the smooth disc of the Pacific Ocean was the island where dwelled their dead. The Bay itself was to them no "harbor," for their small tule rafts never carried cargoes out the Golden Gate. Even the pass through the Coast Range at Carquinez Strait, to which stagecoach and railroad, as surely as the rivers, finally were to gravitate, had no great importance to a fleet brown foot that daily climbed the mountain barrier for rabbits. In all those ways that the contours of the region were to influence the welfare of white inhabitants, the Indians were affected little. But for other reasons the Bay environment impressed its pattern upon them.

It was the Bay that set the sleepy rhythm of the Indians' days. It determined, first, the location of their villages. A few groups lived on the ocean front and a few more on the banks of streams among the wooded hills, but most of them settled at the mouths of estuaries, on the Bay beaches. There the struggle for existence almost was reduced to reaching out a hand for supplies that the waters laid upon their doorsteps: for mussels, soft-shell clams, and seaweed, and the driftwood used to cook them. The marine vertebrates swam so close to shore that the Indians could run into the waters and catch them—a feat noted by Drake.

In developing their handicrafts, the Indians were influenced by the abundance of tule grass in the marshes. They made no pottery, but from woody stems and fibers they constructed water-tight baskets, often decorated with shell beads, which they used as cooking utensils. Their houses were circular structures of poles usually tied together at the top and thatched with brush or tule matting. Rushes were used, too, for the short flaps worn as skirts by the women, though occasionally these garments were made of deerskin or of bark fiber. The men generally went entirely naked, except in the early morning when they sometimes plastered themselves with a coating of thick mud for warmth.

On the basis of their crafts, mythology, or language, the California Indians can be classified in large groups, but such inter-relationships were involuntary. The intense particularism of local communities gave rise to marked variations, even between closely related groups. In small villages, usually comprising about 15 families each, lived the Indians of the Bay region. Each village claimed a well-defined territory with seasonal campsites reserved for its own use. If a deer hunt or a summer wandering took its inhabitants as far as 50 miles, the racial brothers they encountered might be wholly alien to them and their dialects incomprehensible. However, although they recognized no allegiance beyond that which they paid to their village chief, the peoples of the Bay region were all of one linguistic family, the Penutian. The greater

part of the Bay area was occupied by the Costanoan, whose territory
included the San Francisco Peninsula, the coast country as far south as
Point Sur, and the eastern shores of the Bay as far inland as the Mount
Diablo Range.   North of the Bay, as far east as the Sonoma Valley
and as far north as the Russian River, lived the Coast Miwok.   Eastward, beyond the Sonoma Valley, the Wintun held the shores of San
Pablo and Suisun Bays.

Among all the peoples of the earth, no others are known who kept
so long unchanged their ways of living and thinking.   During the last
30 to 40 centuries when western civilization was making its cyclical
and labored rise, time stood still for the Bay Indians.   Early white
visitors remarked that these natives were squalid and listless.   However,
most such observers had seen them after the mission system had begun
forcing upon them an alien civilization.   In 1579 Drake's men had
noted that the Miwok Indians handled their bows and arrows "very
skilfully," that their spokesman was "using sich violent Gestures, and
so strong a Voice, and speaking so fast that he was quite out of Breath,"
and that these Indians "run very swiftly, and long, and seldom go any
other Pace. . . ."   It was after 40 years of mission rule, in 1816, that
the Frenchman Louis Choris described the apathy of the San Francisco
Costanoan: "I have never seen one laugh.   I have never seen one look
one in the face."

Apathetic though they may have seemed to white men who could
not understand their failure to take up arms in their own defense, still
they were not lacking in sensitivity, for they gave lyrical expression to
their feeling for the environment in their mythology and songs.   In the
beginning, the Costanoan told each other, waters covered all of the
earth except the summit of Mount Diablo.   There lived a coyote, a
humming bird, and an eagle, and as the waters receded these three, but
chiefly Coyote, created the world.   Their myths about Coyote's subsequent adventures are a mixture of ribald humor and idealism.   The
Indians worshipped the sun with offerings, and held sacred the towering
redwood trees.   To the Coast Miwok, Mount Tamalpais, whose long
eastward slope resembles the figure of a sleeping woman, was the human
bride of the sun god, who fell from his arms as he was trying to carry
her to his celestial world.   When summer fog wrapped the figure, the
Indians told each other that this was her fleecy blanket, made by the
god from his tears.

Even critical white observers found the Costanoan songs peculiarly
pleasing.   In some of them the singers tried to express the sensibilities
of small woodland animals—of the wood-rat, for instance:

> "I dream of you,
> I dream of you jumping.
> Rabbit, jack-rabbit and quail . . ."

Apparently they were aware that their Bay and its peninsulas were the dramatic western boundary of a great land, for another of their songs began:

"Dancing on the brink of the world . . ."

Such imagery suggests that the native singers were not wholly apathetic and morose. When the white man came, to prove that their coast was not the world's brink and to put an end forever to the dancing, apathy may not have been the only reason they did not laugh.

THE WHITE MEN CAME

Grim, medieval Carlos V of Spain—uncertain of his geography, but with his black eyes fixed on galleons bearing spices and treasure across the vast Pacific—had ordered Hernando Cortez, in the course of the expedition on which he set forth in 1532, to "seek a natural port well north of New Spain" where "my navigators may find refuge, refit and rest." From such a safe harbor, far up the unexplored California coast, His Most Catholic Majesty had hoped that "they may then continue the voyage from Manila to Acapulco with a greater degree of safety from the enemies of my country."

Spanish navigators required 227 years to carry out this royal decree; and even then, it was not his Majesty's sailors but rather his soldiers, led by Don Gaspar de Portola, who early in November of 1769 first discovered the great landlocked anchorage now known as San Francisco Bay. Not even Portola, to whom the glory has gone, was the first actually to see that body of inland water large enough to contain "all the ships of Spain." From the summit of the Montara Ridge Don Gaspar himself saw no more than the Gulf of the Farallones and, purple in the distance, the long headland which the navigator Sebastian Vizcaino, in 1603, had named Punta de los Reyes (Sp., King's Point). It fell to soldiers of his expedition whose names with one exception are unknown to look first on San Francisco Bay.

Finding on the jagged shoreline no resemblance to the huge and sheltered bay described by Vizcaino in 1603, Portola's party had followed the shore of Monterey Bay without recognizing it to the mouth of the San Lorenzo River, present site of Santa Cruz. Pushing on through redwood trees, over ridges, arroyos, and creeks, they trudged past Half Moon Bay. Rising before them in the October rain they saw the rocky barrier of Montara Ridge, and at its base made their camp. The next day being clear, they surveyed from the summit of Point San Pedro the far-off purple cape of Point Reyes.

Gazing at the distant headland christened in honor of the Three Wise Men of the East who had brought gold and frankincense and myrrh to the infant Jesus, Don Gaspar decided it might be worthwhile to search the intervening coastline for that Puerto de San Francisco which shipwrecked Cermeno had happened upon in 1595. Portola therefore put one of his scouts, Sergeant Jose Francisco Ortega, in charge of a party of ten, presumably to explore the region as far north as Point Reyes.

Sergeant Ortega's little band of soldiers never reached their rather ambiguous goal. Precisely what they did, where they went, and what they saw are mysteries which still tantalize the imagination of historians. Some authorities have advanced the theory that Ortega's progress northward was halted by the Golden Gate, for which reason he must have been the first to look into San Francisco Bay from the vicinity of Point Lobos. However probable, the theory is pure conjecture based mainly on the fact that the exploring party, in the three days it was given to accomplish its purpose, had sufficient time to traverse the Peninsula to its end. The diary kept by Padre Juan Crespi, chronicler of Portola's expedition, gives scant information on this vexing possibility. And his diary, overburdened as it is by the padre's preoccupation with the needs of Portola's men suffering from scurvy and diarrhea, is the only reliable record of these events.

The San Francisco Peninsula's abundance of roots, acorns, grasshoppers, sparrows, and squirrels may have been responsible for the tameness of the aborigines, but it hardly served to supply the lack of red meat and green vegetables which had brought Portola's men to the point of starvation. It was therefore mainly a desperate abdominal urge which drove them on to some rather extensive exploration of the area around San Francisco Bay—exploration which would later result in the establishment of the northernmost outpost of Spanish civilization in the New World.

According to Padre Crespi's diary, which is corroborated by Miguel Costanso, Portola's engineer, the second exploring party was allotted four days for their itinerary and "their ration of flour to keep off hunger for that time." They started on the afternoon of November 7. On the night of November 10, wrote Crespi, "the explorers returned, very sad, and no longer believing in the report of the heathen, which they confessed they had not understood. They said that all the territory which they had examined to the northeast and north was impassable because of the scarcity of pasture and especially because of the ferocity and ill-temper of the heathen, who received them angrily and tried to stop their passage. They said also that they had seen another estuary of equal magnitude and extent with the one which we had in sight and with which it is communicated, but that in order to go around it one would have to travel many leagues; and that they saw no signs that might indicate the proximity of the port where it terminates, and that the mountains were rough and difficult."

So well does Crespi's description apply to the *contra costa* (Sp., opposite shore), it is fairly obvious that this exploring party discovered San Pablo Bay, probably from the rugged shoreline of Pinole Point, at that time inhabited by the Wintun Indians, who later proved a menace to Spanish settlers north of San Francisco Bay. Their failure to report having seen the Golden Gate indicates that they may have travelled inland, possibly up the Moraga Valley. Certain it is that famished as they were, and presumably mounted on mules equally famished, they took the easiest route they could find.

Discouraged by their inability to reach the entrance of what they still believed was the port of Monterey, in the vicinity of Point Reyes, Portola's expedition began the long trek homeward to San Diego. The whole course of their explorations had been determined by their first view of the Gulf of the Farallones, which tallied with Cabrera Bueno's description of the old Port of San Francisco, derived originally from reports of Spanish galleons dropping anchor there for wood and water some 200 years before. Even if they had been able to see the Golden Gate from Point San Pedro, however, it is doubtful that they would have followed a different course, so convinced were they that Point Reyes was the headland of a great arm of the sea extending inland east of the rocky peninsula shaped like a plowshare which lies between Bolinas Lagoon and Tomales Bay.

Padre Junipero Serra, father superior of the Franciscan missionaries in California—lean, ascetic, sometimes merciless, but a more efficient administrator than most secular representatives of Spain in the New World—came north by ship the following year (1770) to establish a mission on Monterey Bay, discovered finally at the cost of a second expedition. Even before the founding of this future capital of Alta California, Serra had insisted that surely one of the projected missions in the territory should be dedicated to the patron saint of his order. To this the Visitador-General, Don Jose de Galvez, had answered dryly: "If St. Francis wants a mission, let him show us his port and we will found one." Now that Portola had been led by Divine Grace to St. Francis' port, it became an obvious duty to establish a mission there without delay.

Hence, in the spring of 1772, Portola's young lieutenant, Pedro Fages, and Padre Crespi led a party of 12 soldiers from Mission San Carlos Borromeo (now Carmel Mission) to select a suitable site for the new mission near the entrance to what was now called the Port of Our Father St. Francis. The Fages expedition proceeded up the Salinas and Santa Clara Valleys, and northward around the eastern shore of San Francisco Bay. From the present site of Oakland, which they passed on March 27, they must have had a fair view of the Golden Gate. Next day, from the hills below which Berkeley now stands, they saw through the Golden Gate the peaks of the southeast Farallon Islands rising on the horizon. Though Costanso later claimed that Portola's men were the first to see the famous strait, the honor doubtless belongs to the Fages party.

From the Richmond Hills the explorers travelled northward to the south shore of San Pablo Bay a few miles east of San Pablo Point and then eastward past Carquinez Strait to the present site of Martinez. They skirted Suisun Bay and followed the south bank of the San Joaquin River almost to where Antioch now stands. Finding the San Joaquin too wide to cross, the Fages party decided to return to Monterey. On their homeward journey they passed through the Pacheco Valley, west of Mount Diablo through the San Ramon Valley, and down through Alameda Canyon to the site of the future Mission San Jose. From their camp near the present village of Milpitas they continued down the old trail to Monterey which, beaten by the pack trains of the explorers who came after them, was to extend the great Camino Real (Sp., King's Highway) from Mexico to the northernmost limits of the Spanish Empire.

The new Spanish viceroy at Mexico City, farsighted Antonio Bucareli, was determined, at the risk of losing one of his clumsy little ships on the dangerous California coast, to settle for once and for all the question of San Francisco Bay. He therefore sent Lieutenant Juan Manuel de Ayala on the *San Carlos* with instructions to make a further survey of the Gulf of the Farallones. As darkness fell on August 5, 1775, the *San Carlos,* having sent a launch ahead to find anchorage, sailed cautiously through the Golden Gate and anchored for the night. On August 7 it moved to a new anchorage on the north side of Raccoon Strait and a week later to another in Hospital Cove off Angel Island.

The hardy band of settlers whom Juan Bautista de Anza led through incredible hardships all the way overland from Tubac in Sonora province had arrived on the present site of San Francisco with a platoon of soldiers and two priests by the time the *San Carlos* sailed a second time through the Golden Gate. With the assistance of the ship's carpenters and crew, Lieutenant Jose Joaquin Moraga's soldiers were able, on September 17, 1776, to raise the standard of Carlos III of Spain over the quarters of the *comandante* (commander) in the Presidio. The occasion was celebrated with a high mass, the firing of cannon, and the chanting of a fervent *Te Deum*.

The opening and dedication of the new Mission San Francisco de Asis (later known as Mission Dolores) on the grass-clad slope near a small lake, dolefully named by the padres Laguna de los Dolores (Lake of Sorrows), was delayed until October 8, 1776 because of the absence of Moraga on an exploring expedition. Moraga's expedition observed the feast-day of Saint Francis by proving conclusively that the Golden Gate was the only entrance to San Francisco Bay. "At length," exclaimed Padre Serra on his arrival at the new mission the following year, "our Father St. Francis has advanced the sacred cross . . . to the very last extremity of California; to go further requires ships."

Unfortunately, St. Francis' new mission lacked adjacent arable land. Anza's poverty-stricken settlers, and the few who came after them, soon found the fertile Santa Clara Valley to the south more suitable for them than the wind-swept, flea-infested sandy wastes of the area dedicated to their patron saint. Therefore, on January 12, 1777, the new Mission Santa Clara was founded down the peninsula. And three miles south of it arose the first purely civil settlement in California—the *pueblo* (town) of San Jose.

Before the close of the century two more Franciscan missions had been established in the Bay area: Mission Santa Cruz, on August 28, 1791, and Mission San Jose de Guadalupe, on June 11, 1797. The lands which reminded Anza's settlers of the fertile valleys of Valencia soon brought prosperity to these adobe outposts of Catholicism; their baptismal fonts grew muddy with the dirt of Indians saved from the wrath of God. Only by slow degrees, however, did the reluctant aborigines desert their mud huts and childlike savage habits for the adobe barracks, the lengthy prayers and hard work of the missions. Though the padres occasionally lost patience and punished petty crimes with rawhide when sweet words were of no avail, they did not generally ill treat their converts. On the whole the condition of the Indians was improved by their strange new masters in cassocks with shaved heads whose God hung nailed upon a cross. Of course, they learned to speak Spanish and did the manual labor of plowing and harvesting; they excelled in handicraft and later as herders of cattle and sheep. By 1800 intermarriage had produced many *mestizos* (half-breeds) among the 30,000 Indians converted by the Bay region missions. Within the following decade, however, the neophytes were decimated by measles and smallpox epidemics.

Alarmed by the catastrophic mortality, which was threatening the mission with extinction, the fathers transferred a number of neophytes to the more salubrious climate of the north Bay region. The experiment proved successful; the health of these invalids was greatly improved. On December 14, 1817, the *asistencia* (chapel) of San Rafael was founded at the present site of the town of San Rafael. Young Padre Jose Altimira planned a more radical solution to the problem, namely, complete abandonment of Mission Dolores and transference of its neophytes along with those at San Rafael to a new mission at Sonoma. Accordingly Mission San Francisco Solano was founded in 1823—without, however, the authorization of church dignitaries, who objected. A compromise was reached, permitting the new mission and Mission Dolores and San Rafael as well to remain. It was to be the last mission founded in Alta California.

Even after the outbreak of the Napoleonic wars, when trade with foreigners was declared illegal, *alcaldes* (mayors) and *comandantes* averted their eyes from the illicit traffic with American whalers and traders who brought oil, tea, textiles, silk, and household utensils in exchange for hides and agricultural products piled up in the storehouse of the missions. Rezanof's unromantic followers who settled around Fort Ross on Bodega Bay, and whom Governor Pablo de Sola distrusted, were being welcomed to Yerba Buena Cove with urbane politeness in 1821—while the viceregal regime in Mexico City was being overthrown. The interregnum of General Agustin Iturbide's regency, immediately succeeded by the short-lived Empire of Mexico, passed almost unobserved by the Emperor's subjects in Alta California; and news of the institution of a republican regime, which reached the territory in January, 1824, was received without much enthusiasm. At Mission Dolores, Father Estenaja delivered a sermon praising the constitution of the new Republic of Mexico and said a mass for its future greatness. The Presidio guns were fired, a few cheers went up; and when the echoes of the celebration had died away across the great Bay, the straggling settlement relaxed into its accustomed *siesta*.

YANKEE INVASION

The Bay region, despite a half century of misrule that combined paternalism with neglect, had attained economic independence when on March 26, 1825, Alta California formally was declared a province of the Mexican Republic. The decade which would elapse before the secularization of the missions was to witness the heyday of Hispano-Mexican colonization on the Pacific Coast.

Mission San Jose in 1825 owned 62,000 head of cattle, as many sheep, and other livestock; in 1828 Mission Santa Clara had, besides other livestock, 14,500 head of cattle and 15,500 sheep. Mission Dolores' economic importance was, however, eclipsed by the cove of Yerba Buena to which the Bay area missions and ranchos brought their produce in oxcarts for trade with foreign ships. Besides their great herds, which furnished the hides and tallow sought by European and American traders, the missions owned vast fields planted in wheat and maize and other crops primarily for domestic consumption. Cloth, a coarse kind of serge, was woven from wool; and the *aguardiente* (brandy) distilled from the vineyards of Mission San Jose was the delight of foreign visitors. The missions, designed originally to form the nuclei of *pueblos* and intended to relinquish control of their Indian convert-citizens to the civil authority, had become so wealthy by 1830 that they were reluctant to fulfill a destiny which would deprive them of their power.

This system of monastic feudalism was likewise perpetuated by the vast ranchos, ranging from one-half to more than sixteen square leagues (a league being equal to about 4,438 acres), granted by Spanish governors to soldiers of the Portola and Fages expeditions. During the years of Mexican rule grants were also made to Americans and other foreigners who showed a disposition to settle the country in a neighborly manner. Rancho San Antonio, the 48,000-acre domain within whose former boundaries now stand the cities of Alameda, Albany, Berkeley, Emeryville, Oakland, Piedmont, and San Leandro, and Las Pulgas (the fleas), the 35,000-acre rancho granted in 1795 on which stand almost as many Peninsula towns, were typical of these feudal estates. Here, in their adobe ranch houses, the lordly dons entertained friends and relatives with lavish hospitality. They were grateful for the luxuries brought to Yerba Buena Cove by foreign traders whose followers would one day dispossess them.

When the missions were secularized about 1834, the great landowners came into possession of most of the mission lands—and of their Indian charges as well. The plan had been that the mission communities should be organized as towns, enough land set aside for the support of the clergy, and the surplus divided among the Indians. But to the administrators appointed by the government, rather than to the Indians, went the greater part of the flocks and herds and grain fields. Relieved from the discipline of the monks, the freed neophytes were the easy prey of gamblers and thieves. Without any direction, spiritual or economic, they became scattered on the great ranches whose owners under Mexican grants were getting control of the best of the lands in the coast valleys. All the while tuberculosis and smallpox and a declining birth rate were steadily reducing their numbers. The state of affairs at the Mission Dolores was typical. The *pueblo* did not develop into a prosperous town. Padre Rafael de Jesus Moreno pointed out that the commissioner was acting for his own advantage rather than for the good of the Indians. Likewise there were charges and countercharges at Santa Clara, San Jose and the other missions around the Bay. All of them fell into neglect and decay. There were only 50 Indians at San Francisco when the French explorer and scientist, Duflot de Mofras, was there in 1841.

International rivalries meanwhile were shaping the future of Alta California and the Bay area. Fort Ross, less than 100 miles north of the Bay, was developing into something more formidable than an outpost of Russian hunters of seal and sea otter who chased their prey from the Farallon Islands right into San Francisco Bay. Representatives of Britain's Hudson's Bay Trading Company, who came to make surveys of the Boy region and to twit the *comandante* of Yerba Buena's presidio on the sad state of his defenses, had a knowing political gleam in their eyes.

Least suspect of all were the Americans. Unlike some other foreigners settling in the Bay region, they assumed no official character which could be construed as representing aggressive designs on the part of the United States. The majority of Yankee immigrants, in fact, adopted unhesitatingly the religion and customs of the Mexicans; they renounced their American citizenship and married into leading Mexican families. Not for some years after the first trappers had begun to cross the Sierra were the Yankees regarded by Mexican authorities with suspicion such as the Russian incursion into the Bay area had received since 1812.

Secure behind their stockades and twelve brass cannons at Fort Ross, the Russians ignored repeated orders to leave the country. As early as 1817 Governor Pablo Vicente de Sola had reported to his superiors in Mexico City that he could not drive them out with the forces at his command, whose weapons were effective only against Indians armed with bows and arrows. Now that Mexico was an independent nation she no longer had protection from the Spanish navy, and no supply ships had arrived at Yerba Buena since 1811. Captain William Shaler, describing San Francisco Bay in 1805, found the entrance defended only "by a battery on which are mounted some brass pounders, which afford only the show of defense; and the place could make no resistance against the smallest military force . . ." The Castillo de San Joaquin, here described, was not improved by subsequent decades of neglect.

Whether or not the provincial authorities recognized the fact, from 1823 onward the American government had entered into the long-range struggle of world powers for control of Alta California. Concern over Russian inroads into the Bay region prompted Andrew Jackson's administration to undertake negotiations with the Mexican government for acquisition of Alta California. What "Old Hickory" had his eye on was that portion of Mexican territory north of the 37th parallel, including San Francisco Bay, which had been described to him as "a most desirable place of resort for our numerous whaling vessels . . . in the Pacific, far superior to any to which they now have access." The $3,500,000 which Jackson offered Mexico's President Santa Anna was, however, refused; and the American government's subsequent attempts to bring the Mexicans to terms met with no better success.

American citizens meanwhile were far from idle. From frontier settlements in Missouri, Kentucky and Tennessee, trappers and fur traders in coonskin caps and greasy buckskin had been threading their

way across the plains and mountains of the West.   First of these restless
Yankees to reach Alta California by an overland route was Jedediah
Smith.   In the fall of 1826 this "Pathfinder of the Sierras" had opened
the way for American settlement of the Sacramento and San Joaquin
Valleys.   That his presence in the Bay region was unwelcome is apparent from the fact that, on his arrival at Mission San Jose, Padre
Narciso Duran locked him in an outhouse; and upon his release Governor Jose Maria de Echeandia gave him two months to get his fur
traders out of the country.

The feudal *rancheros* had no great interest in encouraging trade
and industry, but under Governor Jose Figueroa's liberal regime San
Francisco Bay was declared a port of entry and, in 1835, the *pueblo* of
Yerba Buena was laid out on the cove.   Appointment of a harbormaster
and lifting of restrictions on trade with foreign shipping opened for the
Bay area a decade of friendly relations between Mexicans and Yankee
settlers which might eventually have resulted in peaceful annexation of
California by the United States.   The appointment of Thomas O.
Larkin as United States Consul to Alta California in 1843 was made,
apparently, to encourage the *Californios* to sever their ties with Mexico
and seek protection under the American flag.

The loss of Texas to Sam Houston's rebellious settlers in 1836 left
the regime in Mexico City in too perilous a state to cope with the
political intrigue among its representatives in Alta California; and some
of these began to depend upon certain foreign elements in the province
to maintain their despotic rule against rival officials and a citizenry
from which arose the rumblings of revolt.   Their most powerful aide
in the vicinity of the Bay area was Johann Augustus Sutter, Swiss immigrant and adventurer extraordinary, who had established a settlement
in the Sacramento Valley.   At Sutter's Fort were welcomed the American immigrant trains whose oxcarts came straggling down through
passes in the high Sierra after 1841.

In 1841, when the Russians decided to withdraw from Fort Ross,
Sutter had acquired all their territory around Bodega Bay.   In return
for assisting General Mariano Guadalupe Vallejo, *comandante* of
Sonoma, to disperse the roving brigands which General Manuel Micheltorena brought with him from Mexico when he came to displace Governor Juan Bautista Alvarado at Monterey in 1842, the redoubtable
Sutter was left unmolested to play off one rival official against another.
Even when this "Lord of the Marches" threatened to "proclaim California a Republic independent of Mexico" if he were not given leave
to do as he pleased, Vallejo dared not break off friendly relations with
him.   He wrote unhappily at the time, when American immigration was
filling the Bay area with Yankee settlers, that "the only certainty is
that Californians will die," and again, "I dare not assure myself that

California will be saved." He drew what consolation he could from the fact that Sutter had prevented further encroachment of the British Hudson's Bay Company and kept his political rival, Juan Bautista Alvarado, at a safe distance; but he saw the Americans taking over the country.

When the first overland party from Missouri arrived at the ranch of Dr. John Marsh near Mount Diablo in November 1841, they were permitted to settle unmolested. Governor Micheltorena had orders to put a stop to all immigration; but his disreputable army had made him unpopular and he was dependent on American support to put down the conspiracies of rival officials who openly defied his authority. Furthermore, the crafty Alvarado had left the treasury of the province empty; and the secularization of the missions in 1834 had already destroyed the source of funds by which presidio garrisons had been maintained. To aggravate this precarious situation even more, the American and British consuls in Monterey were keeping their respective governments informed of the events leading to a crisis in which intervention of some sort would decide the future of the territory.

Such was the state of affairs in California and the Bay region when, in December 1845, Captain John Charles Frémont entered the province. As United States topographical engineer in command of two previous expeditions sent to survey California's natural resources, Frémont was received on January 27, 1846 in Monterey without serious misgivings by Mexican authorities, who gave him permission to obtain supplies pending his promised departure into Oregon. Little more than a month later, however, Frémont's followers joined him near San Jose, marched across the Santa Clara Valley and through the Santa Cruz Mountains, and camped near Monterey.

Promptly ordered to leave the country, Frémont made a show of resistance, swearing that "if we are hemmed in and assaulted we will die, every man of us under the flag of our country." Being neither hemmed in nor assaulted, Frémont's party withdrew up the Sacramento Valley to Sutter's Fort and proceeded north toward Oregon. His martial depredations caused Larkin to petition Consul John Parrott at Mazatlan to send a warship to Monterey.

Whether acting on secret orders received from the United States State Department or on his own initiative, Frémont suddenly retraced his steps and set up headquarters at Marysville Buttes in the Sierra foothills. From here a party of about a dozen Yankee hunters and trappers —in command of Ezekiel Merritt, a settler from Rancho Barranca Colorado (Red Bluff)—was ordered by Frémont to seize 170 horses being taken from Sonoma to Santa Clara by a party of Castro's men. The captured animals having been delivered to Frémont's new camp on the Bear River, Merritt's party of 20 marauders crossed the hills into Napa Valley, where they were joined by 12 or 13 recruits.

At daybreak on June 14, General Mariano G. Vallejo in his house at Sonoma was roused without warning by this little band of men and called upon to surrender. Somewhat puzzled, but courteous as always, he invited them in. On being informed that they were acting under Frémont's orders, he proceeded to wine and dine his callers to the point of stupor while terms of surrender were being discussed. At length the captors were able to agree on a declaration to which three of them put their names—Ezekial Merritt, Robert Semple, and William Fallon. They presented it to Vallejo: "We, the undersigned having resolved to establish a government upon republican principles, in connection with others of our fellow-citizens, and having taken up arms to support it, we have taken three Mexican officers as prisoners: Gen. M. G. Vallejo, Lieut. Col. Victor Prudhon and Capt. Salvador Vallejo." But dissension then broke the ranks of the insurrectionists, frightened by the magnitude of their exploit. William B. Ide, a Yankee settler with the gift of oratory, saved the day. Cried he: "I will lay my bones here before I will take upon myself the ignominy of commencing an honorable work and then flee like cowards, like thieves, when no enemy is in sight. In vain will you say you had honorable motives. Who will believe it? Flee this day, and the longest life cannot wear out your disgrace! . . . We are robbers, or we must be conquerors!"

Taking possession of the *pueblo* without opposition, the rebels impatiently hauled down the Mexican flag. It occurred to them that a new flag was needed to replace it. On a piece of homespun to which was attached a strip of red flannel they painted a red star and the crude figure of a grizzly bear. "My countrymen," orated Lieutenant Henry L. Ford as the new standard was hoisted up the flagpole, "we have taken upon ourselves a damned big contract." But the insurgents' chosen leader, William B. Ide, who promptly dubbed himself "Commander-in-chief" and later "President of the California Republic," was undaunted. He invited "all peaceable and good citizens of California . . . to repair to my camp at Sonoma, without delay, to assist us in establishing and perpetuating a Republican government, which shall secure to all civil and religious liberty, which shall encourage virtue and literature; which shall leave unshackled by fetters, agriculture, commerce and manufactures."

Though Frémont would admit no direct responsibility for the "Bear Flag" rebellion, he ordered the arrest of Jacob Leese, Vallejo's brother-in-law, because he was a "bad man"; and according to Leese's account, he also threatened to hang Sutter for demanding that consideration be shown a man of Vallejo's pro-American sympathies. It was generally assumed, by both Yankee settlers and *Californios* in the Bay region, that Frémont was in command of a movement to seize the territory.

General Castro, learning of the affair at Sonoma, sent a force of

50 or 60 men under Joaquin de la Torre to attack the "Bears." Marching northward from San Rafael, De la Torre's contingent was joined by Juan Padilla's roving bandits. On the morning of June 24, 1846, the *Californios* were attacked at the Olompali Rancho near Petaluma by 17 or 18 men under Lieutenant Henry L. Ford. After a charge in which one of De la Torre's men was killed and several wounded by Ford's riflemen, the *Californios* retired and the Americans returned to Sonoma.

Until this first battle of the war Frémont had taken no open part in the events which his presence doubtless had precipitated. Now, however, as he says in his *Memoirs*, "I have decided that it was for me to govern events rather than to be governed by them. I represent the Army and the Flag of the United States." Furthermore he realized that "at last the time had come when England must not get a foothold; *that we must be first.* I was to *act,* discreetly but positively." And act he did, though neither he nor his Mexican opponents were as yet aware that their respective countries were already at war below the Rio Grande.

Arriving at Sonoma on June 25, Frémont assumed command of the Bears and with a combined force of 130 men marched to meet De la Torre's detachment at San Rafael. Here occurred an incident which ever since has blemished Frémont's reputation. This was the murder of three innocent *Californios*—the twin sons of Yerba Buena's first *alcalde,* Francisco de Haro, and old Don Jose Berryesa, father of the *alcalde* of Sonoma who was then among Frémont's prisoners at Sutter's Fort. On being informed by Kit Carson that these three were about to land from a boat at Point San Pedro, Frémont is reported to have said: "I have no room for prisoners." Kit Carson, G. P. Swift, and one of Frémont's trappers shot down the three unarmed men.

Outnumbered and badly armed, De la Torre's forces fled across the Bay to join Jose Castro's at Santa Clara. Following Frémont's raid on the old Castillo de San Joaquin, Dr. Robert Semple, participant in the Bear Flag affair at Sonoma, led ten men on a foray into Yerba Buena which captured Robert Ridley, ex-factor of the local Hudson's Bay Company post.

After thus putting down all military resistance of the *Californios* in the Bay region Frémont returned to Sonoma to declare the independence of California and place the country under martial law for the duration of the conflict. While continuing "in pursuit of Castro" in the valley of the Sacramento (actually Castro already had begun his retreat southward from Santa Clara), Frémont received news that the United States naval commander on the Pacific Coast, Commodore John D. Sloat, had raised the American flag at Monterey and had ordered the U.S.S. *Portsmouth* to do likewise at Yerba Buena. Thenceforth the Bay region heard only distant rumblings as the Yankee invasion progressed southward with mild skirmishes in the Salinas Valley, to end at last in a decisive victory for the Americans at San Gabriel, January 8–9, 1847.

The Treaty of Guadalupe Hidalgo, February 2, 1848, gave California to the United States. The Bay region's Bear Flag war was only an incident in the hasty transfer of a vast territory from one nation to another. But it marked the beginning of a new era, and the end of an old one. And Jose Castro himself, *comandante-general* of the forces of the north in the struggle of the *Californios* against the Yankee invaders, foresaw in some degree what that new era would be like when he told an assembly at Monterey: "These Americans are so contriving that some day they will build ladders to touch the sky, and once in the heavens they will change the whole face of the universe and even the color of the stars."

Emporium of a New World

*". . . San Francisco . . . the sole emporium of a new world,
the awakened Pacific . . ."*

—RICHARD HENRY DANA

HARDLY had the dead hand of Mexican rule been lifted from
the Bay region when the Gold Rush struck it like a hurricane.
The thousands who flocked to the shores of San Francisco
Bay in 1848 at first asked little. But when the excitement died down
the little gold frontier town had become a city, and its people demanded
much: wharves, and dry paved streets; homes and stores, with firm
foundations on which to build them; and a transportation system that
would encompass not only the land about the Bay, but the Bay itself.
Almost overnight the fleet of steamers and sailing ships which glutted
with the manufactured products of Eastern merchants the wharves of
San Francisco, Stockton, and Sacramento established the Bay's maritime supremacy on the Pacific Coast.

Mining camps developed into towns and cities amid the rich agricultural lands of the Sacramento and San Joaquin valleys; and around
the old *pueblos* of San Jose and Santa Clara the vast ranchos of the
Mexicans and Spaniards became orchards, fields, and vineyards. From
these, and from the soil of Sonoma County, from Napa Valley and
from the counties of the *contra costa,* would come the "green gold"
which a vast system of canneries and packing houses now prepares for
distribution all over the world. To supply this populous hinterland
with commodities, and to bring down to the harbors of the Bay its tons
of exports, a network of railroads and highways, bridges and improved
inland waterways had to be established. Throughout almost a century
Bay region industrialists, farmers, and shippers have had to struggle
with problems of engineering to overcome deficiencies in an area otherwise ideally suited to the building of prosperous communities and metropolitan centers.

For all its magnificence and its utility, San Francisco Bay was,
until completion of its two great bridges, an obstacle to transportation
which prevented development of large sections of Marin County; and
it isolated the industrial centers of the East Bay from financial and
distribution facilities of San Francisco. Phenomenally rapid as its
progress has been, this new unity, which engineering has accomplished,
assures a future of more intense and orderly development for all communities of the Bay region.

Today, the San Francisco Bay region is the market place and workshop for a population of nearly 2,000,000 people—a great harbor ringed with factory smokestacks, sheltering vessels from all ports of the globe, terminus of transcontinental railroads and airlines and home base of the Pacific Clippers flying to the Orient. Ranking second in value of water-borne commerce of all United States ports, the San Francisco Bay area has become the Pacific Coast's largest distribution center and the West's financial capital. Among 30 industrial areas of the Nation, it ranked sixth as a manufacturing center, with an industrial output of more than $800,000,000 in 1935. Its wholesale trade volume of $1,353,710 for the same year was larger than the value of its water-borne commerce; and the value of its retail trade was half as large.

WORLD PORT

John Masefield's "dirty British coaster with salt-caked smokestacks" is but one of the myriad craft, from nations all over the world, which have come and gone through the Golden Gate since Lieutenant Manuel de Ayala's little *San Carlos* first dropped anchor in San Francisco Bay in 1775. Across the racing tides of that narrow channel have swept the white sails of the clipper ships that brought the Argonauts; through it have steamed sidewheelers and modern freighters, sleek liners and palatial yachts, naval armadas and army transports; and casting brief shadows of the future upon it, and upon the mighty bridge which spans the strait, the silver wings of clipper planes go soaring out across the Pacific.

The pioneer Pacific Mail Steamship Company's 1,000-ton sidewheeler, *California,* already had sailed from New York for the Pacific Coast by way of Cape Horn, with no passengers, when the news of the discovery of gold in California reached the East. When the *California* anchored at Panama on January 30, 1849, she found hundreds of frenzied gold-hunters who had made their way across the Isthmus awaiting her. On February 28, topheavy with several times her capacity of 100 passengers, she steamed through the Golden Gate—the first vessel to round Cape Horn under her own steam and sail into the Bay of San Francisco. Pacific Mail promptly hurried completion of two sister ships; but these were not enough. Its fleet rapidly grew to 29 steamships destined to carry 175,000 people to San Francisco within a decade.

During the height of the Gold Rush, however, demand so far outdistanced supply in the maritime industry that chaos reigned, retarding for several years development of regular and systematic commercial facilities. The rapid increase in population—from about 860 to almost 42,000 by the end of 1852 in San Francisco alone—brought a wide and insistent demand for manufactured goods, tools, machinery and food products which undeveloped local industry could not supply. Eastern shippers, without accurate knowledge of local requirements, sent tons of merchandise for which San Francisco could find no use. The market was glutted; prices crashed; goods of every description were left to rot in the holds of ships, on the wharves, and in the city streets. Fully as demoralizing to maritime commerce was the wholesale desertion of ship's crews, who joined the wild rush to the mines. San Francisco Bay in the early fifties presented a sight seldom seen in the history of the world: a veritable forest of masts rising from hundreds of abandoned ships.

With the gradual stabilization of trading conditions, however, maritime commerce was revived until the rapid increase in shipping made necessary the immediate building of extensive piers and docking facilities. Prior to the Gold Rush all cargoes had been lightered ashore in small boats, usually to the rocky promontory of Clark's Point at the foot of Telegraph Hill. When in the winter of 1848 the revenue steamer *James K. Polk* was run aground at the present intersection of Vallejo and Battery Streets—at that time part of the water front—the narrow gangplank laid from deck to shore was considered a distinct advance in harbor facilities. The brig *Belfast* was the first vessel to unload at a pier: she docked in 1848 at the newly completed Broadway Wharf—a board structure ten feet wide. Others were soon built. By October 1850, 6,000 feet of wharfage had been constructed at a cost of $1,000,-000. As the tidal flats were filled in, the piers were extended: Commercial Wharf, at first extending only 30 feet into waters only two feet deep, became Long Wharf as it was lengthened to 400 feet to provide docking facilities for deep water shipping.

During the boom years of the 1850's competition between Eastern shippers became so sharp that a type of sailing vessel faster than the old schooners and barques constructed on the lines of whaling ships had to be built. Between 1850 and 1854, 160 fast clipper ships were launched on the Eastern seaboard to supply the demand for speed and more speed to the Pacific Coast.

"On to the mines" was the order of the day for both passengers and cargoes landed on San Francisco's water front. The fastest way to the mines was by water—through San Pablo Bay, Carquinez Strait, and Suisun Bay, and up the San Joaquin River to Stockton, or up the Sacramento to the town named for it. The first steamboat in the Bay, the 37-foot sidewheeler *Sitka,* imported in sections from the Russian settlement at Sitka, Alaska, and reassembled, had already attempted the trip to Sacramento, requiring six days and seven hours. Vessels better equipped for the journey were soon imported. Meanwhile, lighter craft were pressed into traveling service. Since 1835, when William A.

Richardson had begun operating two 30-ton schooners with Indian crews to transport the produce of missions and ranches from San Francisco and San Jose to trading vessels anchored in the Bay, a variety of small vessels had plied the waters inside the Golden Gate. In 1850 Captain Thomas Gray's propeller steamer *Kangaroo* began the first regular run, twice weekly, between San Francisco and San Antonio Landing (now Oakland) in the East Bay. On September 2, 1863, the San Francisco and Oakland Railroad Company, first in the Bay region, began running the *Contra Costa* six times daily from its Oakland wharf to Broadway Wharf in San Francisco; and the following year, the San Francisco and Alameda Railroad Company inaugurated train-ferry service from Alameda Wharf with the *Sophie McLane*. At the Alameda Wharf, on September 6, 1869, the steamer *Alameda* took on the first boatload of passengers arriving on the Pacific Coast by transcontinental railroad.

After the opening of ferry slips at the two-mile Oakland Long Wharf in 1871 and at a new San Fransisco passenger station at the foot of Market Street four years later, the ferry fleet grew rapidly in size. In 1879 the world's largest ferry, the *Solano,* began transporting whole railroad trains across Suisun Bay from Benicia to Port Costa. The ferry system was extended until by 1930 the 43 boats operating between San Francisco and Oakland, Alameda, Berkeley, Sausalito, and Vallejo comprised the largest transportation enterprise of its kind in the world; in that year they carried a total of more than 40,000,000 passengers.

The lifting of the Mexican regime's restrictive measures against foreign trading brought the Pacific whalers to San Francisco. As early as 1800, whaling vessels had begun to anchor in sheltered Richardson's Bay, then known as Whaler's Bay, off the site of Sausalito, where they took on wood and water. The first captain of the port, shrewd William A. Richardson, had collected fees for piloting the whalers to their anchorage. But Mexican regulations and tariffs forced the whaling industry to base its operations in the Sandwich Islands. After American occupation, San Francisco merchants, foreseeing profits to be gained from yearly outfitting of the whalers and their crews, made hardy efforts to center the industry here. They succeeded to such an extent that by 1865 a total of 34 whalers, with a combined tonnage of 11,000 tons, anchored in the Bay.

As late as 1888, San Francisco was still Pacific Coast whaling headquarters. But the whaling fleet dwindled rapidly after 1900—as tugboats for pursuit ("killer" ships) and steam-driven processing plants (factory ships) supplanted sailing vessels—until in 1938 the California Whaling Company, sole survivor in the industry, called in for the last time its remaining ships.

Within two decades after the building of its first wharf, the tip of the San Francisco Peninsula was saw-toothed with piers. The water front had been pushed into the Bay as the shallow waters of Yerba Buena Cove were filled in. In 1873, two years after control of the San Francisco water front had been acquired by the State, the construction of a great sea wall was begun by the State Board of Harbor Commissioners; and in 1878, the 200-foot wide Embarcadero was laid out. San Francisco's great era of maritime commerce was entering into the full stride of its phenomenal development.

While shovels and picks and gold pans rusted in thousands of back yards, the State turned from gold mining to agriculture and manufacturing. Sacramento and Stockton, great mining centers during the Gold Rush, became agricultural capitals of northern California. The two great rivers sweeping inland to these cities became arteries of commerce. Barges and river boats stopped at numberless docks and landings to pick up the diversified products of the rich land that swept for miles on either side of the broad rivers. And the products of the great agricultural hinterland, flowing into San Francisco Bay, contributed heavily to its export trade. From 1860 to 1875 exports from San Francisco grew in value from $8,532,439 to $33,554,081. By 1889 the figure had increased to $47,274,090 and imports had grown correspondingly in value.

The era of the clipper ships, which had abandoned the San Francisco run and entered the China trade, had given way to a new phase of shipping which called for the transport of heavy industrial products and for the expansion of foreign trade. Successors to the clipper ships were square-rigged sailing vessels, sturdily built, with spacious holds, for carrying heavy cargoes of freight, fish, and agricultural products. Only when displaced by the fast freight steamers of the late nineteenth century did the square-riggers pass from the shipping lanes and from San Francisco Bay. The ships of the Alaska Packers' fleet, last of these great windjammers, were dismantled early in the 1930's. Meanwhile the first of the roving cargo carriers known as "tramp steamers" had passed through the Golden Gate in 1874. By the end of the following year more than 30 of these vessels had arrived. Their number increased rapidly until the rise late in the century of the great modern steamship lines, which absorbed the independent shippers who had dominated the pioneer era. By the middle 1870's the growth of logging camps and sawmills in the timber regions of the State had also created a demand for large fleets of freighters.

Regular monthly service for freight and passengers was established between San Francisco and the Orient in 1867 by the Pacific Mail Steamship Company, which had for several years prior been transporting thousands of Chinese coolies to supply the demand for cheap labor during the building of the Central Pacific Railroad. By 1878 the Pacific Mail had established regular sailings to Honolulu, carrying merchandise which was exchanged for raw sugar, pineapples, coffee, and hides. Five years later the Oceanic Steamship Company entered this lucrative field of trade, and in 1885 extended its service to the ports of Australia and New Zealand. Within the following decade the names of William Matson and Robert Dollar were becoming known in maritime circles. As sea-borne commerce expanded during the last two decades of the nineteenth century, other lines developed. Among these pioneers of American shipping on the Pacific Coast were the American-Hawaiian, United Fruit, and Panama-Pacific Lines. The Kosmos Line, later absorbed by the Hamburg-American Steamship Company, inaugurated the first monthly sailings to Hamburg and other European ports in 1899. By 1916 the American-Hawaiian Steamship Company's fleet of 26 steamers with a capacity of 296,000 tons was said to be the largest tonnage under single ownership operating under the flag of the United States.

When the Panama Canal was opened in July 1914, the maritime commerce of San Francisco Bay entered its modern epoch of expansion. Along San Francisco's Embarcadero, until the outbreak of the war at the end of 1939, were represented almost 200 steamship companies whose vessels, both of domestic and foreign registry, called at nearly every port of the seven seas. Of these, at least half were engaged in coastwise, intercoastal, or transatlantic trade service (via Panama Canal); the others trade with Mexico and Latin America, Hawaii, Australia and the Orient, the African coasts, or offered round-the-world passenger service. From Puget Sound to Madagascar are known the huge dollar-sign insignia of Dollar Steamship Company ships (lately superseded by the spread eagle of the American President Lines), the blue-and-white smokestacks of California and Hawaiian, and the Matson Line's substantial "M." No less familiar to San Franciscans and other Bay region residents are neat Dutch liners and freighters bound for Rotterdam or Antwerp out of Batavia in the East Indies, for which San Francisco was a regular port-of-call. The ships of Japan, British ships from India and east African ports, ships from the Scandinavian countries and the Balkans were seen alongside piers of San Francisco's water front or in other harbors around the Bay. Most commonplace of all, however, are those coastwise freighters which butt in and out of ports all the way from Vancouver to Valparaiso.

Among San Francisco's chief imports today are copra, sugar, coffee, and vegetable oils; paper and burlap; fertilizer and nitrates. Chief exports are petroleum products; canned, dried, and fresh fruit; lumber; flour and rice; canned and cured fish; explosives and manufactured goods. Between 1926 and 1936 San Francisco shipped 63 per cent of the total volume of canned, and 70 per cent of the dried, fruit exported from the Nation. In return for the goods which it ships away, San Francisco Bay receives from the whole Pacific Basin its products for distribution throughout the West. Of the 35,000,000 tons of inbound and outbound cargo cleared by California ports in 1935, San Francisco Bay handled 17,000,000. In total commerce it ranked fourth among all commercial centers in the country.

The Port of San Francisco is much more than the 17½ miles of berthing space which flank San Francisco's Ferry Building on either side. Actually it consists of the series of bays extending northeast from the Golden Gate to the confluence of the Sacramento and San Joaquin Rivers and southward almost to San Jose. Harbor facilities are supplied by the half-dozen cities and industrial centers scattered along 100 miles of shoreline enclosing 450 square miles of water. These ports within a port are as interdependent as are the economies of the different cities and towns of the Bay region.

Thus a vessel in from the Hawaiian Islands may discharge pineapple at San Francisco and raw sugar at Crockett before proceeding to the Port of Oakland to take on a cargo of canned and dried fruits for the Orient, or a coastwise vessel up from Nicaragua or Honduras with a hold full of green coffee will unload at San Francisco before crossing to Oakland for automobiles for South or Central America. A tanker coming in through the Gate may steam directly to the Standard Oil docks at Richmond, or the Shell pier at Martinez; or it may make for the Selby Smelting Company's wharf at Selby.

An air view of San Francisco Bay's littoral—its miles of public and private wharfage; its manifold industrial plants crowding the water's edge; its deep-water anchorage for warships; its airports and islands and dockyards—will alone reveal the stupendous picture of this port. And in October 1936 travelers to and from San Francisco Bay were provided with such a view when Pan-American Airways launched the first transpacific commercial passenger flight to Manila. To the historic roll call of ships which have sailed through the Golden Gate— *San Carlos, California, Flying Cloud,* galleons and square-riggers, whalers and tramp steamers—was added one more name: *China Clipper.*

SMOKESTACKS AROUND THE BAY

Less than a century spans the interval between the primitive looms and forges, kilns and winepresses of the missions around the Bay and the giant factories, shipbuilding yards, and refineries with their soaring smokestacks that congregate about the water's edge today. Where cattle grazed the lonely hills—almost within the memory of living men—furnishing hides for the illicit trade with Yankee sea captains, now rise Contra Costa's sugar and oil refineries, steel mills, explosive and chemical plants. Where whaling boats embarked from San Antonio Landing to carry wild fowl, bear, and deer across the Bay to market, now spreads the East Bay's crowded belt of canneries and factories. And where whalers and hide traders once tied up on the other side of the water, San Francisco's printing and coffee roasting plants, meat-packing and canning establishments crowd to the shore.

The infant city by the Golden Gate grew rich overnight as industries sprang up to supply and outfit the Gold Rush population. Within little more than a decade after Stephen Smith had established his steam-powered grist- and sawmill—California's first—at Bodega in 1843, San Francisco had built stagecoach and wagon factories, flour mills, and breweries. Boot and shoe factories and plants for the grading and manufacture of wool endeavored to fill the need for clothing and blankets. As was natural in a city which was in the habit of burning down two or three times a year, lumber mills flourished. To supply the miners' demands for picks and shovels and pans, the Donahue Brothers established their foundry (later the Union Iron Works) as early as 1849. Since metal was scarce, San Francisco's pioneer machine shops and iron moulders were soon hammering iron wagon wheel rims and harness chains into miners' tools.

After the overland railroad began providing transportation to and from the East for both freight and passengers in 1869, San Francisco's industries expanded rapidly. The development of quartz mining and the growth of large-scale agriculture spurred the manufacture of mining and milling equipment. Other leading industries during this era, in order of importance, were breweries and malt houses, sash and blind mills, boot and shoe factories, tin-ware manufacturing, flour milling, and wool grading and manufacture. Of lesser importance were the tan-neries, coffee and spice processors (now one of the city's leading indus-tries), rolling mills, box factories, soap works, cracker factories, and packing plants. Over all, annual industrial output for the two decades of 1870-90 rose from $22,000,000 to $120,000,000.

The rapidly expanding mining industry had created a tremendous demand for special mining machinery. By 1860 San Francisco had 14 foundries and machine shops employing 222 men and turning out nearly $1,250,000 worth of products annually. With the development of quartz mining and the growth of mining in Nevada, it became the un-disputed Western capital for mining machinery. But mine machinery did not long remain the sole concern of local industry and soon, with typical audacity, the comparatively inexperienced machine shops of San Francisco blithely were turning out such complex pieces of workmanship as railway locomotives, flour mills, steamships and lesser objects of everyday utility. By the end of the nineteenth century, San Francisco's machine shops constituted an industry of international stature, supplying flour-milling machinery and equipment for the entire Pacific area, including such widely separated places as South and Central America, Japan, China, Mexico, New Zealand, Siberia, and Australia.

When the miners turned away from the creeks and climbed the hills to follow the quartz ledges, they needed explosives. It was in San Francisco in 1867 that Julius Bandmann took over exclusive rights to manufacture dynamite under the Nobel patents. At his plant in Rock Canyon he put together and discharged two pounds of dynamite—the first, so far as can be determined, ever to be manufactured in the United States. In 1888 he moved his plant to Contra Costa County, where it became the Giant Corporation, a subsidiary of the Atlas Corporation. As the West began tearing down whole mountains to dam rivers and blasting highways along granite cliffs, other explosive manufacturing plants were opened—the Hercules at Pinole and the Trojan at Oakland.

In 1865 Thomas Selby, a San Francisco hardware merchant, built a tall tower at First and Howard Streets for the purpose of dropping lead shot. But the lead ore, mined in California and Nevada, had first to make the long trip to Europe for smelting. Selby began to smelt the ore himself in a small plant in North Beach. The business grew and he moved, first to Black Point, then to Contra Costa County. In 1905 the Selby plant was taken over by the American Smelting Company. Its tall chimney can be seen for miles around. Some of the ore from the famous mines of California and Nevada has been treated there—antimony, lead, silver, and gold, including all of the latter two metals needed by the United States Mint in San Francisco.

Another industry which had gained an early foothold in San Francisco was sugar refining. The story of how a German immigrant boy, Claus Spreckels, graduated from his small San Francisco grocery business to become a millionaire sugar tycoon is typical of the swashbuckling manner in which many robust San Francisco pioneers acquired fortune and fame. Captain Cook, discovering the Sandwich Islands—later the Hawaiian Islands—in 1788, commented on the size and fine quality of the sugar cane he found growing there. Until Spreckels became interested, all the cane from the Islands passed through San Francisco on its way to the East to be refined. Acquiring an early interest in Hawaiian plantation lands when he won part of the island of Mauai in a poker game with Kalakaua, the island king, Spreckels built a refinery here in 1863. Dissatisfied with results, he sold out and went to Germany, France, Austria, and Belgium to study the latest methods of refining. Returning to San Francisco, he built a second refinery. In 1882 he moved his plant to the water front at the foot of Twenty-third Street, where ships from the Islands could unload the cane directly into the refinery. There he installed improved methods of refining. It is this plant, enlarged and reorganized, which today is the home of the Western Sugar Refinery.

The California and Hawaiian Sugar Refinery at Crockett in Contra Costa County, a comparatively late comer, has developed into a giant corporation that grows, mills, refines, and distributes—as sugar and sugar products—nearly 80 per cent of all the cane that comes from the Hawaiian Islands.

Men who had come to dig gold in California had remained to farm. Soon California's fertile inland acres were sprouting the "green gold" for which the State was to become world famous. Even before the great wheat farms of the 1870's and 1880's had been supplanted by fruit and vegetable ranches, a few men had foreseen that this "green gold" might be shipped to the whole world if only it could be preserved against perishability, and packaged.

In 1854 Daniel R. Provost, member of an Eastern fruit preserving firm, had stepped ashore in San Francisco to represent his company here. He rented a small building on Washington Street, where he repacked Eastern jellies in small glass containers. Two years later he enlarged the business and began to make preserves and jellies from California fruits. This was the first time native fruit had been preserved commercially on the Pacific Coast.

Francis Cutting came three years later. He went into the fruit and vegetable-preserving business on Sacramento Street, where his unusual window displays attracted hungry customers. He added tomatoes to his line of products and in 1860 received a shipment of Mason jars which were well received in San Francisco. People began to refer to San Francisco as a fruit-packing center.

In 1862 Cutting received from Balitmore his first shipment of tin plate, at a cost of $16 a box. That year he shipped California canned fruit to the Fifth Avenue Hotel in New York City, to the Continental Hotel in Philadelphia and to the Parker House in Boston. He canned 5,400 cases of California fruit in 1862. California's giant canning industry was born. In 1899 eleven pioneer companies merged to become the California Fruit Canners Association. The industry expanded rapidly.

San Francisco developed a luxury line of fruits and vegetables put up in glass containers and the Illinois Glass Company arrived in Oakland to provide the jars. Typical of the canning industry today is the California Packing Corporation—Calpak—which owns 71 canneries, warehouses, and dried fruit plants, and many thousands of acres of fertile California lands. In the delta region, where the two great rivers empty into the Bay, Calpak owns 9,000 acres, 5,000 of which are planted to asparagus. According to a 1937 census the product of Bay area canneries that year was valued at $49,920,161.

Despite the fact that no oil is produced within 300 miles of the Bay, the center of its oil industry, Contra Costa County, has developed, in the brief interval since a China-bound steamer sailed west with a cargo of oil in 1894, into the clearing house for one-eighth of the entire world's supply of gasoline and petroleum products. All the way from the San Joaquin Valley's southern end, where oil was discovered late in the nineteenth century, pipes were laid to connect with Bay shore refineries. Standard Oil was the first of the large companies to build one; its Richmond plant was opened soon after the first ferry connection was made with San Francisco. It put out one of the early wharves at Point Orient, linking the East Bay directly with the Far East by means of its tankers. Today four of the world's largest refineries overlook the water from San Pablo Bay's southern shore.

Sugar, canning, oil—these are the Bay region's industrial giants. For the most part, their operations are centered across the Bay from San Francisco. Long the West's chief industrial center, San Francisco had passed its zenith as a manufacturing city by the turn of the century. In its place, the East Bay came forward as factories found industrial sites cheaper and rail connections more convenient on the mainland. The city of San Francisco itself assumed its present role of financial and marketing center for an industrial area embracing the whole Bay region—that of front office for the plants across the water. Although outranked in economic importance by both wholesale and retail trade, manufacturing nevertheless contributed 22 per cent of the city's annual pay roll in 1935. As befits a commercial and financial center, the printing and publishing industry—important ever since the Pacific Coast's first power press was set up in April 1850—leads all the rest, with an output valued in 1937 at more than $40,000,000. The city's next most important industries are those of food-processing—the coffee and spice (by far the most important), bread and bakery products, meat packing, and canned fruit and vegetable industries.

Along the shores of Alameda and Contra Costa Counties stretches an industrial belt of bewildering complexity. At Emeryville, for instance, are situated no less than 35 concerns of national reputation, with products ranging from light globes to corsets, from canned fruit to preserved dog food. Oakland is coming to be known as the "Detroit of the West," for Eastern automotive tycoons, to pare transportation costs, have built their assembly plants here. There are three General Motors plants in Oakland, a Ford plant in Richmond, and a Chrysler plant in San Leandro. Fageol trucks of Oakland are found high up among the mines of the Andes Mountains; huge tractors built by the Caterpillar Tractor Company of San Leandro are shipped all over the world. In 1921 the Atlas Imperial Diesel Engine Company of Oakland built the first solid injection marine Diesel engine to be manufactured with commercial success in America. The Union Diesel Engine Company, which has been building gas engines since 1885, supplies the means of motive power for boats of the United States Navy, the United States Bureau of Fisheries, and of the Arctic Patrol of the Canadian Northwest Mounted Police. The 400-acre plant of the Bay region's steel center, Pittsburg, recalling the giant mills of its Pennsylvania namesake, provides steel for many of the West's biggest construction jobs. Organized in 1910 by a group of San Francisco financiers, Columbia Steel (now a subsidiary of United States Steel) owns its own coal and iron mines, blast furnaces and coke ovens in Utah.

In 1940, only a few years short of the hundredth anniversary of gold's discovery, more than 3,000 industrial plants crowd the shores of San Francisco Bay, employing nearly 90,000 workers and producing goods valued at more than $1,000,000,000. Almost 71 per cent of central California's population of 3,000,000 people live within a 75-mile radius of San Francisco—still the hub of a great marketing area as it was in Gold Rush days. Now as then it is the San Francisco Bay region's job to supply their needs—and now, too, the needs of millions more beyond the horizons of a wider expanse, the whole Pacific.

ENGINEERING ENTERPRISE

The discovery of gold brought thousands clamoring to the muddy shores of the shallow indentation known as Yerba Buena Cove, which extended in an arc from the foot of Telegraph Hill to the present Montgomery Street and around to the foot of Rincon Hill. One of the first acts of the newcomers as a corporate body was to begin grading away the sand hills along Market Street and dumping them into the mud flats of the cove. The project was many years in completion. Before it was finished, about 1873, they had already begun building a sea wall several blocks east of the shoreline so that ships could unload directly upon the wharves without the aid of a lighter.

The construction of the sea wall, a stupendous project for its time, took many decades to complete. A trench 60 feet wide was dredged along the line of the proposed water front, and tons of rock blasted from Telegraph Hill were dumped into it from lighters and scows. The rocks were allowed to seek bed-rock of their own free weight; when settling ceased, a layer of concrete two feet thick and ten feet wide was laid on top of the resulting embankment.

While this work was going on, the reclamation of the mud-flats and shallows of the original cove was progressing. Some of the city's lesser hills were dumped bodily into the area between the old water front and the new sea wall until the business and financial district of lower Market Street—everything east of Montgomery Street—arose from the sea.

Agitation for rail connections to link the Bay with the outside world had begun as early as 1849. By 1851, $100,000 worth of stock had been sold for a projected line between San Francisco and San Jose. Three successive companies achieved little; but the fourth not only reached Menlo Park, but extended its line down the Peninsula to San Jose and was completed January 16, 1864. September of 1863 had seen completion of the San Francisco and Oakland Railroad Company's line from downtown Oakland to the Oakland ferry wharf.

Meanwhile, San Francisco's "Big Four" were pushing their Central Pacific rails over the mountains to join the Union Pacific in Utah. The first transcontinental railroad, completed in May 1869, extended only as far west as Sacramento. But the "Big Four," determined that San Francisco should be the focal point of a country-wide network of railroad lines, systematically acquired control over every means of entry to the Bay region from all directions. Having bought a short railroad between Sacramento and San Jose, they built a branch to Oakland, purchased the two local roads connecting Oakland and Alameda with the East Bay water front; and taking over another line between Sacramento and Vallejo, they extended it to Benicia, where they inaugurated ferry service to carry their trains across Suisun Bay, installing the world's largest ferryboat for the purpose. Finally they bought the San Francisco and San Jose Line. The Bay was encompassed by the tracks of the "Big Four."

"The railroad has furnished the backing for a great city," reported the San Francisco *Bulletin*, "and the need now is for a thousand miles of local railroads in California." The four went about answering the need. They completed a line southward to Los Angeles through the San Joaquin Valley on September 5, 1876. Their monopoly of rail transportation was unchallenged until completion in 1898 of a competing line financed by popular subscription, which was sold in the same year to the Atchison, Topeka, and Santa Fe Railroad Company. The "Big Four," meanwhile, were gradually extending the original San Francisco and San Jose line until in 1901 it stretched all the way down the coast to Los Angeles. On August 22, 1910 the Western Pacific line from Oakland through Niles Canyon, Stockton, Sacramento, and the Feather River Canyon to Salt Lake City was opened to traffic. By joint agreement in 1904 the Southern Pacific and the Santa Fe began consolidating a group of short lines in the northern coast counties—including the San Francisco and North Pacific from Tiburon to Sherwood and the North Shore from Sausalito to Cazadero—into one line extending from the tip of the Marin Peninsula northward to Trinidad, near Humboldt Bay, finally opened November 17, 1914.

Meanwhile a growing San Francisco had spread beyond the limits set for it in the imagination of its first settlers. Tycoons of mine, ship, and railroad began to build grotesque, grey wooden mansions, tired-looking beneath their burdens of architectural bric-a-brac, on the city's highest elevations. They then were confronted with a new, and purely local, problem of transportation—that of devising a vehicle capable of surmounting hills too steep for horses. The result was the invention, by local manufacturer Andrew S. Hallidie, of the cable car. The inaugural trip of the first car, over the newly laid line on Clay Street between Kearny and Jones Streets, was a civic event. On the morning of August 2, 1873, the unfinished car was sent down the hill and back. That afternoon a public trial trip was made: many people climbed into and upon the car, which was intended to hold only 14, but in spite of the overload, it literally made the grade. Thirty days afterward the line was put into regular operation. The principle of cable traction was not new. The crowning engineering achievement lay in adapting it to street transportation—in solving the problem of how to make a moving cable follow the contour of the street and how to devise a grip which could not tear the cable apart by too sudden a jerk. The cars promised in their day to become the prevailing type of public conveyance in all of America's larger cities. They still survive in the city of their birth, an antique touch in a streamlined world.

Before introduction of the cable car, horse cars and omnibuses had been the prevailing means of street transportation. The first such line, starting in 1852, had been the "Yellow Line," a half-hourly omnibus service which carried 18 passengers at a fare of 50¢ apiece from Clay and Kearny Streets out the Mission Street plank toll road to Mission Dolores. In 1862 the first street railroad on the Pacific Coast had begun providing service from North Beach to South Park. A steam railway began operation on Market Street in 1863, but sand and rain repeatedly filled the cuts, and omnibuses constantly obstructed the tracks and in 1867 horse cars were substituted. Even after cable car tracks were installed on Market Street (hence the name "South of the Slot" for the district south of Market) a horse car line paralleled them until 1906. An electric line was in operation on Eddy Street as early as 1900. In 1902 began the unification of all the city's lines, except the California Street cable, into one system, predecessor of today's Market Street Railway Company. The first line in the long-planned Municipal Railway—first city-owned street railway system in the United States and second in the world—was the Geary Street, put into operation in 1912. There are now 378.35 miles of street railway and bus lines in San Francisco.

On September 11, 1853, the consciously progressive city by the Golden Gate had made another—and very different—stride toward conquering the distances that lay between the communities of men. On that date was opened for use the first electric telegraph on the Pacific slope, connecting the San Francisco Merchants' Exchange with six-mile-distant Point Lobos. It was built to announce the arrival of vessels at the Gate (previously signalled to the town by the arms of the giant semaphore atop Telegraph Hill). Two days later, James Gamble started out from San Francisco with a party of six men to put up wire for the California State Telegraph Company, which had obtained a franchise from the Legislature for a telegraph from San Francisco to Marysville by way of San Jose, Stockton, and Sacramento. On September 25th the wire was in place. On October 24, 1861, the first direct messages between New York and San Francisco passed over the wires of the first transcontinental telegraph line.

One year after Alexander Graham Bell had invented the telephone, in 1876, Frederick Marriott, Sr., publisher of the San Francisco *News-Letter,* had a wire installed between his office and his home. In February 1878 the American Speaking Telephone Company began regular service with 18 subscribers. Soon afterwards the National Bell Telephone Company offered competition. The early switchboard consisted of two boards affixed to the wall, each with a row of brass clips into which holes were drilled to receive the plugs making the connections. In the National Bell Telephone Company's office, bells above these boards notified the operator of a call. Since the bells sounded exactly alike, however, a string had to be attached to each bell tapper and a cork to each string; the antics of the cork called the attention of the operator to the line that demanded attention.

On January 25, 1915, the first transcontinental telephone line was opened. Dr. Alexander Graham Bell in New York spoke to his former employee, Thomas Watson, in San Francisco, repeating his sentence of an even more memorable occasion: "Mr. Watson, come here, I want you!" In December 1938, San Francisco had 282,204 telephones—more connections per capita of population than any United States city except Washington, D. C.

A still greater stride in communication was made on December 13, 1902, when the shore end of the first transpacific cable was laid in San Francisco by the Commercial Pacific Cable Company (organized in 1883 by Comstock king John W. Mackay).

A more homely problem—a vexatious one for San Francisco since 1849—was that of its water supply. In early years water had been brought from Marin County on rafts and retailed at a dollar a bucket. Throughout the latter half of the nineteenth century, local sources of supply were exploited by private companies. When these failed to keep pace with the requirements of the rapidly growing metropolis, the City and County of San Francisco began in 1914, after a long and bitter struggle with monopolistic interests, the construction of the Hetch-Hetchy system.

Heart of the system is O'Shaughnessy Dam, towering 430 feet high across the granite-walled course of the Tuolomne River, high in the Sierra Nevada in Yosemite National Park. The mountain waters impounded are piped to San Francisco by gravity through tunnels and steel pipes over 163 miles of mountains and valleys. Besides the main dam and reservoir at Hetch-Hetchy, the system includes a number of subsidiary storage reservoirs and power stations with a combined capacity of more than 150,000 horse power. The dam was completed in 1923, the aqueduct in 1934.

The East Bay, too, had been faced with a similar situation regarding its water. From several wells in the vicinity and the surface run-off of San Pablo and San Leandro Creeks the region long had drawn a water supply whose quality was impaired by the inflow of salt water from the Bay and whose quantity was estimated at about one-sixth of that soon to be required. In the same year the O'Shaughnessy Dam was completed to impound waters for thirsty San Franciscans, the East Bay Municipal Utility District was organized. Eight years later it had completed the 358-foot-high Pardee Dam on the Mokelumne River in the Sierra foothills, a 93.8-mile aqueduct, two subsidiary aqueducts, and auxiliary storage reservoirs.

Long before the waters of the Sierra Nevada were generating power to light the homes of the Bay region—on the evening of July 4, 1876— Reverend Father Joseph M. Neri presented electricity to San Franciscans, operating on the roof of St. Ignatius College three large French arc searchlights with an old generator that had seen service during the siege of Paris in 1871. This was an occasion surpassing even the lighting of the city's first gas lamps on February 11, 1854—illumination provided by gas manufactured from Australian coal by the San Francisco Gas Company (first of its kind on the Pacific Coast).

George H. Roe, a local money broker whose interest in electricity had been aroused when he found himself owner of a dynamo taken as security for a loan, organized in 1879 the California Electric Light Company and erected a generating station on a small lot near the corner of Fourth and Market Streets. Early consumers paid $10 a week for 2,000 candlepower of light—which was turned off promptly at midnight. By 1900 a number of other companies had been organized. Through a merger of two of the largest, in 1905, was incorporated the Pacific Gas and Electric Company, which now operates four steam-electric generating stations in San Francisco and two in Oakland. Now the third largest public utilities system in the United States, P.G. and

Bay Region: Today and Yesterday

THE BAY AND ITS CITIES

GOLDEN GATE BRIDGED BY WORLD'S TALLEST, LONGEST SPAN

PENINSULA CLIFFS

ORCHARDS CARPET THE VALLEYS

MOUNT TAMALPIS LOOMS OVER MARIN COUNTY

THE PRESIDIO IN 1816

Drawing by Louis Choris

GRAVEYARD, MISSION DOLORES

NORTHERNMOST MISSION AT SONOMA (1824)

RUSSIAN CHAPEL AT FORT ROSS (1812)

VALLEJO'S CASA GRANDE NEAR PETALUMA

PEDRO FONT'S MAP OF SAN FRANCISCO BAY (1777)

E. serves an area of 89,000 square miles on the Central Pacific Coast. It controls 49 hydroelectric generating plants and ten steam generating plants, all interconnected, with a total installed capacity of 1,676,902 horsepower. Radiating from hydroelectric generating stations installed on 30 different streams of the Sierra Nevada and supporting steam powerhouses, the electric system forms an interconnected network of transmission and distribution lines from the mountains to the sea, more than 500 miles in length.

In the meantime, San Francisco's hills again had proven to be—and this time literally—stumbling blocks to the city's progress; for, as they halted further expansion, the town became cramped for space. Answer to the new problem was the construction of a series of five railway tunnels known as the Bay Shore Cutoff; completed in 1907, they brought the Peninsula towns within commuting distance of "the city" and opened up a large new residential area. In 1915 the city's North Beach section was made more easily accessible by a tunnel driven through Nob Hill on Stockton Street. Two years later the completion of the 2¼-mile Twin Peaks Tunnel provided a short-cut to the district west of Twin Peaks, doubled the city's potential residential area, and brought a rich financial return to property owners, business men, and real estate promoters. Another tunnel was bored to carry streetcars under Buena Vista Heights.

By the third decade of the twentieth century the fast-growing East Bay communities were confronted, as San Francisco had been, by the need of making similar improvements on nature. In 1928 a $4,496,000 automobile and pedestrian tube was laid beneath the Oakland Estuary to connect Oakland with the island city, Alameda. The Posey Tube (named for its designer and engineer) is unusual in that it is constructed of twelve prefabricated tubular sections, 37 feet in outer diameter, which were "corked," towed across the Bay, and sunk into a great trench dredged on the bottom of the estuary. The center one of the tube's three horizontal sections accommodates traffic; the lowest is a fresh air duct; the uppermost, an outlet for foul air.

More than 1,000 men toiled three years to build the impressive Broadway Tunnel connecting East Bay cities with Contra Costa County, which cost $4,500,000 before its completion in 1937. This twin-bore automobile and pedestrian tunnel, an extension of Oakland's main thoroughfare, has two additional lateral approaches from Berkeley and East Oakland. A clover-leaf obviates the crossing of traffic lanes. By day, "twilight zones" at each portal accustom the drivers' eyes to the change from natural to artificial light.

But when engineers had created a city where mud flats had been, had surmounted the hills of that city and the hills and valleys of the region beyond, had learned to talk over miles of wires and harnessed mountain streams to provide drinking water and electricity for a people, they had still to span the great body of water on whose shores the people lived. Not until 1927 was the Bay first bridged when the narrowest width at its extreme southern end was crossed by the Dumbarton Drawbridge, connecting San Mateo and Alameda Counties.

Carquinez Strait, the narrow entrance from San Pablo Bay to Suisun Bay, was next to be spanned. Carquinez Bridge is a tribute to the imagination and determination of two business men—Avon Hanford and Oscar Klatt. In 1923 their company secured a toll bridge franchise and—despite the admonitions of engineer and layman that the water was too deep and swift to permit a bridge at the site—construction was begun. In 1927 the $8,000,000 structure was opened to traffic. The great double pier rests on sandstone and blue clay at a depth of 135 feet below mean water level, over which the steel construction towers, for four-fifths of a mile, 314 feet above the strait.

March 3, 1929, saw completion of what was then the longest highway bridge in the world—the twelve-mile San Mateo Toll Bridge, crossing seven miles of water a few miles north of the Dumbarton Bridge. The movable, 303-foot, 1,100-ton center steel span—erected in South San Francisco and floated by barge to its resting place—can be raised 135 feet above water level.

The San Francisco-Oakland Bay Bridge was opened in November, 1936. It has six lanes for automobile traffic on its upper deck; three lanes for truck and bus traffic and two tracks for electric trains, on its lower. Its length is 12 miles, including approaches. Clearance above water at the central pier is 216 feet, sufficient to clear the mast of the largest ships. The west crossing—between San Francisco and Yerba Buena Island—consisting of two suspension bridges anchored in the center to a concrete pier, is unique in bridge construction; it is so built that the roadway forms a single smooth arc. Connecting the east and west crossings is the largest diameter tunnel in the world, blasted through Yerba Buena Island's 140 acres of rock. It is 76 feet wide and 58 feet high; through it an upright four-story building could be towed. Three pioneer tunnels were bored through the rock and then broken out until they became one horseshoe-shaped excavation. A viaduct was built 20 feet above the floor of the tunnel to carry the six-lane automobile boulevard; beneath it pass electric trains and trucks. The extraordinary depth of the bedrock to which concrete supports for the towers had to be sunk through water and clay presented bridge builders with an exceptional problem. To solve the problem, engineers devised a new system of lowering the domed caissons, controlled by compressed air. In the case of the east tower pier of the east crossing, bedrock lay at such a depth that it could not be reached. The foundations were laid at a depth greater than any ever before attained in bridge building.

Six months after the opening of the San Francisco-Oakland Bay Bridge, San Francisco was linked to the northern Bay shore by the world's longest single span, the Golden Gate Bridge. It measures 4,200 feet between the two towers and 8,940 feet in all. Its towers rise 746 feet above high tide; its center span, 220 feet above low water. The tops of the towers rise above the waters of the Golden Gate to the height of a 65-story building. Most spectacular feat in the bridge's construction was the building of the south tower's foundation. Because of the swift tidal flow at this point, spanning the Golden Gate had long been considered impossible. Working on barges tossed continually by swells as high as 15 feet, seasick workmen built from bedrock a huge concrete fender completely enclosing the site. Inside this fender, which later became part of the structure, caissons were sunk.

When the two towers were finished, workmen clambering along catwalks strung between them spun the giant cables from tower to tower. Into the spinning of each of the cables (which measure 36½ inches in diameter) went 27,572 strands of wire no thicker than a lead pencil. To support them, each tower has to carry a vertical load of 210,000,000 pounds from each cable and each shore anchorage block to withstand a pull of 63,000,000 pounds. From these cables the bridge was suspended by traveler derricks invented to perform jobs of this kind.

At about the time the two bridges were being woven into the Bay region's design of living, Treasure Island was rising from the rocky shoals just north of Yerba Buena Island. An outline of the island-to-be was drawn in tons of quarried rock. Inside it were dumped 20,000,000 tons of sand and mud dredged from the bottom of the Bay. When the job was completed a 400-acre island, cleaned of salt by a leaching process, had replaced the shoals once feared by seamen. Built to support the $50,000,000 Golden Gate International Exposition, Treasure Island is destined to become, when the Exposition closes, a terminal for the graceful Pacific Clippers that fly to Hawaii, the Philippines and the Orient.

Golden Era

"Mind before mines ought to be thè motto . . . of every edu-cated Californian."

—Reverend H. W. Bellows

To THINK of its power and influence," marveled Horace Greeley at San Francisco's pioneer literary journal, the *Golden Era,* "when the population is so sparse and the mail facilities so poor." The *Era's* youthful founders, Rollin M. Dagget, who was only nineteen years old when he arrived on the Coast, and J. MacDonough Foard, who was only twenty-one, had followed Greeley's own advice: "Go West, young man!" The phenomenal success of their attempt to spread enlightenment on such matters as education, literature, and the fine arts through the *Era's* columns, beginning in 1852 when the infant city could not yet supply itself with even the common necessities of life, was indicative of that hunger for all the arts and refinements of civilization which inspired the Argonauts almost as much, it would seem, as the quest for gold. "To encourage virtue and literature" had been one of the announced objectives of the founders of the Bear Flag Republic in 1846. Certain it is that "virtue and literature"—and art, and learning, and architecture—have received rare encouragement in the cities around San Francisco Bay. Even the earliest saloons insisted on hanging paintings on their walls and providing *musicales* for their patrons! The Gold Rush may have swept San Francisco's first public school-master, Thomas Douglas, off to the mines six weeks after he called his first class to order, but countless others who took his place would demonstrate a steadier adherence to the motto the Reverend Bellows framed for "every educated Californian."

CENTERS OF LEARNING

To trace the pioneer impetus in the educational field is like watching the man in the old story who brought water on mule-back from the ocean to the Colorado River. One disbelieves, and yet one sees the thing happening: individual after individual carrying obstacles before him that look insurmountable, impelled by nothing but his own belief and courage. There is Colonel Thomas J. Nevins, who first revealed to the Common Council of San Francisco that children were among the products of the gold-bearing State. The council, in those days when only the color of gold could put a man in action, was inclined to distrust Colonel Nevins' report until he thrust under their noses a census of his own taking, and illustrated it by samples of both sexes. The result was an ordinance for the establishing of the free common school system. That was in 1851. Nevins had earlier, of his own accord, set up a school in Happy Valley, south of Market Street, and could be seen each day following an express wagon along San Francisco streets, gathering up children and expressing them to the Happy Valley schoolhouse. And even earlier yet, Yale graduate Thomas Douglas had opened on April 3, 1848 California's first public school in a small shack on Portsmouth Square, beginning with six pupils, whom he taught until the Gold Rush, following shortly afterward, bore him off to the mines.

There is John G. Pelton, who came around Cape Horn from Andover, Massachusetts, determined to lay the foundations of a public school system in the illiterate West. Pelton even brought a school bell with him, which was tied to the mast and rang the watches on the tedious voyage from the Atlantic to the Pacific. He arrived with $1.50 in his pockets, not enough to remove books, globes, maps, and bell from the sandy beach where they had been landed. Some unnamed visionary rescued him and his wife. As soon as a boarding house opened by Mrs. Pelton was under way, he started a free school in the basement of the Baptist Church.

Writes John Swett, who became principal of one of the schools established after the ordinance of 1851: "This school [the Rincon School] was . . . in a small rented house planted in the middle of a sandbank on the corner of First and Folsom Streets. . . . There was neither a blackboard nor map. . . . The only apparatus consisted of a wooden water pail and a battered tin dipper, from which the children drank water brought from a well not far distant, the owner of which allowed the boys to draw one bucket of water a day." An early teacher is pictured scooping the drifted sand from under the pot outside his tent door, proceeding to boil his potatoes and brew his kettle of tea for a solitary supper after his day's work.

Ambitious in the face of difficulties is a list of geography questions propounded by an early school board president who prided himself on being able to teach more in one day than any teacher in San Francisco. The questions were (1) name all the rivers of the globe; (2) name all the bays, gulfs, seas, lakes and other bodies of water on the globe; (3) name all the countries of the world; (4) name all the cities of the world. It is told that when a young man from Texas had worried through the questions in arithmetic and had come to these on geography, he examined them carefully, then walked up to the chairman's table and handed them to him, saying, "If the Board wants me to prepare a primary geography, they must pay me for it."

The first kindergarten was opened in September 1863, by "Professor" Charles and Madame Weil, at 41 South Park Street. Schools sprang up quickly in imitation of the first successful private children's school, and by the end of the century there were easily a hundred of them in the city. Child education, however, did not receive mature attention until the advent of Miss Emma Marwedel in 1878. Miss Marwedel was one of the earliest child educators in the East to teach story-telling and drawing to children, and she left a highly successful school in the Nation's capital to organize a kindergarten in Los Angeles. During this period of teaching and training she instructed Kate Douglas Wiggin in kindergarten work.

Later Miss Marwedel and Mrs. Wiggin were associated in conducting San Francisco's famous Silver Street Kindergarten, parent institution of all Pacific Coast kindergartens. It was located in the notorious Tar Flat district around Second and Harrison Streets where ". . . life is sodden and aimless . . . children are often born of drunken mothers, and show deformities and mental deficiencies and inherited diseases . . . kindergarten teachers in their visiting sometimes find mothers helpless with drink . . ."

Fighting against such conditions, Miss Marwedel and Mrs. Wiggin taught the ever-increasing classes games, music, and the elements of cultural education, and with the help of other assistants made their school one of the most active educational forces in the history of Western child training. When Mrs. Wiggin later gained international fame by writing such books as *Rebecca of Sunnybrook Farm* and *Mrs. Wiggs of the Cabbage Patch,* she continued the crusade for child education. In San Francisco during her last few hours of intolerable illness, Miss Marwedel said to followers: "Have faith in the kindergarten . . . I believe in its power to reform the world."

Jean Parker, who believed the education of a child should include more than arithmetic, history, grammar, and other basic studies, first introduced useful and practical accomplishments—such as domestic science classes, school luncheons, girls' and boys' clubs, manual arts, and physical culture—to California juvenile education. The Jean Parker Grammar School in San Francisco not only follows her now-famous "learning by doing" method, but is a living memorial to the woman about whom was said: "She knew the new education before it poured in a beneficent flood over the land, and she created while others evolved laboratory schemes of advancement . . ."

The rise of colleges and universities followed the same impulse which broke through the apathy of a raw and materialistic civilization to establish the common schools. On the eastern side of the Bay, at a time when Oakland was a cluster of houses and Berkeley but an expanse of neighboring fields, when the first transcontinental railroad had not reached California, and Tiburcio Vasquez was harassing honest men in the San Joaquin Valley, the University of California was opened in 1868.

Leland Stanford came to California in 1852, penniless, to sell salt pork and miners' sieves in a store at Michigan Bluff. After a while he was able to bring his wife out from the East, and for a time they made their own furniture from drygoods boxes—but only for a time. On a November morning in 1885, Senator and Mrs. Stanford gathered a group of men in their Nob Hill home in San Francisco and presented to them the founding grant of Stanford University. Without ostentation and seemingly the least impressed of all present, the Senator deeded over to this board of trustees 83,200 acres of the richest farmlands in California, and declared his intention of bequeathing to the institution the bulk of his estate, then estimated at $30,000,000. The world gasped. Never before had an educational institution come into existence on foundations so munificent. But that was the least cause for astonishment. There was not even a flag stop where the doors of the university were to open, nothing but unbroken stretches of grain. Furthermore, the university at Berkeley had not yet reached the 400 mark in its graduating classes, and, as the *New York Mail and Express* remarked, the need for another university at such close quarters was about as urgent as for "an asylum of decayed sea captains in Switzerland."

Nevertheless, the very daring of the enterprise, and the beauty and fitness of the Romanesque buildings as they arose, arcade on arcade, against the low tawny hills, together with the word broadcast by Dr. David Starr Jordan, "The winds of freedom blow!", drew a student body of 465 in the first year. Among that first generation were Herbert Hoover, Ray Lyman Wilbur, Vernon Kellogg, Holbrook Blinn, Will and Wallace Irwin, and Charles K. Field. It was Senator Stanford's idea that the university he had founded should be a place for specialization, with the primary emphasis on usefulness. In terms of this ideal the growth of the university has been molded, with the gradual elimination of work of general and elementary nature and the expansion of research and graduate studies. On the other hand, Mrs. Stanford's insistence was on the spirit of democracy, an objective aided by the fact that both students and faculty were necessarily resident on the campus, from the very earliest days when the great iron triangle sounded for communal "Grub!" As a consequence, it has become a Stanford claim that no student can consider his college career a success if, when he graduates, he is not known by his first name to at least three professors.

But pioneer education was not reserved for men only. On an acreage in the foothills of Alameda County, ideals of manners and "ladyhood" were taught young women who had no designation to set beside their names but some vague territorial address such as "Nevada." In a society founded by adventurers, this was indeed stemming the stream.

Dr. Cyrus Taggart Mills had reached California in the 1860's, then a man of middle age, his only fortune a small one acquired by missionary toil and close saving. Purchasing the ground where Mills College now stands, he transported to it Benicia Seminary, and under mansard roof and cupola "beautifully frescoed" within with well-meaning cherubs, garlands of roses, and be-ribboned musical instruments, Dr. Mills and his wife taught the daughters of miners "to spell correctly, to read naturally, to write legibly, and to converse intelligently."

Numerous other educational institutions arose during the 20 years after Mrs. Olive Mann Isbell taught her youngsters in a stable where she saw her wedding handkerchief used as a flag of truce to the Mexicans. In 1850 the Sisters of St. Dominic opened St. Catherine's Academy at Benicia; today as the Dominican College of San Rafael, it is particularly noted for its school of music. The University of San Francisco had its beginning five years later as St. Ignatius College, built on land described as "the sand dunes near the little town of San Francisco"—the present site of the Emporium. In 1863 Archbishop Alemany founded St. Mary's College, since transferred from San Francisco to Oakland and more recently to Moraga.

It is primarily in scientific discovery that the pioneer spirit now evinces itself, and it is in science that California scholars have made their greatest mark. In the Radiation Laboratory of the University of California stands a gigantic contrivance that looks like a Brobdingnagian cheese, but has been compared more appropriately to a huge machine gun. This cyclotron Dr. E. O. Lawrence directs against atoms—objects so small that the entire population of the world would require 10,000 years to count the number of them in a drop of water. Before Dr. Lawrence's experiments the only bullets powerful enough, and at the same time tiny enough, to crack through the nucleus of the atom were the natural emanations of radium, an extremely expensive commodity and one available in very small quantity. By means of the cyclotron the nuclei of a special type of hydrogen atom may be utilized for the same purpose. These nuclei, fired at the rate of a hundred thousand billion a second against whatever element is exposed to the machine, satisfy both the necessity for tremendous force and the necessity for infinitesimal smallness.

The reason for this vindictive effort to break up the innocent atom lies in the tremendous energies released by the cracking open of the atomic nuclei, energies which are the most tantalizing forces known to man. Already the atoms of all the available (some 30 different) elements have been blasted by the stream of so-called "deuterons" emitted by the machine. The rearrangement in pattern and size of the atomic nuclei of these elements has resulted in the realization of the old dream of the alchemists—the transmutation of one element into another, of platinum into iridium and gold, of bismuth into polonium and lead. It has resulted also in the creation of substances never yet found in nature, substances whose common characteristic is the fact that they are all radio-active. Several of these new forms show promise in the treatment of certain radio sensitive diseases. Even more sensational is the liberation of the "neutron ray," a ray similar to X-ray but far more effective in the treatment of tumorous and cancerous tissue, and now regarded as one of the most promising developments in the scientific fight against cancer.

Dr. Ernest Linwood Walker, quiet and sincere student, professor of tropical medicine in the University of California Medical School, some years ago swept aside the veil of superstition and fear which for thousands of years had blinded men to the real nature of leprosy. He was able to identify the bacterium cultivable from leprosy as a soil-growing organism, and he suggests, as an alternative hypothesis to contagion, the entrance of this soil bacterium into the human body through soil-contaminated wounds as the primary mode of infection in leprosy. Wild rats are subject to a leprosy-like disease, from which the same soil organism can be cultivated and for which a similar mode of infection is suggested. No longer were bells to be rung as the leper approached, and the dreadful cry, "Unclean!" go from mouth to mouth.

A housewife who opens a can of peaches is protected by a long series of intensive researches carried on in the university laboratories. Dr. Carl Meyer and his assistants, after working on the subject of botulism (food poisoning), were able to reduce poisoning from commercially packed foods to the extent that now there is actually more danger from foods preserved in the home.

In the Engineering Materials Laboratory, preparatory to the building of Hoover Dam, concrete was accorded unusual attention. It was tested by delicate instruments, in turn lovingly coddled and lovingly smashed and given ideal conditions and the worst conditions—in order that one of the engineering projects of the modern world might guard the waters of the Colorado River. Within adiabatic calorimeters—cork-lined rooms with doors like those of the refrigerator of a butcher shop —samples of various types of concrete were housed in cylindrical compartments; electrical resistance thermometers were imbedded in the concrete. The concrete was tested under various stages of dampness, with and without loads; its strength was measured in a universal testing machine of 4,000,000-pound capacity. Its durability was gauged under artificial weather conditions duplicating those to which the dam would be subjected. This testing laboratory has been concerned in an advisory capacity with engineering projects including the Colorado River Aqueduct into Los Angeles, the San Francisco-Oakland Bay Bridge, the

Golden Gate Bridge, Pine Canyon Dam, and Oakland's Broadway Tunnel.

At Stanford University aeronautical research has been carried on since the eve of America's entry into the World War, when Professors Durand and Lesley built their wind tunnel on the campus and started experimentation with airplane propellers on reduced scale models. This was real pioneering, for the problems were then virtually unattacked. Stanford is now recognized as the leading center in the United States for propeller research.

In the same way that research is integrated with the commercial life of the State, so also is it integrated with the life of California farmers, returning to them millions of dollars, saved through improved agricultural methods. In more than one curious instance, experiments carried on for the benefit of agriculture have had their effects in a totally different field of industry. When Charles B. Lipman, now Dean of the Graduate Division, and Dr. Aaron Gordon were engaged in the problem of treating pear-blight by injecting a poisonous solution in the trunks of the trees, it was hoped the solution would act on the bacteria causing the blight. Unfortunately it was not successful with pear trees, but it was remarkably successful with telephone poles. The problem now became a totally different one, that of protecting piles and timbers, used in marine construction and by power companies, from the depredations of various types of borers. The process, which is like embalming, consists in injection of the poisonous solution into the circulatory system of the living tree or cut pole. Practical tests on telephone poles and piles before they are cut have shown it to be a cheap and efficient method of protecting them from marauding organisms, fungi, and molds.

These are a few of the values immediately accessible and easily visualized by the layman who is interested in "results" from the State's educational system. Yet even in the liberal arts department, there is the eternal individual with warmly giving hands and heart fixed on the future. Josiah Royce, one of the truly great "great men" who have come from the University of California, speaks of climbing around under the eaves of Bacon Hall, where the books belonging to the old College of California were stored. There, where deep dust stood on ancient theological and scientific treatises, he gathered, according to his own statement, the most profound intellectual impressions of his life.

The immense collections of the present University Library came into being, step by step, with the gifts of individuals who had felt a similar debt to "book-learning." One of the most delightful of these collections is lodged in the Morrison Library, on the ground floor of the building. The story of its foundation parallels Walter Scott's preface to *Quentin Durward*. Just as Sir Walter was introduced by the fantastic Marquis de Hautlieu, with many apologies for tattered tapestry and tenant owls, to the turret room of a ruined castle where were deposited "the precious relics of a most splendid library," so, demurring in housewifely fashion for the untidiness of the attic, the widow of Alexander F. Morrison led her guests, one evening after dinner, to a garret lit up like an Aladdin's cave with the splendor of 15,000 books which she wished to give to the university as a memorial to her husband. These books, so vital a part of her own life, were not to be swallowed in the catacombs of the stacks, but were to form a room of their own where students, sans notebooks, might genuinely recreate themselves intellectually.

The Bancroft Library is, of course, one of the most important of the individual collections, and becomes each year increasingly the center of research for students of the history of the Pacific Slope and Hispanic America. Scholars in constantly larger numbers come from the East and abroad to consult these rich manuscripts and printed materials. Similarly unique in its own field is the Hoover Library on War, Revolution, and Peace, at Stanford, containing documents relating to the World War—government reports, unofficial publications, periodicals, books, pamphlets, and manuscripts, some of so confidential a nature that they will not be available for use for 40 years.

It has been said that the degree of civilization attained by any nation may be estimated from the provision it makes for study of the stars. Certainly, paradoxical as it may seem, no one has ever asked that Lick Observatory show its credentials in the shape of "practical" benefits. The discovery of a fifth moon in Jupiter or a shadowy duplicate streak across Mars has satisfied the public mind as much as an honest piece of cement or the last meal of a mealy-bug issuing from the university laboratories. This tolerance for sidereal phenomena is, as a matter of fact, a good deal more respectable than the tolerance which James Lick himself felt for starry matters. It is said of him that he "had never looked through anything larger than a ship's spy-glass," and when he was consulted at his Alviso flour mill in 1887 on the subject of a university foundation for scientific studies, he "listened patiently, but it made no more impression on him than on the fruit trees" he was walking under. Yet he founded—for what reason no one can surmise—the observatory on Mount Hamilton, one of the seven branches of the University of California. There, in the base of the pier on which the observatory rests, rests also the body of James Lick.

And there, through telescopes a good deal larger than a ship's spy-glass, have been discovered the several satellites of Jupiter additional to the four discovered by Galileo in 1610. There have occurred the first great successes in photographing comets and the Milky Way, teaching more about the structure, formation, and dissolution of the comet's tail than had been learned in all previous time. There the sulky steps of the young blue stars have been measured, the staid stride of the middle-aged yellow stars, and the fine gallop of the old red stars. There the advance through space of our own solar system has been set at 12.2 miles per second in the direction of the constellation of Hercules. Whether this would have meant much or little to James Lick, no one can say, for he "wot not of it" under his fruit trees at Alviso.

Notoriously unexciting as is the history of education, the hardihood of those first California educators—considered now from a safe distance in time—seems no less awe-inspiring than the hardihood of their contemporaries who forged across the Sierra Nevada, seeking gold. For the apathy they faced and overcame was no less cold and cruel than the Sierra. Nevertheless they opened school in stable and tent. And it is still their day—the day of the pioneer—in the halls now decently clad with stucco and adorned with drinking fountains, while the chimes of Berkeley's Campanile proclaim the international frontiers of education, ringing out, slowly and liquidly, a tune from Heine or an old English carol or "The Goden Bear."

ARGONAUTS OF LETTERS

In 1864 an earthquake damaged San Francisco but left Oakland unharmed. Discussion ensued as to the reason for Oakland's invulnerability. Bret Harte, citing "Schwappelfurt, the celebrated German geologist," endeavored to explain the singular fact by suggesting that there are some things the earth cannot swallow. Whether Harte's affection for Oakland was paralleled by a similar affection for San Francisco is a question; he was given a job in the mint so that he could write stories, but as soon as he had written the stories he left and went to wear his green gloves in Boston and to part his Dundreary whiskers in London.

Bret Harte is not the only writer who, wearing the local label, conducted himself with an astonishing resistance toward this geographical section. Harte left it bodily. Mark Twain, Joaquin Miller, and others found the city's frank money grubbing and social vulgarity unbearable. Boston and New York, London and Paris seemed to offer a more soothing atmosphere for artistic nerves jangled by such excesses of gross materialism. And yet Harte endowed California with its earliest literary prestige. He discovered and romanticized the Argonauts, at a time when it could be said of the urban intellectuals of whom he was one, that, like the Hangtown girls,

> "They're dreadful shy of forty-niners,
> Turn their noses up at miners."

And there is ironic justice in the fact that once he had created the Argonaut of California fiction, he tucked up his mustachios and departed.

It is the California setting, particularly the setting of San Francisco —its place on the sea, facing the Orient, with its back to the mines— which alone has inspired in its writers a continuity of tradition. The region gave elbow room for the unpredictable expansion of certain individual writers, elbow room they would not have had elsewhere. The effect has been what some critics call the "virility" of Californian literature. This is the one tradition to which it is possible to point—the defining effect of the region on its writers.

San Francisco's literary beginnings were its pioneer journals—the first of which, the *Golden Era,* was founded in 1852 by J. MacDonough Foard and Rollin M. Daggett. In March 1857 the *Golden Era* printed a slight, sentimental poem, "The Valentine," signed "Bret." Its author followed with more verses and sketches. Another contributor was Samuel Langhorne Clemens, a young Missourian, signing himself Mark Twain. The two men met soon after May 1864, while Clemens was employed on the *Call,* which shared a building with the local United States Mint. Later Harte became temporary editor of the *Californian,* and engaged Clemens to write regularly for the publication. Harte laid the foundation for Western romance, and Twain crystallized Western humor.

Harte played the more irrational, the more unpredictable part, and in this way the more truly "Californian" part; for scarcely a year before the appearance of *The Luck of Roaring Camp,* he was writing editorials (as editor of *The Overland Monthly*) on the unromantic ugliness of such place names as Poker Flat and Red Dog Gulch, advising young writers to steer away from the appellation "honest miner," since "the less said about the motives of some of our pioneers the better; very many were more concerned in getting away from where they were, than in going to any particular place." And in his editorial in the second number of *The Overland Monthly* he prophesied that it would be 300 years before the red shirts of the pioneers would become romantic and their high boots heroic. One of the worst of prophets, he had just finished writing the story that would do more than anything else to make the red shirts romantic and the high boots heroic. It was contained in the same issue.

The Luck of Roaring Camp had more than its author's own resistance to his environment to overcome. The resistance of proofreader and printer was so strenuous that it was almost still-born—and American local-color with it. Cherokee Sal's profession shocked the young lady who read proof. A reference to obstetrics threw her into hysterics. And finally Kentuck's exclamation over the baby—"The d——d little cuss!"—brought her hurriedly to the printer, who shared her appalled conviction that the story should never see the light. Dictatorial interference alone saved it for the August number of the *Overland.* What happened then was a publishing miracle, which brought offers from the *Atlantic Monthly,* a letter from Charles Dickens, and an announcement from Henry Adams that there was just one hopeful thing in a hopeless world—Bret Harte.

Harte is usually associated with the Argonauts of '49 and '50, whereas he is a writer of the later fifties and the sixties, writing of "the disused ditches, the scarred flats, the discarded levels, ruined flumes, and roofless cabins." His Yuba Bill he very probably rode beside, on some dusty stagecoach, but as he himself says in *A Lonely Ride:* "The road from Wingdam to Slumgullion (that is, in the heart of the mining country) knew no other banditti than the regularly licensed hotel-keepers." Harte's Indians were the Indians whose carcasses he saw floated by the raft-load down to Uniontown after a cutthroat revel of some upstanding citizens inspired by whisky and manifest destiny. His "heathen Chinee," who "for ways that are dark and for tricks that are vain" was so very peculiar, was one of the unfortunates who were being attacked with all the violence of anti-oriental chauvinism.

California "romance" and California "savagery" of the sort that appeared in Harte's writing give striking point to the story told by Mark Twain of how Harte drew the railroad tracks under the grizzly bear for the *Overland's* title-page. A grizzly, the old grizzly that had been the State's totem ever since the Bear Flag days, had been selected as emblem for the *Overland Monthly.* The grizzly was drawn, engraved and printed, but he seemed a very lonely bear. "As a bear, he was a success—he was a good bear—" says Mark. "But then, he was an objectless bear—a bear that *meant* nothing in particular . . . simply stood there snarling over his shoulder at nothing . . . But presently Harte took a pencil and drew these two simple lines under his feet and behold he was a magnificent success! the ancient symbol of California savagery snarling at the approaching type of high and progressive Civilization, the first Overland locomotive!" This, however, was not the only significance of the symbol, as Harte would prove by his almost immediate departure down those tracks for an Eldorado that lay in the opposite direction, the direction of the East and Europe. He left California's "savagery" to John Muir, in whose gentle hands the mining camps were erased from the mountains; and California's "high and progressive Civilization" to Henry George, whose *Progress and Poverty* was to issue from San Francisco.

The unshorn gentry of the mining towns had at first provoked satire among San Francisco wits, and then, by Harte's unpredicted gesture, romance. But satire remained a strong undercurrent. Twain's description of the celebrated jumping frog of Calaveras County might be a typically monstrous understatement for the "honest miner" himself: "You never see a frog so modest and straightfor'ard as he was, for all he was so gifted. And when it come to fair and square jumping on a dead level, he could get over more ground at one straddle than any animal of his breed you ever see." Twain, who had adopted his pseudonym in 1863, mounted as a humorist on the back of this frog, for he wrote the sketch and won his first fame all in one leap. He remained in California from May 1864 until December 1866, and worked on the San Francisco *Morning Call* for a few months. Of the writers with whom he had contact, most were humorists: it was the typical humor of the Comstock Lode era that crystallized in his style at this time— coupling the tall tale of the barroom with excessive understatement. By the time he left California, his popularity in the East had become enormous. And like Harte, he sought those greener pastures.

Besides Harte and Mark Twain, the *Golden Era,* the *Californian,* and the *Overland* had other contributors whose fame spread beyond the local boundaries. Prentice Mulford's rollicking satire of frontier heroics found great favor. Charles Warren Stoddard, the poet, a close friend of Harte, later became the celebrated author of *South Sea Idyls* and *The Lepers of Molokai.* Ina Coolbrith, who contributed poems to the *Californian* under Harte's editorship, was many years afterward named the "poet laureate" of California. *Songs from the Golden Gate* contains many of her finest lyrics. Another distinguished contributor was Edward Rowland Sill, author of *The Hermitage* and other volumes of verse.

Joaquin (Cincinnatus Heine) Miller, "the Poet of the Sierras," was deeply impressed by the city's literary atmosphere when he first came to San Francisco as a young man. "I have seen the world well since," he said many years later, discussing the *Golden Era,* "yet those carpeted parlors, with Joe Lawrence and his brilliant satellites, outshine all things else, as I turn to look back." His name, Joaquin—replacing the ridiculous Cincinnatus Heine—was derived from Joaquin Murrieta, the Mexican outlaw in California. Miller's fame, however, originated not in San Francisco but in London, where he became a nine days' wonder as a fiery poet and a convincing representative of the "Wild West," with his high top boots, red flannel shirt, a sombrero, and his long hair falling, Indian-fashion, upon his shoulders. In his grandiloquent poetry he celebrated the deeds of pioneers, Indians, and bandits amid the natural marvels of the West. Except for "Columbus," which is still in the school boy's repertoire, he is remembered today for his attitudes rather than for his verse. In his hilltop eyrie, "The Hights" (*sic*), overlooking Oakland, he settled down, after his wanderings abroad, to practice his odd histrionics until his death in 1913.

Ambrose Bierce was another who found elbowroom for the development of an even more intense individuality, but the stamp of the region upon him was of a different sort. For a quarter of a century he was a

literary figure, *the* local literary figure, and the years which he dominated stretched into an era vastly different from the era of the Argonauts
as the "unutterably gorgeous" society of the 1860's gave way to the
sand-lot crusades of "the terrible seventies." This was the era of novels
such as *On the Verge,* abounding in voluptuous ladies at the pianoforte,
and in French quotations; of the poets such as Richard Realf, whose
record for bigamy won as much sympathy as his record for bad verse;
of essays on Petrarch and of editions of Heredia. It was the era of the
false front, and it showed even worse propensities in the eighties—Greek
porticos flanked by bay windows, Corinthian columns leading up flights
of wooden steps, conical towers, and Queen Anne flourishes. From
Nob Hill to Barbary Coast, barbarism and greed destroyed the possibility of good work in the arts.

This was Ambrose Bierce's domain. He declared himself in 1877
with the first issue of the *Argonaut:* "It is my intention," he said, "to
purify journalism in this town by instructing such writers as it is worth
while to instruct, and assassinating those that it is not." His column,
appearing consecutively from 1868 to 1900, was a vivid experience in
the lives of innumerable Westerners. He had deliberately set himself
the task of direct attack on individuals. It was his moral function, and
possibly the only function open to him in his time and in San Francisco.
His style he had acquired in the beaver-hat age, an age of gesture and
flourish; and he patched it together with ideas of "elegance" gained in
London, and delivered his opinions with a bludgeon-like ponderosity
suitable for denting the pates of a hoodlum citizenry. He himself
summed up his literary proclivities in a fable: "A rattlesnake came
home to its brood to die—I have been bitten by the editor of a partisan
journal, it said."

Irony indeed—and poetic justice, perhaps—in the career of this
Titan who had San Francisco for his malfeasant Olympus, is the very
name of the column which carried his "homicidal paragraphs": *Prattle.*
Another irony is his mysterious end in Mexico, trailed by apocryphal
tales of an old man shot by a firing squad. Still another is the end met
by those disciples who called him "Master"—Herman Scheffauer, who
took his own life in a Berlin hotel, and George Sterling, who committed suicide in San Francisco's Bohemian Club. But these futilities
cannot be laid at Bierce's door, by calling him, as some critics have done,
a "death man." The style of the time, in a community of contradictions, was morbid. Bierce's own style, if it is measured in terms of the
resistance he put up to those contradictions, was one of tremendous
vitality.

To combat those same contradictions required even more vitality of
Bierce's successors. From an Oakland cannery, where ten hours a day
of taut nerves prevented a moment's attention to the frequent victims

who had their fingers snapped off by the machinery, Jack London was graduated to become "the prince of the oyster pirates." He has indicated the reason for his choice of a profession: "Every raid . . . was a felony. The penalty was state imprisonment, the stripes and the lock-step. And what of that? The men in stripes worked a shorter day than I at my machine." With Whiskey Bob, Joe Goose, Nicky the Greek, Soup and Stew Kennedy, Clam Bart, Irish and Oyster Kelly, Patsy Haggerty, Harmonica Joe, Hell and Blazes, and young Scratch Nelson of the monumental shoulders, he discovered the social conditions which fecundated his talent. Having nearly forfeited his life to a Chinese shrimp poacher who marooned him on an island off the Marin shore—a story he tells in *Tales of the Fish Patrol*—he learned enough wit to leave oyster pirating and seek the primitive salt in a three-topmast schooner bound for a larger universe.

The Sea-Wolf, The Call of the Wild—these titles indicate not only London's place in space, on a bay crowded with ships that offered adventure far from "the man-city and its snarling roar"; they indicate also his place in time, when the romantic gesturer had to turn from Oscar Wilde's hothouse, and go hunting with "huskies" on the last big hunt before the world closed up its frontiers. Lonodon came back from the South Seas and wrote of nut-brown queens, who sat on swan-skins and greeted a chance traveler thus: "Stranger, I reckon you're sure the first white man that ever set foot in this valley. Set down an' talk a spell, and then we'll have a bite to eat. Which way might you be comin'?" And of primitive Teutons in the clothes of James Ward of Ward, Knowles and Company, who dictated to their stenographers by day and chased coyotes on the hills of Mill Valley by night.

But California's most spectacular and widely read California author was much more than a romantic gesturer. London's social philosophy was direct and radical. And the themes he dealt with were those of elemental physical conflict. In the handling of swift action he has scarcely been surpassed. Superlatively strong men stalk through his books, which were based directly on his own experiences. *Martin Eden* and *John Barleycorn* are semi-fictionized accounts of his own life, alternating between infantile romanticism and profound disillusionment. Mostly self-educated, he wrote, in 16 years, 43 volumes, besides acting as war correspondent and cruising in his yacht, the *Snark*. He died at his ranch in Glen Ellen, California, in 1916, of uremia.

He had long been a victim of ill health, disappointments at the hands of his friends, overwork in order to maintain a large establishment, and that battle against drink described in *John Barleycorn*. As a voice of his time and region, a spinner of yarns, a furious prophet, London is remembered by an audience probably larger than that of any other American author.

In this period, Frank Norris comes closest to the accent of greatness. And misses it. While London wrote of James Ward, who puzzled philologists at the University of California by his chants in primitive Germanic, Norris wrote of McTeague of McTeague's Dental Parlors, whose ambition was to have projecting from the corner window over Polk Street "a huge gilded tooth, a molar with enormous prongs, something 'gorgeous and attractive." While London wrote of Klondike huskies, Norris wrote of B Street Station:

"Near the station a bit of fence painted with a cigar advertisement reeled over into the mud, while under its lee lay an abandoned gravel wagon with dished wheels . . . Across the flats, at the fringe of the town, were the dump heaps, the figures of a few Chinese ragpickers moving over them . . . Across the railroad tracks, to seaward, one saw the long stretch of black mud bank left bare by the tide, which was far out, nearly half a mile. Clouds of seagulls were forever rising and settling upon this mud bank; a wrecked and abandoned wharf crawled over it on tottering legs; close in an old sailboat lay canted on her bilge . . ."

In the dynamic fictions of Frank Norris and Jack London an awareness of social forces is more evident than in any earlier Western writing. Norris, who came to California from Chicago at fourteen years of age, laid his early novels, *Blix, Vandover and the Brute,* and *McTeague,* in San Francisco. The essence of the city's life—at North Beach, Telegraph Hill, Nob Hill, Russian Hill, the Polk Street district—is reflected, although not without certain youthful exaggeration, in their pages. Norris determined to explore, on a large scale, the economic mainsprings of society. *The Octopus* and *The Pit* were the two first volumes of an intended trilogy, "The Epic of Wheat." In *The Octopus* is depicted the stranglehold of a railroad on California wheat growers and the entire State. *The Pit* is placed in Chicago, the world's wheat market. The third volume, *The Wolf,* to have been an account of the consumers of wheat the world over, was never written. In the midst of his ambitious plans, Norris died at the age of 32. Although marred by melodramatic excesses, a confusing tinge of mysticism, and an apparent lack of clear understanding of the issues involved, his novels, in their search for truth, in their tone, stand as distinguished landmarks at the threshold of the era of realism in American letters.

The society which London attacked with merciless fury and Norris probed with surgical ruthlessness was gently scolded in *The Lark,* edited by Gelett Burgess in the nineties, which for the whole of its two years sustained a wondrous buoyancy. It was read throughout the country, though Burgess often mocked the staid with such ditties as:

> "I love to go to Lectures,
> And make the Audience Stare,
> By walking 'round upon their heads,
> And spoiling People's hair!"

Conventional readers tolerated his nonsense because Burgess always kept it "clean" and because it was young as they never had been young; its more sophisticated comments escaped them, being whispered, as Albert Parry says, "in exquisite innuendo." Its chief contributors were Ernest Peixotto, Bruce Porter, Florence Lundborg, Carolyn Wells, Yone Noguchi—besides Burgess, whose "Purple Cow" classic first appeared in its pages. The New York *Times* nicknamed the group *Les Jeunes*. It was abandoned while still thriving and making money because, as Burgess wrote to Carolyn Wells, "I wanted it to die young and in its full freshness." Its whole staff, except Noguchi, moved to New York. But Burgess remembered San Francisco, for in *The Heart Line* he satirized both practitioners and victims of palmistry and astrology, cults which have always thrived in a city where so many have lived dangerously.

After the turn of the century an increasing number of young San Franciscans hoping for a career in literature yearned toward the cultural centers in the East and Europe; but many still received their impetus from the local scene. "The Man With the Hoe," published in a San Francisco newspaper, made famous overnight the young San Jose poet, Edwin Markham. The coterie of writers who frequently met at Papa Coppa's restaurant during the years just preceding the earthquake and fire of 1906 included Jack London, Wallace and Will Irwin, the short-story writer James Hopper, the imperious and aging Ambrose Bierce and his two brilliant pupils, poets Herman Scheffauer and George Sterling. Having learned from Bierce nothing of that writer's Swiftian vigor but only his magniloquence, Sterling was invoking in such volumes as *The Testimony of the Suns* a Platonic idea of California scenery, largely in the colors of purple and crystal. The Irwins each celebrated the Chinatown of the pre-fire era—Will in *Pictures of Old Chinatown* and Wallace in *Chinatown Ballads;* after the fire, Will wrote a requiem for "The City That Was," while Wallace, who had gained his early fame with such verses as *Love Sonnets of a Hoodlum,* turned to novel writing.

Charles Caldwell Dobie, 26 at the time of the fire—when he helped his mother transport the family treasures beyond the reach of the flames —was later to describe the more picturesque aspects of the city as it had been in *San Francisco: A Pageant, San Francisco Tales,* and *San Francisco's Chinatown.* Another of those for whom the "days of old, days of gold" have provided a rich vein to tap for literary purposes is Stewart Edward White, author of *The Gray Dawn* and *The Forty-Niners.*

Even before the turn of the century Gertrude Atherton's literary explorations had been leading her back to California's Spanish beginnings. She wrote of Magdalena Yorba, half-Spanish and born tongue-tied, and of her father, Don Roberto, a bank president, who practiced "hip-hip-hooray!" in his study and hanged himself with the American flag. From the Spanish period, which she celebrated in *The Dooms-woman, The Californians, The Splendid Idle Forties,* and *Rezanov,* she went on to the American era in *Ancestors* and *Patience Sparhawk,* and then, having covered California, shifted to Montana, Greece and Africa. *Rezanov,* love story of the visiting Russian officer and the San Francisco Presidio *comandante's* daughter, probably has remained her most popular novel. In *Adventures of a Novelist* (1932) she looks back on the five decades of her literary career.

Charles Norris, like his brother Frank, writes "to make people think." Characteristic of his novels—conceived on a less ample scale than those of his brother—are *Brass,* an attempt to present different phases of "what we understand by marriage"; *Pig-Iron,* concerned with the materialistic influence on American life; and *Bricks Without Straw,* dealing with the ever recurring battle of ideals between parents and children. His wife, Kathleen Norris, who in her early youth was a San Francisco newspaper woman and a contributor to local periodicals, completes the noted family; since her first published volume, *Mother* (1911), which went into numerous editions, she has written almost 50 novels, all observing the proprieties of middle-class family life.

Even Gertrude Stein, when she turned to description of the local scene in *The Making of Americans,* wrote of a vanished yesterday—of her girlhood in an old-fashioned house with verandas amid the tangled rambler roses and eucalyptus trees of suburban Oakland. But the post-war writers have now been succeeded by post-post-war writers who have put nostalgia behind them. William Saroyan might have been born anywhere—anywhere that there was a colony of Armenians—but he happens to have been born in the San Joaquin Valley, and the majority of his earlier stories reflect his goings to and fro about the rich valley earth and that much of the cosmos located between Carl Street, San Francisco, and the Civic Center.

"I want you to know," he writes, "that it is very cold in San Francisco today, and that I am freezing . . ." Or he tries it on another tack: "I am out here in the far West, in San Francisco, in a small room on Carl Street, writing a letter to common people, telling them in simple language things they already know." Out of these trivia—blue fingers for the writer, things they already know for the readers—comes Theodore Badal, the Assyrian barber on Third Street; comes young "Iowa," gone north with his yellow hair and hope; comes the daring young man himself, turning his "lost face to the empty sky."

John Steinbeck has been gathering California local color all his life and has turned it to account in several books, most powerfully and angrily in his recent novel, *The Grapes of Wrath.* In a curious—but perhaps not an accidental—way, Saroyan and Steinbeck recall "with variations" some of the earlier phases of literature in the region. The he-man of the 1890's is re-born in William Saroyan, born with the proper cosmopolitan note of Armenian hair and with the genuine mid-century stamp of a depression-starvation appetite. A virility less flamboyant than Jack London's—because it had no Klondikes in which to exercise—none the less manifests itself in the immediacy of Saroyan's style, in his simple, undetailed human sympathies. And finally, John Steinbeck has made as disturbing a figure in the Nation's literary scene as any California writer by bringing to its culmination that "local-color" fiction for which Bret Harte—and California literature along with him —became famous.

ART AND ARTISTS

Of all Apollo's embattled stepchildren who have attempted to create works of artistic value amid the Bay region's turbulent economic development, few have achieved so much as its painters and sculptors. Enormous is the variety of their work—much of it derivative and mediocre, some of it distinguished by originality. If theirs is not yet a tradition of masterpieces, they nevertheless have put behind them almost a century of aesthetic ferment, of tireless experimentation.

San Franciscans, whatever their qualifications for aesthetic judgment, have always been outspoken critics of their city's art and artists. Before a monument may be erected or a mural finished, citizens from the mayor downwards must have their say. A minority opinion recently delivered by members of the Art Commission—the city's final arbiter of art works and public buildings—condemned the proposed erection of Beniamino Bufano's gigantic statue of St. Francis on Twin Peaks. "It looks like a holdup," they said of the design for this 156-foot figure of stainless steel with arms upraised in supplication; and local factions were aroused anew by a syndicated columnist's Nation-wide crusade against what he termed "God-awful statuary" as represented by Bufano's unorthodox model. This controversy had been preceded by the public turmoil attending the painting of murals in the Coit Tower, which was marked by political tail-twisting such as Diego Rivera practiced on his patrons in his Rockefeller Center murals in New York. To bring this hectic tradition up to date, Hilaire Hiler threatened to leave uncompleted his murals in the lobby of Aquatic Park unless plans were abandoned to install furniture not in keeping with his decorative motif. The files of the *Alta California*, the *Wasp,* the *Overland Monthly,* and the *News-Letter* offer plentiful testimony, in saltier epithets of earlier decades, that such controversies are by no means confined to the present generation.

The plastic arts have been a product and a reflection of the cultural growth of the Bay region, and of San Francisco in particular. As the rough-and-ready decades of the Gold Rush passed, a kind of poker-faced conservatism settled on the metropolis dominated by the bonanza millionaires. Its culture froze in the urbane, ornamental, shock-proof mold of the 1880's and remained always slightly out-of-date until rejuvenated after the calamity of 1906. Its painters, depending wholly on the patronage of a *nouveau riche* society, offered productions acceptable to a clientele whose tastes were dictated by extravagant notions that had nothing to do with art. In their imitation villas and chateaux the families of the bonanza elite wanted interior decoration that would be "elegant" and dazzling and grand, something flamboyant enough to impart an overwhelming impression of social prestige. Whenever these "cultural accoutrements" could not be produced locally in sufficient quantity, all Europe was ransacked for an astonishing assortment of paintings, sculpture, stained glass, tapestries, furniture, and bric-a-brac. The result, as that gaudy generation's sophisticated and refined descendants laughingly acknowledge, was hideous and absurd.

For those Bay region artists who had to put up with such nonsense this was an environment that sorely tested their professional integrity. But despite the perversion of public taste, which characterized American life generally during the nineteenth century, the majority of the Bay region's painters and sculptors devoted themselves to their work with uncompromising sincerity. And eventually, out of all the mass of spurious importations, were established those collections and exhibitions of both European and native art by which the public has been educated to appreciate the significance of local craftsmen and their colleagues abroad. Out of the aesthetic confusion of the bonanza era have evolved those art schools and museums which have helped to create a new synthesis of the welter of artistic influences.

If, as John P. Young's history of San Francisco points out, most of the city's literati in the 1860's ignored the local scene, "no such accusation can be brought against the painters of the period, for their subjects were almost wholly Californian." Pioneer of this California School was the artist of whom the *Alta California's* discerning critic observed: "Few men dare paint flesh, against a pink cushion, Nahl has dared, and won (!)" This was with reference to Charles Christian Nahl's (1818-75) three separate renderings of *The Rape of the Sabine Women.* Painted in the pseudo-classical manner of the Düsseldorf School, this romantic work was long considered his masterpiece. Unfortunately for his reputation, many of his more relevant and minutely authentic studies of Gold Rush scenes have either been scattered among private collections or lost. Though the M. H. de Young Memorial Museum contains some of his paintings, his most representative works, including *The Fandango* and *Sunday at the Mines,* are in the E. B. Crocker Art Gallery at Sacramento. Descendant of a long line of German artists, Nahl was indebted to his ancestry for what talent he had. In subject matter and technique he was influenced by the classic revival and by his early studies under Horace Vernet in Paris.

Expert draughtsman that he was, Nahl revealed in his canvases a love of detail for its own sake which make them primarily exercises in careful documentation: genre paintings in which the sitter for a portrait, accompanied by his favorite domestic animals, appears against a bucolic background of his own countryside. His restless energy and versatility enabled him to make hundreds of drawings for engravers, supplying popular demands for illustrations depicting Gold Rush scenes. His designs for the 18 woodcuts in Alonzo Delano's *The Idle and Industrious Miner, a Tale of California Life* are a marvel of draughtmanship which enliven with droll humor that collection of melodramatic verses. "It was inevitable," says Eugen Neuhaus in his appraisal of Nahl, "that a man of his innate endowments and extraordinary powers of observation should be inspired to depict in his own medium . . . the early California glorified by Bret Harte . . . ; and it is from these pictorial records that we today get by far the best idea of those stirring times. . . . The Nahl who will live in the annals of art is not the painter of remote, academic historical scenes; it is the artist of the life in the California mines, as lived by an adventurous, polyglot society of Americans, Indians, Mexicans, and Europeans, of which he himself was a part."

Painting in California would have remained a purely provincial art had not the literature of the Gold Rush with its wondrous accounts of the natural scenery of the West publicized for the Atlantic seaboard and for Europe the Sierra Nevada's fabulous grandeur. To the "increasing astonishment and reverential awe and rapture" of millions of Americans, the "California School" arose to rival those landscape painters who were glorifying the Hudson River Valley. Prodigious as these Hudson River wonders appeared, they presumably could be put to shame by more gigantic representations of the "magnificent scenery of that marvellous region, where the roar of the cataract and the roll of the thunder reverberate like the tread of the countless millions who evermore march to the westward."

If today the vast landscapes painted by Albert Bierstadt (1830-1902) seem impressive only in size, they nevertheless furnish a commentary on the popular taste which once acclaimed them as masterpieces. Their depiction of cyclopean gorges and mountain peaks—with every detail, down to the minutest leaf and pebble, described with an exactitude approaching photography—have also a certain expansive gusto which must have appealed to a public thrilled by the first full flowering of its national spirit. Bierstadt, born in Düsseldorf and brought to America as a child, came West with General Lander's expedition of

1858. His *Rocky Mountains,* a huge canvas of ponderous detail and uncertain perspective, "threw the people into an ecstasy of delight" and he "bounded at one step to celebrity." S. G. W. Benjamin, whose *Art in America* confutes some of the prevailing artistic credos of his generation, remarks that since Bierstadt was "naturally an artist of great ability and large resources," he "might easily have maintained a reputation as such if he had not grafted on the sensationalism of Düsseldorf a greater ambition for notoriety and money than for success in pure art."

Bierstadt's contemporary, who succeeded him as "artist in waiting to the Yosemite Valley," was Thomas Hill (1829-1908). Beginning his career as a coach painter, Hill depicted panoramic views of entire mountain ranges which constituted the *reductio ad absurdum* of the California School's approach to landscape painting. His celebrity, like Bierstadt's, was spectacular; but today the works of these two boosters of Western natural scenery are looked upon as curiosities of a fabulous epoch.

The reputation of Thomas Moran (1837-1926) has suffered less from the refinement of popular taste than either of these flamboyant representatives of the California School. Having studied abroad, he enriched his canvases with the influence of Turner. If in his own time his works received less vociferous acclaim than inferior productions, his solid talent is today being appreciated. With William Keith's, the landscapes of Moran represent the best accomplishments—almost the sum and substance—of the California School.

Like Bierstadt, Hill, and Moran, Toby Edward Rosenthal (1848-1916) achieved celebrity abroad. Born in New Haven, Connecticut, he studied in San Francisco with the Mexican painter, Fortunato Arriola, in Munich at the Royal Academy, and with Raupp and Piloty. After gaining local fame, he maintained a studio in Munich, where he turned out excellent examples of the solid craftsmanship, the minuteness of literal detail, the sentiment and the "homely philosophy" of the Munich school of genre painters. His method of painting was laborious, scholarly; he spent three years in literary research, travel, and sketching to produce a single canvas, *The Trial of Constance de Beverley* (illustrating Scott's *Marmion*), now in the possession of Stanford University. "I have spared," he wrote in 1882 while at work on it, "no labor, time, nor money in my endeavour to make *Marmion* my greatest work," and the remark reveals his attitude toward painting; to him. it was related to archeology, literature, philosophy. Only incidentally, however, can Rosenthal be considered a Bay region painter. His *The Cardinal's Portrait* and the *Seine Madonna,* both at the California Palace of the Legion of Honor, keep his curious local reputation alive.

It was only natural, once the novelty of wealth had begun to wear off and a new generation had been born to inherit it, that the patrons of art should take their cultural ambitions less casually. It was inevitable, too, that artists of the Bay area should forsake the old methods and adopt the technique of the Barbizon School—exemplified by such painters as Corot and Millet, who strove to render nature in her aspects of light and air rather than in pictorial detail. Yet' of the San Francisco painters who came under the influence of the forerunners of Impressionism, only one seems to have gained a lasting distinction.

William Keith (1838-1911), born in Scotland, came to California in 1859. Eschewing the colossal marvels so loved by Bierstadt and Hill, he translated the more benign aspects of the lower altitudes into turgid, dreamy landscapes, painted with the molasses-like *impasto* that was a fault common to the Düsseldorf School, resulting from the use of bitumen. He was content to paint brooding and tranquil landscapes— the interplay of light and shade in groves of live oaks, forest glades, hillsides, and brooks. His style relates him somewhat to the Barbizon school; his lyric tranquillity, to George Inness, who was his intimate friend. His ambition, like Vincent Van Gogh's, was to achieve with paint the effect of music. Often he succeeded. Unfortunately, his use of bitumen to achieve subtlety of tone has caused many of the paintings to fade into indistinctness. Keith was the only California painter to whom a whole room was devoted in the United States section of the Panama-Pacific International Exposition's Fine Arts Galleries, yet until recently he has remained almost unknown outside the State. At the Keith Memorial Gallery in St. Mary's College at Moraga and at the Bohemian Club in San Francisco are many of his paintings.

The influence of Keith was strong on the minor painters who banded together in the Bohemian Club after its foundation in 1872. Little of the California sunlight is reflected in Arthur Mathews' somber work, but his murals in the Mechanics'-Mercantile Library, in the Lane Medical Library, and in the Masonic Temple illustrate an architect's sense of values. Typical of Gottardo Piazzoni's conventionalized California seacoast and hill country landscapes are his Public Library murals, subdued in tone. A sincere and accomplished landscapist, Xavier Martinez settled in Piedmont to paint the quiet beauties of the East Bay hill country in a number of canvases owned by the Oakland Art Gallery. Other Bohemians were Bruce Porter, architect and mural painter; Charles Dickman and Henry Joseph Breuer, landscapists.

Twenty-three local artists organized in 1871 the San Francisco Art Association and the following year opened headquarters in a loft-like gallery over a market, where as a visitor to their spring exhibitions put it, "Art was pervaded with the aroma of fish and the sound of the butcher's cleaver was heard." With a collection of casts of classic statuary—the gift of the Republic of France to this gallant undertaking of culture in the Far West—the association opened its school in 1874 with Virgil Williams as master. From such humble beginnings the association was elevated when Edward F. Searles, who had married Mark Hopkins' widow, presented it in 1893 with the Nob Hill castle of the railroad tycoon. The house was described by Amelia Ransome Neville as "a mess of anachronisms. One entered portals of a feudal castle to pass into the court of a doge's palace, all carved Italian walnut with a gallery around the second story where murals of Venetian scenes were set between the arches. These were the work of Jules Tavernier, French artist, who stopped in California after a trip to the South Seas, where he painted long before Gaugin." In gratitude, the association named its school the Mark Hopkins Institute of Art.

The first California sculptor whose name reached beyond the State was Douglas Tilden (1860-1935) who, himself deaf from the age of five, studied in Paris with the deaf-mute sculptor Paul Chopin. At intersections along San Francisco's Market Street, the heroic-style commemorative monuments for which he was famous overlook the passing traffic—the *Mechanics' Monument* with its three brawny artisans straining to force a huge mechanical punch through a plate of metal, the *Native Sons' Monument* with its bronze miner waving a flag, the *Spanish War Monument* with its young soldier marching beside an equestrian Victory. Public parks and squares are plentifully adorned with the sculpture of such pupils of Tilden's as Robert Ingersoll Aitken (1878—), sculptor of the *Victory Monument* in Union Square and the *William McKinley Monument* in Golden Gate Park, and M. Earl Cummings (1876-1936), sculptor of the *Hall McAllister Monument* beside the City Hall and the *Robert Burns Monument* in Golden Gate Park.

To the rest of the country until recent years, however, Tilden's self-taught younger contemporary, Arthur Putnam (1873-1930), was almost the personification of California sculpture. From youthful experience in riding, driving cattle, working in the forest, and laboring in a South San Francisco slaughterhouse, Putnam gained a remarkable knowledge of animal life, tamed and untamed. Masterful in composition, his bronze lions, leopards, and pumas show close observation, a thorough knowledge of animal anatomy, and a sensitive feeling for rhythm and movement. His figures of children, rabbits, and fish equal in charm his savage subjects. Among his best known works are *The Snarling Jaguar* in New York's Metropolitan Museum and *The Death* in the Boston Museum. The California Palace of the Legion of Honor has a collection of 130 of his works.

At the Panama-Pacific International Exposition in 1915 (where Putnam was represented only by an ornate mermaid fountain modelled from his designs—described by Sheldon Cheney as "typical of the fine strength of his work, and at the same time appealing by the grace of its sinuous lines") one of his students, Ralph Stackpole, was exhibiting a variety of sculpture, including *The Man with a Pick,* which was "justly admired as a sincere portrayal of a simple laboring type," and an unnamed kneeling figure by the Palace of Fine Arts lagoon, "one of the most appealing bits of all the Exposition sculpture, well expressing devotion and reverence." Another young San Francisco sculptor represented was Haig Patigian, whose bas-relief friezes and four nude male figures —*Steam Power, Invention, Electricity,* and *Imagination*—for the Palace of Machinery served "to carry out the sense of immensity and strength that characterizes the entire building," although "lacking the refinement that would make them interesting as something besides vigorous types."

The wealth of sculpture and painting displayed at the 1915 exposition was to "focus the artistic expression" of San Francisco Bay region artists as the art of the Columbian Exposition at Chicago had done for the artists of the Nation. The "far-reaching effect" of the Panama-Pacific Exposition, wrote Cheney, was to show "the immense value of coordination of all the arts . . . The great thing here is the complete harmony of purpose, of design, and of color, in the combined work of architects, sculptors, painters, and landscape gardeners." It had the farther-reaching effect, perhaps, of educating public taste to the point where for the first time local artists could begin to expect informed criticism of their work.

Judging "the first definite exposition of the new point of view crystallized by the influence of the Panama-Pacific International Exposition," a critic of the San Francisco Art Association's Forty-second Annual Exhibition was pleased to note that at last "the noble lines of the California hills are being painted without pseudo-idealistic, romantic preconceptions." Comparing the canvases on view at the latter exhibition with "previous Western 'animals'," a critic in *The International Studio* found "almost no vestige of the 'brown sauce' school of yesterday" and little which was "reminiscent of Keith, Whistler, and the Barbizon School—three influences which, but a very short time ago, dominated the California annual exhibitions."

In the exposition's Palace of Fine Arts, the French section had exhibited "a number of examples of the new and ultra-new schools, from Monet and Degas to Redon and Puy." During the quarter-century interval before San Francisco staged its next exposition, local artists began to modify their styles under influences even more revolutionary— Cézanne, Van Gogh, Picasso, Rousseau, di Chirico, Dali, and the other godfathers of modern art. Among others, Lucien Labaudt and Jane Berlandina were successful in grafting the best traditions of French art upon the local heritage. Some of the influences were first-hand ones. Henri Matisse, for example, spent some time in San Francisco painting the Steinhart Aquarium's tropical fish. Foujita came to teach some of modern Japanese art's pellucid quality to a group which was naturally receptive to an oriental treatment of local materials. When the Mexican muralist, Diego Rivera, came to paint frescoes for the San Francisco Stock Exchange and the California School of Fine Arts, his influence on many of the local painters—Victor Arnautoff, Ralph Stackpole, and Bernard Zakheim, among others—was tremendous. The visit of German exile Hans Hoffman, the Munich abstractionist, to teach summer classes at the University of California greatly inspired a group of the younger East Bay artists, including Vaclav Vytlacil, Beckford Young, Edgar Dorsey Taylor, and Florence Swift. Hoffman became virtually the spiritual godfather of the East Bay group.

Even the California School of Fine Arts (as the Mark Hopkins Institute of Art had been renamed upon its removal to new quarters on Russian Hill in 1926), which had hitherto exhibited an academic bias, responded suddenly to the new influences. Feeling that the kind of painting they had learned abroad from followers of impressionism or pointillism, of Puvis de Chavannes and Maurice Denis, offered no further promise of development, many of the painters associated with the school became devotees of Cézanne. Two of these, Lee Randolph and Spencer Macky, studied briefly in Paris in 1926 under André Lhote, teacher and exponent of Cézanne's methods. The courses given here by Arnold Blanch and Maurice Sterne furthered the spread of modern influences. Meticulous craftsmen, the painters associated with the School of Fine Arts have come to be characterized, as a group, by a style variously described as neo-classicism and modern realism. Characteristic of the group were the late Rinaldo Cuneo and the late Frank Van Sloun. Otis Oldfield, Randolph, and Macky are still associated with it. Ray Boynton, formerly a member of this group, is now teaching at the University of California.

Aside from a series of exhibitions held at the Palace of Fine Arts following the 1915 exposition, no public galleries presented really comprehensive collections of foreign masterpieces until 1930. Lloyd Le Page Rollins, appointed director of San Francisco's California Palace of the Legion of Honor, then made it his policy to secure traveling exhibits of international importance. After his resignation in 1933 his policies were continued, with certain unavoidable reservations, by Dr. Walter Heil. In 1935 the San Francisco Art Museum in the Civic Center was opened under the competent, dynamic leadership of Dr. Grace McCann Morley. It has become a living center of education and appreciation of modern art. The response of the public has been remarkable; attendance figures at the shows brought from New York by the museum have approached, and in some instances exceeded, those of the larger city.

During the depression the earliest large government-supported mural job. the decoration of Coit Tower, undertaken by the Civil Works Administration in 1933, was a co-operative endeavor involving a number of San Francisco's best-known artists, including Ralph Stackpole, Bernard Zakheim, Lucien Labaudt, Victor Arnautoff, Otis Oldfield, Rinaldo Cuneo, John Langley Howard, William Hesthal, Jane Berlandina, Ray Boynton, and Maxine Albro. The murals, which show principally the influence of Diego Rivera, are as a whole distinguished by a high level of craftsmanship. The WPA Art Project's decoration of the Aquatic Park Casino lobby, the work of Hilaire Hiler and his associates, is, to date, one of the major accomplishments of the WPA Art Program in the West and one of its stellar achievements nationally. It is significant that people come daily to the building simply to look at the radiant fish depicted upon these walls and marvel at the technique by which they are made to seem not at rest, but alive with graceful movement.

Of Matthew Barnes, a San Francisco painter whose genius is now finally achieving national recognition, William Saroyan once wrote in the San Francisco *Call-Bulletin:* "As he sees it, the world is a place where all who live are no more than visitors . . . A lonely place. Earth and sea and sky, mountain and plain and tree. Sun and Moon. And then the places of men: road and gate and house . . . City and streets and the immortal visitor of the earth: yourself. Only when Matthew Barnes paints these places and things they begin to mean just a little more than they used to mean." The ultimate sources of Barnes' terrifying nocturnes, of the eerie realism of such studies as his *Crime in Concrete,* lie in childhood memories of Scottish folklore (he was born in Ayrshire in 1886) no less than in San Francisco streets seen through swirling fog and incandescent lamplight:

> ". . . ghasties and ghoulies and four-legged beasties,
> And things that go 'whoosh' in the night . . ."

Known for his "Westerns," vividly delineating such subjects as the cattle ranch, wild mustangs, the red raw canyons, is Maynard Dixon. Examples of his mural decorations appear at the San Francisco Water Department, the Kit Carson Grill, the United States Building and Loan Association, and the "Room of the Dons" in the Mark Hopkins Hotel.

One of the most disconcerting of painters is Bernard Zakheim, whose paintings are crudely drawn, beautifully designed, at once complex and brutal—somewhat resembling the work of José Clemente Orozco. He has done a number of large murals for both public and private buildings, among the best known of which are those in Coit Tower, in the Jewish Community Center, and at the University of California Medical School.

Ralph Stackpole has been an influence of tremendous value on younger men; he is responsible for a notable local school of sculpture. Stackpole adapts the earthy simplicity of Mayan art to themes which are modern but nearly always elemental. Strong simple masses, figures with big hands, big hips, big feet—these are typical of his technique. His stylized, truly heroic proletarian figures cut in granite on bastions beside the entrance of the San Francisco Stock Exchange show his tendency to make sculpture an appurtenance of architecture. A dominant feature of the Golden Gate International Exposition was his gigantic figure, *Pacifica.*

Beniamino Bufano has been at work for more than a decade on a statue even more tremendous—his *St. Francis,* which has become almost a San Francisco legend. Bufano's use of color, of stainless steel, and other unorthodox media in his sculpture exhibits a daring which has gained him world-wide renown. An excellent example of his work is the majestic *Sun Yat Sen,* in stainless steel with a head of rose granite, which stands in St. Mary's Square in Chinatown.

The bas-reliefs—seen on the facade of the Aquatic Park Casino— and wood carvings of Sargent Johnson are simple and decorative, treating the human figure somewhat abstractly but without violent distortion. Other notable sculptors include Ruth Cravath, Adeline Kent, and Robert Howard, all represented by bas-reliefs at the San Francisco Stock Exchange.

Since the late 1930's a group of East Bay artists—followers of the somewhat forbiddingly named Mural Conceptualist movement—has attempted to express a functional inter-relationship between the arts of painting, design, and architecture. This new idea seems likely to enter the lives of more people in a more direct way than any artistic development since the principles of functionalism were formulated. To the small home-owner this may mean that the materials of which a house is built can have a quality more interesting than that of keeping out the elements. A hitherto blank wall, for example, may be enlivened by a decoration of common bricks incised and arranged in ingenious patterns. Deserting the studio, the conceptualists work with architects, carpenters, and masons; and their materials are the materials of the building trades: concrete, metals, the new plastics, and many kinds of glass.

All this renascence of the plastic arts in the Bay region, while constituting a local "school" only in a geographical sense, exhibits a progressive spirit which is in the best traditions of European and American art. The standard of criticism and appreciation, among the public generally and in the local press, has been raised immeasurably. Encouraging is the atmosphere of healthy, if sometimes violent, discussion now going on among the artists and their public over problems of aesthetics and technique. There is hope for a sound cultural tradition when people can get excited and angry and form factions about the sanity and significance of Georges Braque's *The Yellow Cloth.*

Calendar of Events

Jan. 1	San Francisco	Shrine East-West Football Game
nfd	San Francisco	California Dog Show
nfd	San Francisco	National Match Play Open Golf Championship
nfd	Oakland	Open Golf Tournament
or Feb. nfd	San Francisco	Chinese New Year
Feb. 22	Campbell	Old Settlers' Day
3rd wk.	Cloverdale	Citrus Fair
Mar. 17	San Francisco	South of Market Boys' St. Patrick's Day Celebration
nfd	Saratoga	Blossom Festival
or Apr. nfd	Niles	Annual Outdoor Bulb Show
or Apr. nfd	Petaluma	Redwood Empire Marathon (Footrace)
or Apr. nfd	Lincoln Park, Alameda	Easter Sunrise Services
or Apr. nfd	Cragmont Park, Berkeley	Easter Sunrise Services
or Apr. nfd	Mount Davidson, San Francisco	Easter Sunrise Services
or Apr. nfd	San Rafael Hill, San Rafael	Easter Sunrise Services
or Apr. nfd	Saratoga Summit, Saratoga	Easter Sunrise Services
Apr. 6	Presidio, San Francisco	Army Day (Review)
6	Hamilton Field, San Rafael	Army Day (Air Circus)
1st 2 wks.	South San Francisco	Interstate Livestock and Baby Beef Show
nfd	San Francisco and Oakland	Baseball Season Opens
nfd	Kentfield	Annual Pistol Shoot
nfd	Oakland	Food Show
nfd	San Francisco	Spring Yacht Regatta

nfd	Golden Gate Park, San Francisco	Japanese Cherry Blossom Festival
nfd	San Francisco	Wild Flower Show
and May nfd	Mira Monte Park, Kentfield	Iris Blooming Season
or May nfd	Kentfield	Tamalpais Center Flower Show
or May nfd	Napa	Spring Flower Show
or May nfd	Oakland	California Spring Garden Show
or May nfd	Sebastopol	Blossom Festival
or May nfd	San Rafael	Annual Art Exhibit

May 1	Golden Gate Park, San Francisco	Children's May Day Festival
1	San Anselmo	May Day Festival
12-19	Calero Reservoir, Santa Clara Co.	Motorboat Regatta
16-17	San Jose	Hobby Fair
3rd wk.	Lincoln Park, Alameda	May Day Celebration
3rd wk.	San Jose	Fiesta de las Rosas
3rd Sun.	Mount Tamalpais	Mountain Theater Play
30	Lake Merritt, Oakland	Memorial Day Motorboat Regatta
30	San Francisco	Memorial Day Parade
nfd	Calistoga	Kiddies' Play Day Parade
nfd	Hayward	Rodeo
nfd	Oakland	Mills College Horse Show
nfd	Redwood City	Pet Parade
nfd	Richmond	Fiesta and Horse Show
nfd	San Rafael	Horse Show
nfd	St. Helena	Napa County 4 H Club Fair
or June nfd	Madrone	Rodeo

June 1st wk.	Martinez	Early Days Fiesta
1st wk.	Oakland	Sportsmen's Carnival
1st wk.	Santa Rosa	Rodeo
2nd wk.	Livermore	Rodeo
3rd wk.	Shellville	Sonoma Rodeo
24	Alameda	Scandinavian Midsummer Day Celebration
nfd	Brentwood	Apricot Festival
nfd	Martinez	Soap Box Derby
nfd	Oakland	Gladiolus Show
nfd	San Mateo	Gymkhana Club Horse Show
nfd	San Rafael	Dog Show

July 1st wk.	Calistoga	Silverado Fair and Horse Show
4	Fairfax	Celebration, Horse Show
4	Lake Merritt, Oakland	Fireworks and Motorboat Regatta
4	San Francisco	Fireworks
14	San Francisco	Bastille Day Celebration
nfd	San Francisco	Soap Box Derby
or Aug. nfd	Petaluma	Sonoma-Marin Agricultural Fair
Aug. 2nd wk.	Atherton	San Mateo Horse Show
4th wk.	Pleasanton	Alameda County Fair and Fiesta del Vino
31-Sept. 2	Gilroy	Round-Up and Gymkhana
nfd	Antioch	Contra Costa County Fair
nfd	Berkeley Yacht Harbor	Berkeley Regatta
nfd	San Francisco	Harbor Day
nfd	San Francisco	Dahlia and Flower Show
nfd	San Leandro	Dahlia Show
nfd	Santa Rosa	Sonoma County Fair and Horse Show
or Sept. nfd	Pittsburg	Western Horse Show
Sept. 9	Throughout Bay Area	Admission Day Celebration
1st wk.	San Francisco	Labor Day Parade
3rd wk.	Bay Meadows	San Mateo County Fiesta and Rodeo
nfd	Benicia	Old Timers' Celebration
nfd	Berkeley	Pacific Coast Tennis Championship Tournament
nfd	Napa	Fall Flower Show
nfd	Lake Merritt, Oakland	Outboard Motor Races
nfd	Richardson Bay	Yacht Regatta
nfd	St. Helena	Vintage Festival
nfd	San Jose	Fiesta de las Rosas Golf Tournament
or Oct. nfd	San Jose	Santa Clara Valley Fair
or Oct. nfd	San Rafael	Old San Rafael Days Fiesta
Oct. 12	Lake Merritt, Oakland	Columbus Day Festival and Motorboat Regatta
12	San Francisco	Columbus Day Festival
3rd wk.	San Francisco	Grand National Livestock Exposition
31	Petaluma	Parade of the Witches

nfd	Bay Meadows	Opening Horse Racing Season
nfd	San Francisco	Opening Grand Opera Season
nfd	San Francisco	Opening Symphony Season
nfd	Watsonville	Santa Cruz County Fair
Nov. 11	Mill Valley	Marin County Armistice Day Celebration
11	Oakland	Armistice Day Parade
11	San Francisco	Armistice Day Parade
11	Santa Rosa	Sonoma County Armistice Day Celebration
nfd	Berkeley, Even Years Palo Alto, Odd Years	California-Stanford Big Game
nfd	Hayward	Winter Poultry, Pigeon, Bantam, and Rabbit Show
nfd	San Francisco	Santa Clara-St. Mary's Football Game
Dec. 1st wk.	Oakland	Cat Show
14	Santa Rosa	Lighting of Cedar of Lebanon Tree Marking Luther Burbank's Grave
25	Oakland	Christmas Pageant
31	San Francisco	New Year's Eve Celebration
4th wk.	Piedmont	Outdoor Christmas Tree Display
4th wk.	San Francisco	Outdoor Christmas Tree Display
nfd	Santa Rosa	Christmas Fiesta
nfd	St. Helena	Christmas Festival

PART II
"The City"

General Information

Information Service: Better Business Bureau, 15 Stockton St. California State Automobile Assn. (A. A. A.), 150 Van Ness Ave. Californians, Inc., 703 Market St. National Auto Club, 228 Pine St. Redwood Empire Assn., 85 Post St. San Francisco Chamber of Commerce, 333 Pine St. San Francisco Hotel Assn., 821 Market St. Shell Travel Bureau, 102 Bush St. State Chamber of Commerce, 350 Bush St. State Dept. of Motor Vehicles, 160 Van Ness Ave. S. State Park Commission, 417 Montgomery St. Travelers' Aid, Ferry Bldg. U. S. Forest Service, 760 Market St. U. S. Travel Bureau, 461 Market St. Out-of-town telephone directories at: Telephone Bldg., 444 Bush St., and pay stations, 104 Powell St.; Emporium, 835 Market St.; Roos Bros., O'Farrell St. entrance (near Stockton St.); and several hotels. Reference library information bureaus (limited service): *Call-Bulletin, Examiner, News.* For correct time call ROchester 8900.

Railroad Stations: Atchison, Topeka and Santa Fe Ry., bus connections at 44-4th St.; ticket office, 235 Geary St. Northwestern Pacific R. R., Ferry Bldg.; ticket office, 65 Market St. Southern Pacific R. R., Ferry Bldg. Sacramento Northern Ry., Bay Bridge Terminal, 1st and Mission Sts. Southern Pacific R. R., 3rd and Townsend Sts., and Ferry Bldg.; main ticket office, 65 Geary St. Western Pacific R. R., Ferry Bldg.; ticket office, 287 Geary St.

Bus Stations: Abbott Lines, 85-4th St. Airline Bus Co., 55-5th St.; main office, 1188 Harrison St. All American Bus Lines, Inc., 40 Eddy St. Dollar Bus Lines, 781 Market St. Pacific Greyhound Lines, 75-5th St. Burlington Trailways, Gibson Lines, Key System, Napa Valley Bus Co., National Trailways System, River Auto Stages Co., Sacramento Northern, and Santa Fe Trailways Bus System (main office, 85-5th St.), 44-4th St.

Sightseeing Buses: Gray Line, 781 Market St. Several private limousine stands near Union Square.

Airports: Municipal Airport (Mills Field), 13 m. S. on US 101 Bypass, for United Airlines and TWA. Treasure Island for Pan American Airways; office, 427 Post St. Taxis to Municipal Airport, $3.00-$3.50; time 30 min.

Taxis: 25¢ first 1/3 m., 10¢ each additional 2/5 m.

Streetcars and Buses: Local: California St. Cable Ry., 5¢, Market St. Ry., 7¢, Municipal Ry., 5¢; free transfers. Jitneys (privately owned) from downtown to County line, 10¢. *Interurban:* Trans-Bay electric trains to East Bay, 21¢, round trip 42¢. Market St. Ry. down Peninsula to San Mateo, 25¢. Pacific Greyhound and Northwestern Pacific to Marin County cities. Southern Pacific to southern Peninsula cities.

Bridges: San Francisco-Oakland Bay Bridge approaches: 5th and Bryant Sts. and Fremont and Harrison Sts.; toll 25¢ (1 to 5 passengers), 5¢ for each additional passenger; no pedestrians. Golden Gate Bridge approaches: Marina Blvd. and Baker St., Lombard and Broderick Sts., Lake St. and Park Presidio Blvd. (Presidio Tunnel); toll 50¢ (1 to 5 passengers), 5¢ for each additional passenger; pedestrians 10¢ within turnstiles.

Piers: Embarcadero, foot of Market St. For travel information consult travel bureaus or steamship companies.

Traffic Regulations: Speed limit 25 m.p.h. in business and residential districts. No U-turn in business district. No left-turn on Market St. east of Van Ness Ave. No parking on Market St. 7 a.m.-6 p.m. No parking in central traffic district (bounded by Mission and California Sts., 1st and Taylor Sts.) 8-9:30 a.m. and 4:30-6 p.m. Parking limit varies (see street signs). Right-turn against red light outside business district after full stop and if pedestrian lane is clear.

Radio Stations: KSFO (CBS, 560 kc.), 639 Market St. KPO (NBC red network, 680 kc.), and KGO (NBC blue network, 790 kc.), 111 Sutter St. KROW (some NBC broadcasts, 930 kc.), 505 Geary St. KFRC (Don Lee Mutual Broadcasting System, 610 kc.), 1000 Van Ness Ave. KJBS (Northern California Broadcasting System, 1070 kc.), 1470 Pine St. KSAN (McClatchy Broadcasting System, 1420 kc.), 1355 Market St. KYA (1230 kc.), 5-3rd St.

Motion Picture Houses (only downtown theaters are listed. Box offices are open approximately from 11 a.m. to 10 p.m., except Sat. when first-run houses have midnight showings): First-Run: Fox, 1350 Market St.; Paramount, 1966 Market St.; St. Francis, 965 Market St.; Warfield, 988 Market St.; Golden Gate (with vaudeville), Golden Gate Ave. and Taylor St.; Orpheum, Market and Hyde Sts.; United Artists, 1077 Market St. *Second-Run (only the larger theaters are listed*): California, 4th and Market Sts.; Davies, 934 Market St.; New Embassy, 1125 Market St. *Newsreel:* Telenews, Market St. near Powell St.; The Newsreel, 980 Market St. *Foreign Language:* Clay, 2261 Fillmore St.; Larkin, 816 Larkin St.; Princess, 1584 Church St.; Verdi, 644 Broadway; Vogue, 3290 Sacramento St.

Legitimate Theaters: Curran, 445 Geary St.; Geary, 407 Geary St.

Amateur and Little Theaters: Andre Ferrier Art Theater, 1470 Washington St., productions in French; Children's Theater Association, High School of Commerce Auditorium; Fairmont Hotel, 950 Mason St.; Girl's Club, 362 Capp St.; Jewish Community Playhouse, California St. and Presidio Ave.; Theater Arts Colony, 1725 Washington St.; Wayfarers Playhouse, 1740 Clay St.

Burlesque Theaters: Capitol Follies, 50 Ellis St.; Kearny, 825 Kearny St.; Liberty, 649 Broadway.

Concert Halls: Civic Auditorium, Grove St. between Polk and Larkin Sts.; Community Playhouse, 609 Sutter St.; Opera House (War Memorial), Van Ness Ave. at Grove St.; Scottish Rite Auditorium, Van Ness Ave. at Sutter St.; Veteran's Building (War Memorial), Van Ness Ave. at McAllister St.

Dance Halls (The following list includes only public dance halls.   One also may dance at the larger hotels, in many night clubs, and at fraternal halls):   Avalon Ball Room, 1268 Sutter St., open 8-12:30 nightly except Mon. and Wed., 8-1 Sat., popular and old-fashioned dances. Knights of Columbus Hall, 150 Golden Gate Ave., Sat. nights only, 8-12:30, modern and old-fashioned dancing.   Wolohan's Ball Room, 1319 Market St., open 8-12 Sun., Mon., Wed., Fri.; 8-12:30 Sat.   El Patio Ball Room, 1545 Market St., open 8-12:30 nightly except Mon. and Wed.

Night Clubs (Clubs close at 2 a.m.   It is illegal to sell liquor between 2 and 6 a.m.):   Alabam, 1820A Post St., Negro; short orders, *a la carte;* dancing.
Bal Tabarin, 1025 Columbus Ave., dinner, floor show, dancing.
Beachcomber, 142 Francisco St.; dinner, floor shows Wed., Fri., Sat.
Chinese Sky Room, 605 Pine St.; Chinese; dinner; floor show Sat.; dancing.
Finocchio's, 506 Broadway; no dinner; floor show (female impersonators).

Forbidden City, 363 Sutter St.; Chinese; minimum charge; dinner, all-Chinese floor show; no dinner nor floor show on Sun.

John's Rendezvous, 50 Osgood Pl.; minimum charge; floor show, dancing.

La Conga, 525 Pacific St.; Cuban; dinner, floor show.

La Fiesta, 553 Bay St.; marimba band; dinner, floor show; closed Mon.

Lido, 915 Columbus Ave.; luncheon dances, Thurs. 1-4 p.m., Sat. 1-4 p.m.; minimum charge; dinner, dancing, floor show; closed Tues.

Moderne, 555 Sutter St.; minimum charge; dinner, floor show.

Monaco, 560 Pacific St.; dinner, floor show.

Music Box, 859 O'Farrell St.; minimum charge; dinner, floor show.

Roberts-at-the-Beach, 2200 Great Highway; dinner, dancing.

Royal Hawaiian, 960 Bush St.; minimum charge; dinner, floor show; closed Mon.

Sinaloa, 1416 Powell St.; dinner, floor show.

South Seas, 540 Sutter St.; dinner, entertainment.

Streets of Paris, 54 Mason St.; dinner, entertainment; closed Sun.

Tahitian Hut, 99 Broadway; dinner, all-Tahitian floor show.

Three Six Five, 365 Market St.; minimum charge; dinner, floor show.

Tiny's Embassy, 2766 Taylor St.; minimum charge; dinner, floor show.

HOTEL AND OTHER ACCOMMODATIONS

San Francisco has 1,326 hotels and rooming houses—more per capita, it is said, than any other city in the world. The following list is confined to hotels in the area bounded by Market Street on the south, Bush Street on the north, Grant Avenue on the east, and Larkin Street on the west. Space limitation forbids inclusion of hundreds of lower-price hotels.

Luxury-Class Hotels: Clift, 495 Geary St.; Fairmont, 950 Mason St.; Mark Hopkins, 999 California St.; Palace, 639 Market St.; St. Francis, 335 Powell St.; Sir Francis Drake, 450 Powell St.

Medium-Rate Hotels: Alexander Hamilton, 631 O'Farrell St.; Ambassador, 55 Mason St.; Baldwin, 321 Grant Ave.; Bellevue, 505 Geary St.; Beresford, 635 Sutter St.; Biltmore, 735 Taylor St.; Bristol, 56 Mason St.; Californian, 405 Taylor St.; Canterbury, 750 Sutter St.; Carlton, 1075 Sutter St.; Cartwright, 524 Sutter St.; Casa Nova, 354 O'Farrell St.; Cecil, 545 Post St.; Chancellor, 433 Powell St.; Colonial, 650 Bush St.; Commodore, 825 Sutter St.; Cordova, 521 Post St.; Court, 555 Bush St.; Crane, 245 Powell St.; Dalt, 34 Turk St.; Davenport, 540 Jones St.; Devonshire, 335 Stockton St.; Drake-Wiltshire, 340 Stockton St.; El Cortez, 550 Geary St.

Empire, 100 McAllister St.; Fielding, 386 Geary St.; Franciscan, 350 Geary St.; Gaylord, 620 Jones St.; Glen Royal, 940 Sutter St.; Golden State, 114 Powell St.; Harvard, 685 Ellis St.; Herald, 308 Eddy St.; Herbert, 161 Powell St.; King George, 334 Mason St.; LaFayette, 240 Hyde St.; LaSalle, 225 Hyde St.; Lyric, 140 Jones St.; Manx, 225 Powell St.; Mark Twain, 345 Taylor St.; Maurice, 761 Post St.; Mayflower, 975 Bush St.; New Continental, 127 Ellis St.; Olympic, 230 Eddy St.; Oxford, 16 Turk St.

Padre, 241 Jones St.; Palomar, 364 O'Farrell St.; Plaza, 310 Post St.; Powell, 17 Powell St.; Roosevelt, 240 Jones St.; San Carlos, 811 Geary St.; Senate, 467 Turk St.; Senator, 519 Ellis St.; Shaw, 1112 Market St.; Sheldon, 629 Post St.; Somerton, 440 Geary St.; Springer, 615 Taylor St.; Stewart, 353 Geary St.; Stratford, 242 Powell St.; Sussex, 701 Sutter St.; Travelers, 255 O'Farrell St.; Vanderbilt, 221 Mason St.; Victoria, 598 Bush St.; Virginia, 312 Mason St.; Washington, 342 Grant Ave.; Whitcomb, 1231 Market St.; Willard, 161 Ellis St.; Worth, 641 Post St.

Hotels for Women: Emanu-El Sisterhood, 300 Page St.; Evangeline Residence, 44 McAllister St.; Women's Hotel, 642 Jones St. *The following rent by the week only:* Girls' Friendly Society Lodge, 1590 Sutter St.; Girls' Recreation Home Club, 557 Van Ness Ave., S.; Glide, 322 Ellis St.; Mary Elizabeth Inn, 1040 Bush St.; St. Margaret's Club, 1499 California St.

Apartment Hotels (The following list includes only those offering weekly accommodations): Clifton, 520 Taylor St.; El Cortez, 550 Geary St.; Huntington, 1075 California St.; Keystone, 1369 Hyde St.; Worth, 745 Hyde St.

Y.M.C.A.'s and Y.W.C.A.'s: Y.M.C.A., 220 Golden Gate Ave.; Y.M.C.A. Hotel (for men, women, and families), 351 Turk St.; Y.M.C.A. Chinese Branch, 855 Sacramento St.; Y.M.C.A. Army and Navy Branch, 166 Embarcadero. Y.W.C.A., 620 Sutter St.; Y.W.C.A. Chinese Branch, 965 Clay St.; Y.W.C.A. Japanese Branch (women under 35 only), 1830 Sutter St.

Tourist Camps: Marina Motel, 2576 Lombard St.; Ocean Park Motor Court, 46th and Wawona Sts.; San Francisco Auto Court, 701 Sunnydale Ave. Other courts are located south of the city limits on US 101, US 101 Bypass, and State 1.

RESTAURANTS

(Each establishment has a public or service bar unless otherwise stated.)

Downtown: Bay City Grill, 45 Turk St., *a la carte;* Bernstein's Fish Grotto, 123 Powell St.; Bit of Sweden, 560 Sutter St.; Blue Lagoon, 153 Maiden Lane; Breen's, 71-3rd St., *a la carte;* Cairo (Armenian), 77-4th St., *a la carte,* no liquor; California Inn (German), 600 Turk St.; Charles Fashion Grill (Italian), 243 O'Farrell St.; Collins & Wheeland, 347 Montgomery St.; Diller's Hungarian Kosher Style, 126 Turk St., beer and wine; Famous RKO Grill, 35 Taylor St.; Fly Trap, 73 Sutter St.; Forbidden City (Chinese and American), 363 Sutter St., closed Sun.; Girard's French, 65 Ellis St.; Golden Pheasant, Powell at Geary St.; Hawaiian Paradise, 67A-1st St.; Jacinto (Mexican), 67 Turk St., wine; John's Grill, 63 Ellis St.; Kit Carson, 395 Geary St.; La Buvette, 134 Maiden Lane; Louis' Fashion (French-Italian), 526 Market St.; Madrid (Spanish), 165 O'Farrell St., wine; Maison Paul, 1214 Market St.; Marconi (French-Italian), 241 Pine St.; Mario & Frank's (Italian), 225 California St., closed Sun.; Mayes Oyster House, 531 California St., *a la carte;* Mayfair, 116 Maiden Lane, no liquor; Omar Khayyam (Armenian), 196 O'Farrell St.; Oyster Loaf, 30 Kearny St.; Pierre's (French), 447 Pine St.; Pig'nWhistle, 33 Powell St., 621 Market St., 130 Post St. and 1032 Market St.; Prizer's Hungarian Kosher, 89 Turk St.; Roundhouse, Toll Plaza, Golden Gate Bridge, beer; Russian Tea Room, 326 Sutter St., closed Mon., wine and beer; Ruth's, 333 Sutter St., health food, no liquor; Solari's, 354 Geary St.; St. Julian (French), 140 Battery St.; Temple Bar, 25 Tillman Pl.; Three Musketeers (German), 200 Hyde St.

Historic San Francisco: Blue Fox (Italian), 659 Merchant St.; Jack's (French), 615 Sacramento St.; Manger (Italian), 611 Washington St.; Old Grotto (Italian), 545 Washington St.; Schroeder's (German), 111 Front St.; Tadich Grill, 545 Clay St.; William Tell (German-Swiss), 630 Clay St., dancing nightly.

Chinatown: Cathay House, 718 California St.; Far East, 631 Grant Ave.; Hang Far Low, 723 Grant Ave., beer; Lotus Bowl, 626 Grant Ave., no liquor; Manila (Filipino), 606 Jackson St., no liquor; Shangai Low, 532 Grant Ave.; Sun Hung Heung, 744 Washington St.; Tao Tao, 675 Jackson St.; Universal, 824 Washington St., wine and beer; Yamato Hotel (Japanese), 717 California St., *sake* and beer; Yamato, 562 Grant Ave.; Yee Jun's, 834 Washington St., beer.

North Beach: Aquatic Park Casino, foot of Polk St.; Backyard (Italian), 1024 Kearny St.; Ernie's (Italian and French), 847 Montgomery St.; Globe (Spanish, French and Italian), 771 Broadway; House That Jack Built (Costa Rican), 2014 Grant Ave.; Jai-Alai (Basque), 895 Pacific St.; Julius Castle (Italian), 302 Greenwich St.; John's Rendezvous, 50 Osgood Pl.; Hotel Español (Basque), 719 Broadway; La Favorite (French), 825 Pacific St.; Lucca's (Italian), 405 Francisco St.; Lupo's Pizzeria (Italian), 1942 Kearny St.; New Joe's (Italian), 536 Broadway, wine and beer; New Tivoli (French-Italian), 1438 Grant Ave.; Ripley's (French), 846 Jackson St.; Riviera (French-Italian), Union and Stockton Sts.; Shadows, 1349 Montgomery St., closed Mon.; Sinaloa (Mexican), 1416 Powell St.; Vanessi's (Italian), 498 Broadway; Veneto's (Italian), 389 Bay St.; Xochimilco (Mexican), 1350 Powell St.

International Settlement: La Conga (Mexican-Spanish), 523 Pacific St.; Monaco (French-Italian), 560 Pacific St.; Rice Bowl (Chinese), 555 Pacific St.

Fisherman's Wharf: Fisherman's Grotto, 9 Fisherman's Wharf; Joe Di Maggio's, Fisherman's Wharf; Neptune Fish Grotto, 2737 Taylor St.; Pop-Eye Fish Grotto, 2770 Taylor St.

Western Addition: Cherryland Sukiyaki (Japanese and American), 1650 Post St., *sake* and beer; El Portal, 8th Ave. and Fulton St.; Grison's Chicken House, 2050 Van Ness Ave.; Grison's Steak and Chop House, Van Ness and Pacific Aves.; Jack's Tavern (Negro—Southern cooking), 1931 Sutter St.; Russian (private residence), 1850 Geary St., open 4-8 p.m. weekdays, 9 a.m.-1 p.m. Sun., no liquor; Salad Bowl, 5616 Geary St.; Swedish Applied Arts Sveagard, 2016 Pacific St., open to public 7 p.m. Thurs. and Fri. by reservation, no liquor; Tenkatsu Mikayi (Japanese), 1762 Buchanan St., *sake* and wine.

Beach: Cliff House, Point Lobos Ave. (overlooking Seal Rocks); Topsy's Roost (Southern cooking), 660 Great Highway, open Fri., Sat., and Sun. nights; Robert's, 220 Great Highway.

SPORTS

For information, or further information, about archery, baseball, basketball, cricket, cycling, flycasting, football, handball, harness horse racing, horseshoe pitching, lawn bowling, polo, riding, softball, and tennis, see GOLDEN GATE PARK.

Badminton: Burke Gymnasium, 2350 Geary St.; Palace of Fine Arts, Baker St. near Marina Blvd.

Baseball: Seals Stadium, Bryant and 16th Sts. (Pacific Coast League); season, Apr. 1st to Sept. 15th.

Basketball: Y.M.C.A., Golden Gate Ave. and Leavenworth St.

Billiards (Only downtown parlors listed):   California Billiard Parlor, 1028 Market St.; Cochran and Palm Billiard Palace, 924 Market St.; Ferry Pool Room, 82 Embarcadero; Harvard Billiard and Pool Parlor, 36 Kearny St.; San Francisco Billiard Parlor, 949 Market St.; Waldorf Billiard Parlor, 165 Eddy St.; Wright's Billiard Palace, 82 Ellis St.

Bowling: Bagdad Bowling Alleys, 1641 Ellis St.; Fillmore Recreation Bowling Dome, 1515 Eddy St.; Golden Gate Recreation, 115 Jones St.; Hub Bowling Alley, 1671 Market St.; Powell Street Recreation, 115 Powell St.; Rialto Bowling Bowl, 80 Ellis St.   Bowling greens and facilities for public bowling are maintained by the city at Funston Field, in the Marina; at Julius Kahn Playground, Pacific Ave. between Spruce and Laurel Sts.; and at Rossi Playground, Arguello Blvd. at Anza St.

Boxing: Civic Auditorium, Grove and Larkin Sts.; National Hall, 1975 Mission St.; Coliseum Bowl, 45-11th St.

Cricket: Julius Kahn Playground.

Cycling: Bicycle-renting establishments, Great Highway and Wawona Sts., near Fleishhacker Pool; 3214 Fillmore St.; 1823 Haight St.; 2218 and 2220 Lombard St.; 638, 672, 780 and 854 Stanyan St. Cycling permitted on the Golden Gate Bridge; toll-charge 10¢ per cyclist.

Fishing: Lake Merced, free; Municipal Pier at Aquatic Park, N. end of Van Ness Ave., free; Water-front piers and Mission Rock near foot of Third St., free.

Football: Roberts Field, 15th and Valencia Sts.

Golf: Harding Park Municipal Golf Course, 36th Ave. at Sunset Blvd.; 18 holes and 6-hole practice course; 75¢ weekdays, $1.00 Sat., Sun., holidays; monthly ticket $3.00.   Ingleside Public Golf Course, Junipero Serra Blvd. and 19th Ave.; 18 holes; 75¢ Mon.-Fri., $1.25 Sun., holidays; Sat., 75¢ before 11, $1.25 11-4, 50¢ after 4; monthly $3.00.   Lincoln Park Municipal Golf Links, 33rd Ave. and Clement St.; 18 holes; 50¢ weekdays, 75¢ Sat., Sun., holidays.

Private Golf Courses: Olympic Club Golf Course (Lakeside Golf Club), Skyline Blvd.   Presidio Golf Club, in the Presidio (U. S.

Military Reservation). San Francisco Golf and Country Club, Junipero Serra Blvd.

Gymnasiums: Burke Gymnasium, 2350 Geary St.; Y.M.C.A., 220 Golden Gate Ave.; Young Men's Institute, 50 Oak St.; Y.W.C.A., 620 Sutter St.

Handball: Burke Gymnasium; Y.M.C.A., 220 Golden Gate Ave.

Ice Hockey: Winterland, Steiner and Post Sts.; occasional series of games.

Ice Skating: Sutro Baths and Ice Rink, Point Lobos Ave. near Great Highway; 25¢ afternoons, 35¢ eve. and Sun.; 15¢ extra for skates, children's skates free afternoons except Sun. Winterland, Steiner and Post Sts.; 40¢ mornings, 55¢ eve.; 25¢ extra for skates.

Riding: Bakers Beach and the Presidio, Hunter's Point, John McLaren Park, Lake Merced, and Ocean Beach. Average charge for horses $1.50 first hour, 75¢ each additional hour. *Riding Clubs and Academies.* Hunter's Point Stables, 415 Galvez St.; Bay View Stables, 950 Palou Ave.; Paramount Riding Academy, 317 Broderick St.; Roberts Beach Riding Academy, 2232-48th Ave.; St. Francis Riding School, 701-7th Ave.; San Francisco Riding School, 734 Stanyan St.; Lake Merced Riding Club, Mission Riding Club, Hollywood Riding Stable, in Colma (just south of city limits).

Roller Skating: Ambassador, Fillmore and Geary Sts.; open 2-5 p.m., 7:30-10:30 p.m.; adm.: women 25¢, men 35¢, 10¢ less for men bringing own skates. Burke Gymnasium, Sat. and Sun. afternoons, and every evening; adm. 25¢. Civic Auditorium, occasional six-day derbys.

Rugby Football: Ewing Field, Masonic Ave. and Anza St.

Skeet and Trap Shooting: Lake Merced Field, Skyline Blvd.; competitions, usually Sun.

Softball: Margaret S. Hayward Playground, Golden Gate Ave. and Gough Sts. (night play); Roberts Field, 15th and Valencia Sts. (night play).

Swimming: Municipal Outdoor Pools (open Apr. 1-Oct. 31): Fleishhacker Pool, Sloat Blvd. and Great Highway; adm. 25¢, children 15¢. Mission Pool (children only), 19th and Angelica Sts.; adm. 5¢. North

Beach Pool (children only), Lombard and Mason Sts.; adm. 5¢. *Privately Owned Pools.* Crystal Plunge and Baths, Lombard and Taylor Sts. Fairmont Plunge, 950 Mason St. Sutro Baths, Point Lobos Ave. near Great Highway. Y.M.C.A., 220 Golden Gate Ave. Y.W.C.A., 620 Sutter St. *Surf Bathing.* Aquatic Park, foot of Polk St. . Ocean Beach (undertow dangerous).

Tennis: Municipal courts at 44 recreation centers. Among them are: Clement Courts (4), 30th Ave. near Clement St.; Crocker-Amazon Playground (6), Geneva Ave. and Moscow St.; Funston Playground (4), Chestnut and Buchanan Sts.; Jefferson Square (4), Golden Gate Ave. and Gough St.; Julius Kahn Playground (4), Pacific Ave. between Spruce and Laurel Sts.; Richmond Tennis Courts (5), 8th Ave. between Clement and California Sts.; all free. Fine Arts Courts (18), foot of Lyon St.; $1.00 per hour per court, day or night.

Water Polo: Crystal Plunge and Baths, Lombard and Taylor Sts.; Fairmont Plunge, 950 Mason St.; Fleishhacker Pool, Sloat Blvd. and Great Highway.

Wrestling: Civic Auditorium, Grove and Larkin Sts.; Y.M.C.A., Golden Gate Ave. and Leavenworth St.

Yachting: Municipal Yacht Harbor, Marina Blvd. between Pierce and Baker Sts.

CHURCHES

(Only representative churches of most denominations are listed below.)

Baptist: Chinese Baptist Mission, 15 Waverly Pl.; First, Waller and Octavia Sts.; First Russian, 904 Rhode Island St.; Hamilton Square, 1975 Post St.

Buddhist: Hongwanji Buddhist Mission of North America, 1881 Pine St.; Nichiren, 1860 Buchanan St.; Sokoji Mission, 1881 Bush St.

Christian: First, Duboce and Noe Sts.; West Side, 2520 Bush St.

Christian Science: First Church, 1700 Franklin St.; Fifth Church, 450 O'Farrell St.; Seventh Church, 940 Powell St.

Church of Jesus Christ of Latter Day Saints: Mission Ward, 2668 Mission St.; San Francisco Ward, 1649 Hayes St.

Congregational-Methodist: Chinese, 21 Brenham Pl.; Grace United Church of the Mission, 21st and Capp Sts.; Park Presidio United, 4319 Geary St.; Temple, Post and Mason Sts.

Episcopal: Church of the Advent, 261 Fell St.; Grace Cathedral, 1122 California St.; St. Francis, San Fernando Way at Ocean Ave.; St. Luke's, 1750 Van Ness Ave.; Seamen's Church Institute, 58 Clay St.; Trinity, Bush and Gough Sts.

Evangelical and Reformed: Bethel, 2005 15th St.; St. John's Community, 2041 Larkin St.

Free Methodist: Free Methodist, 985 Golden Gate Ave.

Greek Orthodox: United Greek Church of the Annunciation, 245 Valencia St.; Holy Trinity, 345-7th St.

Hebrew Reformed: Congregation Emanu-El, Arguello Blvd. and Lake St.; Congregation Sherith Israel, 2010 Webster St.

Hebrew Orthodox: Congregation Anshi Sfard, 1140 Golden Gate Ave.; Congregation Beth Israel, 1839 Geary St.; Congregation Ohabai Sholome, 351-4th Ave.

Lutheran: Anzar Danish Evangelical, 152 Church St.; Ebenezer Evangelical, 200 Dolores St.; First English, Geary St. between Gough and Octavia Sts.; First Finnish Evangelical, 14th and Belcher Sts.; Norwegian, 615 Dolores St.

Methodist: First, Larkin and Clay Sts.; Glide Memorial, 322 Ellis St.; Japanese, 1359 Pine St.; St. John's Italian, 756 Union St.; United German, 240 Page St.

Presbyterian: Calvary, 2501 Fillmore St.; Chinese, 925 Stockton St.; First, Van Ness Ave. and Sacramento St.; Mizpah (Spanish), 725 Folsom St.; Welsh, 449-14th St.

Roman Catholic: Church of the Nativity (Slavonian), 240 Fell St.; Holy Family Chinese Mission, 902 Stockton St.; Mission Dolores, 300 Dolores St.; Notre Dame des Victoires (French), 566 Bush St.; Nuestra Señora de Guadalupe (Spanish), Broadway and Mason Sts.; Old St. Mary's (Paulist), California St. and Grant Ave.; St. Anne's, 810 Judah St.; St. Boniface (Franciscan), 151 Golden Gate Ave.; St. Dominic's (Dominican), 1901 Steiner St.; St. Francis of Assisi, 620 Vallejo St.; St. Ignatius (Jesuit), Fulton St. and Parker Ave.; St. Mary's Cathedral, Van Ness Ave. and O'Farrell St.; St. Patrick's, 750 Mission St.; SS. Peter and Paul (Italian), 650 Filbert St.

Russian Orthodox: Holy Trinity Cathedral, Van Ness Ave. and Green St.; Holy Virgin, Fulton St. near Fillmore St.

Salvation Army: Chinatown, Waverly Pl. and Sacramento St.; San Francisco Citadel, 95 McCoppin St.; Waterfront, 38 Commercial St.

Seventh Day Adventist: Central, California and Broderick Sts.; Russian, 878 Rhode Island St.; Tabernacle (Negro), Bush and Baker Sts.

Unitarian: First, Franklin and Geary Sts.

United Presbyterian: First, 1455 Golden Gate Ave.; Stewart Memorial (Second United), 1076 Guerrero St.

Miscellaneous: Apostolic Faith Mission, 749 Market St.; Art of Living, 609 Sutter St.; Bahai Assembly, 620 Sutter St., in Y.W.C.A.; Bethel Full Gospel Assembly, 3811 Mission St.; Church of Christ, 302 Jules Ave.; Church of God, 3718 Army St.; Father Divine Peace Mission, 821 Pacific Ave.; First Russian Molakan, 841 Carolian St.; Glad Tidings Temple, 1441 Ellis St.; "I Am," 133 Powell St.; Lighthouse Full Gospel Mission (Negro), 1905 Sutter St.; New Jerusalem (Swedenborgian), 2107 Lyon St.; Rosicrucian Brotherhood AMORC, 1655 Post St.; Society of Progressive Spiritualists, 2126 Sutter St.; Sufi Movement, 545 Sutter St.; Theosophical Society, 414 Mason St., Native Sons Bldg.; Unity Temple, 126 Post St.; Vedanta Society, Webster and Filbert Sts.; Volunteers of America, 230-9th St.

San Franciscans: 1940

"Nowhere in America is there less in evidence the cold theological eye, the cautious hand withheld, the lifted eyebrow, the distrust of playfulness . . ."

—GEORGE WEST

T O SHARE with San Franciscans their feeling for the city's elusive identity—that prevailing atmosphere which is to San Francisco what dynamic tempo is to New York, what Old World charm is to New Orleans—a visitor does best to wander about its streets. The city has a look of incredible venerability. What remains of the old San Francisco—the roaring boom town of the Argonauts, the Barbary Coast, and the bonanza days—consists mainly of a handful of once proud business buildings, crumbling and obscure, that somehow belie their conversion to modern usage by their appearance of having withstood the passage of an era of violence and romance. Elsewhere, in those parts of the city which survived the calamity of 1906, row on row of Eastlake wooden houses—with their bay windows, corner turrets, and fantastic scrollwork—are reminders of a fabulous past. But although San Francisco is more profoundly steeped in a tempestuous history than any other American city of its age of development, few landmarks of that history remain; the city, for the most part, is the city that rose from the debris of earthquake and fire. Even the rebuilt sections have a look of weathered age. Nor do those sprawling residential districts—real estate developments of more recent years—long escape the mellow tarnish of wind and weather. The very streets, cutting over hill and down valley with resolute forthrightness, are memorials to the men of the Gold Rush, whose roughshod surveys determined the city's main features, imposing on traffic a series of permanent inconveniences which are nevertheless excused for the dramatic vistas they provide. And the old-fashioned cable cars that lurch and sway with clanging bell up and down their precipitous slopes have long since brought to street transportation a spirit of almost festive novelty which it enjoys probably nowhere else.

A tradition which has behind it the most hectic and glamorous epoch of American pioneering is still the factor which determines much of the city's enigmatic charm and governs many of those political, economic, and cultural phenomena by which San Franciscans continue to astonish the world. Every principle of American democracy has been tested here, and what has emerged is a kind of collective wisdom by

which public affairs may be administered with a minimum of interference with personal liberty. The average San Franciscan still adheres
to the pioneer concept of government: the less of it the better. His
Argonaut forbears tried to do without it altogether, but found themselves at the mercy of social evils which nothing short of a harsh popular
tribunal could eradicate. Their subsequent experience with municipal
administrations, reformist and otherwise, led them finally to devise a
city charter of such elaborate checks and balances that corruption on
a grand scale was forestalled. By resounding majorities bond issues of
a dubious nature are voted down, but not appropriations for education,
for parks and playgrounds—or for expositions and bridges.

What is supremely important to San Franciscans is that they be let
alone to think and act as they please. Here the accent has always been
on living, and however much the city has changed in other ways, 1940
sees no let-up in that vigorous search for experience by which San
Franciscans have been enriching their lives since 1850. The difference
nowadays lies in a certain refinement of critical faculties which is having its effect on all phases of the city's social life. The crowds who
attend concerts and art exhibits, movies and cabarets, theatrical performances and the opera constitute audiences whose verdict is something to be respected. What San Franciscans like they applaud with
a sensitive and overwhelming enthusiasm; what they believe will not
please them they simply avoid. Rather than have a mediocre theater
of their own, they still attend dramatic performances imported from
New York. The cuisine of their hotels and restaurants is still renowned the world over; and every San Franciscan is something of an
epicure. The thousand-and-one treasures of the city's shops find a
sophisticated response among San Franciscans to whom luxuries are,
and always have been, aids to graceful living rather than the accoutrements of fashion. All sorts of exotic importations, brought in by the
city's various ethnic groups, contribute to the fun of being a San Franciscan. This universal delight in just being alive here, which has
amazed so many outsiders, has its source very largely in a certain playfulness of spirit—a natural gusto—by which rich and poor alike are
able to draw from some simple experience (a ride on a cable car or a
dinner at Solari's) a sense of *joie de vivre*.

The Genteel Tradition was never able to take root here. The
virile ethics of the Argonauts forbade it. San Franciscans have always
shown an almost universal disregard for the haughtier privileges of great
wealth. Nob Hill was not a social success: the city's sense of humor,
its love of gaiety, its unfailing urbanity have excluded aristocratic exclu-
siveness. Its absentee aristocracy (descendants of the bonanza millionaires who have retired to estates down the Peninsula or in the
Marin hills) continue to make "The City" the hub of their social

whirl; but San Francisco itself has no recognizable "four hundred." The city has not a single public place where formal attire is obligatory; almost the only social requirements are that one hold one's liquor well and behave like a gentleman—or a lady. The predominance of highly skilled workers, professional people, and technicians in its population— inevitable in a city which is much more a commercial than an industrial center—determines the social standard, outweighing even the labor movement's more highly publicized influence. But the middle-class influence is modified, not only by labor's strength, but also by the effects of the city's polyglot mixture of nationalities—its vast number of people who have come from every country under the sun, and while becoming citizens in all respects, have retained nonetheless the customs of their homelands.

The best way to insult a San Franciscan is to slap him on the back. Whatever violates his natural urbanity receives a chilly response. Like his Argonaut predecessors he continues to form friendships and choose business associates in the "partner" tradition of the Gold Rush. This delicate social process, which has repelled countless newcomers, has resulted in a population for whom individuality is the keynote; and those of a more gregarious nature quickly retire to places where their back-slapping propensities will be appreciated. Despite this unkind form of social selectivity, San Francisco is constantly acquiring new citizens from every state of the Union and from abroad. Those who remain partake inevitably of the city's social tradition; and so profoundly will it affect them that, though they may journey to the ends of the earth, this place will always be home to them. The citizen of San Francisco is a citizen of the world.

The City's Growth

"The Yankees are a wonderful people, wonderful. Wherever they go they make improvements. If they were to emigrate in large numbers to hell itself, they would somehow manage to change the climate."
—GENERAL MARIANO G. VALLEJO (to President Lincoln).

AT THE crossroads of the great migrations of antiquity arose such cities as that magical pandemonium the Argonauts inhabited: Nineveh, Babylon, and Jericho. Although the sin and splendor of the bonanza epoch have long since given way to the iron age of corporate industrialism, the successors of the Argonauts have striven mightily to retain their heritage of hilarious action. Somehow it is all here, chastened and dispersed, but no less explosive than in the era before "The Fire": the vigorous delight in living, the susceptibility to tremendous projects, the vengeful spirit of the Vigilantes, the profound sophistication and the capacity for Homeric laughter.

THE VILLAGE OF YERBA BUENA (1835–1848)

Dusty, fleabitten little Yerba Buena was in 1835 an insignificant outpost long frequented by roving seafarers, Russians, and a few nondescript traders who smelled of hides and tallow. But for four redwood posts covered with a ship's foresail which De Haro's harbormaster, William Antonio Richardson, erected on "La Calle" in 1835, San Francisco's original site was little more than a waste of sand and chaparral sloping down to a beach and a small lagoon. *El Parage de Yerba Buena* (The Little Valley of the Good Herb) it had been named long before, because of the aromatic vine (*Micromeria Chamissonis*) found in the underbrush there.

Richardson, young master mariner who had deserted the British whaler *Orion* in 1822, was appointed Captain of the Port of San Francisco by Governor Pablo Vicente de Sola in 1835 when the Bay was declared a port of entry. Stocking his huge tent with wheat, hides, and vegetables, trader Richardson soon supplemented his official duties by raising two sunken schooners which he put into service transporting rancho products from one end of the Bay to the other at somewhat exorbitant rates.

Democratic self-government, of the bureaucratic sort decreed by the Mexican Republic, came to Yerba Buena before the town itself arrived. Citizens of the *partido* (civil district) of San Francisco, on Governor

Jose Figueroa's orders, assembled in the Presidio on December 7, 1834 to choose electors for the *ayuntamiento* (district council). On the following Sunday Don Francisco de Haro was elected to the *ayuntamiento* as *alcalde* for the projected *pueblo* of Yerba Buena. As a gesture toward establishing the town, Don Francisco marked out on the ground, from the site of Yerba Buena to the Presidio, *La Calle de la Fundacion* (Foundation Street) and retired thereafter to Mission Dolores to look after private matters.

Richardson, on July 1, 1836, suddenly acquired a neighbor as resourceful as himself—one equipped to do business in really sumptuous style. Jacob Primer Leese, Ohio-born partner in a Monterey mercantile firm, sailed into the cove aboard the barque *Don Quixote* with a $12,000 cargo of merchandise, a six-piece orchestra, and enough lumber to erect a mansion. By July 4, on a lot adjoining Richardson's property, the amazing Mr. Leese had thrown up a frame house 60 feet long, and 25 feet wide. Borrowing two six-pounders from the Presidio and decking his domestic barn with bunting from ships in the cove, Leese summoned all leading Mexican families north of the Bay to an Independence Day celebration—which lasted two days and a night.

Among the guests at Leese's patriotic housewarming had been Captain Jean Jacques Vioget, of the Peruvian brig *Delmira,* who was also a surveyor and a lively man with a fiddle. In the autumn of 1839 this versatile Swiss was commissioned by *Alcalde* de Haro to make the first survey of Yerba Buena. By 1840 on the west side of Montgomery Street, between Clay and Sacramento Streets, next door to the new Hudson's Bay Company's post and saloon he was serving ship's captains, supercargoes, merchants, and clerks in a tavern.

Thirty families, in 1841, comprised the village population. The most impressive house was that of Nathan Spear, who was running the Bay area's only flour mill. Jacob Leese had now transferred his business to Sonoma. Richardson was living across the Bay on his huge Rancho Saucelito, where he continued to collect customs and pocket the funds, claiming that his salary as harbor master was not paid and that he had no other source of income.

Governor Juan B. Alvarado's decrees, restricting trade with foreigners after 1841, drove the American whalers from San Francisco Bay to a new headquarters in the Sandwich Islands; and by 1844, outrivaled by the port of Honolulu, Yerba Buena had fallen back into obscurity. Though that same year saw the election of its first American-born *alcalde,* William Sturges Hinckley, the village continued to languish.

The mock-heroics of "Pathfinder" John Charles Frémont's raid on the Castillo de San Joaquin were Yerba Buena's first warning of impending change. Slipping over from Sausalito on July 1, 1846, the Yankee adventurer spiked the dismantled guns of the old fort. ("So far as can be known," says Hubert Howe Bancroft, "not one of the ten cannons offered the slightest resistance.") Thereafter, for a week, the habitues of Vioget's hangout gave themselves up to warlike gossip, forgetting to play billiards.

Suddenly, on July 9, the U.S.S. *Portsmouth* quietly dropped anchor in Yerba Buena's cove. The villagers—unaware of Commodore Sloat's flotilla off Monterey—were disturbed at breakfast by a roll of drums and a flurry of fifes. When they rushed to the Plaza, Captain John B. Montgomery's 70 sailors and marines were running up the Stars and Stripes on Mexico's flagpole atop the adobe Custom House. Down in the cove the *Portsmouth's* 21-gun salute rumbled into history across San Francisco Bay.

Captain Montgomery on August 26 appointed Lieutenant Washington Allen Bartlett first *alcalde* of Yerba Buena under the American flag. On September 15 Bartlett was confirmed in office by popular vote, with the same powers enjoyed by his Mexican predecessors. His first important decree ordered revision of Vioget's survey, which had served to locate building lots since 1839. Jasper O'Farrell, civil engineer employed for the job, discovered in 1847 that the Swiss tavern-keeper's streets intersected at two and a half degrees from a right angle. His prompt correction of this error, known as "O'Farrell's Swing," left building frontage and vacant lots projecting somewhat beyond the theoretically proper lines of nonexistent curbstones.

On the last day of July 1846, Samuel Brannan, the bombastic Mormon Elder, sailed in through the Golden Gate aboard the *Brooklyn* with his well-armed flock of Latter-day Saints, a hold crammed with farmer's tools, two flour mills, and a printing press. The Mormons provided all that was necessary to pull Yerba Buena out of its rut once more. Within a year that place which had baffled the urbane and mystical Spaniards for three-quarters of a century would appear on the map of Alta California. Two years later the name of San Francisco would be blazoned in gold on the map of the world.

CAPITAL OF THE GOLD COAST (1848–1856)

"To this Gate I gave the name of 'Chrysopylae' or Golden Gate for the same reason that the harbor of Byzantium was called 'Chrysoceras,' or Golden Horn." Thus Frémont, after gazing at the Bay's entrance from a Contra Costa peak, adorned his report to the United States Congress with an erudite flourish. Little did he suspect how literal was to be the name he had given to that famous strait.

When Brannan's Mormon battalion landed at Yerba Buena in the summer of 1846, the village had 50 or 60 inhabitants. Sam's passengers and crew swelled its population by nearly six-fold. The Plaza, newly named Portsmouth Square, already had its fringe of gambling houses, a hotel and a saloon, and its nucleus of rough characters.

Brannan's bull-throated oratory and domineering personality enabled him to assume leadership of the town's affairs. Within a year he had performed the first marriage and preached the first sermon under American rule, seen to the holding of the first jury trial, established the first newspaper, and sunk all his money in Yerba Buena real estate. In his *California Star,* on January 30, 1847, appeared *Alcalde* Bartlett's ordinance which cut the ground from under the scheme of Thomas Larkin and General Vallejo to adopt the name "San Francisco" for a rival townsite on Carquinez Strait. "It is Hereby Ordained," said the ordinance's clinching paragraph, "that the name of San Francisco shall hereafter be used in all official communications and public documents, or records appertaining to the town [of Yerba Buena]."

Whatever Sam Brannan's original intentions—ostensibly he had brought his cargo of Saints around Cape Horn to establish for Brigham Young a Mormon commonwealth in California—he soon fell somewhat from grace with his followers—and with *Alcalde* Bartlett. The fiery Elder was too deeply involved financially, however, to move on to greener pastures; and though his paper's editor had been rolled down Portsmouth Square in a barrel for lukewarm local patriotism, Sam supported a campaign for public education which resulted in establishment of San Francisco's first school—a frame house on Portsmouth Square which also served successively as town-hall, church, and jail. His own contribution to the spirit of progress was a special edition of the *Star* of which 2,000 copies, carried by horse-borne courier, boosted California all the way to the Mississippi Valley.

The arrival, in the spring of 1847, of Colonel J. D. Stevenson's disbanded regiment of New York volunteers in the Mexican War— "Bowery Boys" schooled in the spread-eagle Americanism of New York's Tammany Hall—so inspired Sam Brannan with faith in California's future that he decided to strike out eastward, meet Brigham Young's stranded pilgrims, and lead them into the Promised Land. This the patriarchal Brigham had already found in Salt Lake Valley, however, and Sam had to retrace his steps to California. Angry and disgusted, he forgot about San Francisco and decided, in the autumn of 1847, to set up a store at Sutter's Fort and help the lord of New Helvetia build a sawmill on the south fork of the American River near the present site of Coloma. When gold was discovered in Sutter's millrace on January 24, 1848, Elder Sam Brannan re-assumed his authority over Mormon miners in the vicinity and began collecting "the Lord's tithes" from them. To the apostle sent to him to claim this illicit revenue Sam retorted: "You go back and tell Brigham that I'll give up the Lord's money when he gives me a receipt signed by the Lord, and no sooner!"

Meanwhile, in San Francisco, Brannan's own newspaper was ridiculing persistent rumors of rich gold strikes in the Sierra foothills. Suddenly the *Star's* owner himself rushed into town with a whisky flask full of the yellow flakes and confounded loiterers in Portsmouth Square with yells of "Gold! Gold! Gold from the American River!" Of the town's 900 inhabitants, only seven were left behind when the renegade Mormon with the bland face and side-whiskers led the first rush to the diggings.

Two hundred and fifty thousand dollars in gold dust came down the Sacramento during June and July of 1848. When news of this reached Mexican and South American ports via vessels from Honolulu, fortune-hunters in thousands swarmed aboard ships bound up the Coast. By New Year's Day, 1849, 6,000 miners were at the diggings. San Francisco was a cantonment of tents with a population of 2,000 excited transients.

On February 28, 1849, the *California,* first steamship to sail through the Golden Gate, arrived with her hold packed with gold-seekers from New Orleans taken on at Panama and her hurricane deck swarming with Peruvians, Chileños and Mexicans. Greeted by San Franciscans with wild cheering and by five American warships in the Bay with broadside salutes, the Pacific Mail steamer was promptly deserted both by passengers and crew in their headlong flight to the mines.

Already embroiled in the slavery issue, the Federal government virtually left California to its own devices for the next four years. The ambiguous powers of San Francisco's *ayuntamiento* were openly flouted by the inrush of fortune-hunters. Many of the town's merchants, who had been quietly getting rich, soon found themselves at the mercy of a lawless mob. Sam Brannan took the chaotic situation in his stride: he returned promptly and did a thriving business selling tacks, canvas, and redwood scantlings to the tent-dwellers who spread out over the sand-hills "like the camp of an army."

The remnants of Colonel Stevenson's regiment soon abandoned the hard toil of the placers and returned to the city, there to style themselves Regulators and enter the employ of shipowners as a police force to track down runaway sailors. In outlandish uniforms, with fiddle, fife, and drum, they soon earned the name "Hounds" for their penchant for "hounding" Mexicans, Peruvians, and others of darker skin to whom they denied all rights in this land "preserved by nature for Americans only, who possess noble hearts." On the night of July 15, 1849, these hoodlums raided the Chilean quarter; in that scene of pillage and general mayhem, one woman was murdered and a Hound stabbed with a bowie knife.

Alcalde T. M. Leavenworth, having neither the legal power nor the courage to make an arrest, let the incident pass; but the town's leading merchants had had enough of lawlessness. Led by Sam Brannan, who stood hurling invective at the Hounds from the rooftop of the *alcalde's* office in Portsmouth Square, San Francisco's first forces of law and order were mobilized. Leavenworth himself was compelled to give them some kind of legal sanction. By sunset 19 of the Hounds had been run down. Next day a grand jury indicted all 19 for conspiracy "to commit riot, rape, and murder." None of these proceedings, of course, had any legal status in California. The verdict was banishment from the territory, but although the Hounds disbanded—and the law-and-order men also—the convicted men could not be deported; and San Francisco's underworld continued to wage a stealthy warfare against the whole community.

W. T. "War-Is-Hell" Sherman presents in his *Memoirs* a graphic picture of the riotous Gold Rush metropolis during the wet winter of 1849 and the spring of 1850: "Montgomery Street had been filled up with brush and clay and I always dreaded to ride on horseback along it. . . . The rider was likely to be thrown and drowned in the mud." Kearny Street was impassable, "not even jackassable," except where it was paved for 25 yards with sacks of flour and bran, tobacco, stoves, and a piano. Drunks, known to stumble into the mire, would suffocate before rescue could arrive.

Portsmouth Square, ringed round on three sides by saloons and gambling dens, was a bedlam that roared night and day. Except for the city's merchants and a few other stationary inhabitants, the population was forever shuttling back and forth between the city and the gold camps. In the period from Christmas Eve, 1849, to June 22, 1851, San Francisco's ramshackle architecture was leveled by six successive fires. Not until after the fifth of these conflagrations did responsible citizens manage to lay charges of incendiarism against the Hounds' successors, the Sydney Ducks.

On June 9, 1851, the first Vigilance Committee was organized in the office of Sam Brannan, who became its president. Two days later, for the theft of a small safe, John Jenkins swung in the moonlight from a gable of the old Customhouse on Porthmouth Square. By July 1 the Vigilantes were so well organized that the city's homicide rate—which nevertheless was to include 1,000 murders between 1849 and 1856—declined temporarily. Among the reputable element, however, duels were common occurrences. Streets and gambling resorts were almost daily the scenes of casual gunfire.

On assuming office in 1850 Mayor John W. Geary had warned the City Council that ". . . we are without a dollar in the public treasury, and it is to be feared the city is greatly in debt. . . . In short, you are without a single requisite . . . for the protection of property, or for the maintenance of order." The warning had little effect. When the public debt had risen to $840,000, it was repudiated. Municipal officials, honest and otherwise, continued to be at the mercy of the Barbary Coast machine which put them in office. Sam Brannan could drum up a lynching as well as any rabble-rouser, but he was no match for those Tammany politicians whose wardheelers stuffed ballot boxes, paid out patronage and bribes, and terrorized voters at the polls. The influx of ticket-of-leave men—ex-convicts from Australia locally known as Sydney Ducks—had brought on a crime wave of alarming violence.

The rich yield of the placers began to run out in 1854. San Francisco went as wild in financial panic as it had been amid the inflation after 1849. One of the victims of the depression, James King of William, vented his chagrin over bad luck on the city's corrupt politicians through editorials in a newspaper he established for the purpose. For his scalping pen, the editor of the *Evening Bulletin* was shot down one day on Montgomery Street by city supervisor James P. Casey.

Already incensed by the failure of a jury to convict the slayer of U. S. Marshal William H. Richardson—one Charles Cora, a gambler, who had resented Richardson's public snubbing of his bagnio-keeping mistress—those San Franciscans grown weary of lawless ways quietly formed the second Vigilance Committee. Under the leadership of merchant William T. Coleman it went about its business with less fanfare, but more efficiency, than the Committee of 1851. Upon the day of James King of William's funeral, the bodies of Cora and Casey dangled from second-story windows of a building on Sacramento Street, later known as Fort Gunnybags.

Since California's admission to the Union in 1850 the new State had made some progress toward stable government. However, the militia recruited in San Francisco on orders from the governor to take over the extra-legal power of the Vigilance Committee was defied with armed resistance. By 1856 the Vigilantes had enrolled most of W. T. Sherman's militiamen within their ranks. At the height of its power the Committee numbered 9,000 men: a military body composed of infantry, artillery, and cavalry detachments. After an altercation with one of its officers a State Supreme Court judge, David S. Terry, was held in Fort Gunnybags, pending recovery of the victim of his bowie knife. During the life of the committee, there had been four executions, and some 30 undesirables had been banished from the State.

On August 18, 1856, the Vigilance Committee disbanded voluntarily. Respect for law and order, which a corrupt government had failed to inspire, was thus established by a popular instrument without legal authority. From the work of this "lawless" body sprang the People's Party which swept the municipal election of 1857 into the hands of men for whom honesty, aside from being the best policy, was a proviso of health and longevity.

BONANZA (1856–1875)

San Francisco's population of 50,000—at no time during the 1850's did it exceed this figure—had been perched on the bandwagon of the Gold Rush for five miraculous years. The roulette wheel was the symbol of its whole economy. When the stream of yellow metal ceased to pour down upon the town, however, the stakes of gamblers and speculators alike vanished into thin air. The crash dealt the relatively small, highly organized community a stunning blow. Inbound shipping decreased by half from 1853 to 1857; liabilities of bankrupt firms totaled more than $8,000,000. Nearly half the city's population was unemployed.

In February and March of 1855 Stockton and Los Angeles papers printed a number of sensational letters giving details of a purported rich strike on the Kern River. Thousands of people abandoned rich claims and steady employment in the rush to the new El Dorado. Additional thousands were preparing to follow when letters from the area brought the discouraging news that there was not work for more than 100 men. The unemployment burden was considerably lightened in 1858, however, when towards the end of summer, 18,000 men joined in a wild exodus to British Columbia's newly discovered Frazier River mines. With recovery came increased commercial activity; and demands from growing agricultural districts for articles of domestic and foreign manufacture laid the foundation of San Francisco's industrial prosperity. More than $4,000,000 a month in gold, besides, was being shipped out through the Golden Gate before the beginning of 1859.

The national controversy over slavery was rapidly dividing Californians into Secessionists and patriots loyal to the Union. As the "irreconcilable conflict" approached a crisis, it became apparent that the State might join the Southern cause. Among San Franciscans this political cleavage was the occasion for personal feuds in which damaging accusations and unprintable remarks led logically to "shooting it out." Consequently when California's champion against slavery in the United States Senate, David C. Broderick, cast aspersions upon Secessionist Judge David S. Terry, chief justice of the State Supreme Court, the latter promptly challenged the somber-faced Senator to a duel. Broderick was killed; 30,000 San Franciscans attended his funeral; Terry was ostracized, and the Senator's martyrdom crystallized Union sentiment among the city's predominantly Yankee population.

Abraham Lincoln's election to the Presidency was acclaimed by San Francisco's Union sympathizers with wild demonstrations in the streets.

Huge mass meetings were addressed by Senator Edward Baker and Unitarian minister Thomas Starr King, both of whom toured the State for the Union cause. Brigadier-General Albert Sidney Johnston, in command of the Presidio and the Department of the Pacific, was displaced by General E. V. Sumner following charges that Johnston was in league with Senator William M. Gwin to turn over California's armed forces to the Confederacy. Sumner's arrest of Gwin left the State's Secessionists without leadership, and their conspiracy collapsed.

With California won for the North, San Francisco proceeded to develop its commerce and industry, in virtual isolation from the War between the States. Its most substantial contribution to the Union cause was the $566,790.66 in gold sent to the United States Sanitary Commission for aid to the sick and wounded among the Northern troops.

The slump in gold production after 1860 found compensation in the growth of new industries and increasing trade. The Nation's treaty with the Hawaiian Islands, permitting free entry of raw sugar, resulted in the establishment of San Francisco's first refinery. The development of transportation brought increasing prosperity to sawmills, foundries, and other enterprises spreading rapidly over the Bay area. On October 24, 1861, San Francisco and New York were connected by telegraph. That same year a young engineer, Theodore Dehone Judah, finally convinced a small group of businessmen that a railroad could be built across the Sierra Nevada.

The possibility of transporting the fabulous silver deposits of Nevada's Comstock Lode to San Francisco by rail inspired even the least imaginative of the city's entrepreneurs. Charles Crocker, Mark Hopkins, Leland Stanford, and Collis P. Huntington—Sacramento merchants with a bare $50,000 among them—saw in Judah's plan their chance to corner for themselves the wealth of California's growing commerce. Prototypes of San Francisco's later financial giants, the predestined "Big Four" organized the Central Pacific Company of California on June 28, 1861. President Lincoln's signing of the Pacific Railroad Bill a year later was the signal for the eight-year race between the Central and the Union Pacific to join the rails of the Nation's first transcontinental railroad.

The completion of this epical undertaking in 1869, though it meant the end of San Francisco's splendid isolation from the national economy, was no occasion for jubilance. The "terrible seventies" were immediately ahead. A goodly portion of the 65,000-odd Chinese coolies whom Crocker and his associates had imported to build the Central Pacific's roadbed came drifting back into the city to compete with jobless whites. Gold production in the State's placer mines, over $44,000,-000 annually until 1860, had shrunk by 1870 to $15,000,000; and unemployment once more became a source of unrest that flared up with increasing violence.   The titanic struggle between the Bank of California and its rivals in Virginia City was a speculator's nightmare in which the brokerage firms of Leidesdorff Street were mobbed by suckers rich and poor who sank savings and borrowed funds in "California" and "Consolidated Virginia." Not until the crash of the Bank of California in August, 1875, did the gambling frenzy reminiscent of the Gold Rush fitfully subside.   When by 1877 the nightmare was over at last, carefree San Francisco's "Golden Age" was irretrievably gone.

With the advent of hard times the labor unions, into which practically every trade in the city had been organized during the decade after 1865, carried their powerful economic struggles into the political field. The rising Workingmen's Party began holding great mass meetings where an Irish drayman, Dennis Kearney, delivered inflammatory harangues which soon made him the leader of a widespread movement to exclude the Chinese from industries employing white labor.   By 1879, however, the Workingmen's Party was coming under the control of cooler heads; and its delegates to the Constitutional Convention of that year brought to Sacramento a program of constructive proposals, several of which were adopted.

For his outspoken charges against local political conditions and for his advocacy of the workingmen's cause, Isaac S. Kalloch, a Baptist minister of considerable oratorical ability, became a candidate for mayor of San Francisco that same year.   His bitterest opponents were the De Young brothers, owners and editors of the *San Francisco Chronicle,* who waged a highly personal war of words with Kalloch until the latter's blistering *riposte finale* caused Charles de Young to blaze away at him with a pistol.   Not fatally wounded, Kalloch was enthusiastically elected; but the feud went on until, on the evening of April 23, 1880, Kalloch's son forestalled further damage to his father's battered reputation by fatally shooting De Young.   With public sentiment in his favor, young Kalloch was acquitted.

BIG CITY (1875-1906)

The city's configuration, minus only its outlying residential districts, is already apparent in Currier and Ives' *The City of San Francisco— 1878* (a bird's-eye view).   The gospel of bigness which William C. Ralston "the Magnificent" had preached by lavish example had caught the city's imagination.   An unkempt metropolis whose nocturnal thoroughfares were still murky with gaslight, a patchwork of paved and cobbled streets with plank sidewalks, San Francisco, by 1885, had ended the first decade of its expansive modern phase.   The decade preceding the panic of 1893 was one of general prosperity in which "The Railroad" was able to gain control of the city through the machinations of

Chris Buckley, blind political boss in its pay, while depositors of savings banks viewed their accounts with satisfaction.

San Francisco's population was nearly 300,000 when, in 1893, a Nation-wide depression caused the closing of 18 local banks. Hundreds of the city's unemployed, forming a local contingent of "Coxey's Army," set out for Washington to demand Federal aid. The following year the Mid-winter Fair, designed to facilitate business revival, was partially successful. But the Southern Pacific's monopoly of transportation still prevented any substantial recovery.

When the Bank of California's old enemy, Adolph Sutro, was elected mayor of San Francisco in 1894, the long-drawn-out struggle to break the power of "The Railroad" began. The public still believed, however, that the prosperity of the community depended on the success of the "Corporation"—and that the Corporation depended for success on special privilege—and Sutro's battle against the Southern Pacific was doomed to be a solitary and thankless feud. His successor in office, James D. Phelan, was somewhat more successful. Despite opposition from the railroad's political machine, Phelan in May 1898 obtained ratification of a new charter which was considered a model for progressive municipal government. In an attempt to beautify the city, numerous parks and public playgrounds were established, and so popular had the "city beautiful" movement become by 1899 that $18,000,000 had been voted for public improvements. In his third and last term as mayor, however, Phelan lost his popularity by attempting to break a city-wide strike of teamsters.

Out of this prolonged and violent teamsters' strike of 1901 arose the Union Labor Party. In the election of 1902 its candidate for mayor, Eugene E. Schmitz of the Musicians' Union, was elected by a sizeable majority. Though Schmitz himself seems to have had honorable intentions, he soon came under the dominance of Abraham Ruef, shrewdest of the city's long succession of political bosses. It became common knowledge within the next four years that the entire structure of municipal government was worm-eaten with graft.

For 50 years San Francisco's tenderloin had been a haven for criminals and prostitutes of every sort; and it had its own crude laws, its definite social gradations. Here, in an area roughly bounded by Clay Street, Grant Avenue, Broadway, and the water front, was that infamous quarter named by seafarers for those pirate-infested shores of North Africa: the Barbary Coast. On November 28, 1869, the *San Francisco Call* had deplored the fact that the region abounded in "scenes of wretchedness and pollution unparalleled on this side of the great mountains"; but since its denizens preyed chiefly upon each other and on such victims as were foolish enough to venture among them, the municipal authorities let them go to the devil in their own way. Leaders

Industry: Arts: Learning

MURAL BY DIEGO RIVERA, SAN FRANCISCO STOCK EXCHANGE

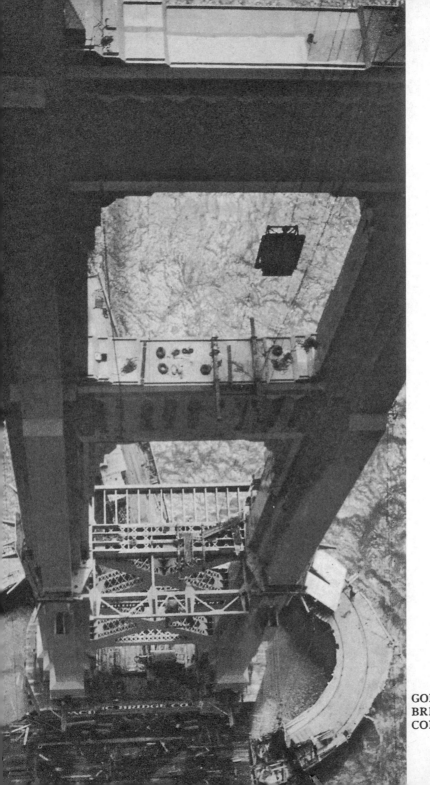

GOLDEN GATE
BRIDGE UNDE
CONSTRUCTIO

WATER AND POWER FROM THE SIERRA: O'SHAUGHNESSY DAM

STEAMERS DRYDOCKED IN OAKLAND

GIANT TOWERS CARRY 165,000 VOLTS ACROSS CARQUINEZ STRAIT

OIL FOR THE WORLD AT POINT RICHMOND

SUGAR REFINING AT CARQUINEZ STRAIT

STANFORD CHAPEL FROM THE QUAD, PALO ALTO

MILLS COLLEGE ART GALLERY, OAKLAND

LICK OBSERVATORY, MOUNT HAMILTON

UNIVERSITY OF CALIFORNIA

SATHER GATE

MEMORIAL BY BENIAMO BUFANO

SUN YAT SEN, IN ST. MARY'S SQUARE

of the Barbary Coast's gang of hoodlums—criminal descendants of the Hounds and the Sydney Ducks of Gold Rush times—forced profits from the myriad resorts of vice, and in their turn paid protection money to the political machine which was exacting tribute from respectable San Franciscans in other ways.

"The Wickedest City in the World" it might be; but its flourishing vice traffic and its scandalous misgovernment notwithstanding, San Francisco in 1906 had attained the stature of undisputed metropolis of the Pacific Coast. With a population of nearly 400,000, with its great hotels and churches and commercial establishments—its numerous fine schools, libraries, and hospitals—the city by the Golden Gate was a recognized world center of trade and finance and a gay capital of international society on a par with London, New York, and Paris.

Five o'clock on the morning of April 18, 1906, and all was well. The majority of the city's population was peacefully asleep. "Families of artisans and mechanics living in homes and lodging houses south of Market Street were be-stirring themselves. Oil stoves were lighted and smoke was lazily curling out of kitchen chimneys . . . when at thirteen minutes past the hour, the deeps of the earth, far down under the foundations of the city, began to rumble and vibrate." Instantly the whole community was awake, transfixed and speechless with alarm. "The earth tremors increased in violence . . . there was a sickening sensation as if everything were toppling. Plaster poured from ceilings . . . heavy furniture moved about banged upon the floor; and then the brick walls gave way . . . Tall structures, ribbed and rocked with steel, swayed like trees in a wind-storm, but stood triumphant at the end with scarce a brick or stone displaced."

Such, in Charles Keeler's description, was the first impact of the earthquake. It lasted only 48 seconds. Few persons, outside the downtown business district, had any idea of the extent of the calamity which had befallen the city. Certainly no one dreamed that this was to be but the prelude to its destruction. The crowds of bewildered citizens who rushed out into the streets in their night-clothing, seeing no more than some fallen masonry and sniffing the pall of dust, straggled back to their rooms to wash their faces and get decently dressed.

Well-constructed buildings were hardly damaged at all. The most appalling ruin was that of the great City Hall, on which $7,000,000 of public funds had been squandered. But San Francisco was 90 per cent frame, a larger portion of wooden buildings than any city in the United States. Old lodging houses of the laboring poor, in the congested area south of Market Street, bore the full brunt of the shock; and as these toppled over upon countless screaming victims, fires from overturned stoves within the wreckage blazed up in a score of widely separated places. A terrific explosion shook the area: the city's gas works had blown up. No alarms were struck owing to complete breakdown of the fire alarm system, and as fire engines went clanging through the streets, a huge cloud of smoke rose over all the southern section of the city.

Crowds of anxious spectators and the horde of refugees from the burning district were amazed at the sight of artillery troops and caissons from the Presidio rumbling down Montgomery Street. The sound of muffled explosions, coming from the edge of the approaching wall of flame, confirmed the rumor that water mains had been disrupted by the earthquake, and that dynamite was being used in a desperate attempt to save the city. As the day advanced the fire swept along the water front, leaped across Market Street. By nightfall Chinatown and all the business district was ablaze. The South of Market area was a charred and smouldering ruin. Endless streams of refugees fled to the hilltops or westward to Golden Gate Park.

By nightfall of the second day, with the raging inferno moving steadily westward as if to engulf the entire city, a last stand was made by the army of fire fighters at Van Ness Avenue. With charges of dynamite they blasted to heaps of rubbish the long line of mansions forming that wide thoroughfare's eastern facade. The heartbreaking destruction, at last, turned the tide. Not until Saturday morning, April 21, however, did the fire finally burn itself out among the scattered houses of North Beach. The center of the city—an area of 512 blocks containing a total of 28,188 buildings great and small—had been demolished in 72 hours. Property losses amounted to $500,000,000. Three hundred and fifteen bodies were recovered from the debris and ashes; 352 persons remained unaccounted for. In the Presidio, in Golden Gate Park, and in parks and lots outside the burned area more than 250,000 homeless citizens were encamped; and 100,000 more had fled to safety across the Bay or down the San Francisco Peninsula.

RISING PHOENIX (1906-1940)

To all intents and purposes, though never by actual proclamation of the mayor, the city was under martial law from the morning of the earthquake until about the middle of May. Besides Federal troops and a naval patrol, State militia and the local police force, a citizen's committee appointed by Mayor Schmitz patrolled the city; and on his authority these various law-enforcing bodies were instructed to "shoot to KILL any and all persons found engaged in looting or in the Commission of Any Other Crime." That remarkable propensity for bringing order out of the howling chaos—or, as Josiah Royce puts it, that American genius for self-government—was never better demonstrated than during the weeks of feverish reconstruction which followed the calamity. Despite the enormity of the disaster, it had the salutary effect of reducing all classes and condition of men to the common denominator of the breadline, wherein the goodnatured camaraderie of the early days of '49 was suddenly restored. For two months following the earthquake and fire the hitherto diverse and antagonistic social elements worked together in jovial accord, and San Francisco was the best-behaved city in America. Night and day the labor of clearing away the rubbish, of laying new foundations, went on at a lively pace. With the opening of a thousand makeshift saloons, however, the city fell from grace; within three months 83 criminal offenses were committed and some 6,000 pistol permits were issued for defense of persons and property.

The ashes of San Francisco were hardly cool when the drive to "clean up the city" that was interrupted by the disaster was resumed. Public-spirited citizens led by ex-Mayor James Phelan and Rudolph Spreckels led the attack against "the System" of Abe Ruef, the municipal government, and the Southern Pacific Company's subsidiary, the United Railways. The graft investigation opened with charges that city officials had granted the United Railways a monopoly of streetcar franchises in exchange for bribes, thus preventing the $11,000,000 municipal railway organized by Spreckels and Phelan from operating traction lines in competition with the private company.

Assisted by Fremont Older, crusading editor of the *Bulletin,* and attorney Francis J. Heney, prosecutor of Oregon's infamous land frauds, the graft investigators established not only the bribe-taking of city supervisors in the matter of railway franchises but also brought to light the complicity of these officials in aiding private corporations to gain control of municipal public utilities. Testimony of the 18 supervisors, who were promised immunity for confessions when faced with proof of their guilt, convicted Abe Ruef and put Mayor Schmitz behind bars.

Despite all this name-calling and legal violence the work of rebuilding the city went steadily on. The $175,000,000 paid to holders of insurance policies furnished a substantial impetus to rehabilitation. Within the year following the disaster construction amounting to more than $80,000,000 was undertaken. By 1909 construction figures had reached $150,000,000; and the devastated area was almost completely rebuilt by the end of the year.

Reformist Mayor Edward Robeson Taylor, who had succeeded the unlucky Schmitz, was displaced in the election of 1909 by the Union Labor Party's candidate, P. H. McCarthy. Despite apparent collapse of the campaign against the "Interests," the sentiment for reform had permeated the whole State; and the election of Hiram Johnson to the governorship saw the appointment of a Railroad Commission that smashed the power of the Southern Pacific's machine which had dominated California for almost half a century. Following the election of James Rolph, Jr., in 1911, the Union Labor Party went into a decline. It is, however, still the political arm of the American Federation of Labor and endorses candidates but does not run its own slate.

Consistently returned to office for the next 20 years, "Sunny Jim" Rolph was a prince of glad-handers in high-heeled polished boots, ten-gallon hats, and Palm Beach suits who brought to San Francisco a bizarre policy of goodwill that was the outward symbol of confidence and prosperity. His prolonged administration saw the extension of streets into residential districts beyond the hills, electrification of street railways and extended municipal ownership of public utilities; the successful Panama-Pacific International Exposition; the hysteria preceding American entrance into the World War and the speculative boom of the early '20's; the eclipse of social conviviality in the morbid Prohibition days of bad gin, sex, and jazz.

When the State's Red Light Abatement Act and the revoking of dance-hall licenses finally brought to an end in 1917 the long career of the Barbary Coast, old-timers watched its passing with aching hearts. Pride in the splendor of the rising city, however, turned the eyes of San Franciscans to the future as great hotels, lofty apartment houses, and skyscrapers brought to the truncated skyline the aspect of a massive American metropolis. Thrilling tribute to a three-quarter century of progress was the city's Diamond Jubilee of 1925, when the Nation's naval forces—forming a procession 25 miles in length—steamed in through the Golden Gate.

The Nation-wide financial crisis of 1929 did not immediately check San Francisco's business boom, and public improvements continued. In 1930 its population passed the 634,000 mark. The great Hetch-Hetchy dam in the high Sierras was nearing completion, and pending availability of its resources of light and power the city augmented its public utilities by purchasing the Spring Valley Water Company. Municipal government cast off its outmoded legal garment and clothed itself in the shining armor of a new charter. Even the onslaught of the depression which struck the city in 1932, while it brought on a decline in shipping and industry and threw some 70,000 workers out of employment, delayed only for another year the initial construction of the San Francisco-Oakland Bay Bridge. The city's sound financial and business structure enabled it to emerge with losses less serious than those of any other major American city.

The Golden Gate International Exposition of 1939-40, planned as a "Pageant of the Pacific" to celebrate the completion of the two great bridges across the Bay and the Golden Gate, was attended in 1939 by 10,496,203 visitors; it gave to the Bay area the impetus needed to raise

San Francisco business indices to pre-depression levels. Even more vast and incalculable appear the cultural influences which may be derived from this "World's Fair of the West" in the new era of increasing relations with the nations of the Pacific and the western hemisphere.

San Franciscans at Work

"No occupation was considered at all derogatory . . . Every kind of business, custom, and employment, was solicited . . . the field was open, and every one was striving for what seemed to be within the reach of all—a foremost rank in his own sphere."
—J. D. BORTHWICK (1857)

WHEN the first streaks of dawn scatter the night, San Francisco awakes, not to the march of early morning factory workers, but to the whir of limousines speeding brokers to the Stock Exchange. For in San Francisco, because of the difference between Pacific and Atlantic time, they must be at work by six of a summer morning to be on the floor of the Exchange when Wall Street begins trading. In winter, when daylight saving has been discontinued in the East, the San Francisco broker may sleep on hour later.

But the stock brokers are not the earliest risers. At two in the morning the area east of Montgomery Street and the financial district already has begun filling, the narrow streets rumbling to the heavy wheels of trucks bringing fresh fruits and vegetables from Peninsula truck farms and valley ranches to the wholesale produce markets. And in North Beach the crab fishermen are hurrying to the wharf, anxious to push their small boats through the Gate on an acquiescent tide.

When the siren at the Ferry Building sounds eight o'clock the water front comes suddenly to life. Longshoremen surge through steel-jawed pier doors, teamsters and trucks at their heels. As loading and discharging of cargo proceeds in the nearby warehouses some eight to ten thousand warehousemen sort, check, and pile the thousands of tons of merchandise for storage, transshipment, or distribution. Here, on or near the water front, congregate the crews of the many vessels from tugboats to passenger liners—sailors and marine engineers, radio telegraphers and bargemen, firemen, oilers, and watertenders. Masters, mates and pilots, cooks and stewards join the groups clambering aboard the ships at dock.

Here too are the shoreworkers: the maritime jitney drivers hauling trucks of cargo from pier to pier, the scalers who scrape and paint the hulls and tanks and holds of the ships, the lumber handlers who pile and unpile the millions of feet of lumber unloaded by steam schooners. Marine machinists and boilermakers, shipbuilders and wharfbuilders, watchmen, checkers, and maritime office employees—all of these come to work in the city within a city that is San Francisco's Embarcadero.

As the men and women who haunt the silent office buildings at night climb aboard outbound streetcars at dawn and stare sleepily out of windows, yawning, anxious only to get home, the trickle of white-collar workers which will soon become a river of humanity is already flowing from the opposite direction. Soon the cars are packed with office workers, doctors, lawyers, stenographers, and salespeople, who populate the downtown area and line lunch counters behind steam-covered windows, seeking the morning cup of coffee. Down the California Street hill come the bulging cable cars to disgorge their human cargoes into the financial district—cars locally dubbed "Stenographers' Specials," loaded with the female office workers whom eastern columnists have called "the most beautiful working-girls in the world." Warehousemen, factory workers, printers mingle with the white-collar workers, clutching transfers, smoking, hurrying to the job. The stream of humanity moving east is joined by another, the commuters coming from the Bay Bridge train terminal, overcoated, packing rumpled newspapers, books, and purses. From the ferries and bridges—from Marin County, Oakland, Berkeley, Alameda, and Peninsula towns—they come. As they pour into the doorways of department stores, shops, and office buildings, there comes to the observer the significance of statistics which say that in San Francisco the ratio of white-collar workers to manual workers is more than that of any other American city.

Meanwhile along the southern shore of the city proceeds the inpouring of the stockyard and industrial workers, the men who sweat in the freight sheds, the sugar refinery in Butchertown, and the fish reduction plant; who toil in the railway repair shops, the shipyards and drydocks, the foundries, the steel and wire and pipe industries, the drab cement and gravel plants. Here more than anywhere else in San Francisco comes the impression of the trek to work of a grimy march of men to the music of necessity—men totaling more than 68,000, equaling in numbers those employed in wholesale and retail trade.

Among the city's 250,000 gainfully employed workers, the greatest concentration occurs in about equal proportion in the manufacturing industries, in the retail and wholesale trades, and in transportation and communication. With an estimated 50,000 dependent upon direct maritime activities, the balance are engaged in the innumerable pursuits of a commercial, financial, and distributing center. More than 21,441 are engaged in real estate, insurance, and finance; 32,565 in service establishments; and 24,642 in professional and semi-professional pursuits.

As the morning wears on, the newsboys shout raucously. The owners of flower stands pack bright, dripping carnations and gardenias in colorful rows along the sidewalks. Suddenly the newsboys are silent, waiting later editions and blacker headlines. The buildings spew forth their crowds to seek a quick lunch in drug store, cafeteria, and restaurant.

Women shoppers throng Market Street after lunch, peering into store windows. Uniformed ushers and doormen stand idly by box offices, awaiting matinee crowds. Finally, the sun ducks behind the office buildings, and the homeward rush begins.

As day merges into night, neon lights flash on. Cocktail lounges begin to fill; darkness brings a dinner rush. Musicians and entertainers, waitresses and night cooks scurry through alley entrances to the centers of the city's night life. Taxis move from hotel to night club, from restaurant to bar. Life becomes a rising tide, hidden behind frosted glass, pulsing to the blare of nickel phonographs or the fevered tunes of swing bands.

And then at two a. m. the lights go out; stools and tables are stacked; doors are closed. Musicians and dancers, kitchen help and customers, going home through dark and empty streets, hear the swish of street-cleaning trucks. The flare of an electric welder busy at a street intersection flashes through the night. Soon come the white milk trucks converging to their distribution points, and the mountainous garbage vans clattering from restaurant back doors loaded for suburban pig farms. Already stirring are the produce workers and fishermen whose work is about to begin.

So the day ends and begins again, and time has drawn another 24-hour circle around the city and its workers.

WALL STREET OF THE WEST

San Francisco's Montgomery Street, "Wall Street of the West," runs north from Market Street between tall, austere office buildings, a canyon of high finance. What men say in offices, staid restaurants, and soft-lighted bars along Montgomery Street is passed on by the ticker tapes of the Nation, is translated into the languages and dialects of Mexico, South America, Australia, the Orient. Great farms, staggering lumber resources, Hawaiian sugar and Guatemalan coffee plantations, broad oil fields with their forests of derricks, Alaskan fish canneries and some of the largest fruit canneries in the world, shipping lines that encircle the globe, mines and power plants—the life blood of all these is regulated in Montgomery Street's board rooms and brokerage firms.

Up the street toward the Plaza in May, 1848, out of breath and dusty after his trip from the diggings, hurried Sam Brannan. Within five years he would become California's first millionaire—and Montgomery Street would be lined with bankers' offices. As gold dust began coming down the Sacramento, some means for handling it had to be found. The first requisites were scales and a safe, to weigh and store the precious metal; and so storekeepers were the first bankers. Soon merchants, assayers, and express companies were buying up gold dust in exchange for drafts on Eastern banks. And before the end of the year, Stephen A. Wright had opened his Miners' Bank with an advertised capital of $200,000 and was collecting interest of from 8 to 15 per cent a month on real estate loans. He was soon competing with others: Henry M. Naglee; Lucas Turner and Company, represented by William Tecumseh Sherman—and even the Rothschilds.

Rich in gold, San Francisco nonetheless found itself poor in money. A pinch of gold dust substituted for a dollar; a "bit piece" of dollar-length gold wire (divided into eight parts), for smaller coins—"two bits," "four bits," "six bits." The coins of every nation were pressed into service, at a rate of exchange based on their size. English shillings, French francs, and Mexican double-reals were as acceptable as American quarters. Peruvian doubloons, Spanish pesetas, Austrian zwanzigers, Dutch florins, Indian rupees changed hands regularly. Even the price of gold fluctuated from $8 to $16 an ounce until 1851, when it was stabilized at $16. In the absence of a mint, assay offices began to coin 5-, 10-, 20-, and 25-dollar slugs; at one time 14 such private mints were operating. Their coins varied widely in value, ranging from the Pacific Company's $10 gold pieces, worth $7.86, to Kohler and Company's, worth $10.10. Not until 1854, when the United States Mint was opened, were standards for coinage fixed.

The methods of Joseph C. Palmer of Palmer, Cook and Company, express agents who became bankers in 1851, reflected the spirit of the times. It is said a depositor once wanted to withdraw $28,000 from his account with the firm. Palmer's consent was necessary. The depositor found him in a lumber yard a mile from the bank. Neither pencil nor paper nor pen was available. Palmer picked up a shingle and on it, with a piece of red chalk, wrote a check for $28,000 which was readily accepted at the bank.

The express companies did a land-office business shipping gold to the east, receiving deposits, selling drafts and making loans. Outstanding among them was Wells Fargo, a name still familiar throughout the West. As early as 1852 this firm was selling exchange on 53 different cities in the country. In many California mining or ghost mining towns Wells Fargo scales on which millions of dollars in gold dust have been weighed are still on exhibit. The company became a bank in 1866, operating its banking activities in conjunction with its express business until 1878, when the two branches were separated.

The Gold Rush boom had so far overreached itself by 1854 that a crisis in mercantile affairs developed which steadily grew worse until the "Black Friday" of February 23, 1855, began a financial panic which forced 20 of the 42 banking firms to shut their doors forever. Real estate values slumped. Bankruptcies increased from 77 in 1854 to 197 in 1855. "Honest" Harry Meiggs, city alderman, fled to Chile, leaving behind $800,000 worth of bad debts, impartially distributed among the financial houses of the city, which were secured only by forged city warrants. Palmer, Cook and Company failed with a loss of $3,500,000.

When in 1859 the flow of colossal riches from the silver deposits of Nevada mines began, however, a new era commenced which established San Francisco finally as financial center of the West. When the Federal government and all of the Eastern banks left the gold standard in 1862, William C. Ralston convinced San Francisco's business men that California must stay on gold. He pointed out that the Union would need gold, which they could ship to the East and exchange for greenbacks. As greenback values dropped—before the war was ended a gold dollar was worth two greenbacks—the merchants and investors profited handsomely.

As mining activities went on booming, San Francisco became again the turbulent city of the Gold Rush, but no longer was it necessary for a man to dig in the earth to make his poke. Fortunes were made daily —and lost as easily—in mining stocks. In 1862 forty men united to organize the San Francisco Stock and Exchange Board.

In the second year of the war, when President Lincoln signed the Pacific Railroad Bill, the "Big Four" began laying the tracks of the Central Pacific eastward.

The Comstock Lode was pouring wealth into San Francisco, and William C. Ralston had a finger in the most important of the mines. On July 5, 1864, his Bank of California opened with D. O. Mills as president. For more than ten years it was to be the power back of the greatest undertakings in the West. Bank money developed the Comstock Lode—and the Lode repaid more than abundantly. When the "Big Four" were blocked in their efforts to put the railroad through, Ralston loaned them bank money on their personal notes, and assumed personal responsibility for their debts.

The collapse of the short boom in real estate prices which followed the driving of the last spike in the transcontinental railroad in May, 1869, left Ralston holding much property in the Montgomery Street extension south of Market. When it began to appear that the Comstock Lode, in which millions of the Bank of California's deposits had been sunk, was worn out, rumors started that threatened to cause a run on the bank. In September, 1869, the night before the run was expected, Ralston managed a stunt which has never been duplicated. During the night, Ashbury Harpending and a man named Dore, exchanged five tons of gold with the United States Sub-Treasury for coined money. These men carried this load by hand throughout the night. In the morning, when the run began, Ralston was able to put on the tables, in sight of the depositors, an inexhaustible supply of coined money. The panic stopped almost as soon as it had started.

During 1865 and 1866, the mines seemed to have played out as one by one they reached the end of visible ore. Adolph Sutro, a German-Jewish emigrant, conceived the idea of building a tunnel under the Comstock Lode to drain flooded shafts and to reach ore that was too deep for the mining methods of that time. Ralston at first was impressed, but the "Ring" was afraid of anyone's else cutting in on the rich profits of the mines. Ultimately Sutro had to fight the whole Bank of California ring to put the Sutro Tunnel through. His epic nine-year struggle against the Bank was the beginning of the fall of Ralston's empire.

By 1870, according to popular opinion, the Comstock had reached bottom rock, and there seemed little chance of further veins being discovered. But several astute miners were quietly buying up the stock of several of the mines. John Jones and Alvinza Hayward got the Crown Point Mine away from the "Ring." In 1872 two young mining men, John W. Mackay and James G. Fair, who had worked in the Comstock mines, formed an association with James G. Flood and William S. O'Brien, San Francisco saloon keepers who for years had dabbled in mining stocks. For less than $100,000, the quartet quietly obtained control of the California and the Consolidated Virginia, two mines which had yet shown little promise. The discovery of a few veins started the stock market booming. By 1872, stocks which had been listed at $10 a share were bringing hundreds. Consolidated Virginia jumped from $160 to $710. San Francisco went stock-gambling mad. Nowhere could one hear anything but names of mines and stocks—Kentuck, Yellow Jacket, Crown Point, Consolidated Virginia, Ophir, Gould and Curry, Savage. Again the feeling that the riches under the Lode were inexhaustible swept San Francisco.

Then, like a flaming comet over the horizon of Montgomery Street, blazed the news that the "Nevada Four's" two mines, known as the Big Bonanza, covered the richest vein of ore in the Comstock Lode. Mackay, Fair, Flood, and O'Brien had already taken the precaution of buying up all available stock before releasing the news. Holding unlimited funds, they settled down to relentless warfare with Ralston and the Bank of California. The objective was control of the incredibly rich Comstock mines. The physical properties lay elsewhere but the blows were struck on the exchanges of San Francisco's Wall Street of the West.

As the struggle proceeded, San Francisco was swept by an unprecedented frenzy of speculation. Gambling tables in the city were practically deserted. On the street curbs in the financial district women brokers, dubbed "mudhens," hawked stock of all descriptions. Women wearing diamonds and expensive clothes joined the morning crowds flocking to the exchanges.

The downfall of Ralston in 1875 brought financial San Francisco down with him. Resolved to break the Bank of California, the Nevada Four planned to open a rival bank. Ralston meanwhile was seeking control of the Ophir mine, valued fictitiously at $31,000,000, in the belief that it covered part of the Big Bonanza. James Keene, presiding member of the Stock Exchange, quietly bought large blocks of Ophir stock for him. "Lucky" Baldwin, hearing the stock was in great demand, secured many shares which he sold, netting himself a nice profit of millions. Ralston alone was overloaded with Ophir stock when it was disclosed that the mine was an empty hole. William Sharon, Ralston's right hand man, had known—and quietly unloaded his shares in the mine, neglecting to tell Ralston. In February, 1875 a rumor swept the city that the Big Bonanza had given out, and the stock market crashed. The drop in market values shook the Bank of California. It began to be rumored that the bank was unsound, and that Ralston was to blame because of his speculations. The new Bank of Nevada withdrew cash deposits from the leading banks of San Francisco, in order to open its own doors with a $5,000,000 reserve in actual coin. The withdrawals sent most of the banks to the edge of insolvency. Ralston began to sell his holdings wherever possible in order to raise money. On August 26, 1875, after weeks of crashing values in mine shares and an exhausting run, the Bank of California closed its doors.

The next day Ralston, as was his habit, went swimming. His drowned body was found in the Bay off North Beach.

The failure of the Bank of California for a time stopped all trading on the Exchange. The bank was reorganized by D. O. Mills and William Sharon, who had profited heavily by sale of Ophir stock. But when it reopened, it found the Bank of Nevada, opened a few days later by the Nevada Four, already dominant in San Francisco.

Montgomery Street's era of crusading capitalists had come to an end. In the period that followed, high finance pursued a steadier course. In 1875 the San Francisco Clearing House, first in the State, was organized; before the year had passed it was fifth in importance in the United States. The year 1877 saw the establishment of a State Board of Bank Commissioners, despite terrific opposition. In 1882 the present San Francisco Stock Exchange was established. The year following, Charles Crocker organized the banking firm of Crocker-Woolworth and Company, which today is the Crocker First National. The 1884 depression in the Eastern States was scarcely felt in San Francisco, but closer financial ties brought the effects of the 1893 panic to Montgomery Street within a few months of the time it was felt in New York.

The fire of 1906 was the occasion for the rise of another spectacular figure. Since 1904, A. P. Giannini, a commission merchant who had retired with a comfortable income at the age of thirty-two, had been trying out his banking theories in the Bank of Italy (now the Bank of America), which he and his step-father had founded. Giannini was able to turn the disaster of 1906 to his advantage when he managed to remove the assets and records from his bank before the advancing fire reached them. They were hauled to his San Mateo home in wagons from his step-father's commission warehouse and camouflaged with a heap of fruits and vegetables. The Bank of Italy was the first in the city to be re-opened.

In 1909, Giannini launched a drive to create a State-wide system of branch banks on the theory that branch banking was the best safe-guard against failure of banks in single-crop or single-industry regions because they served to spread the risk. His streamlined advertising campaign with full-page advertisements in the newspapers was un-precedented in banking history. He added bank after bank to his chain.

When the Federal Reserve System was established by Congress in 1913, San Francisco was selected as center for the Twelfth Federal Reserve District. Established in the following year, the San Francisco Federal Reserve Bank by 1939 had a membership of 282 of the 574 banks in operation in the twelfth district comprising an area including California, Oregon, Washington, Utah, Idaho, Nevada, and most of Arizona. Its resources have grown from $1,965,555,000 in December, 1914, to little short of $6,000,000,000 in 1939.

Of the vast financial network comprising present-day San Fran-cisco's citadels of business, the Wells Fargo Bank and Union Trust Company—Wells Fargo merged with the Nevada National Bank in 1905 and with the Union Trust Company in 1924—and the Hibernia Savings and Loan Society alone have had uninterrupted existence since the feverish days in which they were founded. But San Francisco remains the financial capital of the West. Six of its 21 banking firms are listed among the 50 largest in the country. The Bank of America, operating 506 branch banks throughout the West, ranks as the Nation's fourth largest financial corporation; its earnings in 1938 were $10,000,-000 greater than those of any other banking institution in the country. Only one San Francisco bank has failed in more than 30 years, and that one, a branch of the Bank of Canton, collapsed during a monetary crisis of the Chinese Revolution in 1926. Following the stock market crash of 1929, the leading bankers of San Francisco met and pledged a revolving fund of $100,000,000 to protect the city's banks against failure, with the result that not one cent was lost to depositors. Con-stantly seeking new outlets for investment the city's financial institutions have increasingly assumed closer control of industry and agriculture, of shipping and transportation.

San Francisco's bank clearings for 1938 totaled $7,000,000,000, fifth highest in the United States. Its per capita wealth is the highest in the country.

LABOR'S THOUSANDS

San Francisco workers are proud of their unions and jealous of union welfare. Employers estimate that half the population of San Francisco consists of union members and their families. All major West Coast union organizations maintain offices or headquarters in the city. There are an extensive inter-union sports movement and a junior union movement for the children of union men. The newspaper guildsmen, the warehousemen, the longshoremen, the bartenders, and the waiters and waitresses, among others, hold annual grand balls that are attended by thousands. The labor press, steeped in tradition, has a large following of readers. The CIO broadcasts a radio labor news program that is popular with AFL and CIO members alike. Despite the division between American Federation of Labor and Congress of Industrial Organizations, union men of both groups intermix freely.

Today industry-wide agreements arrived at by bargaining over the round table are becoming fairly common in the Bay area, particularly in the water-front industry, where both labor and employers are strongly organized. Sometimes these conferences are as dramatic in their own way as the strikes or lockouts which they often supplant. Union men and employers, at the appointed hour, crowd into the room, which more often than not is located in one of the city's most modern office buildings. Opponents may exchange guarded jokes. Brief cases are tossed on a table liberally supplied with ash trays. Debate is conducted with an alertness that demands frequent nervous lighting of cigar or cigaret. The press is often admitted. If an agreement is reached, its terms become big news, splashed at once across the front pages of the city's newspapers. When there is a deadlock, newspaper editors offer their own alternatives in front page editorials. Citizens write letters to their favorite papers suggesting solutions which are printed in the public forum columns. Columnists and radio commentators discuss the issues. Heated debates break out on the early morning streetcars.

Twice in recent years a water-front dispute has been taken to the general public by means of "town meetings" held in the Civic Auditorium and attended by thousands. There employers and union representatives debated from the platform and their talks were broadcast over extensive radio hookups. The audience often was as partisan as the chief participants, but a general good humor prevailed.

The city's union consciousness had its beginning in the days of the Gold Rush. "There are evidences of such early trade union activity in San Francisco," writes Lucille Eaves, "that one is tempted to believe that the craftsmen met each other on the way to California and agreed to unite." At least one instance proves the point: in 1864, when the Employers' Association of San Francisco, attempting to smash a strike of iron molders, wired East for strikebreakers, the unions dispatched representatives to Panama who met the men hired to take their jobs; when the ship docked in San Francisco all walked ashore as union brothers. Among the men who came to San Francisco were many from countries of Europe where the struggle for unions already had been in progress for many long years.

To combat an exorbitant cost of living, the unorganized carpenters and joiners struck in 1849, demanding a wage increase, which they won. Before a year had passed the San Francisco Typographical Society had been organized as the first bona fide trade union on the coast. Teamsters, musicians, riggers and stevedores, and building trades workers soon followed suit. These early unions, organized on the basis of immediate demands, appeared and disappeared in bewildering variety until the campaigns for the eight-hour day and against the competition of cheap Chinese labor supplied rallying points around which all could unite with some degree of permanence.

The Chinese, accustomed to a low standard of existence in their homeland, were employed here in many trades at a wage much lower than the Occidentals could afford to accept. The thousands of coolies who helped build the first railroad across the American continent were paid as little as $30 a month. When the railroad was completed, they flocked to San Francisco. In 1872 it was estimated they comprised nearly half of all the factory workers in the city. Occidental workers feared and resented the competition of this cheap labor. To combat it, they joined in an anti-Chinese campaign that sometimes found outlet in violence. It led finally to adoption of the Chinese Exclusion Act by the State legislature in the 1880's. Although anti-Chinese sentiment was widespread for many years after, the admission of Chinese to membership in a number of unions during recent years has marked its passing. A strike here of Chinese girls, members of the International Ladies Garment Workers Union, gained Nation-wide notice in 1937 when the attractive and dainty women pickets were pictured in the press of the country.

Out of the turbulence of the anti-Chinese movement arose Dennis Kearney, one-time vigilante and opportunist extraordinary. For a time his violent talks, made on the sand lots in what is now the Civic Center, captured the imagination of thousands. Opposed to him was a sincere young Irishman, a Fenian exile, named Frank Roney. The group around Roney succeeded in discrediting Kearney, who retired to private trade to be heard from no more. But Roney continued an active member of the trade union movement for many years. He organized the Seamen's Protective Association and became its president.

Largely because of Roney's work the Trades Assembly, a city-wide group, succeeded in doubling its membership. His plan of organizing unions into trade councils was later to be adopted on a national scale by the AFL. When the Trades Assembly sent delegates to a convention of the Federated Trades and Labor Union of the United States (which later became the American Federatioh of Labor), held in 1881, San Francisco labor for the first time became affiliated with an organization national in scope.

Always the lot of American seamen had been a hard one, and San Francisco was known as one of the world's toughest ports. It was common for a seaman ashore after a long trip, his wages in his pocket, to buy a drink at one of the many saloons—and wake up next morning aboard a vessel bound for Shanghai. The practice of kidnapping was so common that the term "shanghai" was applied to it. Against such abuses the Seamen's Protective Association fought.

A fight against wage cuts in 1885 resulted in formation of the Coast Seamen's Union. From this organization came the ascetic Norwegian, Andrew Furuseth. Emotional, sharp-featured, and extremely energetic, Furuseth, who later was known simply as "Old Andy," spent most of his life with the seamen. He was credited with knowing more about sea law than any other man alive. In his later years he helped unite American seamen into the International Seamen's Union, comprising sailors, firemen, and cooks and stewards. Aided by Senator Robert M. LaFollette in 1915, he succeeded in securing passage of the Seamen's Act, a Magna Carta of liberation for these men.

The Employers' and Manufacturers' Association of San Francisco, newly organized, opposed unionization in a campaign that took real effect as the depression of 1893 reached its depths. As union membership dropped to a mere 4,500, at least 35,000 jobless workers tramped the streets of the city in search of food and work. In 1894 the American Railway Unions struck against the Pullman Company in Chicago. Trains stopped and trans-Bay ferry service was paralyzed for ten days. Federal troops marched into San Francisco. In Oakland citizens raided roundhouses to extinguish fires in the locomotives. At this time, too, the Bay area contingent of the famous Coxey's Army was organized. Under the command of "General" Charles T. Kelley the unemployed army, credited with superior discipline, sought refuge for a few days in Oakland, then started on the long box-car ride across the continent.

Meanwhile the men on the water front had organized the City Front Federation. Several times before similar federations had been organized, notably the Wharf and Wave Federation in 1888 and the City Front Labor Council in 1891. But the City Front Federation was the strongest yet to be formed; it was, in fact, one of the best-organized groups of its kind in the country at that time. As the depression gradually became history, other union groups began to show signs of life. Particularly in the building trades did the organizing campaign show results. In December, 1900, the Central Labor Council called a convention of California unions at which a State Federation of Labor was formed. At the same time a State Building Trades Council was set up with P. H. McCarthy as president, an office he held continuously until 1922. Employers, too, were organizing. They built a new association, raised a huge war chest, and instituted a boycott against recalcitrants who recognized union groups. The new association operated secretly.

In 1901 trouble developed between the teamsters and the Draymen's Association that rapidly developed into a lockout. When the City Front Federation came to the aid of the teamsters, Bay area traffic was tied up. After a deadlock lasting two months, Governor Henry T. Gage came to San Francisco and arranged a meeting between employers and workers. A compromise was effected within an hour, the terms of which never were made public. The teamsters became a powerful segment of organized labor. Under the leadership of a broad-shouldered Irishman, Michael Casey, they branched out into fields hitherto untouched by unions. But the City Front Federation, wracked by internal dissension, declined in importance. Sailors, however, emerged in possession of a new agreement with shipowners.

The labor unions, angered by what they considered unnecessary police violence during the teamster struggle, formed the Union Labor Party. Aided by Father Yorke, Catholic priest and intimate friend of Jack London, the new party succeeded in gaining the election of Eugene Schmitz, a member of the Musicians' Union, as mayor. Three labor men were elected to the Board of Supervisors. But Schmitz became the puppet of Abe Ruef, shrewd political boss, and graft, corruption and bribery flourished. Ruef, Schmitz, and the supervisors were indicted by the grand jury in a reform wave that followed the 1906 earthquake. Ruef went to prison, but his henchmen and backers went free. Patrick Calhoun, head of the street railway corporation, which had been implicated in the bribery exposures, engineered a strike of the streetcar workers. Andrew Furuseth, Mike Casey, and Fremont Older attempted to halt the strike but were unsuccessful. When Calhoun imported strikebreakers who terrorized the carmen, it appeared he had saved the city, an impression he deliberately had set out to create. The carmen's union was demoralized.

Meanwhile P. H. McCarthy of the building trades unions had forged to the front. In 1909 he was elected mayor. Under his leadership the Building Trades Council built its own mills and enforced a boycott against mills outside the city, mills with wage rates lower than those of San Francisco.

When the longshoremen struck in 1916 for higher wages, the employers and the Chamber of Commerce organized the Law and Order Committee and issued a lengthy manifesto calling for unity of San Francisco's citizens. The Law and Order Committee succeeded in getting the city to pass an anti-picketing ordinance. Meanwhile, the war in Europe had begun to affect this country, which at the same time was engaged in a punitive expedition against Mexico. The atmosphere was tense. As anti-German sentiment grew, people were seeing spies behind every telephone. The city planned to hold a parade in favor of preparedness.

The parade, held July 22, 1916, had hardly gotten under way when a bomb exploded at Steuart and Market Streets, killing ten persons and injuring many more. Newspapers demanded the arrest of those guilty of the outrage. Among those arrested were Thomas J. Mooney and Warren K. Billings, both of whom were convicted.

Labor in California and throughout the United States was convinced that the two men were innocent. When repeated protests of world-wide scope caused President Woodrow Wilson to request Governor William D. Stevens to exercise leniency, Mooney's death sentence was commuted to one of life imprisonment. Later investigations disclosed irregularity in the conduct of the trial, in the handling and testimony of witnesses, and in the treatment of the jury. Judge Griffin, in whose court the trial had been held, declared in 1929: "The Mooney case is one of the dirtiest jobs ever put over and I resent the fact that my court was used for such a contemptible piece of work." As time wore on Mooney—and Billings—became, for labor, symbols of injustice, until Governor Culbert Olson, fulfilling a campaign promise, was able to pardon Mooney and aid in securing the release of Billings.

In 1921 San Francisco employers again drew closer together, forming the Industrial Association. The building trades unions lost ground when faced with the strong opposition of the new employer group. Metal trades workers and seamen lost strikes in 1921; carpenters, in 1926. Longshoremen, since 1919, had been obligated to become members of the Longshoremen's Association of San Francisco, an organization they considered to be under employer domination. They called it the "Blue Book Union," deriving the name from the color of the membership books. The Industrial Association maintained an employment office, a hotel for non-union workers, and a training school for non-union plasterers, bricklayers, plumbers, and carpenters. The only labor organizations that did not suffer from the general intertia that swept the city's trade union movement during this period were the Railway Brotherhoods. A Brotherhood bank was established in San

Francisco which merged with a non-labor bank after the collapse of the national Brotherhood's banking system.

The depression beginning in 1929 further weakened the organized labor movement until union sentiment began to revive with the passage of the National Recovery Act. The men on the water front were among the first to take advantage of Section 7-a of the act, dealing with labor organization. The longshoremen secured a charter under the International Longshoremen's Association of the AFL and, spurred by the pungent criticism and organizational appeals of an anonymously sponsored mimeograph bulletin, fully 90 per cent of the dock workers joined the ILA. Harry Bridges, wiry Australian longshoreman, came to the front as a leader and spokesman for the new group. A coastwise longshoremen's convention was held in 1934 and demands were made upon the shipowners. Subsequently a strike vote was taken.

On the morning of May 9 longshoremen in San Francisco and other Coast ports walked off the docks in what was to be one of the most dramatic struggles in the history of West Coast labor. On May 13 the teamsters, despite opposition of their leadership, voted unanimously against hauling cargo to or from the docks. On May 15 the seamen joined the strike, presenting their own demands to the employers; licensed officers followed suit. The newspapers reported that on May 15, for the first time in the history of Pacific Coast ports, not a freighter left port. Events were rapidly approaching a climax when the Industrial Association announced to the public that the port would be opened on July 5.

As the morning of July 5 dawned, strikers and police massed in great numbers at the pier from which cargo was to be hauled by non-union truck drivers. The pickets who attempted to approach the pier were forced back repeatedly by police. At Rincon Hill south of Market Street a pitched battle occurred between police and strikers. Two strikers were killed during the day and many were taken to the hospital suffering from wounds and tear gas. A few hours later the National Guard moved into the city and took over the water front.

July 5, now memorialized by the water-front unions each year under the name of "Bloody Thursday," crystallized sentiment for a city-wide general strike in sympathy with the maritime unions. Union after union voted to go out. On July 17, first day of the general strike, it was estimated that 127,000 San Francisco workers had left their jobs. A peculiar silence descended upon the city. Market Street, usually one of the busiest streets in the Nation, appeared deserted.

The general strike was ended July 20 at the instance of the Central Labor Council and thousands returned to their jobs. The water-front unions remained on strike for several days until their demands were given over to mediation. Eventually they gained greatly improved working conditions and, what was most important from their point of view, union hiring halls. A second maritime strike which tied up shipping along the entire coast in 1936 was ended in the first week of the new year with further improved working conditions.

The organization of the Congress of Industrial Organizations in 1935 found San Francisco sentiment divided. The longshoremen and their affiliates voted to join the new group, of which Harry Bridges was later made West Coast Director. The seamen were split; some preferred to remain with the AFL, some for a while maintained an independent status, and some joined the CIO. The effects of the split were felt in the bitter partisanship which appeared in the Maritime Federation of the Pacific, organized following the 1934 strike. But a strong and deeply rooted sentiment for unity in times of crisis prevented disintegration.

During the 1938 gubernatorial campaign in California organized labor united in San Francisco, pointing the way for the rest of the State in supporting candidates and issues favorable to the unions. Culbert Olson, the union-backed candidate, won the election. A State anti-picketing measure was voted down by a large majority. John F. Shelley, president of the AFL Central Labor Council, who was elected State senator from San Francisco, perhaps described the position of organized labor in the Bay area when he said: "When San Francisco labor is faced with a concrete issue, it will unite."

In 1939 the major employers of the city organized an Employers' Council for the purpose of dealing unitedly with the unions. When Almon E. Roth, chosen to head the group, took over his duties, he told the newspapers that "San Francisco actually has had fewer strikes and labor disturbances in recent years than most American cities of comparable size."

Social Heritage

"San Francisco knows how."
—President William Howard Taft

O F ALL the arts San Franciscans have practiced, the one they have most nearly perfected is the art of living, but hedonism is only one of the elements of which San Francisco's civilized social tradition is compounded. Omar Khayyam's "Take the Cash and let the Credit go" has been as freely accepted for a motto, perhaps, as his "jug of wine" and "loaf of bread"—and more freely than the spiritual precepts of the city's official patron, the gentle St. Francis.

Yet all through this materialism runs a fugitive thread of humanitarian tenderness; a reverence for culture, often uncritical; a fundamental urbanity. Every viewpoint has had its say in the city's long succession of journals and newspapers. Enriched also by this democratic quality is the whole history of the city's devotion to the theater, to musical performances and art exhibits, to restaurants and cabarets and bars. Where so much of living has vitalized a popular culture, the social heritage is bound to have a special richness.

HIGH LIFE AND LOW LIFE

A "sort of world's show of humanity"—such was that San Francisco which so impressed the visiting Britisher, J. D. Borthwick, in 1851, with its "immense amount of vitality compressed into a small compass." Around the same table in the gambling saloons he found "well-dressed, respectable-looking men, and, alongside of them, rough miners fresh from the diggings, with well-filled buckskin purses, dirty old flannel shirts, and shapeless hats; jolly tars half-seas over . . . Mexicans wrapped up in their blankets smoking cigaritas . . . Frenchmen in their blouses smoking black pipes; and little urchins, or little scamps rather, ten or twelve years of age, smoking cigars as big as themselves . . ." Along the streets, old miners were to be seen loafing about "in all the glory of mining costume . . . Troops of newly arrived Frenchmen marched along . . . their persons hung around with tin cups, frying-pans, coffee-pots, and other culinary utensils . . . Crowds of Chinamen were also to be seen, bound for the diggings, under gigantic basket-hats . . ."

After the first rush to the mines, most of this mob of immigrants returned to San Francisco to stay. Careless of the professions to which they had been trained, doctors and dentists became draymen, barbers, or shoeblacks. Lawyers and brokers turned waiters or auctioneers or butchers; merchants became laborers and laborers, merchants. Any and all of them kept lodginghouses and gambling saloons, speculated in real estate and merchandise—always ready to embark on some new enterprise.

Not without reason did the Argonauts boast that no coward ever started for California and no weakling ever got there. The Gold Rush was composed almost entirely of young men, many in their 'teens, with a lust for adventure as strong as their lust for fortune. In this adventurers' paradise, ladies of joy reveled in a degree of latitude rarely heard of in American history. While cribs and brothels catered to the unfastidious, more sumptuous parlors enticed the discriminating. When "the Countess," San Francisco's leading courtesan of 1849, opened her establishment, she sent cards of invitation to the town's leading citizens, not excluding the clergy. Full dress was the rule at this fasionable rendezvous, and six ounces of gold dust, or $96, was the price of an evening's entertainment.

Any talents used to entertain the public were handsomely appreciated. Dr. D. G. Robinson, part-owner of the Dramatic Museum, was elected alderman in 1851 to reward him for the pleasure he had given by renditions of his "Random Rhymes." No one thought it strange in 1849 when the Commissioner of Deeds, Stephen C. Massett, resigned from his job to compose songs and to give recitations and imitations. A strolling piper with "cymbal, triangle, accordion and bass-drum" gathered a "harvest," and "Dancing Billy" earned enough to buy drinks all around each time he stopped, and was able to pay his musician $50 an hour. The musicians "blew and scraped, thrummed and drummed, jingled and banged throughout the live-long day and night."

In every saloon were tables for monte and other card games, or for rondo and roulette and chuck-a-luck. Gambling facilities were the main source of revenue in all hotels. Merchants had to bid against their operators for places to do business; the resorts spilled over onto the wharves. Most of the gold which miners brought to town made its final disappearance over the tables, for the men had a superstition that it was bad luck not to be flat broke when they started back to the mines.

In 1853, the editors of the *Christian Advocate* made a survey of the town and "found, by actual count, the whole number of places where liquor is sold in this city to be five hundred and thirty-seven." Of these, 125 places did not even "keep an onion to modify the traffic." Forty-eight were "dance-houses and such like, where Chinese, Mexicans, Chilean, and other foreign women are assembled." Contemporary writers describe the saloons as "glittering like fairy palaces." The outlying taverns were spoken of with no less warmth: "A jolly place to lounge in easy, ricketty, old China cane chairs and on bulgy old sofas" was MacClaren's, on the lane to the Mission. Little inns with similar charm were strung along all the rural roads.

On Sunday, the Spanish village at the Mission was aglitter with the silver trappings of hitched horses, whose owners, having ridden out from the commercial settlement, were spending the day in the Spanish taverns. The Russ Gardens, along the Mission Road, were taken over on holidays and Sundays by national groups who "leaped, balanced and twirled, danced, sang, smoked and made merry."

Though the 1850's saw no abatement in gambling, drinking, and carousing, the more discriminating element of the population was gradually withdrawing from the more popular saloons and restaurants. New hotels and cafes were being established to meet their demands. The Parker House with its elegant appointments, its apple toddy, and its painting of *Eugenia and Her Maids of Honor,* vied for popularity with the Pisco Punch and the *Samson and Delilah* of the Bank Exchange. Around these, the Tehama, and the St. Francis gathered those who were groping toward refinement and that privacy which their lack of homes denied them. Private gambling dens were set up and a process of social selection began.

Steve Whipple's gambling house on Commercial Street was transformed, in 1850, into the first gentlemen's club, its clientèle girded in swallowtails and flashing diamond cuff links. Such devices for "drawing the line" were not without painful consequences to that spirit of camaraderie which the average forty-niner had naively come to expect of his fellow men. An anecdote of this period tells of a miner, wearing the rough clothes of the "diggings," who wandered inside and was politely informed by a waiter that he had strayed into a private club.

"A private club, eh?" retorted the miner. "Well, this used to be Steve Whipple's place and I see the same old crowd around!"

Nevertheless, San Francisco's leading citizens were determined to create some kind of orderly and civilized social pattern; and this tremendous task was finally solved by elevating the saloon, the cafe, and the theatre to places of social distinction. Even before 1851 there had been attempts to stage decorous balls and parties where "fancy dress" was required, but even the most successful of these affairs could not attract more than 25 ladies. A record was set in June, 1851, by the attendance of 30 fair maidens at the first of a series of *soirées* given at the St. Francis; and when 60 ladies showed up at the July *soirée,* the newspapers commended the St. Francis for the "social service" it had rendered.

But this hotel (which also first introduced bed sheets to the city) was to be the scene of an even greater triumph. This was a grand ball organized by the Monumental Six, the city's first company of volunteer firemen, at which no less than 500 ladies were present. It was said that California was ransacked for this array of femininity, and that some of them were brought by pony express from as far east as St. Joseph, Missouri. The press declared that at last "the elements were resolving themselves into social order."

Since the brilliance of this affair was not immediately repeated, the process of social cohesion threatened to give way once more to the rough-shod individualism of the forty-niners. Even the respectable women of San Francisco complained of the high cost of party dresses and avoided going out into the muddy and rat-infested streets. The men started attending the theater, but it offered little attraction. The rainy season set in and brought monotony to the city which, until then, had never known a dull moment.

In this social emergency, some enterprising individuals hit upon the idea of presenting a series of "promenade concerts." "A large crowd was present on the first evening, but . . . there were no ladies present to join in the ball at the close of the concert; and such a scene as was presented when the dancing commenced beggars description. . . . The music commenced; it was a polka; but no one liked to venture. At last two individuals, evidently determined to start the thing, ladies or no ladies, grappled each other in the usual way . . . and commenced stumping it through the crowd and around the hall . . . As dance after dance was announced more and more joined in, until . . . the whole floor [was] covered with *cotillions* composed entirely of men, with hats on, balancing to each other, chassezing, everyone heartily enjoying the exhilarating dance . . ." Whether or not the affair was a "failure," as McCabe's *Journal* called it, the promenade concerts were abandoned.

What civic-minded San Franciscans could never quite accomplish in the battle for social cohesion was brought about by natural and dire necessity. As a result of the conflagrations that had almost destroyed the city on six successive occasions, there had sprung up a number of companies of volunteer firemen, to which it was generally considered an honor to belong. A parade of San Francisco's firemen was the occasion for the whole State to go on a Roman holiday. Preceded by blaring bands and the gleaming engines decked with flags, the parades stretched a mile in length. Each fireman marched proudly to the martial music, attired magnificently in his red shirt and white muffler, his shiny black helmet, and his trousers upheld by a broad black belt. Each firehouse, on parade days, was thrown open to the public. The city's leading breweries gave kegs of beer, and other firms donated crackers, cheese, and sandwiches.

The engine houses themselves were furnished as lavishly as the hotels and restaurants of the later fifties. Howard Engine, to which Sam Brannan gave allegiance, was one of the most splendid of them all and was especially noted for the brilliance of its social functions. The Monumental Six and the High Toned Twelve might boast more elegant houses, but the "Social Three," as Howard Engine was popularly known, had the only glee club and the first piano. Long afterwards, San Franciscans recalled with pride that magnificent dinner the "Social Three" once gave for the visiting firemen from Sacramento. The menu on that occasion, still preserved in the M. H. de Young Museum, was "of cream satin, a foot and a half long and a foot wide, highly embossed, and elaborately decorated in red, pink, and blue, the work of the finest ornamental printers in the city."

So rapidly did the city grow that by 1856 all its aspects of intolerable crudity had disappeared. Plank sidewalks brought a measure of safety to pedestrians, and substantial new buildings were going up in every street. The custom of promenading took hold on everyone; and Montgomery Street became for the next 30 years an avenue filled with the endless pageantry that was old San Francisco.

It was a gay and motley crowd that paraded there every day of the week in the 1850's and 1860's—a crowd utterly democratic and unconventional. From the fashionable quarter at California and Stockton streets came the wives and daughters of San Francisco's wealthy set. "Tall, finely proportioned women with bold, flashing eyes and dazzling white skin" came from the half-world of Pike Street (now Waverly Place). Lola Montez was known to pass along this street, her bold admirers kept at a distance by the riding-whip she carried. Men were still in the majority; bankers, judges, lawyers, merchants, stock brokers, gamblers—all wearing silk hats, Prince Albert coats, ruffled shirts, fancy waistcoats, and trousers fitted below the knee to display the highly polished boot.

Mingling with this passing show were strange public characters whom everyone accepted as part of the parade. "George Washington" Coombs, who imagined himself to be the father of his country, paraded the streets in coat, waistcoat, and breeches of black velvet, low shoes with heavy black buckles, black silk stockings, and a cocked hat. The tall disdainful figure of "The Great Unknown," clad in the height of fashion and impenetrable mystery, was the cynosure for all eyes, but never was he known to stop or talk to anyone in the years he followed this solitary course. The street beggars, "Old Misery" (also known as the "Gutter Snipe") and "Old Rosey" each morning appeared, gathering odds and ends from refuse cans—"Old Rosey" always wearing a flower, usually a rose, in his dirty coat lapel. There were also the two remarkable mongrels, "Bummer" and "Lazarus," whose relationship transcended ordinary animal affection; together they trotted the same course as the paraders.

Also allowed a certain patronage was Oofty Goofty, the "Wild Man of Borneo" in a sideshow, who walked the sidewalks of the Barbary Coast, in a garb of fur and feathers, and emitted weird animal cries. Later he launched into new fields, allowing anyone to kick him for 10¢, hit him with a cane or billiard cue for 25¢, with a baseball bat for 50¢. When the great pugilist John L. Sullivan tried his luck with the bat, Oofty Goofty was sent to the hospital with a fractured spine. After his recuperation, he engaged in freak shows as the companion and lover of "Big Bertha."

The era was a heyday of street preachers: evenings and Sunday mornings would find "Old Orthodox" and "Hallelujah Cox" delivering orations to accumulating multitudes. Stalking them would be "Old Crisis," a vitriolic freethinker of the times, who would mount the rostrum when they had vacated. The itinerant patent-medicine distributors also did a thriving business. Of these, the "King of Pain," attired in scarlet underwear, a heavy velour robe, and a stovepipe hat decorated with ostrich feathers, rode in a black coach drawn by six white horses. Found daily on the sidewalks around the financial district was a greasy figure, old and lonely, displaying a large banner reading, "Money King, You Can Borrow Money Cheap"; he charged his borrowers exorbitant rates of interest.

Last, but by no means least, came the Emperor Norton attired in his blue Army uniform with its brass buttons and gold braid and his plumed beaver hat. Everybody knew and liked this mildly insane little Englishman, who, after heavy financial reverses had wrecked his mind, styled himself "Norton I, Emperor of North America and Protector of Mexico." For two decades, traveling from one part of the city to another, he saw to it that policemen were on duty, that sidewalks were unobstructed, that various city ordinances were enforced. He visited and inspected all buildings in process of construction. The newspapers solemnly published the proclamations of this kindly old man, and his correspondence with European statesman. When in need of funds, he issued 50¢ bonds, supplied by an obliging printer, which were honored by banks, restaurants, and stores. His funeral, in 1880, was one of the most impressive of the times, with more than 30,000 attending the ceremony in the old Masonic Cemetery. When, only a few years ago, his remains were removed to Woodlawn Cemetery, down the Peninsula, an infantry detachment fired a military salute, and "taps" were blown over his grave.

The "golden sixties" saw the flowering of a Western culture, wherein the uncouth, violent San Francisco of Gold Rush days evolved to the tune of Strauss waltzes and polite salutations from carriage windows; and the grand social events of the Civil War period brought to the Oriental Hotel, the Lick House, and the St. Francis a social pageantry, splendid and refined. The tobacco-spitting, gun-toting forty-niner was being taken in hand by such arbiters of propriety as Mrs. Hall McAllister and Mrs. John Parrott. *Nouveau riche* citizens of Northern sympathies were succumbing to the gracious mode of living taught by the Secessionists. The aristocratic Southern set, which insisted on a certain formality, could, however, always forgive those who violated its discipline with charm and wit and good taste. Gradually the fashionable parade of carriages outshone the promenade of Montgomery Street; and the exodus toward Market Street began, which was to erase the most distinguished feature of San Francisco as the city of the Argonauts. But it was in the large ball rooms of private homes that the magnificence of San Francisco's social life was shown to best advantage. Here, seemingly oblivious of the civil strife, San Franciscans gave full rein to their natural gaiety.

The completion of the transcontinental railroad put an end to the splendid isolation in which San Franciscans had reveled for two decades. Soon the fantastic wooden castles of the Big Four were to rise on the summit of Nob Hill, to announce to an astonished citizenry that San Francisco was at last an American city. "California has annexed the United States" was the prevailing opinion, but it was only the final and defiant expression of the pioneer spirit that refused to admit its heyday was over. With money running plentifully, society in the seventies and eighties was tempted to relax, to catch what lavish silver-toned enjoyment emerged from its pompous realm.

Marking the first official get-together of writers, artists, and dilettantes, the Bohemian Club was founded in 1872, with quarters on Pine Street above the California Market. Under the guidance of art-loving Raphael Weill, the club opened its portals to Sarah Bernhardt and Coquelin the Elder and, later, entertained with elegant breakfasts, luncheons, and dinners in the Red Room of its building at Post and Taylor streets. Other notables sampling the Bohemian Club's correct and charming hospitality, which was acknowledged to speak for all San Francisco, were Nellie Melba, Ellen Terry, Rudyard Kipling, Henry Irving, Helena Modjeska, and Ignace Paderewski.

During this era and the "Gay Nineties" San Francisco was to achieve its reputation as "The Wickedest City in the World." The potbellied little champagne salesman, Ned Greenway, led society through the artful steps of the cotillion. Sprightly Lillie Hitchcock, as honorary member of the San Francisco Fire Department, aroused disapproving thrills among smart matrons by wearing the resplendent badge presented her by the Knickerbocker 5. Returning from entertainment furnished in the rose-tinged Poodle Dog at Bush and Dupont Streets or from Delmonico's, famous for its soundproof rooms and discreet waiters, railroad builders and Comstock financiers chatted of rare vintages and made inward plans for "private" suppers.

Along the Barbary Coast, the underworld whirled in fantastic steps to the rhythmic tunes of banging pianos, banjos, tom-toms, and blaring brass horns. It was the era of checkered suits, derby hats, and bright turtleneck sweaters. The police patrolled the district in pairs. Assisted by honky-tonk pianos grinding out "Franky and Johnny," gamblers fleeced their victims with inscrutable calm. From Barbary Coast dives to the Hotel St. Francis came the banjo, with Herman Heller as orchestra leader, soon to be followed by Art Hickman's introduction of the saxophone, which would bring jazz to the modern era.

It was into this phantasmagoric atmosphere that Arnold Genthe brought Anna Pavlowa on a slumming tour. At the Olympia, a glittering dance hall, she watched the rhythmic sway of the dancers. Fascinated, soon she and her partner were on the floor. No one noticed them, no one knew who they were. Feeling the barbaric swing of the music, they soon were lost in the oblivion of the time-beats of the orchestra. One couple after another noticed them and stepped off the floor to watch. Soon they were the only dancers left on the floor, the other dancers forming a circle around the room, astonished, spellbound. The music stopped, Pavlowa and her partner were finished, there was a moment of silence. Then came a thunderous burst of applause, a stamping of feet, a hurling of caps. The air was filled with yells of "More!" Pavlowa was in tears.

San Francisco "remembered" the sinking of the battleship *Maine* with characteristic gusto in 1898. While transports clogged the Bay, the boys in blue camped in the Presidio hills and daily marched down Market Street to the troopships to the tunes of "There'll Be a Hot Time in the Old Town Tonight" and "Coon, Coon, Coon, Ah Wish Mah Color Would Fade." The Spanish War to San Franciscans was almost one continuous fiesta. Too late for the war, the battleship *Oregon* steamed into the Bay to celebrate the victory. Public subscription erected a monument to Admiral Dewey in Union Square.

Soon the "ridiculous" horseless carriage was snorting along the roads in Golden Gate Park; later it ventured timorously downtown to frighten the bearded or bustled citizens, who viewed the "newfangled contraption" only to maintain that horse and cable cars "were fast enough."

Near the corner of Powell and Market streets, in 1914, stood some of the most famous of the cabarets and taverns in the West. On Powell Street were the Odeon, the Portola Louvre, and the Techau Tavern. Around the corner was the Indoor Yacht Club. On Mason Street flourished the Black Cat, the Pousse Café, and Marquard's, and within walking distance were famous bars, such as the Waldorf and the

Orpheum, and innumerable foreign restaurants. While the graft investigation scandals of 1906 had forced the toning down of the city's night life, it was not until the war years and the advent of Prohibition that the death knell of San Francisco's gaiety was sounded.

Most of the cabarets closed, never again to reopen. San Franciscans disdained grape juice and patronized the bootlegger; they escaped, however, the curse of the gangster, who in most cities crept in with temperance. The Odeon became a cafeteria, as did the Portola Louvre. The Techau Tavern became a candy store; Marquard's became a coffee shop. Over old San Francisco, twilight had fallen, from which it never would emerge. San Francisco would be the same city when the era of sobriety came at last to its end, but, like wine in a bottle once opened, then corked and laid away, its flavor would be gone.

BEFORE THE FOOTLIGHTS

Through the ingenuous emotions of a child of the eighties, a famous San Franciscan has tried to lay a finger on the special and intrinsic values that have caused San Francisco to be considered a great theater city: "Actors in those days liked to go out to the Coast, and as it was expensive to get back and not expensive to stay there they stayed . . . Uncle Tom's Cabin . . . was very nearly my first play . . . Then I enormously remember Booth playing *Hamlet* but there again the only thing I noticed . . . is his lying at the Queen's feet during the play . . . although I knew there was a play going on there, that is the little play. It was in this way that I first felt two things going on at one time."

The theater-goer here probing back into her childhood was a longtime resident of San Francisco—Gertrude Stein—later associated with the stage herself as the author of *Four Saints in Five Acts*. And the conclusion she draws may be extended to all the theater-goers and actors of San Francisco, who have never lost the feeling of two things going on at one time: that active co-operation of audience and actor.

The Americans who came with their banjos ringing to the tune of "O Susanna!" were not content for long with wandering minstrelsy. By the middle of 1849, they had lined their pockets with gold, were dressed up, and wanted some place to go. In an abandoned schoolhouse, from which the teacher and trustees had departed for the mines, on June 22, 1849, Stephen C. Massett, "a stout red-faced little Englishman," adventurer and entertainer who also called himself "Jeems Pipes of Pipesville," gave a one-man performance of songs and impersonations, for which the miners were happy to pay him more than $500. Following Massett came the first professional company—"h"-dropping Australians—who presented on January 16, 1850, Sheridan Knowles' touching drama, *The Wife*. The excellence of this performance may be judged from the leading lady's speech, quoted from another play, *The Bandit Chief:* " 'is 'eart is as 'ard as a stone—and I'd rayther take a basilisk and wrap 'is cold fangs around me, than surrender meself to the cold himbraces of a 'eartless villain!" The theater was filled with curious, excitable miners, who paid as high as $5 for admission. Yet the miners soon learned to order such hams out of town at the pistol point.

The circus had already come to town, even preceding the Australians. Wandering by way of Callao and Lima, the enterprising Joseph A. Rowe brought his troop to a lot on Kearny Street, opening October 29, 1849. Here materialized a curious phenomenon, the alternation of circus performances with the tragedies of Shakespeare. Rowe on February 4, 1850, put on *Othello*—the first of a long series of Shakespearean performances.

The early 1850's were noted for a series of off-stage tragedies that periodically snuffed out the stage performances. Six disastrous fires brought theater buildings down with the rest of the city. In the period from 1850 to 1860, there were three Jenny Linds, two Americans, two Metropolitans, two Adelphis, to say nothing of structures not rebuilt—the Dramatic Museum, the National, the Theatre of Arts, the Lyceum, and countless others. But with pioneer courage the city rebuilt.

And struggling through these fires to make theater history in San Francisco were Tom Maguire and Dr. David G. "Yankee" Robinson—utterly unlike except for their power as impresarios. With Dr. Robinson came the first crude stagecraft and the first real satires on the local scene. On July 4, 1850, he opened his Dramatic Museum on California Street, with a localized adaptation of *Seeing the Elephant,* a popular circus deception. He started the first dramatic school in San Francisco. An actor himself and a kind of playsmith, he was the life-blood of his theater. One of his plays, *The Reformed Drunkard,* has had many revivals under the title *Ten Nights in a Barroom.*

Beginning as an illiterate cab driver, gambler, and saloon keeper, Tom Maguire came to be one of the country's great impresarios. This man, like the city itself, was fiery, good-natured, both acquisitive and generous; ignorant, uncouth, eager for novelty and yet animated by a childlike passion to be a patron of "culture." Sleight-of-hand artists, opera singers, sensational melodramas, jugglers, minstrels, Shakespeare, leg-shows: all these succeeded each other swiftly at Maguire's Opera House during its eighteen years of existence. The only man comparable to him in his time was P. T. Barnum.

The roaring fifties saw a cavalcade of exits and entrances on the San Francisco stage: James Stark, that ambitious young tragedian; Mrs. Sarah Kirby Stark, his wife, and a noted actress-manager; the

San Francisco's By-gone Days

AMERICAN FLAG RAISED AT YERBA BUENA (1846)

YERBA BUENA COVE CROWDED WITH SHIPS (1849)

PANORAMA FROM RUSSIAN HILL

George Fanning

EXECUTION BY THE SECOND VIGILANCE COMMITTEE (1856)

BUSINESS DISTRICT IN 1852

ABANDONED SHIPS ON WATERFRONT PRIOR TO 1851

THE FIRST CABLE TRAIN (1873)

J. W. Harris

SHIPBUILDING SOUTH OF RINCON POINT (1865)

GREENWICH STREET CABLE CAR CLIMBING TELEGRAPH HILL (1884)

VALLEJO STREET WHARF IN EARLY SIXTIES

CLIFF HOUSE (1866)

James Hall

BARBARY COAST (1914)

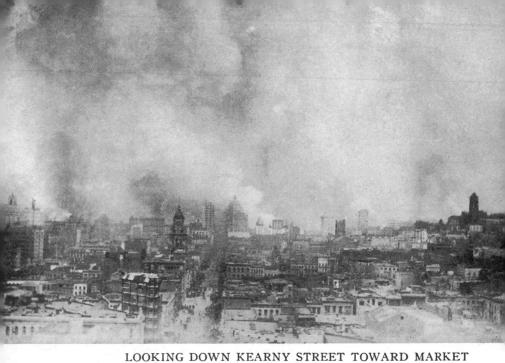

LOOKING DOWN KEARNY STREET TOWARD MARKET

GREAT FIRE OF 1906

AFTERMATH

RUINS OF OLD ST. MARY'S CHURCH (1906)

prolific and talented Chapman family, headed by William, Caroline and George; the perennial Mrs. Judah as Juliet's nurse; and the unsurpassed family of Booth, magniloquent Junius Brutus and the adolescent Edwin. The "Sensation Era" of the 1860's brought Lola Montez, Adah Isaacs Menken, and Lotta Crabtree, those glamor girls of the Gold Coast. And late in the 1860's came Emily Melville, of musical comedy fame, whose subdued style of the French school usurped the place of the "sensation" manner.

It was the "Sensation Era" which saw the rise of the melodeons or variety houses, whose insouciance and camaraderie of atmosphere were to be found nowhere else but in San Francisco. They reflected the life of the city as the more respectable, more resplendent theaters did not. The girls who so cavorted might be found variously at the Bella Union, Gilbert's, and the other melodeons, in such extravaganzas as *The British Blondes, The Black Crook, The Black Rook, or The Black Rook with a Crook.*

The "big time" theaters of the city came and went, and the "inquitous" Bella Union outlived them all, impudently mocking the pretensions of the great. There were other melodeons: the Alhambra (later the Bush Street Theatre); Gilbert's Melodeon (later the Olympic); the Temple of Music (later the Standard); Buckley's Adelphi; the Pacific Melodeon and hosts of others of less importance. But of all these the Bella Union was the prototype. In the burlesques was the healthy spirit of satire; the minstrels alone had the temerity to deflate the balloon pretensions of the tycoon age. Many of the performers are still remembered: Lotta Crabtree, Joe Murphy "The Great," Joseph and Jeff de Angelis, Eddie Foy, Ned Harrigan, Eliza Biscaccianti, Ned Buckley, James Herne, and the incomparable Harry Courtaine. A periodic drunkard, irresponsible, incurable, the despair of managers and the delight of audiences, Courtaine always returned and was always forgiven because there was no performer like him in the city.

The curtain went up on a new era, when William C. Ralston opened his new California Theater in 1869. In the audience were Bret Harte, Leland Stanford, James Fair, James Flood, John Mackay, and Emperor Norton. The name of the play was *Money.* A *Bulletin* reporter said rapturously of the drop curtain: ". . . the lookers-on were held breathless . . . with a thrill of surprised delight . . ." No less thrilling had been the scene outside the building, where *grandes dames* in full silk gowns had been met by the host, Lawrence Barrett. Presently they heard from his lips the dedicatory poem—a rapturous incoherency from the pen of Bret Harte.

The building of the California Theater was the signal for Tom Maguire's decline. The actors for whom Ralston built this sumptuous house, John McCullough and Lawrence Barrett, had both, ironically enough, been brought to San Francisco by Maguire. When his Opera House, on Washington Street, now "out of the way," was destroyed in 1873, along with its rival Metropolitan, Maguire took over two theaters in the Bush Street district. But the old magic touch was gone. Ralston's entry into the theatrical world was the sign for other wealthy men to follow. In 1876 E. J. "Lucky" Baldwin built the Baldwin Academy of Music. Maguire, finding it harder to raise capital than in the old reckless days, became manager of Baldwin's Academy; but, in 1882, he threw up the sponge and departed for the East, never to return. With him departed an era.

Later houses were chiefly notable for their actor-managers, the excellent stock companies which played there, and the world-famous actors who appeared: Edwin Booth, Lawrence Barrett, Adelaide Neilson, Helena Modjeska, John Drew, Maurice Barrymore, and a host of others. San Francisco was, and long remained, the only city in the United States, outside of New York, where a high-salaried player could be assured a long and lucrative stay.

Probably the most dramatic incident in the history of the San Francisco theater attended the production of *The Passion Play* at the Grand Opera House in 1879. Written by Salmi Morse, a Jew, it was announced for March 8 and 9, with James O'Neill, a Catholic, as the Christus. A storm of protest followed—mostly from clergymen—and the Board of Supervisors threatened to prohibit the performance. They were forestalled by the production of the play on March 3. Riots broke out which threatened the safety of any recognizable Jew appearing on the streets. The production of the play continued, however, with interruptions, until April 21, when Morse withdrew it "in deference to public opinion." The storm so affected him that a few months later he took his own life in New York.

The end of the century saw David Belasco, a humble prompter at the Baldwin Theatre, laying the foundation for his career. It saw little Maude Adams, aged nine, in *Fairfax;* Lillian Russell, a youthful unknown, in *Sparks* at the Standard; and Maurice Barrymore's talented daughter, Ethel, with a company including John Drew. Adelina Patti came to count out her $5,000 in cash every night before going on the stage, and Sarah Bernhardt, cooing, cursing, and dying in 130 roles; Anna Held augmented her theatrical prestige with publicity about beauty baths in milk; and Edith Crane, who appeared as Trilby, had full-sized photographs of her number 3 shoes published in the San Francisco papers. And that same Mauve Decade saw Henry Irving and Ellen Terry; a very risqué play at the Baldwin entitled *Lady Windermere's Fan;* and Blanche Bates in *The Darling of the Gods*. Marie Dressler came to dance the buck and wing, and Harry Houdini to make his mystifying escapes.

All but one of the city's theaters, both elegant and rowdy, were eliminated at a single stroke by the fire of 1906. By that time the early millionaire angels were dying and leaving their money to more sedate institutions such as art galleries, so the local drama began its struggle back with less assistance than it had enjoyed before. The possibility of its recovering an important place in the life of San Franciscans was doomed by the advent of moving pictures. Since then there have been many nights when no curtain rose anywhere in a once-great theatrical town.

In most of San Francisco's schools and recreation centers, however, amateur casts are unceasingly busy learning lines, making costumes, and staging performances. Hundreds of young San Franciscans have an exceptional appreciation for the drama because Maxwell Anderson, hoarding a trunkful of unproduced plays, put them through their Shakespeare at Polytechnic High. Many have worked with Dan Totheroh in the Mountain Play on Mount Tamalpais. Babies make their first acquaintance with the theater in fairy stories staged by The Children's Theater Association.

The Theater Union, a permanent amateur organization of the socially conscious type, staged John Steinbeck's *Of Mice and Men* in their Green Street Theater in the Latin Quarter, long before that play became a hit on Broadway. In the fine little theater in Lincoln Park overlooking the Golden Gate, Maestro Guilo presents rarely heard *opera bouffe*. Jack Thomas' Wayfarers have an esthetic slant; Barney Gould's Civic Repertory Theater plays in the Theater of the Golden Bough. The Federal Theater, too, until closed by Congressional law, presented such successes as *Run Little Chillun* and *The Swing Mikado*.

In every section of the city amateur performances may be seen regularly in Russian, German, Yiddish, Italian, Spanish, Greek, Arabic, Czech, Finnish, Polish, Japanese. Of professional interest are the French and Chinese theaters. The Gaité Française, or Théâtre d'Art, of André Ferrier, at 1470 Washington Street, is the only permanent French theater in America. San Francisco's Chinese theater was professional from the outset, and it set out very early—in the 1850's. Two Chinese theaters now operate in San Francisco, the Great China and the Mandarin—the only two in America—and companies still come from China to San Francisco under special permit.

For San Franciscans the theater has never been a shrine for the cult of indifferentism. Many were the nights when Lola Montez heard cries of "Bravo"; and many were the nights when she was pelted with vegetables. The spontaneity of theater audiences continues to draw comment from both sides of the footlights. John Hobart of the San Francisco *Chronicle* has stated succinctly San Francisco's distinction as a theater city: "New York audiences are quick, but easily bored;

in Chicago, they are over-boisterous; in Boston, they are over-refined; in Los Angeles, they are merely inattentive. But in San Francisco the *rapport* between the people out front and the players behind the footlights is ideal, for there is stimulation both ways, and a kind of electricity results."

MUSIC MAKERS

In one of San Francisco's gambling saloons, the El Dorado, a female violinist, "tasking her talent and strength of muscle," alternated musical offerings with exhibitions of gymnastic skill. At the Bella Union five Mexicans strummed the melodies of Spain. At the Aguila de Ora a group of well-trained Negroes gave the city's first performance of spirituals. Meanwhile, from lesser bars and shanties issued a cacophony of singing, stomping, and melodeon-playing.

This was the town with hundreds of suicides a year, the town that stopped a theatrical performance to listen to an infant crying in the audience. It was the town of Australia's exiled convicts, of professors turned bootblacks, of a peanut vendor wearing a jurists's robes. Men outnumbered women twelve to one, had built a hundred honky-tonks but only one school. Here was humanity suspended in an emotional vacuum—or what would have been a vacuum but for the lady gymnast tripping from trapeze to violin and the Negroes harmoniously invoking glory. The demand for music was furious—and furiously it was supplied. Eventually normal living conditions were established; but the stimulus of music had been accepted as one of the permanent necessities.

The Gold Rush ballads had a tranquil prelude in the Gregorian chant taught by the Franciscan friars to the mission Indians. An observer, visiting one of the missions in later years, spoke of these choirs: "The Indians troop together, their bright dresses contrasting with their dark and melancholy faces . . . They pronounce the Latin so correctly that I could follow the music as they sang . . ." The friars next taught the Indians to play the violin, 'cello, flute, guitar, cymbal, and triangle, and their neophytes surprised them by producing a lyrical rhythm unlike either the religious or secular.

Meanwhile, the Spaniards on their ranchos accompanied the day's activities with singing. In the midst of weaving, cooking, planting, and riding, the *rancheros* found time to celebrate at seed time as well as at harvest; they danced at all three meals. But the Spaniards' lively and nostalgic airs were destined to be silenced by lusty throats crying for gold.

As early as 1849, the city's cafes began to cater to their patrons' diverse musical tastes. At the El Dorado, an orchestra "played without cessation music ranging from Mendelssohn and Strauss to the latest dance trot"; and Charley Schultz, who enticed customers into the Bella Union with his violin and singing, brought to San Francisco the Hawaiian tune, "Aloha," to which he sang, "You Never Miss Your Sainted Mother 'Till She's Dead and Gone to Heaven."

More to the miners' liking were songs that celebrated their own exploits, like "The Days of Old, the Days of Gold, and the Days of '49," first sung by Charles Benzel (known on the stage as Charles Rhodes), who came with the Argonauts. Another favorite was "A Ripping Trip," sung to the tune of "Pop Goes the Weasel":

> "You go aboard a leaky boat
> And sail for San Francisco.
> You've got to pump to keep her afloat,
> You've got that by jingo.
> The engine soon begins to squeak,
> But nary a thing to oil her;
> Impossible to stop the leak,
> Rip goes the boiler."

Other concerns of the miners were chronicled with "The Happy Miner," "The Lousy Miner," "Prospecting Dream," "The Railroad Cars Are Coming," "What the Engines Said," "What Was Your Name in the States?" These ballads were supplemented by songs brought from foreign homelands.

But many citizens soon demanded more cultivated fare. San Francisco's first concert was performed at the California Exchange on Monday afternoon, December 22, 1850—an exquisite execution of the classics on a trombone by Signor Lobero. Shortly after this the Louisiana Saloon gave a concert. But the attempt to uplift was only half successful; later the *Alta California* felt it necessary to admonish the audience: "We would respectfully advise gentlemen, if they must expectorate tobacco juice in church or at the theatre that they . . . eject it upon their own boots and pantaloons . . ." The Arcade Saloon announced a series of "Promenade Concerts a la Julien." The Bella Union countered with the following invitation: "Grand vocal Concert with Accompaniment—to the lovers of Music of Both Sexes—"

The Germans of San Francisco contributed their substantial talents to the city's musical development. *Turnverein* organizations became the center and stimulus of choral societies; by 1853, four German singing societies were in full swing and had held their first May Day festival.

Miska Hauser, Hungarian violinist, originated the first chamber music group. His own words, appearing in his collected letters, tell the story: "The Quartett which I organized so laboriously gave me for a long time more pleasure than all the gold in California . . . the Quartett in its perfection as Beethoven saw it, this mental Quadrologue of equally attuned souls. . . . My viola player died of indigestion—and for some time I will miss the purest of all Musical pleasures. . . . Too bad that the other three were not solely satisfied with the harmonies of the Beethoven Quartett. They want a more harmonic attribute of $15 each for two hours. . . ."

Mr. Hauser may have had some difficulty in sustaining enthusiasm among his attuned souls, but, in the fifties and sixties, opera burst the town wide open. Eliza Biscaccianti, Catherine Hayes, and Madam Anna Bishop gave the city its first reputation as an opera-loving community. When Biscaccianti opened her first opera season on March 22, 1852, at the American Theatre, there were more calls for conveyances than the city could provide. According to the *Alta California* of March 24: ". . . the evening marked an era in the musical, social and fashionable progress of the city." Despite such appreciation, Mme. Biscaccianti returned to San Francisco six years later to find that her place had been taken by Kate Hayes, press-agented as the "Swan of Erin."

San Francisco lionized these singers in a manner befitting the legendary heroines whose lives they portrayed. When Madam Biscaccianti sang Rossini's *Stabat Mater,* "Fire companies came out in full uniform to honor her and on one occasion their enthusiasm was so great they unhitched the horses from her carriage and pulled her to her hotel." To Miss Hayes also the volunteer firemen gave undeniable proof of their delight.

How the firemen found time from drilling, fighting fires, and attending luminaries to make music of their own is a record of ingenuity. Several companies, however, gave band concerts both in and outside the city. Many other amateur groups often augmented professional offerings. Instrumental ensembles and singing societies were formed by immigrants from France, Great Britain, Switzerland, and a little later by Italians, Finns, and other Scandinavians. Professional musicians, amateurs, and audiences were *en rapport* during the invigorating epoch of the Gold Rush. Thus, by 1860, a rich musical tradition was well on its way to becoming permanent.

The development of symphony music was given its initial impulse by Rudolph Herold, pianist and conductor, who came to California in 1852 as accompanist to Catherine Hayes. The first of Herold's concerts of notable magnitude occurred in 1865, when he conducted an orchestra of 60 pieces at a benefit concert for the widows and children of two musicians. In 1874 he began his annual series of symphony concerts with an orchestra of 50 pieces, continued, with no financial succor to speak of, until 1880. After Herold's retirement, symphony concerts were given more or less regularly under such conductors as Louis Homeier, Gustav Hinrichs, and Fritz Scheel. Scheel, who later founded the Philadelphia Orchestra, was a musician of genius, esteemed by such renowned contemporaries as Brahms, Tchaikovski, and Von Bülow.

No American theater did so much to popularize opera as the Tivoli, best remembered of all San Francisco's theaters, which Joe Kreling opened as a beer garden in 1875, with a ten-piece orchestra and Tyrolean singers. Rebuilt in 1879, it became the Tivoli Opera House. Its career began happily with Gilbert and Sullivan's *Pinafore,* which ran for 84 nights. For 26 years thereafter it gave 12 months of opera each year, never closing its doors, except when it was being rebuilt in 1904: a record in the history of the American theater. For eight months of the year light opera—Gilbert and Sullivan, Offenbach, Van Suppé, Lecoq—was performed, and for four months, grand opera, principally French and Italian, occasionally Wagner. From the Tivoli chorus rose Alice Nielson, the celebrated prima donna.

William H. Leahy, familiarly known as "Doc," who became manager of the Tivoli in 1893, was a keen judge of musical talent. His greatest "find" was Luisa Tetrazzini, whom he discovered while visiting Mexico City, where she was a member of a stranded opera company. In 1905 Tetrazzini made her San Francisco debut at the Tivoli as Gilda in *Rigoletto* and became forthwith the best-beloved singer in the city. When San Francisco was rebuilt after the earthquake and fire of 1906 (as was the Tivoli), Tetrazzini returned to sing in the street, in front of the *Chronicle* office at Lotta's fountain, on Christmas Eve, 1909. Jamming the streets in five directions was the densest crowd ever seen in the city. She also sang at the fourth Tivoli, opened in 1913. But the heyday of the famous theater was over; and on November 23, 1913, it gave its last operatic performance with Leoncavallo conducting his own *I Pagliacci.*

How permanent was the city's musical tradition was proved some 75 years later, when the citizens of San Francisco made their symphony orchestra the first and only one in the Nation to be assisted regularly with public money. Since its debut concert in 1911, the San Francisco Symphony had enjoyed more than local respect, under the successive direction of Henry Hadley, Alfred Hertz, Basil Cameron, Issay Dobrowen, and Pierre Monteux. But during the 1934-35 season, conditions became so acute that of the playing personnel only the director, concert-master, and solo 'cellist remained. The situation was remedied by taxpayers who gave a half-cent of every dollar that found its way into the municipal coffers.

Pierre Monteux, conductor since 1935, an ex-associate of the Metropolitan Opera and a former conductor of the Boston Symphony and several European organizations, has done much to reaffirm the orchestra's position. Beginning in 1937, the season—curtailed during the depression—was increased to 12 concert pairs, carrying over 18 weeks. The San Francisco Symphony was the first major orchestra to admit women to the playing personnel. It has also taken an interest in such youthful prodigies as Yehudi Menuhin, Ruggiero Ricci, Grisha Goluboff, and Ruth Slenczynski.

The San Francisco Opera Association owes its existence largely to Gaetano Merola, its general director, who came to California with an organization headed by Fortune Gallo, one of the many traveling companies that visited San Francisco following the twilight of the Tivoli. The present San Francisco Opera Company made its inaugural bow before the public in September, 1923, in the cavernous Civic Auditorium, originally built for convention purposes. In 1932, after 20 years of personal and political wrangling, the War Memorial Opera House—first municipal opera house in the United States—was completed.

The season at the present time is divided into a regular subscription series of 11 performances and a popular Saturday night series of three. In its 17 years of existence, the San Francisco Opera Company has produced no single star of the first magnitude from its own ranks, but it has imported such singers as Lawrence Tibbett, Lotte Lehman, Lily Pons, Elizabeth Rethberg, Kirsten Flagstad, Lauritz Melchior, and Giovanni Martinelli. The popular-priced San Carlos Opera Company's performances, during the unfashionable late winter months, invariably sell out.

The "quadrologue of equally attuned souls" that Miska Hauser tried vainly to keep together is come to life in the present San Francisco String Quartet, a lineal descendant of the earlier Persinger, Hecht, and Abas ensembles, which played for many years in and near San Francisco. The San Francisco String Quartet has held the leading position among the city's chamber music artists since 1934.

The Northern California Music Project in San Francisco (formerly the Federal Music Project), now under the direction of Nathan Abas, not only has performed standard choral and symphonic works, but has resurrected with acute musical vigilance the *opera bouffe,* so popular with Europeans. Erich Weiler has given the operas English librettos, their humor pointed up with modern colloquialisms; and the artists have caught their spirit of hilarious pasquinade. The project also maintains a free school of musical instruction for those unable to afford private training.

Gaston Usigli, who directs the Bach festival each summer at Carmel, has been heard as guest-conductor with the project's orchestra, as has Dr. Antonia Brico, one of the few women in the world to wield a baton effectively. Arnold Schönberg directed the orchestra in the San Francisco premiere of his own tone poem, *Pelleas and Melisande.* San Franciscans had to wait for the project orchestra's performances to hear Dmitri Shostakovitch's *First Symphony,* and Paul Hindemith's *Mathis der Maler.* The project's chorus, as well as its orchestra, has composed its programs with imagination and initiative. But perhaps the most significant value of these musical organizations has been the opportunity they have given San Francisco composers and audiences to appraise music written locally. Exciting events were the world premieres of Ernst Bacon's *Country Roads (Unpaved)*, Nino Comel's *The Conquest of Percy,* and Tomo Yagodka's *Sonata for Piano and Orchestra.*

The impact of the modern environment on the sensibilities of the artist has seldom been better expressed than by San Francisco's Henry Cowell. Though most audiences have been staggered, technically trained composers recognize the theoretical value of Cowell's contribution to modern music. In the Marin hills overlooking the city, Ernest Bloch composed his rhapsody *America,* while serving as director of the San Francisco Conservatory of Music. Ray Green and Lew Harrison, local exponents of the modern experimental school, have written instrumental music and brilliant compositions for dance groups. John St. Edmunds, composer of nearly 400 songs somewhat more traditional in technique, received in 1937 the Columbia University Bearns Prize.

To many, the Barbary Coast's unbroken hum of melodeon, piano, Mexican orchestra, and singer was only San Francisco's brawling night voice. But one man caught in these sounds the musical implications of a future rhythm. This man was Ferdinand Rudolph van Grofe—Ferde Grofe—incomparable arranger of jazz, composer of *Grand Canyon Suite* and other notable interpretations of the American scene. As an extra piano player on call at the Old Hippodrome and Thalia, Barbary Coast resorts, he recorded in his mind a medley of folk songs, Negro dance tunes, and sailor's chanties. "The new music in the air along Pacific Street . . . did something to me!"

When Grofe left the Barbary Coast to play the piano with Art Hickman's band at the St. Francis Hotel, the two arranged music that was different and sparkling. Other orchestra leaders who played in San Francisco—Paul Whiteman, Rudy Seiger, and Paul Ash—became conspicuous exponents of this new music. Recent band leaders who have taken off from San Francisco on their musical flights include Paul Pendarvis, Dick Aurandt, Frank Castle, Carl Ravazza, and Ran Wilde.

Home music makers in San Francisco often aspire to the highest professional standards. Amateur groups frequently meet to forget the tensions of the day in the sanity of Brahms or Bach, or in the work of local composers. Both the playing and the composing are marked with a strong beat of self-reliance, in whose echo can be heard the promise of San Francisco's musical future.

SAN FRANCISCO GOES TO CHURCH

For 60 years before the founding of Yerba Buena, the *padres* of Mission Dolores heard their Indian converts recite the *Doctrina Chris-*

tiana, watched their Mexican parishioners lumbering over the sand hills in oxcarts to celebrate saints' feast days. And hardly had the first Argonauts pitched their tents around Portsmouth Square before a Protestant clergyman rose to deliver the doctrine of Methodism. Today nearly 300 churches, representing more than 50 denominations, exert a vast influence over the lives of thousands of San Franciscans. Many were founded amid the turbulence of the Gold Rush, others in the era of industrial expansion. Some have accepted high responsibilities in the city's struggles for public order. Issues of the Civil War, of State and municipal politics were declared from their pulpits.

Sam Brannan's Latter-Day Saints assembled in harbor master William A. Richardson's "Casa Grande" in 1847, but internal dissension—and the Gold Rush—soon caused them to lose their influence. Throughout the winter of 1848 Elihu Anthony, a layman, preached to packed audiences in the Public Institute. His rival, who drew a like number of listeners to this town meeting-house in the Plaza, was the Reverend Timothy Dwight Hunt, a Congregationalist missionary who followed his Argonaut flock from the Sandwich Islands. On his arrival in San Francisco, an enthusiastic citizenry elected him chaplain of the city for one year at a salary of $2,000.

Gold-mad San Francisco offered opportunities for conversion only to such heroic missionaries as that Reverend William "California" Taylor, who conducted open-air meetings on Portsmouth Square in 1849 and became the most renowned of the city's host of street preachers. This resourceful Methodist's approach to the adamantine hearts of his listeners he described later in his memoirs: "Now should a poor preacher presume to go into their midst, and interfere with their business, by thrilling every house with the songs of Zion and the peals of Gospel truth, he would be likely to wake up the lion in his lair. . . . I selected for my pulpit a carpenter's work-bench, which stood in front of one of the largest gambling houses in the city. I got Mrs. Taylor and another lady or two comfortably seated, in the care of a good brother, and taking the stand, I sung on a high key, 'Hear the royal proclamation, the glad tidings of salvation', . . ." The good Reverend Taylor's summons brought people tumbling out of saloons and dancehalls "as though they had heard the cry 'Fire!' 'Fire!' 'Fire!'" Many remained to listen with respect.

In 1854, the Reverend William Anderson Scott, D.D., LL.D., preached his first sermon in San Francisco to a crowd in a dancehall. Neighboring resorts closed during the services, while bartenders, card-dealers, and female entertainers flocked to hear this scholarly Presbyterian from one of New Orleans' largest churches. Subsequent meetings resulted in the construction in 1854 of a church on Bush Street, in a district then notorious for its dancehalls, gambling saloons, and dens of vice. In 1869 this neighborhood became so boisterous that the congregation had to seek a new home. But the Reverend Dr. Scott was no longer on hand to lead them. At the outbreak of the Civil War, he had preached the right of secession to an outraged membership, while a mob of Northerners stormed the front door of his church. Spirited out a rear exit by a loyal female supporter, he was whisked away in a carriage to a ship that took him to safety in New York.

Among claimants to the honor of having erected the city's first Protestant church, Baptists point with pride to that makeshift affair of lumber and sailcloth into which the Reverend Osgood C. Wheeler led his little flock in March, 1849. The Baptist pastor closed his sermon in the spring of that year with a prediction of the city's great commercial future, urging his listeners to build an organization able to cope with so portentous a destiny. The Baptists were to prove equal to their obligations when the Reverend Isaac S. Kalloch headed the reform movement that elected him mayor in 1879.

Meanwhile the six loyal followers of the Reverend Albert Williams, a Presbyterian clergyman, had met in a tent and laid plans for establishing a church of their own. When the prefabricated place of worship arrived from the East and was dedicated, thirty-two ladies attended the proceedings, much to the amazement of the male population.

Just as the Gold Rush offered opportunities for every profession, it welcomed every creed. In such an atmosphere the timid religionist was as lost as the timid gambler, but for the resourceful there was a place. When the luckless miner or workman had nowhere else to turn, he could find a champion of his rights in the pastor of some friendly church. Even the last hours of the Vigilantes' victims were cheered by spiritual consolation.

Of the Protestant sects which have accepted leadership in public affairs, none has had so decisive an influence on San Francisco and the State as the Unitarians. This denomination, during the critical period of the Civil War, had as its Abolitionist representative in California the fiery young evangelist, Thomas Starr King. He was only 35 when, in 1860, he took over the pastorate of San Francisco's Unitarian Church. David Broderick, leading opponent of the State's powerful secessionist minority, had been killed the previous year; and Colonel E. D. Baker, having been elected United States Senator from Oregon, had left California with a ringing appeal for the election of Lincoln. Thus the task of holding the State in the Union column fell on the frail shoulders of the young preacher from Boston, whose personal charm and spellbinding oratory were instrumental in saving California with the election of Leland Stanford as governor in 1861. King's death four years later was due to his strenuous efforts collecting funds for the United States Sanitary Commission, the Red Cross of the Northern armies.

While Lincoln hesitated to proclaim the issue of freedom for the slaves, Thomas Starr King appealed with Abolitionist fervor: "O that the President would soon speak that electric sentence,—inspiration to the loyal North, doom to the traitorous aristocracy whose cup of guilt is full!" That King's idealism went beyond the issues of his day is revealed in his lectures in defense of both the Chinese in California and those white laborers whose hand was raised against them.

The Nation observed King's passing with the firing of minute guns in the Bay; flags hung at half mast on foreign vessels in the Bay, on consulates and all public buildings in San Francisco. In 1927 the California Legislature bracketed his name with Junipero Serra's, and, with the $10,000 appropriated for the purpose in 1913, erected companion statues of these two official California heroes in Statuary Hall, Washington, D. C.

The Episcopal Church can lay claim to the most romantic origin of all local religious institutions. Its *Book of Common Prayer* was used for the first time on American soil by the *Golden Hinde's* chaplain Francis Fletcher, in the service held on the shore of Drake's Bay on June 17, 1579 (old style). Two hundred and seventy years later, in 1849, the Reverend Flavel Scott Mines from Virginia established Trinity Church; and in the same year Grace Church was founded. When Bishop Kip, in 1863, placed his Episcopal Chair in the latter, he thereby made it the first Episcopal cathedral in the United States. Perhaps no other religious leader in the city's history has occupied quite such social prominence as was accorded Bishop Kip. To a gay generation he represented a serenity of faith and a Christian liberalism in which the innocent frivolities of social life might be reconciled with religion. His successor, Bishop Nichols, lived to see the realization of his dream of a cathedral which, when finally completed, would be worthy of his church's ancient tradition. After the 1906 fire, which destroyed the original Grace Cathedral, wealthy families donated sites of their charred mansions on Nob Hill to the Episcopal diocese; and in 1910 the cornerstone of the present majestic Grace Cathedral was laid.

To Gold Rush San Francisco also came leaders of the Roman Catholic faith; and the establishment of American rule offered an opportunity for the Catholic diocese in Oregon to found a pastorate of the Jesuit Order in San Francisco. That the prospects for this venture were more of a challenge than an invitation is clear from the record kept by a colleague of that Father Langlois who, in 1849, arrived to plant his faith "on the longed-for shores of what goes under the name of San Francisco but which whether it should be called the mad-house or Babylon I am at a loss to determine . . ." So hopeless appeared all but a handful of French-Canadians among the Argonauts that the good

Father resolved to depend on these few strayed parishioners to form the nucleus of his congregation.

With the establishment of Bishop Joseph Sadoc Alemany's diocese at Monterey, however, and the early arrival in San Francisco of Father Maginnis to aid in the work, Father Langlois was able to say Mass and baptize the first convert in a new parish chapel. Soon after the arrival from Ireland, in 1853 and 1854, of several Sisters of Mercy, the city's first parochial school had enrolled 300 pupils. Once St. Patrick's Church was established, the firm foundation was laid for the progress of Catholicism in San Francisco. On Christmas Day, 1854, St. Mary's Church was dedicated as the cathedral seat of newly consecrated Archbishop Alemany, whose spiritual domain included California and Nevada.

Despite its history of missionary achievements antedating the signing of the Declaration of Independence, the Catholic Church in San Francisco had to start from scratch, after the 80 years of comparative prosperity in which Mission Dolores had shared. Though title to the land and buildings of Mission Dolores was not restored to the Church until 1860, it was occupied almost continuously by Franciscan or Picpus Fathers between the date of its secularization (1833) and the advent of American rule. The St. Thomas Aquinas Diocesan Seminary, operated at Mission Dolores between 1853 and 1866, was a pioneer in the revival of education; but its efforts to teach white children resemble the arduous pedagogy of the colonial period. Thus matters stood until, in 1855, the Jesuits began the establishment of the College of St. Ignatius, from which the present University of San Francisco has grown. However great the debt owed by Catholicism to the missions and to Junipero Serra, the church in San Francisco has derived its present prosperity from the Gold Rush and bonanza wealth in which it shared.

Two of the city's Hebrew congregations first assembled near Portsmouth Square in 1849. Temple Emanu-El, founded by German Jews, and Temple Sherith Israel, whose original congregation was composed mainly of English and Polish elements, constitute today San Francisco's chief citadels of reformist Judaism. These congregations provide magnificent and modern cultural centers for the city's liberal Jewry. Rabbi Nieto, leader of Sherith Israel congregation for 32 years, played a prominent part in the restoration of the city after 1906. His advocacy of welfare facilities in connection with synagogues resulted in the establishment of "Temple Centers" throughout the Nation. Today in San Francisco the Jews share with the Catholics, in institutions for public welfare which they have separately established, a major responsibility for the city's orphans and aged and destitute; most of the city's hospitals owe their origin and maintenance to Catholic or Hebrew congregations.

Especially characteristic of San Francisco is a host of lesser sects.

From few city directories could be compiled such a list of denominations and churches as this: Seventh Day Adventists (both Greek and Chinese), Mexican Baptists, Buddhists (American and Japanese), Molokans (Russian Christians), Armenian Congregationalists, the Christian Spiritualist Church, the Father Divine Peace Mission, the Glad Tidings Temple, the Golden Rule Spiritualist Church, Jehovah's Witnesses (Negro), the Rosicrucian Brotherhood, the Society of Progressive Spiritualists, the Spanish Pentecostal Church, the Theosophists' United Lodge, the Tin How Temple (Chinese), and the Vedanta Society.

From San Francisco's diverse population, tens of thousands (50,000 in 1940) each Easter morning make the difficult pilgrimage up the city's highest hill, Mount Davidson, to worship at the foot of the great cross on the peak. And, here, all forget their differences of creed in a common reverence to that religious spirit which has remained a social force since the city's earliest days.

GENTLEMEN OF THE PRESS

"Some contend," said Yerba Buena's first newspaper in 1847, "that there are really no laws in force here, but the divine law and the law of nature; while others are of the opinion that there are laws in force here if they could only be found." This polite apology for a state of anarchy may have caused some speculation among readers of Sam Brannan's *California Star,* but it foretold nothing of the militant and decisive role journalism was to play for half a century in the public affairs of San Francisco.

More indicative of this role was California's pioneer newspaper, the *Californian,* established in Monterey in 1846 and removed to Yerba Buena a year later. Its editor and publisher, when it became the *Star's* competitor, was that formidable Robert Semple who had helped lead the Bear Flag revolt and published manifestoes of the American occupation. Hardly, however, had Brannan's little sheet begun to ridicule the *Californian's* mild reports of "Gold Mine Found" and "Doc" Semple's patriotic oratory, when news from Sutter's mill race caused both papers to suspend publication. Their publishers and printers joined the stampede to the diggings.

Late in 1848, Edward C. Kemble acquired the *Star,* of which he had been editor when its weekly circulation "outside town and other parts of the globe" was a hundred copies; and, soon after, he bought the defunct *Californian* and combined the two papers under the name *Star and Californian.* With two new associates, printers from New York, Kemble issued in January, 1849, the *Alta California,* which became San Francisco's leading source of news for the next 30 years. Not until

1891 did it finally pass from the scene, having published, in its time, the letters written from Europe by Mark Twain in the 1860's that were compiled in *Innocents Abroad*. Among its managing editors was Frank Soulé, co-author of the *Annals of San Francisco*.

The growth of rival journals, which by 1850 forced the *Alta* to become the first daily, continued throughout the decade with a luxuriance propagated by political factionalism and homesickness among the immigrant population. Not to be outdone, the *Daily Journal of Commerce* was issuing daily editions within 24 hours after its elder rival began doing so. Before the end of 1850, daily editions of *The Herald*, the *Public Balance*, the *Evening Picayune*, the *California Courier*, and the *California Illustrated Times* had appeared.

Despite the high mortality of the press of the Gold Rush era, Kemble in 1858 listed 132 periodicals as having appeared in San Francisco since 1850. Only dailies to survive the decade, however, were the *Alta* and *The Herald*.

That the majority of these organs were rather journals of opinion than newspapers is not surprising. Crime, gold strikes, and other sensational matters were so much the subjects of common knowledge that the press had to search far and wide for news of interest to its readers. The huge influx of immigrants from Eastern communities compelled numerous San Francisco papers to employ correspondents on the Atlantic seaboard, who dispatched bulletins by the steamers that brought also large batches of Eastern newspapers. The Overland Stage, reducing communication between St. Louis and San Francisco to 21 days after 1858, somewhat improved news-gathering facilities; and when a telegraph line was strung in 1861, news of national significance was available. The quality of printing, with the introduction of the Hoe cylindrical press in the 1850's, likewise was improved; and by 1860 a grade of paper better than foolscap was obtainable.

Editorials and classified advertising, however, continued to be the main features of weeklies and dailies alike. Though articles were rarely signed, the style of each editor was instantly recognizable to readers who, according to John P. Young's *History of Journalism in San Francisco*, "looked not so much for intelligence as to see who was being lambasted." This highly personal tone was employed also by editors of less slanderous journals, such as the columnist of the *Golden Era* who addressed his correspondents by their initials and gave fatherly advice. Perhaps this friendly policy had something to do with making the *Golden Era* the city's leading weekly for 30 years after its establishment in 1854.

In the San Francisco of the Gold Rush era, newspaper editors had to be printers, writers of verse, and hurlers of insults; they had to take sides in political controversies, during which their opponents might at any moment attack them in a fist fight or challenge them to a duel. Catherine Coffin Phillips, in her history of Portsmouth Square, states that above one editor's desk was hung this laconic placard: "Subscriptions Received From 9 to 4; Challenges From 11 to 12 only."

Bitterness over the slavery issue was the cause of frequent brawls and armed encounters. Duels were of such common occurrence that newspapers mentioned them only in passing, unless they involved prominent persons. A. C. Russell, an editor on the staff of the *Alta California,* having escaped harm in a duel with pistols, was subsequently stabbed in an "affair of honor" fought with bowie knives. The *Alta's* managing editor, Edward Gilbert, was killed in 1852 by a henchman of Governor John Bigler, who defended his boss against an item intended to make him appear ridiculous. In that same year, the *Alta's* support of David Broderick, campaigning for election to the State Senate on an anti-slavery platform, caused the wounding of another of its editors by an editor of the pro-slavery *Times and Transcript.* An editor of *The Herald,* a daily fighting corruption in municipal politics, was shot in the leg by a city supervisor. James King of William (a distinction invented to avoid confusion with other James Kings), who founded the *Evening Bulletin* in 1855, did not survive his first encounter with a spokesman for the embattled politicians. His death, from a wound inflicted by the supervisor who was editor of the *Sunday Times,* was, however, the signal for mobilization of the Vigilance Committee of 1856. The office of the *Morning Herald,* the *Alta's* most potent rival, was stormed by a mob, who burned its editions in the streets for opposing the committee's work.

The close of the Civil War saw the establishment of the only two morning dailies that have survived since 1865: the *San Francisco Examiner* and the *San Francisco Chronicle.* The *Dramatic Chronicle,* edited by two brothers in their teens, was so well received after "scooping" the news of Lincoln's death that Charles and M. H. de Young, in 1868, were able to transform it into the daily *Morning Chronicle.* For the next 15 years, under the management of the belligerent Charles, the *Chronicle* entertained its readers with scandal and political onslaughts, while its editor defended himself in duels and libel suits. Following a bitter campaign against the Workingman's Party and its candidate for mayor in 1879, Charles de Young was killed; and for the next 45 years the *Chronicle* was under the direction of his younger brother. Throughout his long career, M. H. de Young, through his managing editor, John P. Young, made his paper a force for political conservatism and social order. Follower of an anti-slavery tradition, the *Chronicle* remained staunchly Republican, its viewpoint attracting to its staff such writers as Will and Wallace Irwin and Franklin K. Lane, who was Secretary of the Interior under President Wilson. Not until the 1930's, however, did it suddenly recapture, under the management of young Paul Smith, the sophisticated quality of its earliest editions.

Leading rival of the *Chronicle* for morning circulation, William Randolph Hearst's *Examiner* was founded on the ruins of the pro-slavery *Democratic Press,* which a mob, provoked by news of President Lincoln's assassination, had wrecked beyond repair. Despite popular indignation, the staff of the *Democratic Press* was carried over intact to the *Daily Examiner.* From its appearance on June 12, 1865, until a wealthy miner named George Hearst bought it in 1880, the *Examiner* defended the interests of Southern Democrats who remained entrenched in California politics. With its transfer to young William Randolph Hearst in 1887, however, began that sensational career which made the *Examiner's* owner a storm center of American journalism for 50 years.

With bonanza millions at his disposal, and a genius for showman-ship, Hearst gathered together a staff that included some of the best newspaper talent that money could buy. S. S. (Sam) Chamberlain, protégé of James Gordon Bennett and founder of the first American newspaper in Paris, became managing editor. The daring resourceful-ness of the *Examiner's* reporters delighted its readers and filled its rivals, especially the *Chronicle,* with alarm. Unheard-of was its print-ing of two full pages of cablegrams from Vienna, relating the mysterious death of Crown Prince Rudolph of Austria and the Baroness Marie Vetsera. *Examiner* correspondents dispatched news from the ends of the earth. Announced with glaring headlines and illustrated with photographs, this dramatization of the news caught the imagination of the public. To the reporting of local news the *Examiner* brought innovations no less startling. One of its editorial writers, the cynical Arthur McEwen, once remarked that reporters risked their necks for the sake of a story to make the public exclaim: "Gee whiz!"

Jack London was on the *Examiner's* brilliant staff in the closing decades of the last century. The modern comic strip was born as cartoonists James Swinnerton, Bud Fisher, Rube Goldberg, R. Dirks, and Homer Davenport labored side by side creating the "Katzenjammer Kids," "Little Jimmy," and "Mutt and Jeff" (created by Fisher from habitués of the old Tanforan Race Track). Ambrose Bierce's "Prattle" made him the most feared of the *Examiner's* columnists. One of his malevolent verses, predicting the assassination of President William McKinley, was interpreted afterwards as an incitation to the act. This gave the popularity of the Hearst papers a setback, but Hearst was already on the way toward establishing his powerful chain. Though the *Examiner* remains one of the leading newspapers on the Coast, it has long since dropped its original pro-labor policy. Vanished also from its offices is that droll atmosphere wherein Hearst himself "would

sometimes preface his remarks to his editors by dancing a jig . . ."
And not since H. D. ("Petey") Bigelow wangled an interview out of
three train robbers in a mountain hideout has the *Examiner* found a
sensation to equal either that story or its author.

Of the city's two surviving afternoon dailies, the *Call-Bulletin* has
the longer history. Its ancestor, James King of William's militant
Bulletin, fought corruption in politics and finance for half a century.
It was saved from oblivion in 1859, three years after its first editor's
untimely death, by a publisher from New Orleans, G. K. Fitch, who
later sold half his interest to Loring Pickering. Soon afterwards, the
partners acquired the *Morning Call,* a cooperative paper issued by a
group of printers claiming to be "men without frills." Fitch became
editor of the *Bulletin;* Pickering, of the *Call.* Though both papers were
published under the same roof and ownership, their policies were deliberately antithetical. At a time when violent taking of sides was
evidence of red blood, Pickering's *Call* dared to be nonpartisan. Not
less outrageous than its objective reporting was its society page, on
which the doings of "the Colonel's lady and Mrs. O'Grady" were
chronicled side by side. For 30 years Fitch kept the *Bulletin* alive with
caustic editorials and reportage in the crusading spirit of its founder.
He fought waste in municipal administration and gambling on the stock
exchange, assailed big corporations, and attacked political corruption in
both Democratic and Republican parties.

When, in 1897, the *Bulletin* became the property of R. A. Crothers,
it engaged as managing editor a hard-working journalist from Wis-
consin, whose name was to be associated with San Francisco for the next
two decades. Fremont Older had come West with an ambition to "be
like Horace Greeley," and while he introduced in the *Bulletin* all the
sensational tricks of "yellow journalism," he was genuinely motivated
by hatred of injustice and ardor for decency in public affairs. Banner
headlines, cartoons of politicians in striped uniforms, and editorials
solidly documented and barbed with irony revealed the corruption of
the Ruef-Schmitz machine. Triumph of the graft prosecutions made
Older so popular that he was able to name the reform candidate who
was elected mayor. The *Bulletin's* subsequent aid to Hiram Johnson
enabled him to break the railroad monopoly and win the gubernatorial
race of 1910. Older's discovery of perjured evidence in the Thomas
Mooney case, which led him to denounce the prosecution, failed to meet
with such popular acclaim, however. Rather than agree to the milder
policy advised by Crothers, Older resigned from the *Bulletin* in 1918.
Until its merger with the *Bulletin* in 1929, he was managing editor of
the *Call and Post* and thereafter, until his death in 1935, of the combined *Call-Bulletin,* which became another link in the Hearst chain.
The merger of the two papers brought an end to the *Post,* which since

1871 had been first the mouthpiece of Henry George of Single Tax fame and then spokesman for the United Railways.

The city's other afternoon daily, the *San Francisco News,* was founded, in the spring of 1903, as the 18th link in the Scripps-Howard chain. It adhered to Scripps' declared intention "to put into the homes of workers who had little time to read, honest, fearless thought impartially incorruptible by social, political, or financial influences." Issued originally as the *Daily News* from a mouldy little office "South of the Slot," its penny editions were eagerly bought by workingmen. As late as 1919, a strike of railroad yardmen, though outlawed by union leaders, was headlined with the caption: "Starvation Pay is Cause of Strike Men Say." A boxed resumé enlarged upon this theme.

In 1923, the *News* (now under Roy Howard and the United Press) acquired a new managing editor, W. N. Burkhart, and in 1930 moved to its present plant on Mission Street. Its pro-labor policy became less uncompromising, and it "saw both sides" of the struggle over municipal ownership of public utilities. Thus it was able to cross the social equator of Market Street without losing its circulation in "the Mission." Where the Bill of Rights is at stake, however, the *News* foregoes the sweetness of compromise. In this, it manages to preserve that pioneer integrity which died hard in San Francisco, when, as elsewhere, in William Allen White's words, "the trade which became a profession turned into a business and there it is today."

PART III
Around the World in San Francisco

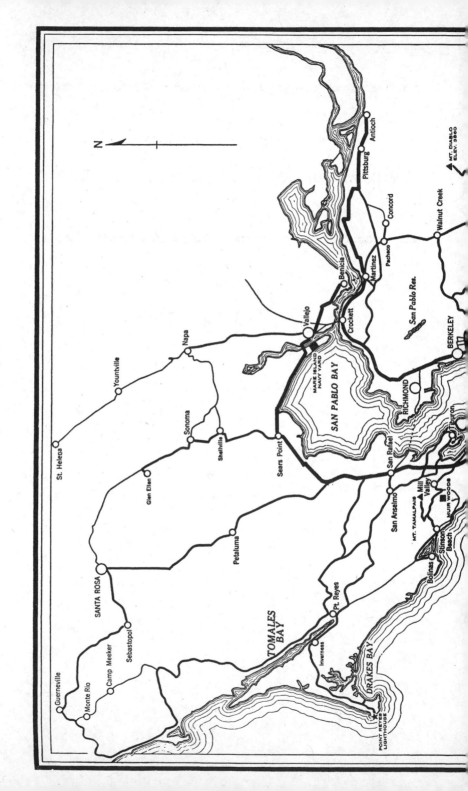

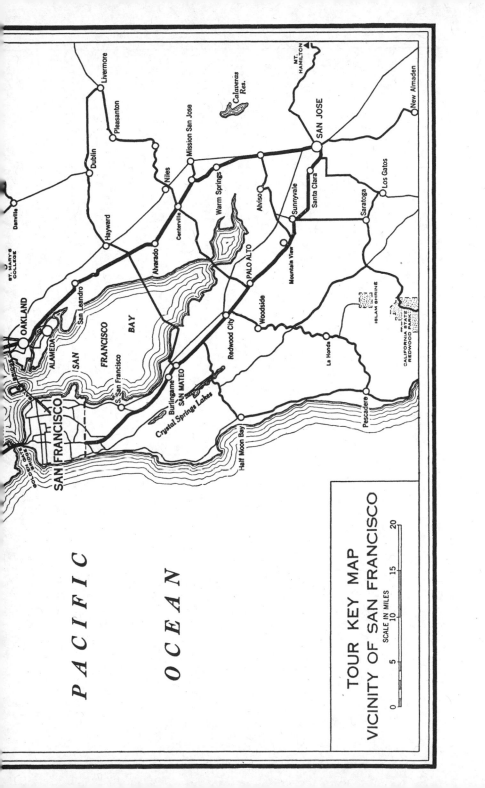

TOUR KEY MAP
VICINITY OF SAN FRANCISCO

SCALE IN MILES

0   5   10   15   20

Civic Center

"Above all the dome, seen so often like that of St. Paul's but dimly through the fog."

—MAURICE BARING

SAN FRANCISCO'S Civic Center constitutes a Beaux Arts monument to the city's cultural tradition, its achievements in democratic government, and its proud position among the commercial centers of the Nation. Dominated by the massive, symmetrical pile of the City Hall—whose dome, surmounted by a gilded lantern, soars high above the city—the wide plaza with its fountains, its trim shrubbery and acacias, its central concourse paved with red brick has been for the last quarter-century the focal point for all public demonstrations. The Civic Center has been the scene of welcome for so many celebrities and so many parades that henceforth—as Charles Caldwell Dobie has suggested—it is likely to become the most popular and historic of the city's landmarks.

The present group of eight buildings, built of California granite in variations of the massive style of the French Renaissance, is an example of city planning to contradict the city's once-famous reputation for letting things run wild. One by one these substantial structures have risen on those blocks within the apex of that angle formed by the convergence of Market Street and Van Ness Avenue which was cleared of debris and ashes after 1906. The $8,000,000 bond issue voted in 1912 laid the foundation for the project. As further funds become available and a need for new units arises, other structures will be added. Perhaps in time the dream of the Civic Center's original designer, D. H. Burnham, will be realized by the extension of its monumental plan to include the entire city.

Municipal government in San Francisco was not always so well-housed or so well-ordered. For more than a half-century after 1776 the seat of local government was a tiny dirt-floored two-room hut, home of the military *comandante* at the Presidio. Here in 1834 met the voters of the district of San Francisco to decide on eleven electors—who later chose the first *ayuntamiento* (town council), consisting of an *alcalde,* two *regidores,* and a *syndico.* These officials entered upon their duties on January 1, 1835. In 1839 the council was abolished. When the State came under American rule in 1846 Lieutenant Washington A. Bartlett of the United States Navy was appointed *alcalde.* Publicly charged in 1847 with misappropriating town funds (amounting to

$750), he was acquitted but nevertheless was withdrawn to the Navy. At a meeting of the common council of six members elected a few months later—which first convened in September 1847—the *alcalde* was permitted to preside over, but not participate in, the discussion. The governmental situation was so confused that the editor of the *California Star* complained plaintively, "we have alcaldes all over . . . who claim jurisdiction over all matters for difference between citizens."

There were to be many complaints, more vociferous, before the government of the growing town became orderly and predictable. At one time no less than three councils each claimed sole right to govern. In 1847 an ordinance provided that two constables should "strictly enforce the law" and "receive for the service of any unit or other process, one dollar, to be paid out of the fines imposed upon cases." In 1848 an ordinance was passed ordering the seizure of all money found on gambling tables, the money to go into the town coffers, but in that same year the lure of gold drained the town of so many inhabitants that at one time not a single officer with civil authority remained. Only 158 people were on hand to cast votes at the election held in October to reestablish some kind of civic administration. Too impatient to wait for the reestablishment of State government, the people met at a public mass meeting in February 1849, organized the Legislative Assembly, and proceeded merrily to make their own laws. The Assembly met 35 times before it was dissolved on June 4 by decree of the military governor of the State, General Bennet Riley. At an election held on August 1, 1,516 votes were cast, all for John W. Geary for *alcalde.* Later that month the *ayuntamiento* purchased the first public building under the American regime—the brig *Euphemia,* which it converted into a jail.

Anticipating by more than four months California's admission to the Union, the city was incorporated April 15, 1850. Under the charter adopted by the already functioning State legislature, a mayor, recorder, and council of aldermen were elected on May 1. The police department was enlarged—but "not to exceed 75 men"—and a fire department headed by a chief engineer was established.

At its first meeting on May 9 the council members promptly rifled the treasury by voting to pay the mayor, recorder, marshal, and city attorney annual salaries of $10,000 and other officials including themselves, $4,000 to $6,000. Later in the year, anticipating the celebration of the admission of the State into the Union, they each awarded themselves a handsome gold medal to cost $150, the expense to be borne by the city. Unfortunately the medals were not completed in time for the celebration; when they did arrive, the town fell into such an uproar that the councilmen prudently paid for the medals out of their own pockets and promptly melted them into "honest bullion." Despite this, sacrifice, the city was $1,000,000 in debt before the end of the year.

The adoption of a new charter by the Legislature in 1851 did little to halt the extravagance of the officials or the depredations of the increasing criminal element. But the Consolidation Act passed by the State Legislature in the same year, which authorized merger of the City and County of San Francisco, creating a Board of Supervisors to replace the double board of aldermen provided for by the charter of 1851, served to establish a more stable civic government. It was to be San Francisco's organic law for 44 years. When the heat of the vigilante movement had subsided, a reform movement headed by the People's Party gained power and held it long enough to put comparatively capable men into office.

When the old city hall burned down, the idea of transforming the Plaza into a reputable center of municipal government moved the council, in 1852, to purchase the Jenny Lind Theater, at Washington and Kearny Streets, for a new seat. So exorbitant was the $200,000 paid for the theater, however, that a storm of public criticism broke out. But the building had to serve. In 1865 the Board of Supervisors refused to pay the city's gas bill. The company promptly removed its lanterns from the street posts and turned off the gas at the city hall. That evening the city fathers, each carrying a flickering candle, stumbled upstairs to discuss the lighting situation.

Finally, in 1870, construction was begun on a new city hall "away out on Larkin Street" at a site then known as Yerba Buena Park (now the site of the Public Library). Originally a tangle of chaparral, this tract had become in 1850 Yerba Buena Cemetery. Economy was the watchword. The city fathers planned construction on the installment basis, paying each installment out of an annual special tax levy. But the piecemeal method of construction boosted costs to more than $7,000,-000, far beyond original estimates, and delayed completion for many years. As the city grew it became apparent that the Consolidation Act no longer sufficed to serve its needs. Twice James Phelan, who headed the reform movement that swept him into the mayor's chair in 1897, attempted, with the aid of a Committee of One Hundred, to secure adoption of a new charter, but without success. But in 1900 the electorate accepted at last a freeholders' charter which loosened the State Legislature's grip on municipal affairs, outlined a definite policy of municipal ownership of public utilities, and substituted civil service for the spoils system in civic administration.

But the new charter was not enough to protect the city government from the Ruef-Schmitz ring, into whose hands it fell in 1902. When the old city hall came tumbling down in less than 60 seconds at the first shock of the earthquake on April 18, 1906, municipal wrath gave impetus to the already gathering movement for cleaning house. In 1908 a supervisors' committee solemnly reported that "so far the most rigid inspection of the standing and fallen walls . . . have (*sic*) failed to disclose any large voids or enclosed boxes, barrels or wheelbarrows that have been told in many an old tale as evidence of lax supervision and contractors' deceits." But many San Franciscans went on believing "many an old tale." And when they decided to build a new city hall, they were determined that its occupants should be more worthy of the public trust and more responsible for the public welfare.

The urgency of rebuilding the ruined city defeated the city planning efforts of Daniel H. Burnham, whose vision of a system of great boulevards encircling and radiating from the intersection of Market Street and Van Ness Avenue (and the extension of the Golden Gate Park panhandle) was not to be realized, but when the city began, in 1912, to plan for the Panama-Pacific Exposition, a part of the scheme was revived in modified form. A permanent staff of architects for the Civic Center (John Galen Howard, Frederick H. Meyer, and John Reid, Jr.) was appointed and a bond issue of $8,800,000 voted for purchase of land and construction of buildings.

Under the municipal ownership provisions of the new charter, Mayor Phelan's dream of "a clean and beautiful City" began to be realized. San Francisco became the first large municipality in the Nation to establish a city-owned street railway system, which opened December 28, 1912. Under the supervision of veteran City Engineer Michael Maurice O'Shaughnessy, construction was begun at Hetch Hetchy of the great dam which bears his name and of the 168-mile aqueduct which brings Tuolumne River water to the city. The work continued over the next two decades until 1934. In 1913, under O'Shaughnessy's direction, the first comprehensive system of boulevards was formulated. In 1927 the San Francisco Municipal Airport was opened. By 1940, the city-owned utilities system was valued at approximately $167,000,000.

Meanwhile the park system was increased to a total of 45 parks covering 3,170 acres (one-ninth of the city's area). Since the establishment in 1907 of a Playground Commission (since 1932 the Recreation Commission), municipal playgrounds have increased to a total of 45 (exclusive of 28 school playgrounds), where during the fiscal year 1937-38 nearly 4,500,000 persons participated in such activities as athletics, gardening, handicrafts, music, and dramatics. The San Francisco Unified School District in the same fiscal year (its 87th) was operating 102 public schools, including ten junior high and eight high schools and a junior college, enrolling an average of 81,297 students. The library system was extended to a total of 22 branches serving 130,000 persons. The M. H. de Young Memorial Museum and the California Palace of the Legion of Honor, a city-subsidized symphony orchestra and the only city-owned opera house in the Nation, San Francisco Yacht Harbor, Aquatic Park, and the municipal Fleishhacker Zoo —all added to San Francisco's attractions. And meanwhile, as San Francisco became a more healthful and attractive city, it also was becoming a safer one. Its decreasing crime rate—between 1938 and 1940 it was the only large city to register a decrease—attested to the efficiency of its police department; a study of 86 cities made in 1935 showed that San Francisco, although 11th among American communities in population, stood 20th in number of robberies and 35th in homicides.

Just as the city had outgrown the Consolidation Act of 1856, drawn up for a city of 40,000, so it outgrew the freeholders' charter of 1900, drawn up for a city of 325,000. Beginning as a comparatively short document, the old charter had grown by process of amendment to 304 pages of articles, chapters, and subdivisions. In 1930 the voters elected a board of 15 freeholders to frame a new charter. Having studied the various forms of municipal government, the freeholders formulated a "strong mayor" plan which was adopted in March 1931 and put into operation in January 1932, under the administration of Angelo J. Rossi. Under the new charter the mayor—writes Chief Administrative Officer Alfred J Cleary—is made "a strong and responsible executive, with the power of appointment of the principal officials and members of boards." Officials whose duties are primarily governmental (policy-making) were continued in elective positions; those whose duties are primarily ministerial (carrying out policies), in appointive positions. To the Chief Administrative Officer was entrusted responsibility for supervision of departments headed by the latter and for long-range planning; to the Controller, responsibility for financial planning, management, and control. Under the new charter's provisions, the city's business must be conducted on a cash basis and its budget balanced annually. An eleven-member Board of Supervisors was retained as the legislative branch of government and relieved of administrative duties.

POINTS OF INTEREST

1. Dominating the Civic Center, the CITY HALL, Van Ness Ave., Polk, McAllister, and Grove Sts., lifts its gold-embellished dome 308 feet above ground level—16 feet 2⅝ inches higher than the National Capitol in Washington, D. C., as Mayor James Rolph used to boast. It was Rolph who broke ground for the new structure with a silver spade April 5, 1913. Second unit of the Civic Center to be completed, the City Hall was dedicated December 28, 1915, having cost $3,500,-000. In the great rotunda under the dome, Rolph welcomed the world, receiving a long procession of celebrated visitors: the King and Queen of Belgium, Queen Marie of Rumania, Eamon de Valera, William

Howard Taft and Woodrow Wilson. Here San Francisco made merry all night long to celebrate the Armistice in 1918. Here the funeral of President Warren G. Harding took place in 1923, and here, in 1934, Rolph himself lay in state.

Of gray California granite with blue and gold burnished ironwork, the building conforms to the French Renaissance style of the Louis XIV period, its east and west facades consisting each of a central pediment supported by Doric pillars and flanked on either side by Doric colonnades. Rising four stories high and covering two city blocks, it was

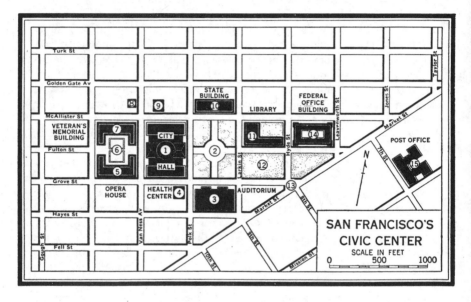

designed by architects John Bakewell, Jr. and Arthur Brown, Jr. as a hollow rectangle, 408 by 285 feet, enclosing a square centerpiece covered by the dome.

On the Polk Street pediment, the symbolic statuary represents San Francisco standing between the riches of California and Commerce and Navigation; on the Van Ness Avenue pediment, Wisdom between the Arts, Learning, and Truth and Industry and Labor. The interior, with its marble tile flooring, is lavishly finished in California marble, Indiana sandstone, and Eastern oak. Grouped around the great central court are the offices of the Registrar, Tax Collector, and Assessor. From the center of the lobby a wide marble staircase leads to the second-floor gallery, off which are the Mayor's office and the chamber of the Board of Supervisors. Similar galleries overlook the court from the third and fourth floors. The vast dome, 112 feet in diameter, weighs approximately 90,000 tons and will withstand a wind load of 30 pounds per square foot.

On the fourth floor is the SAN FRANCISCO LAW LIBRARY (*open. Mon.-Sat. 9 a.m.-10:45 p.m., Sun. 10:30-4:30*), a free, city-supported, reference and circulating library of about 30,000 volumes.

Near the Polk Street entrance is a bronze STATUE OF ABRAHAM LINCOLN (Haig Patigian, sculptor), seated in meditative pose, one hand resting on his knee. Facing the street named for him is a bronze STATUE OF HALL McALLISTER (Earl Cummings, sculptor), a distinguished pioneer attorney.

2. The CIVIC CENTER PLAZA, Grove, Polk, McAllister, and Larkin Sts., with its broad red .brick walks, its fountains playing in circular pools, its great flocks of pigeons, its flowerbeds and box hedges, is surrounded by a row of acacia trees and lined, along Larkin Street, by flagstaffs.

3. Since the CIVIC AUDITORIUM, Grove St. between Polk and Larkin Sts., was presented to the city by the Panama-Pacific International Exposition, events as diverse as political rallies, automobile shows, balls, prize fights, operas, symphony concerts, bicycle races, and circuses have been held here. Memorable have been the "Town Meetings," where employers and union men met in amicable debate; the "dime" symphony concerts of the WPA Music Project; monster mass meetings demanding freedom for Tom Mooney; the National conventions of the Democratic Party in 1920 and of the American Federation of Labor in 1934; and Max Reinhardt's presentation of *The Miracle,* for which the main auditorium was converted into a gigantic cathedral. Designed by Arthur Brown, Jr., the structure is four stories high, with a facade of California granite ornamented in carved stone and a pyramidal tile roof topped by a great tile-covered octagonal dome. Besides the main auditorium, seating 10,000, and the two companion auditoriums—Polk Hall and Larkin Hall, each seating 1,200—which flank it, it contains 21 smaller halls and twelve committee rooms. Overhanging the vast arena, 187 by 200 feet, which can be enlarged to include the two companion halls or diminished by use of electrically operated curtains, is a spectacular canvas canopy painted to simulate sky and clouds, bordered by Gleb and Peter Ilyin's mural insets. From three sides great balconies overlook the 90-foot stage. The four-manual console of the great organ controls the six distinct parts: great, swell, choir, solo, pedal, and echo organs. The largest pipe is 32 feet long and 20 inches in diameter.

4. The city's public health supervision centers in the four-story HEALTH CENTER BUILDING (*open weekdays 8-5*), corner Grove and Polk Sts., erected in 1931-32. It houses various clinics, the

Central Emergency Hospital, and offices of the Health Department of the Bureau of Inspection.

5. Twin structures—the OPERA HOUSE (*open weekdays 10-4*), NW. corner Van Ness Ave. and Grove St., and the Veterans' Building (*see below*)—form the War Memorial of San Francisco, erected in 1932 as a tribute to the city's war dead. The buildings are similar in external appearance, patterned in classic style to conform with other Civic Center structures. Against the rusticated terra cotta of their facades, rising from granite bases and steps and surmounted by mansard roofs, are placed free-standing granite columns.

This, the Nation's only municipally-owned opera house (Arthur Brown, Jr., architect; G. Albert Lansburgh, associate), represented the achievement of years of struggle by San Francisco music lovers for an opera house of their own. It was opened on October 15, 1932 with Lily Pons singing *Tosca*. The auditorium, seating 3,285 persons, is richly decorated. The floor of the orchestra pit can be raised and lowered. The stage is 131 feet wide, 83 feet deep, and 120 feet from floor to roof. At the 30-foot-long switchboard, all the lighting combinations required for an entire performance can be set in advance and released in proper order by the throwing of a single switch.

6. Beyond massive gilt-trimmed iron fences stretch the green lawns of MEMORIAL COURT, separating the Opera House and the Veterans' Building. Severely formal, it was designed by Thomas Church with planting in long flat masses to conform to its architectural setting.

7. The four-story VETERANS' BUILDING (*open 8 a.m. to indefinite hour*), SW. corner Van Ness Ave. and McAllister St., houses over 100 veterans' organizations. From the vestibule on the main floor of the building (Arthur Brown, Jr., architect), a long, columned Trophy Gallery with cast stone walls, vaulted ceiling, and marble floor leads to the Souvenir Gallery. Here the coffered ceiling and stone walls give quiet sanctuary to a display of military medals and souvenirs. Over a granite cenotaph with a bronze urn containing earth from four American cemeteries in France, a light burns perpetually. In the auditorium, seating 1,106 persons, arched panels between the pilasters of the side walls contain eight murals by Frank Brangwyn depicting earth, air, fire, and water. The maple floor can be tilted to afford a clear view of the stage or levelled into a dance floor. On the second floor is the genealogical library of the Sons of the American Revolution. The corridors on both second and third floors are lined with meeting and lodge rooms.

The 13 galleries of the SAN FRANCISCO MUSEUM OF ART (*open weekdays 12 m.-10 p.m.; Sun. 1-5*), on the fourth floor, are gained by elevator from the McAllister Street side. The permanent collection of painting and sculpture is predominantly the work of modern artists including Van Gogh, Cézanne, Matisse, Hofer, Bracque, Roualt, and Picasso. The Diego Rivera collection, not on display at present (1940), is one of the most important in the United States. There are frequent loan exhibits of the work of contemporary artists. Here also are an art library and lecture room. The San Francisco Art Association opened the museum in 1935 with Dr. Grace McCann Morley as director.

8. The STATE BUILDING ANNEX, 515 Van Ness Ave., a six-story building, houses offices of the California Nautical School; of several divisions of the Departments of Education and of Industrial Relations; and of the Department of Professional and Vocational Standards. Here also is the Hastings College of Law (University of California), founded and endowed in 1878 by Serrano Clinton Hastings, first Chief Justice of the California Supreme Court.

9. In two-story PIONEER HALL, 456 McAllister St. (*open Mon.-Fri. 10-4; Sat. 10-12*), occupied jointly since June, 1938 by the Society of California Pioneers and the California Historical Society, an exhibit of firearms, mining implements, and poker chips keeps alive memories of the days of '49. The Society of California Pioneers, founded in 1850, limits its membership to direct descendants of the early settlers. The California Historical Society, founded in 1852, publishes books, pamphlets, and a quarterly on Western history. The two organizations maintain libraries of some 40,000 volumes and own many manuscripts, documents, and historic prints and illustrations concerning California.

10. The block-long, five-story granite STATE BUILDING, McAllister, Polk, and Larkin Sts., in the Italian Renaissance style, was built in 1926 at a cost of $1,800,000. It houses offices of the Governor and Attorney General and other divisions of the State government.

11. A ragged senate of unemployed philosophers gathers daily along the "wailing wall' by the south entrance of the SAN FRANCISCO PUBLIC LIBRARY, Fulton, Larkin, and McAllister Sts. (*open weekdays 9 a.m.-10 p.m.; Sun. 1:30-5 p.m.*). Around the corner, Leo Lentelli's imperturbable heroic-size statues symbolizing Art, Literature, Philosophy, Science, and Law, posed between Ionic columns, wear a calmer mien. Across the granite facade are carved the words: "May this structure, throned on imperishable books, be maintained and cherished from generation to generation for the improvement and delight of mankind." The 140,000 books on which the library was "throned" in 1906, however, were unfortunately no more imperishable than was the old City Hall's McAllister Street wing, in whose wreckage they were destroyed. For the design of its new home, the architect, George W. Kelham, selected Italian Renaissance as "seeming best to represent the scholarly atmosphere which a library should attempt to convey."

Ground was broken in March, 1915 and dedication ceremonies held February 15, 1917. Of the $1,152,000 expended on construction and equipment, $375,000 was contributed by Andrew Carnegie (he contributed a like amount for construction of branch library buildings).

The board of trustees who organized the library in 1878 boasted among its 11 members Andrew S. Hallidie (inventor of the cable car) and at least one renowned writer—Henry George, author of *Progress and Poverty.* With an appropriation of $24,000 from the Board of Supervisors, the trustees bought 6,000 books, installed them in a rented hall, and invited the public to come and read (but not to borrow) them. The library opened its doors June 7, 1879. During the third fiscal year, when books were first circulated, 10,500 persons held cards. The number had almost tripled by the eve of the library's destruction in the wreckage of the City Hall, where it had been installed in 1888. With about 25,000 volumes, returned from homes and branches after the disaster, it continued operations in temporary quarters. The library's collection had grown by 1940 to 520,000 volumes, the number of card holders to 140,000, and the annual circulation to more than 4,000,000. Besides the main library, the system includes 21 branch libraries and 5 deposit stations.

From the main entrance vestibule, where a bronze bust of Edward Robeson Taylor, who was both poet and mayor (1907-10), stands in an alcove, a corridor leads to the exhibit hall, juvenile rooms, and newspaper room along the south side of the building. A monumental staircase rises to the high-ceilinged delivery room, on the second floor, finished —like both the entrance vestibule and the staircase—in soft beige-colored Roman travertine and an imitation travertine made locally. The main reading room, opening from it, extends along the south side, leading to the Max John Kuhl Memorial Room. Above the desk in the reading room is *Pioneers Arriving in the West,* one of two large murals by Frank Vincent Du Mond painted for the Panama-Pacific International Exposition. From the head of the staircase, colonnaded galleries—on whose walls are Gottardo Piazzoni's murals of the California landscape, in low-keyed blues and browns—lead to the reference room and art library along the west front. Both the reading and the reference rooms are finished with cork-tiled flooring, dark oak woodwork, and painted beam ceilings. On the east wall of the reference room is Du Mond's mural, *Pioneers Leaving the East.* On the third floor are the periodical room, music library, assembly room, patent room, secretary's office, and Phelan Memorial Room. Along the north side of the building are the stacks.

The library's collection is notable chiefly in the fields of music, fine arts, costume, and world literature. The music library, containing 7,400 volumes of music, 8,000 pieces of sheet music, and 5,000 pictures, is one of the largest in the United States. In the Max John Kuhl Memorial Collection of examples of fine printing and bookbinding are books from the presses of such San Francisco typographical artists as Helen Gentry, John Henry Nash, and Edwin Grabhorn. The collection includes a Kelmscott Chaucer, an Asbendene Spenser, and a Dove's Press English Bible. The collection of Californiana, housed in a room made possible by James D. Phelan, who willed $10,000 for establishment of the Phelan Memorial Room, contains manuscripts, autographs, and first editions of California authors including Bret Harte, Mark Twain, Joaquin Miller, Ina Coolbrith, Ambrose Bierce, Jack London, George Sterling, and Gertrude Atherton.

On condition that they never be removed from San Francisco, the heirs of Adolph Sutro—San Francisco mining engineer, philanthropist, and one-time mayor—presented in 1913 to the State from his private library 70,000 volumes which escaped the fire of 1906. This collection, now in the SUTRO BRANCH OF THE CALIFORNIA STATE LIBRARY (*loan desk and catalogue N. end of reference room*) is open to qualified scholars. It includes 45 of the 3,000 incunabula in the original collection, among which are the letters of St. Jerome printed by Peter Schoeffer in 1470. In the collection of many thousand Spanish and Mexican books are a compilation of Mexican laws published in 1548 and 42 volumes bearing American imprints of the seventeenth century. There are copies of the first, second, third, and fourth folios of Shakespeare and first and second folios of Ben Jonson. The religious works include the prayer books of James I and Charles II and a Bible used by Father Junipero Serra. Well-known to Hebrew scholars is the collection of Hebrew manuscripts obtained in Jerusalem, at least one of which—a 90-foot scroll, probably of sheepskin—is attributed to Maimonides. The library also owns a notable collection of pamphlets on biographical, political, and religious subjects—Latin, German, Mexican, Spanish, and English—of the seventeenth, eighteenth, and nineteenth centuries, including the thousands of English pamphlets, documents, and parliamentary journals collected by Lord Macaulay in writing his history of England.

12. Women air their babies and exercise their dogs, schoolboys play football, and down-and-outers snatch a bit of sun and sleep on MARSHALL SQUARE, Grove, Larkin, Hyde, and Fulton Sts., named for James W. Marshall, discoverer of gold in California. The last of the coffins was removed from the sandy graves of the old cemetery here in 1870. During the following decade the "sand lots" were the meeting place for gatherings addressed by fakirs, phrenologists, and socialists. Unemployed workmen applauded the harangues of an Irish drayman with shouts of "The Chinese must go—Dennis Kearney tells us so!"

Sixty years later, in the depression of the 1930's, the unemployed met here again in great mass meetings.

13. The PIONEER MONUMENT, Grove, Hyde, and Market Sts., keeps alive the memory of James Lick, who came to San Francisco in 1847 and died a multimillionaire in 1876. He left the city a bequest of $3,000,000, of which his will earmarked $100,000 for "statuary emblematic of the significant epochs in the history of California . . ." The Pioneer Monument (Frank Happersberger, sculptor), whose cornerstone was laid September 10, 1894, is a great central pediment upholding a bronze figure symbolizing California, with her spear and shield and bear, from whose base project four piers, each supporting subsidiary statuary: *Early Days, Plenty, In '49,* and *Commerce.* The central pedestal is ornamented with four bronze bas-reliefs—depicting immigrants scaling the Sierra, traders bargaining with the Indians, cowboys lassoing a steer, and California under the rule of the Mexicans and the Americans—and with five relief portraits of James Lick, John Charles Frémont, Francis Drake, Junipero Serra, and Johann August Sutter.

14. The grayish-white granite walls of the massive five-story, block-square FEDERAL BUILDING, Hyde, Fulton, McAllister, and Leavenworth Sts. (*open 8-5 Mon.-Fri.; 8-1 Sat.*), newest of the Civic Center group, was completed in 1936 at a cost of $3,000,000 (Arthur Brown, Jr., architect). Its 422 rooms house approximately 1,275 employees of 33 divisions of the Federal government.

15. Situated just outside the orbit of the Civic Center, the weathered four-story UNITED STATES COURTHOUSE AND POST-OFFICE BUILDING (*open 6 a.m.-12 p.m.*), NE. corner Seventh and Mission Sts., glittered in new white granite grandeur late in 1905. The building on its foundation of piling withstood the earthquake and fire of the following year, but the sidewalk and street—built over the bed of a former stream—sank several feet, and the building now obviously stands higher than the original sidewalk level. Having withstood the flames, it was easily refurbished. The building, designed in Italian Renaissance style by James Knox Taylor, cost $2,500,000, to which $450,000 was added for improvements after 1906. (In 1933 a $750,000 annex was added.) After Congress had appropriated the original funds, the price of steel dropped sharply below original estimates and in the absence of any law providing for its return to the Treasury, the surplus was spent in lavish interior decorations. Not only were Carrara, Pavonezza, Sienna, and Numidian marble imported but skilled Italian artisans were imported with them to install the verd antique trimmings of the corridors, the elaborate mosaics of the columns and vaulted ceilings. The court chambers were panelled in California curly redwood, Mexican Prima Vera mahogany, antique oak, and East Indian

mahogany, and immense ornate fireplaces (which never have been used) were installed.

San Francisco's central post office, with its financial and executive offices, occupies the first floor. On the second floor are the offices of the Railway and Air Mail Services; district chief clerks of the third and fourth post office districts and superintendent of the eighth division; and Post Office Inspector in Charge, whose department includes Arizona, California, and Nevada; Hawaii, Guam, and Samoa.

The United States Circuit Court of Appeals, on the third floor, has the widest territorial jurisdiction of any circuit court in the Nation, hearing cases from Arizona, California, Idaho, Montana, Oregon, and Washington, from Alaska and Hawaii, and from the United State extraterritorial court in Shanghai. Here also are the chambers of the United States District Courts and the offices of divisions of the Department of Justice, of the Mineral Production and Economics Division of the Bureau of Mines, and of the Naturalization Service.

A far cry from these splendid marble corridors was the city's first post office, the frame building housing C. L. Ross and Company's New York Store at Washington and Montgomery Streets, where in April, 1849 postmaster John White Geary removed a pane of glass from the front window and began dealing out the 5,000 letters he had brought with him on the *Oregon*. Following the arrival of the fortnightly mail steamer from Panama, wrote the British traveler, J. D. Borthwick, in 1851, "a dense crowd of people collected, almost blocking up the two streets which gave access to the post-office. . . . Smoking and chewing tobacco were great aids in passing the time, and many came provided with books and newspapers. . . . A man's place in the line . . . like any other piece of property . . . was bought and sold . . . Ten or fifteen dollars were frequently paid for a good position . . . There was one window devoted exclusively to the use of foreigners . . . and here a polyglot individual . . . answered the demands of all European nations, and held communication with Chinamen, Sandwich Islanders, and all the stray specimens of humanity from unknown parts of the earth."

"Steamer Day," the beginning and middle of each month, which brought not only the mail but also the Eastern papers—only source of news of the outside world—became a San Francisco institution. For a week the population prepared its letters and its gold dust—of which millions of dollars' worth were shipped East—for the fortnightly outgoing steamer. Even after 1858, when the Overland Stage Line to St. Louis began carrying eight mails each month and the Pony Express to St. Joseph two a week, the custom continued, and business men paid their accounts on Steamer Day. Not until the 1880's did the custom end.

Metropolitan Scene

"There are just three big cities in the United States that are 'story cities'—New York, of course, New Orleans, and best of the lot San Francisco."

—FRANK NORRIS

TIMES SQUARE and Picadilly Circus recall the metropolitan grandeur of New York and London. Although San Francisco has no single spectacular landmark by which the world may identify it, the greatest cities have long since welcomed it into their company. Portsmouth Square, the Palace Hotel, and the Ferry Building, which served successively as symbols of civic vanity, no longer resound with much more public clamor than many another plaza, hostelry, or terminal. Only Market Street accents for the casual observer San Francisco's metropolitan character.

Southwestward from the Ferry Building to Twin Peaks Tunnel, Market Street's wide, unswerving diagonal bisects the city. To Market Street, as to Rome, lead all downtown streets, converging from north, southeast, and west at wedge-shaped intersections where traffic tangles bewilderingly. Northward, where slopes rise steeply to hilltops, are shops, clubs, theaters, office buildings, luxury hotels, and apartment houses—the center of San Francisco's commercial activities and vortex of its social whirl. Southward—in what is still "South of the Slot" to old-timers—abruptly begin the row upon row of pawn shops, fly-specked restaurants, and shabby lodginghouses that stretch over level ground to the warehouses, factories, and railroad yards along the Bay's edge.

Jasper O'Farrell's survey, a century ago, laid the foundation for Market Street's development. Long before the forty-niners paved it with planks, the tallow and hides of Peninsula ranchos rolled down its rutted trail in Mexican oxcarts to Yerba Buena Cove. Hundred-*vara* lots along the street's southern side were considered ideal business locations; and the width of the thoroughfare determined its future. Steam-cars, in the 1870's and 1880's, brought along it passengers to be deposited in frock coats and crinolines before the Palace Hotel. Before the disaster of 1906, cable cars went careening up the street, like diminutive galleons riding on waves of basalt pavement whose sand foundation sank unevenly beneath the traffic.

A hundred and twenty feet wide, Market Street epitomizes Western spaciousness. At its upper end soar the crests of Twin Peaks, green with grass in spring. Flooded with sunlight on clear days, it contrasts sharply with the dingy canyons of neighboring streets devised for shopping and finance. After dark, gleaming with neon fluorescence of lighted signboards, it is a broad white way. Thanks to the fire of 1906, which piled the thoroughfare high with debris of baroque monstrosities, its contours are obstructed by few grotesque domes and fantastic facades, once the pride of the bonanza generation. With its streamlined array of neon signs, movie-theater marquees, neat awnings, and gleaming windowglass, Market Street's predominant tone is one of settled progress housed in masonry and concrete.

To millions of visitors who have ventured through the portals of the Ferry Building at its southern end to set foot for the first time in the city of St. Francis, Market Street must have seemed a little frightening. After a calm leisurely ferryboat voyage from the main railroad terminals across the Bay, the visitor plunged into what was obviously a traffic engineer's nightmare. A huge three-track trolley loop—encircling a forlorn plot of bush and grass—routes a succession of clanging electric juggernauts past the Ferry Building and back up Market Street. Unfortunately for streetcar riders, Market Street is wide enough to accommodate four tracks—a pair for each of the city's two systems. Boarding cars which ride the inner pair calls for a dauntlessness peculiar to San Francisco pedestrians. When two cars come thundering abreast down the tracks, the cautious commuter waits for both to stop, then darts around the back of the outside car to board the inside one; but hardier souls take a firm stand in the narrow gap between tracks, breathing in as two cars roar by on either side. Market Street at five o'clock on a workday afternoon is a deafening concourse of streetcars plunging through swirling eddies of pedestrians, passengers bulging from doors and agile youths swarming over rear fenders.

Along both its upper and lower reaches, Market Street has little of that dynamic tempo which marks its middle stretch. The first few blocks southwest of the Ferry Building pass between low buildings— railroad and steamship offices, nautical supply stores, transient hotels— before skyscrapers begin flinging lofty heads heavenward. Beyond the reach of shoppers, this section is never crowded; late at night, it is gloomy and deserted except for an occasional streetcar, a lone roisterer, or a solitary patrolman. Where it skirts the Civic Center on its southwestward route, the solid phalanx of office buildings, theaters and stores begins to show gaps, thinning into strings of paint stores, second-hand book shops, and parking lots, until the black mouth of Twin Peaks Tunnel swallows the streetcar tracks. That Market Street along whose broad sidewalks moves the informal pageant of San Franciscans on parade comprises nine blocks between Hyde Street on the west and Montgomery Street on the east.

The windswept corner at Powell and Market begins a gay, devil-may-care street that has for better than half a century fascinated and delighted both native and visitor. Unlike the tiny slow cable cars that clang up and down the Powell Street hill to be reversed on the turntable at Market Street, life always has run fast and a little loose along this narrow urban canyon. On the east corner of Powell and Market stood the Baldwin Theater, housed within a hideously ornate hotel of the period. Around the corner on Eddy Street was the Tivoli Theater, where patrons sat at tables and ate and sipped refreshments while watching the performance. Although the fire of 1906 razed the entire area, Powell Street and environs maintained their reputation by immediately rebuilding. The district became known as the "Uptown Tenderloin." Until the Eighteenth Amendment relegated pleasure spots to back rooms, it was replete with lively restaurants, saloons, and cabarets—whose names make older residents yearn for the "good old days." Techau Tavern stood on the site of the present bank at the southwest corner of Powell and Eddy; the Portola Louvre, across the street. Around the corner at 35 Ellis Street was the Heidleberg Inn, and at 168 O'Farrell Street, the famous old Tait-Zinkand cabaret, across from the Orpheum Theater where vaudeville was born. Fabulous Tessie Wall kept her red plush and gilt bagnio on the southwest corner of Powell and O'Farrell Streets—Tessie Wall, who reigned before Prohibition as "Queen of the Tenderloin," whose answer to her husband, gambler Frank Daroux, when he asked her to move to a suburban home in San Mateo is still quoted: "San Mateo! Why I'd rather be an electric light pole on Powell Street than own all of the county." Mason Street, one block west of Powell, was the "White Way," sparkling with the lights of Kelly's place, Jimmy Stacks' cabaret, the later Poodle Dog, and Billy Lyons' saloon, "the Bucket of Blood."

Powell Street, now relieved of suggested rowdiness by smart hotels, shops, and bars, has outlived its past. The hilarious uptown tenderloin which rivalled the Barbary Coast has receded to streets immediately west. This newer, downtown tenderloin is a district of subdued gaiety that awakens at nightfall—a region of apartment houses and hotels, corner groceries and restaurants, small night clubs and bars, gambling lofts, bookmakers' hideouts, and other fleshpots of the unparticular. Techau's, the dine-and-dance place renowned for "an appearance of Saturnalia," is today the name of an ultra-modern cocktail bar at another Powell Street address. The old Portola-Louvre at Powell and Market—described as "that which takes the rest out of restaurant and puts the din in dinner"—is now a quiet cafeteria more modestly named. Whatever remains of the great tradition of such theaters as the Baldwin is preserved at the city's only two legitimate houses, on Geary Street west of Powell.

Between Geary and Post Streets, where Powell Street begins its climb up Nob Hill—that climb which leads it up, up, and up to where stood gaudy mansions of the bonanza "nabobs"—the solemn gray-green stone facade of the St. Francis Hotel faces eastward over the sloping green turf and venerable palms of Union Square. Here the benches are packed the day long with successful men and failures feeding pan-handling pigeons or humming together at one of the semi-weekly WPA Music Project's noonday concerts. Clerks and nurses, salesmen and stenographers, eat their lunches on the grass. Chinese boys scurry along the paths, shouldering bootblack kits, alert for dusty shoes. Along the wrought-iron picket fence on the south side, drivers of long limousines lounge in their cars, waiting for sightseeing customers.

Union Square is the heart of that area of shops and hotels which represents to an international clientele and to San Franciscans the city's traditional demand for quality. Here department stores have for so many decades been custodians of public taste—their founders being patrons of the arts and *bon vivants*—that their very buildings are con-sidered public institutions. Along Grant Avenue, Geary, Stockton, Post, and O'Farrell Streets, the gleaming windows of perfume and jewelry shops, travel bureaus, art goods and book stores, apparel and furniture shops entice throngs of shoppers. Near these stores flower-vendors have the sidewalk stands so dear to San Franciscans. Along Sutter Street are offered rugs from India and Afghanistan, books, art objects from Europe and the Orient, household fixtures and antiques. Here San Franciscans pay gas bills and see dentists, and here are the commercial art galleries.

Kearny Street is the shopping district's eastern boundary. At its wide, windy intersection with Market Street the new San Francisco meets the old. Glowering down upon Lotta's Fountain stands the un-gainly red-brick De Young Building (San Francisco's first "sky-scraper"), and facing it across the intersection is the modernized tower of the old Spreckels Building. "Cape Horn" the city's rounders dubbed this breezy crossing, back in the era of free lunches and beer for the common run and champagne for the elite. Here lounged young wastrels whose delight it was to observe the skirts of passing damsels wafted knee-high by sudden gusts.

"All bluffs are called on Kearny Street," wrote Gelett Burgess. Running north from Market Street to the Barbary Coast, it was an avenue of honky-tonks and saloons frequented by racetrack tipsters and other shady professionals. On election nights it was the scene of torch-light parades and brass bands. Of early theaters, the Bush, the Stand-ard, and the California were situated near Bush and Kearny Streets. Among the restaurants that gave San Francisco a name were the Maison Dorée on Kearny between Bush and Sutter Streets, the Maison Rich, a block west at Grant Avenue and Geary Streets, the Poodle Dog at Grant Avenue and Bush Street, and Tortoni's, two blocks west at O'Farrell and Stockton Streets. All served French dinners that were gastronomical delights to a city that always has known how to eat. Another famous restaurant was Marchand's, at Grant Avenue and a little two-block alley called Maiden Lane. Now chaste and obscure, Maiden Lane has been renamed a half-dozen times, but the original name sticks, inducing a wry smile from old-timers who remember when its "maidens" were ladies of little or no virtue.

The inglorious past is slipping fast from Kearny Street. Streamlined clothing establishments for men, smart shops, and cocktail bars are marching northward against the tawdry remains of an era of architectural horror and moral obliquity. Its awakening comes late but it comes with a vengeance. A few blocks northward its businesses and buildings decline in class and size to pawnshops, bailbond offices, and the hangouts of dapper, black-haired Filipinos.

Not even the most farseeing mind could have imagined, in San Francisco's toddling days, the narrow canyon between skyscrapers that is present-day Montgomery Street. Being then the water front, it was the city's doorstep to the world. The doorstep was gradually moved eastward as filled-in land pushed back the Bay waters, but San Francisco went on doing business in the original location. Into Montgomery—and later Kearny Street, one block west—were compressed most of what the city possessed—banks, customhouse, post office, business houses, newspaper offices, dance and gambling halls, theaters, livery stables, saloons, and restaurants. The streets were ungraded. Kearny was paved with sticks and stones, bits of tin, and old hatch coverings from ships that had tramped the world. The going was difficult, if not downright dangerous, for both pedestrian and rider. In 1849 the site of the Palace Hotel's present magnificence, across from the southern end of Montgomery Street, was Happy Valley—host to a tent settlement of poor immigrants. Market Street was a dream in the brain of young Jasper O'Farrell, who was to engineer San Francisco's street design.

Montgomery Street has thrown off its old boisterous and willful ways. Neat and austere between sheer walls of stone, glass, and terra cotta, it is visible evidence of San Francisco's financial hegemony over the far West. But the past that dies hard in San Francisco still lingers on. Old-fashioned and with clanging bell, the cable cars go lurching through the cross streets that intersect Montgomery, past insurance companies and foreign consulates. All day the street's great office structures are beehives, humming with business; its sidewalks are populated with businessmen carrying briefcases, and lined with parked shiny automobiles. But at dark, when the skyscrapers are deserted but for their watchmen and scrubwomen, the deep canyons are black and silent, and the clank of cables, pulling their freight uphill toward the lighted hotels and apartment houses atop Nob Hill, echoes in the stillness.

POINTS OF INTEREST

16. Looming over the Civic Center and uptown San Francisco, the soaring shaft of the 28-story HOTEL EMPIRE, NW. corner Leavenworth and McAllister Sts., embodies the spirit of a new era rising from the old, like the Phoenix of the municipal seal. Built through the united efforts of the city's Methodist churches, it was opened in the late 1920's as the William Taylor Church and Hotel, named for the noted street preacher of the 1850's, since it housed a built-in Methodist Church.

17. Founded a decade after '49 by John Sullivan, the HIBERNIA SAVINGS AND LOAN SOCIETY (*open 10-3*), NW. corner McAllister and Jones Sts., has survived eight decades of prosperity and panic to become one of San Francisco's oldest banks. Its classic, one-story building (Albert Pissis, architect)—whose granite facades were gleaming white when finished in 1892 but have been weathered to a dull gray—survived even the fire of 1906. It is topped by a gilded dome surmounting the Corinthian colonnade which rises at the head of the curved granite steps of the corner entrance. Inside, marble pilasters spring from a floor inlaid with mosaic to represent a mariner's compass card.

18. The bronze angel atop the NATIVE SONS MONUMENT, Market, Turk, and Mason Sts., holds aloft a book inscribed with the date of California's admission to the Union: September 9, 1850. Beside the granite shaft a youthful miner shouldering a pick, armed with the holstered six-shooter of his day, waves an American flag. Gift of James D. Phelan, the monument (Douglas Tilden, sculptor) was unveiled on Admission Day, 1897.

19. The austere UNITED STATES BRANCH MINT (*not open*), NW. corner Fifth and Mission Sts., now houses temporary offices of various departments of the Federal government. Its basement walls of Rocklin granite and upper facades of mottled British Columbia bluestone, its pyramidal flight of granite steps climbing to a portico of Doric columns are blackened with grime. Built in 1870-73 to supplant the first branch mint, established in 1854 on Commercial Street, the $2,000,000 structure (A. B. Mullett, architect) was itself supplanted in 1937 by a still newer mint. In 1906, while flames gnawed at its barred and iron-shuttered windows, mint employees aided by soldiers fought a seven-hour battle with a one-inch fire hose and saved $200,000,000 from destruction. One-third of the Nation's entire gold reserve was housed here in 1934.

20. "Industrial Gothic" is the three-story CHRONICLE BUILD-

ING (*visitors shown through plant by appointment*), SW. corner Fifth and Mission Sts., with tall arched windows and high corner clock tower. A morning paper with a circulation of approximately 110,000, the *Chronicle* issues five regular editions daily, the first appearing on the streets at about half past seven o'clock in the evening.

21. On the highest assessed piece of land in the city is San Francisco's largest department store, THE EMPORIUM (*open 9:45-5:25*), 835 Market St. The massive, gray sandstone facade, its three arched entrances opening onto a quarter-block-long arcade, is ornamented with columns in half-relief rising from the fourth-story level to the balustrade at the roof edge. Inside, an immense glass-domed rotunda, 110 feet in diameter and 110 feet high, ringed by a pillared gallery, rises through four stories to the roof garden. Its present building, replacing one built in 1896 and destroyed by the 1906 fire, stands on the site of St. Ignatius College, now the University of San Francisco.

22. Traffic waits goodnaturedly at the CABLE CAR TURN-TABLE, Market, Powell, and Eddy Sts., where a careening southbound car comes to a halt every few minutes, while conductor and grip man dismount and push the car around until it faces north.

23. Traces of discoloration in the sandstone near the entrances of the FLOOD BUILDING, NE. corner Market and Powell Sts., recall the earthquake and fire of 1906, which broke windows and blackened the walls of the structure a year after its completion. Named for bonanza king James C. Flood, the building stands on the site of the Baldwin Hotel and Theater, built by his contemporary, E. J. ("Lucky") Baldwin in 1876-77 and destroyed by fire in 1898. Of gray sandstone, the 12-story structure is wedge-shaped to fit the site, its two facades converging in a rounded corner ornamented with columns in half-relief.

24. Head office of the Nation's fourth largest bank is the BANK OF AMERICA (*open Mon.-Fri. 10-3, Sat. 10-12*), NW. corner Market and Powell Sts., whose resources topped $1,500,000,000 at the end of 1939. "Statewide organization, Worldwide scope" is the motto carved beneath Giovanni Portanova's bas-relief, personifying the bank as a female figure enthroned between a Mercury (commerce) and a Ceres (agriculture), above the corner entrance. The seven-story structure, faced with white granite and decorated with Corinthian pilasters, was erected in 1920.

25. A grassy haven in the midst of the downtown bustle, UNION SQUARE, Powell, Geary, Post, and Stockton Sts., spreads 2.6 acres of green lawns around the 97-foot-high granite shaft of the NAVAL MONUMENT (Robert Ingersoll Aitken, sculptor), whose bronze female Victory, armed with wreath and trident, commemorates "the Victory

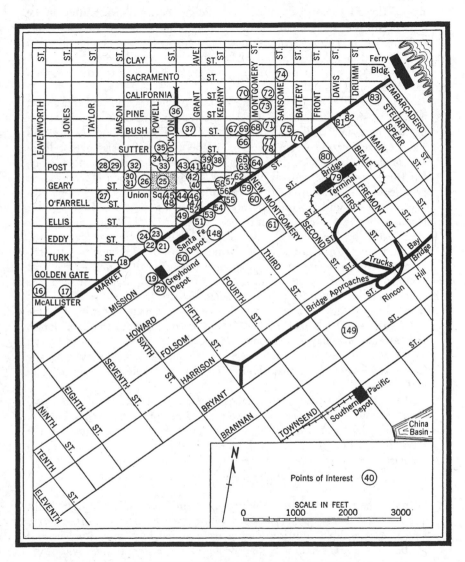

DOWNTOWN SAN FRANCISCO

of the American Navy under Commodore George Dewey at Manila Bay, May First, MDCCCXCVIII." President William McKinley broke ground for the monument in 1901 and President Theodore Roosevelt dedicated it in 1903. Union Square was presented to the city in 1850 by Mayor John White Geary. Mass meetings held here on the eve of the Civil War by Northerners demonstrating their loyalty to the Union gave the square its name.

26. The ST. FRANCIS HOTEL, Powell, Geary, and Post Sts., is the 14-story, block-long, steel-and-concrete successor to the hotel opened here in 1904 and razed in 1906. The building (Bliss and Faville, architects), is an adaption of the Italian Renaissance style to the modern skyscraper. Its main facade, weathered a somber gray, has three wings, the central one flanked above the second story by deep open courts separating it from the others. The spacious lobby with vaulted ceiling and Corinthian columns is one of the city's most popular meeting places. Near the entrance to the Mural Room, under the great Austrian clock which controls 50 smaller clocks throughout the building, under-graduates from Stanford and the University of California—who sometimes refer to the hotel as "The Frantic"—have kept appointments for three decades. In the Mural Room (named for Albert Herter's seven murals, *The Gifts of the Old World to the New*), whose black columns, mirrored walls, and blue and gold ceiling provide a pleasant setting, socialites have met for two decades to dine, dance, and attend Monday luncheons and fashion reviews. Occupying an entire wall of the largest of the hotel's banquet and meeting rooms, the Colonial Ballroom, is Albert Herter's mural portraying American Colonial life.

On the second floor are the headquarters and library of the COMMONWEALTH CLUB (*open to members and certified students Mon.-Fri. 9-5, Sat. 8:30-12*), founded in 1903 by Edward F. Adams of the *Chronicle*. The club's motto is "Get the Facts"—and it maintains a permanent fund of $270,000 for research in subjects of public interest. More than 1,500 distinguished visitors have addressed the club during its career.

27. The modern 17-story white-brick and stone CLIFT HOTEL, 495 Geary St., was opened in 1915 by attorney Frederick Clift. Three new stories and an additional wing were added in 1926. Lobbies and public rooms are combined Spanish and Italian Renaissance with high beamed ceilings. The Redwood Room is panelled with highly burnished 2,000-year-old California redwood and its 30-foot bar is made entirely of redwood burl.

28. "Weaving spiders come not here" admonishes an inscription over the Taylor Street entrance of the five-story red brick Italian Renaissance home of the BOHEMIAN CLUB (*private*), NE. corner Post

and Taylor Sts., erected in 1934. Across J. J. Mora's bronze bas-relief on the Post Street facade troop a procession of Bret Harte's characters. The club grew in 1872 from informal Sunday breakfasts at the home of James Bowman, editorial writer on the *Chronicle*. Artist friends sketched so freely on Mrs. Bowman's tablecloths her husband decided that San Francisco intellectuals needed an official club.

For the first few years, quarters were shared with another club, The Jolly Corks. The atmosphere was casual, the furnishings meager. Members who complained of the lack of tables and chairs were reminded that "when a man gets tired of holding his drink all he has to do is to swallow it." The club's monthly "High Jinks"—their name derived supposedly from Sir Walter Scott's *Guy Mannering*—were debates followed by suppers. The more or less serious "High Jinks" (later burlesqued by "Low Jinks") were sometimes exciting occasions. The story persists that one speaker opened his manuscript to show a wicked-looking revolver, which he placed on the table in front of him, saying: "This is to shoot the first Bohemian galoot who stirs from his seat before I end this paper." In 1877 the Bohemians moved into quarters of their own on Pine Street. Among the honorary members elected to the club have been Mark Twain, Bret Harte, and Oliver Wendell Holmes.

The Bohemian Club now has a world-wide membership of about 2,000 and a waiting list of hundreds. Once a year they come together for a midsummer frolic in the club's Bohemian Grove, where an original play has been produced since 1880, when the first Midsummer Jinks —an open-air picnic accompanied by speeches and celebrations—was held.

29. The winged "O" of the OLYMPIC CLUB (*private*), 524 Post St., oldest amateur athletic organization in the United States, has been worn by many star athletes, including "Gentleman Jim" Corbett, the San Francisco bank clerk who became world's heavyweight champion after practice as the club's boxing instructor, and Sid Cavill, one of a famous family of Australian swimmers, who introduced the Australian crawl to America as the club's swimming instructor. Nucleus of the Olympic Club, formed May 6, 1860, was the group which Charles and Arthur Nahl invited to use the gymnastic apparatus they had assembled in their Taylor Street backyard. The organization now has 5,000 members. The five-story brick clubhouse is equipped with a gymnasium, a solarium, squash and handball courts, an indoor track, a billiard room, a marble plunge piped with ocean water, dining halls, a library, and a lounge.

30. The Corinthian-pillared FIRST CONGREGATIONAL METHODIST TEMPLE, SE. corner Mason and Post Sts., was founded in 1849 in the schoolhouse on the Plaza, led by a missionary

from Hawaii, the Reverend T. Dwight Hunt. Having outgrown the frame structure built at Jackson and Virginia Streets in 1850, the congregation spent $57,000 raised largely by pew rentals on a structure at Dupont (Grant Avenue) and California Streets. In 1872 it moved into a tall-spired red brick Gothic Church on the present site, and in 1915 into the present building; here it was joined in 1937 by the Temple Methodist Church, which gave up its William Taylor Church.

31. The eight-story red brick and buff tile NATIVE SONS OF THE GOLDEN WEST BUILDING (*open daily 7 a.m.-12 p.m.*), 414-30 Mason St., houses an organization founded in 1875. J. J. Mora's terra cotta bas-reliefs between the upper windows depict epochs in pioneer history. Above the entrance are bas-relief portraits of Junipero Serra, John Charles Frémont, and John D. Sloat. Around the balcony of the auditorium, which seats 1,250, are intaglios portraying California writers.

The (fourth-floor) FRENCH LIBRARY (*open 1-6, 7-9; fee, 50¢ monthly*), conducted by L'Alliance Française, the largest French library in the United States, contains 21,000 volumes. It was founded in 1874 as the Bibliothèque de la Ligue National Française, under the patronage of Raphael Weill, through the efforts of a society of French residents formed after 1871 to protest appropriation of Alsace and Lorraine by Germany.

32. Against the dark panelling of the JOHN HOWELL BOOK SHOP (*open 9-5:30*), 434 Post St., gleam the rich colors of the rare old volumes which line the walls. The collection is especially rich in early Californiana and Elizabethan literature. Beyond the main room, a large studio displays the West's largest collection of rare Bibles. It includes a Venetian Latin Bible printed in 1478; the Bible printed by John Pruss at Strassburg in 1486, one of four in America; one of the nine copies of the first issue of the Martin Luther Bible, printed at Wittenberg in 1540-41; the Great "She" Bible of 1611; and the family Bible of Sir Walter Scott, hand-ruled in red. Also displayed is the first American edition of the Koran, printed in 1806. On the wall is a rare parchment containing 24 panels painted by a Buddhist priest which depict the story of Buddhist worship.

33. NEWBEGIN'S BOOK SHOP (*open 8:30-6*), 358 Post St., was founded in 1889 by John J. Newbegin, friend of Ambrose Bierce, Ina Coolbrith, Jack London, and George Sterling. Mr. Newbegin is an authority on rare books; his collection of material dealing with shipping is said to be the world's largest.

34. The vertical lines of the 22-story SIR FRANCIS DRAKE HOTEL, 450 Powell St., culminate in a six-story, set-back tower overlooking city and Bay. The structure (Weeks and Day, architects) was completed in 1928. Four great panels by local muralist S. W.

Bergman, depicting the visit of Sir Francis Drake to the Marin shores, decorate the English Renaissance lobby. Name bands play nightly in the Persian Room, whose low illuminated ceiling plays changing lights on the Persian murals of A. B. Heinsbergen.

35. Looming in monumental grandeur above the business district, the FOUR-FIFTY SUTTER BUILDING, 450 Sutter St., rises—a massive shaft with rounded corners, faced in fawn-colored stone—25 stories above the street. A striking adaptation of Mayan motifs to functional design, the structure (Timothy L. Pflueger, architect), completed in 1930, required more than two years and $4,000,000 to build. Its wide entrance, topped by a four-story grilled window in a tree-like Mayan design, is in nice proportion to the facade's severe lines. Large windows, flush with the exterior, flood the offices with light—especially the corner suites, which have six bay windows. The building provides its tenants—doctors, dentists, pharmacists, laboratory technicians, and others of allied professions—with a solarium, a doctors' lounge, and a 1,000-car garage.

36. December, 1914 saw completion of the $656,000 STOCKTON STREET TUNNEL (Michael O'Shaughnessy, engineer), boring 911 feet through Nob Hill from Bush almost to Sacramento Street to connect downtown San Francisco with Chinatown and North Beach. The tunnel is 36 feet wide and 19 feet high; sodium vapor lights were installed in 1939.

37. NOTRE DAME DES VICTOIRES (Our Lady of Victories), 566 Bush St., serves San Francisco's French colony. The church, completed in 1913, is of Byzantine and French Renaissance architecture, constructed of brick with groined twin towers and high arched stained-glass windows.

38. Since 23-year-old Leander S. Sherman in 1870 bought the shop where he had been employed to repair music boxes, SHERMAN, CLAY AND COMPANY, SW. corner Kearny and Sutter Sts., has ministered to the city's musical wants. Since the 1870's, the firm— known as Sherman, Hyde, and Company until Major C. C. Clay bought out F. A. Hyde's original interest—has been selling music lovers their supplies and tickets to concerts and recitals.

39. *Ici on parle Francais* (French spoken here) was the legend which Messrs. Davidson and Lane, founders of THE WHITE HOUSE (*open 9:45-5:25*), Grant Ave., Sutter, and Post Sts., hung in the window of their small shop on the water front when they hired 18-year-old Raphael Weill as a clerk in 1854. When Richard Lane went into gold mining in 1858, young Weill took his place as partner of J. W. Davidson and Company. As San Francisco grew rich, the store began to dazzle shoppers with costly and daring Paris importations. When Raphael Weill asked one of the newspapers for a full-page

advertisement, he was indignantly refused. "What does he think we're running, a signboard or a newspaper?" demanded the editor. "He gets two columns, no more!" But Weill got his full-page advertisement, the first in the history of the retail business.

When the store moved to its own three-story brick building at Kearny and Post Streets, Weill persuaded his partner to name it after the famous Maison Blanche in Paris. By 1900, when The White House was outfitting the women of the city in high-button shoes and ostrich boas and filling homes with sofa pillows and table throws, its fame had spread up and down the Coast. The 1906 fire reduced it to a heap of ashes. Weill promptly wired New York for carloads of merchandise, which he distributed to 5,000 women. Having vowed that he would not shave until the store reopened, he let his beard grow for three months while quarters on Van Ness Avenue were prepared. When the present five-story structure, faced with white terra cotta (Albert Pissis, architect) opened March 15, 1909, it was one of the first to reopen in the old shopping section. Weill lived to see the store overflow into two adjoining buildings before his death in 1920 at the age of 84.

Philanthropist, epicure, and patron of the arts, Weill left his impress on the organization. Employees celebrate his birthday annually and the store still closes on the birthday of Abraham Lincoln, whom he greatly admired. In the street-floor MEMORIAL OFFICE (*open business hours*), which Weill set aside as a place to greet his old friends, fresh flowers are still placed among the honors heaped on Weill: old photographs, citations, and plaques—a little museum of old San Francisco.

40. Around the show windows of the florists' shop of PODESTA AND BALDOCCHI (*open weekdays 8-6, Sun. 8-11 a.m.*), 224 Grant Ave., passersby cluster to admire flaunting sprays of rare orchids, exquisite lilies, or rich-textured camellias, arranged with spectacular artistry among many kinds of blossoms. In the early spring, the shop is embowered in pink and white flowering branches of fruit trees; at other seasons, in great masses of trailing greenery.

41. One of the Nation's oldest jewelry establishments, SHREVE AND COMPANY (*open 9-5*), NW. corner Grant Ave. and Post St., have been dealing in precious stones and rare objects of gold and silver since 1852. It is the only large downtown store still operating whose advertisement appeared in the San Francisco City Directory of 1856—when its address was No. 139 Montgomery St.

42. Book and art lovers frequent PAUL ELDER AND COMPANY (*open 9-5:30*), 239 Post St., established in 1898. Elder not only sells current literature, rare editions, and used books in a shop whose Gothic decorative motifs were suggested by Bernard Maybeck—

designer of the Palace of Fine Arts—but also presents lectures, dramatic readings, and book and art exhibits in the second-floor galleries.

43. To collectors the world over, the name of S. G. GUMP AND COMPANY (*open 9:45-5:25*), 250 Post St., means jade, but the firm's agents have scoured the world for more than jade. Show rooms are styled to conform with the rare objects they contain. Since Solomon and Gustave Gump founded the firm in 1865, it has grown into an institution whose buyers gather items for collectors throughout the Nation. In its show rooms are displayed modern china, pottery, glass, linens, silverware, and jewelry; silks, brocades, and velvets; Siamese and Cambodian sculpture; porcelain and cloisonné, rich-textured tapestries, bronze temple bells, hardwood screens ornamented with jade, and rugs from Chinese palaces acquired after the overthrow of the Manchu government. In the Jade Room all of the eight colors and 45 shades of the stone are represented, including the rarest, that most nearly resembling emerald; pink, so rare that only small pieces have been found; and spinach green, a dark tone flecked with black, used for large decorative pieces. The collection of tomb jade, recovered from mounds in which mandarins were interred, includes pieces 2,000 years old. The Jade Room also contains figurines carved of ivory, crystal, rose quartz, white and pink coral, rhinoceros horn, and semiprecious stones.

44. *Fluctuat nec Mergitur* (It floats and never sinks), Paris' own municipal motto, has been the slogan of the CITY OF PARIS (*open 9:45-5:25*), SE. corner Stockton and Geary Sts., since the spring of 1850, when Felix Verdier hung up—over an edifice constructed largely of packing cases the sign:

"LA VILLE DE PARIS
Felix Verdier, Proprietor
Fluctuat nec Mergitur"

The motto was appropriate, for the contents of "La Ville de Paris" had been afloat ever since Verdier had left France in a ship whose cargo he bought with profits from his silk-stocking factory at Nimes. (A republican, he had preferred exile to the new emperor.) Destroyed several times by fire, the store moved each time to larger quarters. When Felix was succeeded, at his death in the late 1860's, by his son Gaston, it was moved into its own building at Geary Street and Grant Avenue. It came to its present location in 1896.

Twenty-four-year-old Paul Verdier had scarcely taken over in 1906 when the building was destroyed. First store in town to reopen, it resumed business in a mansion on Van Ness Avenue. The present six-story building—with its glass dome rising above balconies, its Louis

XVI window frames of white enamel and carved, gilded wood—was opened in the spring of 1909. At the peak of the dome appear the original crest of Paris, a ship in full sail, and the motto. Author of *A History of Wine,* Paul Verdier personally selects the more than 1,000 choice vintages which stock the cellars.

45. When the NATHAN-DOHRMANN COMPANY (*open 9:45-5:25*), SW. corner Stockton and Geary Sts., opened in 1850 (as Blumenthal and Hirsch), it sold mining equipment. By 1886, when Bernard Nathan, manager since the founder's death, took as his partner Frederick W. Dohrmann, the firm was stocking oil lamps, basins, ewers, and shaving mugs. Still managed by descendants of Nathan and Dohrmann, it now sells wares and utensils of all descriptions.

46. In a studio penthouse the COURVOISIER GALLERIES (*open 9-5:30*), 133 Geary St., present shows of contemporary American and foreign art. Founded as an art shop in 1902 by Ephraim B. Courvoisier, the business was burned out in 1906. Courvoisier recouped his losses by restoring the fire-damaged paintings of wealthy collectors. The friend of such artists as Charles Rollo Peters, Thomas Hill, and William Keith, he developed a large clientele which followed him even when reverses forced him for a while to a Kearny Street alley. The firm was taken over by his son in 1927. After its exhibition in 1938 of the original water colors on celluloid for Walt Disney's *Snow White and the Seven Dwarfs,* it acquired the exclusive agency for sale of the originals from Disney's future productions.

47. Behind a shining all-glass three-story facade, the ANGELO J. ROSSI COMPANY (*open weekdays 8-6:30, Sun. 8-12 a.m.*), 45 Grant Ave., streamlined florist's establishment owned by the Mayor of San Francisco, displays masses of fragrant bloom against mirrored walls.

48. A neo-Gothic eight-story building houses O'CONNOR, MOFFATT AND COMPANY (*open 9:45-5:25*), NW. corner O'Farrell and Stockton Sts., founded in 1866 by Bryan O'Connor, newly arrived from Australia. O'Connor was so impressed with the city's prosperity that he sent to Melbourne for his friend, George Moffatt. Since the death of O'Connor and retirement of Moffatt in 1887, the business has been carried on by descendants of the first employees. The original dry-goods store moved in 1929 to its present building and expanded, becoming a department store.

49. Young Adolphe Roos, who founded the clothing firm of ROOS BROTHERS (*open 9:45-5:25*), NE. corner Stockton and Market Sts., arrived in San Francisco from France in time for the stampede to the Virginia City (Nevada) mines, where he made his stake by outfitting miners. Returning to San Francisco, he sent for his younger brother, Achille; together they opened the first Roos Brothers store on Leidesdorff Street in 1865. Since 1908 the firm, now guided by the

founder's son, Robert Roos, has occupied its present five-story building. Remodeled (1936-38) at a cost of $1,000,000 (J. S. Fairweather, building architect; Albert R. Williams, interior architect), it was transformed into a series of individually designed shops, its street entrances equipped with doors automatically opened by electric beams and its interiors with fluorescent illumination simulating daylight. The various shops are panelled with rare woods—hairwood from the British Isles, Yuba wood from Australia, Jenisero from Central America; in one shop is a mosaic in which more than 48 varieties are used.

50. Largest daily circulation in the city is boasted by the paper published in the SAN FRANCISCO NEWS BUILDING (*visitors shown through plant by appointment*), 812 Mission St., whose twelve presses grind out eight regular editions daily. The first edition is released at 11 a.m., the last at 5:30 p.m. The paper is one of the Scripps-Howard chain.

51. The 18-story gray-green HUMBOLDT BANK BUILDING, 785 Market St., capped by a fantastically adorned dome, was built in 1907 (Meyer and O'Brien, architects). Under construction when the earthquake and fire destroyed it, it was completely rebuilt—the first architectural contract placed after the disaster. Bronze doors lead into the banking room of the Bank of America (*open Mon.-Fri. 10-3:30, Sat. 10-12*), ornate with white Ionic columns, warm Sienna marbles, and buff mosaic floor.

52. The domed, granite AMERICAN TRUST COMPANY BUILDING (*Savings Union Office; open 10-3 Mon.-Fri., 10-12 Sat.*), NW. corner Market St., Grant Ave., and O'Farrell St., was erected in 1910. The pediment above the Ionic-pillared portico is adorned with Haig Patigian's bas-reliefs of the head of Liberty between flying eagles (based on Augustus St. Gauden's design for $20 gold pieces). Corinthian columns, Travernelle marble pilasters, and Caen stone walls lend richness to the 65-foot-high banking room. The American Trust Company was formed through successive mergers of older institutions, one of which, the Savings Union Bank and Trust Company, was the city's oldest surviving savings bank, dating back to foundation of the San Francisco Accumulating Fund Association in 1854.

53. The ageing six-story buff-brick BANCROFT BUILDING, 731 Market St., is named for the Bancroft brothers—historian Hubert Howe and publisher Albert L.—who conducted in its five-story predecessor (second brick building erected on Market Street) a book-selling and publishing firm. In partnership with George L. Kenny, Hubert Howe Bancroft previously had gone into the book-selling business in quarters on Montgomery Street. Joining the firm, his brother Albert planned the new Market Street office building, opened in 1870. In 1875 the firm announced: "Bancroft's Historical Library is the basis

of important scientific and descriptive works of a local nature, and maps or books of reference relating to the Pacific Coast." In the same year appeared the first of Hubert Howe Bancroft's histories, Volume I of his *Native Races of the Pacific Coast of North America.* In the fifth-floor publishing department, Bancroft went ahead with his prodigious labors of compiling in detail the history of all Western America. One of the pioneers of mass production methods in literature, he directed a large staff of anonymous collaborators. In 1884 he published the first of his seven volumes on the history of California—carrying a list of quoted authorities 66 pages long. Before his death in 1918, he had accumulated a library of 500 or more rare manuscripts and 60,000 volumes, now housed in the Bancroft Library at the University of California.

54. The 22-story steel-and-concrete CENTRAL TOWER, SW. corner Market and Third Sts., defies detection as the old Claus Spreckels Building. It was remodeled along functional lines in 1938. The simply decorated entrance relieves the severity of the unornamented vertical shaft with its six-story tower. In the lobby, the walls are vitriolite brick. In 1895 Claus Spreckels bought the site and erected a 19-story building in which the *Call* was published for a time. During the Spanish-American War, a cannon thundered news of American victories from the roof. Only bright spot in a darkened and devastated area, during the days after April 18, 1906, was the light kept burning in the partly destroyed cupola. In its report the Geological Survey said "the general behavior of this structure demonstrates that high buildings subject to earthquake can be erected with safety even on sand foundations."

55. The 12-story HEARST BUILDING (*visitors conducted on two-hour tour 7-9 p.m.*), SE. corner Market and Third Sts., of white terra cotta with polychrome ornamentation, houses the *San Francisco Examiner,* first paper in the Hearst chain. The first of its five regular daily editions appears on the streets about seven o'clock in the evening. On this site was the Nucleus Hotel, first brick building on Market Street, which surprised everyone—contrary to the woeful predictions of skeptics—by surviving the earthquake of 1868 almost unscathed.

56. Beloved to old-timers is LOTTA'S FOUNTAIN, corner Market, Geary, and Kearny Sts., the cast-iron shaft presented to the city in 1875 by little laughing, black-eyed Lotta Crabtree, who won the adoration of San Francisco in the era of gallantry and easy money that followed the age of gold. The 24-foot fountain within its granite base, conventional lion heads, and brass medallions depicting California scenes is commonplace, but its donor was one of the sensational personages of the last century.

In 1853 when Lola Montez visited Rabbit Creek, a small gold

camp near Grass Valley, she taught singing and dancing to the eight-year-old daughter of one of the prospectors. Not long afterward her pupil made a sensational first appearance in a Sierra mining town: gold as well as applause was showered upon the young Lotta by generous Argonauts. Her subsequent debut in San Francisco was no less encouraging. At the age of 17 she appeared on the New York stage, and at 44 she retired. Fortunate real estate investments augmented her fortune, which at her death (1924) exceeded $4,000,000. After her retirement her fountain was neglected, and its site, a busy downtown intersection, became known as Newspaper Square from the large number of newsboys who congregated there. In 1910, however, another—and perhaps a greater—singer brought Lotta's Fountain once more into prominence. At midnight on Christmas Eve, hushed thousands massed as Louisa Tetrazzini sang "The Last Rose of Summer" beside the fountain. In remembrance of the event, a bas-relief portrait of the singer by Haig Patigian was added to the monument.

57. When the De Young brothers, proprietors of the San Francisco *Chronicle,* decided in 1890 to put up the ten-story red brick DE YOUNG BUILDING, NE. corner Market, Geary, and Kearny Sts., they were considered optimistic. On a site then rather far west of the business district, they proposed to erect a steel-frame structure—the first in San Francisco. Chicago architects Burnham and Root designed an edifice whose simple lines reveal the Romanesque style of their teacher, Henry Hobson Richardson. Wiseacres were convinced the structure would not survive an earthquake—but the disaster of 1906 proved them to be wrong. A 17-story annex just completed at the time was repaired and the interior of the original structure rebuilt. Here, until 1924, was the home of the *Chronicle.*

58. One of the dozen sidewalk booths shaded by gay umbrellas which enliven the streets of the shopping district is the FLOWER STAND, Market, Geary, and Kearny Sts., standing on the location where the first flower vendors stood in the 1880's. When the De Young Building was erected, Michael de Young allowed the vendors—most of whom were boys of Italian, Belgian, Irish, or Armenian descent—to sell their flowers in front of the building, protecting them from the policemen. The curbside stands were first licensed in 1904. All attempts to suppress them have been halted by storms of protest from press and public. Their wares change with the seasons—from January, when the first frilled golden-yellow daffodils and great armfuls of feathery acacia with its fluffy tassels make their appearance, to December, when hosts of flaming crimson poinsettias and great bunches of scarlet toyon berries herald the advent of the holidays.

59. The original PALACE HOTEL, Market and New Montgomery Sts., was (according to Oscar Lewis and Carroll Hall) "at

least four times too large for its period and place, but the town had
never had a sense of proportion and no one was disturbed." Least
disturbed was its builder, William C. Ralston. This "world's grandest
hotel" would cover two and one-half acres; it would soar to the impressive height of seven stories and contain 800 rooms; its marble-paved,
glass-roofed Grand Court (about which the rectangular structure was
designed) would face Montgomery Street through an arched driveway;
artesian wells drilled on the spot would supply its storage reservoirs
with 760,000 gallons of water; its rooms would contain "noiseless"
water closets and gadgets designed to make life at the Palace effortless
and luxurious.

But three years' advance publicity satiated even a town reared on
superlatives, and before the hotel opened San Franciscans had chuckled
at the announcement of local columnist "Derrick Dodd": "The statis-
tician of the *News Letter* estimates the ground covered . . . to be eleven
hundred and fifty-four square miles, six yards, two inches . . . A contract is already given out for the construction of a flume from the
Yosemite to conduct the Bridal Veil fall thither, and which it is designed to have pour over the east front. . . . The beds are made with
Swiss watch springs and stuffed with camel's hair, each single hair
costing eleven cents. . . . There are thirty-four elevators in all—four
for passengers, ten for baggage and twenty for mixed drinks. Each
elevator contains a piano and a bowling alley . . ." Of the dining room
the *News Letter* predicted: "All the entrees will be sprinkled with
gold dust . . ."

For once, San Francisco was to be treated to reality that exceeded
even the exaggerations of its humorists. Ralston, desirous of developing local industries, financed many factories to supply the hotel's needs
until his cautious associate, Senator William Sharon, finally asked: "If
you are going a buy a foundry for a nail, a ranch for a plank, and a
manufactory to build furniture, where is this going to end?" Ralston
continued to pour millions into the structure—and died before its completion, owing the Bank of California $4,000,000. Sharon, who had
wondered "where it was going to end," found himself in possession of
the hotel.

Through the doors of the Palace, opened in October 1875, passed
"the great, the near-great, and the merely flamboyant . . . bonanza
kings and royalty alike . . . Grant, Sheridan, and Sherman were feasted
in the banquet halls; and the Friday night Cotillion Club danced . . .
in the ballroom . . ." Here the graceful manners of Oscar Wilde
charmed a local "lady reporter," and James J. Jeffries gave a champagne
party for a sweater-clad coterie. Here royalty was impressed (said
Brazil's emperor, Dom Pedro II, in 1876: "Nothing makes me ashamed

of Brazil so much as the Palace Hotel.") and royalty died (King David Kalahaua of Hawaii, January 20, 1891).

For more than a quarter of a century the Palace played host to the world. As its marble halls became less fabulous its reputation grew more so. Tales related of its "great and near-great" were echoed in a hundred cities. Climax to them all were the stories told of the early morning of April 18, 1906 when the hotel's scores of guests were shaken violently from slumber and sent wide-eyed into debris-strewn streets. Among the most alarmed was Enrico Caruso; the great tenor joined fellow members of the Metropolitan Opera Company carrying a portrait of Theodore Roosevelt and wearing a towel about his famous throat. Although it suffered only minor interior damage by the 'quake, the Palace succumbed, its elaborate fire-fighting system useless against the raging inferno.

Rebuilt in 1909 on the same site, the present eight-story tan-brick and terra cotta structure is in the Beaux Art tradition. There are low grills at the windows and several ornate iron balconies. The eighth floor is surmounted by an elaborate frieze. Reminders of the past are a porte cochere on the site of the carriage entrance to the Grand Court, facing (across the lobby) the present glass-roofed Palm Court; the Comstock Room, a duplicate of the room wherein the "Nevada Four" opened their poker sessions with a "take-out" of $75,000 in ivory chips; the Happy Valley cocktail lounge with its Sotomayor murals of Lotta Crabtree and "Emperor" Norton; and the Pied Piper Buffet (*for men*) with its mahogany fixtures and Maxfield Parrish painting (modeled by Maude Adams). No less illustrious than the guests of the old Palace have been the patrons of the new. In 1923 the hotel was the saddened host to Warren G. Harding, who died in the presidential suite.

A corridor leads from the Palace lobby to the studios of KSFO (entrance at 140 Jessie St.), constructed in 1938 at a cost of $400,000. The interior is effectively decorated in soft blues and grays highlighted by chromium trim. A circular staircase leads to the second-floor reception lounge, executive offices, master control room, and broadcasting studios. The third floor is devoted to the engineering, script, music, art and advertising departments.

To prevent vibration, each studio is suspended on springs, with walls and ceilings constructed so as to form no parallel lines, thus eliminating echoes. A layer of spun glass fibre underlying perforated walls soundproofs each studio.

60. San Francisco's oldest surviving newspaper, the *Call-Bulletin,* is published at the CALL BUILDING (*visitors shown through plant by appointment*), 74 New Montgomery St., its presses turning out four daily editions (the first appears about 10.45 a.m.) with an average circulation of 110,000.

61. The gray stone walls, sometimes floodlighted in gleaming yellow splendor by night, of the monolithic PACIFIC TELEPHONE AND TELEGRAPH BUILDING, 140 New Montgomery St., enclose the head offices of a telephone network embracing all the far West. Largest building on the Pacific Coast devoted to one firm's exclusive use at the time of its completion in 1925, it was built at a cost of $3,000,000 (J. R. Miller, T. L. Pflueger, and A. A. Cantin, architects). From each of the four facades of its four-story tower, two huge stone eagles survey the city from their 26-story perches. The terra cotta facade, with its lofty piers and mullions tapering upward in Gothic effect, cloaks but does not hide the structural lines. The building's 210,000 square feet of floor space provide working room for 2,000 employees.

62. A monument to San Francisco's early-day regard for learning is the nine-story MECHANICS INSTITUTE BUILDING, 57 Post St., erected in 1910 (Albert Pissis, architect), which houses the Mechanics-Mercantile Library (*open weekdays 9 a.m.-10 p.m., Sun. 1-5*). On December 11, 1854, a group of citizens met in the tax collector's office to found a Mechanics' Institute for the advancement of the mechanic arts and sciences; and on March 6, 1855, they adopted a constitution providing for "the establishment of a library, reading room, the collection of a cabinet, scientific apparatus, works of art, and for other literary and scientific purposes." With four books presented by one S. Bugbee—*The Bible, the Constitution of the United States,* an *Encyclopaedia of Architecture,* and *Curtis on Conveyancing*—the library began its activities in June, 1855.

Progress of the association began with the inauguration of annual Mechanics' and Manufacturers' Fairs, September 7, 1857, in a pavilion on Montgomery Street between Post and Sutter Streets. As the fairs became civic events of prime importance, one sprawling wooden pavilion after another was built to house them—six in all, of which the third and fourth occupied Union Square; the fifth, Eighth Street between Mission and Market Streets; and the sixth, the site of the Civic Auditorium. The last of the fairs was held in 1899.

In 1866 the Institute built its first structure on the present site. By 1872 it had collected a library of 17,239 volumes. In January, 1906 it merged with the Mercantile Library Association, organized in 1852 by a group of merchants. The merger of the two associations, whose combined library numbered 200,000 volumes, had scarcely been affected, however, when the fire of 1906 destroyed books, equipment, and building. Hard hit, the Institute nevertheless had acquired a new library of 40,000 volumes by 1912, when it realized from the sale of its pavilion lot to the city the sum of $700,000. Its present (1940) collection of 195,000 volumes is especially notable in the fields of science and technology. The Mechanics' Institute also provides for its members a chess and checker room and a lecture series.

63. The 13-story CROCKER FIRST NATIONAL BANK, NW. corner Post and Montgomery Sts., stands on the site of the old Masonic Temple. Oldest national bank in California, it is a merger of the First National Bank, opened in 1871 with James D. Phelan as president, and the Crocker National Bank, organized in 1883 by Charles Crocker (one of the "Big Four"). The two banks were consolidated in 1926. Of Italian Renaissance style, its entrance is distinguished by a rotunda supported on granite pillars (Willis Polk and Company, architects).

64. Prosaic monument to a story-book past is the 12-story granite NEVADA BANK BUILDING, NE. corner Montgomery and Market Sts., housing the Wells Fargo Bank and Union Trust Company. A lively chapter in the history of the West is the story of its parent institution, Wells Fargo and Company. A year before its incorporation in New York the express firm was buying and selling "dust," receiving deposits, and selling exchange. One of the few institutions to survive the "Black Friday" of February 1855, it operated its banking business until 1878 in conjunction with its express activities. In 1905 the Wells Fargo Bank was consolidated with the Nevada Bank and in 1924, with the Union Trust Company. The present building, built in 1894, was raised to a height of ten stories in 1903 and to twelve in 1907-08. The History Room on the tenth floor houses a historical library and a museum of pioneer relics including a stagecoach, veteran of the Overland Trail; the golden spike which Leland Stanford drove at Promontory, Utah, in 1869; and a gold scale that weighed $55,000,000 worth of the gold dust mined in the Mother Lode.

65. The neo-Gothic, gable-roofed ONE ELEVEN SUTTER BUILDING, SW. corner Montgomery and Sutter Sts., since 1927 has reared its buff-colored terra cotta facades 22 stories above a site which was worth $300 when James Lick bought it and $175,000 when he died. The marble-inlaid lobby and corridors of the interior (Schultze and Weaver, architects)—the pillars adorned with green and white Verde Antique from Greece, the lobby floor with Hungarian red, the corridor floors with Italian Botticino, Tennessee pink, and Belgian black marbles—rival the luxurious interior of the Lick House, which Lick built here in 1862. The latter hostelry boasted $1,000 gas chandeliers, mirrored walls, and mosaic floors of rare imported woods. Trained as a cabinet-maker, the eccentric millionaire finished with his own hands the woodwork of the luxurious banquet hall.

The building houses offices and studios of the National Broadcasting Company's stations KGO and KPO (*open 8:30 a.m.-11 p.m.*). On the second and third floors are the reception lobby, executive and business offices, and production departments. The broadcasting studios, each with its own control room and monitor's booth, occupy the 21st and 22nd stories. Sharing these top floors respectively are the music library, largest of its kind west of New York, and the master control room, distributor for incoming broadcasts.

66. Because of well-balanced construction, the 16-story ALEXANDER BUILDING, SW. corner Montgomery and Bush Sts., a simple shaft faced in buff-colored brick and terra cotta whose vertical lines give it a towering grace, is considered ideal for studies of earthquake stresses on skyscrapers. Seismographs installed at top, center, and bottom of the structure by the U. S. Geodetic Survey furnish research data for the University of California and Stanford University. The building was erected in 1921 (Lewis Hobart, architect).

67. "The Monument to 1929"—thus have financial circles, since the stock market crash, referred to the three-story granite SAN FRANCISCO CURB EXCHANGE BUILDING, 350 Bush St. (J. R. Miller and T. L. Pflueger, architects). Scene of the frenzied speculation of the 1920's, it housed the San Francisco Mining Exchange until 1928, when it was taken over by the newly organized San Francisco Curb Exchange. Remodeled in 1938, when the Curb Exchange was absorbed by the San Francisco Stock Exchange, it now houses the California State Chamber of Commerce.

68. "An example to all Western architects of a model office building," wrote Ernest Peixotto in 1893 of the MILLS BUILDING, 220 Montgomery Street, built in 1891 for banker Darius Ogden Mills (Burnham and Root, architects). "It is an architectural composition, and not mere walls pierced by window openings . . . It consists of a two-story basement of Inyo marble, carrying a buff brick super-structure of seven stories, crowned by a two-story attic. The angle piers . . . are massive and sufficient; between them piers spring from the third story, crowned in the eighth by arches . . . The effect of height is strengthened by the strongly marked lines of the piers . . . The focus for ornament is the Montgomery Street entrance, which rises to an arch . . . as large and ample as it should be . . ." So sound was the building's construction that it survived the fire of 1906 with little damage to its exterior. Adhering to the original design, Willis Polk supervised its restoration in 1908 and the erection of additions in 1914 and 1918. When the adjoining 22-story MILLS TOWER (entrance at 220 Bush St.)—to which all but the second of the older building's ten floors have direct access—was erected in 1931, architect Lewis Hobart also followed Burnham's design. The same buff-colored pressed brick especially manufactured for the original building was used on its facade. The combined buildings contain 1,300 offices and 350,000 feet of floor space.

On the site of the Mills Building in the 1860's stood Platt's Hall, a great square auditorium where people flocked for lectures, concerts, and political conventions. On its stage, Thomas Starr King lifted Bret Harte from obscurity by reading his poem, "The Reveille." Among the attractions which drew crowds were Henry Ward Beecher and General Tom Thumb and his wife.

69. Largest office building on the Pacific Coast, the block-long RUSS BUILDING, 235 Montgomery St., stands on the ground where Christian Russ, in 1847, established a residence for his family of twelve. Here in 1861 the owner of Russ' Gardens built the Russ House, a hotel long favored by farmers, miners and merchants. Still owned by his heirs, its site, nine decades after Russ acquired it at auction for $37.50, was assessed at $675,000. Construction of today's $5,500,000 skyscraper, begun in July, 1926, was completed in September, 1927. Modernized Gothic, the massive, sandy-hued edifice rises 31 stories, its three wings deployed in the shape of an "E" (George W. Kelham, architect). Its 1,370 offices, comprising 335,245 square feet of floor space, house 3,500 persons. With its 400-car garage and its eleventh-story complete shopping department, the building provides its personnel with every service from a Public Library branch to a language translation bureau.

70. The 15-story FINANCIAL CENTER BUILDING, NW. corner Montgomery and California Sts., marks the SITE OF THE PARROTT BUILDING. The latter, San Francisco's first stone structure, was built in 1852 by Chinese masons of granite blocks quarried in China. When the Chinese struck for higher pay they won their demands because no other available workers could read the markings on the blocks. The old building survived earthquake and fire but was torn down in 1926 when the present skyscraper was built.

71. Ten lofty granite Tuscan columns flanked by massive pylons dominate the temple-like Pine Street facade of the SAN FRANCISCO STOCK EXCHANGE BUILDING (*open Mon.-Fri. 7-2:30, Sat. 7-11*), SW. corner Pine and Sansome Sts. (public entrance 155 Sansome St.). The pylons, carved by Ralph Stackpole, symbolizing Mother Earth's fruitfulness and Man's inventive genius, stand on either side of the steps. Above the Pine Street wing, which houses the Trading Room (*members only*), rises the 12-story gray granite tower of the administration wing. Above its doorway, carved in high relief, is Stackpole's *The Progress of Man,* and on the lintel, a sculptured eagle with outstretched wings. The walls of the public lobby are inlaid with dusky red Levanto marble and the ceiling with gold leaf in a geometric star design. A marble stairway ascends to the visitors' gallery overlooking the Trading Room.

Above the high windows of east and west walls of the Trading

Room are Robert Boardman Howard's two groups of three sculptured panels—one portraying development of electric power; the other, development of gas power. Along north and south walls extend the quotation boards, their markers' galleries equipped with ticker receiving instruments and headset telephones. Beneath, an annunciator signal system summons members to their booths along the sides of the room. At the center of the brown rubber-tiled trading floor is stationed the telegraph ticker transmitting station, which sends reports of every transaction to brokers' offices along the Pacific Coast. Around it are stationed four oak-panelled hollow enclosures for nine trading posts, each equipped with electrically synchronized stamping devices that indicate the time of every order to a tenth of a minute. Essential to the rapid handling of orders is the telephone exchange, busiest in San Francisco, which handles an estimated total of 5,000 calls per hour of trading. It can handle 1,800 calls at one time, with a peak capacity of 180,000 words per minute.

The ninth floor of the administration wing houses headquarters of the Governing Board and exchange officials. The solid oak door to the walnut-panelled Governing Board room is carved with a bas-relief by Robert Boardman Howard depicting the steps in construction of a building. The Lunch Club quarters (*not open to the public*) on the tenth and eleventh floors are decorated with frescoes by Diego Rivera depicting California history.

In the basement of a building a block northward, the Stock and Bond Exchange was organized September 18, 1882, by 19 pioneer brokers. It succeeded several earlier exchanges, of which the first, the San Francisco Stock and Exchange Board (contemporaneously referred to as "The Forty Thieves"), had been established in 1862. Since 1882 the present exchange has stopped functioning as the pulse of business life on the Pacific Coast on only three occasions: April 18, 1906, because of the earthquake and fire; July 31, 1914, because of the World War; and March 2-14, 1933, because of the National bank holiday. Its memberships, which sold for $50 in 1882 and rose to an all-time high of $225,000 in 1928, today sell for varying sums, the most recent sale price having been $16,500.

72. The BANK OF CALIFORNIA (*open Mon.-Fri. 10-3, Sat. 10-12*), NW. corner Sansome and California Sts., was erected in 1908 (Bliss and Faville, architects). The gray granite building has tall and finely proportioned Corinthian colonnades. The immense banking room, 112 feet long and 54 feet high, faced in Tennessee marble, resembles a Roman basilica. In the rear on either side of a large clock are carved marble lions (Arthur Putnam, sculptor). Less subdued in its magnificence was the palatial edifice erected on this site to house the bank in 1867, three years after its establishment with Darius Ogden Mills as

Downtown

CITY HALL

EXPOSITION AUDITORIUM

SAN FRANCISCO'S JAGGED TERRACES FROM THE BAY © *Gabriel Moulin*

SKYLINE FROM A SKY WINDOW

MARKET STREET AT 5:15

LABOR DAY PARADE UP MARKET STREET

A FIVE-MINUTE WALK FROM THE BUSINESS DISTRICT

FOUR-FIFTY SUTTER BUILDING AND SIR FRANCIS DRAKE HOTEL

PORTSMOUTH PLAZA

MONTGOMERY BLOCK

MONUMENT TO ROBERT LOUIS STEVENSON, IN PORTSMOUTH PLAZA

president and William C. Ralston as cashier. To clear the site they moved the Tehama House—which humorist "John Phoenix" celebrated in *A Legend of the Tehama House*—a popular hostelry among Mexican *rancheros* and military and naval officers. Ralston built a handsome two-story structure with tall arched windows surmounted by medallions and framed in marble columns, a cornice crowned with a stone balustrade supporting fretted vases, doors and balcony railings of bronze, and a burnished copper roof. For a decade the bank was the financial colossus of all the territory west of the Rocky Mountains. It reached into Nevada, during the Comstock Lode boom, to establish four branch banks. When the collapse of the silver boom brought it crashing from financial dominance in 1875, the whole State was shaken. But the reorganized bank survived and grew, taking over in 1905 the London and San Francisco Bank, Ltd., with branches in Oregon and Washington.

A glass case in the main office contains the scales on which Darius Ogden Mills weighed some $50,000,000 of miners' gold in the tent which he set up at Columbia in 1849, before coming to San Francisco to become president of Ralston's bank.

73. Venerable home of a parent organization of the San Francisco Chamber of Commerce was the 14-story MERCHANTS' EXCHANGE BUILDING, NE. corner California and Sansome Sts. Here until 1911 the city's moguls of industry and agriculture congregated to regulate and put through huge deals in hay, grain, and shipping. In bonanza days Robert Louis Stevenson used to haunt the Exchange's central board room, where he found material—in such men as John D. Spreckels—for heroes of *The Wreckers*.

Since 1851 the main-floor MARINE EXCHANGE (*always open*) has operated continuously except during 1906 and though much of its romantic element was lost with the passing of sailing ships, its function remains virtually the same. Outgrowth of the old Merchants' Exchange and Reading Room established in 1849 by Messrs. Sweeny and Baugh, who operated the signal station on Telegraph Hill, the Exchange is connected with lookout stations which report every movement of local shipping. It receives and compiles complete information from every Pacific Coast vessel from start to finish of every voyage. Files on the Exchange's mezzanine floor record launchings, cargoes, crews, disasters, sales, weather reports—all marine information required by shippers, ship owners, ship chandlers, warehousemen, exporters, and importers. Before the advent of the telephone a messenger boy on horseback rushed news of incoming ships from the Exchange to the city's major hotels.

At one end of the Exchange, beneath an arch set at right angles to the south wall, hangs the original Vigilance Committee bell which hung on top of Fort Gunnybags in 1856. The bell, which once tolled the death knell of Cora and Casey, now clangs to announce to the Exchange some mishap to a ship whose home port is San Francisco.

Though grain, shipping, insurance, and similar firms still occupy this building, which survived the fire of 1906, its chief interest lies in such features as evoke its past. Something of its lusty social tradition survives in the Commercial Club occupying three top stories and in the Merchants' Exchange Club in the basement. Reminiscent of other days are Nils Hagerup's paintings on walls of the main lobby depicting Amundsen's explorations in the *Gjoa* and W. A. Coulter's ships in port and at sea. The latter's huge painting of the San Francisco fire hangs, draped with red velvet, in the billiard room of the Merchants' Exchange Club.

74. From ground above the hulls of long-buried sailing ships, the FEDERAL RESERVE BANK (*open Mon.-Fri. 8:30-4:30, Sat. 8:30-1*), NE. corner Sansome and Sacramento Sts., rears its eight white granite Ionic columns, rising up three of its seven stories to a classic pediment (George W. Kelham, architect). When steam shovels excavated the basement vaults in 1922, they exposed the oaken skeleton of the city's first prison, the brig *Euphemia,* moored at Long Wharf in the 1850's. The Sansome Street entrance leads into a Travertine marble lobby with murals by Jules Guerin. From the Battery Street side, ramps descend to the vaults, where trucks discharge treasure for deposit behind 36-ton doors, under the hawk-eyed gaze of guards.

75. By day, bathed in sunlight, the 30-story SHELL BUILDING, NW. corner Battery and Bush Sts., San Francisco headquarters of the Shell Oil Company empire, is a buff, tapering shaft; by night, floodlight-swept, a tower looming in amber radiance. Its Bush Street entrance is enriched with a filigree design in marble and bronze. Erected in 1929 (George W. Kelham, architect), it broke Pacific Coast records for rapid construction, rising three stories each week.

76. With heroic vigor, the bronze figures of the DONAHUE MONUMENT, Battery, Bush, and Market Sts. (Douglas Tilden, sculptor)—five brawny, half-naked workmen, struggling to force by lever a mechanical punch through plate metal—are poised on their granite base, in a triangular pedestrian island. Executed in 1899, the monument is James Mervyn Donahue's memorial to his father, Peter Donahue, founder of San Francisco's first iron foundry, first street railway, and first gas company. A bronze plaque etched with a map in the pavement at its base marks the shoreline as it was before Yerba Buena Cove was filled in, when Market Street from this point northeast was a 1,000-foot wharf.

77. On what was the shifting sand of a Yerba Buena beach lot towers the 22-story, gray granite STANDARD OIL BUILDING,

SW. corner Sansome and Bush Sts., erected in 1921 (George W. Kelham, architect). Its cornice-overhung facade, the upper stories adorned with Doric columns, is a modern adaptation of the Florentine style. The two-story vaulted entrance leads into an ornate lobby of bronze and marble.

78. To trace the origins of the ANGLO CALIFORNIA NATIONAL BANK (*open Mon.-Fri. 10-3, Sat. 10-12*), 1 Sansome St., is to follow the ramifications of international finance. One of its parent institutions, the Anglo Californian Bank, Limited, organized in London in 1873, took over the San Francisco branch of J. and W. Seligman and Company of New York, London, Paris, and Frankfurt. Three years later Lazard Frères, silk importers and exchange dealers of New York, London, and Paris, opened a San Francisco branch, out of which grew, in 1884, the London, Paris, and American Bank, Limited, of Great Britain. The two were consolidated in 1909 under the latter name and a new bank, the Anglo-Californian Trust Company, emerged to handle the older bank's savings business. The Fleishhacker brothers, Herbert and Mortimer, gained financial prominence as presidents of the two institutions. By 1920 the Anglo-Californian Trust Company had absorbed four San Francisco banks, and by 1928 it had opened eight local branches. From the merger of the two Fleishhacker banks in 1932 came today's Anglo California National Bank, which soon reached into the rest of the State. By 1939—when the number of banks absorbed by it and its parent institutions had grown to 15—it was operating branches from Redding in the north to Bakersfield in the south.

79. Of the thousands of commuters who once poured daily through the Ferry Building, for six decades San Francisco's chief gateway from the east, most now enter the city through the BRIDGE TERMINAL BUILDING, Mission, First, and Fremont Sts. The low-spreading three-story steel-and-concrete structure, completed in 1939 at a cost of $2,300,000, is the terminal for electric interurban trains carrying passengers over the San Francisco-Oakland Bay Bridge to the East Bay. Through the terminal pass an estimated number of 60,000 persons daily, 21,000,000 annually. During the rush hour, between 4:45 and 5:45 p.m., when 37 trains arrive and depart, the building resounds with the din of shouting newsboys, taxi barkers, and streetcars clanging up the wide ramp from First and Mission Streets to discharge passengers at the entrance. Ramps and stairways ascend to the loading platforms which separate the three pairs of tracks. To diminish noise, the rails are laid on timber ties embedded in concrete which rests on a two-inch insulated cushion. A viaduct carries the trains high above streets and buildings onto the lower bridge deck. Their speed is governed by a code picked from the tracks by a receiver attached near the front axles and

transmitted to an indicator in the motorman's cab. If the motorman fails to slow down within two and one-half seconds after a warning bell indicates a slower speed, the train automatically stops.

80. Exponent of fine printing is the firm of TAYLOR AND TAYLOR, 404 Mission St., established in 1896 by Edward DeWitt Taylor, who, since the death of his brother and co-partner (Henry H. Taylor) in 1937, remains sole owner. *Types, Borders & Miscellany of Taylor & Taylor,* included in the American Institute of Graphic Arts' "Fifty Books of the Year" for 1940, has been described by Oscar Lewis as having a "classical simplicity of typographical design." Besides limited editions of Californiana, catalogs for art exhibits, and items for various cultural institutions, Taylor and Taylor are printers of much distinctive commercial advertising. Edward Taylor gained local fame for his work in the installation of the Denham cost-finding system among the printing trades of the Bay region.

In the firm's composing room stands an ornamental Columbian hand press (1818), a reminder of Taylor's first printing venture in 1882: *The Observer*—a journal "devoted to general literature and the interests ot the Western Addition."

The firm's typographical library contains two centuries of European type specimens and examples of fine printing from the fifteenth century to the present. Included are such rare editions as the Kelmscott Chaucer from the press of William Morris and one of the world's most comprehensive collections of the works of Homer.

81. On wooden piles driven into the mud of what was Yerba Buena Cove rest the 17 steel-and-concrete stories of the PACIFIC GAS AND ELECTRIC BUILDING, 245 Market St., headquarters of the Nation's third largest utilities system, which originated with Peter Donahue's gas company (1852) and the California Electric Light Company (1879), both Pacific Coast pioneers. Designed by John M. Bakewell, the building was opened in March, 1925. Over the three-story arched entrance is Edgar Walter's bas-relief symbolizing the application of electric power to man's needs. The granite keystones of the first-story arches, carved by the same sculptor, represent the rugged mountain country whose rushing torrents have been tapped for hydroelectric power.

82. Memorial to the company's founder, Swedish sea captain William Matson, is the Viking vessel in bas-relief above the main entrance of the 16-story MATSON NAVIGATION COMPANY BUILDING, 215 Market St. Into Hilo, Hawaii, in 1882, Matson sailed his 200-ton schooner, the *Emma Claudine.* His line grew from one vessel to a great fleet of freighters transporting the sugar and the pineapple of the Islands to the Pacific Coast. When financial ties linked the Matson line with the "Big Five" who controlled Hawaiian sugar, the company

achieved a monopoly of Hawaiian shipping. In 1925 its general manager, Matson's son-in-law, William P. Roth, built the $7,500,000 luxury liner, *Malolo,* to carry tourists to the Islands; began construction there of a luxury hotel, the Royal Hawaiian; and inaugurated a Nation-wide advertising campaign to popularize "The Paradise of the Pacific." Having bought out two competing lines, he constructed three more liners— the *Lurline* for the Hawaiian service and the *Mariposa* and *Monterey* for service to Australia and New Zealand. Beside the headquarters of the Matson shipping and real estate empire, the Matson Building houses the offices of four of the firms comprising the so-called "Big Five" which dominate finance, trade, transportation, and utilities of the Hawaiian Islands.

83. The ten-story SOUTHERN PACIFIC BUILDING, 65 Market St., constructed in 1917, is headquarters for the railroad system inaugurated by the "Big Four's" Central Pacific in 1869. The building's 506,000 tons of steel and concrete (Bliss and Faville, architects) rest on 60 miles of cedar piling. It stands on the SITE OF THE PRE-PAREDNESS DAY PARADE BOMBING, where ten persons were killed July 22, 1916, in an explosion which led to the conviction and imprisonment of Thomas Mooney and Warren K. Billings.

Landmarks of the Old Town

*"Cities, like men, have their birth, growth and maturer years.
Some are born Titans, and from the beginning promise to be
mighty in their deeds, however wilful and destructive."*
—*The Annals of San Francisco* (1852)

THE MARVEL is not that so little but that so much of the city's
venerable and homely architecture has escaped time's vicissitudes
— of which not the least was the fire of 1906. Recalling the
great fire of 1851—in which the El Dorado gambling saloon was saved
by the citizenry's desperate stand—one may suppose that the area around
Portsmouth Square was spared, less by a shift of wind, than by San
Franciscans stubbornly defending the cradle of their traditions. Unlike
the carefully preserved Vieux Carré of New Orleans, however, it survives, not through care, but through sheer neglect.

On the muddy shores of a little cove at the southeastern base of a
rocky hill (Telegraph Hill), San Francisco was born. A short distance
inland, Francisco de Haro marked out his Calle de la Fundacion, skirting the shore on its way north-northwest over the hill toward the Presidio (along the present Grant Avenue). Just north of Washington
and Montgomery streets was an inlet from which the shoreline ran
diagonally southeast to Rincon Hill (western terminus of the San Francisco-Oakland Bay Bridge). From the rocky headland north of the
inlet, first called Punta del Embarcadero and later Clark's Point (now
the intersection of Battery Street and Broadway), William S. Clark
built the first pile wharf in 1847. The line of anchorage was the present Battery Street, where the Russians loaded grain and meat for their
Alaskan colonies, where the frigate *Artemisia*—first French ship to enter
the Bay—anchored in 1827, and the *San Luis*—first American warship
to enter the harbor—in 1841. When the warship *Portsmouth* dropped
anchor July 8, 1846, Captain John B. Montgomery disembarked at
what is now the southeast corner of Montgomery and Clay streets (*see
plaque on Bank of America Building, 552 Montgomery St.*). The
Plaza (later Portsmouth Square) was only 500 feet west of the water's
edge.

West of the Plaza, facing the Calle de la Fundacion between the
two cross streets (now Clay and Washington streets) which ran eastward to the line of Montgomery Street along the water's edge, "the
first tenement" (reports *The Annals of San Francisco*) had been "constructed in the year 1835 by Captain W. R. Richardson, and up to the

year 1846, there might not be more than twenty or thirty houses of all descriptions in the place." Richardson's dwelling (*see plaque between 823 and 827 Grant Avenue*) was "a large tent, supported on four redwood posts and covered with a ship's foresail." Near by on July 4, 1836, Jacob Primer Leese completed Yerba Buena's first permanent dwelling—"a rather grand structure, being made of frame sixty feet long and twenty-five feet broad." (The plaque at the southwest corner of Clay Street and Grant Avenue states incorrectly that here Leese "erected the first building in San Francisco," birthplace of "the first white child in San Francisco . . . April 15, 1838." The first building was erected at the Presidio in 1776, and the first white child was born at the site of Mission Dolores August 10, 1776.) Not to be outdone by Leese, Richardson erected his adobe "Casa Grande."

Soon after United States conquest, Americans had built a sprawling town on the cove; by 1847 there were "22 shanties, 31 frame houses, and 26 adobe dwellings." City Engineer Jasper O'Farrell laid out the streets in checkerboard fashion, swinging De Haro's Calle de la Fundacion into line with the north-and-south streets, and extending the town's limits far beyond the district surveyed by Jean Vioget in 1839 (bounded by Montgomery, Dupont, Pacific, and Sacramento Streets)—westward to Leavenworth Street, north to Francisco, south to Post, and southeast beyond Market Street. The year 1848 marked the first building boom. According to *The Annals of San Francisco,* "A vacant lot . . . was offered the day prior to the opening of the [Broadway] wharf for $5,000, but there were no buyers. The next day the same lot sold readily at $10,000." Long before lots could be surveyed, the area was "overspread with a multitude of canvas, blanket and bough covered tents,—the bay was alive with shipping . . ."

The community soon pushed eastward beyond the shore line, supporting itself with piles above the water and over rubble dumped into the tidal flats. Most of Commercial Street was then Long Wharf, built 2,000 feet into the Bay from Leidesdorff Street in 1850. A narrow plank walk, connecting Long Wharf with the Sacramento Street pier, was the beginning of Sansome Street. Into abandoned ships, dragged inland and secured from the tides, moved merchants and lodgers. Of these vessels, perhaps the most famous was the windjammer *Niantic*— one of the first to sail through the Golden Gate after 1849—abandoned by crew and passengers bound for the "diggin's." Doors were cut, the hold was partitioned into warehouses, and offices were built on deck. When the superstructure was destroyed by fire in 1851, the Niantic Hotel (replaced in 1872 by the Niantic Block) was erected on the site (*see plaque at NW. corner Clay and Sansome Sts.*). Among other vessels claimed were the *General Harrison,* at the northwest corner of

Clay and Battery streets, and the *Apollo,* at the northwest corner of Sacramento and Battery streets.

On Christmas Eve, 1849, fire destroyed the ramshackle city. By May 4, 1851, it had been burned five times. So reluctant were men to invest in San Francisco building enterprises that the East Bay enjoyed a tremendous growth. To restore local confidence, bankers and realtors combined to erect fire- and earthquake-proof buildings. First was the Parrott Block, built of granite blocks imported—cut and dressed—from China, on the present site of the Financial Center building at the northwest corner of Montgomery and California streets. Along Montgomery and adjoining streets arose a series of office buildings—solid, dignified, well-proportioned—which still remain.

The life of the town for more than three decades revolved around San Francisco's first "Civic Center," Portsmouth Square—the Plaza of Mexican days. At its northwest corner stood Yerba Buena's government building, the adobe Customhouse, where Captain John B. Montgomery quartered his troops in 1846. Authorized by the Mexican Government in 1844, the four-room, attic-crowned structure with veranda on three sides, was not finished at the time. Soon afterwards occupied by the *alcalde* and the tax collector, it became the seat of city government. (From the beams of the south veranda, in 1851, the first Vigilance Committee hanged the thief, John Jenkins.) At the behest of the newcomers from the *Portsmouth,* Captain John Vioget, the town's first surveyor, changed the name of his Vioget House, the town's first hotel, to Portsmouth House. In the bar and billiard saloon of the wooden building, at the southeastern corner of Clay and Kearny streets, hung Vioget's original map. Across the street on the southwest corner was the long, one-story adobe store and home of William Alexander Leidesdorff, the pioneer business man from the Danish West Indies, of mixed Negro and Danish blood, who was the American Vice-Consul under Mexican rule. At the first United States election held here on September 15, 1846, Lieutenant Washington A. Bartlett was chosen *alcalde.* Leidesdorff's house was transformed in November by John H. Brown into a hotel, later known as the City Hotel. On the west side of the square was built in 1847 the first public schoolhouse, which soon served also as jail, courthouse, church, and town hall, grandiloquently called the "Public Institute."

Around Portsmouth Square clustered in the early 1850's the noisy saloons, theaters, and gambling houses of the city's first bawdy amusement zone. Not only the first public schoolhouse and the first hotel, but also the first theater faced the plaza: Washington Hall, on Washington Street along the north side, where the city's first play was presented in January, 1850. In the same block were built the Monumental Engine House No. 6, and the Bella Union Melodeon. The famous Maguire's

Opera House (*see Social Heritage: Before the Footlights*) rose on the east side of the square. To the east, on the site of the present Hall of Justice, were the rowdy Eldorado gambling house and the Parker House, which became the Jenny Lind Theatre in 1850 and the first permanent City Hall two years later.

Today the cradle of old San Francisco is a half-mile inland. Its ageing landmarks, hemmed in by Chinatown and North Beach on the north and west, by the financial and commission districts on the south and east, are all but overlooked. Persistent indeed must be the observer who can discover the few remaining landmarks of the vanished village of Yerba Buena.

Montgomery Street, the water front of '49, commercial artery of the roaring boom town, relaxed into a bohemian quarter long before 1906; artists' studios still occupy buildings which housed journalists and bankers, gamblers and merchants and bartenders, miners and sailors and stagecoach drivers. Realtors, printers, lawyers, and pawnbrokers occupy outmoded structures wherein their forbears speculated on fabulous "deals" in a boom era. Here, Chinese, Filipinos, Italians, Frenchmen, all sorts of Americans, still congregate and engage in business. But sailors from the seven seas gather no more on the slope of Portsmouth Square.

Something of the relative simplicity of the Argonauts—not the gaudy pretentiousness of their bonanza successors—survives in those old buildings with square cornices and simple facades, whose cornerstones were laid upon redwood piling and filled-in land during 1849 and the early 1850's. A few bronze plaques here and there are all that identify San Francisco's memorable landmarks of the Gold Rush era. A few names of defunct firms, in obscure letters across weatherbeaten facades, tell legends which only those knowing the city's lore may fully comprehend. A few steep and narrow streets, a quiet plaza, an odor of decay, and a few scattered relics are all that remain of that once crowded area.

POINTS OF INTEREST

84. Upon the green, sloping lawns of PORTSMOUTH PLAZA, Kearny, Clay, and Washington Sts., Candelario Miramontes, who resided at the Presidio, raised potatoes in the early 1830's. When the plot became a plaza is not known. Until 1854, when it was graded and paved, it had been graced only with a speakers' platform and a cowpen. Most of the stirring events from the 1840's to the 1860's took place here —processions, flag raisings, lynchings, May Day fetes. When news of the death of Henry Clay was received, all the buildings surrounding the plaza were draped in black. To hear Colonel E. D. Baker's funeral oration here for Senator David Broderick (fatally wounded in a duel

September 13, 1859, by Judge David S. Terry) 30,000 people gathered. From 1850 to 1870 the square was headquarters for public hacks and the omnibus which ran from North Beach to South Park. In 1873 crowds gathered to gape at Andrew Hallidie's pioneer cable car climbing the hill on its first trip from the terminus at Clay and Kearny streets. Before 1880 the square ceased to be the center of civic gravity, as the business district moved south and west. Into abandoned buildings moved the Chinese on the west and north, the habitues of the Barbary Coast to the northeast, the residents of the Latin Quarter on the east. Here terrified Chinese ran about beating gongs to scare off the fire demons during the earthquake and conflagration of 1906; here came exhausted fire fighters to rest among milling refugees; here shallow graves held the dead; and thousands camped during reconstruction. The Board of Supervisors, in December, 1927, restored the square's Spanish designation of "plaza."

Under the boughs of three slender poplars stands the ROBERT LOUIS STEVENSON MONUMENT, the first shrine ever erected to the memory of the man who sought the sunshine here in 1879. A simple granite shaft surmounted by a bronze galleon in full sail, the *Hispaniola of Treasure Island* (Bruce Porter, architect; George Piper, sculptor), the monument is inscribed with an excerpt from Stevenson's "Christmas Sermon." Around it are clumps of purple Scotch heather.

Near the square's northwest corner, the MONTGOMERY FLAG POLE marks the site on which Captain John B. Montgomery first raised the United States flag, July 9, 1846. Erected in 1924 by the Daughters of the American Revolution, it has at its base a plaque inscribed in commemoration of the event.

85. On historic ground stands the HALL OF JUSTICE, SE. corner Kearny and Washington Sts., facing Portsmouth Plaza. Here stood the famous Eldorado gambling house, and here, too, was Dennison's Exchange Saloon, where the first official Democratic Party meeting was held October 25, 1849, and where the first of the city's fires broke out two months later. Destroyed in this fire, the Parker House next door, built by Robert A. Parker and John H. Brown, was rebuilt—only to be twice burned again. Destroyed a third time in 1851, the year after Thomas Maguire had converted it into the Jenny Lind Theater, it was reconstructed. When a fifth fire reduced it to ashes in the same year, it was replaced by the third Jenny Lind Theater, built of stone. This the city purchased in 1852 for a City Hall (*see Civic Center*), to which it annexed the four-story building on the site of the Eldorado for a Hall of Records. Razed in 1895, the two buildings were replaced by the first Hall of Justice, which in turn was replaced after 1906 by the present somber gray-stone structure (Newton J. Tharp, architect),

housing the city police department and courts, Superior Court criminal division, city prison, and morgue.

S. on Kearny St. to Commercial St., E. from Kearny on Commecrial.

86. "To take some worthy works that are in danger of extinction and perpetuate them in suitable form" is the aim of the GRABHORN PRESS, 642 Commercial St., as stated by Edwin Grabhorn. Since 1919 he and his brother Robert—whom the English book expert, George Jones, has declared the world's greatest printers—have been issuing their rare and valuable books in San Francisco. Of the books which first gave them renown, their edition of Walt Whitman's *Leaves of Grass*, illustrated with Valenti Angelo's woodcuts, is especially remembered. They have reproduced such items as *New Helvetia. Diary. A record of events kept by John A. Sutter & his clerks, at New Helvetia, California, from September 9, 1845 to May 25, 1848* (1939); and *Naval Sketches of the War in California*, reproducing 28 drawings made in 1846-47 by William H. Meyers, gunner on the U.S. Sloop-of-war *Dale* (1939). Each year since 1919, at least one of their books (in 1939, three) has been chosen by the American Institute of Graphic Arts as one of the 50 best books published in the United States. The ground-floor office of the old two-story brick building is a repository of Grabhorn publications and historic photographs, prints, and posters dating from Gold Rush days.

87. The massive first-story walls of the UNITED STATES SUB-TREASURY BUILDING, 608 Commercial St., erected in 1875-77 on the SITE OF THE FIRST UNITED STATES BRANCH MINT, have resisted earthquake, fire, and dynamite. Of the original structure's three stories of red brick, erected over the mint's steel-lined vaults, only the first remains, now roofed over, its square red-brick columns crowned by weathered gray curlicues. The basement houses still the old vaults with their steel-lined walls and intricate locks.

Here, in what was the young city's financial district, the United States Government in 1852 purchased the property of Curtiss, Ferry and Ward, Assayers, for $335,000, and reconstructed the building as a fireproof, three-story brick structure. On April 3, 1854 San Francisco's first mint was opened, equipped to issue $100,000 worth of currency daily. By 1887 San Francisco had coined $242,000,000—almost half as much money as the Philadelphia mint had issued since 1793. As early as 1859, the first mint proved to be far too small; and, finally, the old building was razed, following completion of a second mint, in 1874.

In 1877 the new United States Subtreasury was opened on the site of the first mint. In April, 1906, the structure was dynamited in an effort to halt the flames. Unshaken by the blast, the 30-inch-thick first-story walls also withstood the fire, as did the basement vaults, which were crammed with $13,000,000 in gold. When, in 1915, the subtreasury was moved to its new building on the site of the San Francisco Stock Exchange, the old building was taken over by private firms.

88. At the heart of the old financial center stands the B. DAVIDSON BUILDING, NW. corner Montgomery and Commercial Sts.,

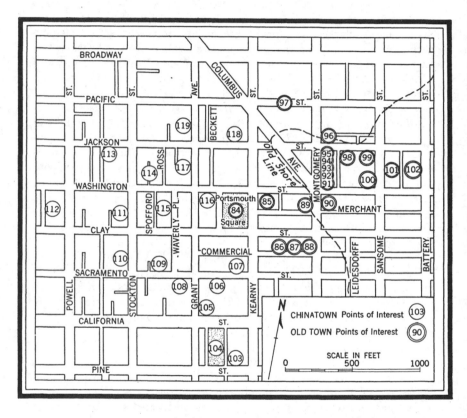

whose first story was built soon after the fire of May 4, 1851 for merchant William D. M. Howard. A few years later, two more stories were added. On the walls of the first-floor tobacco shop are pictures of the structure taken in Gold Rush days. The iron vaults, where pioneer bankers stored their treasure, remain in the basement—so stoutly constructed that they long defied attempts to open them for the present owner.

In excavating a sewer along the Commercial Street side, in 1854, workmen uncovered a coffin with a glass-covered aperture in its lid, through which could be discerned a man's features. A coroner's examination revealed that the man was Hudson's Bay Company's agent, William Glenn Rae, son-in-law of Chief Factor John McLoughlin. Arriving at Yerba Buena in August, 1841, Rae opened his post in the store room, with $10,000 worth of goods. To rebels against Governor Manuel Micheltorena in 1844, he furnished $15,000 worth of stores and munitions. Worried over collapse of the revolt and fearing punishment, Rae took to drinking heavily. On January 19, 1845 he shot himself. He was buried in the garden outside his house.

When the Americans took California in 1846, the Hudson's Bay Company sold its property to the merchants and realtors, Mellus, Howard and Company. Seeing a prosperous future for San Francisco, the Rothschilds of London authorized Benjamin Davidson to open an agency for their banking firm. Of the five banking firms which, according to the *Annals of San Francisco,* were operating in the city at the end of 1849, three were situated on Leese's old 100-vara frontage—Davidson; Thomas Wells and Company; and James King of William. Early in 1850, when Long Wharf opened into Montgomery Street, the Hudson's Bay Company's old post was the United States Hotel.

When all of the old building but Leese's original adobe kitchen was destroyed by fire in 1851, William Howard had the room roofed with Australian bricks by Chinese laborers. Soon Howard erected a new brick structure (now the first story of the present B. Davidson Building), into which moved the Rothschilds' agent.

N. from Commercial St. on Montgomery St.

89. Oldest business building in San Francisco is the BOLTON AND BARRON BUILDING, NW. corner Montgomery and Merchant Sts., a three-story fortress-like edifice, with rusty iron fire-escapes hanging wearily from its flat roof. Built in 1849, its brick and cast-iron walls withstood successive fires. Today, geraniums peep from boxes in the deep-set windows of upper-floor studio apartments, and a gaudy black-tile facade adorns the ground-floor tavern.

90. "Halleck's Folly" and "The Floating Fortress," people called the four-story MONTGOMERY BLOCK, Montgomery, Merchant, and Washington Sts., when Henry W. Halleck (later General-in-chief of the Union Army) began building it in 1853. Wiseacres predicted it either would sink into the ooze of the tidelands or float across the Bay on its foundation of redwood logs. But the structure is still in good repair, though shorn of its heavy iron shutters, the carved portrait heads which adorned its facade, and the wrought-iron balcony which ran along its second story.

Conceiving of a building constructed upon military lines, Halleck consulted architect G. P. Cummings; together they drew up a design combining the principles of the fortress with those of the Florentine court: four connecting buildings around a courtyard. The four buildings were then linked by wrought-iron bands and adjustable turnbuckles inserted between the floor levels. The building defied every accepted principle of construction.

Dedicated as the Washington Block on December 23, 1853, it was the largest building on the Pacific Coast. It was popularly called the Montgomery Block, and its builders officially changed the name the following year. Within the year it was San Francisco's legal center, housing the city's first law library. Most of the Adams Express Company's gold bullion was placed in the basement vaults. The second floor housed a huge billiard parlor. Here were the offices of the Pacific and Atlantic Railroad, of the United States Engineers Corps, of the *Alta California* and the *Daily Herald*. For 30 years, the block housed the portion of Adolph Sutro's library (now in the San Francisco Public Library) that escaped the 1906 fire.

As James King of William lay dying in one of the rooms in 1856, prominent citizens organized the Vigilance Committee that hanged his assassin, James P. Casey. King was shot in front of the Bank Exchange Saloon on the ground floor, where brokers did business until establishment of a stock exchange in 1862.

On that April morning in 1906, when flames were bearing down upon the block, soldiers stood powder kegs against the walls, ready to blast a fire-break. Oliver Perry Stidger, agent for the building, begged them to wait, appealing to their civic pride in an impassioned speech. Soon the danger had passed. Since this was the only downtown office building undamaged by the fire, it again became a center of business activity.

In the 1890's various artists of the West had begun setting up their studios in the Montgomery Block. With them came Frank Norris, Kathleen and Charles Norris, George Sterling, and Charles Caldwell Dobie. Known affectionately as the "Monkey Block" today, the old building consists largely of offices converted into studios.

91. The SHIP BUILDING, 716-18-20 Montgomery St., supposedly owes its origin to the gold-seeking master and crew of the *Georgean,* who deserted her in the spring of '49. The schooner lay abandoned in the mud near Sansome Street, her cargo of Kentucky "Twist" (chewing tobacco) and New Orleans cotton molding and unsold, until a speculator claimed salvage rights and beached her on the present site. Today the supposed "foc'sle head" of the old schooner houses a Chinese laundry and a plumbing shop; the second floor, artist's studios.

92. Gay blades haunted the MELODEON THEATER BUILDING, 722-24 Montgomery St., awaiting companions for a "bird-and-

bottle" supper. Opening December 15, 1857, the Melodeon drew sea-faring men and miners, who delighted in its musical and minstrel shows. After the Melodeon closed about 1858, the hall was rented infrequently to various groups. Here in 1883, according to *Disturnell's Strangers' Guide to San Francisco and Vicinity,* was the "extensive bathing establishment of Dr. Justin Gates. . . . Special apartments have been nicely fitted up for ladies and families."

93. San Francisco's oldest sign, hanging from the GENELLA BUILDING, 728 Montgomery St., states in faded black and gold letters that "H. and W. Pierce . . . Loans and Commissions" once did business here, exchanging paper and coins for gold bullion. The struc-ture was built about 1854 by Joseph Genella, who dealt in chinaware in an upstairs room. On the second floor the International Order of Odd Fellows had its first hall, where Yerba Buena Lodge No. 15 met every Thursday evening. Since the early 1920's, the second floor has housed PERRY DILLEY'S PUPPET THEATER, which presents an annual season of performances, beginning usually in April. Dilley creates all of his own figures, designs and paints his sets, writes the musical scores, and re-writes classical and modern plays to suit his medium.

94. Named for the first of San Francisco's literary periodicals, the GOLDEN ERA BUILDING, 732-34 Montgomery St., housed on its second floor for more than two years the weekly established in Decem-ber, 1852, by youthful J. Macdonough Foard and Rollin M. Daggett (*see Golden Era: Argonauts of Letters*). Its circulation among a Gold Rush populace, starved for reading matter, grew enormously. A "weekly family paper," it was devoted to "Literature, Agriculture, The Mining Interest, Local and Foreign News, Commerce, Education, Morals, and Amusements." On March 1, 1857, appeared a poem by an unknown author, "The Valentine"—first preserved published work of Bret Harte. Among other contributors were Ina Coolbrith, Thomas Starr King, Joaquin Miller, Mark Twain, and Charles Warren Stoddard. It sur-vived nearly four decades. Beneath the *Era's* original offices, on the ground floor, was Vernon's Hall, rented to fraternal societies and theatrical troupes; today it houses a Chinese broom factory. The *Era's* old rooms are now artists' studios.

95. Disguised beneath its cream stucco finish and its gay red and blue canopies, the PIOCHE AND BAYERQUE BUILDING, SE. corner Montgomery and Jackson Sts., now occupied by an Italian restaurant, is the same structure that was erected in 1853 by the pioneer merchants and bankers, F. L. A. Pioche and J. B. Bayerque. It stands on the SITE OF THE FIRST BRIDGE, a sturdy wooden structure—the town's first public improvement—which *alcalde* William Sturgis Hinckley constructed in 1844, over the long-vanished slough connecting the Laguna Salada (Sp., salty lagoon) with the Bay, thus enabling

people to cross to Clarke's Point. In the Pioche and Bayerque Building were housed the offices of the city's first street railroad, of which both Pioche and Bayerque were directors. Horses drew the first car up Market Street on July 4, 1860 (soon replaced by steam).

96. Not since 1857 has the LUCAS, TURNER AND COMPANY BANK BUILDING, NE. corner Montgomery and Jackson Sts., housed banking offices. When the firm of Lucas, Turner and Company, a branch of a St. Louis bank, desired property on which to erect its own building in 1853, William Tecumseh Sherman, then the resident manager and a partner in the firm, found (he later wrote) that "the only place then available on Montgomery Street, the Wall Street of San Francisco, was a lot . . . 60 x 62 feet . . ." For this he paid $32,000, then contracted for "a three-story brick building, with finished basement, for about $50,000." As manager of the new institution, Sherman was overprudent. He refused to allow the occasional overdrafts his depositors demanded and declined to grant credit except on the soundest securities. Finally in 1857 the bank closed.

W. from Montgomery St. on Jackson St. to Columbus Ave.; NW. from Jackson on Columbus to Pacific St.; E. from Columbus on Pacific.

97. The "Terrific Street" of the 1890's—that block of Pacific Street, SITE OF THE BARBARY COAST, running east from the once-famous "Seven Points" where Pacific, Columbus Avenue, and Kearny Street intersect—is set off now at each end by concrete arches labelled "INTERNATIONAL SETTLEMENT." As Barbary Coast it was known round the world for half a century, more notorious than London's Limehouse, Marseilles' water front, or Port Said's Arab Town. The enterprise of Pierino Gavello, restaurateur and capitalist, is today's "International Settlement," developed in 1939, streamlined with the stucco facades and gleaming windows. Where gambling halls, saloons, beer dens, dance halls, and brothels once crowded side by side, a Chinese restaurant, a night club and cocktail bar, a Latin American cafe, and an antique shop now appear.

One resort of the old "Coast" remains in business—TAR'S, 592 Pacific St., the former Parente's saloon (newly painted and decorated), whose walls are still plastered from floor to ceiling with Parente's famous collection of prize-fight pictures—including champions from James Figg, bare-knuckle artist of 1719, to Joe Louis, 1940 title holder.

"Give it a *wide berth,* as you value your life," warned the *New Overland Tourist* of Barbary Coast in 1878, describing "the precise locality, so that our readers may *keep away."* Since the 1860's it had worn the name Barbary Coast, derived probably from sailors' memories of the dives of North Africa. But even in the early 1850's, when the neighborhood was Sydney Town, inhabited by Australian outlaws known as "Sydney Ducks," the "upper part of Pacific Street, after dark"—reported the San Francisco *Herald*—"was crowded by thieves, gamblers, low women, drunken sailors and similar characters . . ." The block bounded by Kearny, Montgomery, and Broadway was known as Devil's Acre, and its Kearny Street side as Battle Row (here stood the Slaughterhouse, later renamed the Morgue).   The district contributed a new word, "hoodlum," applying it to the young ruffians who roamed the "Coast" armed with bludgeons, knives, or iron knuckles (it is thought that the word comes from "huddle 'em!" the cry of the boys as they advanced on a victim).   So too the expression "to shanghai" originated here.

The employment of women in the "Coast's" resorts was strictly forbidden by law as early as 1869, but the "Coast" paid no heed. Besides the brothels of three types—cribs, cow-yards, and parlor houses, all advertised by red lights and some even by signboards—the district contained call houses, cheap lodgings patronized by street-walkers, bagnios over saloons and dance-halls, where variety show performers entertained between acts.   Among the most renowned of the "Coast's" attractions in the 1870's were the "Little Lost Chicken," a diminutive girl who concluded her songs by bursting into tears (and picked the pockets of her admirers); the "Waddling Duck," an immensely fat woman; "Lady Jane Grey," who decked herself in a cardboard coronet, convinced she was of noble birth; the "Dancing Heifer" and the "Galloping Cow," whose sister act made the boards of the stage creak. "Cowboy Maggie" Kelly, a large blond known as "The Queen of the Barbary Coast," was proprietress, and bouncer, of the Cowboy's Rest.

Wiped out in 1906, the Barbary Coast was revived for another decade of gaudy life.   "The quarter did what every courtesan does who finds her charms and her following on the wane," wrote Charles Caldwell Dobie.   "It decided to capitalize its previous reputation, buy a new false front and an extra pot of rouge.   The result was a tough quarter maintained largely for the purpose of shocking tourists from the Chatauqua circuit."   Almost every dance hall put on a good show for the benefit of gaping visitors in "slummers' galleries."   "Take me to see the Barbary Coast," said John Masefield—and he was taken, as was nearly every other visiting celebrity, including Sarah Bernhardt and Anna Pavlowa.

"The most famous, as well as the most infamous" of the resorts, reminisced photographer Arnold Genthe, "was the Olympia, a vast 'palace' of gilt and tinsel with a great circular space in the center and around it a raised platform with booths for spectators . . . Below us on the floor . . . a medley of degenerate humanity whirled around us in weird dance steps."   Of the same description was the Midway (downstairs at 587 Pacific Street)—a training ground for vaudeville acts—its walls decorated with large murals by an unknown Italian artist.

The Seattle Concert Hall (574 Pacific Street), later known as Spider Kelly's, first important resort to reopen after the fire, won local fame for its "key racket." On the promise of keeping a rendezvous after work, the dance-hall girls sold, for five dollars, the keys to their rooms; the dupes wandered about until morning, vainly seeking doors their keys would fit. The "slummers' gallery" of the Hippodrome (570 Pacific Street) was crowded nightly by visitors. Chief claim to fame of the Moulin Rouge (540 Pacific Street) were Arthur Putnam's sculptured panels on its facade, depicting figures of complete nudity until churchwomen forced the sculptor to drape the ladies.

No resort was better-known than Lew Purcell's So Different Saloon (520 Pacific Street), a Negro dance hall, where the "Turkey Trot" is said to have originated. The Thalia (514½ Pacific Street), on whose immense rectangular floor the "Texas Tommy" was first danced, lured patrons with a sidewalk band concert every evening. The Thalia's *pièce de resistance* was hootchy-kootchy dancer Eva Rowland.

But the Barbary Coast's assets as a tourist attraction did not outweigh its liabilities as a crime center. The Police Commission's revocation of dance-hall licenses in 1913 was a hard blow, but the "Coast" recovered, and two years later licenses had to be revoked again. The Thalia went on operating as a dancing academy. Once more liquor permits were cancelled. As late as 1921, Police Chief Daniel J. O'Brien thought it necessary to forbid slumming parties in the area—but the Barbary Coast was dead.

S. from Pacific St. on Montgomery St. to Jackson St.; E. from Montgomery on Jackson.

98. Once noted for its paintings and well-stocked library, the iron-shuttered HOTALING BUILDING, SE. corner Jackson St. and Hotaling Pl., housed the warehouses and stables of the Hotaling distillery. Narrow Hotaling Place, running south to Washington Street, was known as Jones' Alley between 1847 and 1910. Loaded drays rumbled over the planked street to the Broadway wharf; heavily guarded express coaches of the Wells Fargo and Company bore their cargoes to sailing ships; and under the dim gaslights silk-hatted dandies waited in hansom cabs for the beauties from the Melodeon. The Hotaling Building survived the fire of 1906 almost unscathed.

99. The hulls of abandoned ships were piled into the mud flats of Jackson Slough to make solid footing for the three-story brick PHOENIX BUILDING, SW. corner Jackson and Sansome Sts., which from 1858 to 1895 housed the factory of Domingo Ghirardelli, pioneer choco-

late manufacturer (*see Rim of the Golden Gate*). Survivor of the 1906 fire, it hides its smoked and weathered facade under a thick coat of buff paint.

S. from Jackson St. on Sansome St.

100. Reared from the mud on a brick and pile foundation, GOVERNMENT HOUSE, NW. corner Sansome and Washington Sts., was constructed some time before 1853, when it was known as Armory Hall. The *Golden Era* in February of that year carried an advertisement of "Buckley's Original New Orleans Serenaders." Known thereafter as the Olympic Theater, the hall led, according to the *Annals of San Francisco,* "a brief and sickly existence." After 1860, the building appeared in city directories as the "Government House Lodgings." For a time Adolph Sutro lived in one of its furnished rooms.

Still illuminated by gas, Government House shows its age. The first floor was forced underground when Sansome Street was regraded early in the present century; its basement rooms are now entered through narrow stairways leading from iron trap doors in the sidewalk. Shorn of its once ornate cornices, which began to crumble, the facade is shabby, its faded green paint and grey plaster cracked and peeling.

The oldest drugstore in the city, ALEXANDER MCBOYLE AND COMPANY, still housed on the ground floor of Government House, was opened in 1866. McBoyle, although not a dentist, managed to fill a window of his curious shop waist-deep with the extracted teeth of seafarers. Grateful seamen repaid with curios and treasures from other lands and with ship models, painstakingly carved and fitted. While other druggists beckoned to the public with green and red globes, McBoyle drew three times the trade with a display of model ships sailing in the sea of teeth. He compounded for years the bulk of medicines shipped to the Orient. The present owners have retained a few faded pictures of sailing ships, and they sell Alexander McBoyle's "Abolition Oil," to alleviate sprains and bruises, mixed according to the original formula.

101. Oldest structure still used by the Federal Government in San Francisco is the five-story brick and wrought-iron UNITED STATES APPRAISERS BUILDING, Sansome, Jackson, and Washington Sts., erected (1874-81) as one of the Army Engineer Corps' most boasted construction achievements. Here, until after 1850, the tides lapped at the narrow row of piles marking the line of present Sansome Street. "Upon the head of these piles," recalled Barry and Patten, "was nailed a narrow plank walk . . . without rail or protection of any kind . . . pedestrians passed and repassed in the dark, foggy nights, singing and

rollicking, as unconcernedly as if their path was broad Market Street . . ."

On piles projecting eastward from what is now the corner of Sansome and Washington streets stood the wooden shanty where in August, 1850, Pedar Sather and Edward W. Church—joined nine months later by Francis M. Drexel of Philadelphia—opened a bank. When fire destroyed the structure, their safe fell into the water; it was fished up, however, and installed in a new building at the end of Long Wharf. (The only bank in the city founded as early as 1850 to see the twentieth century, it was reorganized in 1897 as the San Francisco National Bank and finally absorbed by the Bank of California in 1920.)

Into the blue mud of the old cove bottom, Army engineers in 1874 began driving 80-foot piles, over which they laid a seven-foot thickness of "rip-rapped" concrete. On this foundation they erected the three-foot-thick walls of the Appraisers Building. The roof, fabricated of wrought iron in the manner of a truss bridge, rested on the outside walls, supporting a heavy slate covering. The 90 offices had hardwood doors and bronze hardware. The hydraulic elevator with ornately carved cage, installed in 1878, the first passenger elevator on the Pacific Coast, is still in use.

Having survived the 1906 earthquake, the building was threatened by the fire but saved by the Navy. From two tugs anchored below Washington Street, sea water was pumped through fire lines to save the old structure. In 1909, mud began to ooze from beneath its foundations into a sewer excavation along Sansome Street; the southwest corner sank 11 inches, but the structure remained intact.

In the Appraisers Building, dutiable imports were appraised and stored for payment of duty until 1940, when the structure was ordered razed to make way for a new 15-story building.

E. from Sansome St. on Washington St. to Battery St.; N. from Washington on Battery.

102. The UNITED STATES CUSTOMHOUSE (*open 9-4:30*), Battery, Washington, and Jackson Sts., has occupied this site for more than 75 years; but the block-long, five-story edifice of Raymond granite, its interior resplendent with marble and oak, erected (1906-11) at a cost of $1,600,000, is a far cry from the three-story customhouse and post office, built of cement-plastered brick in 1854, which stood here until 1903. The town's first customhouse on the Plaza was abandoned in 1849; it survived—its porch railings carved by the jacknives of Yankee newcomers—until 1851, outlasting the second, William Heath Davis' four-story structure with its white-painted balconies, to which the collector of the port had removed his offices.

From the ruins of this second customhouse, nearly $1,000,000 in specie was rescued from a large safe, which had preserved it from the flames. The removal of the treasure by the collector of the customs, T. Butler King, "created some little excitement and much laughter," as the *Annals of San Francisco* reported. "Some thirty gigantic, thick-bearded fellows, who were armed with carbines, revolvers and sabres, surrounded the cars containing the specie, while the Honorable T. Butler King stood aloft on a pile of ruins with a huge 'Colt' in one hand and a bludgeon in the other . . . The extraordinary procession proceeded slowly . . . Mr. King marching, like a proud drum-major, at the head . . . peals of laughter and cries of ironical applause accompanied the brave defenders of 'Uncle Sam's' interests to the end of their perilous march. . . ."

Chinatown

"Wherever, in any channel of the Seven Seas, two world-wanderers met and talked about the City of Many Adventures, Chinatown ran like a thread through their reminiscences."
—WILL IRWIN

A QUARTER of old Canton, transplanted and transformed, neither quite oriental nor wholly occidental, San Francisco's Chinatown yields to the ways of the West while continuing to venerate a native civilization as ancient as the Pyramids. Grant Avenue, its main thoroughfare, leads northward from Bush Street through a veritable city-within-a-city—alien in appearance to all the rest of San Francisco—hemmed within boundaries kept by tacit agreement with municipal authorities for almost a century.

Chinatown enjoys a measure of civil autonomy unique among San Francisco's foreign sections. Though police protection, public education, and public health are directed by municipal authorities, local affairs are controlled largely by the powerful Chinese Six Companies. Labor relations, family regulation, traditional customs, and commercial activities are the province of this unusual body.

Along Grant Avenue bright display windows, neon signs, and glazed tile form a foreground wholly modern for merchandise which conforms to the age-old pattern of China's craftsmen. The street's smart cocktail lounges defy ancestral gods by adding American swing to the inducements of oriental atmosphere and native waitresses in brocaded gowns; its fashionable cafes, while they serve genuine native foods, advertise more familiar dishes. Beneath the pagoda-like cornices, electric chop suey signs perpetuate the popular notion that this dish, imported from the Atlantic seaboard, is something more exotic than its name—the Chinese word for hash—indicates. Side by side with curio shops offering inexpensive articles of oriental design are bazaars, wherein the discerning may buy objects genuine and costly. Within recent years, however, many sources of supply have been cut off by the Japanese occupation of China. Scattered along Grant Avenue also are Japanese-owned shops that sell goods manufactured in Japan.

Grant Avenue's commercial area is only the bland and somewhat cynical face the settlement turns to the world. More oriental are the avenue's northern reaches and the streets that run crosswise from Nob Hill to Chinatown's eastern boundary, Kearny Street. Along these congested sidewalks, among cheap shops and restaurants, are the market places whose distinctive sounds and odors give Chinatown its atmosphere of the unchanging East. A curious bazaar of foodstuffs are the poultry markets, the displays of dried and pickled fish, and the odoriferous tubs of snails along the curbstones. Roast ducks packed in rice; roast ducks from Canton, glazed with a salty wax—many of them flattened as if starched and ironed—hang in golden rows in grocery stores; and beside them are whole hogs—steaming hot from the barbecue pits—from which portions are cut and sent to Chinatown's dinner tables. Eels and octopi, shark, and other unusual sea foods are displayed in the many fish markets. Bakery windows are crowded with cakes of almost limitless variety, of which even the most common are decorative and of evasive flavor. The vegetables of Chinatown are a marvel to the stranger: string beans slender as blades of grass and 12 to 14 inches long; peas with sweet, tender edible pods; and many Chinese greens. Bitter melons to be added to soups, fuzzy melons resembling cactus fruit, bamboo shoots, bean sprouts, and lotus roots hang festooned in market windows. The artistry of the oriental cook is nowhere in the Western world better demonstrated than in San Francisco's Chinatown. In the numerous and inexpensive little Chinese restaurants that crowd the slopes of Jackson, Clay, and Washington streets above and below Grant Avenue, the occidental dines with relish on the meats and vegetables he has looked upon with disfavor in the markets around the corner.

About half Chinatown's population of 16,000 are immigrants from the mother country, many of whom still cling to the ancient customs and ancestral religion. Amid the modern throng appear in diminishing number those who still conform to the age-old styles of dress. Little old women pass by, their shiny black hair brushed tightly back and knotted, their black pantaloons showing beneath black gowns; and benign old men in loose jackets and black skullcaps. The upper-class women of the old generation reveal their bound feet—the "golden lilies" of Chinese literature—beneath the long narrow native costume covered by a coat of American make. Upon rare occasions, dignified Chinese gentlemen gracefully thread their way through the crowded streets in elegant custom-tailored attire, leisurely wielding fans.

Young Chinatown preserves its language and the more democratic of its national customs, while adopting the dress, the slang, and the commercial methods of its American compatriots. Grant Avenue is its creation. The shops of its elders, where the abacus is still used for calculation, are being forced to the side-streets. Even the little wall-shops, where for generations dreamy-eyed old men sitting in the sun have reluctantly bestirred themselves to sell occasional bags of candied melon, ginger, or lichee nuts, are being taken over by alert youngsters, who have stocked these narrow tables and outdoor shelves with souvenirs for the tourist.

The children of Chinatown, most modern element of all, are benefiting most by the inroads of the West. Education is one of the colony's primary interests. Besides its regular public grade school, Chinatown has a dozen or more public and private schools. The children, expert negotiators of traffic, scamper in small bands from sidewalk to sidewalk on shopping tours for their parents. Children of the poorer families swarm the sidewalks nightly, armed with shoe-shine kits. Many of the older boys spend their evenings at the Chinese Y.M.C.A.; and many of the girls (whose families allow them to accept modern ways), at the Y.W.C.A. Chinese youth of both sexes frequent the various family clubs. Fong-Fong's on Grant Avenue (a soda fountain, lunchroom, and bakery) is a widely patronized "Joe-College" hangout.

Old Chinatown watches with silent disapproval the departure of its youth and its children from the ancient customs, brought here from Canton and preserved inviolate for three-quarters of a century. And Chinatown's elders still maintain customs of oriental feudalism, long since abandoned throughout China.

Though practically every religion has built churches and gained adherents here, the native Chinese temples, or joss houses, are still centers of Chinatown's spiritual life. (The word "joss" is a corruption of *Dios,* Portuguese word for God, which the Cantonese learned from early Portuguese traders at Macao.) Many of the furnishings have a history intimately associated with the Chinese immigration, during the Gold Rush, to this land they called *Gum Sahn* (Golden Hills).

Barometers of public sentiment in Chinatown are the sidewalk bulletins before the shops of its five newspapers. If the oblong strips of Chinese characters denote light news of local interest, a lively chattering ensues; but let the bulletins be of more serious import, concerned perhaps with events in their embattled homeland, and silence settles over the groups of 50 or more, as each man reads and goes his way without a word of comment.

The one ancient festival in which all Chinatown is united annually is the Chinese New Year, celebrated—according to the lunar calendar and the ancient philosophy of Tung-Fang-So—on the first day of the new moon after the sun enters the sign of Aquarius (between January 20 and February 20). This is the occasion to propitiate the gods and banish the evil spirits abroad each Yuen Tan (New Year's Day). It is also the season for the cancellation of debts, during which failure to meet obligations is considered a confession of inability to do so.

The first day of the new year, Yuen Jih (Day of Beginnings), often is called the "Three Beginnings"—the start of the year, of the month, and of the season. On the eve of Yuen Jih, joyous throngs crowd the streets of Chinatown. Gay lanterns sway in a blue haze of gunpowder smoke; a barrage of firecrackers continues far into the night. Houses must be cleaned thoroughly before midnight; then brooms are hidden until dark of the following day—for sweeping during the ensuing daylight hours brushes all luck out of the house for the entire year. No one sleeps on New Year's Eve; even the youngest children are awake until two or three o'clock in the morning. Incense burns throughout the colony to invite the good spirits.

The only food served on this birthday of Confucius is *gai gum choy,* a meatless stew eaten after one o'clock in the morning of the Day of Beginnings, and oranges, which have been arranged in perfect pyramids for days in anticipation. Throughout New Year week the children of the household will be unusually dutiful, for this is the season of the "red package." These packages, wrapped in red paper and containing silver coins, all unmarried children—regardless of age—are entitled to receive from each visitor to the home.

On the second day of the new year, as on the first, no meat is served, for this day is dedicated to worship of Ta'ai Shen (God of Wealth). But from the third day onward, feasting and merrymaking are unrestrained, as pastries, sweet cakes, and candies are set out to satisfy the proverbial Kitchen God when he makes his annual report on family behavior.

The festivities end usually on the seventh day (Day of Human Beginnings) with the Dance of the Dragon. Unless events worthy of a highly spectacular celebration have occurred during the year, the Lion of Buddha substitutes for the traditional dragon. The lion requires but two men to operate; the dragon, trailing innumerable yards of tinsel and colored silk, must be borne along Grant Avenue on the stooping shoulders of from 10 to 50 persons. Since its first appearance here in 1850, the dragon has been Chinatown's official protector. Homes and stores are decorated with green vegetables and red packages to attract his attention, for where he dances prosperity remains throughout the year. As the glittering monster weaves his way from sidewalk to sidewalk, coins, wrapped in lettuce leaves or red papers and suspended from doors and windows by strings, are snatched by an alert hand that darts from beneath the dragon's gaping jaws.

Chinatown today is the Chinatown that was rebuilt after 1906; the dim, narrow alleys so famed in melodrama are as safe now as brightly lighted Grant Avenue. But it occupies still little more than the cramped space in which the Chinese of Gold Rush days settled. The American brig *Eagle,* in the spring of 1848, brought San Francisco's first three Chinese immigrants, two men and a woman. Clipper ships in the China trade during the following decade brought 25,000 coolies and peasants from Kwangtung Province. Eager to escape the famine succeeding the disastrous Tai Ping rebellion, and lured by prospects of sudden wealth, they arrived to do the menial work of the Gold Rush. Though many went to the mines, the majority settled in San Francisco. Despite the racial hostility they faced, they early became sellers of wares imported from China, peddlers of fresh vegetables, fishermen, servants, gamblers, and real estate owners.

As the Yankee first settlers, following the expanding water front in the 1850's, moved down the slope toward Montgomery Street, the Chinese inherited their abandoned locations adjoining Portsmouth Square. Because of their value as laborers in the boom years when white labor was at a premium, they were allowed to entrench themselves in what was known to be an ideal residential district sheltered from wind and fog. The growing commercial district below Kearny Street formed the colony's eastern barrier; to the north Pacific Street's course between the Presidio and the water front was a natural boundary; south of California Street, almost in the shadow of Old St. Mary's Church, was a white *demi-monde* dominated by French prostitutes; along the higher slope of what is now Nob Hill, Stockton Street's respectable residential quarter forbade encroachment farther west. Destroyed by the successive conflagrations of the 1850's and 1860's, Chinatown rose repeatedly on old foundations that no sufficient majority of San Franciscans cared to reclaim.

Old Chinatown had neither the native architecture nor the glitter of lights characteristic of its streets today. Dim lanterns, hung on the iron balconies of tenements, furnished by night the only illumination, until gaslights brought their flickering radiance. Overcrowding compelled the Chinese to enlarge their quarters with cellars which were to add many a legend to the colony's ill repute. Even before its traffic in vice and its tong wars reached the alarming proportions of the 1870's, 1880's, and 1890's, Chinatown was a stage set for criminal drama—a place of eerie shadows and flitting figures, of blind alleys and obscure passageways, of quiet stabbings and casual gunfire.

Subjected to increasing racial discrimination, the Chinese inherited the full measure of stigma that had been visited only incidentally upon the Hounds and Sydney Coves. When, during the building of the Central Pacific Railroad, additional thousands were imported by the Big Four to swell the already unwelcome horde of competitors with white labor, "Crocker's pets" became the objects of abuse throughout California. Dennis Kearney's sand-lot Workingmen's Party drove the hapless orientals from factories, burned their laundries, and threatened their white employers with violence.

The resulting Chinese Exclusion Act of 1882 made no provision, however, for deportation of Chinese lawfully within the country; and San Francisco's "Little China" remained to outlive half a century of agitation against it. But the exclusion of orientals from their former respectable pursuits made them more than ever the prey of criminal

elements. From the bonanza days until 1906, the district was synonymous with the Barbary Coast. The two decades between 1906 and
1927 (when the last tong war occurred) were required to eliminate its
opium dens, its vice and gambling rackets, and its menace to public
health.

The municipal czardoms of "Blind Chris" Buckley and Abe Ruef
subjected Chinatown to domination by their oriental henchman, Fong
Chong—better known as "Little Pete"—and his blackmailing society,
Gi Sin Seer. Little Pete operated in a Chinatown where rival tongs
fought over the profits of a vice traffic as old as the colony itself. In its
most flourishing days, thousands of slave girls with bound feet were
crowded into brothels along Grant Avenue—then the notorious Dupont
Street—and adjacent alleys. The bloodiest of the tong feuds, lasting 7
years and costing 60 lives, was fought over "Lily-Foot" Wan Len,
queen of the slave girls. It was Little Pete's Gi Sin Seer and a rival
outfit of similar hired assassins, Bo Sin Seer, which finally settled the
enmities of this oriental underworld and opened the way for Chinatown's modern phase.

For his bribing activities in the case of Lee Chuck, one of his
hatchetmen whose ready six-shooter sent a rival sprawling in Spofford
Alley, Little Pete served five years in San Quentin Penitentiary. Once
back in his old haunts, he began extending his activities beyond the
confines of Chinatown. His gang cleaned up $100,000 in a racetrack
swindle, which made enemies who swore to get him the instant he
should appear without his usual bodyguard of white men. Their chance
came in January, 1897. Impatient to learn the latest racetrack results,
Little Pete entered a Waverley Place barber shop without his bodyguard and paused to have his forehead shaved, his queue plaited, and
his ears cleaned of wax. Then, "Two figures as swift and black as
crows dart from nowhere into the doorway. There is a crackle of
sound like the sputtering of a string of firecrackers ushering in the New
Year: Little Pete falls forward in a crimson pool . . ."

In true gangster tradition, Little Pete's cohorts attempted to give
him a magnificent funeral. After two hours of intricate last rites,
performed by four priests from his favorite joss house, his casket was
placed in a resplendent hearse drawn by six black-draped white horses.
Hired mourners preceded the hearse, burning joss sticks and wildly
beating the air with uplifted arms. From a carriage, four Chinese
busily tossed out bits of paper punched with square holes—to confuse
the devils seeking to make off with the spirit of the departed. The
fantastic cortege, led by a popular orchestra playing the funeral march
from *Saul,* proceeded through streets lined with spectators to the Chinese
Cemetery down the Peninsula. Here a mob of onlookers—not hoodlums, but respectable San Franciscans indignant over losing bets on race

horses doped by Pete's henchmen—greeted priests and mourners with hoots and clods of earth. The Chinese were compelled to haul the coffin back to the city where, at the old Chinese cemetery Little Pete's remains were interred pending arrangements for shipment to China. The wagonloads of roast pig, duck, cakes, tea, and gin left beside the grave were guzzled by the crowd of white onlookers.

The Chinatown of Little Pete and his rival tongs was the Chinatown that shared with the Barbary Coast a worldwide notoriety. But always there was the sober, industrious Chinatown of respectable merchants and hard-working coolies; of ancient native customs and religion; and of traditional family life. Quietly this larger element was accumulating wealth, gradually co-operating with the Protestant and Catholic missions, and—after 1906—with the city's police. When it became necessary to erect the new Chinatown upon the charred foundations of the old, Chinese capital and enterprise accomplished the task promptly and with good taste. The colony's southern boundary was extended to Bush Street, claiming the block now occupied by St. Mary's Square.

The last three decades have seen various improvements on the district's sudden reconstruction after 1906. But not until recent years has its past—assiduously kept alive by pulp magazines and newspaper supplements—been lived down. Naive visitors still expect to be shown opium dens and underground passages. The new Chinatown, alert and progressive, is without nostalgia for its long era of dirt and crime. The second largest Chinese settlement outside the mother country (Singapore has the largest), it prefers its modern role as meeting place of East and West.

POINTS OF INTEREST

103. The red-brick KONG CHOW TEMPLE (*suggested visiting hours 6-10 p.m.*), 520 Pine St., is entered through bright red doors opening onto the Passageway of Peace, a bare corridor ending in a blank wall—protection against evil spirits, who travel only in straight lines. From an inner courtyard, stairs lead to the third-floor sanctuary, just beneath the green double-tiered oriental roof—for worship of the ancestral gods permits nothing more created by human hands to be above the deities. Decorating the room are richly brocaded silken hangings and, extending its full breadth, hand-made wood carvings bearing stories of the Six Dynasties (589-317 B.C.); the upper part of one, a priceless, glass-enclosed work, depicts scenes from the Court of the Dragon King. From the articles of divination in the temple, religious Chinese determine those days auspicious for instituting business ventures and trips. Strips of red paper in the temple anteroom record the amounts of recent contributions—heavily swelled on such special occa-

sions as the Day for Sweeping the Graves and the Feast Day to Quan Ti.

Pioneer Chinese from the district of Kong Chow first established their temple locally in 1857; after the buildings of the Kong Chow Association (one of the Chinese Six Companies) were dynamited to check the fire of 1906, they rebuilt their joss house here. Rescued from the doomed temple was the figure of Kuan Ti, patron deity and head of the 17 gods and goddesses of the temple, now enthroned in the reconstructed shrine.

104. Where the soft crunch of gravel underfoot or the snores of a drowsing panhandler disturbs the quiet of green-terraced ST. MARY'S SQUARE, Pine, Anne, and California Sts., the raucous solicitations of the inmates of brothels once mingled with the bark of rifles in shooting galleries below, and American and British sailors met periodically for bouts and brawls. But the little park was not always so bawdy. In the 1890's, the women of San Francisco petitioned the city, and the prostitutes were removed from Dupont Street (Grant Avenue) to the comparative isolation of the square (hidden from Dupont by a row of business establishments, as it is today). Here they remained for several years to distress the Paulist Fathers of Old St. Mary's, who faced them across California Street. In 1898, the Fathers organized the St. Mary's Association, whose purpose was to remove the bagnios and have the area set aside as a park. Between 1898 and 1904, money was appropriated on more than one occasion to buy the property for the city, but each time County Treasurer Sam Brooke used it for other purposes. A series of lawsuits resulted in the decision in 1904 that taxes should be levied to make the necessary purchases; but, before this was done, the fire of 1906 wiped out the offending red light area. A step in replanning the city was the creation of the present park.

From the high western slope of the square a STATUE OF SUN YAT-SEN faces the East toward China. The 12-foot figure, with head and hands of rose-red granite, wearing a long robe of bright stainless steel, was created by sculptor Beniamino Bufano under the sponsorship of the WPA's Northern California Art Project (formerly the Federal Art Project). Dr. Sun Yat-sen (1866-1925), organizer of the Kuomintang—whose local branch supplied materials for the memorial— visited San Francisco on several occasions. China's present (1940) president, Lin Sen, in 1937 wrote the words that appear on the steel disc in the granite base of the monument: "Father of the Chinese Republic and First President . . . Champion of Democracy . . . Proponent of Peace and Friendship Among Nations . . ."

N. from Pine St. on Anne St. to California St.; W. on California.

105. The construction of OLD ST. MARY'S CHURCH, NE. corner Grant Ave. and California St., was inaugurated in 1853 by Archbishop Joseph Sadoc Alemany, and at midnight Mass on Christmas Day, 1854, the edifice was dedicated as the cathedral seat for the Roman Catholic diocese of the Pacific Coast. Until completion of St. Mary's Cathedral in 1894, Old St. Mary's remained the most powerful stronghold of Catholicism in California and Nevada. Respected for its rich tradition and the simple dignity of its services, this stately old structure for the last 45 years has been the parish church of the Paulist Fathers.

Old St. Mary's stands on land donated by pioneer banker John Sullivan, whose wife (Catherine Farrell Sullivan) lies buried in the crypt of the church. Architects Crane and England are thought to have modeled the purely Gothic structure after a church in the Spanish birthplace of Archbishop Alemany. Its red brick and ironwork was shipped around the Horn; granite brought from China was hoisted into place with improvised wooden derricks by Chinese workmen. The two large clocks in the 90-foot-high square Gothic tower were long the community timepieces of early San Franciscans. Beneath the frontal dial still appear the gold letters on black bronze, whose warning was intended to put the fear of God into the roisterers of Dupont Street: "Son Observe the Time and Fly from Evil." As early as 1855, an angry correspondent to the *Alta California* made irreverent protest against the booming bell of Old St. Mary's: "Those who want their sins washed off by those daily ablutions may as well be aroused by their own consciences, without annoying the whole neighborhood."

Completely gutted by the fire of 1906, the interior of the church was rebuilt on its original plan. In January, 1929, the basement was remodeled to form a modern auditorium, Paulist Hall; two months later a five-story structure adjoining St. Mary's on the north was razed and the church building extended to its present length of 153 feet. This latter wing, which maintains the architectural features of the original (Edward A. Eames, architect), houses the PAULIST CIRCULATING LIBRARY (*open weekdays 11-6, Sun. 10:30-1:30*).

Each night for more than a decade, a long line of needy migrants has waited patiently at the side entrance to Old St. Mary's for the food and lodging tickets supplied them by the Paulist Fathers.

N. from California St. on Grant Ave. to Sacramento St.; E. on Sacramento.

106. The NOM KU SCHOOL (*open 5-8 p.m.*), 765 Sacramento St., for children between the ages of 6 and 15, supplements the public

school curriculum, offering a purely cultural program designed to foster Chinese traditions and customs in American-born Chinese. No commercial subject is taught; emphasis is placed on Chinese language, calligraphy, literature, history, and philosophy (particularly that of Confucius).

Built in 1912 by a group of wealthy Chinese, the school building follows the official courthouse design of China. A pair of sacred lions guard the set-back upper story. High, narrow windows in many small panels give myriad light reflections to the interior, whose simple teakwood furnishings are relieved by the lavish use of decorative colors: vivid green, yellow, red, and turquoise.

107. More than its name implies is the CHINESE CHAMBER OF COMMERCE (*open Mon.-Fri. 10-5, Sat. 10-12*), 730 Sacramento St., the only organization of its kind when established in the 1880's. In addition to fostering Chinese business and commerce, the organization aids in solving the housing problem of Chinese in San Francisco; enlightens its countrymen on legal matters; and aids in the liquidation of bankruptcies of Chinese merchants by negotiation rather than by court procedure.

The Chamber of Commerce has assumed commercial arbitration over matters once handled by the Chinese Six Companies, settling disputes among merchants and members of their families, and—rarely— among trade organizations (such as the Jewelry Guild or Laundry Workers Association). Since establishment of a similar chamber in New York in 1910, this bureau no longer serves Chinese throughout the United States. Executive Secretary Chee Lowe, educated at San Francisco public schools and the University of California, worked for 20 years as a mining engineer in China, and returned to San Francisco in 1938.

Retrace on Sacramento St.

108. Outwardly occidental are the businesslike offices of the KUOMINTANG HEADQUARTERS IN AMERICA (*open 10-12, 2-4*), 827 Sacramento St., from which are supervised the activities of the 3 regional and 50 branch offices of the Chinese Nationalist Party in the United States. The San Francisco headquarters was the second established outside China (the first was in Honolulu). Party activities in this country (according to National Chairman Dr. K. D. Lum) consist of establishing good will between the people of the United States and the people of China and sponsoring the spread of the democratic idea by following the principles laid down by Sun Yat-sen. The Western Regional Office of the Kuomintang, with jurisdiction over branches in

California, Nevada, and Utah, also is located in San Francisco (846 Stockton St.).

The party publishes two Chinese-language newspapers in the city: The *Chinese Nationalist Daily* (809 Sacramento St.) and the *Young China* (881 Clay St.), founded by Dr. Sun Yat-sen.

109. The irregular series of rectangular terraces forming the CHINESE CHILDREN'S PLAYGROUND (*open weekdays 10-10; play apparatus*), Sacramento St. between Waverly Pl. and Stockton St., are walled by the dark brick of surrounding buildings. Brightly lighted at night, the playground is the occasional scene of evening entertainment and concerts (on gala occasions the children wear their native dress). The upturned cornices of the small pagoda-like stucco clubhouse are brightly painted.

N. from Sacramento St. on Stockton St.

110. The CHINESE CONSOLIDATED BENEVOLENT ASSOCIATION (*open to visitors 1-5*), 843 Stockton St., also called the Chung Wan Wui Goon and the China Association, is best known as the Chinese Six Companies—despite the fact that it long has represented seven companies. These seven associations, each representing a province or district of old China, are the Kong Chow, Ning Yung, Sam Yup, Sue Hing, Yan Wo, Yeung Wo, and the Hop Wo—formed when so many persons had come from one district that it was advisable to make two companies of one. (The Chinese system of organization follows three lines: family—of which there are about 100; geographical—hence the 7 associations listed above; and fraternal—the tongs, of which there are about 40, composed of people with common interests, such as trades.)

With Nation-wide jurisdiction, the Six Companies functions as a board of arbitration, settling disputes among organizations and individuals. Chinatown's civic activities, such as the annual Community Chest drive and Rice Bowl parties, are under its management. It assists in maintaining the Chinese Hospital and Chinese schools. A particularly important function is its supervision of the removal of the bones of Chinese dead from American cemeteries to China for reburial or repository in shrines.

The Six Companies at one time engaged in commercial activities—such as the importation of bonded Chinese laborers—but is today a nonprofit organization supported by popular subscription, special taxes, and the income from its properties. From among its officers (representatives of the seven associations named above) a new president is elected every three months. The brief presidential term is designed to prevent the acquisition of undue power or influence by any one officer.

The organization occupies a three-story stuccoed building roofed with red tile. White marble steps lead to a first-floor veranda guarded by giant Chinese lanterns. Contrasting with the facade of sky-blue tile are green- and gold-trimmed balconies opening onto the second and third floors. The interior is sumptuously furnished in the Chinese motif, from the large main-floor meeting hall to the rooms and offices of the upper floors.

111. A pioneer of Protestant faith in Chinatown is the CHINESE PRESBYTERIAN CHURCH, 925 Stockton St., founded in 1853. The present building was erected after the 1906 fire upon the ruins of the original structure. The simple, uncarpeted interior resembles that of a country church, with its rough, beamed ceilings, its long pews, and the rows of chairs behind the pulpit; yet its atmosphere is that of the Orient. Three red velvet panels behind the rostrum carry inscriptions, in gold Chinese characters, of the Ten Commandments, the Lord's Prayer, and the Beatitudes.

The Chinese Presbyterian Church, in 1854, published San Francisco's first Chinese and English newspaper (probably the first in the United States), *The Oriental,* which is said to have done much to counteract the local hostility between Chinese and the white race during its two-year existence. A copy of the paper is preserved in the Presbyterian Theological Seminary at San Anselmo. The church conducts day and evening classes in English for Chinese of all ages.

W. from Stockton St. on Washington St. to Wetmore St.; S. from Washington on Wetmore.

112. Today's CHINESE (PRESBYTERIAN) MISSION HOME, 144 Wetmore St., occupying a small double flat—home of a staff of Chinese girls—is far removed from the busy mission that moved to larger quarters four times after its establishment in 1874. In 1894, a building was erected at 920 Sacramento Street to house the crowded home. The following year its management was assumed by Donaldina Cameron, who became "Lo Mo" (The Mother) to the scores of Chinese girls she rescued from slave operators. Long before her retirement at the age of 70, Miss Cameron had achieved an international reputation. The mission moved to its present quarters in 1939.

Retrace on Wetmore St. to Washington St.; retrace on Washington to Trenton St.; N. on Trenton.

113. The CHINESE HOSPITAL, SE. corner Trenton and Jackson Sts., built in 1924 by public subscription by and for the residents of Chinatown, occupies a four-story, many-windowed gray concrete build-

ing, decorated by ornamental iron grill work and topped by a large sunroom. Chinatown continues to support its little 58-bed hospital, aided only by the Community Chest, while white patients in increasing numbers take advantage of its reasonable rates—low in comparison to those of other modern hospitals of the same standing. The institution consists, in addition to its general medical department and surgery, of emergency and maternity wards; an eye, ear, nose and throat department; and a clinic with in- and out-patient departments. It is staffed by both Chinese and white employees and officials.

Retrace on Trenton St. to Washington St.; E. on Washington.

114. What is now OLD CHINATOWN LANE, extending a half-block northward from its entrance near 868 Washington Street— a narrow paved thoroughfare of bazaars and shops characteristic of Chinatown—was once the "Street of the Gamblers," a crowded little lane notorious for its gaming rooms and brothels. Later, it became Cameron Alley (honoring Donaldina Cameron) and kept this name until 1939, when, oddly enough, its dingy tenements were modernized to resemble the untouched Chinatown of a generation ago.

At the street's entrance stands a 40-foot edifice embodying a watch tower, in authentic design, such as guards temple or palace gates and public grounds in China. The alleyway is decorated with bright Chinese lanterns, flowers, and shrubs. Among its shops is THE PAVILION OF THE SEVEN MAIDENS. Here, beyond a store offering oriental handcraft, is the first women's temple in the United States, dedicated to the Queen of Heaven (T'ien Hou) and watched over by the goddess of mercy. The legend of the temple is the story of a lovely goddess, who fell in love with a shepherd. She was allowed to marry him but, as punishment, was permitted to join him only on the seventh day of the seventh moon, at which time magpies formed a bridge with their wings that the goddess might descend. One of the tapestries in the temple depicts the goddess in the act of descending thus to meet her waiting lover.

In the CHINGWAH LEE ART STUDIO (*12 m. to 12 p.m.*), reached by a narrow stairway at the far end of the lane, are exhibited a rare collection of porcelain, bronzes, ancient snuff bottles, paintings, ancient weapons of warfare, and a large collection of Chinese gods (many from temples formerly situated in towns and camps throughout California, which eventually will be housed in a new temple).

Extending from the north end of Old Chinatown Lane westward to Stockton Street is the STREET OF THE LITTLE BAZAARS, an indoor passage whose model was a street of old China. Midway in it is a wishing well surrounded by a small garden.

S. from Washington St. on Waverly Pl.

115. The main floor of the four-story, yellow-brick building housing the TIN HOW TEMPLE (*suggested visiting hours 6-10 p.m.*), 125 Waverly Pl., is occupied by the Sue Hing Benevolent Association, by whom the temple is maintained.   Maroon-colored balconies run the length of the three upper floors.   A wrought-iron gate on the top floor (*summon attendant by bell*) guards the temple of T'ien Hou, Queen of the Heavens and Goddess of the Seven Seas.

It is believed by many Chinese that one of the present altars was brought to San Francisco in 1848, by one of the few Chinese who arrived that year, transferred from a sailing vessel to a house at First and Brannan Streets, and later moved to Waverly Place.   When a larger temple erected in 1875 was ravaged by the flames of 1906, the altar and the goddess T'ien Hou were removed temporarily to Oakland. The following year, workmen excavating for the basement of the present building discovered the great temple bell, and it too was reinstalled.

The main altar of the temple presents an intricate carving representing the life story of Confucius.   To the left of T'ien Hou sits Moi Dii, god of military affairs, and Ni-Lung, one of the goddesses of motherhood.   In front of T'ien Hou are three massive bronze urns containing prayer sticks and a tiny altar light, which is never permitted to burn out.   Along the walls are 16 ceremonial wands, resembling ancient Chinese battle-axes, used in early times as implements of warfare against evil spirits.   With the altar, set in the center of the sanctuary, are two urns inlaid with Cantonese enamel and precious stones; their designs depict scenes from the life and work of Confucius, whose teachings are especially revered, although Buddhism and Taoism are also represented.

Retrace on Waverly Pl.; E. on Washington St.

116. A pagoda-like, green-fronted, little one-story structure houses the CHINESE TELEPHONE EXCHANGE, 743 Washington St., only exchange of its kind outside China.   The interior is elaborate with gilt and wood carvings; dragons in bas relief decorate the ceiling. Intricately carved grillwork screens shield the 20 girls operators from observation.   Some of the present (1940) operators are descendants of the men who handled the original exchange in 1894; unusual memories are required of them, since the 2,100 subscribers include many who insist upon asking for one another by name rather than by number.

The exchange stands on the SITE OF THE CALIFORNIA STAR.   Here Sam Brannan, renegade Mormon and organizer of the first Vigilance

Committee, published the *California Star,* first newspaper in San Francisco.

Retrace on Washington St. to Grant Ave.; N. on Grant.

117. Guiding the destiny of the ORIENTAL BRANCH OF THE BANK OF AMERICA (*open Mon.-Fri. 9-3, Sat. 9-1*), 939 Grant Ave., are its California-born manager, Dorothy Gee, and eight Chinese women department heads. (Only one other bank in the world, in Shanghai, is operated entirely by women.) The branch is proud of an unusual record: not a single loan defaulted during the entire period of the depression.

The establishment occupies the ground floor of a four-story yellow-brick building. The facade is enlivened by black and red marble, the windows bordered with carved black teak. Customers' desks in the lobby—some of which are of teakwood—are supplied with the abacus, still used for mathematical calculations by many of the branch's 9,000 depositors.

E. from Grant Ave. on Jackson St.

118. Motion pictures made both in Hollywood and China (Chinese films predominate) have been shown at the GREAT CHINA THEATER (*open 7-12 p.m., adm. 35¢*), 636 Jackson St., since it abandoned legitimate productions in 1938. In the small ornate foyer—orange-fronted and covered by a blue ceiling dotted with gilt stars—stills of Chinese cinema stars are displayed beside scenes from such attractions as "Ray 'Crash' Corrigan in Part 3 of *Undersea Kingdom."* The names of current attractions, in Chinese characters on cheap wrapping paper, are elaborately framed with floral designs.

Retrace on Jackson St. to Grant Ave.; N. on Grant.

119. Everyone is a first-nighter at the MANDARIN THEATER (*open 7:30 p.m.-12:30 a.m.; adm. 25¢-50¢*), for the play changes each evening. With few props and little scenery, the native dramas seem to flow on endlessly, while the orchestra (seated onstage out of range of the play) and the audience consume melon seeds, ice cream, and "pop." For late arrivals, the programs carry detailed synopses of the play. The actors are unperturbed by the antics of children scampering up and down the aisles or by the intrusion of prop men, who casually walk off and on supplying needed properties—often by placing a table between two bamboo stools to form a bridge, over which the actor walks sedately

to meet his foe in the dramatic sword fight that highlights every performance.

Only within late years were curtains introduced into Chinatown's legitimate theaters. These usually were supplied by some Chinese manufacturer, who devised this method of advertising local wares to a foreign public. The following notice recently appeared on the rather gaudy drapery of the Mandarin's proscenium:

> "Heart Brand Disease Solution Dependable for curing all kinds of Skin Disease. 'The Wai Shang Yuk Ching' Tonic Juice. Safely and Highly recommended for nourishing the Blood and Brain.
>
> Aukah Chuen   Canton, China."

Latin Quarter:
Telegraph Hill and North Beach

"The city is full of bold hills, rising steeply from the deep water. The air is keen and dry and bright like the air of Greece and the waters not less blue . . . recalling the cities of the Mediterranean . . ."

—JAMES, VISCOUNT BRYCE

BETWEEN the two steep hills that loom abruptly from the Peninsula's northeastern bulge—on the east, Telegraph Hill; on the west, Russian Hill—ringed with their tiers of buildings, a narrow valley runs northwestward from the fringes of the financial district to the water front of North Beach. Along its bottom cuts the diagonal of Columbus Avenue, which begins among the clustering shops, cafes, and night clubs at the southern base of Telegraph Hill and ends among the gasworks, warehouses, and smokestacks at the northern base of Russian Hill. Up from this traffic-crowded artery, where stucco-fronted commercial buildings with their awnings and signboards string in long rows, climb endless blocks of weathered frame flats, staggered—step-like—one above another. Here and there a round-bellied window, a red-tiled roof, a patch of green garden breaks the monotony of their ranks. In the salt-fresh, sun-baked air of a clear day, each building stands out sharply, tarnished with a mellow patina of sun, fog, and soot. Seen in such weather, under a hot blue sky, the district is reminiscent of some Mediterranean seaside village spilling to the water from steep heights. And seen when the billowing mists of a smoky twilight stream down the slopes, it has the look of a sprawling hillside town of northern Italy.

Whether imagined or actual, such resemblances could not have failed to suggest themselves to San Franciscans who know that this is San Francisco's "Little Italy." It could only have been an imagined resemblance that prompted Ernest Peixotto's often-quoted remark: "If you want to behold a bit of the Bay of Naples, go some misty morning to Fisherman's Wharf." To Robert Louis Stevenson the district was "Little Italy . . . a favorite haunt of mine . . ." In his time, too, it was called "Little Mexico" (a part of it still is Mexican). And it might once have been named "Little Ireland," for as Wallace Irwin wrote of "Telygraft Hill":

"The Irish they live on the top av it,
   And th' Dagoes they live on th' base av it,
   And th' goats and th' chicks and th' brickbats and shticks
   Is joombled all over th' face av it . . ."

Through the years, the face of hill and beach have changed almost
beyond recognition, but since the town's beginnings the steep slopes of
these northeastern limits have been peopled with a many-tongued foreign
colony. And like Latin Quarters everywhere, the district came in the
end to be the traditional haunt of bohemia.

The visitor who boards a streetcar for North Beach will no more
find an ocean beach at the end of the line than will the pedestrian who
toils up Telegraph Hill find a telegraph station at the end of his climb.
The beach along which bathhouses clustered—in the days when the
famous wharf built by "Honest Harry" Meiggs in 1853 still extended
into the Bay from the foot of Powell Street—was buried more than
half a century ago when tons of earth were dumped into the water, out
as far as the sea wall extending along the present water front, finished
in 1881. And long since vanished is that telegraph station on the
summit of the hill which was a city landmark for decades after it was
connected by wire in 1853 with a lookout station at Point Lobos. The
station replaced the still older semaphore of which Bret Harte wrote in
"The Man at the Semaphore": ". . . on the extremest point of the
sandy peninsula, where the bay of San Francisco debouches into the
Pacific, there stood a semaphore telegraph . . . it signified to another
semaphore farther inland the 'rigs' of incoming vessels, by certain uncouth signs, which were passed on to Telegraph Hill, San Fraincisco,
where they reappeared on a third semaphore . . . and on certain days
of the month every eye was turned to welcome those gaunt arms widely
extended at right angles which meant 'side-wheel steamer' (the only
steamer which carried the mails) and 'letters from home.' "

The road to the Presidio, which wound over Telegraph Hill's
western shoulders and past North Beach, was a track through unsettled
wilds until the later 1850's. For years the only house between Yerba
Buena and the Presidio was the hospitable adobe which Juana Briones
built in 1836 near the hill's western base, at what is now the intersection of Powell and Filbert Streets. In the shelter of that Loma Alta
(high hill) of the Spanish discoverers, the buxom dark-featured widow
of Apolinario Miranda supplied milk and green vegetables to visiting
ship's crews, administered to the sick, and sheltered an occasional refugee
from the wretchedness of life before the mast. The travelers of the
1850's found the "old Presidio road . . . neither safe nor pleasant,"
recalled pioneers T. A. Barry and B. A. Patten. "The hard adobe soil
in summer was like stone, and in the rainy season gummy, sticky and
disagreeable. The steep, shelving, uneven way [made] the carriage per-

petually seem as if it were just toppling over. . . . Like all primitive roads, it wound up over the highest, most toilsome way, past cattle-pens, corrals, brick-yards and butcher's shambles, the ground all the way looking as baked and hard as slag or adamant, with no sign of vegetation . . ."

Around Telegraph Hill's southern slopes—no more than a stone's throw from the town's first landing place at Clarke's Point—congregated in 1849 exiles from Australia's penal colonies in a district of grog shops, brothels, and gambling dives known as "Sydney Town." Along the hill's western base spread the shacks and tents of "Little Chile," settled by Chilenos and Peruvians. At weekly intervals, usually on Sundays, the organized hoodlums who called themselves "Hounds"— many of their number recruited from Sydney Town—used to raid the Chileno quarter, pillaging the houses, robbing and beating the inhabitants, attacking the women. The depredations were only halted by the Vigilance Committee of 1851.

For decades the North Point Docks under the brow of Telegraph Hill, built in 1853 from the foot of Sansome Street, were the landing place for immigrants from France and Italy. From the beginning they settled around the slopes of the hill. The section became a polyglot community, where Irish, Germans, French, Italians, and Latin Americans mingled easily. Although the first Italians had arrived as early as the 1830's, they began to overwhelm the other nationalities with their numbers only toward the end of the nineteenth century. By the thousands they came—laborers, artisans, mechanics, farmers, shopkeepers. As soon as they were well established, they lent passage money to countrymen in the homeland. The majority settled in the North Beach-Telegraph Hill section because it reminded them of their native land, because rents and land were cheap there, and because it was near the Bay where many of them earned their living by fishing. The Irish, the Germans, and the French moved to other parts of the city. When the fire of 1906 began to creep up the slopes of the hill, it was the Italians who saved it. From their cellars they rolled out barrels of red wine and, forming a bucket brigade, protected their houses against the flames with blankets soaked in the wine. The district has been theirs ever since, shared for the most part only by the Latin American colony at its southwestern fringes, near the base of Russian Hill, and by the bohemian colony (succeeded lately by sympathizers of more affluent means) on the crest of Telegraph Hill.

"Little Italy" is no longer so little, for the Italians, 60,000 strong, are San Francisco's largest and most powerful national minority. And North Beach is home not only for the Italians who live there but also for those who have moved to other parts of the city or the Bay region. On Sundays and feast days they come back to North Beach to visit relatives and revive old friendships. They fill the bay-windowed flats, lounge in the doorways, and gather in groups for sidewalk discussion. They crowd the lawns and benches beneath the weeping willows in Washington Square. In their eyes is little regret for the vanishing past; in their rich laughter only a hearty appreciation for the present. What if the old stores are beginning to disappear—the dingy shelves and counters stacked with dried mushrooms, anchovies, and the Italian cheeses: Parmesan, Roma, Gorgonzola—the dusty rafters festooned with yards of rich moldy sausages and bunches of aromatic dried herbs: rosemary, thyme, sage and sweet marjoram—the boxes of creamy smooth chocolates from Turin and Perugia? Are not the great new markets, dazzling with refrigerated show cases and white tile, filled with the same good things to eat?

In the spring the markets, both old and modern, proclaim the virtues of *capretti,* fresh suckling kid. The young goats' heads, replete with tiny horns, are displayed in the windows. Brown and white candy lambs, with little brass bells hung about their necks and Italian flags thrust in their backs, appear in all the confectionaries. Beside them lie huge Easter eggs with *Buona Pasqua* written on them in sparkling sugar. The pre-Lenten season is also the occasion for elaborate displays in shops devoted to imported gravure prints of a religious nature and Carrara marble images of the Virgin.

Formerly this season was marked by the rivalry between the Garibaldi and Bercigliari Guards. Sponsored by competing undertaking establishments, these two drill companies contested at Easter parades and pre-Lenten carnival balls for the choice of a queen and for trophies. Today the Italian Family Club and other social organizations hold pre-Lenten balls, but the maskers are missing, being confined to Italian celebrations of such Anglo-Saxon festivities as Hallowe'en and New Year's Eve.

Keen rivalry still exists, however, among the colony's residents in the choice of a queen for the annual fete on Columbus Day. Elected usually by votes secured through purchases at various North Beach stores, she reigns briefly each October 12. A special mass at the Church of Saints Peter and Paul honors the great discoverer, as does a parade to the Municipal Pier at the foot of Van Ness Avenue. At the pier a pageant in fifteenth century costumes re-enacts Columbus' momentous landing on the shores of San Salvador.

In the fall, when truckloads of ripened grapes have been piled in cellars, North Beach waxes heady with the smell of fermenting wine. The owners of portable winepresses move from one cool basement to another, crushing grapes for the red *vino.* Besides beverages of domestic manufacture, North Beach merchants offer wines and liquors imported from Italy; and *vov* of Padua has converted many not of Latin blood to the colony's gastronomy and its casual way of life.

To industry, finance, sports, and politics the city's Italians have made distinguished contributions. The names of Amadeo Giannini, founder of the Bank of America, Armando Pedrini, and James A. Bacigalupi are known to the world's stock markets. (Until the 1929 stock market crash scarcely a North Beach Italian, from cook's helper to crab fisherman, did not own shares in Giannini's corporation.) Mayor Angelo J. Rossi is of Italian descent. Of National reputation in the world of sports are the Di Maggio brothers; Fred Apostoli, the boxer; Charlie Ferrara, golf champion; Vic Bottari and Angelo "Hank" Luisetti, football and basketball heroes. (With great pride North Beach residents point out the playground at Lombard and Mason Streets where they say Joe Di Maggio learned to play baseball.)

Mostly immigrants from Italy's northern provinces, the robust inhabitants of North Beach maintain their attachment for the soil in spite of their urban mode of living. The Peninsula truck gardens owned by their compatriots supply the city's wholesale vegetable and flower markets. The colony's other roots, particularly for its Neapolitan and Sicilian elements, are in the fishing industry; and herein is revealed a communal strain that is in marked contrast to the individualism apparent in other Italian enterprises. Members of the Crab Fishermen's Protective Association own their boats and gear in common and share among themselves the profits of the catch they bring in to Fisherman's Wharf.

Ever since Juana Briones established her home here, Spanish-speaking people have lived in North Beach. Although most of them now live farther west near the base of Russian Hill, many still cling to their older habitat on the slopes of Telegraph Hill. Here an ill-concealed and profound antagonism exists between them and their Italian neighbors. They patronize small butcher shops and grocery stores owned by their own countrymen. At the base of the hill a barber shop finds it expedient to hire barbers of each nationality, with separate chairs, for its factional clientele. That the sins of the fathers may not be visited upon the coming generations, however, a third chair is provided, with a hobbyhorse mounted on its seat, which is shared by children of both nationalities.

The small colony of Spanish-speaking people in the vicinity of Powell Street and Broadway likewise share with some misgivings the larger domain of their Italian neighbors, who own most of their property, and even their weekly newspaper, *El Imparcial*. The Mexicans and other Latin Americans maintain a separate life and a separate culture that clings to customs of their homelands. Although a common religion is their strongest bond with their immediate neighbors, Nuestra Señora de Guadalupe differs in aspect from the Italian church which overlooks Washington Square. Along the base of Russian Hill they have also their restaurants and social clubs, their *abarrotes* which offer Mexican candies, pastry, *huaraches,* and pottery. Spanish phonograph records are sold in a store which displays Spanish books, South American and Mexican periodicals, and American "pulp" magazines reprinted in Spanish.

Despite its Spanish origins, San Francisco has today only about 8,700 Mexicans, of whom approximately 7,000 are native born. Other scattered Spanish-speaking groups bring the total Latin American minority to about 14,000. Many old families live in North Beach. The majority of the Mexicans are laborers; the Peruvians and others have clerical jobs in the export and import trade. They have no native theater, but a North Beach movie shows a Spanish motion picture once each week. The Basque sheep-ranchers who come occasionally to North Beach are still to be found about the Español and Du Midi hotels. Mexican folk dances such as the *jarabe tapetillo* are seen only in cafes like La Fiesta. A little curio shop on Pacific Street sells baskets woven of maguey fibre, the vivid handicraft of Yaqui Indians, and various native wares imported from below the Rio Grande.

As North Beach clings to its traditions in spite of physical and social change, so does Telegraph Hill; and the hill has a tradition all its own which is not altogether incidental to the history of the Latin elements that have claimed all but its summit and its eastern side. The "Telygraft Hill" of the Irish who believed themselves descendants of Gaelic kings and littered the hill with their shanties, their washing, and their goats exists today only in the reminiscences of old-timers, but their influence is still there—with a few of the Irish themselves to keep it alive. The French, who shared the hill with them, have also moved elsewhere, and their old locations have been claimed by the Italians.

Gone, too, is that fervent assemblage of bohemians to whom Telegraph Hill was an oasis of Art in the wasteland of the 1920's. Scattered now to fame, hack work, or cheaper quarters are all those blasé girls and sad young men who talked interminably in Freudian overtones of Picasso and T. S. Eliot, Stravinsky and Isadora Duncan, and read with bated breath in *transition* and the *Dial* the expatriate communiques from Rapallo and Trieste, and Paris editions of Joyce's *Ulysses* smuggled in from Mexico. That they painted little and wrote less was beside the point: they represented for Telegraph Hill the cultural frustration of an epoch, Gertrude Stein's "lost generation" before it found itself in the rebirth of National bohemianism somewhat more affluent, less real.

The passing of the days when the summit of "the Hill was not inhabited save by flocks of goats"—as Charles Warren Stoddard, who once lived there, wrote—was bitterly resisted by the little group of professional bohemians who had labored to create a Greenwich Village of the West. When one of the first of the hill's more pretentious homes began to rise from concrete foundations perched uncertainly on the steep slope, it was threatened by intermittent barrages of rocks, tin cans, and dead cats until, during the last weeks of construction, the owner was obliged to camp out in the unfinished building to protect it from vandalism. As improvements encroached, rents rose. When Montgomery Street was paved through to Julius' Castle and towering concrete bulkheads were erected to dam up the treacherous clay hillsides, three- and four-story stucco apartment buildings with rents running into fancy figures began to appear. As rents soared, property owners began to rebuild and remodel the weatherbeaten shanties clinging to the eastern slopes or to demolish them and erect ultramodern studio apartments in their places. The artists retreated to lands of cheaper living. To take their places on the crest of the hill came brokers, minor executives, and other part-time bohemians.

Filbert Street's long flight of weather-blackened stairs, climbing over the hill's grassy-edged shoulders and up its scarred brown rocky face, gouged out long ago to fill in the water-front tidelands below, still affords glimpses of the hill as it was. Mounting the grassy slopes, where torrents of rainwater still gush down the ruts in spring, it passes tiny cottages hanging against cliff sides, narrow alleys laid with planks, steep little gardens behind picket fences. Remotely sound the rattle of winches along the docks, the puffs and snorts of the Belt Line Railroad locomotives, the sirens, whistles, and bells of the water front below, from which float upward whiffs of the odors of roasting coffee, of cinnamon, cloves, and nutmeg from spice and coffee houses. Through the haze over the Bay, where gulls wheel, shimmer Yerba Buena Island with its pillared causeway below the wooded crest; the radiant white walls and towers of Treasure Island; and the bluish slopes—with their tumbled white buildings—of the East Bay shore. Over the weatherbeaten board walks and fences tumble matted hedges of geraniums; around green-shuttered windows, over the railings of balconies on stilts, up weather-stained shingled walls clamber creeping vines. And from the summit of the hill, banked in greenery, soars the gleaming white fluted shaft of Coit Tower.

The crest of the hill is another land. Around the park's patch of green, hemmed in by concrete walls, soaring modern apartment houses rear their blank stuccoed facades. Ragged eucalyptus trees shed their leaves on jumbled, varicolored roofs. From facades painted pink, green, blue, or yellow, expansive windows look out across the Bay. Behind heavy wooden doors, narrow brick-flagged passageways lead into courtyards sheltered from the cold blustering breezes off the ocean, where caged canaries sing in the sun. The building fronts are adorned with gaily painted doors and brass knockers, with windows revealing Indian pottery and blankets, with window boxes colored sea green, aquamarine, and lemon yellow. And only a half-block down the western slope, where gloomy flats border narrow Genoa Place, begins Little Italy, with its sour smell of bread dough fermenting; its pillows, mattresses and bedding hung out to air from open windows; its screaming children tobogganing down the steep pavements on the broken-out sides of fruit boxes.

Along the Latin Quarter's southern boundary, Broadway, where it turns its face toward the rest of San Francisco, denizens of hill and beach—Italians and bohemians—meet and mingle with the rest of San Francisco. Gaily bedizened with glaring electric signs after dark, Broadway and its cross streets in the four blocks between Kearny and Powell Streets are bordered continuously with restaurants and night clubs whose food, wine, and entertainment draw nightly throngs: Vanessi's, Finocchio's, the Fior d'Italia, and New Joe's—where crowds wait for seats at three in the morning; the Xochimilco and the Sinaloa; the Jai-Alai and the Español. At the opposite end of North Beach, near the water front with its wharves and warehouses, the bright lights of the Club Lido, the Bal Tabarin, Lucca's and the Fiesta Club dispel the gloom. And to the water front at Fisherman's Wharf, where the crabs brought in by the fishermen are cooked on the sidewalk in steaming caldrons, comes all of San Francisco for sea food at Joe di Maggio's, Fishermen's Grotto, or one of a dozen open-fronted cafes.

To those who love it best North Beach will remain the Latin Quarter: bohemia between the hills and neighbor to the sea, hospitable with the musical linguistics and the gracious folkways brought hither by *paisanos* from the hot countries. And the hill will still stand, with its crown of wind-swept eucalyptus, through the fog and the rain and the sun. And people will still come there at sunset to watch the long shadows creep upward from the trees of Washington Square and to feel in the stir of the gathering darkness the touch of George Sterling's "cool grey city of love."

POINTS OF INTEREST

120. Probably the best-known and best-loved bar in a city of countless streamlined cocktail lounges is ISADORE GOMEZ' CAFE, 848 Pacific St. A small lantern before an inconspicuous door marks the entrance to a narrow flight of dirty wooden stairs. Upstairs is a long, smoke-filled room—a room (describes the *Almanac for Thirty-Niners*) ". . . dilapidated as in speak-easy days, retaining the broken plaster of the ceiling, the insecure chairs, the cracked oilcloth on the tables, the

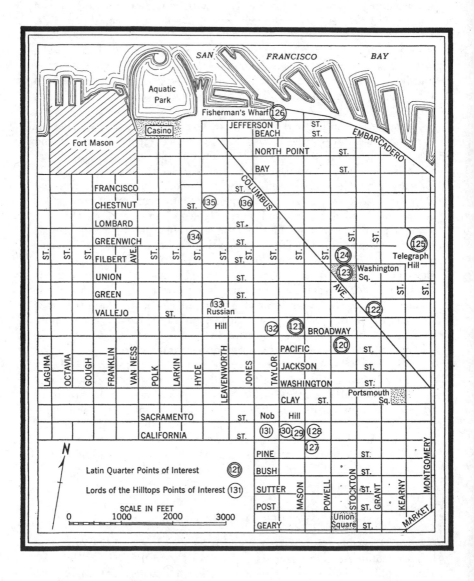

long pine bar . . . Idle behind the bar, leaning across it with leisurely amusement, is Izzy Gomez in a black fedora . . . a coffee-colored fat man . . . elaborately feted on his birthday by San Francisco's Press Club . . . an illiterate fat man painted, photographed, written and sung about . . ." Here 63-year-old Isadore greets his closest friends, or anyone who may wander in, and tells tall, witty tales of life in his native Portugal—or dances Portuguese folk-dances with incredible grace despite his massive bulk. On occasion he expounds—punctuating with a ponderous forefinger—the three principles of his philosophy: "When you don't know what to say, say nothing"; "Life is a long road; take it easy"; "When you come to a pool of water on that long road, don't make it muddy; maybe you'll pass there again, and you'll be thirsty."

Since 1900 Izzy has been running his bar, since 1930 in its present location. Famed in a city noted for good things to eat are his thick, juicy steaks and great platters of French-fried potatoes. And drinks are not measured here, but poured with casual generosity from the bottle. Repeal has not changed the house of El Gomez; red chalk marks left by a spotter during Prohibition days are still preserved, and a peep-hole still overlooks the stairs. The same famous mural back of the bar records the faces of Izzy, of Joe and "Dad" (who have served Izzy's customers for many years, casually polite, vastly unhurried), and of the more colorful characters who once gathered here. The initials of hundreds of them appear, cut into woodwork and tables.

N. from Pacific St. on Powell St. to Broadway; E. on Broadway.

121. Only church in San Francisco whose services are conducted in the Spanish language is NUESTRA SEÑORA DE GUADALUPE, 908 Broadway, which derives its name from the shrine erected near Guadalupe, Mexico, in commemoration of the appearance before the peon, Juan Diego, of the Virgin Mary. One of its two stained-glass windows, softly lighting the rich interior, portrays Juan Diego kneeling before Bishop Sumaraga. The chastely simple Romanesque church building, its twin domes topped by gold crosses, was built in 1912. The first church in the United States to be constructed of reinforced concrete replaced the old frame structure (dating from 1875) destroyed by the 1906 fire. In April, 1939 Father Antonio M. Santandreu had rounded out his fiftieth year as the church's pastor. Oldest living priest on the Pacific Coast, totally blind and partially deaf, he now (1940) is assisted by three younger men, all trained in Mexico or Spain.

In sharp contrast to the austere facade is the ornate interior, approached from stone steps which lead to a sheltered patio bordered with flowers. On the arched ceiling of the nave, supported by twelve pillars, is portrayed in fresco the Holy Sacrament and the Coronation of the

Blessed Virgin. Behind the flood-lit white marble altar, standing at the end of the exquisitely tiled main aisle, is a mural depicting the Last Supper and the Multiplication of the Loaves and Fishes. By day, light streams through stained-glass windows portraying the miracle at Guadalupe and the Sermon on the Mount; by night, from massive and ornate candelabra. Every year during the nine days before Christmas, when Mexican families are commemorating the birth of Christ with the ceremonies of Las Posadas (the lodgings) in their homes, the church holds a novena with special singing and prayers.

N. from Broadway on Mason St. to Vallejo St.; E. from Mason on Vallejo.

122. First Roman Catholic parish church in San Francisco, ST. FRANCIS' CHURCH, 620 Vallejo St., owes its origin to the religious zeal of a group of the Gold Rush town's French residents, who persuaded a young officer of the United States Army to give them the use of a small room for services. Father Langlois, on his way from Oregon to eastern Canada by way of Cape Horn, was persuaded to remain as their pastor. In a new adobe chapel on the church's present site, on July 19, 1849, Father Langlois said Mass for the first time in the new building and administered the town's first Roman Catholic baptism. The French soon were joined by worshippers of so many other nationalities that in 1856 they withdrew to found a church of their own, Notre Dame des Victoires.

In the adobe chapel's schoolroom, on December 7, 1850, a reception was given for young Bishop Sadoc Alemany, just arrived to take charge of a diocese extending from the Rocky Mountains to the Pacific Ocean. Since St. Francis' congregation was still smarting from the indignity of having been embezzled by an impostor of funds, Father Langlois is said to have insisted on the Bishop's credentials. When it appeared that San Francisco, rather than Monterey, would be the chief city of the diocese, he returned as Archbishop Alemany, his formal translation to the Metropolitan See of San Francisco occurring July 23, 1853. Here he took up residence in a wooden shanty adjoining the church, which served as his cathedral until dedication of St. Mary's on Christmas, 1854.

Construction of a new St. Francis Church was begun five years later. Dedicated March 17, 1859, the fourteenth-century Gothic structure of cement-faced brick survived the 1906 fire with little enough damage to permit restoration. The interior is an aisled nave of seven bays with a shallow apse. In the apsidal arches above the ornate altar and reredos are a series of frescoes depicting events in the life of St.

Francis. Two larger frescoes over the side altars portray the death of St. Francis and the showing of the Stigmata.

NW. from Vallejo St. on Columbus Ave.

123. In the heart of the teeming Italian section, WASHINGTON SQUARE, Columbus Ave., Union, Stockton, and Filbert Sts., a quadrangular oasis of lawn, cypresses, and weeping willows, is an out-of-doors refuge from the close-set flats of the locality. In the center of the square is a bronze STATUE OF BENJAMIN FRANKLIN, bequeathed by Henry D. Cogswell, wealthy philanthropist and eccentric, to: "Our boys and girls who will soon take our places and pass on." A plaque in its base bears the curious inscription:

"P. O. Box With
Mementos
For The
Historical Society
In 1979
From H. D. C."

Inscriptions as curious—"Vichy," "Congress Water," and "California Seltzer"—proclaim the virtues of the ordinary drinking water (Cogswell was a determined temperance advocate) which spouts from the fountain. On the east side of the park a granite UNITED STATES COAST GEODETIC SURVEY MARKER carries the legend: "Astronomical and telegraph longitude, United States Coast and Geodetic Survey: Lat. 37.47′, 57″ N. Longitude 122.24′, 37″ W. Station Washington Square, 1869-1880." Facing Columbus Avenue is the VOLUNTEER FIREMEN'S MONUMENT (Haig Patigian, sculptor), a bronze group of three volunteer firemen—one holding a supine woman in his arms—dedicated to the "Volunteer Fire Department of San Francisco, 1849-1866." It was erected in 1933 through a bequest of Lillie Hitchcock Coit. Washington Square, which served as a campground for homeless citizens after the 1906 holocaust, occupies land donated to the city January 3, 1850 by its first mayor, John W. Geary.

E. from Columbus Ave. on Filbert St.

124. The Roman Catholic CHURCH OF SS. PETER AND PAUL, 660 Filbert St., of concrete construction, lifts its two spires high above the Italian district it serves. Its cornerstone laid in 1922 by Archbishop Hanna, all but the exterior of the church was completed the following year. In 1939 and 1940 its facade again was shrouded in

scaffolding. When finished the terra cotta exterior will be embellished on each side of the doorway by a mosaic of Dante at work on his *Paradiso* and another of Columbus landing in America. In the ornate interior seating 1,000, the Roman altar and many gilded images reflect the soft light filtering from the stained glass windows. Brought from Italy, the richly ornate altar, inlaid with mosaic and framed in white Carrara marble, bears a sculptured reproduction of Leonardo da Vinci's *The Last Supper.* The church's large statuary collection also includes a statue of patron saint John Bosco and a sixteenth-century carved wood figure of Jesus Christ.

Up Filbert St. steps to Telegraph Hill Blvd.; N. from Filbert on Telegraph Hill (by motor, N. from Filbert on Stockton St. to Lombard St.; E. from Stockton on Lombard to Telegraph Hill Blvd.; S. from Lombard on Telegraph Hill).

125. Crowning the brow of Telegraph Hill is PIONEER PARK, whose paved esplanade and parkway command a stirring panorama of the vast Bay and its shores and the city crowding to the edge of the Peninsula. Grown from loam-filled crevices on the bare rocky summit, its yellow broom, cypress trees, and stately eucalyptuses bank in greenery the base of COIT MEMORIAL TOWER (*open Wed., Sat., Sun. 10-4 and 8-10; elevator 25¢*), a slim, fluted concrete column (Arthur Brown, Jr., architect) whose glass-enclosed observation gallery is 540 feet above the waters of the Bay. The tower is named for a life-long friend of San Francisco's firefighters, Lillie Hitchcock Coit, who in 1929 left funds to the city to be used for a memorial to the volunteer firemen of the 1850's and 1860's. As a girl of 15, she had been the mascot of the crack Knickerbocker Company No. 5. To the end of her life she wore the diamond-studded gold badge given her by the firemen, whether she attended a formal evening function or an early morning blaze. Where Coit Memorial Tower now rises stood, in the middle of the nineteenth century, the telegraph station for which the hill is named—"A place of much resort" in the fifties, reminisced Barry and Patten. ". . . it was good exercise to walk up there, and the view repaid the trouble. There were . . . refreshing milk-punches to be had in the room beneath the lookout on the roof, where privileged visitors could ascend and use the telescope."

A landmark in the history of government-subsidized art are the COIT TOWER MURALS, reflecting the contemporary scene in California city, factory and field in 1934, which were the result of the first work relief project for artists sponsored by the Federal government in the United States. Covering the walls of first and second floors and the stairway between them, they were executed by 20 members of San

Francisco's art colony. On the main floor, above the entrance to the elevator room, a pair of Cyclopian eyes look down from Ray Boynton's mural symbolizing the mystic forces of nature, man in search of sustenance, and man in search of wealth. Other walls of the first floor graphically portray the characteristic activities of California life with their ten-foot figures by Malette Dean and Clifford Wight; industrial plants by Ralph Stackpole; a department store interior by Frede Vidar; a San Francisco street by Victor Arnautoff; and rich agricultural fields by Maxine Albro. A library cross-section by Bernard Zakheim shows readers scanning the headlines in contemporary newspapers. A mural by John Langley Howard depicts unemployed "snipers" panning gold and grim-faced workers massed in front of a smelter plant. The murals in the elevator room, executed in oil, show views from Telegraph Hill and rolling California landscapes by Otis Oldfield, Rinaldo Cuneo, and Moya del Pino. A spectacular portrayal of the Powell Street hill by Lucien Labaudt decorates the stairway walls ascending to the second floor, where are found illustrations of California sports and outdoor life and Jane Berlandina's scenes of domestic life in egg tempera.

The MARCONI MEMORIAL, at the foot of the steps leading to Lombard Street, a modern, simply carved bench of Raymond California granite containing a bronze plaque (Raymond Puccinelli, sculptor) of Guglielmo Marconi, was erected to commemorate the inventor of the wireless in July, 1939. A Latin inscription reads: "Outstripping the lightning, the voice races through the empty sky."

N. on Telegraph Hill Blvd. to Lombard St.; W. from Telegraph Hill on Lombard to Columbus Ave.; NW. from Lombard on Columbus to Taylor St.; W. from Columbus on Taylor.

126. Twentieth-century commercialism and Old-World tradition go hand in hand at FISHERMAN'S WHARF, foot of Taylor St., where are moored in serried ranks the tiny, bright-painted gasoline boats of the crab fishermen and the tall-masted 70-foot Diesel-engined trawlers of the sardine fleet. The high-sterned junks with square sails of the Chinese shrimp fishermen who supplied the forty-niners with seafood have long since disappeared. The colorful craft of the Italians who supplanted them—rigged with triangular lateen sails like the fishing boats of the Gulf of Genoa or the Bay of Naples—have disappeared too, supplanted in turn by trim vessels powered with combustion engines. And the fish markets to which San Francisco housewives once drove in buggies have become neon-lit shops offering "curb service" to motorists. But the gulls still fight over morsels thrown into the lagoon; small boys still impale sardine bait on the troll lines; the oldsters of the crab fleet

still sit cross-legged, mending their nets by hand with long wooden needles.

Heedless of onlookers, the sun-browned fishermen go about their work, tossing their fish from the holds to the wharves, where they are trundled off in hand trucks, hanging up their nets to dry in great brown festoons, painting and repairing their vessels, haggling with fish buyers. Sicilian in origin, many of the barrel-chested crab fishermen sport the tam-o-shanter, the knit jersey, and the heavy sea boots of their Mediterranean homeland.

The boats of the crabfishing fleet, like their larger sisters of the sardine fleet, are brightly painted, with blue and white the predominating hues. During the fishing season (November through August) the crab fleet usually leaves the wharf with the tide—between two and three o'clock in the morning—bound for fishing grounds between three and six miles outside the gate, where each boat anchors within hailing distance of its neighbor. In mid-afternoon they return, laden with from one to four dozen crabs apiece, accompanied by screaming hordes of gulls. When not at sea, the crab boats are anchored at the inner harbor at Fisherman's Wharf, where the walks and planking are often plastered with nets drying in the sun.

Usually anchored outside the square lagoon of the crab fishermen are the sardine and bottom fish boats—large schooners and trawlers with deep after holds, their blue and yellow masts and booms towering above the smaller craft. In the sardine fleet, Norwegians and Slavonians predominate—excellent seamen, tanned by sun and wind, their faces wrinkled. Powered with 200- and 300-horsepower Diesel engines, the vessels venture northward as far as Alaskan waters and southward to Mexican shores. The dark of the moon between August and February is the best time for sardine fishing, because the sardine schools then are sighted most easily by the iridescent flash they create as they move through the water. The sardine fishermen use the net known as the purse seine, which is maneuvered in a circle by means of a skiff and then drawn together in much the same fashion as a tobacco pouch. The bottom fish vessels use the paranzella net, dragged between two boats, which revolutionized the industry when Pedro Costa introduced it in 1876. In these nets they trap sole, sand dab, rock cod, and flounder— which comprise 90 per cent of their catch—and occasionally starfish, octopi, and even sharks. The trawlers of the bottom fish fleet—which number about 20—rank in size with those of the sardine fleet. It was the bottom fish fleet which first used steam-powered boats, also introduced by Costa—for which reason sole were first known around San Francisco Bay as "steamerfish." More than 2,000 men and 350 vessels are engaged in the fishing industry throughout the year; the annual catch totals nearly 300 million pounds. Ranking first in size of catch is the sardine; second, the crab. The shore community at the wharf includes blacksmiths, boatbuilders, tackle menders and net repairers, and the dock includes a marine service station where the tanks of the gasoline-powered crab boats are filled. Fishing fleet boats are available for hire at an average cost of $3.00 per person—which often includes *cioppino* (fish stew) with red wine.

Along the wharfside, the sidewalk is lined with huge iron cauldrons simmering over open fires of boxwood, where live crabs are boiled after the buyer has selected his choice from the dripping stacks on display. Behind the kettles are squirming piles of lobsters, trays of shrimp and prawns, shelves decked with rainbow-hued abalone shells, and little turtles with brightly painted designs on their backs for sale as souvenirs. Automobiles line the curb, their occupants eating seafood delicacies from trays. Other diners sit by restaurant windows looking out over the masts of the boats moored in the lagoon.

Lords of the Hilltops

"I estimate that a dime dropped on the crest of California Street would gather speed enough to kill a horse on Market Street, unless it hit a Chinaman on Grant Avenue."
—Philip Guedalla

WHENEVER the builders of San Francisco could not go forward, they went up. In Currier and Ives' bird's-eye view, *The City of San Francisco—1878,* they already had leaped that crescent-shaped barrier of hills which swings from Telegraph Hill on the northeast to Twin Peaks in the middle of the Peninsula. Persistently the long files of houses climbed to the crests and down the other side. Where the heights defied scaling even by the cable car, the city's uphill progress was facilitated by steps.

No San Franciscan was amazed to behold even that doughty railroad builder, Collis P. Huntington, being towed uphill to his mansion by the California Street grip. The pinnacle to which a man's rise in riches might carry him had a name in those days—Nob Hill, inspired by those "nabobs" of commerce and finance who looked down from its crest. To Robert Louis Stevenson, the "great net of straight thoroughfares lying at right angles, east and west and north and south over the shoulders of Nob Hill, the hill of palaces, must certainly be counted the best part of San Francisco. It is there that the millionaires who gathered together, vying with each other in display, looked down upon the business wards of the city."

When Dr. Arthur Hayne, having made a comfortable fortune at his medical practice, desired to settle down with his bride, actress Julia Dean, he chose Nob Hill and, hacking a trail through the brush to the summit, built in 1856 a house of wood and clay on the future site of the Fairmont Hotel. A short time later, a merchant, William Walton, erected a more pretentious dwelling at Taylor and Washington Streets. Not until late in the 1860's, however, when the mass exodus of the elite from Rincon Hill began, was Nob Hill populated extensively.

Among the first men of wealth to settle there was Maurice Doré, banker William C. Ralston's confidante, who bought Walton's house. The first palatial homes built by millionaires—recalled Amelia Ransom Neville, chronicler of San Francisco's social elite—were Richard Tobin's, "distinguished by reason of having what might be termed a hand-picked library"; James Ben Ali Haggin's, "a large gray mansard with stables behind it where were all the most fastidious horses one could

desire"; Lloyd Tevis', where "wonderful parties were given . . ."
Later William T. Coleman built "a white Roman villa in a walled
garden" and Senator George Hearst, "a long Spanish palace of white
stucco."

The Hill's inducements as a residential site were greatly augmented
by the advent of the cable car in the 1870's—that curious vehicle whose
means of locomotion puzzled the visiting English noblewoman, Lady
Duffus Hardy, almost as much as the "newly arrived Mongolian" whose
remarks she quoted: " 'No pushee, no pullee, no horsee, no steamee;
Melican man heap smart.' "

And from the summit of Nob Hill were rising, in the 1870's, those
"really palatial residences, the homes of the railway and bonanza kings,"
of which Lady Hardy wrote. To advertise their new-found wealth, a
half-dozen "get-rich-quick" millionaires—Leland Stanford, Mark Hopkins, and Charles Crocker of the "Big Four"; David Colton, who was
known as the "½" of the "Big 4½"; James C. Flood of the "Nevada
Four"; and E. J. ("Lucky") Baldwin—lavished their railroad and
mining millions in unbridled display. Of wood treated to resemble
stone they built their palaces, and stuffed them with *objets d'art* imported from Europe in shiploads. In their ostentation they were anything but discreet, as they must have realized when Dennis Kearny led
an army of "sand-lotters" up the hill one autumn day in 1877 to shake
angry fists at the mansions. For three decades the vainglorious display
continued to dazzle all beholders—until one by one, the mansions burst
into blaze as fire swept the hill in April, 1906.

Risen from the ashes, Nob Hill continues to justify its proud epithet,
"Hill of Palaces." Where the bonanza mansions stood, luxury hotels,
aristocratic clubs, and towering apartment houses overlook the Bay.
Fastidious old gentlemen still reach their homes on the heights by cable
car. Nob Hill ladies out airing their dogs, doormen resplendent in
uniform before gleaming entrances, shining limousines attended by
liveried chauffeurs perpetuate the traditions of the hill's golden age.
But the days of reckless ostentation passed with the fire; the Nob Hill
of today breathes an air of subdued gentility.

Nob Hill was but one of the summits claimed and held by the rich.
As the rest of the city began to swarm around, the vanguard of the
"Four Hundred" moved northward to Russian Hill or westward to
Pacific Heights, where they could dwell surrounded by gardens looking
down upon the Golden Gate.

What part the Russians played in the naming of Russian Hill
remains a mystery. According to one legend, a colony of Russian farmers
raised vegetables on its slopes for the seal catchers of the Farallones;
according to another, certain Russians of unknown identity were buried
there; and according to still another, a Russian sailor of prodigious

drinking habits fell into a well on the hill, where he drowned. The place made its earliest appearance in the city's annals as the site of a gibbet, where on December 10, 1852, one José Forni was hanged in the town's first official execution.

When Joseph H. Atkinson built his house in 1853 on the south side of Russian Hill, it stood alone. But Charles F. Homer, a government contractor, soon built next door; and next to Homer, W. H. Ranlett erected his "House of Many Corners." William Squires Clark, who had constructed the town's first wharf, built the two-story house later purchased by William Penn Humphreys. And not far away were erected two of the city's eight octagonal houses.

One of the first panoramas of the city, drawn and lithographed from daguerreotypes made from the summit of the hill about 1862 by C. B. Gifford, shows a few straggling fences and a handful of isolated houses among unpaved streets on the hill's northern and southern slopes. From its summit rises the "observatory"—somewhat resembling an oil well derrick with a spiraling stairway—which Captain David Jobson erected in 1861. From the crow's nest atop this structure (known as "Jobson's Folly"), picnickers who had toiled uphill from Harbor View Park on the Bay could survey, for 25¢, the landscape and seascape through a telescope.

Almost from the beginning, Russian Hill was the haunt of the city's artists and writers. Of their number, however, Robert Louis Stevenson —whose "homes" are almost as numerous as the beds "in which George Washington slept"—was not one, although his widow came here to live after his death. Ambrose Bierce's cynicism found vent there. Joaquin Miller composed poetry there, as did Ina Coolbrith and George Sterling. Frederick O'Brien lived there when he wrote *White Shadows of the South Seas.* There Peter B. Kyne wrote many of his "Cappy Ricks" stories, and Stewart Edward White, his novels. Will and Wallace Irwin, in the days when Will was co-editor with Frank Norris and Gelett Burgess of *The Wave,* found refuge on the hill. It was because he lived there that Burgess conceived his "Ballad of the Hyde Street Grip":

> "Rush her at the crossings, catch her on the rise,
> Easy round the corners when the dust is in your eyes!"

Of the colony were John Dewey, before he acquired his fame in the East; Mary Austin and James Hopper, before they went to join the colony at Carmel; Kathleen and Charles Norris, before they deserted the city for the Peninsula. On the crest of the hill, Rose Wilder Lane found inspiration. And here Inez Haynes Irwin wrote *The Californians* and Charles Caldwell Dobie, *San Francisco: A Pageant.* Sculptors

Douglas Tilden and Haig Patigian have lived here, and the painter Maynard Dixon. In a walled cavern built from an old cistern, "Dad" Demarest, high priest of Russian Hill's bohemia since 1872, lived for two weeks after the fire in 1906—and he still keeps it fitted up as a den, "just in case." Tall apartment buildings began invading bohemia's province on the Hill long ago. Higher and higher the newcomers have lifted their steel-and-concrete shafts. But despite this invasion, Russian Hill is still a world removed, where steps climb and brick-flagged lanes twine up sheer heights between green hedges. Gracious homes and rambling studios perch among gardens spilling downhill on its slopes. Among the Tudor villas and the neo-French chateaux, chastely simple dwellings of plywood and glass brick, designed with corner windows and sun decks to admit sunlight, air, and the view, have begun to appear of late years.

POINTS OF INTEREST

(From Market and Powell Sts., the Washington and Jackson cable car crosses Nob Hill via Powell and Jackson Sts.; from Market and California Sts., the California St. cable car via California; from the Ferry Building, the Sacramento St. cable car via Sacramento. From Market and O'Farrell Sts., the O'Farrell, Jones and Hyde Sts. cable car crosses Russian Hill via Hyde; from the Ferry Building, the Municipal Railway "E" car via Union St.)

127. From the verge of the hill, the 20-story MARK HOPKINS HOTEL, SE. corner California and Mason Sts., above a triangular plaza entered between pylons and enclosed by balustrades, lifts its beacon-tipped minarets 563 feet above sea level. Opened in December 1926, it looks down on one of the city's most magnificent panoramas.

Famous orchestras broadcast nightly beneath painted peacocks flaunting their plumage on the ceiling of Peacock Court. Adjoining is the Room of the Dons, decorated with the murals of Maynard Dixon and Frank Van Sloun, depicting the story of California with its recurrent theme of "Golden Dreams." "The Mark" is the scene of such established cults as the Friday night dance and the annual Junior League dance and fashion show.

To guests of sybaritic tastes, the solid gold bathroom fixtures of several of the tower apartments may recall the overwhelming lavishness of the mansion which railroad magnate Mark Hopkins built on the site in the 1870's. Presented after Hopkins' death to the San Francisco Art Association, the mansion became the scene of extravagant annual Mardi Gras balls.

128. On the foundations laid by James G. ("Bonanza Jim") Fair for a Nob Hill mansion which would outshine all others, the FAIR-

MONT HOTEL, California, Mason, Sacramento, and Powell Sts., rears its lordly pile of white granite. Only the granite walls enclosing the grounds had been built when domestic troubles interrupted Fair's plans. To memorialize her father, "Tessie" Fair Oelrichs undertook the erection of a de luxe hotel. The Fairmont stood complete but for its windows—and crates of sumptuous furnishings had been moved into the lobby—when the fire of 1906 demolished everything but the walls. Under the direction of Stanford White the hotel was repaired and refurnished, and on April 17, 1907—one day short of the anniversary of the fire—it was opened with a banquet for 500 guests. It at once became the resort of the elite, led by Ned Greenway, self-appointed arbiter of the city's "Four Hundred."

From a semicircular drive flanked by lawns and shrubs, a porte-cochère leads to the entrance, marked by six gray stone columns rising six stories to the roof. From the walls of the vast, white-columned lobby, splashed with vivid red furnishings, look down panelled Florentine mirrors mounted in carved frames inlaid with gold leaf, imported from the Castello di Vincigliata in Italy. From the lobby open the Gold Room, scene of brilliant Army and Navy balls; the Laurel Court, fashionable at tea time; and the Venetian Room, where guests dance to "name bands." In the Circus Lounge, against a background of gold leaf, eight murals by Esther, Margaret, and Helen Bruton depict men and animals performing under the "big top." Popular Fairmont diversions are swimming in the fresh-water Terrace Plunge (*open 10-10*) and sun-bathing on the Terrace Lawn overlooking the Bay.

129. The PACIFIC UNION CLUB, NW. corner California and Mason Sts., occupies the only residence on the hill to survive the fire of 1906—the massive $1,500,000 Connecticut brownstone mansion built by James C. Flood after his return from a trip to New York, where he was impressed by the brownstone mansions of the rich. Flood's "thirty-thousand-dollar brass fence," recalled Amelia Ransome Neville, "flashed for the entire length of two blocks on the square . . . and it was the sole task of one retainer to keep it bright." The foundations of the Flood fortune were laid in the "Auction Lunch" kept by Flood and his partner, W. S. O'Brien, "where an especially fine fish stew drew Patrons from the Stock Exchange nearby. Daily the proprietors heard talk of stocks and mining shares and together decided to invest. Results were overwhelming."

In Steve Whipple's saloon on Commercial Street was founded the Pacific Club, first "gentlemen's club" in San Francisco, of which Cutler McAllister, brother of New York's social arbiter, Ward, was a founder. It was amalgamated eventually with the rival Union Club, founded in 1854. Its memberships, restricted to 100, pass like inheritances from father to son. Near Point Reyes, in Marin County, members hunt and fish in a preserve of 76,000 acres.

130. Where nursemaids trundle streamlined prams along the shrubbery-bordered paths of HUNTINGTON PARK, California, Taylor, and Sacramento Sts., Collis P. Huntington used to stride up to his front door from the cable car stop on California Street. Huntington bought his mansion from the widow of his one-time friend, David D. Colton, legal counsel for the "Big Four." After Colton's mysterious death in 1878, the "Four" brought pressure upon her for the return of securities on the grounds that Colton had embezzled funds from their properties. Mrs. Colton vindicated her husband's name by introducing at a subsequent trial the famous "Colton Letters" exposing the machinations by which the four partners had acquired their railroad properties. From his enemy in court, Huntington bought Colton's house. Unlike the mansions of most of his contemporaries, the railroad lawyer's was in good taste, copied (wrote Mrs. Neville) "from a famous white marble palace of Italy . . ." Its site was bequeathed by Huntington's widow to the city in 1915.

131. Like those Gothic churches of the Middle Ages under construction for generations, GRACE CATHEDRAL, California, Taylor, Sacramento, and Jones Sts., is not finished, although its cornerstone was laid by Bishop William Ford Nichols 30 years ago. Its spire— from which an illuminated cross will rise some day 230 feet above the hilltop—is still a gaunt skeleton of orange-painted girders. The dream which inspired its founders has been nurtured since September 1863, when the Right Reverend William Ingraham Kip, first Episcopal Bishop in California, placed his Episcopal Chair in Grace Church (founded 1850), thus establishing the first cathedral seat of the Protestant Episcopal Church in America.

The Grace Cathedral of Bishop Kip's day (California and Stockton Streets) was destroyed in the 1906 fire. On January 27, 1914, the Founders' Crypt of the new church was opened. Halted by the War, construction was resumed toward the end of the next decade, to be delayed again by the economic depression. Present (1940) completed units include the sanctuary, choir, north and south transepts, three bays of the nave, and the Chapel of Grace. When completed the north tower will support a carillon whose 44 bells—weighing from twelve pounds to six tons each—were cast in Croydon, England. The carillon is the gift of Dr. Nathaniel Coulson.

The cathedral is 340 feet long and 119 feet wide (across the main front). The towers rise 158 feet from the street; the 87-foot-high nave extends 300 feet. The use of undisguised concrete for the exterior gives the massive, buttressed walls an air of enduring strength. In the Chapel of Grace are an altar from tenth-century France, an altar rail of Travertine marble, and a reredos of fourteenth-century Flemish wood carving.

Property on which the cathedral stands was deeded to the diocese by the heirs of Charles Crocker, whose mansion stood here until 1906. Attempting to acquire possession of the whole block in 1877, Crocker was defied by a Mr. Yung, whose home occupied a 25-foot strip on Sacramento Street. In revenge, Crocker had Yung's property hemmed in by a fence that shut out the sunlight. During the ensuing deadlock gripmen stopped their cable cars at the spot, hackmen brought ogling tourists, and souvenir seekers removed pickets from the "spite" fence. It was not until after the death of the principals that the Crocker family obtained the property.

132. Second oldest surviving residence in San Francisco, the AT-KINSON HOUSE (*private*), 1052 Broadway, was built by Joseph H. Atkinson and his wife in 1853. Entered through an iron gate from the grass-grown cobblestones of the street, the gray plaster two-story house clings to the steep hillside, its narrow second-story balconies level with the terrace at one side. Through creepers and ferns wind narrow brick-flagged paths. The old house was occupied by Atkinson's relatives until recent years.

133. The OCTAGONAL HOUSE (*private*), 1067 Green St., first of a number of such architectural oddities conceived by an early Eastern builder, has been occupied continuously by descendants of the French settler, Feusier, for whom it was built in 1858. With every room a front room, the large double windows on all sides stare like so many Argus eyes upon a world of rapid change.

134. Overlooking the Golden Gate from the end of a graveled walk between interlacing plane trees, half-way down the hill from the Lombard Street Reservoir, the GEORGE STERLING MEMORIAL, Hyde, Greenwich, and Lombard Sts., is a simple bench inlaid with warm-hued tiles, dedicated by the Spring Valley Water Company June 25, 1928, "To Remember George Sterling, 1869-1926." The bronze tablet is inscribed with a stanza from the "Song of Friendship" (a musical composition whose lyrics were written by Sterling) and a quotation from the poet's "Ode to Shelley":

> "O Singer, Fled Afar!
> The Erected Darkness Shall But Isle the Star
> That Was Your Voice to Man,
> Till Morning Come Again
> And Of the Night That Song Alone Remain."

Sterling's death by his own hand marked for many of his admirers the passing of that bohemia of which he had been one of the chief representatives.

135. An abandoned rain-filled cistern saved San Francisco's oldest surviving residence, the WILLIAM PENN HUMPHRIES HOUSE (*private*), NE. corner Chestnut and Hyde Sts., from the 1906 fire. The owner's sons and neighbors cleared the debris from the unused backyard reservoir and drenched the house with buckets of water. The handiwork of William Squires Clark, who built the town's first wharf, the house was constructed in 1852 of heavy white oak timbers brought around the Horn. Its broad verandas resemble the decks and its third story, the captain's bridge of a ship. Into the garden at its feet, flagstones lead from wooden gates, one shadowed by a towering eucalyptus, the other by a twisted acacia. Along its western side gnarled cypresses border the tall latticed fence built for a windbreak. Honeysuckle climbs about the verandas, weeds glut the yards, lattices and fences are falling. Like many another ancient residence, the mansion now is a "guest house"; efforts to secure its purchase by the City and County of San Francisco for preservation as a museum have been unsuccessful.

136. Above a hillside garden overlooking the Bay soars the tile-roofed tower of the CALIFORNIA SCHOOL OF FINE ARTS (*open Mon.-Sat. 9-4; Mon., Wed., Fri., 7-10 also*), Chestnut and Jones Sts., dominating the rambling, three-story structure of painted concrete, which surrounds a patio with a tiled fountain at its center. A constantly changing student exhibit of murals and frescoes covers the interior walls. In one of the studios is Diego Rivera's *Age of Industry,* one of two Rivera murals executed in San Francisco. The school was built in 1923 by the San Francisco Art Association, from profits derived by the sale of the Mark Hopkins property on Nob Hill, where since 1893 it had conducted the Mark Hopkins Institute of Art. It houses the ANNE BREMER MEMORIAL LIBRARY (*open to students Mon.-Fri. 10-5*), endowed by art patron Albert Bender, which contains fine prints, current art publications, and valuable books on ancient and modern art. A full program of courses in fine and applied arts is conducted for an annual enrollment of about 650 students.

Embarcadero

". . . that harbor so remarkable and so spacious that in it may be established shipyards, docks, and anything that may be wished."

—FATHER PEDRO FONT (1776)

THE story of San Francisco is largely the story of its water front. As if it had grown up out of the sea, the original town clung so closely to the water's edge that one might almost have fancied its settlers—newly landed from shipboard, most of them—were reluctant to take to dry land. For years all the city's traffic passed up and down the long wooden wharves, sagging with business houses that ranged from saloons to banks. Many of the old ships lie buried now beneath dry land. Above the level of the tides that once lapped the pilings, streetcars thunder. Even old East Street, last of the water-front thoroughfares, has gone the way of the sailing vessels which once thrust proud figureheads above the wharves' wooden bulkheads. Around the Peninsula's edge, from Fisherman's Wharf to China Basin, sweeps the paved crescent of the 200-foot-wide Embarcadero, lined with immense concrete piers. Where the four-masters and square-riggers once disembarked, cargo-ships and luxury liners rest alongside vast warehouses, unloading their goods from all the corners of the earth.

By night the Embarcadero is a wide boulevard, dimly lighted and nearly deserted, often swathed in fog. Its silence is broken by the lonely howl of a fog siren, the raucous scream of a circling seagull, or the muffled rattle of a winch on a freighter loading under floodlights. The sudden blast of a departing steamer, the far-off screech of freight-cars being shunted onto a siding by a puffing Belt Line locomotive shake the nocturnal quiet. The smells of copra, of oakum, raw sugar, roasting coffee and rotting piles, and mud and salt water creep up the darkened streets.

Even before the eight o'clock wail of the Ferry Building siren, the Embarcadero comes violently to life. From side streets great trucks roll through the yawning doors of the piers. The longshoremen, clustered in groups before the pier gates, swarm up ladders and across gangplanks. The jitneys, small tractor-like conveyances, trailing long lines of flat trucks, wind in and out of traffic; the comical lumber carriers, like monsters with lumber strapped to their undersides, rattle along the street. Careening taxis, rumbling underslung vans and drays, and scurrying pedestrians suddenly transform the water front into a traffic-thronged artery.

Street Scenes

CALIFORNIA STREET STILL CHALLENGES THE CABLE CAR

CHINESE NEW YEAR CELEBRATION

CHINATOWN

CHINESE CHILDREN AT THANKSGIVING PLAYGROUND PARTY

HOTEL 中興旅舘

GRANT AVENUE

FISHERMAN'S WHARF

SS. PETER AND PAUL CHURCH

PACIFIC UNION CLUB, MARK HOPKINS
AND FAIRMONT HOTELS ON NOB HILL

TELEGRAPH HILL FROM THE PRECIPITOUS SIDE

OCTAGONAL HOUSE ON RUSSIAN HILL, BUILT IN 1854

PACIFIC HEIGHTS

A never-ending stream of vehicles brings the exports of the Bay area and the West and the imports of both the hemispheres. Stored in the Embarcadero's huge warehouses are sacks of green coffee from Brazil; ripening bananas from Central America; copra and spices from the South Seas; tea, sugar, and chocolate; cotton and kapok; paint and oil; and all the thousand varieties of products offered by a world market. Here, awaiting transshipment, are wines from Portugal, France, and Germany; English whisky and Italian vermouth; burlap from Calcutta and glassware from Antwerp; beans from Mexico and linen yarn from northern Ireland.

North of the Ferry Building dock the vessels of foreign lines. Here, too, are berths for many of the old stern-wheelers, and of barges and river boats of the Sacramento and San Joaquin Rivers which bring to San Francisco the products of central California's great agricultural plains.

South of the Ferry Building dock the big transpacific passenger ships. Near China Basin are several piers from which sail the around-the-world boats of the American President Line (formerly Dollar Lines). Sailing and docking days bring a fleet of taxis to the pier head with flowers, passengers, and dignitaries. When the Pacific Fleet is anchored in Man-o'-War Row, the bluejackets disembark from the tenders at Pier 14.

Around China Basin and the long narrow channel extending inland from the Embarcadero's southern end are railway freight yards, warehouses, and oil and lumber piers. Of the bridges that span the channel, most important is the trunnion bascule lifting bridge at Third and Channel Streets, built in 1933, one of the largest of its type. On the south side of the channel entrance are the Santa Fe Railway Company's wharves, with a mechanically adjustable ramp that can be raised or lowered with the level of the tide. To adjoining piers are moored many large purse-seiners, driven south by winter storms, whose home ports include such places as Chignik, Nome, Sitka, Juneau, and Gig Harbor. Fishing in southern latitudes during winter, they utilize San Francisco as their base.

Busiest section of the Embarcadero is the stretch between the Ferry Building and the Matson Line docks. Opposite the great concrete piers is a string of water-front hotels, saloons, cafés, billiard parlors, barber shops, and clothing stores. The one sail loft which remains has turned long since to making awnings. In the block between Market and Mission Streets the atmosphere of the old water front lingers in the saloons, lunch rooms, and stores where seafaring men and shore workers gather.

As on most American water fronts, store windows are stuffed with dungarees, gloves, white caps, good luck charms, cargo hooks, and accordions. A tattoo artist decorates manly arms and chests with glamour girls, cupids, and crossed anchors. Gone today are the bum-boatmen, who once climbed aboard incoming ships from rowboats with articles to sell; but peddlers patrol the Embarcadero, some pushing carts with candy and fruits, mystic charms and shoestrings, lottery and sweepstakes tickets. In many cafes or saloons a longshoreman can cash his "brass," the small numbered metal token given him for presentation at the company pay windows. For cashing it, the charge is usually five cents on the dollar.

Scalers, seamen, longshoremen, warehousemen—all have their hiring halls and union headquarters in the small area bounded by the Embarcadero, Market, Clay, and Drumm Streets, known to seafaring men and dock workers as the "Front." Here the men congregate between shifts and between jobs awaiting their turn for new jobs handed out through union dispatchers. Their talk is interminably of union contracts, politics, jobs, lottery tickets, and horse racing. From the various hiring halls the men are sent out, the longshoremen sometimes hurrying to docks and ports as far away as Crockett in Contra Costa County and the seamen packing their suitcases of working "gear" to the ships. All dispatching is done by rotation: this is the hiring hall system for which the men fought in the 1934 maritime strike.

The longshoremen with their white caps and felt hats, their black jackets and hickory shirts, their cargo hooks slung in hip pockets, outnumber the workers of any other craft in the maritime industry. As soon as a ship is tied up, they go aboard, and as the winches begin to rattle, unloading is under way. The jitney drivers pull up alongside with their trucks; checkers keep track of every piece of cargo. Meanwhile, ship scalers are aboard cleaning out empty holds, boiler tubes and fire boxes, painting sides and stacks, scraping decks, and doing the thousand jobs required to make a vessel shipshape.

The produce commission district, a stone's throw from the water front in the area bounded by Sacramento, Front, Pacific, and Drumm Streets, also bustles with activity in early morning. A district of narrow streets lined with roofed sidewalks and low brick buildings, it is the receiving depot for the fresh produce that finds its way into the kitchens, restaurants, and hotels of the city. Long before daybreak— in the summer, as early as one o'clock—trucks large and small begin to arrive from the country with fruits and vegetables. From poultry houses come the crowing and cackling of fowls aroused by the lights and commotion. The clatter of hand-trucking and a babel of dialects arise. About six o'clock the light delivery trucks of local markets begin to arrive. By this time a pedestrian can barely squeeze past the crates, hampers, boxes, and bags along the sidewalks.

The stacks of produce dwindle so rapidly that by nine o'clock the busiest part of the district's day is over. Then come the late buyers, known as "cleaners-up," to take advantage of lowered prices; street peddlers with dilapidated trucks, and poverty-stricken old men and women, carrying bags, to search the gutters for fruit and vegetables dropped or flung away. By afternoon this district is almost deserted.

"San Francisco is the only port in the United States," reports the United States Board of Engineers for Rivers and Harbors, "where the water front is owned and has been developed by the State, and where also, the public terminal developments have been connected with one another and with rail carriers by the Belt Line, owned and operated by the State." In 1938, the State Board of Harbor Commissioners, celebrating its control of the water front since 1863, reported the port of San Francisco had "43 piers available for handling general cargo; 17.5 miles of berthing space; 193 acres of cargo space; terminals and warehouses for special cargo—a grand total of 1,912 acres owned by the State of California. A shipside refrigeration and products terminal equipped with modern facilities for handling and storing agricultural products and perishable commodities in transit; a grain terminal for cleaning, grading and loading grain for export; special facilities for the promotion and development of the fishing industry at Fisherman's Wharf; tanks and pipelines for handling Oriental vegetable oils and molasses; fumigating plants for cotton; lumber terminals. The entire water front and adjacent warehouses and industries are served by the State Belt Railroad, which has 66 miles of track and direct connection with all transcontinental and local railroads. . . . The Port's ensemble of wharves, piers, terminals and commercial shipping facilities virtually as they exist today, have been constructed during the last 28 years and are valued at close to $42,000,000. All the facilities of the port are appraised at $86,000,000."

Before there was an Embarcadero the shoreline of a circling lagoon swept inward from Clark's Point at the base of Telegraph Hill and outward again to Rincon Point near the foot of Harrison Street. From August, 1775, when Lieutenant Juan Manuel de Ayala first sailed the *San Carlos* through the Golden Gate until September, 1848, when the brig *Belfast* docked at the water-front's first pile wharf, cargoes were lightered from vessel to shore. The favored landing place was Clark's Point, the small, rocky promontory sheltering Yerba Buena Cove on the north, first known as the Punta del Embarcadero (Point of the Landing Place). Here in September, 1847 William Squires Clark persuaded the Town Council to authorize construction of a public pier (*see bronze plaque on wall of Montevideo and Parodi, Inc. Building, 100-110 Broadway*). Sufficient only to pay for the pier's foundations, the $1,000 appropriated was exhausted by the following January. In 1848 the Town Council agreed to appropriate $2,000 more for continuance of the work. This, when completed, was the first wharf built on piles on the Pacific Coast north of Panama.

"The crowd of shipping, two or three miles in length, stretched along the water . . ." wrote globe-trotter Bayard Taylor before the end of 1849. "There is probably not a more exciting and bustling scene of business activity in any part of the world, than can be witnessed on almost any day, Sunday excepted, at Broadway Street wharf, San Francisco, at a few minutes before 4 o'clock p.m. Men and women are hurrying to and fro; drays, carriages, express wagons and horsemen dash past. . . . Clark's Point is to San Francisco what Whitehall is to New York."

First wharf for deep-water shipping was Central or Long Wharf, built along the line of Commercial Street, which by the end of 1849 had been extended to a length of 800 feet. It was used by most of the immense fleet of vessels from all the world which anchored in the Bay in the winter of 1849-50. By October, 1850, an aggregate of 5,000 feet of new wharves had been constructed at an estimated outlay of $1,000,000. The wharf building was accomplished in haphazard fashion. Not until May 1851, when the State legislature passed the Second Water Lot Bill, was the city empowered to permit construction of wharves beyond the city line. No less than eight wharves, however, had been built by this time. Nearly one half of San Francisco rose on piles above water. The moment a new wharf was completed, up went frame shanties to house a gambling den, provision dealer, clothing house, or liquor salesman.

Soon, however, more substantial structures were being erected. Of these, perhaps the most famous was Meiggs' Wharf, built by Henry Meiggs in 1853. From the water line (then Francisco Street) at the foot of Mason Street, Meiggs' L-shaped pier, 42 feet wide, ran 1,600 feet north to the line of Jefferson Street and 360 feet east. Long after its builder had absconded to Peru (where he made a fortune building a railway through the Andes), following discovery of his embezzlement of $800,000 in city funds, the wharf was a terminal for ferryboats plying to Alcatraz and Sausalito. From the foot of Sansome Street, in the shadow of Telegraph Hill, ran the North Point Docks, built in 1853, where for many years landed most of the city's French and Italian immigrants.

The ten-year leases under which most of the important wharves operated expired in 1863—and in that year was appointed a State Board of Harbor Commissioners, which refused to grant renewals. Not until 1867, because of litigation with wharf-owners, was the board able to proceed with harbor development. A channel 60 feet wide was dredged 20 feet below low tide level, in which loads of rock dumped by scows and lighters were piled up in a ridge reaching the level of mean low tide. On top of the embankment were laid a foundation of concrete and, on top of the concrete, a wall of masonry. But the protracted litigation with water-front property owners, the decline in shipping caused by competition of the newly completed transcontinental railroad, and the grafting of private contractors who had undertaken to build the sea wall—all combined to hold up the work. Within two years after construction had been resumed in 1877, a thousand feet of the wall west of Kearny Street had been completed. From the scarred eastern flanks of Telegraph Hill, long lines of carts transported rock. In the course of construction, tons of rock were gouged from the hill's slopes, and tons more (more than 1,000,000) were ferried from Sheep Island, off Port Richmond. Not until 1913 was the sea wall finally completed.

The Belt Line Railroad was first debated in 1873, but not until 1890 was a mile-long line with a three-rail track built for both narrow- and standard-gauge cars. At first confined to the section north of Market Street, the road was extended southward in 1912 to link the entire commercial water front with rail connections to the south and thereafter westward through the tunnel under Fort Mason to the Presidio and southward to Islais Creek Channel.

Revolutionary as the port's physical changes have been in the past century, no less marked have been the differences wrought in the lives of the men who earn their livelihood on its ships and shores. During the years after '49, "the Front" gained the reputation of being one of the toughest spots in the world. In the last half of the century the shortage in sailors was so great that kidnapping or "shanghaiing" was practiced. The very expression "shanghaiing" originated in San Francisco in the days when voyages to Shanghai were so hazardous that a "Shanghai voyage" came to mean any long sea trip.

Notorious among the crimp joints of the 1860's was a saloon and boarding house conducted on Davis Street by a harridan named Miss Piggott. Here operated one Nikko, a Laplander whose specialty was the substitution of dummies and corpses for the drunken sailors the ships' captains thought they were hiring. Miss Piggott had a rival in Mother Bronson, who ran a place on Steuart Street. She would size up a likely customer, smack him over the head with a bung-starter, and drop him through a trap door to the cellar below where he awaited transfer to a ship.

Shanghai Kelly, a red-headed Irishman who ran a three-story saloon and lodging house at 33 Pacific Street, was probably the most notorious crimp ever to operate in San Francisco. The tide swished darkly beneath three trap doors built in front of his bar. Beneath the trap doors, boats lay in readiness. Kelly's most spectacular performance came in the middle 1870's. Three ships in the harbor needed crews. One was the notorious hell-ship *Reefer,* from New York. Kelly engaged to supply men. He chartered the paddle-wheel steamer *Goliath* and announced a picnic with free drinks to celebrate his "birthday." The entire Barbary Coast responded. Once in the harbor, Kelly fed his guests doped liquor, pulled alongside the *Reefer* and the other two ships, and delivered more than 90 men.

During the 1890's six policemen sent successively to arrest a Chilean, Calico Jim, were kidnapped in turn and put aboard outward bound boats. Ultimately, all six returned to San Francisco, swearing vengeance. The crimp had gone to South America. The policemen raised a fund and sent one of their number to Chile to wreak vengeance. Having found Calico Jim, he pumped six bullets into him, one for each policeman, and returned to duty.

The most famous runner for sailors' boardinghouses was Johnny Devine, the "Shanghai Chicken," who had lost his hand in some scrap and had replaced it with an iron hook. Devine was a burglar, footpad, sneak thief, pimp, and almost everything else disreputable. His favorite stunt was to highjack sailors from other runners.

Of all that lively collection of crimps, highjackers, burglars, pimps, and ordinary rascals, the least vicious—if not the least dangerous— seems to have been Michael Conner, proprietor of the Chain Locker at Main and Bryant Streets. Deeply religious, he boasted of never telling a lie. When ships' captains came seeking able seamen, Conner could swear that his clients had experience—for he had rigged up in his backyard a mast and spars whereon his "seasoned sailors" were put through the rudiments. On the floor of his saloon was a cow's horn, around which Conner would make the seamen walk several times so that he might truthfully say they had been "round the Horn."

The Embarcadero's reputation for toughness rapidly is being woven into legend, along with the doings of the pioneers. San Francisco's water front is no longer a shadowy haunt, full of unsuspected perils. Today, it occupies a place in the forefront of the city's industrial, commercial, and social life. The water-front men take an informed interest in civic affairs—and many of them own comfortable homes out on the avenues.

POINTS OF INTEREST

137. The MARINE EXCHANGE LOOKOUT STATION, Pier 45, Embarcadero and Chestnut St., whose glassed-in, hexagon-shaped cubicle, equipped with a powerful telescope, commands a sweeping view of the Golden Gate, has been called "The Eyes of the Harbor." At the dock below lies the launch *Jerry Dailey,* ready to carry its crew of old-timers through the Gate to meet incoming vessels whenever telephonic reports from the Marine Exchange's other lookout station at Point Lobos announce that a vessel has been sighted on the horizon. The lookout delivers mail and instructions for docking, receives cargo statistics, running time, and other marine news. Returning to the station, he telephones the information to the Marine Exchange, where news of the ship's arrival is listed on the blackboards.

Since its organization in 1851, the Marine Exchange has kept its day-and-night watch for inbound ships, at first with the aid of the lookout station erected by Messrs. Sweeney and Baugh in 1849 on Telegraph Hill, to which signals were relayed from the Point Lobos lookout.

138. A relic of the old days is FLINT'S WAREHOUSE, Filbert, Battery, and Sansome Sts., built in 1854 when the Bay washed at the piles of the Battery Street wharf. Originally two stories high, it was

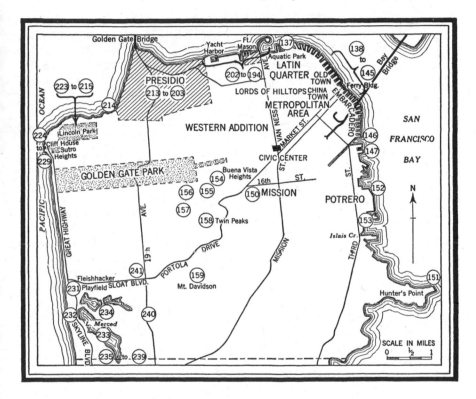

constructed of stone torn from near-by Telegraph Hill; but when the tide lands were filled, the first floor became the basement. Loading beams that served the sturdy square-rigged sailing ships of the 1850's still hang above the Battery Street doorways. Today, the venerable structure, steel-braced and patched with variegated brick but still equipped with its ancient red iron shutters, is a storage plant for automobiles.

139. One police boat, the *D. A. WHITE*, moored at Pier 7, serves the entire San Francisco water front. It is a 66-foot, shallow-keeled vessel powered by two Diesel motors of 190 horsepower each which develop a speed of 16 knots; its two-way radio enables it to keep in contact with the Harbor Police Station, under whose jurisdiction it

operates. Chief duties include rescuing amateur yachtsmen from the mud flats and grappling corpses from the murky waters of the Bay.

140. The HARBOR POLICE STATION, NE. corner Drumm and Sacramento Sts., a compact, two-story, gray stone building, is head-quarters for police control over the water-front area. One of its main concerns is thievery on the docks, commonly known as "poaching the cargo."

141. The HARBOR EMERGENCY HOSPITAL, 88 Sacramento St., is largely a field hospital for derelicts. Here, prisoners from the City Jail and water-front "sherry bums," as well as injured sailors and longshoremen receive treatment in two twelve-bed emergency wards. The present hospital, at this location since 1926, is staffed by a surgeon, nurse, steward, and ambulance driver. Its equipment includes a Drinker respirator for use in drowning cases.

142. The oldest maritime organization on the Pacific Coast has its headquarters at the BAR PILOTS STATION, Pier 7, Embarcadero and Broadway; for 90 years, from 1850 to 1940, the San Francisco Bar Pilots have been steering vessels over the San Francisco bar and through the Golden Gate to anchorage in the Bay. All master mariners, the 20 pilots are former sea captains of long experience on the Pacific Coast. They maintain three auxiliary schooners as pilot boats, each of which carries an engineer, a boat keeper, a cook, and three sailors. Day and night one of these vessels stands by, about six miles off the Golden Gate, with sails spread to keep an even keel in high seas. During its five days at sea, the crew is on constant call. To the schooner at sea, the shore station reports ship movements by means of a wireless telephone system—the only one in the world maintained by a pilotage service. Whenever an approaching vessel requires a pilot, the schooner is brought around to its lee. In a small boat the pilot is rowed over to the inbound ship. On the bridge of the vessel, he takes charge, steering a safe course into the harbor. Under the jurisdiction of the State Pilot Commission, the bar pilots are obliged to keep a 24-hour watch on the bar and to provide pilotage service without undue delay to any ship requesting it.

143. More universally accepted as a symbol of San Francisco than any other single landmark, the FERRY BUILDING, Embarcadero and Market St., has served to identify the city in the minds of countless travelers throughout the world. Before the completion of the two bridges across the Bay, this was the gateway to San Francisco, its high clock tower the most conspicuous feature of the skyline to passengers on the lumbering ferries which churned the waters for nearly nine decades. In the years immediately preceding the opening of train service across the San Francisco-Oakland Bay Bridge, the long hallways of the historic structure echoed to the footsteps of as many as 50,000,000 passengers in a single year—a volume of traffic exceeded only by Charing

Cross Station in London. For 40 years the flower stand on the ground floor was a favored rendezvous where San Franciscans met visiting friends in the midst of a hubbub of talk, newsboys' shouts, slamming taxicab doors, and rumbling streetcars. Now the stairways and corridors are all but deserted, since only overland railroad passengers and Treasure Island pleasure-seekers come and go from the ferry slips.

Erected by the State Board of Harbor Commissioners (1896-1903) on a foundation of piles beyond the edge of the original loose-rock sea wall, the Ferry Building was hailed at its opening in July, 1898 as the most solidly constructed edifice in California. It was built to replace the old Central Terminal Building erected in 1877, a wooden shed over the three ferry slips operated by the Central Pacific, Atlantic and Pacific, and South Pacific Coast Railways, when the volume of traffic across the Bay dictated an improvement in terminal facilities.

Architect Arthur Paige Brown designed a two-story building with an arcaded front extending along the water front for 661 feet. The clock tower, rising 235 feet above the ground—a respectable height in its day—was modeled after the famous Giralda Tower of Spains' Cathedral of Seville. Like the rest of the building, it was faced with gray Colusa sandstone until the 1906 earthquake shook off the stone blocks and they were replaced by concrete. Into the grand nave extending the whole length of the building on the second floor lead corridors giving access to the upper decks of the ferryboats.

For a year after April 18, 1906, the great hands of the clock dials on the tower pointed to 5:17—the time at which the earthquake struck. When first installed, the clock was operated by a long cable wound on a drum, and a 14-foot pendulum; it has since been equipped to run by electricity. Each of the four 2,500-pound dials on the four sides of the tower measures 23½ feet in diameter; each of the numerals, 2½ feet in height. The hour hands are 7 and the minute hands 11 feet long.

Extending the entire length of the grand nave on the second floor is a PANORAMA MAP in relief of the State of California, modeled from United States Geological Survey maps by 25 artists, engineers, electricians, and carpenters, who spent two years (1923-25) fabricating it from cardboard, magnesite, and paint at a cost of $100,000. An automatic electric control regulates a lighting system simulating daylight, sunrise, and sunset and operates a miniature Mount Lassen in eruption. The map is 600 feet long and 18 wide, on a scale of 6 inches to the mile. It is backed by a cyclorama of the Sierra Nevada.

Opposite a huge mosaic of the Great Seal of California in the floor of the nave is the mezzanine stairway leading to the CALIFORNIA STATE MINING BUREAU MINERAL MUSEUM (*open Mon.-Fri. 9-5, Sat. 9-12*), its laboratory, and the John Hammond Mining Library of 9,000 volumes. The museum, fifth largest of its type in the United States, contains specimens of minerals from every part of the world, facsimiles of all of the important nuggets unearthed in California, and models of gold and diamond mines and ore crushers. The institution has been supported by the State and by individual contributors ever since its inception in 1897. J. C. Davis, member of the first board of trustees, has been the principal donor.

Flanking the main entrance to the Ferry Building are two short SECTIONS OF BAY BRIDGE CABLES, the Golden Gate Bridge section to the north and the San Francisco-Oakland Bay Bridge section to the south.

144. From the NAVY LANDING, Pier 14, Embarcadero between Mission and Howard Sts., launches ply back and forth between landing stage and shipside, transporting crowds of blueclad Navy men and sightseeing visitors, whenever the United States Pacific Fleet is tied up along "Man-o'-War Row."

145. Alongside the two-story engine house of the EMBAR-CADERO FIRE DEPARTMENT, Pier 22, Embarcadero between Folsom and Harrison Sts., are anchored one of the harbor's two gleaming red and black, brass-trimmed fire boats, and one of its two auxiliary tugs. The harbor firefighting unit of 23 men is maintained jointly by the State Board of Harbor Commissioners and the city. The fire boats are each equipped with monitor batteries, more than 5,000 feet of hose, and water towers which can be raised to a height of 55 feet above deck. They respond to emergency calls from all parts of the Bay and its islands.

146. Overlooking the China Basin Channel, the STATE REFRIG-ERATION PLANT, between Embarcadero and Third Sts., offers storage and transfer facilities for immense quantities of fresh fruit and vegetables awaiting shipment to foreign markets. In the refrigeration plant's 450,000 cubic feet of space, more than 200,000 packages of fruit can be precooled simultaneously. The fruit is unloaded from trucks on a second-floor platform along the land side and loaded aboard ship from a platform on the water side.

147. At the UNITED FRUIT COMPANY DOCKS, south side of China Basin Channel west of Third St. Bridge, one of the fruit company's banana boats from Central America ties up each Thursday. Occasionally, a frightened monkey or small boa constrictor, half frozen from long hours in refrigerated hatches, comes out of the dark with the fruit. The firm operates three freight and passenger steamships between San Francisco and Puerto Armuelles, Panama. Of Danish registry, the vessels are specially constructed for transporting bananas, each having a cargo capacity of 60,000 stems. The unloading equipment on the pier includes electrically operated traveling conveyors and belts. Issuing from the vessel's holds in endless streams, the banana stems are sorted according to degrees of ripeness and then loaded into refrigerator cars. The capacity of the unloading equipment is 30,000 stems in eight hours.

South of Market

". . . from all around, the hum of corporate life, of beaten bells,
and steam, and running carriages, goes cheerily abroad . . ."
—ROBERT LOUIS STEVENSON

HISTORY has played fast and loose with that great segment of the city which sprawls southward from Market Street to the San Francisco-San Mateo County line. Athwart historic Rincon Hill, fashionable residential quarter of Gold Rush days, the streamlined approach to the San Francisco-Oakland Bay Bridge rises from an area of factories, machine shops, railroad terminals, "skid-road" hotels, and Greek restaurants. Westward from the water front—lined to Hunter's Point with warehouses, stockyards, and shipbuilding plants—the district spreads across Potrero Hill to the heights of Twin Peaks, Buena Vista Park, Mount Olympus, and Mount Davidson. A broad residential district whose most venerable landmark is Mission Dolores, occupying a sheltered coastal plain and adjacent hillsides, "The Mission" is San Francisco's workshop, where live most of the city's working-class population. Here were the ranchos of Spanish dons, the suburbs of the Argonauts; but today this is the city's most "American" section, an area as socially homogeneous as an Iowa town.

POINTS OF INTEREST

148. Shimmering green fingers of ivy cling to the face of ST. PATRICK'S CHURCH, Mission between Third and Fourth Sts., "the most Irish church in all America." Considered to be one of the finest examples of early Gothic ecclesiastical architecture outside Europe, it was rebuilt after 1906 from the charred shell of Old St. Patrick's (1868). First mass was celebrated in 1851 by Father John Maginnis in a little room on Fourth and Jessie Streets; from this chapel grew St. Patrick's Parish, whose first church building was erected in 1854 on the present site of the Palace Hotel.

To rebuild the gutted interior of the present church, Father John Rogers, successor to its founder, brought from Ireland Caen stone and green translucent marble of Connemara. Restored stained glass windows depict the visions of St. Patrick, the Four Apostles, and scenes from Irish mythology. Irish artist Mia Cranwill designed the main altar's metal crucifix inlaid with precious stones and the vestments of cloth-of-gold, embroidered in ancient Gaelic patterns.

149. Dusty and threadbare is the landmark of old SOUTH PARK, Third between Bryant and Brannan Sts., once enclosed by an ornamental iron fence to keep the "shovelry" from the retreat wherein scions of the Gold Rush "chivalry" scampered in seclusion. Today it is an obscure little parkway dominated by the approach to the San Francisco-Oakland Bay Bridge. Surrounded by cheap rooming houses and machine shops, only a narrow elliptoid of turf remains of the project which the enterprising "Lord" Gordon laid out in the early 1850's after the plan of London's fashionable Berkeley Square. Factories and machine shops occupy the sites of the sedate Georgian houses which encircled the park. Here, among others, lived cattle king Henry Miller; the grandparents of Gertrude Atherton; Hall McAllister—until he lost his house in a poker game to a Captain Lyons; Senator and Mrs. William M. Gwin; and "Lord" Gordon's family. After the exodus of their fashionable tenants in the 1870's, the abandoned mansions fell into the hands of Japanese immigrants. Deterioration, the 1906 fire, and conversion to mundane uses have been the fate of this pioneer real estate development.

150. Venerable MISSION DOLORES (*adm. 25¢ including cemetery; open daily May to Sept. 9-5, Oct. to April 9:30-4:30*), Dolores, between Sixteenth and Seventeenth Sts., its heterogeneous architecture well preserved after more than 150 years, was founded by Padre Francisco Palou. Father Palou has told how the pioneer chapel, dedicated on June 29, 1776 to "our seraphic Father San Francisco," was founded just five days before the signing of the Declaration of Independence. With the aid of sailors from the Spanish supply ship *San Carlos* "a building was completed which . . . was made of wood plastered over with clay and roofed with tules. To this was built of the same material . . . a church eighteen varas [or about fifty feet] long. Adjoining it was, in the rear of the altar, a small room which served as a vestry. The church was adorned in the best manner possible with various cloths, flags, bunting, and pendants from the transport ship." Dedicated on October 3, 1776, it was formally opened October 8. Here were performed the first marriage, the first baptisms of Spaniards and of Indians, and the first Christian burial on the San Francisco Peninsula.

On April 25, 1782, in the presence of Padre Jose de Murguia from Mission Santa Clara, Lieutenant Joaquin Moraga and officers from the Presidio, and an assemblage of priests and soldiers, Padre Palou laid the cornerstone of the present church. "Into the sepulcher of the first said stone," he wrote, "were placed the image of our Holy Father San Francisco, some relics from the bones of St. Pius and other holy martyrs, five medals of various saints, and a good portion of silver money to signify the Treasures of the Church."

Perhaps some of these sacred objects are still buried beneath the adobe walls, four feet thick, which support the old mission's low-pitched roof of brown tiles surmounted by a plain Franciscan cross. It has survived the years in remarkably good condition, marked neither by the decay nor the extensive restoration which have befallen some other California missions. The main entrance of the mission is flanked by pairs of engaged semi-Doric columns resting on massive stylobates, which support six pillars rising from the wooden balcony to the widely projecting eaves. Between the four middle columns, in niches cut in the wall, are hung with plaited rawhide the three bells brought from Mexico in 1780—Bret Harte's lyric "Bells of the Past" which once summoned from field and shop the Indian neophytes to midday meals. Measuring 22 feet in width and 114 feet in depth, the mission is a compact and well-proportioned structure in an architectural style whose eclectic Moorish and Classic features are conditioned by adaption to raw native materials and primitive craftsmanship. The joints of doors and windows throughout are secured with manzanita pegs; the struts and ridge-joints of the rafters are bound with thongs of rawhide.

Approached by a low flight of stone steps, its entrance is a wide Roman arch with double doors of panelled wood. The interior reveals Mexican churriguerresque design as interpreted by Indian craftsmen. As vivid as when painted by the neophytes a century and a half ago are the triangular designs of alternating red and white which cover the ceiling between its heavy beams. The beams and sanctuary arch bear chevrons of alternating red, yellow, gray, and white, painted—like the ceiling decoration—with vegetable pigments.

Hand-carved are the main and side altars brought with other furnishings from Mexico. In panels at the bases of the lavender-tinted side altars are bas-relief vases of roses which suggest the Italian influence in Mexican rococo art. In churriguerresque pattern is the large reredos behind the main altar, with its elaborate niches and lavender panels framed with ornamental gilt scrolls, garlands, and other conventional decoration. The door of the revolving tabernacle brought from Manila bears an old Italian-school painting of Christ, blessing the bread He holds before a table bearing a tall silver wine chalice. Over the tabernacle and the Crucifixion are two small paintings in oval frames, one depicting in faded hues a cross; the other, a cross and a soldier's bare arm and clenched hand upholding it. The monstrance is of French origin dating from 1757; Indian neophytes made the Pascal candle; the confessional doors came from Mexico. In their respective niches on the reredos are the original 13 statues of saints carved in wood, of which the St. Michael with staff and uplifted sword is the dominant figure. This soldier of the cross, between Franciscan and Dominican coats of arms, wears red drapery, gilded boots, and a green tunic with gilt flowers. A crowned figure of the Virgin stands to the right of the tabernacle; an exquisitely carved Mater Dolorosa, to the left. In brilliant costume over the right side altar stands St. Anthony, holding in one hand a sheaf of lilies and in the other an open volume on which rests a kneeling child. Side niches are occupied by kneeling figures of St. Francis Solano and San Juan Capistrano. On the opposite altar are represented St. Joseph, St. Bonaventure, and San Luis Rey.

When all this ecclesiastical furniture was installed is not known, but at the end of 1810 the *padres* reported to their superiors in Mexico the aquisition of the two side altars, the statue of St. Michael, several paintings on canvas in gold and silver frames, various silver vessels, a reliquary, and a pyxsis for sick calls. Although the records of the mission's construction are incomplete, it is believed to have been completed by 1800. The huge granary, built in 1794, adjoining a long low residential building of earlier construction which connected it with the church, appears in old prints and photographs to form a wing of the main building. The adjacent pasture and grain field were enclosed "to the distance of half a league" by a ditch. In 1795 twenty adobe homes for an equal number of neophyte families were erected. The closing decade of the eighteenth century also saw enclosed in the mission quadrangle a bathhouse, a tannery, and other structures.

For half a century, says, Fr. Zephrin Engelhardt's authoritative *San Francisco or Mission Dolores,* this "community formed a kind of co-operative association, a sort of Christian Communism, of which the missionaries were the unsalaried managers and the neophytes the beneficiaries." In return for giving up their liberty and such pagan customs as polygamy and accepting the daily routine of religious services, the converts were assured of a regular diet and decent homes as long as they faithfully performed their baptismal vows of labor and devotion. "They were informed that all the land they occupied with the herds belonged to themselves; that even to the missionaries nothing more was due of the property accumulated by the industry of the neophytes than the food and the clothing their guides needed; and that eventually, when they were capable of managing it, the property acquired by the community would be turned over to them exclusively, as was done in Mexico. . . . The priests would after that attend only to their spiritual wants."

Despite its somewhat unhealthy site near the marshes of Mission Creek, Mission Dolores remained fairly prosperous until its property was confiscated for the public domain by the Mexican government and promptly granted to private individuals. During the 57 years of its independent existence the Franciscan Fathers baptized 6,536 Indians and 448 Mexican children, married 2,043 Indians and 79 Mexicans, buried 5,187 Indian and 150 Mexican dead. "The community," declares Fr. Engelhardt, "at the end of the last general report, December 31, 1832, consisted of 204 Indians of all ages, which would mean about 50 families. The herds, on the same date, consisted of 5,000 cattle, 3,500 sheep, 1,000 horses, most of which were of no use, and 18 mules. Owing to the scarcity of able-bodied neophytes, the fields had yielded, in the year 1832, only 500 bushels of wheat, 400 bushels of barley, 50 bushels of corn, and 140 bushels of beans and peas. This harvest was about two-thirds of the usual product."

Twenty-two years later the *Annals of San Francisco* described the mission as a ruined relic of a bygone day: "The Mission has always been a favorite place of amusement to the citizens of San Francisco. Here, in the early days of the city, exhibitions of bull and bear fights frequently took place, which attracted great crowds; and here, also, were numerous duels fought, which drew nearly as many idlers to view them. At present (1854), there are two race-courses in the neighborhood, and a large number of drinking houses. . . . On fine days, especially on Sundays, the roads to the Mission show a continual succession, passing to and fro, of all manner of equestrians and pedestrians, and elegant open carriages filled with ladies and holiday folk." The mission's career as a "place of amusement" was a brief one, however, for in 1857 it was restored to the Roman Catholic archdiocese.

Enclosed by a white stuccoed adobe wall with red tiles, adjoining the mission, the old cemetery is a secluded little garden with clean-swept lawns whose headstones and monuments evoke memories of another era. Many of the graves are unmarked; others are overgrown with tangled ivy and myrtle.

Among the headstone inscriptions which revive for San Franciscans their city's Spanish days is one which reads: "*Aqui Yacen los Restos del Capitan Louis Antonio Arguello. Primer Governador Alta California Bajo el Governiero Mejicano. Nacio en San Francisco el 21 de Junio. 1784 y murio en el Mismo Lugar el 27 de Marzo. 1830*" (Here Lie the Remains of Captain Louis Antonio Arguello. First Governor of Alta California Under the Mexican Government. Born at San Francisco June 21, 1784 and Died At the Same Place March 27, 1830). "Sacred to the memory" of those victims of Vigilante justice, Charles Cora and James P. Casey, are other headstones. Casey's reads: "May God Forgive My Persecutors." Buried also in the cemetery is James ("Yankee") Sullivan, early-day champion pugilist, who while awaiting trial by the Vigilance Committee of 1856, hanged himself in Fort Gunnybags. A statue of Padre Junipero Serra by Arthur Putnam looks down upon the west end of the cemetery. In the center is a large rock shrine, the "Grotto of Lourdes," containing an old redwood cross— erected in 1920—which bears the inscription: "Dedicated to the Neglected and Forgotten Who Rest Here."

The "neglected and forgotten" include mostly the 5,515 Indians interred here and in the rear of the mission between 1777 and 1848. The Burial Register of the *padres* contains the short and simple annals of many a neophyte who died from smallpox, measles, and other epidemics whose periodic toll brought about the establishment of the "Hospital Mission" at San Rafael. Of the 196 white persons recorded in the old register, the most notable is Lieutenant Jose Joaquin Moraga, whose remains rest within the sanctuary of the mission beside those of the Very Reverend Richard Carroll, its pastor from 1853 to 1860. Beneath the paved courtyard behind the mission is buried Jose Noe, last Mexican *alcalde* of Yerba Buena, whose family headstone is set in the red tile floor within the mission entrance. Here too, is the resting place of William Leidesdorff, pioneer San Franciscan who was associated with Jacob Leese and Thomas Larkin during the Bear Flag revolt.

151. Biggest drydock on the Pacific Coast for vessels of the merchant marine is the larger of the two HUNTER'S POINT DRYDOCKS, foot of Evans Ave., in which the biggest oceangoing ships can be lifted high and dry for reconditioning. In great cement-lined troughs, the rusting sides of a ship are exposed from deck to keel. Both docks are graving docks, equipped to permit scraping of the bottoms as well as the sides of vessels, and both are equipped with electric pumps and steam cranes. Graving Dock No. 2, built in 1901, is 750 feet long, has a depth at high water of 28 feet 6 inches; Graving Dock No. 3, built in 1919, is 1,020 feet long, has a depth at high water of 45 feet 6 inches. When filled, the larger dock holds 42,000,000 gallons of water, which its four 750-horsepower pumps can empty in nine and one-half hours. Only dock on the Pacific Coast for merchant marine vessels with a draft of more than 24 feet, Graving Dock No. 3 will accommodate the largest capital ships of the United States Navy. After nearly five years' agitation for acquisition of the docks as a repair base for naval vessels, President Franklin D. Roosevelt signed on June 3, 1939 a bill approving their purchase from the Bethlehem Steel Company Shipbuilding Division.

First drydock at Hunter's Point was built in 1868 by William C. Ralston, then a director of the California Steam Navigation Company, upon the suggestion of civil engineer Alexander Von Schmidt, whose newly invented process of drilling granite under water was employed in excavating the entrance. The cavity was carved almost entirely out of solid stone. From Puget Sound, Ralston imported immense timbers to line the excavation. For the keel blocks, California laurel was used. From the Rocklin quarries in the Sacramento Valley, ox teams pulled enough huge granite blocks to cover 13,000 yards. Cost of the dock, including mechanical equipment, was $1,200,000. Measuring 465 feet in length, 120 in width, and 22 in depth at high water, it was large enough to accommodate any ship afloat at the time except the *Great Western*. Before the stone dock had been completed, Ralston and his associates, who had formed the California Dry Dock Company with a capital of $1,000,000, already had begun construction of a floating dry-dock built of Oregon pine. The stone dock lasted until 1916, when it was removed and the present Graving Dock No. 3 built on its site.

152. From the foundries of the WEST COAST YARDS OF THE BETHLEHEM STEEL COMPANY SHIPBUILDING DIVISION (*private*), Twentieth and Illinois Sts., have come ships, machinery, dredges, railroad locomotives, and endless tons of steel equipment shipped to all parts of the world. Origin of the 30-acre establishment dates back to 1849, when Peter and James Donahue opened a blacksmith shop on Mission Street, which in 1862 became the Donahue Iron and Brass Company and a few years later—when H. J. Booth, Irving M. Scott, and George W. Prescott joined the firm—the Union Iron Works. The first steam locomotive built on the Pacific Coast, for the old San Francisco-San Jose Railroad (1865), was constructed here. Between 1865 and 1870 thirteen railroad locomotives, including two 30-tonners, were built. The plant manufactured practically all the machinery and dredges used in California and Nevada gold fields and shipped tons of equipment to Alaska during the Yukon gold strike.

Following acquisition in the early 1880's of the present plant site, the Union Iron Works began a heavy program of shipbuilding. The *Olympic,* Admiral Dewey's flagship at Manila, and the *Oregon,* equally famous in the Spanish-American War, were built with a speed and thoroughness that amazed Eastern competitors and established San Francisco as a major shipbuilding base. Since the Spanish-American War period, cruisers, gunboats, destroyers, and submarines have been built in these yards, particularly for South American countries. When the shipbuilding boom of war days collapsed, the plant lapsed into a semidormant state. Nevertheless, in the eleven years between 1919 and 1938 it constructed 142 vessels, including submarines, oil tankers, freighters, ferries, and passenger and freight ships. With the revival of interest in the merchant marine, the plant was modernized in 1938 in anticipation of new orders.

The Union Iron Works was acquired in 1906 by the Bethlehem Steel Company but held to its old name until 1917, when it became the Bethlehem Shipbuilding Corporation Ltd.; in November 1938 it was merged with the parent company.

153. The two stone rollers on either side of the ten-story building housing offices of the WESTERN SUGAR REFINERY (*open to visitors 9-11, 1-3*), foot of Twenty-third St., were made in China for use in the "Philippine primitive 2-roll Muscovado Sugar Mill." In sharp contrast to a primitive mill is the plant beyond the entrance, one

of the two cane sugar refineries in the West, equipped to produce 2,500,-000 pounds of raw sugar within 24 hours. Working at full capacity, the plant employs 1,000 men and produces 20 different grades of refined sugar. The Sea Island brand is the staple. The factory consumes daily 1,500,000 gallons of water, 1,600 barrels of fuel oil, and 8,500,000 feet of natural gas—as much as is used by the entire city of Sacramento.

The plant, built in 1861, still utilizes several of the original buildings which survived the 1906 earthquake. Claus Spreckels, founder of the firm, established his first plant at Battery and Union Streets in 1863. When he died in 1903 he had revolutionized the sugar industry in the United States. His sons, John D. and A. B. Spreckels, continued the work begun by their father and expanded the San Francisco plant into the present huge refinery.

154. On the peak of steep Buena Vista Heights, heavily wooded BUENA VISTA PARK, with its deeply shaded nooks smelling always of dampness, was set aside in 1868 as the first plot of the city's now extensively developed parks system. The view from the parking lot atop the hill is far-sweeping. Beyond the line of the East Bay shore are the white homes of Berkeley and Oakland; nearer, in the middle distance, Yerba Buena and man-made Treasure Island. The massive San Francisco-Oakland Bay Bridge swings in a graceful arc from shore to island to shore. In the foreground lies downtown San Francisco, a jumble of pointed skyscrapers and climbing streets.

Mount Tamalpais, a slumberous dark blue, rises high above the rolling Marin County hills across the Golden Gate, beyond the great orange-painted towers of the Golden Gate Bridge rising high above the Bay. Angel Island and Alcatraz break the smooth blue waters. Northwest, the water breaks white against the rocky shore of Point Bonita.

In the foreground lie the Western Addition and Haight-Ashbury residential districts, pierced by the narrow, wooded lane of the Panhandle. North and west dark Strawberry Hill rises out of green Golden Gate Park. In the immediate foreground a portion of Kezar Stadium with its shelf-like seats shines whitely in the sun at the eastern end of the park.

Bare of trees, the two summits of Twin Peaks point to the sky in the west. Tiny roads with yellow embankments cross and wind along the mountainsides. In the distant south the rolling hills of the Bay Shore district hide the horizon, while in the middle distance and foreground the populous Mission District lies flat, cut by streets into severe squares. In the immediate foreground is Corona Heights, a bare peak of rocks, unimproved, with a great red gash in the eastern slope.

155. In 1926 MOUNT OLYMPUS was made a city park. According to legend, the hill received its name from the crippled milk peddler named Hanrahan, who familiarly was known as "Old Limpus"

in the adjoining residential area in the 1860's. A partly ruined statue, *The Triumph of Light,* brought to this country in 1887 by Adolph Sutro, is mounted in the tiny hilltop square in the geographical center of the city; 12 feet in height, it stands on a pedestal 30 feet high. In the Brussels original (by Antoine Wiertz) the standing woman holds a torch in her right hand and a sword in her left; in this copy the right arm is broken off at the elbow and the left is without a sword. Unsubstantiated is the popular story that both sword and arm were removed by irate seamen who declared the statue threw them off their course as they steered through the Golden Gate.

The view from Mount Olympus is similar to that from Buena Vista Park, but offers a more complete picture of Twin Peaks, with the residential section climbing halfway up its eastern slopes. Nearer, also to the southwest, Sutro Forest caps Mount Sutro. Northwest in the distance is the sweeping lawn of Lincoln Park; to the east, Buena Vista Park, encircled by the red-tile-roofed houses of Buena Vista Heights.

156. The white, brick-red, and grey concrete buildings of the MEDICAL CENTER OF THE UNIVERSITY OF CALIFORNIA, Parnassus and Third Aves., occupy a 13½-acre natural amphitheater backed against the dark eucalyptus forest of Mount Sutro and Parnassus Heights. The Center (formerly known as the Affiliated Colleges) includes the University of California Hospital and Clinic; the Colleges of Medicine, Dentistry, and Pharmacy; a training school for nurses and the George William Hooper Foundation for Research supplements the work of the school. Among the Foundation's notable achievements have been the discoveries of Vitamin E and Vinethene, a new anesthetic. Canning and fishing industries have profited greatly by its discoveries.

The colleges date from 1862, when Dr. H. H. Toland founded the Toland Medical School in North Beach. In 1872 the school became affiliated nominally with the University of California, but continued to be supported by the fees of medical students. In 1895 Adolph Sutro donated the present site, and with money provided by the State legislature several buildings were opened here in 1898. In 1902 the properties were taken over by the University of California and support of the college was assumed by the university.

Few private patients are admitted to the 300-bed University of California Hospital, which is maintained almost exclusively for its research in medicine and surgery. Those who crowd the clinic daily come from all parts of the West Coast, some on funds supplied by the State.

157. Clarendon Avenue passes through SUTRO FOREST, over a dark ridge of MOUNT SUTRO (920 alt.). Here Adolph Sutro in the late 1870's—after returning from the Comstock Lode a million-

aire—purchased part of the old Rancho San Miguel. Sutro, who called his mountain "Parnassus," planted trees here in 1887, after the legislature provided that property converted into forest land should be tax-exempt for five years. For years he employed a gardener who not only tended these trees, but those scattered over a 12,000-acre area which included Mount Davidson.

During Sutro's lifetime the forest was open to the public, but it was closed after his death when fires started by careless visitors several times threatened to destroy it. In 1911 realtors Baldwin and Howell purchased 724 acres for $1,417,377 and planned to subdivide the land into homesites.

Today Sutro Forest is a rough wildwood in the heart of a modern residential district. The ground is covered by tangled undergrowth. Ivy clings to the trunks of the tall eucalyptus trees and sugar pines. Each spring it is brightly colored by wildflowers and blossoming brushwood.

158. Twin Peaks Boulevard encircles the TWIN PEAKS in a broad figure "8." The windy summits also are reached by trails and earthen steps that lead up steep, grassy slopes. To the east and south can be seen the bright-colored roofs and smoking chimneys of row upon row of apartment houses, laced together by a network of streets. Mount Davidson, topped by its giant white cross, forms a somber pile against the background of the western sky. Beyond is the long line of the Pacific. Distance lends a serene quality to the Marin hills and bays, darkly blue in the northwest. The long expanse of the East Bay shore rolls as far as the eye can reach.

Legends cloud the history of Twin Peaks. Once, said the Indians, the mountains were one: man and wife. But they quarreled long and bitterly and in time the Great Spirit heard them, and with thunder and lightning smote them in twain.

The Spaniards called the peaks Los Pechos de la Choca (*The Breasts of the Indian Girl*) in memory, so the story goes, of a beautiful maiden. She was softly beautiful, tall and slender. When one spoke to her she dropped her eyes in modesty. N. P. Vallejo, son of Mariano Vallejo, in describing her said, "Never have I seen a cultured maiden half so fair as this untaught, uninstructed daughter of the wilds."

159. The highest point in San Francisco is heavily-wooded MOUNT DAVIDSON (938 ft. alt.), where on bright days the sunlight filtering through the treetops throws bright patches of light on the grassy leaf-covered ground. From its summit rises a great cross, illuminated during Easter week, which was dedicated March 24, 1934 at 7:30 p.m., when President Franklin D. Roosevelt pressed a golden key that sent electrical impulses across the Nation to light the floodlights. The cross, 103 feet in height, is built of concrete and steel. Resting

upon solid rock, its base contains a crypt in which are relics from the Holy Land, including a jug of water from the River Jordan. The concrete which seals the crypt itself was mixed with this water. The first of four crosses preceding the present one was erected atop the mountain in 1923, the year of San Francisco's first sunrise Easter service. Each year since thousands of people have climbed the steep slopes in the hours before dawn of Easter Sunday to gather about the cross for services which, in recent years, have been broadcast to the Nation over radio hook-ups.

Once a part of the Rancho San Miguel, Mount Davidson formed part of the 12,000-acre estate of Adolph Sutro. When George Davidson of the Coast and Geodetic Survey surveyed it in 1862, it was known as Blue Mountain. It remained a barren rocky peak until trees were planted on its slopes. In 1911 A. S. Baldwin purchased the mountain and spent $2,000 in building trails to its summit. In that year too it was named Mount Davidson in honor of its early surveyor.

When in 1926 the encroachment of real estate subdivision threatened it, Mrs. Edmund N. Brown, a member of the State Park Commission, secured the help of the Commodore Sloat Parent-Teachers' Association and other public agencies in a warm publicity campaign which persuaded the city to purchase 26 acres. The area was dedicated as a city park on December 20, 1929, the 83rd birthday of John McLaren (*see Golden Gate Park*).

Western Addition

". . . monotonous miles of narrow-chested, high-shouldered, jimber-jawed houses strongly reminiscent of the scroll-saw period of our creative artistry . . ."

—Irvin S. Cobb

LIKE the backyard of some imposing but superannuated mansion, the Western Addition is cluttered with the discarded furniture of the city's Gilded Age. It is a curious district whose claim to distinction is its disdain of all pretense. It is not beautiful, and yet San Franciscans refer to it almost affectionately as "The Fillmore," the name of its busiest thoroughfare, and love it, as Charles Caldwell Dobie says, "for its supreme grotesqueness."

Once it was what its name implies—the "western addition" to the old town—but now it lies in the very middle of the city. Its eastern boundary is the broad traffic-thronged artery of Van Ness Avenue, "automobile row." Westward it spreads as far as Lone Mountain's vanishing old graveyards, once far out of town in a sandy brush-grown wilderness. Northward it extends to the heights above The Marina, and southward almost to Market Street.

The preposterous old houses built here in the 1870's and 1880's when San Francisco was expanding westward, and spared by the flames of 1906, are monuments to the bonanza era. In them the *nouveau riche* of the Gilded Age attempted to outdo the fantastic wooden castles on Nob Hill. What the jigsaw and the lathe could not accomplish the builders supplied with Gothic arches and Corinthian pillars, with Norman turrets crowned by Byzantine domes, with mansard roofs, balconies, gables, and stained-glass windows. Interiors were resplendent with horsehair divans, marble-topped tables, and bronze statuary. Gaslight flickered in dim vestibules and up redwood staircases. No longer fashionable, the old mansions have been converted into boarding houses and housekeeping rooms.

In the days before the fire, while the Western Addition was still the abode of fashion, Fillmore Street was a suburban center of commerce. After 1906 it had a brief and sudden boom. Before the charred wreckage of Market Street could be cleared off and stores rebuilt, the flow of commerce ran into Fillmore Street—and its delighted merchants sought to keep it there. Arches supporting large street lamps were erected over each intersection from Sacramento to Fulton Street and festooned with electric lights. Through five or six years the great days lasted, but when Market Street reclaimed its commercial prestige after 1910, Fillmore Street was doomed. Today its ornate arches are incongruous reminders of its hour of greatness. Fillmore Street, however, is more than a commercial thoroughfare. It represents a way of life, and is the stronghold of San Francisco's cosmopolitan tradition. Raffish, optimistic, blissfully vulgar, Fillmore Street keeps alive that inimitable social spirit of which San Francisco is the larger expression.

From The Marina, north of the Western Addition, Fillmore Street climbs the precipitous slope of Pacific Heights scaled by two diminutive cable cars. Down the slope below Sacramento Street are stores, movie theaters, and restaurants, a scene of lively disorder. Chaste little antique shops stand next door to radio stores; hamburger joints thrive beside the austere facades of branch banks. Past the sidewalk vegetable stands stroll housewives, pinching grapefruits, tomatoes, and peaches with the fingers of connoisseurs. At convenient intervals are neighborly little bars offering the tired shopper a moment's refreshment while the understanding bartender wheels her offspring's carriage to a quiet corner at the end of the counter. And day or night pass laughing Negroes, dapper Filipino boys, pious old Jews on their way to *schule,* sturdy-legged Japanese high school girls, husky young American longshoremen out for a quiet stroll with the wife and kids.

Near the southern end of Fillmore Street's lengthy market place, where its noisy turbulence gives way again to prosaic respectability at the foot of another hill clustered with turrets, bay windows, and mansard roofs, lies the city's Jewish commercial center, the heart of the before-the-fire section, where bedizened old houses of the 1880's advertize housekeeping rooms on grimy signs. Yet, paradoxically, here is a gourmet's paradise; along adjacent blocks of Golden Gate Avenue and McAllister Street the atmosphere is spicy with the odors of delicatessen shops, bakeries, and restaurants. In a dozen strange tongues, bargaining goes on along McAllister Street—San Francisco's "second-hand row"—for begrimed statuary, ancient stoves, Brussels carpets with faded floral patterns, chamber pots and perambulators, Dresden figurines and fishing tackle, gilt-framed oil landscapes and canary bird cages. Gathered in this district are a large number of the city's 30,000 Jews, most of them immigrants from eastern Europe, many being recent arrivals. But Fillmore Street's Jewish quarter is scarcely representative of the city's Jewish citizenry as a whole. Not confined to any one district, profession, or mode of life, they have played a leading role in the city's development since the first of them came during the Gold Rush. Scattered throughout the Western Addition, as elsewhere in the city, are numerous synagogues, both orthodox and reformed, and their charitable institutions and fraternal organizations. Though the city's Jews have no native theater, they support a Yiddish Literary and Dramatic Society and numerous social clubs, musical societies, and schools.

East of Fillmore Street, north and south of Post Street, is "Little Osaka," home of a vast majority of the city's 7,000 Japanese. Unlike the Chinese, they have made almost no attempt to establish in miniature the graceful scenes of their native land. For the most part, they have simply moved in and put up their electric signs on faded facades. The older generation still clings to religious beliefs and folkways, and schools the second and third generations in the ways of the homeland. Little Osaka's young attend not only the city's public schools, but also one of the colony's half-dozen native schools, of which the Golden Gate Institute, on Bush Street near Buchanan, is the second largest in the country. At the Japanese branch of the Y.W.C.A., in a modern building on Sutter Street near Buchanan, young girls practice *cha-no-yu,* the age-old tea ceremony, and *ike-bana,* the ancient art of flower arrangement. Young men are taught *jiu-jitsu* and *kendo,* in which armor-clad participants fence with bamboo sticks.

The Japanese New Year is celebrated throughout the colony on January 1 when the polite pay calls and partake of *sake* (rice wine) and foods dedicated to the occasion. On March 3 the Doll Festival (*Hinamatsuri*) is observed with ceremonious display of exquisite miniature figures dressed in the costumes of old Japan and the serving of flavored rice, with *seki-han, sakura-mochi,* and rice dumplings wrapped in cherry leaves; the display of dolls during *Hinamatsuri* at the downtown Western Women's Club is reputed to be the finest of its kind in America. The Birthday of Buddha is observed on the Sunday nearest April 8 in the Japanese Tea Garden (*see Golden Gate Park: Points of Interest*). The colony's other Buddhist festival, observed as well by Buddhists of other races, is *Ura-bon* (Festival of Souls), celebrated with a religious dance in the Buddhist Church at Pine and Octavia Streets on the Sunday evening nearest to the sacred day. At the celebration of Boys' Day (*Osekku*) on May 5, intended to inspire young males to swim against the current of life with vigor and courage, *kashiza-nochi* (rice dumplings wrapped in oak leaves) is served ceremoniously and native folk dances are staged.

In Little Osaka's restaurants on Post and Sutter, between Octavia and Buchanan Streets, are served such delicacies as *soba* and *undon* (noodles); roasted eel and rice; chicken soup, amber-clear, with seaweed, fish, or red beans; and *tempura,* concocted of deep-fried fish and prawns with such vegetables as leeks, soya bean cake, gelatin strings, and bamboo shoots. San Francisco's Japanese have no native theater, though occasionally a troupe of actors or dancers presents the dramatic art of both modern and old Japan. Japanese music, played on native instruments, may be heard at the colony's various church auditoriums and language schools. Two Japanese daily newspapers are published in the city, each with its section in English for the benefit of younger readers. Imported Japanese films, both silent and vocal, are shown at a local bookshop.

Throughout the Japanese settlement is scattered a Filipino colony, smaller than the quarter on upper Kearny Street but distinguished by the same social features. Wherever these jaunty, small-statured people congregate at social functions, the *carinosa,* their national dance which resembles the tango, is danced to the orchestral accompaniment of *bandores,* twelve-stringed mandolins of native origin. The disparity of the sexes among the city's 3,000 Filipinos lends a pathetic note to their social life.

West of Fillmore Street and south of Sutter Street live many Russians although their folkways are more apparent in their other and tighter little colony on Potrero Hill. Divided by opposing political loyalties, the city's Russians never have created a distinctive colony of their own. The older immigrants came to escape the Tsar, the newer to escape the Soviet regime. The ways of both are the ways of exiles who strive to keep alive the customs of their forbears among alien surroundings. In the Western Addition the Russian residents are chiefly *émigrés* from the Russian Revolution. The older generation is defiantly monarchist in politics and orthodox in religion. Until recently they kept up the courtly ceremonials of their former life, appearing in faded regimentals of the Imperial Army to pay each other elaborate respects over vodka, tea, and caviar. Annually they squandered the savings of a twelvemonth on a grand ball in honor of their Petrograd days. Easter is still celebrated as gaily as ever at the Russian Orthodox Church on Green Street at Van Ness Avenue.

The greater number of San Francisco's 7,000 Negroes live in the neighborhood west of Fillmore between Geary and Pine Streets. Among them are representatives of every State in the Union, of Jamaica, Cuba, Panama, and South American countries. Of those from the South, the greater number are Texans who arrived after the World War; these still celebrate "Juneteenth," Emancipation Day for the Texas Negroes, who did not learn of the Emancipation Proclamation until June 19, 1863. The colony's social life revolves around its handful of bars and restaurants, its one large and noisy night club, its eight churches of varying faiths, and the Booker T. Washington Community Center on Divisadero Street, where trained social workers guide educational and recreational activities for children and adults. Occasionally, in churches and clubs, are heard old Negro folk songs surviving the days of slavery.

With its confusion of customs from half the world, the Western Addition is more entitled than any other section of the city to be called

San Francisco's International Quarter.   But the Western Addition abhors labels.   It is just "The Fillmore," and proud of it.

POINTS OF INTEREST

160. The stately, white, six-story MASONIC TEMPLE, SW. corner Van Ness Ave. and Oak St., was dedicated on October 13, 1913. Of Romanesque design (William B. Faville, architect), the building is faced with Utah marble and adorned with sculptural decorations representing Biblical and allegorical figures by Adolph A. Weinman and Ralph Stackpole. A small rotunda leads into the main lobby of polished gray and white marble.   In the large halls on the second and fourth floors are portraits of past grand masters, many by Duncan C. Blakiston.   The great Commandery Hall on the third floor is surmounted with a dome rising 85 feet above the floor; two large murals on religious subjects are by Arthur F. Matthews.

SW. from Van Ness Ave. on Market St. to Haight St.; W. from Market on Haight.

161. A collection of frame and stucco structures, the five variously styled buildings of SAN FRANCISCO STATE COLLEGE, main entrance SE. corner Haight and Buchanan Sts., stand closely together on a two-block hillside campus bare of trees.   Above the arched main entrance to stuccoed, tile-roofed Anderson Hall is a fresco, Persian in style, picturing California flora and fauna.   The frescoes depicting children at play on the patio wall of the Frederick Burk Grammar and Training School, at the southeast corner of the campus, are by Jack Moxom and Hebe Daum of WPA's Northern California Art Project. A teachers' college, San Francisco State grants teaching credentials in kindergarten-primary, elementary, and junior high school fields.   Average yearly attendance is slightly more than 2,000 students.   The Frederick Burk Training School, accommodating about 450 children, follows a modern progressive philosophy of education.   Launched in 1862 in one room of the city's only high school, San Francisco College was housed in the Girls' High School until 1899, when the Legislature provided for foundation of the San Francisco Normal School in a red brick building on Powell Street, between Clay and Sacramento Streets.

S. from Haight St. on Buchanan St. to Hermann St.; W. from Buchanan on Hermann.

162. The $1,000,000 UNITED STATES MINT (*not open to public*), Hermann, Buchanan, and Webster Sts. and Duboce Ave. (Gil-

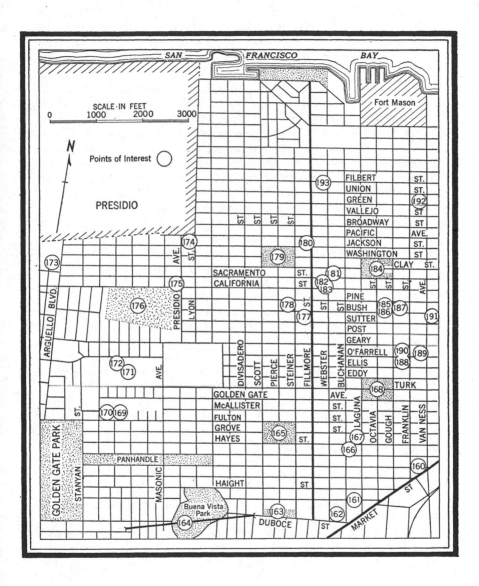

bert Stanley Underwood, architect), rears its fortress-like walls from the solid stone of steep Blue Mountain. Constructed of steel reinforced with granite and concrete, the building's severe facades are pierced by three sets of windows, the middle tier barred with iron. Above and between the middle sets are large bas-reliefs in concrete of United States coins of various denominations. On the first floor are a marble lobby and large storage vaults for gold, silver, copper, and nickel, with concrete walls two feet thick. Second and third floors hold offices, minting rooms, an assay laboratory, and a women's lunch room. On the fourth floor particles from the vapor given off by melting and refining furnaces is recovered in a series of tubes; the vapor is electrified with a 75,000-volt current which causes the metal particles to cling to the tubes' sides. A guards' pistol range occupies the fifth floor, and all approaches to the mint are covered by gun towers; the surrounding area can be illuminated by batteries of floodlights set in the walls. A network of pipes entering all key points of the building is designed to discharge a flood of tear gas at the sounding of an alarm. Both front and rear entrances are barred by electrically operated doors made of heavy double steel, only one of which can be opened at a time; the door guarding the main vault weighs 40 tons.

163. The landscaped terraces of 4-acre DUBOCE PARK, W. end of Hermann St., rise gradually to the row of old-fashioned frame dwellings on its western side; once a mound-dotted wasteland on which tons of rock had been dumped, the park was opened to the public in 1900.

164. In the city's western residential districts real estate prices shot skyward when SUNSET TUNNEL, E. Portal at S. side of Duboce Park, was opened October 21, 1928, with Mayor James Rolph at the controls of the first streetcar to make the tunnel trip. Piercing Buena Vista Hill, the tunnel is 4,232 feet long, 25 feet wide, and 23 feet high.

N. from Hermann St. on Steiner St.

165. In 1860, Charles P. ("Dutch Charlie") Duane, undaunted by threats of the Vigilance Committee, fought for his squatter's rights to ALAMO SQUARE, Steiner, Fulton, Hayes and Scott Sts., 12 acres of smooth green lawn and rustling pine and cypress trees on the top of a hill. Wide cement steps ascend to a palm-fringed circular flower bed, and shrubbery-lined paths lead to an adjacent picnic grove and children's playground. Squatter "Dutch Charlie," chief fire engineer from 1853 to 1857, gained the attention of the Vigilance Committee of 1851 for his shooting, two years earlier, of a theater manager. He was later exiled from the city under penalty of death by the Vigilance Committee of 1856 for the then greater crime of stuffing a ballot box. Returning in 1860, he waged an unsuccessful suit until 1877 for the property, which

had been acquired by the city in 1853. Refugees from the fire of 1906 lived on the hill, and some of the victims, it is believed, were buried here.

E. from Steiner St. on Hayes St.

166. The old Wesleyan Methodist Episcopal Church was converted in 1930 into the HAYES VALLEY RECREATION CENTER AND COTTAGE (*open Mon.-Fri. 2:30-5, 7-10; Sat.-Sun. 10-12, 1-5*), SE. corner Hayes and Buchanan Sts. Open to all boys over 14, it provides facilities for indoor games, dancing and theatricals, a camera club, a band and orchestra, and study groups in arts, crafts, cooking, gardening, and sewing. More than 2,500 children weekly attend the center in a district once noted for its high ratio of juvenile delinquency. The property was leased in 1930 through a legacy left by Adolph Rosenberg, merchant and philanthropist, and established as a recreation center under the jurisdiction of the Recreation Commission.

N. from Hayes St. on Laguna St.

167. Five days after the 1906 fire the Board of Supervisors assembled in what was MOWRY'S OPERA HOUSE, SW. corner Grove and Laguna Sts., a three-story red-brick and frame building erected in 1879, on whose gaslit stage appeared "Gentleman Jim" Corbett to be acclaimed for his victory over John L. Sullivan. At subsequent secret sessions of the supervisors, during which Abe Ruef issued his instructions, detective William J. Burns gathered evidence leading to the graft prosecutions that destroyed the Ruef machine. Since December, 1906, when it ceased to serve as a city hall, the sturdy old building, with its triangular wooden parapet decorated with a harp in bas-relief and its brick ground floor with huge double doors, has been occupied by various mercantile firms.

168. Sometimes referred to as San Francisco's Hyde Park, JEFFERSON SQUARE, Golden Gate Ave., Laguna, Gough, and Eddy Sts., is noted for the stormy character of its political meetings. On pleasant Sunday afternoons every shade of political and religious thought is expounded in open-air forums by old-age-pension advocates, single taxers, and fanatical champions of religious cults. In 1906 the park was used as a refugee camp. The park slopes downhill, its green sward broken by tall eucalyptuses, evergreens, and shrubs planted along graveled walks. In the playground, named for Margaret S. Hayward, for many years a city recreation commissioner, are tennis courts, volley and basketball courts, baseball diamonds and stands. In the center of the park is the low stucco building housing the San Francisco Fire Depart-

ment's Central Alarm Station with its aerial and high-tension electric transformer towers. Situated in a congested area, the park is a favorite recreation center for youngsters of many national groups.

W. from Laguna St. on Golden Gate Ave. to Masonic Ave.; S. from Golden Gate on Masonic to Fulton St.; W. from Masonic on Fulton.

169. Founded in 1855 as St. Ignatius Church and College, the UNIVERSITY OF SAN FRANCISCO, Fulton St., Parker and Golden Gate Aves., stands beside St. Ignatius Church on part of the site of the Masonic Cemetery, one of four burial grounds encircling the base of Lone Mountain. Conducted by the Jesuits, the university is open to male students of all denominations; only its law and evening classes are co-educational. On the broad hillside campus stand the gray three-story Faculty Building, which houses the priests of the teaching staff; the four-story Liberal Arts Building of gray reinforced concrete; a one-story, stucco tile-roofed structure containing classrooms; and the sole surviving cemetery structure, a small wooden edifice resembling a Greek temple, once the tomb of a San Francisco brewer, in which students now attend classes. Offering liberal arts, premedical, law, economics, and commerce and finance courses, the institution has an enrollment of more than 1,000 students and a faculty of more than 80. Established as St. Ignatius Church and College in 1855, it was empowered by the State Legislature in 1859 to grant degrees and honors. The school won fame in 1874 when Father Joseph Neri, a professor, introduced San Francisco to the arc light with an exhibition on the roof of the school building; during the centennial celebration of American Independence in 1876, he strung three arc lamps of his own invention across Market Street. The university was renamed at the request of prominent San Franciscans in 1930.

170. Standing on Ignatius Heights, the buff-colored brick structure of SAINT IGNATIUS CHURCH, NE. corner Fulton St. and Parker Ave., with its campanile, twin towers, and golden dome glinting in the sun, is a San Francisco landmark. Dedicated in 1914, the church is seventeenth-century Renaissance in design (Charles Devlin, architect). The interior is still unfinished, with exposed loudspeaker system and racks bulging with religious tracts. Under the dome is the sanctuary, bordered by fluted pillars; above the white marble altar, flanked by filigreed gilt candelabra, is suspended an ornate gold sanctuary lamp. On the right are the altar of St. Joseph and the crucifix; on the left, the altar of the Blessed Mother and the pulpit. The altars, both of marble, stand against blue wall panels ornately filigreed with gold. The two murals of the altar, by Tito Ridolfi, are dedicated to St. Robert Bellarmine and depict the seventeenth-century Cardinal of Milan in two

poses. Ridolfi also painted the series of murals in the frieze above the colonnades on either side, depicting the 14 stations of the cross, in which Christ is shown in mediaeval tradition wearing an under cloak of dull red and an outer cloak of dull blue. Above the frieze are round windows, to be replaced with stained-glass representations of Catholic scholar saints; the two installed depict St. Ives, patron of lawyers, and St. Augustine, doctor of theology. In the campanile is the old bell, now battered and rusty, that hung in the original church of 1855, obtained from a local volunteer fire company which had ordered it from England but was unable to pay for it.

Saint Ignatius Church was founded in 1855, when Father Anthony Marachi dedicated a small wooden building in the waste land of what was then known as the Valley of St. Anne, south of Market Street between Fourth and Fifth Streets. The present buildings, both church and college, were begun in 1910 and completed in 1914.

N. from Fulton St. on Parker Ave.

171. From the top of Lone Mountain, the Spanish Gothic tower of the SAN FRANCISCO COLLEGE FOR WOMEN, Parker and Masonic Aves. and Turk St., lifts an iron cross 115 feet above the mountain's flattened crest. A curving road winds up from Turk Street, past newly planted trees, shrubs and flower beds, to the flight of wide stone steps leading past terraced lawns to an ornamental arched doorway. The three-story building, Spanish-Gothic in design, has vaulted halls richly furnished with tapestries, paintings, statues, and wood carvings. In the east wing is the oak beamed library; its 100,000 volumes, the majority donated by Monsignor Joseph M. Gleason, pastor of the St. Francis de Sales Church of Oakland, include rare manuscripts and first editions. Here are such rarities as the sermons of Pope St. Leo the Great; a set of wills and indentures covering the reigns of the English sovereigns from James I to George III; several papal bulls, óne signed by nine cardinals who attended the Council of Trent in 1566, and the second by Pope Pius V, before the battle of Lepanto; a copy of the Nuremburg Chronicle; and what is probably the most complete collection of bookplates in the United States. Americana include a newspaper published in the South on wallpaper during the Civil War, an unpublished and autographed poem by Henry Wadsworth Longfellow, and letters written by Ulysses S. Grant, Andrew Jackson, Andrew Johnson, and other notables.

Having purchased Lone Mountain in 1860, Bishop Joseph Sadoc Alemany, Roman Catholic Archbishop of San Francisco, had a giant wooden cross erected on the mountain top. When the city acquired all "outside lands" west of the former city boundary in 1869, Lone Mountain was reserved as a future park site; but Bishop Alemany, through the persuasive abilities of his secretary, John Spottiswoode, succeeded in regaining title to the property. The old cross was replaced by a new one in 1875, and in 1900 a storm blew the great cross down, for the boys of the neighborhood had tunnelled under its base to make a cave in which they gathered to bake potatoes and banquet on other stolen delicacies. Again restored, the cross remained on the mountain top until grading for the college began in 1930. When Archbishop Edward J. Hanna of San Francisco suggested in 1929 that a Roman Catholic women's college be opened in San Francisco, the Lone Mountain site was purchased by the Society of the Sacred Heart. When construction was completed in 1932, the present iron cross at the top of the tower replaced the cross erected in 1900. The college has increased its enrollment from 60 to 223 students.

W. from Parker Ave. on Anza St. to Lorraine Court; N. from Anza on Lorraine Court.

172. In the old Odd Fellows Cemetery at the base of Lone Mountain, the only burial place within the corporate limits of San Francisco, is the SAN FRANCISCO MEMORIAL COLUMBARIUM, 1 Lorraine Court, originally erected at the entrance of the pioneer burial ground in 1898. It contains the cremated remains of more than 7,000 San Franciscans. Of modified Mediterranean design, the green-domed building of white concrete is noted for its stained-glass windows. From the rotunda marble stairways wind upward; on its four floors are galleries of niches, each named for a stellar constellation. Following removal of the Odd Fellows Cemetery to Lawndale, San Mateo County, the columbarium fell into neglect and decay. Acquired by the Bay Cities Cemetery Association in 1933, the structure has been remodeled and restored.

Retrace on Lorraine Court; W. from Lorraine Court on Anza St. to Arguello Blvd.; N. from Anza on Arguello.

173. Dominating most of the city's western residential area, the massive orange-domed TEMPLE EMANU-EL, NW. corner Lake St. and Arguello Blvd., is the religious and cultural center of Reformed Judaism in San Francisco. Of steel and concrete, faced with cream-colored stucco, the temple (Sylvain Schnaittaker and Bakewell & Brown, architects) is designed in the form of an "L" about on open court with low cloisters and fountain. The auditorium seats 1,700; besides assembly halls and Sunday school classrooms, the temple contains facilities for study groups and lectures, social halls, and a huge gymnasium.

Set in colored tile in the pavement before the main entrance is the familiar six-pointed star, the Seal of Solomon, surrounded by the seals of the Twelve Tribes of Israel. The vestibule of the auditorium is a low vaulted gallery finished in light blue to contrast with the ivory tones of the interior walls. In solitary splendor, contrary to custom, the Ark of the Covenant, a gilded bronze cabinet with cloisonné enamel inlay, stands out under its stone canopy against the undecorated walls and vaults around the altar. It contains two ornate scrolls of the Torah, one for regular services, the other for special occasions.

Like other reform congregations, Temple Emanu-El does not require observance of strict dietary laws, wearing of hats or skull caps by male members, and segregation of the sexes on opposite sides of the auditorium during services. Contrary to orthodox ritual, music accompanies worship here. Some 750 heads of families constitute the Temple's regular congregation, though attendance is much larger. An important part of the temple's program are its classes for boys and girls.

E. from Arguello Blvd. on Washington St.

174. Tucked away in a tree-shaded garden behind high walls overrun with climbing vines and rose bushes, the little tiled-brick ivy-bowered CHURCH OF THE NEW JERUSALEM (*services Sun. 11 a.m.*), NW. corner Jackson and Washington St., is a reproduction of a village church near Verona, Italy. Surrounding a clear pool of water are trees from many lands. Completed in 1895, the church is a monument to its founder, the Reverend Joseph Worcester, who lived in close association with the artists of Russian Hill. Its heavy-timbered coffered roof is supported by great hewn madrone trees. The square-framed, tule-bottomed chairs on mats of rushes from the Suisun marshes, the open fireplace ablaze with pine knots, and the wax tapers in wrought iron sconces reinforce the outdoor atmosphere. On the windowless north wall four allegorical landscapes of seedtime and harvest by William Keith are set against plain dark-stained panels of pine. The two beautifully executed stained-glass windows are by Bruce Porter. Following the doctrines of Emanuel Swedenborg (1688-1772), the simple services are opened and closed with a Bible ritual.

S. from Washington St. on Lyon St. to California St.; W. from Lyon on California.

175. The JEWISH COMMUNITY CENTER (*open Mon., Thurs., Sat. 9:30 a.m.-11 p.m.; Fri. 9:30-6; Sun. 9:30-1*), NW. corner California St. and Presidio Ave., is headquarters for communal activities of Hebrew organizations. The two-story structure of smooth tan con-

crete with red tile roof was opened in 1933 and houses an art gallery, library and reading rooms, a little theater workshop, swimming pool and gymnasium, and classrooms and lounges. The multicolored mosaic of glazed household tiles decorating the fountain and pool in the patio is by Bernard Zakheim of the WPA Northern California Art Project. A fresco in the patio, also by Zakheim, depicts the gaity and color of ancient Palestine's festivals. The educational program includes courses in law, journalism, languages, arts and crafts, and philosophical and religious subjects. There are book chats, play readings, open forums, concerts, musical recitals, and dancing.

176. Known to generations of San Franciscans as Laurel Hill Cemetery, PIONEER MEMORIAL PARK, California St., Presidio and Parker Aves., a 54-acre area at the base of Lone Mountain, contrasts strangely with the apartment houses surrounding it. Sorrel, oxalis, and clover cover this graveyard of tottering stones and forgotten tombs, and offshore winds stir the branches of cypress, laurel, pine, and oak trees. In 1854, San Franciscans established Laurel Hill Cemetery here far out in the sand dunes so that it would not interfere with the city's growth. On a wooden board was inscribed a memorial to the first person buried: "To the Memory of the First Inhabitant of This Silent City . . . John Orr . . . interred June 10th, 1854." Some inscriptions were laconic, as in the case of Silas W. Sanderson, judge and lawyer, whose stone simply recorded: "Final Decree." Others, as this over an unknown woman, were elaborately "poetic":

> Pain was my portion,
>   Physic was my food,
> Groans were my devotions,
>   Drugs did me no good.
> Christ was my Physician
>   Knew which way was best,
> So to ease me of my pain
>   He took my soul to rest.

A long list of names important in the city's history have appeared on the headstones: Fire Chief Dave Scannell; Mayor James Van Ness; smelting works founder Thomas Selby; barrister and bon-vivant Hall McAllister; William S. Clark, who drove the first piles in San Francisco Bay; Senator David C. Broderick, killed in a pistol duel with State Supreme Court Justice David S. Terry; *Bulletin* editor James King of William, whose murder by James Casey revived vigilante organization; Samuel Woodworth, author of "The Old Oaken Bucket"; Edward Gilbert, California's first Congressman, slain in a duel by General James W. Denver, for whom Colorado's capital was named; Colonel E. D. Baker, killed with his regiment at the battle of Ball's Bluff in 1861; William Sharon and James G. Fair of Comstock Lode fame.

In 1912, when four cemeteries, Laurel Hill, Calvary, Odd Fellows, and Masonic, were grouped around the base of Lone Mountain, the Board of Supervisors, heeding the protests of the living, ordered the area vacated. All of the cemeteries save Laurel Hill were moved to San Mateo County. The controversy which ensued lasted for 28 years. In 1937 the people of San Francisco voted that the ground be cleared and emptied by the end of 1940. Coffins are being transferred at the rate of more than 2,000 each month to Cypress Lawn Cemetery in San Mateo County to be interred in catacombs and vaults until a mausoleum can be constructed at Lawndale.

N. from Geary St. on Fillmore St.

177. Hot spot of the "Gay Nineties," headquarters of city government following the holacaust of 1906, and meeting place of political, language, and unemployed groups in its declining years, FRANKLIN HALL, 1859 Fillmore St., now wears a general air of neglect with its faded gray walls and unwashed windows. Built in 1895, the four-story wooden building with its auditorium and stage was popular as a public dance hall. Here "Professor" Bothwell Brown, "California's Greatest Female Impersonator," held his audiences with his "art" up to the earthquake and fire in 1906, when the premises were occupied by the San Francisco *Examiner,* Mayor Eugene Schmitz, and the Committee of Fifty, composed of the city's financial leaders. The building later housed a dancing academy.

W. from Fillmore St. on Bush St.

178. The eight-spired Tudor Gothic tower of ST. DOMINIC'S CHURCH, NW. corner Bush and Steiner Sts., rises to a height of 175 feet, dominating the neighborhood. The present structure was completed in 1928 on the site of the original church destroyed in 1906. Stretched across the tallest of its interior vaulted arches is a rood screen bearing in its center the figures of a Crucifixion group. In the chief shrine along each side of the church is a figure of Christ, wearing a regal sceptre and robed in priestly garments. Woodwork of the altar rails and confessional doors is the work of the master carvers of Oberammergau, Bavaria, and of Bruges, Belgium.

N. from Bush St. on Steiner St.

179. ALTA PLAZA, Steiner, Scott, Clay, and Jackson Sts., was reclaimed by John McLaren when he filled a deserted rock quarry with rubbish, topped it with soil, planted lawns, and laid out walks and

tennis courts. The stairway on the south side's steep terraced slope is a reproduction of the grand stairway in front of the gaming casino at Monte Carlo.

E. from Steiner St. on Jackson St.

180. The city's largest Protestant congregation worships in the CALVARY PRESBYTERIAN CHURCH, NW. corner Jackson and Fillmore Sts., founded in 1854 by the Reverend William Anderson Scott, who was hanged in effigy in 1861. A supporter of the original church, William C. Ralston, is reported to have scattered $20 gold pieces among its pews.

The cornerstone of the present classic structure with Corinthian features was laid July 4, 1901, to the accompaniment of fireworks and Protestant hymns. Offering its spacious facilities to other religious congregations and to the city government after the 1906 fire, Calvary had services conducted in its lecture room by the presiding Rabbi of Temple Emanu-El, concerts by the Loring Club in its auditorium, and sessions of the Superior Court in its gymnasium.

S. from Jackson St. on Webster St.

181. The buildings, old and new, of the STANFORD-LANE HOSPITALS, Webster St. between Clay and Sacramento Sts., are the visible record of the institution's last half-century of progress. The huge five-story red-brick Lane Hospital was erected in 1893; the reinforced concrete Stanford Hospital, adjoining on the east, in 1917. The former contains medical, surgical, pediatric, neuropsychiatric, and obstetrical wards, and a clinical nursery, and is operated by a medical faculty chosen by a clinical committee appointed by Stanford University. Stanford Hospital, controlled by the same staff, contains 70 private rooms, a private surgery and a gynecological clinic ward, delivery rooms, hydro- and electro-therapeutic departments, a private clinical laboratory, and X-ray, diagnostic, and therapeutic departments. On the opposite side of Clay Street stands the seven-story gray cement Stanford School of Nursing. Lane Hospital is an outgrowth of the first medical college established on the Pacific Coast in 1858 by Dr. E. S. Cooper.

Containing 90,000 volumes, the LANE MEDICAL LIBRARY, SE. corner Sacramento and Webster Sts., occupies a three-and-one-half-story fireproof building erected in 1912. It contains an early collection of valuable works from the New York Academy of Medicine and 5,000 volumes of medical history, which includes works by ancient or medieval authorities in the Turkish, Arabic, and Persian languages. The library is named for Dr. Levi Cooper Lane, a brilliant surgeon, nephew of the principal founder of Lane Hospital.

W. from Webster St. on Sacramento St.

182. In the DRAMA WORKSHOP, 2435 Sacramento St., a pale green one-story building with wide canary yellow door, costumes of every country of the world are designed, assembled, and stored for use of the San Francisco Recreation Department. Within the skylighted room are doll models and mounted water color paintings of the dress of the world's far places. Recreational activities sponsored by the workshop include puppetry, dance and drama, and adult story-telling groups. Here, too, is housed the extensive library of the Northern California Drama Association, for which the Drama Workshop is head-quarters.

183. Its ponderous limestone mass capped with a gray Levantine dome, TEMPLE SHERITH ISRAEL (*open daily 9-5*), NE. corner Webster and California Sts., is a pioneer stronghold of reformed Judaism which has played a colorful role in the city's political history. Its stern main facade is distinguished by an entrance recessed behind a Roman arch which curves above a vast rose window. The interior auditorium is a huge square, surrounded by two tiers of galleries, from which a domed ceiling rises 80 feet above the floor. The present building was erected in 1904 for a congregation organized in 1850.

Serving as a temporary Hall of Justice immediately after the 1906 fire, the auditorium here was the courtroom in which Abraham Ruef was indicted on 65 counts of extortion by a grand jury. (During a recess, a juryman named Haas, who had been exposed as an ex-convict, shot and wounded Francis J. Heney, chief prosecutor and leader of the graft investigations.) Barely saved from lynching, Ruef was convicted and sentenced to 14 years in San Quentin. Asked by newspaper reporters how he liked exchanging his natty attire for a convict's striped gray uniform, the dethroned political boss of San Francisco replied: "The zebra is one of the most beautiful and graceful of animals. Why, therefore, should I cavil at my attire."

E. from Webster St. on California St. to Laguna St.; N. from California on Laguna.

184. Site of the first observatory in California, LAFAYETTE SQUARE, Washington, Gough, Sacramento and Laguna Sts., is a sloping green hill crisscrossed with hedges and graveled walks, topped with tennis courts and a small playground. Erected in 1879, the observatory was maintained privately for 20 years by George Davidson,

geodesist and astronomer. The park was created in 1867, but the top of the hill was owned by Samuel W. Holladay, ex-Oregon stage driver and owner of the famous Overland Stage Line, whose glistening white home on "Holladay's Hill" was a mecca for literary and Gold Rush aristocracy. Repeated suits by the city failed to dislodge Holladay, and the old mansion, with weathered timbers that had come round the Horn, was not razed until 1936, when the site was incorporated into the park.

E. from Laguna St. on Sacramento St. to Octavia St.; S. from Sacramento on Octavia.

185. Three tiny fragments of bone, each no larger than a grain of rice, repose in three little glass balls enclosed in a glass temple on a beautifully carved altar at the HONGWANJI BUDDHIST MIS-SION OF NORTH AMERICA (*open daily; English services, Sun. 1 p.m.; Japanese services, Sun. 8 p.m.*), 1881 Pine St., first Buddhist church in America and national headquarters of the mission. These sacred relics, reputed to be portions of the body of Buddha, were presented to Bishop Masuyama in 1935 by the King of Siam. The temple is a pearl gray, two-story concrete building, occidental in line; its slender dome is topped with an odd spearlike spire. Beautifully handwrought brass lanterns flank its three entrances.

In the auditorium filigreed black and gold folding panels shield the altar and inner shrine, decorated with pastel and gold leaf friezes representing Buddhist angels in heaven and birds of paradise. The screen panels, when unfolded, disclose the *maejoku* (altar table), with its candelabra, incense burner, and cut flowers in massive bronze urns, flanked on either side by a *rinto* (lantern) of heavily garlanded brass, suspended from a bell-like hood. Behind the altar rises the pagoda-topped shrine with heavily carved columns of gold-leaf; in the inner chamber is a reclining golden image of Buddha under a golden canopy.

The members of the temple are of the Shin sect, with headquarters at the Nishi Hongwanji Temple in Kyoto, Japan. This sect was founded in Japan in the year 1226 by Saint Shinran; its North American adherents number about 70,000. A modest two-story flat at 532 Stevenson Street served in 1898 as the first Buddhist Church in America. The present temple was dedicated in 1938.

186. On the northern fringes of the Japanese quarter a hospital marks the SITE OF THE THOMAS BELL RESIDENCE, corner Octavia and Bush Sts., long known as the "House of Mystery." The house itself was torn down about 1927 but a short row of eucalyptus trees that once hedged it remains. Here, during the heyday of the Comstock period, lived that formidable sorceress known to every San Franciscan as Mammy Pleasant. Ostensibly, the great mansion with

its mansard roof, its inner courtyard, and its mirror-lined ballroom, which was never used for dancing, was the private residence of Thomas Bell, reputedly the power behind William C. Ralston's throne in the Bank of California. Mammy Pleasant was to all appearances his housekeeper. There was scarcely a man in public life who did not treat the scrawny little Negress with utmost deference.

The truth was, of course, that she was a procuress of unusual resources and connections, and a remarkable cook. On her arrival in San Francisco in 1848, she quickly attracted to her boarding house the leaders of the town. The entertainment she provided soon enabled her to open a whole chain of boarding houses. Obeying the injunction of her dead first husband she devoted part of her legacy received from him to the Abolitionist cause, traveling to Boston, where she presented John Brown with a draft for $30,000. When Brown was captured at Harper's Ferry, a note was found on him, signed with illiterate Mammy Pleasant's "M. P." It read: "The ax is laid at the foot of the tree. When the first blow is struck, there will be more money to help."

To ensure this, Mammy returned to San Francisco, set up her *ménage* in the mansion among the blue gum trees, and settled down to her long career of forwarding the infidelities of the city's men of affairs. She squandered Thomas Bell's fortune on her weird schemes, turned his wife against him, kept him virtually a prisoner, and starved his children. When he died of a fall into the courtyard from a third-story balcony, it was believed that his "housekeeper" had pushed him over. She carried on for years a bitter legal duel with members of his family. She died at the age of 92, penniless, asking only that her tombstone bear this epitaph: "She was a friend of John Brown."

E. from Octavia St. on Bush St.

187. First of its denomination on the Pacific Coast, TRINITY EPISCOPAL CHURCH, NE. corner Gough and Bush Sts., was founded in 1849. The present structure, built of rough-hewn Colusa sandstone, Norman in style, is flanked at either end of its main facade by bastions with conical turrets which contribute to the massive effect imposed by the square central belfry (Hobart, Cram, and Ferguson, architects). The interior nave of three bays contains lancet windows of stained glass portraying Biblical subjects, the work of Belgian craftsmen. Buried beneath the chancel is the Reverend Flavel Scott Mines, founder of the church, who died in 1852. Beside the altar stands a bronze angel with folded wings who bears aloft a flat brass scroll on which rests a large Bible. Until 1867 services were held in a private house. From that date until the erection of the present church in 1892,

its congregation met in a large frame building at Post and Powell Streets.

S. from Bush St. on Gough St. to O'Farrell St.; E. from Gough on O'Farrell

188. Its peaked gray roof rising between a cone-topped turret and a square pyramid-roofed bell tower, ST. MARK'S EVANGELICAL LUTHERAN CHURCH (*services Sun. 8:30 and 11 a.m.*), O'Farrell St. between Gough and Franklin Sts., was the first Lutheran Church in California, founded in 1849. The red brick facade of the present structure, dedicated in 1895, is of Romanesque design. In 11 stained glass windows, which shed rich red, blue, and purple light on an interior decorated in French ivory and gold, are represented *The Pascal Lamb, The Holy Writ, The Sacred Chalice, The Cross, The Crown of Christ the King, The Ten Commandments,* and the name "Jehovah" in Hebrew. Behind the ornate altar rise the gilded pipes of the great organ, distinguished for its trumpet brass reed with clarion martial tone. One of the first pipe organs built in San Francisco, it was installed by Felix Schoenstein in 1886 in the church's former building on Geary Street. Until 1864, when orthodox members of its congregation withdrew to found the Church of St. Paulus, Masons and others belonging to secret orders were barred from membership. Following the 1906 disaster the slightly damaged church served as a refugee and hospital center. Until 1931 services were conducted in German.

189. Seat of the Roman Catholic Archbishopric of Northern California, ST. MARY'S CATHEDRAL OF THE ASSUMPTION, NW. corner O'Farrell St. and Van Ness Ave., is a huge ungainly red-brick structure of German Gothic design; its octagonal tower and spire and massive flight of granite steps are out of proportion to its severe and unimposing facade. The interior offers a contrasting aspect of simple magnificence. Royal Bavarian windows of stained glass lend it an atmosphere of symbolic grandeur. The three sections of the *Assumption* rise behind the archbishop's green and gold throne by the high altar, under a rose window in four segments. Behind the two small galleries are rose windows in 12 divisions. Along the north side of the nave are four larger windows representing the *Wedding Feast at Cana, Christ in the Garden of Gesthemane, The Good Shepherd,* and *Peter Receiving the Keys.* On the south side are *The Meeting of Mary and Elizabeth, The Nativity, The Presentation in the Temple,* and *The Flight Into Egypt.* The Stations of the Cross on either side of nave and transept are represented in white, gold, and blue enamel.

N. from O'Farrell St. on Van Ness Ave. to Geary St.; W. from Van Ness on Geary

190. Rich in historic tradition, the FIRST UNITARIAN CHURCH, SW. corner Geary and Franklin Sts., an ivy-covered, gray stone edifice of modified Romanesque and Gothic design, with a square turret in place of the bell tower demolished by the earthquake of 1906, is reminiscent in its quiet dignity of the churches of the English countryside. In the little strip of churchyard is an oblong white marble sarcophagus bearing the simple inscription, "Thomas Starr King, born December 17, A. D. 1824—Died March 4, A. D. 1864"; here repose the remains of the militant pastor of the Civil War period with whom the church long has been identified. The church has a great circular rose window and perpendicular Gothic windows of stained glass. Bruce Porter's allegorical painting, *Lo At Length The True Light,* appears over the altar, which is flanked on either side by winged angels sculptured by Arthur Putnam. The marble baptismal font with rows of finely chiseled cherubs, under a spired Gothic canopy rising to the vaulted ceiling of the church, is the gift of the First Congregational Church of New York to the First Unitarian Church in San Francisco, made in 1864.

The city's first Unitarian religious service was preached on October 20, 1850, by the Reverend Charles A. Farley. A Unitarian society was soon formed and by 1852 was holding services in Armory Hall, then the largest auditorium in town. In a church of its own on Stockton Street the society began meeting in 1853. To this church in 1860 came a young Boston clergyman, Thomas Starr King. When the Civil War began a year later, he canvassed the State, helping to swing California to the side of the Union with his cloquence. Through King's efforts the cornerstone of a new church on Geary Street was laid in December, 1862. Only two months after its dedication January 10, 1864, King died of diphtheria. The Reverend Horatio Stebbins succeeded him and during the 35 years of his pastorate, many distinguished visitors spoke from the pulpit, among them Ralph Waldo Emerson, Julia Ward Howe, Edward Everett Hale, Charles Eliot, and David Starr Jordan. Since the dedication of the present church on February 10, 1889, its pastor and membership have carried on the tradition of Thomas Starr King, playing a leading role in movements for political, economic, and social reform.

N. from Geary St. on Franklin St. to Post St.; E. from Franklin on Post to Van Ness Ave.; N. from Post on Van Ness

191. The chaste white granite and limestone SCOTTISH RITE TEMPLE, NW. corner Van Ness Ave. and Sutter St. (Carl Werner,

architect), was dedicated in 1911 by the Masonic Order of Scottish Rite, first established in San Francisco in 1868. It has been used by clubs, political groups, and trade unions for grand annual balls, public forums, and convention headquarters. Beyond the lobby is the lodge room, seating 1,500, a vast two-storied chamber of English Tudor design, with high stained-glass windows lighting the dark walnut panels of the room. On the fourth and top floor is a library (*open to members only*) of 2,500 volumes, including a copy of Albert Magnus' *Sermons,* printed in 1479, bound in leather with covers of thin wood; the *History of St. Joan,* printed in 1722; and what is perhaps the only complete *Catholic Encyclopedia* on the Pacific Coast.

192. Home of the Russian Orthodox Church in North America is the HOLY TRINITY RUSSIAN EASTERN ORTHODOX CATHEDRAL, NW. corner Van Ness Ave. and Green St., where on Orthodox Sunday (first Sunday in Lent) deep-voiced Russian singers intone their centuries-old laments for the godless. The first Russian cathedral in the United States and the oldest Russian church in San Francisco, the present structure is authentically Byzantine in design, a buff-colored frame building, its green dome surmounted with a gold Greek cross. It faces east in the tradition of the Greek Orthodox Church. Within the belfry hang five bells, the largest of which, weighing two and one-half tons, was made expressly for the church in commemoration of the miraculous escape from death of the "little Father of all the Russias" in 1884. The church has two richly decorated auditoriums, one for daily services, the other for Sundays and holy days. Its murals depicting religious subjects are by Gleb Ilyn. The cathedral has no benches or pews, the congregation being obliged to stand or kneel on the bare floor while priests in colored vestments, thin and frayed from decades of use, intone the mass and vespers. Ikons are usually kept covered on a special table except during Easter, when they are placed on the altar for 40 days.

The first known services of the Russian Greek Orthodox Church held in San Francisco were conducted in 1863, when a priest from a Russian ship in the Bay baptized a Serbian infant in a private house. With the arrival of many Russian immigrants from Alaska, Father Ioann Metropolsky came in 1871 and organized the St. Alexander Russian Orthodox Church. In 1882-83 a cathedral was established on Powell Street; the memorial bells hung in the church were rescued during the fire and earthquake of 1906 and installed in the present structure after its dedication in 1909. The present titular head of the cathedral, Bishop Metropolitan Theopolis Bashkrovsky, former Tsarist army chaplain during the World War, was appointed bishop of San Francisco in 1932 and Metropolitan of the Russian Church in North America in 1934.

W. from Van Ness Ave. on Union St.

193. Of polyglot design, the HINDU TEMPLE (*open Wed. 8 p.m.*), SW. corner Filbert and Webster Sts., rears from its third story a bewildering array of minarets, cupolas, and towers of Gothic, Hindu, Shiva, and Moslem design. The upward-pointing architectural features of the temple, headquarters of the Vedanta Society, are intended to symbolize the goal of Vedanta teachings, ultimate perfection. To each of the six towers is attached a symbolic meaning: one, decorated with crescent, sun, and trident, symbolizes the path to knowledge through devotion and work. In the chapel and auditorium on the first floor, above the altar, hang two life-size portraits, one of Ramakrishna, patron saint of the Vedanta movement, the other of Swami Trigunatita, head of the temple at the time of its completion in 1904. Beside the platform is a large portrait of Swami Vivekananda, who brought Hinduism to the West and under whose guidance the temple was founded.

Rim of the Golden Gate

"Thou seest the white seas fold their tent,
O Warden of two continents.
Thou drawest all things, small and great,
To thee, beside the Western Gate."

— BRET HARTE

194. Facing a little cove within the sheltering arm of Black Point, protected on the north and west by the semicircular sea wall that is Municipal Pier, is 34½-acre AQUATIC PARK (*open 9-4; 10¢ for use of dressing room, locker, shower; suits not furnished*), foot of Polk St. This $1,500,000 municipal recreation center was made possible by WPA funds, laborers, and artists. To create its quarter-mile stretch of clean sand and smooth surf, workmen excavated (1935-38) a large part of that area into which had been dumped in 1906 the debris from the ruins of Chinatown, uncovering jewelry and watches, pieces of jade, and coins from a dozen nations.

The triple-decked white concrete CASINO (William Mooser, Sr., and William Mooser, Jr., architects), resembles a streamlined battleship riding at anchor. Spectators' galleries facing seaward flank its convex ends. Its main entrance on Polk Street, a broad modern doorway and heavy lintel of greenish-grey slate, is the work of Sargent Johnson; the design and incised sculpture of conventionalized marine subjects are modern in conception. Decorating the 100-foot-long main lounge are large murals by Hilaire Hiler depicting undersea flora and fauna. Mr. Hiler's use of brilliant shades of violet, blue, vermillion, orange, rose, and gold against a sober blue-green background has produced a beautifully luminous effect. Outside the lobby a long veranda overlooks the water; at either end are circular chambers: The Rainbow Room—a ladies' lounge with a ceiling decorated in prismatic colors, and the Blue Room. The motif is nautical throughout, from the ground floor—whose dressing rooms and lunch counter face the broad concrete promenade—to the oval-shaped Pilot Room, a cocktail lounge occupying the fourth floor. At each end of the Pilot Room and of the spacious third-floor banquet hall are large sun decks.

The view from the casino decks is superb. The red-leaded Golden Gate Bridge contrasts sharply with the blue Bay and the buff and purple hills of the opposite shore. To the east are the abandoned Golden Gate Ferry slips, the smokestacks of foreign steamships, and—frequently—the tall masts of sardine purse-seiners at anchor. Grim Alcatraz is closest to this part of the mainland.

Notable among the park's ultramodern conveniences are those designed for its bathers. Each person returning from the water passes through a photo-electrically operated chlorinated shower and foot bath on his way to the dressing rooms and fresh-water showers. He dries himself in currents of warm air and retrieves his street clothes from metal containers that will be sterilized with live steam before they are reissued.

On this site in the 1870's were the Neptune Baths, from which William C. Ralston swam to his death in 1875, and industrial units of a woolen mill and smelting company.

195. Popular with fishermen of all ages and Sunday promenaders is the 1,850-foot-long white concrete MUNICIPAL PIER, foot of Van Ness Ave. The semicircular sea wall, constructed in 1929-34, swings northeastward to protect Aquatic Park's little harbor. From adjacent TRANSPORT WHARF NUMBER 4, steamers operate daily to and from Alcatraz and Angel Islands.

196. Neighbor on the south to Aquatic Park is the adjoining city block of red-brick buildings housing the D. GHIRARDELLI AND COMPANY CHOCOLATE PLANT (*private*), 900 North Point St., organized in the 1850's by Domingo Ghirardelli, three of whose eleven grandchildren are active in the firm today. The plant moved here from its original location in the old Phoenix Building in 1897, that it might be near the Belt Line Railroad and utilize the brick building abandoned by the Pioneer Columbia Woolen Mill. Mrs. Marie Oetzel, an early resident, says: "The first woolen mill on that site burned in 1861 and a new one was built. This closed down in 1883. I remember it well. They hired Chinese and housed them in two high narrow buildings down by the water, just about where the park clubhouse [Aquatic Park Casino] now stands. When they were dyeing wool the Chinese would run the finished batch down a long ramp, made of redwood logs, into the salt water to set the color. The whole beach would change color for a few hours; shells, rocks, and sand would look like a colored picture." Also in the immediate vicinity from about 1865 to 1885 were the smelters and refineries of the Selby Company. Said Mrs. Oetzel: "When the old Selby Smelter closed, a Mrs. Kelly put up some bathhouses. There were also some arks along the beach in which some artists and musicians lived. One or two of them were used by the Tivoli Artists, who played in the old Tivoli Theater. Kenori's Boat House was there also. He made some fine oars and small boats for the rowing clubs: the *Ariel, South End,* and *Dolphin.*"

Nucleus of the rapidly expanding chocolate plant was the old woolen mill's building. Today the firm is one of the largest of its kind in the West, its range of distribution reaching from the Mississippi River to the Orient and the islands of the Pacific. The 50 varieties of its product include the ground chocolate originated by Domingo Ghirardelli. In the main office of the plant is a large mixing machine brought round the Horn from France in the 1860's—a heavy circular chocolate mill three feet in diameter with stone rollers used for grinding the raw cacao—and a primitive Mexican hand mill used by the Aztecs. (No better medium for the grinding of chocolate than stone has yet been discovered.)

S. on Polk St. to Bay St.; W. on Bay

197. Thrust northward into the Bay, its land boundaries Van Ness Ave., Bay and Laguna Sts. (main entrance Van Ness Ave. and Bay St.), is FORT MASON UNITED STATES MILITARY RESERVE (usually open 24 hrs.; subject to close without notice), whose 68½ acres enclose the site of Spanish fortifications built nearly 150 years ago. On April 4, 1797, Governor Diego de Borica instructed engineer Alberto de Cordoba to complete certain necessary repairs of Castillo de San Joaquin and to construct another battery where it would "further impede the anchorage of any hostile vessel in La Yerba Buena." Location chosen by De Cordoba for his Battery San Jose was Point Medanos (later called San Jose), today's Black Point, northernmost natural promontory of the reserve. Original defense for the little battery was five brass eight-pounders; by 1798 it had achieved a sixth cannon; but by the turn of the century it was virtually abandoned. When General and Mrs. John C. Frémont in the 1850's moved to Black Point—said to have been so named because of its dense, somber laurel thickets—there was no trace of Battery San Jose.

The area was set aside for military purposes by President Millard Fillmore in 1850-51, but not until 1863 were troops quartered in the area. Meanwhile lawsuits had been waged over boundaries, water rights, and private claims which were to reduce the original 100-acre reserve to its present size.

Unsuccessful in their fight to gain possession of the area were Frémont and four friends who claimed it by squatters' rights. Colonel Richard Barnes Mason carried out the Presidential order to dispossess, thus incurring an enmity that culminated in a challenge by Frémont to a duel, which was never fought. In 1882 the reservation was named for Colonel Mason (California military governor 1847-49).

Fort Mason today contains 102 frame buildings, including several commissary warehouses, a supply depot and 13 units occupied by officers. Residential headquarters of the commander of the Fourth Army (Seventh and Ninth Corps Areas), a rambling old house overlooking the Bay, incorporates the little one-room headquarters built by Major Leonidas Haskell about 1850.

Point of embarcation and arrival for troops stationed abroad are the three ARMY TRANSPORT DOCKS in the northwestern corner of the reserve (foot of Laguna St.). A primary port of the United States Army Transport Service, Fort Mason is the home of the Army transports *Grant, Somme, Cambrai,* and *Meigs.* Annually provisions valued at more than $12,000,000 are shipped to Army outposts in Alaska, Panama Canal Zone, Hawaii, the Philippines, and the Far East. Through a tunnel under the reservation Belt Line locomotives haul freight cars between the Embarcadero and the docks. More than 25,000 replacement troops leave here each year to relieve garrisons in service overseas.

N. from Bay St. on Laguna St. to Marina Blvd.; NW. on Marina (or NW. from Bay St. and Van Ness Ave. on a Fort Mason road to Marina Blvd.; NW. on Marina)

Comparatively new and fashionable is that residential district of stuccoed flats and broad-windowed apartment buildings known as The Marina, extending from Van Ness Avenue west to the Presidio and north from Lombard Street to Fort Mason and the Bay. The older part of the district was built up during the Panama-Pacific International Exposition of 1915; the newer, since 1922, on some 50 of the several hundred blocks on which the exposition was located.

198. Lying north of broad Marina Boulevard between Webster St. and Yacht Harbor, are the block-wide, level lawns of MARINA PARK (*parking area; comfort stations*). Baseball and football players, picnickers, and kite and model airplane enthusiasts have replaced the local amateur aviators who made the park their unofficial landing field until 1925. In that year Marina residents objected so strenuously to the aerial menaces to their lives and property that the Park Commission decided to use the land for its originally intended recreational purposes. The tiny cove at the eastern end of Marina Park, near the Army Transport Docks, is crowded with small fishing craft (*boats rented*). Where the oil-covered pilings of the abandoned wharves push up from the water, implacable fishermen stand guard over bobbing corks or haul oily crabnets from the cove. Cleaner is the small enclosed bathing lagoon at the park's western end.

199. Berthed in municipally owned YACHT HARBOR, Marina Blvd., Scott, and Lyon Sts., are about 200 craft, ranging in size from the tiniest of catboats to Templeton Crocker's black-hulled, two-masted schooner *Zaca,* veteran of far-ranging scientific expeditions. Sail and motor boats moored here dot the Bay on pleasant Sundays and participate in periodical regattas.

200. On the 1,500-foot-long breakwater that shelters the harbor is

the home of the ST. FRANCIS YACHT CLUB (*private*), a two-story cement-faced structure roofed with red and orange tile, all but obscured from the mainland by green pines. Spanish in both exterior and interior—with beamed ceilings looking down on rooms furnished in heavy dark wood and warmed by great open fires—the decorative motif is nevertheless marine. A large glass-enclosed lounge affords an unusually fine view of the Bay and its shores. Among the clubrooms open to its 300 members are a dining room, a bar, steam and locker rooms, and courts for badminton, handball, and squash. Active in formation of the organization (1928) was Hiram Johnson, Jr. Non-profit and given to the promotion of frequent social events, the club's primary interest is yachting. Its annual open racing season (for craft of all classes) attracts sportsmen from the entire Bay region.

201. Beyond the club, at the eastern tip of the breakwater, stands a MINIATURE LIGHTHOUSE of stone and granite once publicized by Robert ("Believe-It-or-Not") Ripley as the only municipally owned lighthouse in the world chartered by a national government. The granite in the 30-foot-high tower came from tombstones in an abandoned Lone Mountain Cemetery. A small park area guarded by reclining stone lions surrounds the little building.

S. from Marina Blvd. on Baker St.

202. Where indoor tennis courts are covered by the long roof of the PALACE OF FINE ARTS (*open weekdays 8:30-11:30; Sun. 8-5; courts $1 an hour; lighted*), foot of Lyon St., visitors to the Panama-Pacific International Exposition of 1915 enjoyed the art treasures of the fair. The tan stuccoed facade of the semicircular building (outer circumference 1,100 feet; width, 135 feet) and its fronting peristyle of terra-cotta Corinthian columns follow the curve of a lagoon in which water fowl glide about two anchored gondolas. In the center of the colonnade, opposite the main entrance, is an ornamental domed rotunda supported by eight pairs of columns flanking as many arches. The palace's designer, Bernard Maybeck, is said to have been inspired by Brocklin's painting, *The Island of the Dead.*

After the fair, in 1918, the palace again housed an art collection—that of the San Francisco Art Commission; but after 1921, when the group moved its exhibit, the building was allowed to deteriorate. In 1927 the Government deeded that ten-acre portion of the Presidio on which the palace stood to the City of San Francisco, but not until 12 years later did San Francisco begin to expend the $500,000 necessary for its restoration.

The restored palace mirrored in the placid waters of the lagoon is all that remains of the $50,000,000 exposition that reached from Fort

Mason to the Presidio. President William Howard Taft broke the first earth on the site October 14, 1911, and four months later issued an invitation to all nations to participate in this great celebration of the opening of the Panama Canal. On the early morning of February 20, 1915, more than 150,000 noisily enthusiastic persons marched through the city streets to the fairgrounds. Only celebrants who did not walk to the Scott Street gates were a group of pioneers whose carriage followed slowly behind the marching leaders of the two-and-one-half-mile-long parade: Mayor James Rolph, Jr., Governor Hiram W. Johnson, and fair official Marshall Hale (whose brother, Robert, first had suggested the celebration to Congress in a letter dated January 12, 1904).

Said a contemporary writer of the exposition: "From the city's heights one looks down on a facade three-quarters of a mile long, dominated at its center by the lofty seven-storied . . . Tower of Jewels, 432 feet in height, and broken on either side by an open court ornamented with lesser towers. As the eye rests upon the rectangular group, eight great domes claim the attention, distinguishing the location of an equal number of exhibit palaces, domes of sea-green color, pale against the intense blue of the sky and the bright red of the tiled roofs. One notes that the avenue bisects the group at right angles, widening along the lateral axis into three courts . . .

"And now the eye withdraws from this central group-building, attracted by the two domed structures in the South Gardens, Festival Hall and the Palace of Horticulture. To the east, rests the Palace of Machinery . . . To the west across the still lake, and curving to its shores . . . stands the Palace of Fine Arts. . . . Passing through the main entrance, underneath the Tower of Jewels, we enter the Court of the Universe. Elliptical in shape, 700 by 900 feet, it contains a sunken garden capable of seating seven thousand persons, is entirely surrounded by handsome colonnades . . . the facades of the four palaces being modified to form the walls of the court. The entrance from the lateral avenue on the east and west are surmounted by magnificent archways. . . . Passing westward along the avenue between the palaces of Agriculture and Liberal Arts, the visitor enters the Court of the Four Seasons. . . . The corresponding court on the east is the Court of Abundance. Two minor courts open to the south, that on the east, the Court of Flowers; on the west, the Court of Palms.

"To the north . . . stretches the long Esplanade, threaded with walks and driveways . . . while over beyond the superb Palace of Fine Arts in bewildering array the dignified Foreign Pavilions and imposing buildings of the states arrest the attention . . ."

Twenty-five foreign nations contributed to the "bewildering array," many duplicating famous structures of their lands—such as Turkey's mosque of Sultan Ahmed I and Japan's sacred temple at Kioto, Kin Ka

Ku Ji. The 43 states and territories represented showed equal imagination: New York built a Fifth Avenue mansion; New Jersey, George Washington's Trenton Barracks; California, a Spanish mission.

Dedicated to sheer fun was the "Zone," with its $10,000,000 worth of amusement concessions. And in the background the 3,600,000-candlepower scintillator on its special pier at Yacht Harbor swept the night skies with color, painting the fog that rolled in from the Bay with every hue of the rainbow.

W. from Baker St. on Lombard St., which leads into Lincoln Blvd.

THE PRESIDIO OF SAN FRANCISCO, UNITED STATES MILITARY RESERVATION (*usually open 24 hours; subject to close without notice; speed limit 20 m.p.h.; night parking prohibited*), entered at Lincoln Blvd. and Lombard St., is a wooded tract of 1,540 acres extending from Lyon St. west to the ocean and from West Pacific Ave. and Lobos Creek north to the rim of the Golden Gate. Largest military post within a city's limits in the United States, the reservation includes general headquarters of the Ninth Corps Area, fortifications hidden by sand dunes and heavily forested hillsides, barracks for enlisted men, officers' quarters, a guard house, recreation centers, a hospital, a cemetery, sleek parade grounds, aviation field and hangars, warehouses, and supply depots. A fortified area since 1776—when it was chosen by Juan Bautista de Anza as military headquarters of the soldiers of Charles III of Spain—the Presidio has been occupied by Spanish garrisons, was host to Frémont's buckskin-clad followers, welcomed volunteers during the Spanish-American War, and trained doughboys for service in the first World War. In 1906 the Presidio became a tent city of refugees of the fire. In 1917-18 it played host in an even grimmer way, housing a concentration camp for enemy aliens.

Associated with the Presidio are some of the most illustrious names of the United States Army. Stationed here were Generals William Tecumseh Sherman, P. H. Sheridan, E. V. Sumner, Winfield Scott, Irvin McDowell, and A. S. Johnson. Brigadier-General Fred Funston commanded the post during the reconstruction of the city in 1906 and General John J. Pershing was in command for a short time before leading the Punitive Expedition into Mexico.

203. Largest military hospital in the West and one of five Army general hospitals in the country is 1,000-bed LETTERMAN GENERAL HOSPITAL. Its 48 acres—on which are 56 permanent structures—are in the eastern end of the Presidio, that part of the reservation most protected from fog and wind. Wide lawns and a profusion of palm trees and shrubs surround the yellow and white buildings. Staffed entirely by Army medical officers, it is the hospital for reception and

definitive treatment of the Army's seriously ill stationed on the Pacific Coast and in near-by States, and for the sick returned from the Canal Zone, Alaska, and transpacific stations. In the Red Cross "hut" on the hospital grounds vaudeville and motion pictures are provided. Further recreational facilities are tennis courts and a library of 10,000 books and periodicals.

The institution was less pretentious when built in 1898 and named in honor of Jonathan Letterman, Medical Director of the Army of the Potomac. One of the finest medical officers of the Civil War, Letterman designed the pavilion type hospital used (with slight modification) by many countries.

204. Still in use is the old STATION HOSPITAL (near the Administration Building) constructed in 1854 of materials shipped around the Horn.

205. West of the hospital grounds, bordered on the north by Lincoln Blvd., is the MAIN PARADE GROUND, flanked by great red-brick barracks and their background of eucalyptus trees. At the northern end of the parade ground a sentry walks his post before the red-brick Guardhouse.

206. Nearby stands the OFFICERS' CLUB (*private*), only survival of the adobe buildings erected by the Spanish. In 1776 it was the headquarters of Lieutenant Jose Joaquin Moraga of the De Anza expedition (*see A Frontier To Conquer: The White Men Came*), who completed the garrison and dedicated the Presidio on September 17 of that year. A plaque on the building reads in part:

> ". . . Officers Quarters
> Under
> Spanish, Mexican, and American Rule
> Oldest Adobe Building in
> San Francisco."

Bronze cannons cast 250 years ago in Madrid, veterans of Pizarro's conquest of Peru, flank the club's entrance. A third, pointing at a marker honoring Lieutenant Moraga, bears on its breech the royal arms of Spain and the date 1679.

207. The NATIONAL MILITARY CEMETERY, Infantry Ter. and Lincoln Blvd., 25 acres of landscaped hillside overlooking the Golden Gate, is surrounded by groves of laurel, cypress, and eucalyptus trees. Among the remains of more than 16,000 men buried here are those of officers and enlisted men from abandoned cemeteries at Fort Klamath, Oregon; Fort Colville, Washington; the Modoc Lava Beds (scene of California's Modoc Indian Wars of 1872-73); and Old Camp Grant in Arizona. Headstones bear the well-known names of Mc-

Dowell, Shafter, Funston and Ligget. "Two Bits October 5 1873" is the inscription on a marble stone over the grave of an Indian interpreter from Fort Klamath. A huge heart-shaped plot with a granite monument, dedicated to the "Unknown Soldier Dead," marks the burial place of 408 soldiers of the World War. "Pauline C. Tyler—Union Spy" is engraved on the headstone of the grave of Pauline Cushman Tyler, young actress who was in the Union services during the Civil War and later received the honorary commission of brevet-major.

208. CRISSY FIELD, stretching along the Golden Gate between Marine Blvd. and Mason St., is the scene of the weekly (*Tues. 2:30 p.m.*) "Retreat Formation" by troops of "San Francisco's own," the 30th Infantry, and the annual encampment of the Citizens' Military Training Camp. On Army Day, the maneuvers, parades, artillery demonstrations, and anti-aircraft bombardments held here are open to the public, as are the divisional reviews of all troops of the post. The eastern end of the field is occupied by polo grounds and the numbered supply depots and warehouses of the Quartermaster Corps. Named in honor of Major Dana H. Crissy, Air Service pilot who was killed in the Transcontinental Air Races of 1919, the field was used as an army aviation base from 1919 until supplanted in 1936 by Hamilton Field (*see North Bay Tour*).

N. from Lincoln Blvd. on Long Ave. to Marine Dr.; W. on Marine

209. FORT WINFIELD SCOTT, near the northern limits of the Presidio, is headquarters of both the Ninth Coast Artillery District and the harbor defense distributed among Forts Barry and Baker (*see North Bay Tour*), Forts Miley and Funston. Within its area are the heavy gun units of the Coast Defense. In 1921 the fort was officially designated as a saluting station to return the salutes of foreign vessels of war visiting the Port of San Francisco. Officers and enlisted men occupy new grey stucco buildings, among them the Signal Corps Radio Station.

210. Fort Point, the promontory (*parking space*) beyond Fort Winfield Scott, is the northernmost point of the San Francisco Peninsula. On the shoreline below is OLD FORT SCOTT (*private*)—called until 1882 Fort Point—marking the Site of Castillo de San Joaquin, beside the southern anchorage of the Golden Gate Bridge. December, 1794 saw completion of the early *castillo* by the Spanish. It is recorded that the adobe walls trembled on their foundations of sand at the mere firing of a salute, that the guns "were badly mounted, and, for the most part, worn out." By July 1, 1846 the guns were dismounted and useless, although Frémont in his *Memoirs* relates that on that date he and 12 of his men spiked the "large, handsome pieces."

Designed after Fort Sumter, the present old brick fortress, with walls 36 feet thick, encloses a paved courtyard at the waters' edge. Today as obsolete as the square-riggers which were its enemies, its only modern facilities are a powerhouse and searchlight.

Retrace on Marine Dr. to Lincoln Blvd.; W. (then S.) on Lincoln to Washington Blvd.; S. on Washington to Park Blvd.; S. on Park

211. Occupying 162 acres in the southern and central part of the reservation are the PRESIDIO GOLF LINKS (*greens fee $2; $1 to officers and their guests Mon.-Fri.; $2 Sat. and Sun.*), Washington and Park Blvds.

212. Adjoining the golf links on the west are the grounds of the six-story, white granite MARINE HOSPITAL, foot of Fourteenth Ave., with its surrounding staff quarters (the medical and nursing staff of 82 live on the premises), laboratories, laundries, and greenhouses. Number 9 of 25 similar institutions operated by the Federal Public Health Service, its 500 beds are open to merchant sailors and all Federal employees except those in the Army and Navy.

This hospital was built in 1932. The city's first Marine Hospital, a four-story brick building, had been erected 79 years earlier on Rincon Point. The first such institution in the country, said to be the oldest Government service, was founded at Norfolk, Virginia, in 1798, to combat cholera and yellow fever, and occupational diseases caused by unsanitary living conditions aboard early American merchant vessels. A merchant sailor's ticket of admission to these hospitals is a certificate from his ship's master and surgeon presented within six months of his discharge.

213. Just east of the hospital and within the Presidio is little MOUNTAIN LAKE, Government-protected sanctuary for ducks and gulls. In 1939 the lake was reduced to half its former size when earth excavated in lowering the grade of the Funston Avenue approach to the Golden Gate Bridge was dumped into it. Mountain Lake Park (*play apparatus*), Lake St. between Eighth and Funston Aves., stretches along the lake's southern shore outside the Presidio.

Retrace on Park Blvd. to Lincoln Blvd.; S. on Lincoln, which leads into El Camino del Mar

214. Property of the War Department, but open to picnickers, bass fishermen, and sunbathers is BAKER'S BEACH, foot of Twenty-fifth Ave., a long sandy strip along the western edge of the Presidio (accessible by trails from the southwestern corner of the Presidio and from the foot of Twenty-fifth Ave.). The beach was named for

Colonel Edward Dickinson Baker (for whom Fort Baker in Marin County; Baker, Oregon; and San Francisco's Baker Street also were named). An eloquent orator and lawyer, Baker came here in the 1850's and canvassed the State in the cause of the Union. After making himself unpopular by defending Charles Cora during the Vigilante trial of 1856, he moved to Oregon, where he became a United States Senator, but returned to command the first regiment of California volunteers in the Civil War. He was killed in battle in 1861. Near Sea Cliff, the impassible promontory at the southern end of the beach, is an old red-brick pumping station which long ago pumped water from Lobos Creek (southern boundary of the Presidio) through a tunnel at Fort Point to downtown San Francisco, but which now supplies only the reservation.

N. from El Camino del Mar on Twenty-seventh Ave. to Sea Cliff Ave.; W. on Sea Cliff, which leads into a footpath; N. on the footpath

215. Toward purchase of the short, irregular crescent of JAMES D. PHELAN MEMORIAL BEACH STATE PARK (*barbecue pits; comfort stations*), the man for whom the park is named left a bequest of $50,000. A five-year wrangle over the property by the city, the State, the Allen Company (Sea Cliff development group), and the newspapers culminated in its purchase in 1933 by State and city for $160,000. It still popularly is called China Beach, a name applied since Chinese fishermen camped on the protected inlet—their nightly bonfires giving rise to the legend that the cove was a rendezvous of pirates. Announced by the Recreation Commission as the only spot on the city's ocean frontage between Fort Point and Fleishhacker Pool safe for bathing, plans call for "terraced gardens for the sloping hillsides; leafy walks; an alluring tea house; tennis courts; and an artificial pool . . ."

Retrace on footpath to El Camino del Mar; W. on El Camino del Mar

In the extreme northwestern corner of city and peninsula are the 270 green-lawned acres of city-owned LINCOLN PARK, facing seaward on the north and west, bounded on the east by Thirty-third Ave. and on the south by Clement St. and Fort Miley Reserve. The terrain slopes gently to the south and east and drops abruptly to the sheer cliffs above the Golden Gate. El Camino del Mar winds the length of the park, at one point skirting high above the rugged rock-strewn shore. Across the Bay, beyond the Golden Gate Bridge, lie the soft Marin Hills and Point Bonita (*see North Bay Tour*); closer are Land's End and Phelan and Baker's Beaches.

Beneath Lincoln Park's smooth lawns lie the graves of thousands of San Franciscans who died during the latter half of the nineteenth century. Among the cemeteries here were the burial grounds of Chinese and Italians, and here was Potter's Field. The city has kept its promise made when it purchased the property in 1910, and has not disturbed the graves.

216. On the formally landscaped summit in the northern section of the park stands the city's largest art museum, the CALIFORNIA PALACE OF THE LEGION OF HONOR (*open daily 10-5; parking area; organ concerts Sat. and Sun. 3-4*), a memorial to California's dead in the first World War, the gift (1924) of Adolph B. and Alma de Bretteville Spreckels. The cream-colored palace, closely resembling the eighteenth-century classic Palais de la Légion d'Honneur (Paris, France), is approached through a Roman arch flanked by two porticoes with double rows of Ionic columns. The porticoes abut the two wings of the palace to form a rectangular court. The wings are flanked by peristyles, each with 22 columns, and the main facade is fronted by a portico with six Corinthian columns. One of the five original bronze casts of Auguste Rodin's *The Thinker* occupies the center of the court. The entire building is set off by a stone balustrade. Bronze equestrian statues (Anna Hyatt Huntington, sculptress), *El Cid,* and *Jeanne d'Arc,* flank the path leading to the entrance. A marble plaque beside the doorway, the gift of France, reads: *"Hommage de la France aux héros Californiens morts pour la défense du droit et la liberté"* (France's homage to the California heroes dead in defense of right and liberty).

Of the museum's 19 main-floor galleries, those to the left and rear of the central foyer contain the permanent collection, which includes a series of fine seventeenth-century Flemish tapestries, French tapestries of the seventeenth and eighteenth centuries—many from the Gobelin works, and a set of modern Gobelins presented by the French government. The paintings include a few of the early Italians, Vivarini, Beltraffio, and Fra Bartolemmeo; there are two fine Guardis, among them the *Rialto Bridge;* a Caneletto, and other eighteenth century Venetians. The Dutch school is represented by Rubens, Cuyp, David Teniers, de Vos, and Ruisdael; the Spanish, by Murillo, Velasquez and El Greco's *St. Peter.* The English eighteenth-century paintings number portraits by Raeburn, Lawrence, Reynolds, Hoppner, and Romney. There are two Constables and Turner's *Grand Canal at Venice.* The French eighteenth-century school, including Fragonard, de Troy, and Boucher, is well represented; the work is hung in galleries containing some fine pieces of French furniture of the same period. Among the works of sculpture are bronzes and marbles by Rodin and others influenced by him, including Arthur Putnam, and a bronze bust by Jacob Epstein.

The galleries to the right of the main foyer are used for loan exhibits. The lower floor houses a little theater and the Albert Bender collection of oriental painting, sculpture, and ceramics.

In the center of the driveway before the museum a 120-foot wooden flagpole marks the western terminus of the Lincoln Highway (US 40). A few yards east is *The Shades,* three nude male bronzes by Rodin, standing with heads bowed and arms outstretched. The group is a memorial to Raphael Weill, pioneer merchant and philanthropist. The semicircular stone balustrade at the edge of the parkway overlooks a curious obelisk of bronze, rising 24 feet from a 7-foot-square granite base bearing the information that it was "presented to the Ladies Seamen's Friend Society by Dr. Henry Cogswell. A landmark of the seamen's last earthly port and resting-place in which he waits the advent of the Great Pilot of his eternal destiny. . . ."

S. from the Palace of the Legion of Honor on an unnamed drive

217. Facing the driveway near one of the main entrances (Thirty-fourth Ave. and Clement St.), in the southeastern section of the park, is headquarters of the 18-hole LINCOLN PARK MUNICIPAL GOLF COURSE. LINCOLN PARK CLUBHOUSE (*greens fee 50¢ Mon.-Fri.; 75¢ Sat. and Sun.; $2 monthly; clubs 50¢ a set; locker $1 a month; restaurant*), a large one-story white frame building resembles a comfortable country home. Near by is the CHILDREN'S PLAYGROUND (*play apparatus; handball courts*).

Retrace on unnamed drive to El Camino del Mar; NW. from El Camino del Mar on a footpath

218. A WPA-built trail, below El Camino del Mar just northeast of the Palace of the Legion of Honor, skirts the cliffside to LAND'S END, the wave-dashed headland forming the northwest rim of the city.

219. From the rocky shoal waters the hoarse siren of MILE ROCK LIGHTHOUSE, a few hundred feet offshore on the larger of the two Mile Rocks, echoes along the cliffs when fogs shroud the Bay; its light, atop a white cylindrical tower 78 feet above the water, is visible for 14 miles. Before the construction of the light (1903-06) the S. S. *Rio de Janeiro* foundered on Fort Point Reef (*see The Harbor and Its Islands*) in 1901 and sank with a loss of more than 100 lives and a reputed fortune in bullion and silk. Visitors intrepid enough to undertake the extremely rough passage and climb a rope ladder—or be hoisted, like the stations' supplies, by a rope swung from a boom—make arrangements for the trip with the Coast Guard at the Customhouse.

220. The path around Land's End follows the shore beneath the

MARINE LOOKOUT STATION OF THE CHAMBER OF COMMERCE, a buff-colored, three-story, towerlike, stuccoed structure equipped with a telepscope with a 30-mile range. The purpose of the station is to report vessels entering the harbor to their owners, the Immigration Department, the Customhouse, the press, supply houses, taxi companies and hotels. Craft are identified after they pass the lightship near the Farallones. The waves below the station wash over the boilers and hull of the lumber schooner *Coos Bay*. Farther west the skeletons of the *Frank H. Buck* and the Standard Oil tanker *Lyman Stewart* lie in the surf.

221. Near the wreckage of the *Lyman K. Stewart,* a few stark, jutting beams compose the remaining FRAMEWORK OF PELTON'S TIDE MACHINE—formerly referred to as "Pelton's Folly" —a structure built on an isolated rock facing the sea. Here Alexander Pelton planned to harness the tides and thus develop electric power. An experimental plant costing $250,000 was three times swept out to sea. When his backer (said to be Adolph Sutro) would advance no further funds and his own were exhausted, Pelton abandoned the project.

Retrace on footpath to El Camino del Mar; W. on El Camino del Mar to Seal Rock Ave.; E. on Seal Rock

222. The UNITED STATES VETERANS' ADMINISTRATION FACILITY (*open Mon.-Fri. 8-4, Sat. 8-12*), Seal Rock and Forty-fifth Aves., is housed in a group of ultra-modern hospital buildings constructed of terra cotta and reinforced concrete, combining pyramidal motifs of Mayan Temple architecture with modern design. Built in 1933 as a diagnostic center, the facility serves all veterans' hospitals west of the Mississippi River. (By special arrangement, a limited number of Canadian veterans are admitted for treatment.) One of 81 such institutions in the United States, it is more than a hospital, serving as a clearing house for veterans seeking compensation adjustments, physical examinations, and similar services. A consulting staff of 39 of the Pacific Coast's best-known physicians and surgeons augments the staff of 27 doctors and three dentists. There are 41 nurses, 90 ward attendants, and 35 kitchen workers (all lesser employees are Civil Service). Among the subsidiary buildings—in addition to laboratories and clinics—are quarters for nurses and married attendants, two duplex buildings for physicians, surgeons' homes, and a library, recreation hall, and canteen.

With a capacity of 336 beds, the facility serves more than 2,000 patients annually and examines about 4,000 more for pension and disability purposes. The principal work is done in the clinical and patho-logical laboratories, the X-ray diagnosis laboratory, and the physiotherapeutic division.

223. The facility is in the extreme southern section of FORT MILEY UNITED STATES MILITARY RESERVATION (*private*), whose 50 acres were set aside in 1900 and named in honor of Lieutenant Colonel John D. Miley, who had died at Manila the preceding year. A fortified reserve, it is surrounded by a strong wire fence and patrolled day and night by sentries. In 1911 Fort Miley was made a subpost of the Presidio.

Retrace on Seal Rock Ave. to El Camino del Mar; S. on El Camino del Mar to Point Lobos Ave.

224. SUTRO HEIGHTS (*open daily 9-5; no vehicles permitted*), Pt. Lobos and Forty-eighth Aves., once the home of Adolph Sutro, is now a public park. One of many enterprises of the Comstock millionaire who invested a fortune in the preservation of the city's natural beauty, the Heights are his most intimate memorial.

Sutro Heights commands a view of three miles of ocean beach below. Among the tall groves of trees in the park are scattered statuettes representing characters of folklore and fiction, among them a group from the stories of Charles Dickens. A white-painted wooden arch and gateway flanked by reclining stone lions marks the park's entrance. Directly within are an octagonal-shaped station house formerly used by a gatekeeper, and twin life-sized iron figures of guards in seventeenth-century cuirasses and helmets. A graveled central pathway, formerly a driveway, leads southward into the center of the garden under trees of a myriad variety, among them palms, firs, monkey trees, Monterey cypresses, and several from the islands of the South Pacific; a Norfolk Island pine, a Hawaiian *cazana,* and an *aurecara* of New Zealand. A smaller path, branching from the main pathway, leads to the top of the heights on the garden's western edge, a steeply descending cliff with terraced rock gardens planted in evergreens and perennials. A low granite wall on the edge of the terrace serves as a base for statues and urns placed alternately. Here also are two large muzzle-loading cannon, near each of which, as if in readiness, stand piles of huge iron shot. These ornaments originally decorated one of the city's earliest pleasure resorts, Woodward's Gardens.

A few paces back from the cliff's edge stood Adolph Sutro's home, built in the late 1870's and condemned and demolished in 1939. Only evidence today that a mansion once was here is a small stone strongroom, fitted with a heavy iron door and furnished with a safe bearing the imprint, "Adolph Sutro."

A native of Germany but a resident of California since 1850, Sutro had achieved wealth and prominence as a mining engineer. Visiting the property for the first time in the early 1880's, accompanied by his small daughter Emma, he was attracted by its possibilities, and forthwith purchased it from Samuel Tetlow, onetime proprietor of the Bella Union. He at once erected a new home on the site, acquired a stable of thoroughbred horses, imported statuary from Europe, and collected rare plants from many parts of the world. In the following years he spent more than $1,000,000 improving the estate, which at one time employed fifteen caretakers and three gardeners, in addition to a corps of house servants.

The Heights quickly became a fashionable gathering place, and its owner's hospitality a thing of renown. On one occasion a performance was given of Shakespeare's *As You Like It,* the cast of which included Ada Rehan and John Drew, both of Augustin Daly's company. It proved eminently successful, although the footlights were only Japanese lanterns; the stage, one of the lawns in front of the mansion.

An uncommon foresight moved Sutro to acquire properties adjoining the Heights, and his estate eventually embraced much of the city which now skirts the sea-front. With Edward B. Pond, then mayor of San Francisco, he planned the magnificent system of boulevards from Thirty-third Avenue westward to the ocean, an area which included the sites of what is the present Lincoln Park and the Veterans' Facility, the Cliff House, and Sutro Heights. Sutro's public-spiritedness was perpetuated by his descendants. "Open house" was always maintained at Sutro Heights; a sign placed near the entrance gate for many years invited the public "to walk, ride, and drive therein." Sutro Heights in 1898 came into the possession of Sutro's daughter, Dr. Emma Sutro Merritt, who left it as a public park to the city on her death in 1938.

W. from El Camino del Mar on Point Lobos Ave.; N. from Point Lobos on Merrie Way to a footpath; W. on footpath

225. Easternmost tip of San Francisco is POINT LOBOS, called Punta de los Lobos Marinos (Point of the Sea Wolves) by the Spanish because of its proximity to the sea lions on Seal Rocks. Lieutenant Juan Manuel de Ayala, who had sailed past the point and through the Golden Gate in the *San Carlos* on the evening of August 5, 1775, had charted the promontory as Angel de la Guarde (Guardian Angel). Somewhere on the heights above, on December 4, 1774, Captain Fernando de Rivera y Moncado and Father Francisco Palou, with four soldiers from their exploring party climbed a summit from which they saw "a great bay . . . its waters were as quiet as those of a great lake." On a rocky headland, "which up to this time had never received the

footprint of Spaniard or Christian," they set up a cross, supporting it by two rocks.

Seventy-nine years later enterprising Yankees were erecting a cross of a different nature on Point Lobos: that carrying the Pacific Coast's first telegraph wires to the Merchants' Exchange by way of Telegraph Hill. A lookout signalled news of the arrival of vessels to the several-mile-distant city.

Retrace to Point Lobos Ave.; W. on Point Lobos, which becomes Great Highway

226. The sprawling buildings of the SUTRO BATHS AND ICE RINK (*open Mon.-Fri. 10 a.m.-11 p.m.; Sat., Sun., holidays 9 a.m.-11 p.m.; skating 35¢ Sun. afternoons and every evening, 25¢ other times; skate rental 15¢; swimming 50¢*), Point Lobos Ave. near Great Highway, covering three acres of sloping beach in the lee of Point Lobos, were built in 1896 by Adolph Sutro. Long advertised as the world's largest are the six indoor pools; of both fresh and salt water, these vary in size, depth, and temperature. Also here are a floodlighted ice rink and an outdoor sand plot for sunbathing. It is said that 25,000 persons have visited "Sutro's" in one day. Wide-tiered galleries and promenades—bordered with palms, tropical plants, natural history specimens, and gay-colored tables and chairs—accommodate 7,000 spectators. One of the resort's numerous decorative palms attained such proportions that it became necessary to cut a hole in the floor above, through which the tree extends to the ceiling of the second story.

Seen from the windows of the resort is a part of the battered hull of the American-Hawaiian freighter *Ohioan*, which—reported the *Chronicle* on October 8, 1936—lost its bearing "in a peasoup fog off the Golden Gate . . . [and] with 42 officers and crew ran aground between Point Lobos and Seal Rocks, below Sutro Baths, just before midnight last night. . . ." The *Ohioan's* 1,500-ton cargo of general merchandise was valued at $450,000; the ship itself, at $350,000. Most of the cargo was saved, much of it undamaged, but the vessel was lodged so firmly on the rocks that it could not be refloated. Much of the steel in the hull was salvaged. Hundreds of curious visitors flocked to view the wrecked steamer. Two years later they again crowded the same stretch of beach to stare at the body of a large whale washed up near the *Ohioan* during a severe storm.

The carcass of a 120-ton whale had been deposited near by several years earlier. The *Chronicle* facetiously advertised on May 16, 1919: "Wanted—Somebody to remove . . . one huge, ancient and long-dead whale . . . before . . . Sunday." Towed to sea, the mammal had returned with the tide. Finally it was destroyed by fire. Said the

Chronicle: "Mourners stand away off as last sad requiem sobbed by winds."

227. The CLIFF HOUSE, Point Lobos Ave. at Great Highway, a white stuccoed building terraced along the edge of the cliff south of Sutro Baths, is a modern restaurant, bar, and gift shop. Both the barroom and the Sequoia Room—a cocktail lounge—are finished in redwood, from smooth walls to rustic beamed ceilings, and both house huge brick fireplaces in which open fires glow on chill days. From the lounge and the blue and white dining room in the rear of the building guests seated at the great plate glass windows on clear days look beyond Seal Rocks for miles across the Pacific.

The present Cliff House is the third to occupy the site. (Contrary to popular opinion, the first Cliff House was not built by Samuel Brannan of lumber salvaged from a wrecked ship. A roadhouse called Oceanside House was built elsewhere by Bela Brooks of the salvaged materials.) The first was built in 1863; its first tenants were, according to the *Morning Call* of February 26, 1894, "a couple of Frenchmen, whose names and memories are lost in obscurity." Traffic to the cafe in the 1860's was by way of the Point Lobos Toll Road, built by James Phelan, William Herrick, John Buckley, and Salem Burdell. A horse-drawn omnibus made the trip from Portsmouth Square to the beach; the fare was 50¢. The road followed Point Lobos Avenue (most of which has been renamed Geary Boulevard). Second tenant was retired seaman Captain J. R. Foster, who leased and managed the Cliff House for nearly two decades. Foster's resort was at first highly successful, for "it was for many years the only recreation point the inhabitants of our then sparsely settled city had when they wished to take the fresh air. Previous to the building of this palace a 'ride to the Mission' was the only luxury of the kind indulged in and this was performed on horseback over the sandhills. . . ." When the Cliff House became less fashionable and less attended, Foster made it a rendezvous of politicians and (continued the *Call*) "of the hetairie of San Francisco. The plazas used to be thronged with these gaily dressed nymphs, the rooms resounded with their carousals, and Captain Foster . . . winked the other eye when he directed the attention of a surprised visitor to the beauty of the ocean view. . . ."

When Adolph Sutro purchased the property about 1879 it was known as the Cliff House ranch. Said Sutro: "I believe there was a dilapidated little farm house down on the beach." On the same beach in earlier years had been Seal Rock House (also confused by some historians with the Cliff House)—"a curious architectural conglomeration" formed by frequent additions to an original "nondescript building"—said to have been managed by Captain Foster.

The Cliff House's first mishap occurred in January, 1887, when the schooner *Parallel,* with her cargo of 80,000 pounds of dynamite, was driven into the bluff below; abandoned by captain and crew, the vessel was pounded against the rocks until the dynamite exploded and seriously damaged the building's foundations. On Christmas, 1894, the Cliff House burned to the ground. Reported the *Call:* "The fire was a hidden one between ceiling and walls . . . started from a defective flue. . . . Toward midnight hacks began to arrive from the city with those curious to view the destruction of one of the most noted resorts in the world. . . . Jets of flame followed it until the bold brow of the cliff shone out . . . It lit up the white forms of the plaster gods and goddesses on the parapet, and revealed the low house of the master and the ghastly figures under the trees [of Sutro's Heights]. . . . The hoarse bellowing of the frightened seals as they fled from the rocks to the depths was heard. . . . The corpulent king of the herd, Benjamin Harrison Cleveland, who succeeded Ben Butler, was first to seek refuge from the falling embers. . . ."

Adolph Sutro erected the second Cliff House two years later—a picturesque structure in the design of a chateau with spiralling towers. The dedication of what jokingly was called "Sutro's gingerbread palace" occasioned great celebration. With this auspicious start began another era of popularity for the resort. It was a favorite of James Flood, James Fair, John Mackay, and Claus Spreckels; played host to Presidents Hayes, Grant, McKinley, Roosevelt, and Taft; and was a rendezvous of such theatrical and literary lights as Sarah Bernhardt, Adelina Patti, Mark Twain, and Bret Harte. In 1901, E. D. Beylard of Burlingame (wrote Oscar Lewis and Carrol Hall) "inaugurated a tally-ho service for the benefit of the Palace [Hotel] guests. Beylard borrowed his idea from the East, where . . . smart hotels were offering daily rides on the tops of coaches driven by young men of social importance. The Beylard tally-ho . . . each afternoon . . . proceeded, via Golden Gate Park, to the Cliff House; there the four horses were changed and the return trip was made by a different route. Twelve passengers were carried and the charge was two dollars per person."

The Cliff House withstood the earthquake and fire of 1906, only to be destroyed by fire the following year. Immediately rebuilt by Sutro, its popularity continued until Prohibition. One attempt to operate it on a temperance basis was unsuccessful. In 1937 the abandoned Cliff House was purchased by concessionaires George K. and Leo C. Whitney, who modernized and reopened the famous old cafe. Their gift shop adjoining the building is said to be the largest curio shop in the world.

228. Legal residents of the city and wards of the Park Commission since 1887, when their hauling ground was deeded by Congress to the City and County of San Francisco, are the sea lions on SEAL ROCKS, 400 feet offshore below the Cliff House. Known as Steller sea lions,

The City's Sights

FERRY BUILDING AND BOATS

SHIPS AT DOCK

HIGHWAY AND OCEAN BEACH

PANAMA PACIFIC INTERNATIONAL EXPOSITION (1915)

SUTRO HEIGHTS

AQUATIC PARK

M. H. DE YOUNG MEMORIAL MUSEUM, GOLDEN GATE PARK

MISSION DOLORES

CARPENTERS' GOTHIC

BAY WINDOWS CATCH THE SUN

THE PRIDE OF ANTIQUARIANS
(ENGINE COMPANY NO. 15—2150 California Street)

U.S.S. *CALIFORNIA* IN DRYDOCK AT HUNTER'S POINT

SEA ISLAND SUGAR REFINERY

they are closely related to the fur seal; both are of the eared seal family. Unlike the more modest leopard (or harbor) seal, also found along the California coast, they are polygamous, gregarious, and noisy—filling the air with their raucous roaring and barking. These Seal Rock lions breed during the latter half of June (the cow produces only one pup in a season) at their rookery on Ano Nuevo Island, about 25 miles south. Once slaughtered almost to extinction—both by fishermen, who believed that the animals interfered with their nets and depleted the fish supply, and by hunters, for their oil and hides—they are protected today by State and Federal laws. Hardly had they recovered from their alarm at the burning of the Cliff House in 1894 when the earthquake of 1906 provided a more serious disturbance—one so great that they retreated to the Farallones and did not return for several years.

Crowds have gathered on occasions to watch swimming races around the Seal Rocks. More thrilling were performances by tightrope walkers James Cooke and Rose Celeste, who balanced to the rocks and back on different occasions in the 1860's. A suspension bridge to the rocks constructed later was abandoned after it overturned with about 20 pedestrians, injuring several.

229. The OCEAN BEACH, between the Cliff House and Sloat Blvd., is thronged on pleasant days with picnickers, surf and sun bathers, equestrians, and sightseers. The pedestrian esplanade bordering the seawall affords a broad view of the Pacific. A vicious undertow is created by the sudden drop beyond the edge of the surf and annually takes its toll of the unwary.

230. At the northern end of the Ocean Beach is PLAYLAND AT THE BEACH, an amusement area consisting of 22 various "rides," a score of games of chance and "skill," shooting galleries, fun houses, many eating places (ranging from tiny hamburger stands to the well-known Topsy's Roost, a fried chicken and dance establishment), a penny arcade, and other concessions familiar to modern amusement zones. In 1929 George and Leo Whitney, professional concessionaires, forced to return from operating Melbourne, Australia's Luna Park by the outbreak of the World War, were successful in taking over this entire area from its several owners. Born in Kansas about 1890, the Whitney brothers' careers began early with their perfection of a "quick-finishing" photographic process. Their first small photography shop was so successful that they began operating penny arcades; profits from these financed their concessions at the Alaska-Yukon Exposition of 1909, in Seattle, Washington.

One and one-half million dollars raised by bond issue in 1927 financed the two-year construction of the Great Highway, which extends along Ocean Beach from the Cliff House south to Sloat Boulevard, a distance of nearly three miles. Construction of the 4,298-foot-long Esplanade, extending from the highway's northern end to Lincoln Way, had begun as early as 1916, but was not completed until the new funds were acquired. Several methods of protecting the road along the ocean had failed until City Engineer Michael O'Shaughnessy designed the present tight cut-off wall of reinforced concrete interlocking sheet piling, which extends 13 feet below extreme low tide. Extending shoreward from the parapet wall, the Esplanade consists of flanking 20-foot sidewalks, 15 feet of lawn, and a paved highway between 150 and 200 feet in width. For a stretch of 3,000 feet, opposite Golden Gate Park, the Great Highway is the widest boulevard in the United States. Paralleling the road between Lincoln Way and Sloat Boulevard is a bridle path—a link in the continuous pathway from the Presidio to Fleishhacker's by way of Golden Gate Park.

Great Highway becomes Skyline Blvd.

231. Set in a little valley encircled by wooded hills are the 128 landscaped acres of FLEISHHACKER PLAYFIELD AND ZOOLOGICAL GARDENS, foot of Great Highway at Sloat and Skyline Blvds. This recreation center dates from 1922, when the city acquired from the Spring Valley Water Company 60 acres on which to construct a playground and pool. Only 37 acres at first were developed; opened in 1924, the park was named for Herbert Fleishhacker, then president of the Park Commission, who had donated the pool and the Mothers' House.

Said to be the world's largest outdoor plunge is the SWIMMING POOL (*open daily 9-5; suit, towel, and locker rental: adults 25¢, children 15¢; 20 life guards*); 1,000 feet long, 150 feet wide, with a graduated depth of from 3 to 14 feet, several thousand persons can swim at one time in its 6,500,000 gallons of warmed salt water. Considered a noteworthy achievement is the system of heating the sea water. Nearby under windblown cypresses are plots for sunbathing.

The PLAYFIELD (*open daily 9-5; free*), in addition to an unusually large variety of play apparatus, boasts a merry-go-round, a miniature railway, and donkey rides (*small fee*). Larger children and adults use the tennis courts, baseball diamond, and sporting greens. Facing the one-foot-deep wading pool for tots is the MOTHERS' HOUSE, a low, stuccoed, tile-roofed building providing a resting place for mothers and children; the gift of Fleishhacker, it is a memorial to his mother. Interior murals and mosaics are the work of WPA artists.

Adjoining the playground is the Zoo (*open daily 10-4:30; free*). Begun in 1929 with a few lion cubs and monkeys, gradually more animals were acquired (by purchase and donation), until the animal, bird, and reptile population reached 1,000. Noted is the fine collection of "cats," which includes lions, tigers, leopards, lynxes, and panthers. In 1935 sixty-eight acres adjoining the zoo were purchased, and here WPA labor constructed the fine ZOOLOGICAL GARDENS (Lewis Hobart, architect), modeled after Germany's famous Hagenbeck Zoo. Here, among man-made streams, waterfalls, islands, cliffs, and caves, are simulated natural habitats of many animals—separated (where practical) from spectators only by moats and designed to give the animals the illusion of freedom. The concrete of the bear pits resembles natural rock. The aquatic bird building stands on the shores of a specially built lake; the "flight cage" is 220 feet long, with rocky refuges, nesting places, trees, shrubs, and a running stream. Also in the gardens are Monkey Island; the pachyderm house, with its separate enclosures and private swimming pools; lion dens; and a lake built for beavers and thoughtfully supplied with "chewy" logs. The gardens are (1940) only 80 per cent completed.

Heated local controversy attended the trial of Wally, the elephant, who in 1936 attacked and killed his keeper. Only intensified by Wally's execution by court order, the discussion continued for several months.

232. Adjoining Fleishhacker Playfield and Zoo on the south is FORT FUNSTON (*private*). Bordered on the east by Skyline Blvd., it stretches for about a mile and a half along the coast. Established as a military reservation during the Spanish-American War (1898), it was known as the Laguna Merced Military Reservation until 1917, when it was renamed in honor of Major-General Frederick Funston, commander of the Army troops who policed San Francisco after the 1906 disaster. During the 1940 "war games" the reservation was the scene of spectacular practice firing in which machine gun tracer bullets "repulsed" a night landing of the "enemy."

233. Historic LAGUNA DE NUESTRA SEÑORA DE LA MERCED (Sp., Lake of Our Lady of Mercy), Lake Merced and Skyline Blvds., is about five acres of fresh water surrounded by sand dunes and golf courses; one of the latter divides the lake into north and south parts by a narrow neck of filled-in land. Wild flowers grow in profusion on the shores, and among nearby rolling sand hills vegetable gardens flourish. The city-owned lake was abandoned as a source of water supply in the 1930's. In 1939 it was leased to Thomas P. Cusick, whose improvements have made it popular with fishermen and devotees of skeet shooting. The lake's original depth was lowered 30 feet on the night of November 22, 1852, by a mysterious disturbance surmised to be a temblor; in Spanish colonial days the water flowed westward through a narrow channel to the ocean.

234. Spreading between the north and south waters of Lake Merced

is HARDING PARK GOLF COURSE (*greens fee 75¢ Mon.-Fri.; $1.50 Sat., Sun., holidays; $3.00 monthly*), a 200-acre tract included in property purchased by the city from the Spring Valley Water Company. The 18-hole course is operated by the Park Commission, which began to improve the property in 1922 and opened it to the public in 1924.

235. In the extreme southwest corner of the city, bisected by Skyline Boulevard, is the OLYMPIC GOLF CLUB AT LAKESIDE (*private*), country club of the Olympic Club. Enclosed within its 278 acres purchased in 1920 are two 18-hole golf courses and four tennis courts, although athletics here are subordinated to social functions.

Retrace on Skyline Blvd. to Lake Merced Blvd.; SE. on Lake Merced

236. The PACIFIC ROD AND GUN CLUB (*private*), near Lake Merced Blvd. on the southwest shore of Lake Merced, is housed in three wooden buildings made of six schoolhouses purchased from the city. Waters of the south lake abound in black bass, blue gills, and other fresh-water fish; these are replenished from the north lake breeding ground, which is closed to fishing and boating.

237. In a little hollow surrounded by rolling hills and vegetable gardens is the SITE OF THE BRODERICK-TERRY DUEL, Lake Merced Blvd. at the San Francisco-San Mateo County Line. Two granite shafts mark the positions of the contestants in the encounter which welded California's political factions on the eve of the Civil War. About ten yards north a granite memorial bears the information that "United States Senator David C. Broderick and Judge David S. Terry fought a duel on this ground in the early morning of Tuesday, September 13, 1859. Senator Broderick received a wound from which he died three days later. The affair marked the end of dueling in California. . . ." Terry, Chief Justice of the California Supreme Court, had accused Senator Broderick of defeating his candidacy for re-election. (Previously Broderick had befriended the fiery Southerner, who in 1856 had been imprisoned for stabbing an officer of the Vigilance Committee.) On learning of Terry's arraignment of him before the 1859 State Convention of the Democratic Party, the "grand, gloomy and peculiar" Broderick remarked: "I have said that I considered him the only honest man on the supreme bench, but now I take it all back." Informed of this statement, Judge Terry demanded a retraction; and when this was refused, "the satisfaction usual among gentlemen. . . ."

Arriving at the appointed spot with their respective seconds in the raw foggy dawn, each contestant was provided with a Lafoucheux dueling pistol (these hair-trigger weapons had been chosen, according to custom, by the challenger). With his back to the rising sun, nervously fingering his weapon, Broderick fired at the count of "one," his bullet striking the ground midway between him and his adversary. Terry, with deliberate aim, shot Broderick through the right breast. Followed by a crowd of some 60 spectators, a carriage bearing the fatally wounded Senator drove the ten miles to Black Point where he died in the home of Leonidas Haskell.

238. A wooden plaque among rolling hills marks the northernmost CAMP SITE OF THE RIVERA Y MONCADA EXPEDITION, Lake Merced Blvd. just north of the San Francisco-San Mateo County Line; here at eleven o'clock on the morning of December 4, 1774, headquarters were established by the third Spanish party sent to explore San Francisco Bay. It consisted of 16 soldiers, Father Francisco Palou, and a muleteer (with mules laden with provisions for 40 days), under the command of Captain Fernando Rivera y Moncada. An hour later Rivera, Palou, and four soldiers proceeded up the coast, where they planted a large wooden cross on Point Lobos. Returning to their hillside camp—which then overlooked a small stream running into Lake Merced—the whole party followed Portola's old route back to Monterey without having chosen a site for the projected Mission San Francisco de Asis—the selection of which had been one of the chief purposes of the expedition.

E. from Lake Merced Blvd. on an unnamed western extension of Stanley St. to Junipero Serra Blvd.; S. on Junipero Serra

239. Organized in 1895, the SAN FRANCISCO GOLF CLUB, LTD. (*private; greens fee $2*), Junipero Serra Blvd. and Palmetto Ave., occupies an 18-hole course of 184 acres bordered on the south by the city and county limits. Located here is the INGLESIDE MEN'S CLUB (*private; bar, restaurant*).

Retrace and continue N. on Junipero Serra Blvd.

240. The INGLESIDE PUBLIC GOLF COURSE, INC. (*greens fee 75¢ Mon.-Fri.; $1 Sat. until 11, $1.25 11-4, 50¢ after 4; $1.25 Sun. until 1:30, $1 1:30-4*), Nineteenth Ave. and Junipero Serra Blvd., has been operated privately since 1926 on 140 acres leased from the Spring Valley Water Company. The San Francisco Golf Club occupied this site until 1919.

NW. from Junipero Serra Blvd. on Nineteenth Ave.; W. from Nineteenth on Sloat Blvd.

241. SIGMUND STERN MEMORIAL GROVE (*barbecue pits; picnic tables; sanitary facilities*), Sloat Blvd. between Nineteenth

and Twenty-fifth Aves., occupies a natural amphitheater 100 feet below street level. The grass-carpeted glade is sheltered by eucalyptus trees planted nearly 70 years ago by homesteader George Greene, a New England horticulturist who came around the Horn in 1847. When it became known in the early 1850's that Congress was to pass an act giving title of this property to those holding land there, Greene and several other homesteaders erected a fort, and for weeks guarded their property day and night against encroachers. In 1892 Greene established the Trocadero Inn; boasting an open-air dance pavilion and trout lake, it was until 1916 a popular resort. The inn was used in 1907 as a hideout by ousted political boss Abe Ruef, and it was here that he was captured.

Mrs. Sigmund Stern purchased about 12 acres of the land and presented it to the city in 1931 as a memorial to her husband, with the provision that it be used only for recreational and cultural purposes. Enlarged later by the purchase of additional acreage by the Recreation Commission, and again in 1937 when another gift of Mrs. Stern made possible the acquisition of still more land, the park today covers more than 33 acres. The remodeled Trocadero Inn is a clubhouse available to organized groups for social and recreational usage (*reservation must be made at the San Francisco Recreation Commission office, Room 370, City Hall*).

Golden Gate Park

"I'd go out into the country and walk along a stream until I came to a bonnie brook. Then I'd come back to the park and I'd reproduce what Nature had done."

—JOHN MCLAREN

FEW demonstrations of man's mastery over nature have been more convincing than the creation of Golden Gate Park: that long stretch of evergreen outdoors—nine city blocks wide and four and a half miles long—cutting a swath from the heart of the city to the ocean's shore. Its grassy meadows and limpid lakes, its forested hills that alternate in the apparent confusion of a natural wilderness, interlaced with winding roadways, bridle paths, and foot trails—all are man's handiwork. When the city set out to create a park here in 1870, these 1,017 acres were a windswept desert. "Of all the elephants the city of San Francisco ever owned," said the Santa Rosa *Democrat* in 1873, "they now have the largest and heaviest in the shape of 'Golden Gate Park,' a dreary waste of shifting sand hills where a blade of grass cannot be raised without four posts to support it and keep it from blowing away." A scant 70 years later that "dreary waste" is a sylvan retreat in the midst of the city, where herds of sheep graze placidly along rolling pastures, darting squirrels, scurrying rabbits, and chattering blackbirds fill the air with forest sounds, and haughty peacocks flaunt their plumage across velvet lawns. Thousands eat Sunday and holiday lunches on the shady slopes soft with leaf mold and sprawl in the sun on the wide lawns. The oldsters, conservatively dressed, listen to the afternoon band concerts, visit the museums, or gather around the checker boards at the eastern end of the park. The youngsters, clad in bright-colored sports clothes, play tennis, ride bicycles, crowd the children's playground, or tumble after footballs.

Today as one walks among the innumerable flower beds and gardens, past lakes, brooks, and waterfalls, over rolling hills and pastoral meadows, he can hardly believe this magnificent evergreen playground entirely artificial. Buffalo, deer, and elk roam in paddocks landscaped to give an impression of fencelessness. So numerous are foxes and other small predatory animals that a hunter is required the year round to prevent destruction of other animal life. The dozen lakes of the park afford feeding and resting places for thousands of waterfowl.

Within the park's confines grow more than 5,000 kinds of plants. One may wander through groves of eucalyptus and conifers, through wild, brush-filled canyons or shaded glens luxuriant with ferns and blackberries, across hillsides riotous under a blanket of yellow chrysanthemums, violet wild radishes, brilliant orange poppies, snapdragons, and purple cestrum. One may find yellow daisies from South Africa or silverleafed ones from Teneriffe, fuchsias from Mexico and Peru, abelias from Mexico and the Himalayas, brooms from the Canaries and South Africa, cypress from Kashmir. Here grow the exotic crimson Waratah from New South Wales, blooming in the United States for the first time, and centuryplants, staggered in development so that at least one plant blooms every three years. The 109 varieties of eucalypti include the rare *alpina* from Australia, which rarely attains more than 12 feet in height. The acacias, as varied as the eucalypti, include a rare pink variety. More than 100 species of conifers are represented, including the Monterey pine and Monterey cypress, the Torrey pine, and the New Zealand kauri-pine. The native live oak is also prominent, as is the *Quercus ilex* from Italy. The principal shrubs are of the genus *Veronica* from New Zealand and the genus *Escalonia* from Chile. Of rhododendrons, which grow in unnumbered thousands throughout Golden Gate Park, there are more than 300 varieties— some from Thibet, India, Japan, Java, Portugal, Siberia, and Yunnan— and from 300 to 400 hybrids, many of which have been developed locally; the display is unrivaled except in Kew Gardens, which boasts more varieties but fewer specimens.

When public demand for a large recreation ground in San Francisco began to arise in the early 1860's, claimants to the area of the present park were asked to give up some of their land in exchange for an absolute title to the land which they retained. During the ensuing long battle over land titles in the courts and the legislature, Mayor Frank McCoppin, twice led delegations to the State Capitol to demand that the area be saved for a park. Finally, in 1868, $801,593 were paid for the desired 1,017 acres. In 1870 Governor Henry H. Haight appointed the first San Francisco Park Commission. The following year, when he had completed a preliminary survey of the proposed Golden Gate Park, William Hammond Hall was appointed Park Superintendent and authorized to proceed with the development.

To most people, the project of growing trees and grass on shifting sand was a foolish dream—and for years it appeared they were not mistaken. When in 1887 a new superintendent was appointed—a sandy-haired young Scottish landscape gardener, John McLaren—cultivation had been confined largely to the eastern end of the park. The Park Commission told McLaren: "We want you to make Golden Gate Park one of the beauty spots of the world. Can you do it?" He answered: "With your aid, gentlemen, and God be willing, that I shall do." And he kept his word.

With the treescape of the eastern part well established, the great task of improving the park proper remained. The two chief problems were to discover an economical and consistent source of fresh water and to fix in position the constantly moving sand dunes. The first was solved when subterranean streams were tapped south of Strawberry Hill. The second demanded infinite patience in experiment.

When native lupine and barley were found to be unable to hold the sand, McLaren resorted to the *Ammophila arenaria,* "sand-loving sand grass," a beach grass common to the coast of Northern Europe. Sending out a mass of roots well below the surface, this grass continues to grow as fast as the wind covers it over, refusing to be buried, until the dune has reached such a height that the wind velocity will no longer carry sand to the top. Second plant to be utilized in fixing the contours of the sand was the Australian tea-tree, a soil-holding shrub closely related to eucalyptus; third was the Australian acacia, a leguminous shrub, a soil-builder as well as holder. The few blue gums planted by settlers in the early 1850's and a few native live oaks were augmented by systematic planting of additional blue gums (eucalypti), manzanita, madrone, and laurel. Principal grasses to follow were Kentucky bluegrass, Australian ryegrass, fescue, and *Poa annua.*

The first years were hard for "Uncle John" McLaren. Time after time he awakened to find thousands of young trees covered with sand. Patiently he dug them out and nursed them back to life. Needing fertilizer, he asked for, and was given, the sweepings from the city streets. (When the automobile drove the horses from the streets, "Uncle John" was annoyed.) Allowed by tacit agreement with city officials to do his own hiring and firing, McLaren refused consistently to employ relatives or friends of the men in power. Neither would he tolerate interference in his plans. When he discovered the three young oaks planted in the parking area before the Park Police Station being dragged away with a steam roller, he replaced the trees. Later that day, when he found the oaks gone again and workmen paving the parking space, "Uncle John" had his own men shovel out the cement as fast as it was poured in. The Board of Public Works gave up its attempt to pave the area, and today three sturdy oaks hide the police station as McLaren had intended they should.

An attempt to retire McLaren when he reached 60 occasioned a minor uprising by the people of San Francisco; "Uncle John" stayed on. When he was 70 the people again came to his defense. In 1922 the Board of Supervisors adopted a resolution that not only exempted him from enforced retirement but raised his wages. On December 20, 1939 he celebrated his 93rd birthday—still superintendent of the park and still active in its development.

Despite its semi-miraculous development, Golden Gate Park was not easily to supplant Woodward's Gardens in the affection of the public. Woodward's in early years had been the established mecca for lovers of outdoor amusement. However, an elaborate children's playground (1886) and free municipal Sunday concerts in the "shell" built in the huge open-air tree-flanked Music Concourse added to the park's popularity. With the celebration of San Francisco's Midwinter Fair within its borders in 1894, Golden Gate Park came permanently into its own. Some of the special features of the Chicago World's Fair, including John Philip Sousa's band and Fritz Scheel's Vienna Orchestra, gave repeat performances at the Midwinter Fair. Thousands visited the conservatory to see the world's largest flower, a pond lily that came to be known as the *Victoria regina*. The famous Japanese Tea Garden, built for the fair, was so popular that it never was torn down.

Throughout the resplendent "gay nineties," the park became the rendezvous for the "horse-and-buggy" social set. Each Sunday they came dressed in the latest fashion. Some rode dog carts, some bicycles—built for one, two, three, or four—but most drove carriages. Trumpeting importantly for right of way, the tally-ho, with its complement of gaily caparisoned riders, cut across bicycles and dog-carts alike. Carriage occupants bowed politely to acquaintances, the men lifting their shining silk toppers. Less dignified were the bicyclists, one of whom inspired a columnist's rude comment, "ocean breezes reveal that—she pads." Tandem bicycles were eclipsed by four-passenger "bikes," seating two pairs of young men and women astride. A female "scorcher" arrested for speeding at the reckless rate of "ten miles an hour," also had committed the heinous crime of wearing the "new-fangled Bloomers." When the noisy horseless carriage first appeared, those seeking to heighten their social prestige by appearing in the park in these gasoline or electric "buggies" were chagrined when Golden Gate Park remained proscribed territory for vehicles mechanically self-propelled (the rule was enforced for several years).

Still observed is McLaren's early refusal to allow "Keep Off the Grass" signs. As in the days after the earthquake and fire of 1906, when the park provided haven for countless refugees, whole families still seek relief on its green swards whenever the city is engulfed by one of its rare heat waves. Indicative of the importance of the park in the life of San Franciscans today are such signs in local streetcars as: "The Rhododendrons are blooming in Golden Gate Park"—signs heeded by thousands.

And meanwhile, as the never-ending stream of visitors continues, the park grows in beauty. What today is a dry canyon tomorrow may be a sparkling brook. For the past few years the WPA, under the guidance of "Uncle John," has been helping him shape the park as he wants it. Today he is most proud of his redwood forest, which he started growing from seeds when he was 80. People laughed. But today the trees are 30 feet high. In his half century as the park's creator, "Uncle John" has planted a million trees. Now he is planting his second million and watching them grow.

PARK INFORMATION

Information Service: Information and maps at Park Lodge, near Stanyan and Fell Sts.

Streetcars and Buses: Municipal Ry. cars B, C, K, L, and N connect with Municipal bus Route #1 which crosses park; fare 5¢. Market Street Ry. cars 4, 5, 7, 17, 20, and 21 pass northern, southern, and eastern entrances; fare 7¢.

Traffic Regulations: Seventeen miles of auto roads. No trucks, drays, and delivery vehicles except on transverse drives, Ninth Ave. and Twenty-Fourth Ave. Speed limit 15 m.p.h. Parking allowed anywhere, except where forbidden by signs, provided general traffic is not disturbed (special parking area, South Drive near Kezar Stadium). No double parking.

Accommodations: Drinking fountains and comfort stations throughout park. Meals and beverages at Beach Chalet; lunch, tea, and tray service for picnickers at Children's Quarters; tea and rice cakes at Japanese Tea Garden. Picnicking allowed on all lawns; barbecue pits near Horseshoe Courts; tables near Children's Playground, Pioneer Log Cabin, and in George Washington Bicentennial Grove. Emergency Hospital (always open) near Stanyan and Frederick Sts.

Art Collections and Museums: M. H. de Young Memorial Museum; lectures on permanent collection Sun. 2-4; puppet plays for children alternate Sat. 10-12; children's puppet classes, Sat. 10-12, 1-3. North American Hall. Simson African Hall. Steinhart Aquarium.

Band Concerts: Music Concourse, Sun. and holidays 2-4:30.

Archery: Local, regional, and National tournaments in Golden Gate Park Stadium; participants provide own equipment (storage facilities for targets).

Baseball: 9 diamonds between 5th and 7th Aves., near Lincoln Way; additional grounds in Recreation Field and near Golden Gate Park Stadium.

Basketball: Pavilion in front of Kezar Stadium.

Bowling: 3 greens for men and women accommodating 64 players each (open only to members of San Francisco Men's Bowling Club or Women's Golden Gate Bowling Club).

Card Games, Chess, Checkers: Ghirardelli Pavilion near Haight and Stanyan Sts.; tables accommodate 200 players.

Cycling: Bicycles rented outside park on Stanyan St., at south end of Ocean Beach amusement area, and on Balboa St. near 4th and 5th Aves.

Fly Casting: Pools south of Main Drive between Golden Gate Park Stadium and Middle Lake. Tournaments October-June.

Football: Recreation Field. Golden Gate Park Stadium. Intercollegiate and high school games, Kezar Stadium.

Handball: 4 courts adjoining baseball fields near 7th Ave.; spectators' gallery.

Horseshoe Pitching: 16 courts (barbecue pits, tables and chairs, and small clubhouse) on North Ridge Dr.

Miniature Yachting: Spreckels Lake (clubhouse maintained by San Francisco Model Yacht Club, with work benches where members may build boats). Regattas Sun. and holiday afternoons.

Polo: Golden Gate Park Stadium; see newspapers for dates.

Riding: 25 miles of bridle paths. Hurdles for leaping in Equitation Field near 41st Ave. and Lincoln Way. Mounts not available in park.

Tennis: 21 courts near Children's Playground, fee 25¢ per hour per court Sat., Sun., holidays; free other days; 8 courts in Recreation Field (players provide own nets).

Volley Ball: Court near Children's Playground.

CALENDAR OF PARK EVENTS

(Note: "nfd" means *no fixed date*)

Jan. 1	Kezar Stadium	East-West Football Game
Mar. nfd or Apr. nfd	Spreckels Lake Children's Playground	Miniature Yacht Regatta Easter Egg Hunt
Mar.-May	Golden Gate Park Stadium	Track meets and tournaments
Apr. Sun nearest 8	Japanese Tea Garden	Festival of birthday of Buddha
May 1	Children's Playground	May Day celebration
Sept. nfd	Kezar Stadium	University of San Francisco-St. Mary's Football Game
Oct. nfd	Kezar Stadium	St. Mary's-Santa Clara Football Game

Nov. Thanksgiv- ing Day	Kezar Stadium	Polytechnic and Lowell High Schools Football Game
Dec. nfd	Lindley Meadow	During holiday season the Three Wise Men are enacted by attendants who tend their flocks dressed as ancient shepherds
20		John McLaren's children's Christmas party and Christmas tree lighting

POINTS OF INTEREST

242. At the entrance to the block-wide Panhandle, the cypress- and eucalyptus-shaded strip extending eight blocks eastward from the main area of the park, stands the McKINLEY MONUMENT (Robert Ingersoll Aitken, sculptor), Baker St. between Fell and Oak Sts., a bronze heroic female figure, emblematic of the Republic, towering 35 feet above a granite base. President Theodore Roosevelt broke ground for the memorial May 13, 1903.

W. from Panhandle park entrance on Main Dr.

243. The sandstone, tile-roofed PARK LODGE, N. of Main Dr. near Panhandle park entrance, stands on a slight elevation surrounded by wide lawns. Although only a few steps from hurrying city traffic, the lodge has the quiet appearance of a country estate. Built in 1896 at a cost of $25,000, it is occupied jointly by Park Administration offices and the household of Park Superintendent "Uncle" John McLaren. A huge Monterey cypress in front of the lodge is known as "Uncle John's Christmas Tree."

244. The FUCHSIA GARDEN extends S. of Main Dr. near the Panhandle entrance, between a double row of tall cypresses. The collection includes fuchsias of a great variety of sizes and colors.

N. from Main Dr. on North Ridge Dr.

245. Steps made of old basalt paving blocks lead from North Ridge Dr. to the HORSESHOE COURTS, surrounded by trees and a stone retaining wall. The sixteen playing courts and the grounds were reconstructed in 1934 by the State Relief Administration. On the cliffs to east and south are giant bas-reliefs of a running horse and a man tossing a horseshoe, carved by "Vet" Anderson of the Horseshoe Club.

Retrace on North Ridge Dr.; W. from North Ridge Dr. on Main Dr.

246. On a wide green against a background of oak and acacia stands the HALLECK MONUMENT, S. of Main Dr., a tribute to the memory of Major-General Henry W. Halleck, General-in-chief of

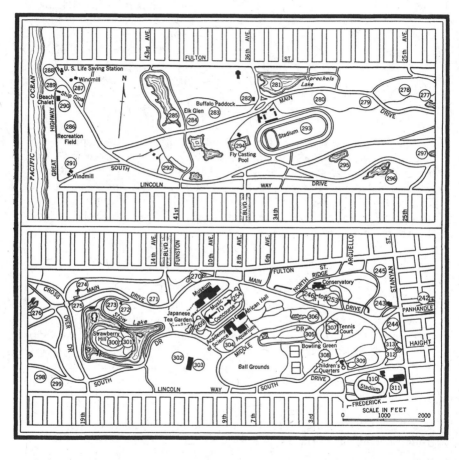

the Union Armies in 1862-64, "from his 'best friend'." It was erected in 1886 by Major-General George W. Cullum. The granite pedestal supports a heroic-size granite figure of Halleck in full uniform, wrapped in his military cape (C. Conrads, sculptor).

247. THE BASEBALL PLAYER, S. of Main Dr., an early bronze by Douglas Tilden depicting a mustachioed player of the eighties throwing a ball, cast in Paris in 1889, was erected in 1892 by W. E. Brown as tribute to Tilden's "energy, industry and ability."

248. In the shade of Monterey pines and cypresses the BOWLES RHODODENDRONS, N. of Main Dr., border the approach to Conservatory Valley on the east. They were given by Mrs. Philip E. Bowles, as a memorial to her husband. Of the park's thousands of rhododendrons, some are always in bloom from February through June, although the largest number appear in full bloom in April.

249. The JAMES A. GARFIELD MONUMENT stands on a knoll N. of Main Dr. On the steps of a granite base sits a mourning female figure holding a broken sword and a wreath. Above stands a heroic-size bronze statue of the martyred president. Modeled by Frank Happersberger and cast in Munich, the work was unveiled July 4, 1885.

250. N. of Main Dr. from the broad lawns of shallow Conservatory Valley—where formal flower beds are gay with bloom the year round—a broad flight of steps leads to a marble fountain and the CONSERVATORY (*open 8-5 daily*). This glass structure whose two wings flank a central octagonal rotunda and dome, modeled after the Royal Conservatories at Kew Gardens, is the successor to one constructed in 1878 of materials purchased in England by James Lick. Destroyed by fire in 1822, it was replaced with funds donated by Charles Crocker. A glassed-in vestibule leads into the rotunda, where rare palms from the Norfolk Islands, Central and South America, Sumatra and Java, China and Japan lift their green fronds above semitropical plants from Australia, New South Wales, and Lord Howe's Island. The center room of the east wing harbors a jungle-like growth of palms, vines, and ferns from Malacca, India, South Africa, Japan, Brazil, and Mexico. In the end room is a rockery green with ferns and other plants and a small pool stocked with gold fish. Plants from Peru, China, and South Africa grow in a hot and humid atmosphere. Floating on the waters of the pool here from July to January are the giant pads of the *Victoria regia,* a water lily native to the waters of the Amazon River, whose petals open in mid-afternoon and close in mid-morning when it blooms in September. In the center room of the west wing grow semitropical plants from Africa, China, India, Central and South America, and a small collection of orchids. The end room offers rotating seasonal exhibits of potted flowering plants. In the hothouse nurseries behind the Conservatory gardeners have developed a collection of about 7,000 orchids.

251. The LIBERTY TREE, a redwood planted by the Daughters of the American Revolution April 19, 1894, on the anniversary of the Battle of Lexington, stands in this area.

252. The McKINNON MONUMENT, S. side of Main Dr. (J. McQuarrie, sculptor), depicting the uniformed figure of Father William D. McKinnon, chaplain of the First California Volunteers of

the Spanish-American War, is set against a background of evergreen shrubs and cypresses.

253. The ROBERT BURNS MONUMENT (M. Earl Cummings, sculptor), S. of Main Dr. near McKinnon Monument, a heroic bronze of the Scotch poet, stands on a sloping lawn against a background of cypresses and tall pittosporum. Here the birthday of "Bobby" Burns, January 25, is observed annually by enthusiastic Scots.

SE. from Main Dr. on drive encircling Music Concourse

254. The MUSIC CONCOURSE (*band concerts Sun. and holidays 2-4:30*), S. of Main Dr. near Eighth Ave. park entrance, a sunken, outdoor auditorium seating 20,000, is 12 feet below the surface of the surrounding roadway. It is bordered by clipped hedges and terraced lawns and roofed by formal rows of trees. In line with the central aisle are three circular fountains. Around the concourse were grouped the buildings of the California Mid-Winter International Exposition of 1894.

255. A memorial to the Unitarian minister who fought to keep California in the Union during the Civil War is the THOMAS STARR KING MONUMENT, Main Dr. and Music Concourse Dr. (Daniel Chester French, sculptor). On the granite base bearing the bronze figure is inscribed: "In Him Eloquence Strength and Virtue were Devoted with Fearless Courage to Truth Country and His Fellow-Men. 1824-64."

256. The CERVANTES MONUMENT, NE. corner Music Concourse, a bronze head of Miguel de Cervantes (Jo Mora, sculptor), looks down gravely from a rugged pile of native rock upon the kneeling figures of Cervantes' fictional creations, Don Quixote and Sancho Panza.

257. Portrayed advancing with a tall cross, the *padre-presidente* of the California missions is memorialized by the JUNIPERO SERRA MONUMENT, opposite the Cervantes Monument. Dedicated November 17, 1907 by the Native Sons of the Golden West, the bronze is the work of Douglas Tilden.

258. The ULYSSES S. GRANT MEMORIAL, NE. corner Music Concourse, is a bronze bust of Grant (R. Schmid, sculptor). On the base are listed his principal battles.

259. On the NW. side of the Music Concourse, flanked by trim lawns and stately Irish yews, is the M. H. DE YOUNG MEMORIAL MUSEUM (*open daily 10-5*). Of sixteenth-century Spanish Renaissance design, the building's pale salmon-colored facades are burdened with rococo ornamentation. Its two wings extend from either side of a 134-foot tower, facing a landscaped court. In the court, before

the main entrance, lies the POOL OF ENCHANTMENT (M. Earl Cummings, sculptor), in which a sculptured Indian boy pipes to two listening mountain lions on a rocky island. At the building's southeast corner, a bronze SUN DIAL (M. Earl Cummings, sculptor) commemorates "the first Three Navigators to the California Coast: Fortuno Ximenes, 1534—Juan de Cabrillo, 1542—Sir Francis Drake, 1579." In front of the west wing stands the VINTAGE, designed by Paul Gustave Doré, a massive three-ton bronze vase depicting in bas-relief the story of the grape. The symbolic sculptures above the main entrance to the museum are by Haig Patigian; other exterior sculptures, by Leo Lentelli.

The museum is a heritage of the California Mid-Winter International Exposition, whose guiding spirit, Michael de Young, publisher of the *Chronicle,* proposed that the $75,000 profits of the fair be used to house a permanent collection of art. In the fair's Egyptian-style Fine Arts Building the museum was opened March 25, 1895. A collection of 6,000 objects bought from the fair was the nucleus of the present collection of more than 1,000,000 items. Throughout Europe De Young searched for treasures, while pioneer-minded citizens sent grandfather's boots and grandmother's sunbonnets, until the museum was congested with "historical curiosities"—so great in number that many have not yet been cataloged. The small, dark rooms were heaped to the rafters with Italian marbles, bric-a-brac, and *objets d'art* of the bonanza period. When the original Fine Arts Building became too crowded to hold anything else, construction was begun in 1917 on the first unit of the present building (Louis Mullgardt, architect)—erected with funds donated by M. H. de Young—to which a second wing was added in 1925, and a third (Frederick H. Meyer, architect) in 1931. Condemned as unsafe in 1926, the old building was torn down. All that remains as a reminder of the old structure are the two sphinxes and bronze lion to the east of the museum.

The museum's galleries enclose the sunken Great Court beyond the main entrance and extend through the wings on either side. Around the Great Court are galleries 1-21. A transverse corridor leads right to galleries 22-49 and left to galleries 50-60. (A floor plan near the main entrance aids visitors.) Exhibits in galleries 1-21 are arranged in chronological sequence:

1. Egyptian: mummies, carved figures in stone, statuettes, vases
2. Greek: red-figured amphorae, vases
3. Roman: pottery, jewelry, a marble sarcophagus
4. Northern Europe, fourteenth and fifteenth centuries: a large Flemish tapestry, wood carvings
5. Northern Europe, fourteenth to sixteenth centuries: German and

Flemish primitives, including Isenbrant's *Madonna and Child,* Van Cleve's *Lucretia,* French limestone statue, *Virgin and Child* (c. 1340)

6. Southern Europe, fourteenth and fifteenth centuries, Italian primitives, including Vivarini's *Madonna and Child* and a small Veronese ecclesiastical chair of wrought iron and brass covered with Genoese velvet

7. Southern Europe, sixteenth and seventeenth centuries: furniture, Veronese's *Virgin and Angel of the Annunciation*

8. Italian, seventeenth and eighteenth centuries: furniture and paintings

9. A wood-panelled room (north Italian of the late seventeenth century), polychrome decorations

10. English and Dutch, seventeenth and eighteenth centuries: furniture and paintings

11. European decorative arts, sixteenth and seventeenth centuries: Delft ware, German armor, Conca's *Adoration of the Lamb*

12. French, eighteenth century: furniture, harpischord, Beauvais tapestry, Sèvres porcelains

13. European decorative arts, seventeenth and eighteenth centuries: glass, china, furniture

14. English and American, eighteenth century: portraits by Kneller, Reynolds, Romney, Gainsborough, Copley, and Raeburn's *Portrait of Sir William Napier;* furniture

15. Northern European, eighteenth century: an Aubusson tapestry, furniture, Vernet's *Seaport at Dawn,* miniatures

16. French, early nineteenth century: Napoleonic furniture, including a throne chair of Napoleon I

17. American, eighteenth and early nineteenth centuries: portraits, one by Benjamin West; mahogany furniture

18. American, mid-nineteenth century: portraits of California pioneers by Nahl, Martinelli, and unknown artists

19, 20, 21. American decorative arts, eighteenth century: silver, pewter, luster ware, glass, early American portraits

22-29. Loan exhibits

30. Print room

31. Textile study room

32. Musical instruments

33. Eastern art

35. Chinese art: sculpture, porcelains

36 and 41. Japanese art: porcelains, priests' robes

42. Indo-China, Java, Bali

43. South Sea Islands

44. Peru and Mexico: Mayan food and ceremonial vessels, Aztec oil

and pulque jars, water and drinking vessels, vases, incense burners; Peruvian jugs, bowls, and effigy vessels

45-46. North American Indians: jars of Ácoma Indians of New Mexico, of California Pomos; weapons, utensils and ornaments of other California aborigines; bead work

47-48. Textiles

49. Reproductions of classical sculpture

50. Paintings and prints of early California

51. California interior (c. 1850), bed-sitting-room

52. California interior (c. 1865), drawing room

53. Changing exhibits of Californiana

54. Study room for history of California

55. Nineteenth-century paintings

56. California interior, 1870, parlor

57. California interior, 1885, lady's boudoir

58. Costumes; portraits of California pioneers

59. Ship models; eight-foot timber from *Natalie* (which took Napoleon from Elba to France), beached near Monterey, 1843; Fire Engine No. 1, 1850

60. Arms, military equipment: cannon used in Thirty Years' War; bronze mortar, Peru, 1780; relics of U. S. S. *Maine;* Civil and World War items

260. The CIDER PRESS MONUMENT, NW. side Music Concourse, represents a nude male in heroic size operating a cider press; a child kneels at his feet holding an apple. Purchased from the French Commission, the statue (Thomas S. Clarke, sculptor) was presented to the park by the Executive Committee of the California Mid-Winter International Exposition in 1894.

261. In the $75,000 Italian Renaissance MUSIC PAVILION, SW. end Music Concourse, gift of sugar magnate Claus Spreckels in 1900, Sunday afternoon band concerts are presented. Built of gray Colusa sandstone, it has a high proscenium arch over the music platform flanked by balustraded colonnades.

262. Arching over the eastern entrance to the JAPANESE TEA GARDEN (*open daily 10-5*), W. of Music Concourse, is a two-storied *ro-mon* (gate) carved of *hinoki* wood, used in Japan before temple entrances. Precipitous, bamboo-railed paths wander through the five-acre garden, over grassy slopes planted with camellias, magnolia trees, cryptomeria, and red-leafed Japanese maples. Between lichen-covered rocks, little streams crossed by small stone bridges descend to a chain of five small pools planted to water iris and stocked with goldfish. Over a still pool curves a "wishing bridge" whose reflection in the water completes a perfect circle. In spring, flowering quince, plum, and cherry trees burst into sprays of blossom. Here and there grow a

hundred or more fantastically gnarled *bonsai,* misshapen conifers, some a century old but none more than three feet in height (to stunt their growth roots and branches are constantly pruned, and only a minimum of water is allowed).

In the thatched tea house near the eastern gate girls in kimonos serve pale green tea and wafer-like cakes to guests sitting at tables made of tree trunks. Along one side of the pavilion, sunlight falls through a lattice arbor burdened with fragrant blossoms of white and lavender wistaria in season. Beyond the tea house is a two-story, four-room *zashiki* (house) with wooden walls, sliding panels, and window panes of rice paper. The interior is severely simple. The floors are covered with matting. There is a *tokonomo* (alcove) for the display of flower arrangements. A huge, red, black, and gold Buddha sits in serene contemplation at the foot of a slope on whose summit is a copper-roofed Shinto shrine. One of the chief attractions of the 1894 exposition (it was the Japanese Village), the garden is operated by descendants of its original proprietor.

263. The GIUSEPPE VERDI MONUMENT, SW. corner Music Concourse, was designed and executed in Milan (Orazio Grossoni, sculptor) and presented by the local Italian colony in 1914. On the granite base below the bronze bust of the composer a male figure holds an hour glass and a laurel wreath, and two children unfurl an Italian flag.

264. The BEETHOVEN MONUMENT, SE. side Music Concourse, a portrait bust in bronze, rests on a formal granite column at whose base stands Music, a draped female figure holding a lyre. The gift of the Beethoven Männerchor of New York, it was dedicated August 6, 1915.

265. The ROBERT EMMET MONUMENT, SE. side Music Concourse, a life-size bronze of the Irish patriot, bears in gold letters simply his name, in conformance with his last wish before he was executed: "When my country takes her place among the nations of the earth, then, and not till then, let my epitaph be written." The work of Jerome Connor, the statue was presented by Senator James D. Phelan in 1919. Here gather the United Irish Societies for yearly observances of Robert Emmet's birthday, which always includes a rendition of his "Speech Before the Dock."

266. Erected in 1887 with a $60,000 bequest of philanthropist James Lick, the FRANCIS SCOTT KEY MONUMENT, SE. side Music Concourse, represents the author of "The Star Spangled Banner" sitting on a travertine pedestal inscribed with the words of his song under a canopy upheld by four Corinthian columns and crowned by bronze eagles, buffalo heads, and a heroic-sized bronze female figure of Liberty bearing a banner and a sword.

267. On the SE. side of Music Concourse are the three buildings of the CALIFORNIA ACADEMY OF SCIENCES, the oldest scientific institution in the West. Supported partly by endowments and bequests and partly by city funds, the institution maintains North American Hall, Steinhart Aquarium, and Simson African Hall, buildings in harmonizing architecture whose white concrete walls enclose three sides of a paved quadrangle. The Academy's exhibits of flora and fauna are only one of its many activities. Its scientific expeditions (on many Templeton Crocker's yacht *Zaca* has been employed) have gone to Alaska, Panama, Asia, Africa, Australia, New Zealand, South America, and many of the Pacific Islands. More than 3,000,000 separate specimens have been collected. It has furnished materials and facilities for original research in the biological and physical sciences, maintaining research departments in the fields of botany, entomology, herpetology, ichthyology, invertebrate zoology, ornithology and mammalogy, and paleontology. Its activities are primarily concerned with the natural history and geology of the lands bordering the Pacific Ocean and its islands.

On April 4, 1853, seven men interested in science met at Lewis W. Sloat's Montgomery Street office; on June 27, 1853, they incorporated as the California Academy of Natural Sciences. For many years their meetings were held in the office of Colonel Thomas J. Nevins, one of the seven founders and San Francisco's first Superintendent of Schools. The "Proceedings," first published in a newspaper, began to appear in illustrated volumes. The library and museum grew and moved in 1874 to larger quarters in a church. In 1891 the Academy established itself on property at Fourth and Market Streets deeded to it by James Lick. Under the terms of Lick's will it became one of two residuary legatees, receiving one-half of whatever remained after all other bequests had been paid. With the $20,000 given by Charles Crocker in 1881 and additional funds from Leland Stanford, it created a large natural history exhibit. Other benefactors included John W. Hendrie and William Alvord. When the Market Street home of the Academy was demolished by the earthquake and fire of 1906, San Francisco citizens voted to reestablish it in Golden Gate Park.

NORTH AMERICAN HALL (*open daily 10-5*), popularly called the Museum of Natural History, is approached by a wide entrance stairway before which are embedded four old millstones from early California flour mills. Opened in 1916, it was the first unit of the California Academy of Science group. In the vestibule are displays of freshly cut flowers and growing plants labeled with both their botanical and common names. The vestibule leads into Mammal Hall, which, illuminated by skylights, has 15 large and many small habitat groups, each glass-enclosed and backed by a painted cyclorama. Of the animals shown here, collected especially because of the threat of their extinction, all but the grizzly bear and the fur-bearing seal are still to be seen in California. Beginning at the right of the entrance hall, the large habitat groups are: Roosevelt elk, near a forest stream of the Olympic Mountains west of Puget Sound; San Joaquin Valley elk, dwarf elk, tule elk, and wapiti, found in Kern County, in the long tule grass bordering a river; Northern and Columbian black-tailed deer, in a shaded dell of Mendocino County; Imperial grizzly bear, in a lakeside valley of Yellowstone Park below towering Wyoming mountains; Rocky Mountain mule deer, in a snow-covered bit of Sierra Nevada forest; prong-horn antelope, in a barren mountain landscape of Modoc County; desert mountain or bighorn sheep, in the San Jacinto Mountains of Riverside County; mountain lions, found in Humboldt County; northwestern black, brown, and cinnamon bears, found in Humboldt County; Alaska fur seal, on a rocky coast of St. George Island in the Bering Sea; leopard and California harbor seals, in a rookery at Cypress Point near Monterey Bay; California sea lions, in a rookery on Santa Cruz Island, Santa Barbara County; Steller sea lions, in a rookery on Ano Nuevo Island, San Mateo County; California raccoon and California skunk; California valley coyote and prairie wolf, found in Moraga Valley, Alameda County.

Mammal Hall opens into Bird Hall. The larger habitat groups are, beginning left of the entrance, in order: Western meadow lark, San Joaquin waterfowl, Nuttall sparrow, sharp-shinned hawk, California condor, California vulture and desert birds. In the condor group, a nest high on a cliff near the headwaters of the San Antonio River in Monterey County is shown. Among the smaller groups are one showing 14 species resting on the rocky cliffs of a rookery on the Farallon Islands and one showing a flock of white pelicans in their breeding colony on Anaho Island in Pyramid Lake, Nevada. Other birds include the California linnet, quail, and clapper rail; coast bushtit; Lazuli bunting; Western robin; water ouzel; and many varieties of sea gulls and wild ducks.

Parallel to Mammal Hall is a corridor displaying a cross section of a California big tree (*Sequoia gigantea*), from Sequoia National Park. The tree is estimated to have been 1,710 years old when it fell in 1917. It was 330 feet high and 25 feet in diameter at the base. In this same corridor are collections of fluorescent minerals, semiprecious stones, butterflies and water colors of California wild flowers.

The other rooms of the building are occupied by the 65,000-volume library of the California Academy of Sciences and its research departments in botany, herpetology, mammalogy, ornithology, and paleontology. These departments house study collections including about 8,000 mammals, 57,000 birds, and 69,000 reptiles (among which is a notable collection of reptiles from the Galapagos Islands). The herbarium of 275,000 mounted plants has grown from 1,000 specimens saved from the earthquake and fire of 1906 by Alice Eastwood, curator of the botany department. The collection of the department of paleontology includes 1,600,000 specimens.

STEINHART AQUARIUM (*open daily 10-5*) houses its collection of fresh- and salt-water life behind a gray stucco facade ornamented with white classic pillars. Facing the entrance to the aquarium are three outdoor pools for sea lions, otter, and other aquatic mammals (*feeding time 4 p.m.*). In the high, pillared lobby is a sunken tank where turtles, water snakes, giant bullfrogs, and alligators move about in an imitation tropical swamp. Along the lobby walls glass cases contain hundreds of small tropical fish of brilliant hues, indigenous snakes, Gila monsters, colorful sea anemones, star fish, sea urchins and mollusks.

From the lobby extend corridors lined with glass tanks built into the walls. Specimens from American streams and Pacific waters include giant sea turtles, crested and speckled eels, fantastic sea horses, periscopic flounders, turkey fish, and electric and bat sting-rays. Among the most unusual are the climbing perch, an oriental fish which climbs the submerged roots of trees and is able to exist out of the water, and the two varieties of lung fish, Australian and African, which breathe through lungs and gills. Trout and other game fish are well represented.

Founded in 1923, the gift of Ignatz Steinhart, the aquarium contained 500 species and 12,000 individual fish in 1940. Its collection has been increased by a system of exchange with the Sydney, Australia, aquarium. In 1939 alone, the institution received 3,000 gifts; among its donors have been Templeton Crocker and Capt. G. Allan Hancock.

In the rear of Steinhart Aquarium a graveled walk leads to a shed sheltering the 75-foot skeleton of a SULPHUR BOTTOM WHALE, captured off the coast of Vancouver Island in 1908. Native to the California coast, the Sulphur Bottom is the largest and swiftest of whales. The skulls of a finback, a Baird's beaked, and humpbacked whale, all obtained on the California coast in 1925, are also on display.

SIMSON AFRICAN HALL (*open Sun. and Wed. 1-5*), newest of the Academy buildings and similar in design to North American Hall, was built by Leslie Simson, retired mining engineer and sportsman who collected specimens of African wild life from expeditions to Kenya. The habitat groups are shown with scrupulous accuracy of detail, against mural backgrounds representing African scenery in the localities where the specimens were collected. Simson as a boy learned to prepare bird and mammal skins from his father, who had received similar instructions from the son of John J. Audubon, the great artist-ornithologist. The predominant habitat group represents an African water hole on the edge of the veldt with distant mountains under clear blue skies in the background. Around the oasis in naturalistic pose are gathered several specimens each of the impalla, the Masai giraffe, the zebra, the white-bearded gnu or wildebeest, the Grant's gazelle and the Coke's hartebeest. The trees, shrubs, rocks, and plants stand in sharp contrast to the grassy plains stretching away to the foothills. In twenty-three other groups—ten large, one intermediate, and twelve small in size—are grouped several specimens each of such exotic creatures as the Beisa oryx, black lechwe, bushback, bush duiker, cheetah, dik-dik, Dorcas gazelle, gerenuk, Hunter's hartebeest, klipspringer, mountain nyala, oribi, steinbok, and waterbuck, as well as specimens of the better-known African lion, baboon, gorilla, Grevy's zebra, African leopard, monkey, roan and sable antelope, and hunting dog.

On the second floor of African Hall is the Department of Entomology, containing more than a million mounted insects, largest research entomological west of the Smithsonian Institution. The Department of Ichthyology in the basement has a collection of about 200,000 specimens of fish, especially rich in South American fresh water fish.

268. In a bower of English laurel is the GOETHE-SCHILLER MONUMENT, E. of Simson Hall, a pedestal of red Missouri granite supporting bronze figures of the two German poets. A reproduction of a monument in Weimar, Germany (Ernst Rietschel, sculptor), it was presented by citizens of German descent in 1901.

269. Facing the Music Concourse against a background of tall pines is the GENERAL PERSHING MONUMENT, NW. side Music Concourse, a bronze statue of General John J. Pershing (Haig Patigian, sculptor) in khaki field uniform with a crushed German helmet at his feet, presented by Dr. Morris Herzstein in 1922.

W. from drive encircling Music Concourse on Main Dr.

270. A shaded road winds through HEROES GROVE, N. of Main Dr., a 15-acre tract of redwoods dedicated to San Francisco soldiers killed in the World War. Their names are inscribed on a large obelisk-shaped boulder.

271. The REDWOOD MEMORIAL GROVE, N. of Main Dr., was dedicated by the Native Sons and Daughters of the Golden West and the Gold Star Mothers of America to the San Francisco men and women who lost their lives in the World War. In the Grove of Memory, a section of the main grove, a redwood for each of the dead towers high above the DOUGHBOY MONUMENT, a bronze figure of a young soldier who stands, hatless and bare-armed, on a 20-ton rock base. Once part of the Panama-Pacific International Exposition, this statue (M. Earl Cummings, sculptor) was purchased by the 52 San

Francisco parlors of the Native Sons and Daughters of the Golden West.

272. The PIONEER LOG CABIN, S. of Main Dr. on an unnamed drive W. of Redwood Memorial Grove, was built in 1911 of logs floated down from Mendocino County. The structure, set in a redwood grove (*picnicking facilities*), is the property of the Association of Pioneer Women of California, who convene there monthly around the huge brick fireplace.

273. Composed of one tree for each of the Thirteen Original Colonies, a group of HISTORIC TREES, planted along a path leading south from the intersection of Main Drive and the drive to the Pioneer Log Cabin, commemorates the surrender of Cornwallis at Yorktown in 1785. Notable are a cedar from Valley Forge and a tree from Thomas Jefferson's grave. The trees were planted in 1896 by the Sequoia Chapter, Daughters of the American Revolution.

274. The sandstone PRAYER BOOK CROSS, N. of Main Dr., modeled after an ancient Celtic Cross on the Scottish island of Iona, towers 57 feet above the edge of a bluff. It was erected in 1894 by the Northern California Episcopal diocese in commenoration of the first use of the Book of Common Prayer on the Pacific Coast by Francis Fletcher, Chaplain to Francis Drake, who conducted a service on the shore of Drake's Bay June 24, 1579.

275. On Sundays and holidays, tiny RAINBOW FALLS, N. of Main Dr., rush over a cliff at the base of Prayer Book Cross into a fern-bordered pool. Artificially fed from a reservoir atop Strawberry Hill, they were named when colored electric lights were strung along the cliff to make rainbows appear in the spray.

276. LLOYD LAKE, N. of Main Dr., fed by a tiny stream that ripples over a rocky ledge, is encircled by a graveled path.

277. The PORTALS OF THE PAST, six white marble Ionic Pillars reflected in the tranquil surface of Lloyd Lake, are all that remain of A. N. Towne's Nob Hill residence burned in the 1906 fire.

278. Nine-acre MARX MEADOWS, NW. of Lloyd Lake, were named for Mrs. Johannah Augusta Marx, who bequeathed $5,000 for beautification of the park in 1922.

279. BROOM POINT, S. of Main Dr., since early days has been a landmark identified by the bright yellow blossoms of Scotch broom that grow there in profusion.

280. Within the confines of 25-acre LINDLEY MEADOW, S. of Main Dr., grazes a herd of sheep. Each December the meadow becomes a living Christmas card, with shepherds in biblical costume herding grazing sheep.

281. Homing ground for migratory game and domestic waterfowl, SPRECKELS LAKE, N. of Main Dr., supplies much of the water

for the park irrigation system. Each Sunday from March to late September the miniature sail and speed boats of the San Francisco Model Yacht Club clip their trim way across its rippling waters, some attaining a speed of 40 miles an hour.

282. The MODEL YACHT CLUBHOUSE (*members only*), W. of Spreckels Lake, a one-story structure of concrete and glass brick, is headquarters for miniature yacht enthusiasts. The Model Yacht Club members, in its fully equipped workshop, build tiny boats which duplicate in every detail their full-sized models.

283. The fences of the BUFFALO ENCLOSURE, N. of Main Dr., are so cleverly concealed in the surrounding forest that the herd of about 15 buffalo seem to be roaming at large.

284. Within the buffalo enclosure are the DEER PADDOCKS, occupied by small herds of Belgian deer and California elk.

285. The CHAIN OF LAKES, N. and S. of Main Dr., is a series of artificial lakes bordered by wilder and more rugged vegetation than is found elsewhere in the park. North Lake, N. of Main Dr., largest of the three, is dotted with several islands planted with birches, rhododendrons, and other shrubs. Waterfowl preen their plumage on the surface of the water and feed among the wild grasses in the shallows. Middle Lake, S. of Main Dr., is framed by 800 camellia and Japanese cherry trees.

286. A 150-yard-long RECREATION FIELD, W. of Main Dr. facing the ocean, includes facilities for football, softball, soccer, and tennis players, and a dressing room with showers.

287. The white, cedar-shingled NORTH WINDMILL (*not open to public*), E. of Main Dr. near NW. corner of park, is an authentic copy of a Dutch windmill. Seen from the Pacific, the structure is in astonishing contrast to the greenery of Golden Gate Park and the skyline of the city beyond. Constructed in 1903 to pump water for the park's irrigation system, it since has been equipped with electric pumps; but sails are attached during the summer months.

288. Reminiscent of the Maine Coast is the UNITED STATES COAST GUARD STATION (*open after 3 p.m.*), NW. corner of park, occupying three white buildings enclosed by a picket fence. A force of 11 men are stationed here to aid distressed vessels. One of the three buildings was constructed in 1870 when the station was established.

S. from Main Dr. on Great Highway

289. The stumpy, schooner-rigged 47-ton sloop *GJOA*, E. of Great Highway near NW. corner of park, only ship to negotiate the ice-bound Northwest Passage, rests in its rocky dry dock behind an iron-

spiked fence overlooking the Pacific. The *Gjoa* was given to San Francisco in 1909 by her commander, Arctic explorer Roald Amundsen. The sloop was built at Hardanger Fjord, Norway, in 1872. After 29 years of active service as a herring boat and sealer, she was purchased by Amundsen. With her superstructure strengthened, her hull sheathed in hardwood, and iron strips bolted to her bow, she was equipped with a 13-horsepower motor. On June 16, 1903, the *Gjoa* set sail from Christiana (now Oslo), Norway, bound for the Arctic and that Northwest Passage, the existence of which for centuries had troubled the minds of the adventurous. Aboard were Amundsen, six companions, Eskimo dogs, scientific instruments, and enough stores for five years.

Disaster soon struck at the expedition. A fire broke out in the engine room. A mysterious malady killed many of the dogs. In the Northwest Passage the sloop was grounded on a reef and her false keel ripped off. Only after precious deck cargo had been tossed overboard was she refloated. At long last the *Gjoa* halted in King William Land, in a bay later named Gjoahaven.

For three years Amundsen remained in the Arctic, with the temperature often "60 degrees below." Completely cut off from civilization, the expedition nevertheless went busily about its work of gathering scientific data. In addition to discovering the Passage, they succeeded in fixing the location of the magnetic pole. Finally the *Gjoa* set sail once more, passing through the Bering Sea and thence into the Pacific Ocean and down the Coast to San Francisco. She dropped anchor off Point Bonita one October day in 1906. In the celebration that followed, American warships dipped their flags to the men who had at last sailed the near-legendary Northwest Passage.

290. The two-story BEACH CHALET (*open daily except Mon. 10-6*), E. of Great Highway, has a large glassed-in dining room overlooking the ocean and the Great Highway. The foyer is ornamented with murals and mosaics by WPA artists.

E. from Great Highway on South Dr.

291. The MURPHY WINDMILL (*not open to public*), N. of South Dr. near SW. corner of park, the second of the park's two Dutch mills, is one of the largest sail-type structures in the world, having a wing spread of 114 feet. Erected in 1905 to supply water for irrigation, it was equipped with electric pumps in 1927. At the present time the sails are operated only as an "exhibit."

292. In the EQUITATION FIELD, N. of South Dr., a fenced, sandy area 25 by 75 yards, skilled equestrians urge their horses over practice hurdles. The adjacent Beach Stables house the horses used in the park.

NE. from South Dr. on unnamed drive

293. Not since early in the century has the three-quarter-mile track of GOLDEN GATE PARK STADIUM, N. of South Dr., thundered to the hoofbeats of thoroughbreds. A bicycle track, a cinder path, a football field, and a polo field occupy the space within the hedge that borders the inner rim of the trotting track. At the end of the last century two driving clubs dominated equestrian activities in San Francisco: the Golden Gate Driving Club, composed of men of wealth, and the San Francisco Driving Club (the "Steam Beer Club") of members in more moderate circumstances. The organizations built the track by private subscription according to the designs of Park Superintendent John McLaren and Park Commissioner A. B. Spreckels. Chief use of the trotting track at present is for training purposes. The stables were replaced in 1939 by the WPA-built Polo Sheds, a group of four gray concrete tile-roofed buildings. The sheds house not polo ponies, but race horses in training for track events throughout the country. In return for free quarters owners put their horses in for one trotting race each season, the proceeds of which go toward upkeep of track and grounds.

294. The angler finds an ideal practice pool in the cement-lined, WPA-built FLYCASTING POOL (*free*), W. end of Golden Gate Park Stadium, hidden in a woodland setting with eucalyptus and evergreen trees mirrored in its placid surface. With an overall length of 450 feet and a width of 185 feet, the pool is divided into three sections, one of which is used for distance casting, one for accuracy, and the third, provided with graduated steps rising above the surface, for improving skill in difficult overhead shots. Overlooking the pool is Anglers' Lodge, a wooden building with hand-hewn window frames and wrought-iron fittings, headquarters of the Golden Gate Angling and Casting Club, which, as the San Francisco Fly Casting Club, functioned as early as 1890. Of its open tournaments from October to June, largest is the Washington's Birthday Handicap.

E. from unnamed drive on Middle Dr.

295. METSON LAKE, S. of Middle Dr., part of the park irrigation system, with its grassy shores, large boulders, and background of conifers, has the appearance of a lake in a mountain meadow.

Retrace on Middle Dr. to unnamed drive; SE. from Middle Dr. on unnamed drive to South Dr.; E. from unnamed drive on South Dr.

296. Rock-rimmed MALLARD LAKE, S. of South Dr., with its wooded islet and tiny falls, is a favored stopover for September's south-

bound duck traffic. Here thousands of transient mallard and canvasback graciously fraternize with their stay-at-home cousins, the drab little mud-hens for whom the lakelet is "home." For years this was known as Hobo Lake, because transient workers on the roadways during the 1894 Mid-Winter Fair rested here between labors on the patches of seagrass.

297. A head-high wire fence encloses ELK GLEN, N. of South Dr., a wooded dell where the hoofs of elk, Scotch sheep, East Indian deer, and buffalo have churned into dusty waves the brown earth around their miniature lake. The elk herd has grown from a pair of the animals given to the city by Alvinza Hayward in 1890. Although death-struggles between the bucks during mating time have occurred on the reservation, the animals are gentle enough to nibble leaves from the hands of visitors.

298. The redwoods of the GEORGE WASHINGTON BICENTENNIAL GROVE, S. of South Dr., were planted February 22, 1932, in honor of the bicentennial anniversary of Washington's birth.

299. The HERBERT HOOVER TREE, adjoining George Washington Grove, a redwood tree planted by the Daughters of the American Revolution in 1935, commemorates the ex-president's work in conservation.

300. Encircling the base of steep, wooded Strawberry Hill is STOW LAKE, N. of South Dr., bordered by tree-lined walks and winding driveways. Central reservoir for the park's irrigation system, it is the largest of the park's artificial lakes. On the wooded islets that dot its surface nest waterfowl, both wild and domestic—brant, pelicans, black and white swans, and wild ducks, arriving in the autumn on their migration southward from as far north as the Arctic. Strawberry Hill, reached by two stone bridges across narrow parts of the lake, is the highest elevation in the park. The steep slopes are covered with cypress, eucalyptus, and long-leafed acacia. From the summit (428 alt.) are visible on clear days the Farallon Islands, gray dots on the horizon, 26 miles out in the Pacific.

301. HUNTINGTON FALLS leaps 75 feet from the summit of Strawberry Hill down a bed of glistening, fern-lined rocks. It was named for Collis P. Huntington, railroad magnate, who contributed $25,000 for the beautification of the bleak sand dunes of the city's new park. The water for the falls is pumped to the top of the hill at the rate of 1,600,000 gallons a day.

302. Plants rare and useful from far-away places grow in the ARBORETUM (open Mon.-Fri. 8-4), S. of South Dr., a 40-acre plot of which a fourth is under cultivation. A bequest by Mrs. Helen Strybing has made possible plans which will include several acres of native California plants and a building housing a laboratory, library,

and botanical collections. The new outlay also provides for classrooms where gardeners will be trained for their work in the park.

Plants are arranged in geographical groupings. Near the entrance, off South Dr., grow shrubs and trees from South Africa, including the aloe, which often reaches a height of 60 feet. South of this group is the Australian and New Zealand section, where grows the kauri, a primitive pine nearly extinct. West of the Australian group is the Mexican area with its Mexican or Montezuma cypress which is said to reach an age of 3,000 years. In the Chinese, Japanese, and Himalayan area, south of the Mexican section, are rare varieties of rhododendrons, including some brought from remote parts of Western China, Thibet, and the Himalayas. There are numerous trees and plants from South Africa. One area is given over to medicinal plants, including one from China from which recently was developed ephedrine. More commonly known are digitalis, from which the drug of the same name is derived; the recinus, or castor oil plant; the Arabian kath, whose leaves are made into a narcotic; and the white Chinese poppy, from which opium is made.

303. South of the Arboretum on gently sloping ground is the ROSE GARDEN, a large collection of standard, hybrid perpetual, and tea roses. Climbing roses cover the fences enclosing the garden. South of the garden, close to a tall stuccoed brick chimney resembling a castle tower, is a fine collection of iris and Kurumi azaleas.

NE. from South Dr. on Middle Dr.

304. A low, clipped hedge of myrtle fronts the GARDEN OF SHAKESPEARE'S FLOWERS, N. of Middle Dr., wherein grow specimens of every flower, shrub, and tree mentioned in the writings of William Shakespeare. Flower beds bordering a lawn include pansies, marigolds, columbines, primroses, yellow crocuses and daffodils, and dainty bluebells. Trees shading the garden include the alder, apple, ash, cedar, chestnut, laurel, lemon, locust, orange, pine, pomegranate, walnut, and yew. There are beds of sweet briar, rue, and thyme. On either side of the plot facing the entrance, where an English holly stands, are marble benches backed by dense growths of box. In the ivy-covered brick wall along the east end of the garden is a glass-enclosed niche holding a bust of Shakespeare, a copy of the Gerard Jensen bust in the Stratford-upon-Avon church. The garden was established by the California Spring Blossom and Wildflower Association.

305. DE LAVEAGA DELL, S. of Middle Dr., is a secluded glen, whose jungle foliage and fern-choked stream are the haunt of squirrels and birds. Giant tree ferns, some 20 feet high, grow among moss-covered rocks, mottled with shadows. Along each side of the twisting

stream run footpaths carpeted with leaves and flanked by shrub-filled artificial gullies. At the dell's eastern end is one of the park's largest collections of rhododendrons and azaleas.

306. The LILY POND, N. of Middle Dr., a long winding pool nestling at the foot of steep overhanging cliffs, was once a quarry. A walk bordered by huge rocks and tree ferns skirts the edge, and rushes and water grasses line the shores of the pond. Ducks paddle among the green pads of water lilies.

S. from Middle Drive on unnamed cross drive

307. From the 21 tree-protected, asphalt TENNIS COURTS, E. of cross drive, have been graduated such players as Maurice Mc-Laughlin, Bill Johnston, the Griffin brothers, and Alice Marble. It was here on some of the world's first asphalt courts, that McLaughlin developed the well-known "American twist" serve. The asphalt courts called for a much faster pace than clay and grass courts. Such pioneers as McLaughlin, after developing their games here, swept all before them in the East and Great Britain.

308. On quiet afternoons the BOWLING GREENS (*open 1-4*), E. and W. of cross drive, first public bowling greens in the United States, present a picture of another era. White-clad men and women bowl on the well-kept turf, while spectators watch from benches on terraced slopes. A row of the rare Torrey pines protects the greens on the west.

E. from unnamed cross drive on South Dr.

309. The CHILDREN'S PLAYGROUND, N. of South Dr., occupies a secluded valley sheltered by thickly planted trees and shrubbery. The first established in a public park in America, it was founded with $50,000 left by William Sharon in 1886. Its playground equipment, donkey course, and merry-go-round center about the Children's House, a two-story building of buff sandstone in Romanesque style.

310. When high, oval-shaped, municipal KEZAR STADIUM, S. of South Dr., was opened with a track meet May 2, 1925, Paavo Nurmi, Finnish marathon champion, was a feature attraction. At first seating 22,000, it was enlarged in 1928 to a capacity of 60,000. Mary Kezar, for whom the stadium was named, gave $100,000 of its total cost of $450,000. It is of articulated reinforced concrete, with a deck of wood, covered by asbestos felt coated with sanded asphaltum.

Kezar Stadium is used chiefly by football teams of San Francisco high schools and the Catholic universities, St. Mary's, Santa Clara, and San Francisco. Main events of the year are the annual clashes between Santa Clara and St. Mary's and the New Year's Day East-West game between picked stars from Eastern and Western university teams. Average annual attendance is more than 300,000.

311. The BASKETBALL PAVILION, E. of Kezar Stadium facing Stanyan St., is a long, low, buff-colored cement building roofed with red tile. Its interior, lighted by great skylights, seats 5,500. During the basketball season high school teams play four afternoons weekly and college teams at irregular intervals at night.

312. The GAMES ENCLOSURE AND GHIRARDELLI PAVILION, N. of South Dr. near Haight St. park entrance, a hedged retreat almost hidden by flowering shrubs, half of which is walled on three sides and roofed by glass, contains tables painted with chess and checkers markings and benches to accommodate about 200 players.

313. ALVORD LAKE, near Haight and Stanyan Sts. entrance, is a small lake sheltered from winds by tall cypresses and clumps of Coast live oak, the only tree native to the park area.

Part IV
Around the Bay

The Harbor and its Islands

FOR two centuries before discovery of the Golden Gate the navigators of Portugal, Spain, and England carefully avoided the sea approaches to the Port of San Francisco. The forbidding coastline and frequent fogs were not alone responsible for its prolonged obscurity: the outer islands indicated the danger of submerged rocks and shoals in the Gulf of the Farallones. Although soundings were taken by Sebastian Cermeno in 1595, not until 180 years later was any mariner bold enough to steer his ship through the Golden Gate. When the master of the *San Carlos* ventured through the strait in 1775, he sent a pilot boat ahead to chart the depth of the channel. Even within the Gate, Lieutenant Juan Manuel de Ayala's little packet proceeded with extreme caution: only too obvious was the danger of being swept out to sea by the ebb tide, whose current had permitted passage only after the vessel's third attempt at entry.

Although modern aids to navigation long since have made San Francisco's harbor one of the safest in the world, incoming ships must begin exercising caution about six miles from shore. Outside the Gate is deposited the silt brought down from inland valleys and carried through the Bay by force of the current. Fanning from the entrance is an undersea delta whose rim, tilted upwards, forms a wide semicircle, the San Francisco Bar, lying only about 30 feet under the surface—on its north side, where it widens out in the "Potato Patch," only 22 feet. During storms the waves break upon these rock-strewn shoals with disastrous force, and even in calm weather they are impassable to large vessels. Three channels cross the bar: the artificially-dredged Main Channel opposite the Golden Gate, kept open by the Army's 3,015-ton *Mackenzie* to a depth of approximately 50 feet, and the narrow North and South Channels, close to shore. The entrance to the Main Channel is guarded by *San Francisco Lightship*, a 129-foot schooner with a flashing light visible in clear weather for 13 miles. Equipped with a foghorn and a transmitter for radio beacon signals, it is serviced by the Yerba Buena station. In the area between the lightship and the bar, the pilot boats cruise, waiting for incoming vessels. When contact with a ship is made, a bar pilot puts out from the lightship in a ten-foot dory to which a rope ladder is thrown over the inbound ship's side. From the lightship in, the Main Channel is outlined with eight buoys, all equipped with flashing lights, three with bells, one with a whistle, and one with an electric trumpet.

In strict nautical terms, the Golden Gate is the three-mile strait between the San Francisco and Marin Peninsulas. At its western end, lights and foghorns on the headlands and buoys in the North and South Channels (some equipped with lights and fog signals), make the entrance to the Bay more conspicuous in any weather than it was when mariners like Sir Francis Drake passed by without guessing the existence of an inland body of water. Radio beacon signals are flashed from the light on Point Bonita; between the cliffs stands Mile Rock Lighthouse. The Golden Gate itself is illuminated by two additional lighthouses, at Point Diablo and at Lime Point. And three life-saving surf stations are maintained along the strait, each with a staff of 9 to 22 men on duty 24 hours a day.

The efficiency of men and machinery in the modern life-saving service of San Francisco Bay is indicated roughly by comparing the casualties of two shipwrecks 39 years apart. The *Rio de Janeiro,* which sank in the Golden Gate during a fog in 1901, carried 128 people down with her. But when the *Pinto* was shattered on the "Potato Patch" in 1939—under circumstances that made rescue particularly difficult—not a life was lost. Even a ferryboat, the *Golden City,* has gone down in the harbor without loss of a single life. At Land's End may still be seen the rusty scraps of four hulks which testify to hazards of the Golden Gate, but no one drowned in any of these disasters.

The islands of San Francisco Bay, besides contributing to its natural charm, have played a notable part in its history. Yerba Buena, Alcatraz, the Farallones, and part of Angel Island were included in the huge Mexican grant claimed by Joseph L. Limantour, a Frenchman who swore that he received it in return for $4,000 he had advanced Governor Manuel Micheltorena in 1843. Besides the several islands the notorious Limantour Claim included about half the present area of San Francisco. Described by United States Attorney General Jeremiah S. Black, who prosecuted the case, as "the most stupendous fraud, the greatest in atrocity and magnitude the world has ever seen," the claim was finally denied in the 1850's after expenditure of $200,000 for litigation and the arrest of Limantour. Gradually, since their recovery by the Federal government, Alcatraz, Angel, and Yerba Buena Islands have been incorporated in the harbor defenses maintained by the Ninth Corps Area, United States Army.

Less prominent are the Bay's two other tiny islands, but they too have had their uses. Brooks Island, the larger of these, lies about half a mile off Point Potrero. Some 46 acres in area, rocky and very sparsely wooded, it is (1940) uninhabited. Once known as Sheep Island, it was exploited several years ago by a construction company operating a rock quarry there. Just off Pier 50, near the San Francisco water front, is Mission Rock, occupied only by a warehouse and a wharf, both partially destroyed by fire in 1936. According to water-front legend a Portuguese fisherman once stocked the rock with sheep; he rowed out to it once a year to harvest his crop with a shotgun, pulling the slaughtered sheep aboard with a boathook.

THE FARALLONES

Almost as remote as Guam or Samoa to most San Franciscans is that chain of islands known as The Farallones, which lie about 32 miles off Point Lobos. Despite their inclusion since 1872 in the City and County of San Francisco, their inaccessibility to the average citizen has invested them with the unfamiliarity of a foreign land. Even to sportsmen, for whose annual yacht races they are a hazardous goal, their history and conformation have little intimate significance.

The Farallones lie in two groups separated by seven and three-quarter miles of open sea. Seven isles constitute the southern group: Southeast Farallon Island, Sugar Loaf Isle, Aulone Isle, Seal Rock, Arch Rock, Finger Rock, and Sea Lion Islet. Of these, Southeast Farallon Island is the most important of the entire chain, and Sugar Loaf Isle (185 alt.) is the highest. Except for one island which rises to an altitude of 155 feet, the North Farallones are small and unimportant. Noonday Rock, marking the northern end of the chain, is a submerged peak so named for the clipper *Noonday* which struck it and sank in 1863. Midway between the two groups lies "lonely little Four Mile Rock." The Gulf of the Farallones, the stretch of water between the chain and the California coast, was called La Bahia de los Pinos (the bay of the pines) by the Cabrillo expedition in 1542 and Bahia de Puerto de San Francisco (bay of the port of San Francisco) by Vizcaino in 1603.

The Southeast, or South, Farallon, about 32 miles west of the Golden Gate, is about one mile long, half a mile wide, three and one-half miles in circumference. A rocky ridge runs its entire length, broken by gorges and a swift-running sea stream called "The Jordan" which separates the portion known as West End. The highest peaks of this island are Tower Hill (on which the lighthouse is built), and Main Top. In some places the slope from the ridge to the water's edge is too steep for a foothold; in others, there are ledges where sparse vegetation makes patches of green. The soil on these flats is a mixture of guano and granite sand. The forbidding coastline of the South Farallon is edged by grotesque rocky cliffs and caves. The contours of the island are suggested by some of the names given various parts: Indian Chief Cliff; Lost World Cave; Great Murre Cave; Giant's Bath, a natural swimming pool on Breaker Hill; Great West Arch, a natural arch with the sea swirling under it; and Breakers Bay, also called Franconia Bay for the *Franconia,* a wooden vessel of 1,462 tons which went ashore on West End June 4, 1881. Fisherman's or Tower Bay is the present (1940) anchorage.

Despite a popular belief to the contrary, the Farallon Islands support vegetation. Besides a group of 20 Monterey cypresses growing in one sheltered spot and the small gardens cultivated by the lighthouse keepers, there are scattered growths of rock flowers, moss, and grass. The largest of several varieties of clinging weeds is the Farallon Weed, bearing a small yellow blossom, which grows in a mat formation, sometimes torn loose in sheets by the winds. It is used by the cormorants and other island birds in constructing their nests. Other weeds have been introduced through seeds contained in the hay shipped in for the solitary island mule.

Around the islands gather great hordes of Steller sea lions, the largest congregations being on Saddle Rock and Sugar Loaf. The California Harbor seal and Pribilof fur seal are seen occasionally. There are also numbers of hares, descendants of a few given by an English sea captain to a former lighthouse keeper. These animals increased so fast that they surpassed the supply of food (weeds) and at one time died of starvation in great numbers. During the last century, when tender service to the islands was less regular than now, the rabbits furnished the only supply of fresh meat for the keepers during periods of protracted storms.

The bird population of The Farallones includes California murres, Western gulls, cormorants, pigeons, guillemots, tufted puffins, Cassin's auklets, ashy petrels, and rock wrens. During the early 1850's, when fresh eggs were almost worth their weight in gold to San Franciscans, the pear-shaped eggs of the murres were gathered here and sold in San Francisco markets. The thick, tough shells of the eggs enabled their collectors to handle them with shovels and eliminated the necessity of packing, but gathering them was a dangerous occupation. So precipitous are the cliffs of these islands that the collectors, besides being liable to arrest as poachers, frequently fell off into the sea. The trade in murres' eggs continued until the late 1880's, when the supply had so decreased that the profits of collecting them no longer outweighed the risks involved.

According to some historians, the first white man to see the Farallon Islands was Bartolemeo Ferrola, who took command of Cabrillo's expedition after Cabrillo's death, although other authorities question the authenticity of the old Spanish chronicles which credit the discovery to him. However, Sir Francis Drake not only saw but landed on one of the Farallones on July 24, 1579—24 hours after leaving "Nova Albion" (Drake's Bay), where the expedition had been repairing their *Golden Hinde* since June 17. Drake named the islands the "Islands of St.

James" and described them as having "plentiful and great stores of seals and birds." Sebastian Cermeno and his companions apparently visited the Farallones in 1595 when they were proceeding down the coast from Drake's Bay in their launch, the *San Buena Ventura,* after their *San Augustin* had been wrecked.

According to Mildred Brooke Hoover, the islands had already been designated as The Farallones: "The name Los Farallones is derived from the Spanish nautical word meaning 'cliff or small, pointed island,' and was fixed on this particular group during the years when the Spanish galleons plied between the Philippines and Mexico." The implication that the islands were well known to mariners of the time is substantiated by the chronicle of Sebastian Vizcaino, who described them in 1603 as a mark for finding Punta de los Reyes and the harbor of Drake's Bay. The first to name individual islands of the group, he called the Southeast Farallon La Isla Hendido [*sic*] (the cleft isle) and the Northwest Farallon, Las Llagas (the wounds) to commemorate the stigmata of St. Francis.

First white inhabitants of The Farallones were fur-gatherers from the Russian colony at Bodega Bay. At a cost of much sickness and death due to improper food and water, they took 200,000 fur seals in three seasons. Although the supply of fur seals was seriously depleted at the end of that time, the Russians continued to keep hunters on the islands. In 1819 a new colony was planted there, including a number of Aleuts. They lived in huts made of stone, planks, canvas, and the sea lions' skins (some of the stone walls still stand). Lacking wood for fires, they used the fat of sea lions and seals. Only once did a Russian brig call at the island for their products. After several months most of the men, too weak to kill the seals, were barely subsisting on raw birds' eggs. By 1825 not one fur seal was left on the island and only one Russian family and 23 Kodiaks (northwest Indians) were living there.

Since 1855 the islands have been under the supervision of the United States Lighthouse Service and closed to the public. In 1909 bird lovers, aided by Admiral George Dewey, succeeded in having the islands declared a bird sanctuary. At the present time (1940) the Southeast Farallon is inhabited by four lighthouse keepers, six Navy men in charge of the Radio Beam Compass Station, and their families. Still standing, though remodeled, is "Stone House," the structure put up during the 1850's when the first lighthouse was built. The original light has been replaced by a modern one, raised 358 feet above mean tidewater and visible for 26 miles. To reach the light, the keepers climb a zigzag path along steep bluffs. It is said that during winter gales they have to crawl on hands and knees along the unsheltered stretches of this path.

ALCATRAZ

Resembling a huge battleship lying just within the Golden Gate, grim Alcatraz Island is known as "The Rock" to the Nation's underworld, whose most desperate criminals are confined within its practically inescapable walls. With a capacity of 800, normally two-thirds filled, this prison for incorrigibles has had such notorious inmates as Al Capone, kidnapper "Machine Gun" Kelly, and mail robbers Albert Bates, Gene Colson, and Charles "Limpy" Cleaver. Amid the riptides of the Golden Gate, a mile and a quarter from the San Francisco mainland, the island consists of barely 12 acres of solid rock rising in sheer gray cliffs from the water's edge. Above its stone walls jut the watchtowers of guards armed with machine guns; and below them the waterline is equipped with barbed-wire entanglements. The wall separating prisoners from the water is 20 feet high; the massive prison gates are electrically operated. In the main building the steel cell-blocks are three tiers high, arranged back to back in four double banks. In the mess hall, above the heads of the prisoners as they eat, hang drums of tear gas that can be released by the pushing of a button.

When visitors call (they are allowed only once a month), they face the inmates across tables through sheets of bullet-proof glass reaching to the ceiling. Conversation is carried on by means of microphone and loudspeaker, over which whispers cannot be transmitted. Since all incoming mail is censored and recopied, inmates never see the original of any letter sent to them; they are allowed to send only one letter a week each to a blood relative. Industries employing prisoners on the island include a laundry, mat factory, clothing factory, model shop, and dry cleaning plant, in one or another of which more than half the prisoners are employed. The inmates are allowed to receive elementary musical instruction and to enroll for correspondence courses sponsored by the University of California.

Less widely publicized by the movies and the press than the island's more forbidding aspects is its little civilian community comprising facilities for 51 families. These quarters, some of which were built half a century ago, are inhabited chiefly by families of prison guards. Some 60 children of these families commute daily between Alcatraz and San Francisco during school terms, being carried by Army boats plying between Angel Island and the Fort Mason Transport Docks.

The history of Alcatraz Island begins with its discovery in 1775 by Lieutenant Juan Manuel de Ayala of the *San Carlos,* who named it Isla de los Alcatraces (Isle of the Pelicans) because of the great number of these birds he found nesting there. In 1846, Pio Pico, last Mexican Governor of California, sold the island to Julian Workman. In March, 1849 Alcatraz was resold to John Charles Frémont, who acted as representative of the United States Government. Before the $5,000 was paid for the property, however, Frémont disposed of the island to the banking firm of Palmer, Cook and Company which subsequently brought suit to recover possession of it. Because Frémont had acted as a Government agent, the suit was denied and the island was retained as Federal property.

When the United States began to fortify the harbor in 1854, a lighthouse and lantern were installed on Alcatraz. Temporary buildings were erected, a wharf was built, and construction of batteries was begun. The building erected at that time as the engineer's office is still standing. Between 1854 and 1882 the Government appropriated $1,697,500 for fortifications on the island. Powder magazines were blasted from the rock and a citadel built on the crest. In 1859 the first Army detachment, Company "H," Stewart's Third Artillery, arrived on Alcatraz, commanded by Captain Joseph Stewart.

The island was designated a disciplinary barracks for prisoners having long sentences to serve in 1868. From the early 1870's on, troublesome Indians were sent to this post from time to time. A company of Indian scouts accused of mutiny at Cibicu Creek, Arizona Territory, were incarcerated here, as were five Indian chiefs who mutinied at San Carlos, Arizona Territory, in June, 1887, among them Kae-te-na, friend of Geronimo. Of the many prisoners who arrived from the Philippines (one transport alone brought 126) in 1900, most had deserted the United States forces and joined the Filipino insurgents. Civilians who committed crimes against the Army in China also were brought here. During the 1906 disaster, 176 prisoners removed from San Francisco jails were transferred to Alcatraz.

From 1895 to 1907 several Coast Artillery detachments were stationed here. In the latter year, when Alcatraz was designated the Pacific Branch of the United States Military Prison, the third and fourth companies, United States Military Prison Guard, were organized as its permanent garrison. It became a Federal prison for civilian incorrigibles in 1934.

Escapes from the island are nowadays seldom attempted and rarely successful. The most ingenious of these get-aways was engineered in 1903 by four prisoners, all trusties for good behavior, of whom one was a professional forger and another a printer by trade. Between them they succeeded in drawing up and printing a document recommending leniency in their cases, to which they forged the name of the commanding officer. Through a friend in the post office department they succeeded in having the document slipped into the outgoing mail. It made its way through all departments to the Department Commander, who then ordered the four released. They were given a military escort to the mainland. No sooner had they landed in San Francisco than they forged four checks to the sum of $125 on the quartermaster department, whereupon they repaired to a grog shop for liquid refreshments. Three of the men, fearing drunkenness, fled; but the fourth was picked up by police on a San Francisco street and promptly returned to the island. More successful were Roy Gardner, the "gentleman bandit," who escaped alone from the island in the early 1920's, and two prisoners who made a sensational get-away in 1938 and never were found. In 1926 a plot for a mass exit was halted when the warden, learning of the plans, pointed to the Bay and told the rebels to "go ahead and swim." The invitation was unanimously declined.

Alcatraz' grim reputation has caused San Francisco civic bodies recently to demand its abandonment; but though former United States Attorney General Frank Murphy in 1939 advised removal of its felons, "The Rock" continues to make San Francisco Bay the locale of the most fearsome of American prisons.

ANGEL ISLAND

Largest island in the Bay, mile-square Angel Island, roughly triangular in shape, rears its central peak (771 alt.) across Raccoon Strait from Point Tiburon. Once the site of a detention camp for hostile Indians captured during the Arizona campaign, it has served since 1892 as San Francisco's Quarantine and Immigration Station (*adm. by pass only to relatives of station employees; boats leave Pier 5, 8:40 and 10:30 a.m. and 1 and 3:30 p.m.*). The grassy green of the island's slopes is broken by darker patches of trees and brush. In some places outcroppings of rock lend a fantastic color to the predominating gentleness of the landscape. The shoreline, nearly six miles in circumference, rough and steep in places, curves inward here and there to narrow strips of white sand. Above it a military road circles the island at elevations varying from eighty to three feet. A Federal game refuge, the island is stocked with deer, quail, and pheasant.

When the *San Carlos* dropped anchor in Raccoon Strait, Lieutenant Juan Manuel de Ayala named the adjacent island Nuestra Señora de los Angeles (Our Lady of the Angels). After a century and a half of consequent neglect, Angel Island was granted in 1839 to Antonio Mario Osio by Governor Juan B. Alvarado, who took this means to prevent its occupation by the Russians and other foreigners. Osio raised horses and cattle there, although he never lived on the island himself. However, his claim generally was recognized until California became American territory, whereupon Osio went to Mexico. When he returned in 1855 with a claim to the island, he found it had already been set aside in 1850 for military purposes by executive order of the United States Government. The island was occupied by Federal troops in

1863. By 1865 a battery of three guns had been established on the west slope of the island, commanding the approach through the Golden Gate, which was later increased to 18 pieces; and in 1867 a general depot for receiving and discharging recruits from the Atlantic Coast was established on the east shoreline.

Before the end of the 1850's, Angel Island had won local fame as the site of a celebrated duel, which grew out of a stormy conflict involving the slavery issue. One Charles A. Stovall had brought with him to San Francisco from Mississippi a Negro slave boy known simply as Archy. When Stovall decided to return home, Archy refused to go and escaped from a Sacramento river boat. His master had him arrested but the Sacramento police refused to hand him over, whereupon Stovall carried the matter to the State Supreme Court. Justice Peter H. Burnett ordered the Negro returned to him. Archy's case then was taken to United States Commissioner George Penn Johnson, who ruled on April 14, 1858 that he no longer was a slave. One of Johnson's closest friends, State Senator William I. Ferguson, a Southerner, challenged Johnson's decision. Feeling ran so high between the two that arrangements were made for a duel. On a tiny piece of level ground on the eastern side of Angel Island the principals met at five o'clock on the afternoon of August 21, 1858. Dueling pistols having been chosen, it was agreed the combatants would start firing at ten paces, this distance to be reduced to ten feet if the first fire ineffective. When neither contestant was hit on the first exchange, or on the second and third, Johnson demanded an apology or a fourth encounter. The latter course was chosen. Ferguson was hit in the right thigh and Johnson in the left wrist. Ferguson was taken to San Francisco, where he died on September 14 while his leg was being amputated.

Near Angel Island a prison brig had been anchored in 1852 with 35 convicts aboard, 17 of whom escaped at different times, overpowering or bribing the keepers. The island itself served as a prison camp during the 1870's for hostile Arizona Indians. A part of its eastern shore was set aside in 1900 as a detention and quarantine camp for soldiers returning from the Philippines. In 1900 the post was named Fort McDowell (*adm. by pass only to relatives of persons at fort; boats leave Pier 4, Army Transport Dock, Fort Mason, at 7:20, 8:30, 10 a.m.; 12 noon; 4, 6 p.m.*). From December 1, 1901 to June 30, 1902 a total of 10,747 soldiers passed through the Angel Island station on their return from Manila.

By an act of Congress in 1888 the building of a permanent quarantine station on the island was authorized and an appropriation of $103,-000 set aside for the purpose. Constructed on the shores of a sheltered indentation north of Fort McDowell, known as Hospital Cove, the quarantine station was opened May 1, 1892. In 1909 the Angel Island

Immigration Station was established. Quarantine and immigration officers board ships from foreign ports for inspection. Individuals who do not pass inspection are taken to the Angel Island Station for further examination. An Oriental Division is in charge of matters relating to vessels from China and Japan (a majority of cases handled at Angel Island are Chinese and Japanese). A hospital at the station operates under jurisdiction of the Public Health Service Department. Besides the Quarantine and Immigration Station, the Government operates a lighthouse, established on the southwest portion of the island, under license to the Treasury Department, in 1886. Its two keepers operate the light, a fog bell, and (by remote control) two fog sirens at other points on the island.

YERBA BUENA

Stepping stone for the bridge builders in spanning the Bay, cone-shaped Yerba Buena Island (*open for official business only by pass from Headquarters 12th Naval District, Federal Office Bldg., San Francisco*), rising between the eastern and western shores, is the anchorage for both the suspension and the cantilever spans of the San Francisco-Oakland Bay Bridge. Through a rock formation of the island passes a bore tunnel connecting the two (*see Emporium of a New World: Engineering Enterprise*). East of the tunnel, the first of the bridge's East Bay spans passes over the buildings of the island's naval reservation on a narrow tongue of land projecting into the bay, terminated by a barren low hill. Winding paved side roads lead to all parts of the island's landscaped and heavily wooded slopes, dotted by the neat dwellings of navy and lighthouse personnel.

Known to early navigators and whalers as Wood Island, Yerba Buena Island was indicated on old Spanish charts as Isla del Carmen. The English navigator, Frederick W. Beechey, gave it the present name in 1826, but it was known locally as Goat Island in the early 1830's when Gorham H. Nye pastured his goats on its slopes. Until after the 1850's, when the Land Commission denied the Limantour claim to the island and gave title to the Government, other early settlers raised goats there. Despite the subsequent disappearance of all goats from the island the colloquial name persisted, although various official documents referred to it as "Yerba Buena." (An 1858 map of California had called it "Ghote" [*sic*] Island.") In 1895 the United States Geographic Board officially adopted the local name.

Not until December 19, 1866 did the Government first take possession. First used as an infantry station, the island served in the early 70's as an artillery post, until fire destroyed the buildings, leaving as the only remaining Government service the lighthouse station established in 1875.

On April 12, 1898, President William McKinley signed an executive order setting aside a part of the island for a naval training station. At a cost of $74,400 barracks were erected to house 500 apprentices. The additional water supply necessary for the training station was piped under the bay from Contra Costa County. The island slopes were cleared and landscaped and a road built to its highest point. A fully rigged training ship, the *Boston,* was attached to the station for use in a six-months cruise of sea duty, following a like training period on shore. Stocks of quail and pheasant turned loose on the island thrived until in 1916 an executive order signed by President Woodrow Wilson set aside 141 of the island's approximately 300 acres as a National game preserve. The naval training station was officially closed in August, 1923. The remaining buildings and old training ship continued to be used as a receiving station for transfer of naval units to and from the Asiatic fleet and various naval bases.

The campaign to change the name of the island, begun in 1916 by historian Nellie van der Grift Sanchez, succeeded in 1931 when the United States Geographic Board made the name "Yerba Buena" official. A newspaper account of the ceremonies held on the island in June, 1931 states: "The day's legend was that there was one remaining goat on the island, and he was to be thrown overboard to free Yerba Buena, like St. Patrick did Ireland. Jack Love, radio operator on the island, dressed up as a goat and was twice fed to the crocodiles, figuratively speaking."

Below the eastern entrance to the Bay Bridge tunnel, a road winds down around the island past a marine sentry post to the Naval Receiving Station on the southeastern shore. Commissary buildings, warehouses and a carpenter shop, a building marked "General Court Martial and Brig," and the old barracks with its colonial portico stand below a span of the bridge. At a nearby dock, beyond a tennis court, the gray-painted receiving ship rides at anchor. Its interior has been altered and its superstructure changed to conform with modern naval construction, so that only the hull and the decks of the original ship remain.

Below the high bluff on the southwest shore are the six buildings of the Yerba Buena Lighthouse Depot, where a force of about 25 men service and supply all lighthouses, lightships, buoys, and fog signal stations on the California coast. A white-painted lighthouse tender, used to maintain contact with the various lighthouses and with *San Francisco Lightship,* is stationed at the depot's dock alongside the red-painted lightship, *Relief.* Equipped with complete radio beam facilities, the *Relief* carries a crew of nine while in port and seventeen while on station. It is used to relieve the regular lightships stationed off San Francisco Bar and Blunts Reef during annual vacation and check-up periods.

Above the island's southwestern point, visible from the San Francisco span of the Bay bridge, is the octagonal grey and white frame tower of Yerba Buena Light, erected in 1875. One of the smallest in the service, it is supplied by a 1,500-watt globe magnified to 12,000 candlepower by its prism shade, which operates at calculated intervals from sunrise to sunset. An astronomical clock regulates the light automatically to conform with changes in the daylight hours. The gray and white frame building with gabled red roof above the tower, occupied by the lighthouse keeper and his assistant, houses a radio-beacon monitor control station. Here radio beams from lighthouses and lightships are checked twice daily with naval observatory time for frequency and strength. (California lighthouse stations are grouped in south, central and northern districts. In clear weather, the southern district broadcasts its beam only during the first and fourth ten seconds of each hour; the central district, during the second and fifth ten seconds; the northern district, during the third and sixth. The monitor station checks all districts to guard against lag or overlap between broadcasts.)

TREASURE ISLAND

"It ought to be in the West, and have a tang of the Orient about it . . . at the last frontier of civilization's forward march, yet looking out upon the most ancient lands and the most exotic peoples." So was hailed—by Lewis Rex Miller in the *Christian Science Monitor*—the concept and construction of the Golden Gate International Exposition (1939-40) on Treasure Island. Approached by a filled-in causeway from Yerba Buena Island, Treasure Island (*see Emporium of a New World: Engineering Enterprise*) appears like a "stately pleasure dome" conjured up by the magic of modern science from Kublai Khan's Xanadu. By night this unearthly effect is enhanced by panchromatic floodlighting which transforms the exposition's towers and pavilions into a floating city of emerald and vermilion palaces.

The architectural commission to whom goes much of the credit for the exposition's dominant features included such outstanding Western architects as Lewis P. Hobart, Ernest Weihe, Timothy Pflueger, William G. Merchant, and Arthur Brown, Jr. Until his death in 1937, George W. Kelham, supervising architect of the Panama-Pacific International Exposition (1915), was chairman of the commission. Under its direction the goal which Kelham described as an attempt "to strike a golden medium between pageantry and structural beauty" was realized to a degree of perfection witnessed by the millions of spectators who have marvelled at the spectacular charm of the exposition's array of courts and pavilions. Working in close harmony with its designers of buildings, landscape architects such as Mark Daniels, Thomas D.

Church, Butler S. Sturtevant, and the Misses Worn, under the supervision of John McLaren, chief landscape architect of the 1915 exposition and of Golden Gate Park, created floral designs and arranged for the planting of evergreens indigenous to the Pacific Coast. Besides rhododendrons and azaleas, native annuals, and perennials from all over the Far West, landscaping brought to this riot of color the exotic hues of flowers and plants imported from far countries of the Pacific area.

Midway down the Avenue of Palms rise two massive Mayan-Incan pyramids (Weihe) supporting huge stylized elephant figures—the exposition's main gateway to its great circular Court of Honor. Here the slim octagonal Tower of the Sun (Brown), pierced by airy embrazures and surmounted by a spire, rises 400 feet to dominate with a Renaissance gesture the conglomerate eclecticism of the surrounding architecture. Northward from the belvederes and statuary about its base stretches the immense oblong Court of the Seven Seas (Kelham). From the facades of the pavilions which enclose it protrude the rearing prows of galleys with carved figureheads, suggestive of travel and adventure. This *via triumphalis* set with standards and lanterns opens into the Court of Pacifica (Pflueger), across whose fountain and sculptures gazes Ralph Stackpole's amazonian statue, *Pacifica,* symbolic of peaceful co-operation between the Americas and their Pacific neighbors, stationed against a gleaming backdrop of tubes and metal stars designed to produce melodious sounds under certain climatic conditions. Eastward from the Tower of the Sun lies the long Court of Reflections with its serene sculptures and still pools, separated by a lofty arch (Hobart) from the adjoining Court of Flowers. Olof C. Malmquist's *The Rainbow* rises from the fountain dominating this enclosure, whose eastern entrance is guarded by twin Towers of the East (Merchant). The Court of the Moon and Stars (Kelham) adjoining the Court of Honor on the south presents a decorative vista of fountain, urns, and bas-reliefs. Beyond, in the direction of Yerba Buena Island, lies the sunken Enchanted Garden, where landscaping plays unconfined about a huge fountain. Overlooking this verdant area, William Wurster's Yerba Buena Clubhouse achieves that gay and functional quality associated with this architect's rejection of ornament and fondness for modern materials.

Throughout the exposition's ensemble of almost a hundred buildings, as various in design as the purposes they serve, are many whose architecture is notable either for beautiful modernity or for features suggestive of cultures ranging from Alaska to Argentina, from Missouri to French Indo China.

The exposition has proved a gigantic workshop for all but a few of the more renowned Bay region sculptors and mural painters. From Sargent Johnson's grotesque Inca Indians astride llamas beside the fountain in the Court of Pacifica and Adeline Kent's evanescent *Air and Water* above the arched west walls of the Court of Honor to Robert Howard's gamboling *Whales* in the fountain of the San Francisco Building and Herman Volz's gigantic mural *The Conquest of the West* on the facade of the Federal Building—the statuary and murals run the gamut of the Bay region's artistic achievements. The academic tradition predominates in Olof C. Malmquist's *Fauna,* in Ettore Cadorin's *Moon and the Dawn,* in Haig Patigian's *Creation.* Purely decorative are Jacques Schnier's gold-finished panel, *Dance of Life;* Raymond Puccinelli's restrained *Flora;* Ruth Cravath's fountain group, *North America.*

When the exposition buildings are demolished and Treasure Island is transformed into an air terminal, the semi-circular Administration Building will remain, and the two huge pavilions housing fine arts and aviation exhibits will become hangars for clipper planes linking San Francisco and the Nation with Latin America, the Orient, and Australasia.

East Bay: Cities and Back Country

I N SPANISH times the distant shoreline opposite the Golden Gate was *"la contra costa"* (the opposite coast), to the *conquistadores.* Today between the shimmering cables and steel girders of the San Francisco-Oakland Bay Bridge, the eastward traveler sees a continuous panorama of home and industry, extending north and south with hardly a break and almost to the crest of the wooded hills in the background. The "opposite coast" is now the East Bay, a heterogeneous urban area comprising ten municipalities in two counties. The bridge is itself both a practical and a symbolical evidence of its close relationship to the other metropolitan areas on the western shore.

The hills seem to recede as the traveler speeds down the eastern half of the bridge: he sees a flat rectangular strip of land on which most of the industrial and business sections of the East Bay rest, as on a stage to which the residential hills are the backdrop. Ahead and to the right are the tall buildings of downtown Oakland, key city of the area, where the industrial district crowds down to the Outer Harbor in the foreground. Across the water to the far right a ferryboat dock— reminiscent of a vanishing era in Bay transportation—affords the only glimpse of Alameda, the island city. Far to the southeast, beyond the traveler's range of vision, are San Leandro and Hayward. Although the vast panorama of homes and business buildings shows no visible gaps, it is a jig-saw puzzle of independent communities closely fitted together—Piedmont, a residential community in the hills almost directly ahead; Emeryville, an industrial town crowding to the shore in the left foreground; Berkeley to the left, best identified by the white campanile and stadium on the university campus, spreading up the slopes beyond; El Cerrito, and Richmond, residential and industrial towns far to the left. With a combined population of over a half-million, these municipalities form a continuous urban unit, yet maintain their political independence.

Its scenic attractions and garden climate—slightly more extreme in summer and winter than San Francisco's—make the East Bay the family homesite of more than 30,000 commuters, who ebb and flow daily across the bridge to business and professional offices. The panoramic setting of the entire Bay region is nowhere better seen than from the Grizzly Peak and Skyline Boulevards, which follow the crest of the hills above Berkeley and Oakland. With impressive authority, a noted traveler has cited this tour as "the third most beautiful drive in the

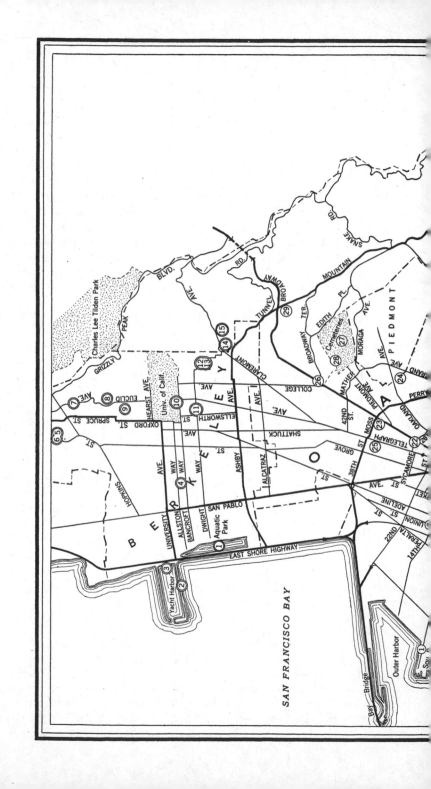

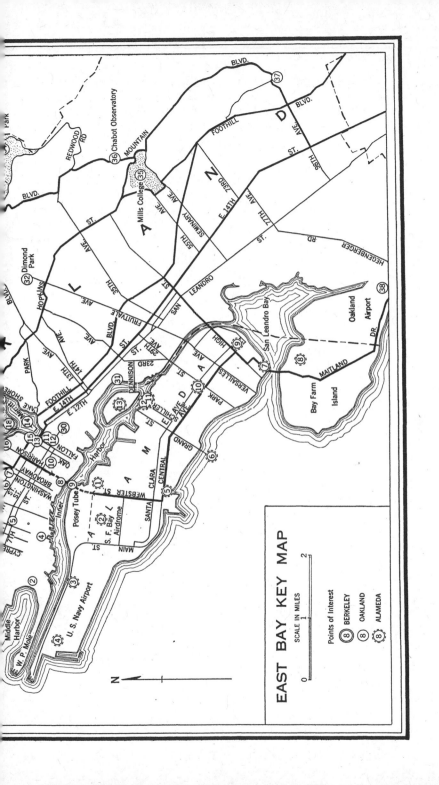

EAST BAY KEY MAP

SCALE IN MILES
0   1   2

Points of Interest

⑧ BERKELEY
⑧ OAKLAND
⑧ ALAMEDA

N

world." It follows for a distance the boundary line between the two counties which share the east side of the Bay—Alameda and Contra Costa, the old Spanish name having adhered to the latter, although its meaning is generally lost on the monolinguistic inheritors of the ranchos.

Oakland

Information Service: Oakland *Tribune,* 13th and Franklin Sts. Chamber of Commerce, 14th and Franklin Sts. Dep't of Motor Vehicles, 1107 Jackson St. California State Automobile Assn., 399 Grand Ave. Alameda County Development Commission, County Courthouse.

Railroad Stations: Atchison, Topeka and Santa Fe. Ry., San Pablo Ave. and 40th St. Sacramento Northern Ry., Shafter Ave. and 40th St. Southern Pacific R. R., W. end of 16th St. and Broadway and 1st St. Western Pacific R. R., Washington and 3rd Sts.

Bus Stations: Greyhound and Peerless Lines, Union Stage Depot, 2047 San Pablo Ave. Santa Fe and Burlington Trailways, 1801 Telegraph Ave. All American Bus Lines, 1901 San Pablo Ave. Dollar Lines, 2002 San Pablo Ave.

Airports: Oakland Municipal Airport, Bay Farm Island, for United Air Lines (about Jan., 1941 base will be moved to San Francisco) and TWA. Treasure Island for Pan-American Airways.

Taxis: Average rates 20¢ first ¼ m., 10¢ each additional ½ m.

Streetcars and Buses: East Bay Transit Co. to all points in Oakland, Berkeley, and Alameda, 10¢ or one token (7 for 50¢); to Hayward, El Cerrito, or Richmond 20¢ or 2 tokens; transfers free. Transbay electric trains to San Francisco, 21¢.

Bridge: San Francisco-Oakland Bay Bridge approaches: 38th and Market Sts. and 8th and Cypress Sts.; toll 25¢, 1 to 5 passengers.

Traffic Regulations: Speed limit 25 m.p.h. in business and residential areas, 15 m.p.h. at intersections. Parking limit 40 min. in business district. No all-night parking.

Accommodations: Eight medium-priced hotels downtown; apartment hotels; Y.M.C.A., 2501 Telegraph Ave.; Y.W.C.A., 1515 Webster St.; eight tourist camps.

Radio Stations: KLX (880 kc.), Tribune Tower; KLS (1280 kc.), 327 21st St.; KROW (930 kc.), 464 19th St.

Concert Halls: Auditorium Theater, Civic Auditorium; Women's City Club.

Motion Picture Houses: Five first-run theaters downtown.

Amateur and Little Theaters: Oakland Theater Guild, Women's City Club, 1428 Alice St.; Faucet School of the Theater, 1400 Harrison St.; East Bay Children's Theater, Junior League, Hotel Oakland.

Burlesque: Moulin Rouge, 485 8th St.

SPORTS

Archery: Peralta Park, 10th and Fallon Sts.
Auto Racing: Oakland Speedway, E. 14th St. and 150th Ave.
Baseball: Oakland Baseball Park (Pacific Coast League), San Pablo and Park Aves. Auditorium Field, 8th and Fallon Sts. Bay View, 18th and Wood Sts. Bushrod, 60th St. and Shattuck Ave.

Boating: Lake Merritt.

Boxing: Oakland Civic Auditorium (Wednesday nights).

Cricket: Golden Gate Playgrounds, 6142 San Pablo Ave.

Golf: Knoll Golf Course, Oak Knoll and Mountain Blvd. Lake Chabot Municipal Golf Course, end of Golf Links Rd.

Ice Skating: Oakland Ice Rink, 625 14th St.

Lawn Bowling: Lakeside Park, N. shore Lake Merritt.

Riding: Bridle paths in hills; horse rental $1.00 per hour up.

Softball: Exposition Field (lighted), 8th and Fallon Sts. Wolfenden Playgrounds (lighted), 2230 Dennison St. Allendale School, Penniman and 38th Aves. Goldengate Playground, 6142 San Pablo Ave. Manzanita School, 24th Ave. and E. 26th St. Poplar Playground, 32nd and Peralta Sts.

Swimming: Lion's Pool, Dimond Park, Fruitvale Ave. and Lyman Rd.; children 15¢, adults 25¢; no suits or towels furnished. Lake Temescal . Forest Park Pool, Thornhill Dr.; children 15¢, adults 25¢; suit 10¢, towel 5¢, caps 10¢ to 25¢.

Tennis: 31 municipal courts; daytime free, 25¢ per court per ½ hour nights. Athol Plaza, Lakeshore Blvd. and Athol Ave. Bella Vista, 10th Ave. and E. 28th St. Brookdale Plaza, High St. and Brookdale Ave. Dimond Park, Fruitvale Ave. and Lyman Rd. Mosswood Park, Moss Ave. and Webster St. Davie Tennis Stadium, 188 Oak Rd.

Wrestling: Oakland Civic Auditorium (Friday nights).

Yachting: Oakland Yacht Harbor, foot of 19th Ave.

CHURCHES

(Only centrally located churches of most denominations are listed)

Baptist. First, 530 21st St. *Buddhist.* Japanese Buddhist Temple, 6th and Jackson Sts. *Christian.* First, 29th and Fairmount Sts. *Christian Science.* First Church of Christ, Scientist, 1701 Franklin St. *Church of Jesus Christ of Latter Day Saints.* Church of Jesus Christ of Latter Day Saints, 3757 Webster St. *Congregational.* First, 26th and Harrison Sts. *Episcopal.* St. Paul's, Bay Place and Montecito Ave. *Evangelical.* St. Mark's, Telegraph Ave. and 58th St. *Free Methodist.* First, 459 61st St. *Greek Orthodox.* Holy Assumption, 920 Brush St. *Hebrew Orthodox.* Temple Sinai, 28th and Webster Sts. *Lutheran.* St. Paul's, Grove and 10th Sts. *Methodist.* First, 24th and Broadway. *Presbyterian.* First, 26th and Broadway. *Roman Catholic.* St. Francis de Sales, Grove and Hobart Sts. *Salvation Army.* Salvation Army Citadel, 533 9th St. *Seventh Day Adventist.* Oakland Central Church, 531 25th St. *Unitarian.* First, 685 14th St.

OAKLAND (0-1600 alt., 304,909 pop.), seat of Alameda County, occupies roughly the central part of the East Bay metropolitan area. Berkeley and Emeryville to the north and Alameda, across the Estuary, limit its expansion, but to the east and southeast it sprawls without let or hindrance over hills and Bay-shore flats.

From the tall white City Hall in the heart of the city, streets, once country roads, radiate: San Pablo Avenue striking northwest to industrial Emeryville and West Berkeley; Telegraph Avenue and Broadway, north through the newer residential sections to the University of California; Fourteenth Street, west through shabby neighborhoods toward the Bay, and east and southeast by zigzags past Lake Merritt and an interminable series of local retail shops supplying the small, neat but monotonous rows of white houses which make up East Oakland, Fruitvale, Melrose, and Elmhurst.

Closely hemming the downtown section, where a few tall office buildings loom over squat business structures, are two- and three-story homes of the "gingerbread" era, slightly down-at-the-heel. Spreading north and east toward the hills from Lake Merritt in the heart of the city are thousands of wood and stucco houses, each with its shrubs and lawn. The one reminder of Oakland's Spanish heritage is the modern homes in the restricted districts—Rockridge, Broadway Terrace, and Claremont Pines—constructed in a modified Mediterranean style of architecture, tile-roofed and stuccoed, with wide arches, studio windows, and sunny patios. Semitropical trees—camphor, acacia, pepper, dracena, and palm—ornament city parks and sidewalks, and figs and citrus fruits ripen in the warm sunshine in many backyards.

Warmer in the summer than its metropolitan neighbor across the Bay, Oakland's climate is nevertheless tempered in summer by cooling winds and fogs from the ocean. This has attracted many San Francisco business men and office workers who, even before the building of the great bridge, came here.

In the springtime, the hills become green backgrounds for wildflower mosaics of scarlet and purple, blue and yellow. Besides the Coast liveoak for which the city was named, the Monterey pine and the eucalyptus are abundant, the latter introduced from Australia in 1856 and planted by thousands in the hills to create a wooded watershed. Vivid with color during the spring months, the uplands are seared to silverbrown through summer and fall because of lack of rain.

Around the City Hall spread the 70 blocks of the retail shopping district. Oakland's department stores and speciality shops draw patronage from the entire East Bay region, but they also yield a certain percentage of such trade to the transbay metropolis, as San Francisco trade names on the doors of local shops indicate. Influenced by the close commercial tie-up between the two cities, Oakland's tempo of living varies with the time of day: by dawn commuters are on the move, feeder highways to the San Francisco-Oakland Bay Bridge are alive with speeding cars, and interurban trains clang through the streets, crossing and re-crossing the great span. After the early morning rush, life in the downtown section settles into a somewhat more moderate pace. At the end of the day, as automobiles, buses, and streetcars carry thousands home from work, the main thoroughfares come to noisy life again.

South of the central business district, the section between Tenth Street and the shore of the Estuary, oldest quarter of the city, is now given over to bargain stores, second-hand shops, and workers' homes. On lower Broadway is a section of honky-tonk beer parlors and skid-road soup houses, where a burlesque show with lurid lobby portraiture is neighbor to a hole-in-the-wall pawnshop and an old-clothes emporium, where panhandlers linger on street corners and at entrances to penny arcades. Southward, interspersed with unpainted, grimy dwellings, are wholesale houses.

Along the Estuary itself, resounding to the grating squeak of winches and the staccato chug of wharf tractors are huge docks, a part of the Port of Oakland's Inner Harbor—one of the three on the city's 32-mile water front: Outer Harbor, between San Francisco-Oakland Bay Bridge approach and the Southern Pacific mole; Middle Harbor, bounded by the Southern Pacific and Western Pacific Railroads; and Inner Harbor, comprising the six miles of tidal estuary between Oakland and Alameda. Into the narrow Inner Harbor come freighters from the seven seas. Here are held crew races of the University of California, and here pleasure craft and fishing boats nose in and out.

West of downtown Oakland, extending from Market Street to the Bay and from the Estuary to Twentieth Street, is the West Oakland district. Crowding close about railroad yards and manufacturing plants are unsightly and dreary-looking dwellings. On some of the streets spacious old homes still maintain an air of shabby and aloof gentility, but many have been partitioned into crowded, rabbit-warren housekeeping rooms. Throughout the district are rows of ugly cottages with blistered paint and rickety stairs and porches, many of which are now being demolished to make way for new projects of the United States Housing Authority. Along Seventh Street, intersecting this district east and west, rumble the interurban trains.

In West Oakland is the city's Harlem, home of the large Negro population attracted by Oakland's position as the western terminus of two overland railway systems, which employ in great numbers waiters, cooks, and porters. West Seventh Street is the center of Negro life. Here are dance halls, restaurants, markets, barber shops, and motion picture theaters for Negroes.

Although Oakland's population includes thousands of Portuguese, Italians, Mexicans, and Chinese, its various national groups are scattered throughout the city rather than settled in well-defined foreign quarters. But their customs and their cuisine lend colorful variety to the city's life.

The Portuguese have been here for three generations, and yet they still hold to such national customs and festivals as the Feast of the Holy Ghost, celebrated annually. A large number of Portuguese-Americans in the environs are truck farmers and dairymen. The Italians, largest foreign language group, have influenced the culinary art of the community. Numerous Italian restaurants feature various *antipasti* with which to whet the appetite; *polenta,* a thick porridge of corn meal; and such delicacies as fried artichokes or squash blossoms dipped in batter and fried in deep olive oil. The Mexican population maintains a few restaurants which serve native Mexican foods—*enchiladas, tacos en tortillas,* and *chili rellena*—and an occasional hole-in-the-wall shop where strings of *chorizo* (Mexican sausage) hang from gray rafters and three-bushel jute bags of purple and crimson peppers stand in corners. Chinatown, with its dangling lanterns and picture word signs, houses its 3,000 Chinese in a loosely knit community centering in the wholesale district near Eighth and Franklin Streets. Up and down its sidewalks the soft-soled slippers of Old China shuffle along beside Young China's tapping occidental heels. On market pegs hang exotic fruits and vegetables, dried ducks and transparent octopuses; from gaudy chop suey establishments issue strains of modern "swing."

Although the site of Oakland was first visited by white men in 1770, when Lieutenant Pedro Fages led an expedition here seeking a land route to Point Reyes, a half century passed before the land was first colonized. In 1820 Spain's last governor of Alta California, Pablo Vicente de Sola, granted to one Sergeant Luis Maria Peralta a tract of land in recognition of conspicuous military service in the Spanish Colonial Army. This grant became known as the Rancho San Antonio. Covering 48,000 acres, it included the area now occupied by Oakland, Berkeley, and Alameda. Threescore years of age at the time he received this prodigious grant, Don Luis never actually lived on it, preferring to remain at his home on a grant he had obtained in 1818, Portados la Rancheria del Chino, near the *pueblo* San Jose. He had four grown sons whom he placed in charge of Rancho San Antonio.

Not only was this the first, but it was also the most valuable, of the land grants on the east shore of San Francisco Bay. Lean years were few. The soil was rich, and herds multiplied rapidly; but agriculture was confined to the raising of a few staples grown in limited quantities.

In 1842 Don Luis, then past 80, divided his grant among his sons. To Jose Domingo he gave what is now Berkeley; to Vicente, the Encinal de Temescal (now central Oakland); to Antonio Maria, the portion to the south (East Central Oakland and Alameda); and to Ignacio, what is now Melrose and Elmhurst. Realizing the danger of future family altercations, he adjured them: "I command all my children, that they remain in peace, succoring each other in their necessities, eschewing all avaricious ambitions, without entering into foolish differences for one or two calves, for the cows bring them forth each year; and inasmuch as the land is narrow, it is indispensable that the cattle should become mixed up, for which reason I command my sons to be friendly and united."

To this sage advice his sons listened with respect. During the golden years of the Peraltas' reign over Rancho San Antonio, business was seldom allowed to interfere with pleasure. There were innumerable fiestas, and, on Antonio's share of the grant, bull fights were held. But while the Spaniards complacently watched their grazing herds of fat cattle "without entering into foolish differences for one or two calves," a new economic order was emerging. Gold had been discovered. Across the Bay the sleepy settlement of Yerba Buena had become a lusty brawling town crowded with men of all descriptions, including trigger-quick adventurers.

Shaken by the momentous events which were threatening the destinies of the Peralta clan, Don Luis called its members together—sons and grandsons—and spoke with grave earnestness, imparting final words of wisdom: "My sons," he said, "God has given this gold to the Americans. Had He desired us to have it, He would have given it to us ere now. Therefore, go not after it, but let others go. Plant your lands and reap; these be your best gold fields, for all must eat while they live."

In 1849 there arrived the first American settler in this region, a former sea captain, Moses Chase. Soon thereafter three newcomers, Robert, William, and Edward Patten, who had leased land from Antonio Peralta, added Chase to their group and became the first American farmers in this district, raising good crops of hay and grain.

With these tenants the Peraltas had come to terms, but a steady stream of new squatters also dotted their holdings. Unsuccessful in several attempts in 1850 and 1851 to eject the newcomers, they were forced at length to compromise by granting leases. Among these squatters was a man whose name was to be closely linked with the early history of Oakland—Horace W. Carpentier, who recently had been graduated from Columbia College in New York. Associated with him in the enterprises that were destined to make him many times a millionaire were A. J. Moon and Edson Adams. Having acquired with his partners a townsite where present downtown Oakland is situated, Carpentier in 1852 succeeded in having the town of Oakland incorporated, with himself seated securely in the mayor's chair. When the citizenry, who were seldom advised of what their mayor was doing, awoke, he held—among other concessions—a franchise for a ferry to San Francisco, the fare to be one dollar a trip.

Carpentier obtained absolute title to the entire water front in exchange for building a small frame schoolhouse and three tiny wharves. The water-front deal resulted in prolonged litigation, known as the "Battle of the Waterfront," by which the city tried to regain title to its doorstep. The fight was not ended until 1910, when assignees of Carpentier agreed to waive title to the water-front property in exchange for long-term leases.

The first combination rail and ferry service began operation to San Francisco in 1863, although ferry service alone had started as early as 1850. During the 1860's the "Big Four"—Stanford, Huntington, Crocker, and Hopkins—started building the Central Pacific Railroad, for which Oakland was the proposed western terminus. When in 1867 they asked the city for water-front rights, the city was unable to comply, having presented all such property to Horace Carpentier. However, the next year Carpentier founded a corporation known as the Oakland Waterfront Company. Associated with him in this enterprise, among others, was Leland Stanford, one of the "Big Four." Carpentier deeded to the corporation his water-front holdings and the corporation in turn conveyed to the railroad 500 acres of tideland. The railroad later appeared as the chief defendant, and loser, in the suit wherein Oakland regained these properties.

At one time the railroad officials had considered the Government-owned Yerba Buena Island as a western rail terminus. The citizens of San Francisco objected violently. It was feared "that the real intention was, by leveling the island and constructing causeways to Oakland, to rear up a rival city on the opposite shore that would be in substance owned . . . by the railroad company." The plan died when the Senate refused to approve the scheme. All obstacles finally surmounted, the first overland rail service began in 1869.

By 1870 there were two banks, three newspapers, and a city directory. Gas lamps illuminated lower Broadway. The first paving had been laid—at a cost of $3.40 per square foot. The University of California (later moved to Berkeley) was "spreading light and goodness," and a seminary for young ladies—now Mills College—was about to open.

The Central Pacific had entered the city, and the Oakland Railroad, already connecting with ferries to San Francisco, had been granted the right "to run horse-cars from the end of Broadway to Temescal Creek, and thence to the grounds of the College of California, for thirty years." Southeast of Lake Merritt the villages of Clinton, San Antonio, and Lynn had been consolidated into the town of Brooklyn—now East Oakland.

The social life of the town, also, had seen great change. No longer were posters seen such as the one which had announced in earlier days:

> "There will be a great bear fight in front of the American Hotel, Oakland, between the red bear Sampson and a big grizzly on Jan. 9th."

By 1870 this form of entertainment had been banned, and less sanguinary pleasures had taken its place: baseball instead of bullfights and typically Yankee "dime parties," socials, and church bazaars instead of Spanish fiestas.

In its growth as a suburb, it gained some distinction from the artists and writers who lived here. Jack London was developing from a water-front loiterer into an internationally known novelist. Joaquin Miller, the "Poet of the Sierras," was vaingloriously displaying his long hair and longer beard. Edwin Markham, while teaching in an Oakland school, awoke to find himself famous for "The Man With the Hoe." William Keith was painting the East Bay hills and trees. George Sterling, the lyric poet of whom London, his contemporary, said, "he looked like a Greek coin run over by a Roman chariot," lived in Oakland from 1890 to 1905, and Ina Coolbrith, who as librarian of the Oakland Public Library guided the early reading of Jack London, and who was a poetess in her own right, was here from 1873 until 1897.

Oakland's growth was greatly accelerated by the earthquake and fire that overwhelmed San Francisco in 1906. Although itself damaged by the earthquake, it escaped the fire which overwhelmed the neighboring city.

Up to 50,000 refugees fled to the East Bay region in one week. Not a few remained as permanent residents. This influx caused such a building boom that by the following year the population had jumped to 125,000. Industrial growth also was stimulated. During the World War, industry boomed as four large shipbuilding companies operated at peak capacity. By 1920 the population was 216,000.

The rapid growth of Oakland shortly after 1900 is credited largely to Francis Marion "Borax" Smith, of Death Valley fame. With the huge profits from his borax mines, Smith invested heavily in the future of Oakland. He tied together the numerous street railway systems of the East Bay and founded the Key Route Ferry System in opposition to the Southern Pacific; he acquired control of the East Bay Water Company, and in partnership with Frank C. Havens, pioneer capitalist, established the Realty Syndicate as a holding company for their many real estate properties. Land in every region of Alameda County was bought and developed, residential and industrial tracts were opened up, and interurban train service was extended into each new era. Smith came to own an estimated one-sixth of Alameda County.

In December, 1910 the $200,000,000 United Properties Company was formed by a merger of money and properties owned by Smith, William S. Tevis, and R. G. Hanford. This corporation, perhaps the largest in California history (excepting the Eastern-controlled Southern Pacific Railroad), was to absorb and develop the railways, ferry system, public utilities, and real estate of the East Bay. However, the company collapsed in 1913 because of unsound financial methods, carrying with it the fortunes of the three founders. Smith, the heaviest loser, saw $24,000,000 slip from his fingers almost overnight. But the company's loss was the city's gain, for its developments remained.

In the Bay region, Oakland's port ranks second to San Francisco in value of cargo handled, and third to Richmond and San Francisco in tonnage. Coordinated water-rail-truck facilities handle the 3,500,000 tons of cargo that pass over the water front annually. Principal exports are dried and canned fruits and vegetables, lumber, grain, salt, and petroleum. Imports include copra, coal and coke, paper, iron and steel, and fertilizer. Fir, pine, cedar, spruce, and redwood arrive from the Northwest and the interior of California to be made into finished lumber or wood products before distribution.

Oakland's water front is well-equipped not only to repair bay, river, and oceangoing vessels but also to lay down such craft and to launch and outfit them. Yachting, commercial fishing, towing, and general boat-building and repairing call for many smaller shipyards. Construction work on large yachts and other boats is facilitated by the proximity of large Diesel engine works.

Fortunate in having ample room for residential expansion, Oakland is still growing. On the outskirts, where garden space is available, files of newly built homes spread into the countryside. Thus Oakland, despite the encroachment of industry, retains its identity as a city of homes.

POINTS OF INTEREST

1. The ALBERS BROTHERS MILLING COMPANY PLANT (*tours for visitors Tues., Wed., Thurs., 10 a.m., 2 p.m*),

west end of Seventh St., manufactures a wide variety of packaged food products and feeds for animals.

2. The NAVAL SUPPLY DEPOT, end of Middle Harbor Rd., will be the largest in the Nation when completed sometime after 1942 at an estimated cost of $15,000,000. It will have 49 buildings; immense warehouses will provide storage space sufficient to hold a two-year supply of food, clothing, equipment, and other materials for the entire United States Navy. Two wharves, capable of handling six battleships, will be reached through a channel and turning basin.

3. The PACIFIC COAST SHREDDED WHEAT COMPANY PLANT (*visiting hours 9-11, 1-4; guides furnished*), Fourteenth and Union Sts., ships much of its large output to countries around the Pacific. In the process of making shredded wheat, hard wheat is dry-cleaned, steam-cooked, and stored in steel tanks for ten hours. Shredded between grooved rollers under 1,700 pounds pressure, it emerges in twenty-nine threadlike layers which are cut into biscuits and baked for twenty minutes at 550° F.

4. The MOORE DRYDOCK (*no visitors*), foot of Adeline St., in 1939 laid keels for four cargo steamers under a $12,000,000 contract with the United States Maritime Commission—the first sizable vessels to be built in San Francisco Bay since the World War. The concern's 300- and 500-foot floating drydocks and marine railway docks provide for building and repairing vessels and for such special jobs as constructing the caissons used in the piers of the San Francisco-Oakland Bay Bridge. This firm, since it laid in 1909 the keel of the first steel ship built in Oakland, has launched 200 such craft. During the World War 58 vessels were constructed, six of them sliding down the ways in 1918 on a single morning tide.

5. At ST. JOSEPH'S CHURCH, Seventh and Chestnut Sts., occurs the annual Portuguese Festival of the Holy Ghost, which originated in Portugal in the thirteenth century when Queen Saint Isabel had a vision of the Holy Ghost. To her He indicated a desire that a church be built in His honor. The ceremonial of the dedication of that church, with its procession, its crowning of a queen, and its placing of the crown on the Altar of the Third Person of the Blessed Trinity, has survived among the Portuguese to this day. The festival, centering around Pentecost Sunday, is celebrated with feasting on barbecued meats and *sopas* and dancing of the *chamarita*.

6. The OAKLAND PUBLIC LIBRARY, Fourteenth and Grove Sts., contains 275,000 volumes and 200,000 pictures and prints. Over the main stairway and on the walls of the second floor are murals by Marion Holden Pope and Arthur Matthews.

7. Oakland's tallest structure, the CITY HALL, Washington St. between Fourteenth and Fifteenth Sts., is a 17-story building rising

360 feet, completed in 1914, and was designed by the New York firm of Palmer, Hornbostel, and Jones, winner in a National competition. Faced with white granite and terra cotta in mingled Doric and Corinthian design, it has three set-back sections, capped by a baroque cupola adorned with four clock faces. The clock was donated by Dr. Samuel Merritt, former mayor.

Opposite the City Hall, overlooked by towering downtown buildings, is the triangular MEMORIAL PLAZA, dedicated to American war heroes.

8. Famed as the cradle of Jack London's genius, the FIRST AND LAST CHANCE SALOON, 50 Webster St., near the Oakland Estuary, has also warmed many another literary celebrity, including Robert Louis Stevenson, Joaquin Miller, and Rex Beach. A guest book bears the signatures of hundreds of the great and near-great. The small, weathered, dilapidated structure, built over 60 years ago from the timbers of an old whaling boat, was first used as a bunkhouse for men working the oyster beds along the East Bay shore. As a saloon, especially in the 1890's, it was a popular hangout for ready-fisted seafarers who crowded its bar and gambled at its card tables. Jack London, in his early teens, found a friend in the proprietor, the late Johnny Heinold, through whose encouragement and financial assistance his genius flowered in adventure tales woven around the lives of South Sea traders, Arctic whalers, and Alaska sourdoughs. Today the tinder-dry boards of the old building are blotched with cracked grey paint. The scarred mahogany bar is still in service. The old gambling tables on which young London often wrote are used for refreshments. On a wall, guarded from souvenir hunters by chicken wire, are letters and photographs, including a picture of Jack in knickerbockers poring over Heinold's tattered old dictionary, and a letter, written years later, inviting Heinold to the author's famous Glen Ellen home.

9. The POSEY TUBE, 4,436 feet long, passing under the 42-foot-deep channel of the Oakland Estuary between Harrison St. in Oakland and Webster St. in Alameda, when completed at a cost of $5,000,000 in 1928 was the world's largest under-water tube for vehicular traffic (its 32-foot diameter has since been surpassed by the Mersey Tunnel at Liverpool, England). It is still the only such bypass west of Detroit, Michigan. Its unusual method of construction drew the attention of engineers the world over. In the Oakland Portal, administrative and operating center, are meters that automatically count passing vehicles, control boards that govern the ventilating system, and delicate instruments that register the percentage of carbon-monoxide gas from automobile exhausts in every part of the tunnel. A staff of 17 engineers, mechanics, and traffic policemen is always on duty. Only

two fatal accidents occurred in the tube during its first 11 years, in which time 70,500,000 trips were recorded.

10. The BUDDHIST TEMPLE, Sixth and Jackson Sts., with its courtyard and school, is the center of Buddhist social and religious life in the East Bay. Here American-born Japanese children, after attending public schools, spend two hours daily learning their mother tongue and old-country customs.

11. The 32-acre PERALTA PARK, facing Lake Merritt across Twelfth St., is dominated by the $1,000,000 steel and concrete, granite-finished MUNICIPAL AUDITORIUM, built in 1915 on ground once occupied by a group of houses collectively known as the "House of Blazes"— a not very select bagnio. The building is in classical style, the main facade facing the lake ornamented by a series of bas-reliefs in terra cotta set in the alcoves above the entrance doors. Besides the arena, seating 10,000, which is used for conventions and sports events, it contains a large theater for dramatic and musical performances. The ART GALLERY (*open 1-5*) on the upper floor houses a permanent collection of paintings. Except for about 30 canvases by Russians, the work is chiefly that of California artists, including Charles Rollo Peters, Xavier Martinez, and William Keith.

12. Across Tenth St. from the auditorium, in Peralta Park, is the EXPOSITION BUILDING, a one-story, concrete and steel structure used chiefly as an armory by the California National Guard, and for civic events. Within the park are a playfield, a militia drill ground, and the shooting ranges and lodge of the Oakland Archery Club, whose members meet and shoot every Sunday morning.

13. The ALAMEDA COUNTY COURTHOUSE, facing Lake Merritt on Fallon St. between Twelfth and Thirteenth Sts., is a steel and concrete structure of neoclassic design, built in 1936 at a cost of $2,500,000. Inside the main entrance, on opposite walls, are two murals designed by Marian Simpson and executed by the WPA Federal Art Project, which depict Alameda County in Spanish days and in Gold Rush times in more than 50 colors of marble.

14. LAKE MERRITT, a 155-acre body of tidal water extending northeast from Twelfth St., named for Dr. Samuel Merritt, ex-Mayor of Oakland who helped create it, occupies the once marshy, muddy lagoon adjacent to San Antonio Creek, dammed and dredged in 1909. Hydraulic gates control the water level. A boulevard, a macadam footpath, and a chain of lights encircle the lake. Directly north of the Oakland Public Museum is the large, concrete, brown-gabled BOAT-HOUSE (*open 8-12 midnight; rowboats, canoes; around-the-lake water tour, 10¢, children 5¢*), containing a dining room, crew quarters and meeting rooms.

15. The OAKLAND PUBLIC MUSEUM (*open weekdays 10-5,*

Sun. and holidays 1-5), beside the lake at 1426 Oak St., housed in a brown, two-story frame building, contains exhibits in natural science and the ethnology of the Pacific Coast. The American history display includes relics of the Nation's wars. Indian, Spanish, and pioneer articles are shown in the California room. In the two Colonial rooms are reproductions of that period, and a "whatnot" once owned by Abraham Lincoln.

16. The SNOW MUSEUM (*open 10-5 weekdays, 1-5 Sun. and holidays*), 274 Nineteenth St., displays habitat groups of birds, animals, and other native life collected on various expeditions by the donor, Henry Adelbert Snow. In 1919-21, on one of these field trips, *Hunting Big Game in Africa,* the first wild-animal picture to be released by a major exchange, was filmed. A recent addition is the Cave Room, whose miniature dioramas of prehistoric animal life portray dinosaurs, mammoths, mastodon, great long-horned bison, saber-toothed cats, and other beasts. The collection includes about 50,000 bird eggs.

17. Amid gardens of Old-World tranquillity, the COLLEGE OF THE HOLY NAMES, 2036 Webster St., stands in an eight-acre campus on Lake Merritt's western shore. This liberal arts Catholic college for women grew from a high school founded in 1868 by the Sisters of the Holy Names of Jesus and Mary, through the efforts of Reverend Michael King, pioneer Catholic priest, and received in 1880 a charter to award bachelor of arts degrees. Its scholastic department issued in 1872 the first high school diplomas granted in Oakland.

18. The 88-acre LAKESIDE PARK (*bowling greens, tennis courts, golf putting greens, boating*), Grand Ave. between Harrison St. and Lakeshore Ave., covers a blunt peninsula thrust between two arms of the lake. A granite boundary marker of the old Rancho San Antonio stands near the Bellevue and Perkins Sts. entrance. In a grassy amphitheater near the beach the Municipal Band gives concerts (*Sun. 2:30, July-Oct.*). A mounted torpedo porthole from the battleship *Maine* and a memorial tablet cast from metal recovered from the vessel stand about 200 yards northeast of the bandstand. The nine-foot McELROY FOUNTAIN of white Carrara marble on the south-central part of the esplanade walk was built in "Commemoration of the Public Services of John Edmund McElroy," Oakland attorney. Near the southern end of the peninsula is a brown-gabled canoehouse (*canoes for rent*) and landing, where privately owned sail boats of the Lake Merritt Sail Club are quartered.

19. East of the canoehouse and landing is the LAKE MERRITT WILD-FOWL SANCTUARY (*feeding hours Oct.-Mar., 10 and 3:30*). In 1869 the California Legislature designated Lake Merritt as a migratory water-fowl sanctuary, and in 1926 it became a banding station of the United States Biological Survey. From four to five thou-

sand fowl are present during the winter months, and many nest on the small wooded island built in the lake by the city in 1923. Besides many species of ducks and geese, other visitors to the lake include the coot, egret, cormorant, grebe, gull, killdeer, loon, heron, swan, tern, plover, and snipe. Fowl tagged here have been shot as far afield as Siberia and Brazil.

20. From the site of EAST SHORE PARK at the easternmost tip of the lake, the Peraltas shipped hides and tallow. Their *embarcadero* is marked by concrete columns bordering a crescent-shaped brick wall, built in 1912.

21. The VETERANS MEMORIAL BUILDING, N. side of Grand Ave., adjoining Lakeside Park, has an auditorium seating 700 and a collection of war trophies.

22. The FIRST PRESBYTERIAN CHURCH, Broadway at Twenty-sixth St., a fine modern adaptation of perpendicular Gothic architecture (William C. Hays, architect), has stained-glass windows designed by Stetson Crawford, a pupil of James McNeill Whistler.

23. A public recreation center, MOSSWOOD PARK (*8-8 daily*), Moss Ave. between Broadway and Webster St., contains playfields, tennis, roque, and croquet courts, horseshoe-pitching ranges, and a shrub-bordered garden theater. A little arroyo spanned by rustic bridges and bordered by flowering shrubs and ferns meanders beneath fine old oaks past the RESIDENCE OF JOHN MORA MOSS, built in the 1860's, which is now used as a clubhouse and tea room.

24. The MUNICIPAL ROSE GARDENS, in Linda Vista Park, Oakland and Olive Aves., eight acres in area, contain approximately 8,000 bushes.

25. The STATE INDUSTRIAL HOME FOR ADULT BLIND, 3601 Telegraph Ave., occupies a group of white concrete buildings in mission style. In the display room are reed furniture, baskets, pottery, brooms, and other articles made by the blind.

26. Founded in 1907, the CALIFORNIA COLLEGE OF ARTS AND CRAFTS, 5212 Broadway, which occupies several buildings on a four-acre campus, claims distinction as "the only art institution on the Pacific Coast authorized to grant college degrees" and as the only one in California "where, on a single campus, students may complete their work for state teaching credentials . . . [while] gaining their professional art training." As the former California School of Arts and Crafts, a nonprofit, coeducational institution, it served the West from 1907-37. In the Divisions of Fine Arts, of Applied Arts, and of Art Education are studios and exhibition halls. The campus with its flowers, shrubs, and trees, its native birds and small animals for art models is the setting for outdoor sketching and painting. Since 1909 the Aztec Indian pupil of Whistler, Xavier Martinez, born in 1873

in Guadalajara, Mexico, has taught painting here. Dressing primitively in hand-woven materials, his black hair bound by a leather thong, "Marty" is unconventional as a teacher, bold and direct as a painter.

27. Entered through a massive stone gateway, MOUNTAIN VIEW CEMETERY, head of Piedmont Ave., on a beautifully landscaped hillside, has a fine view of San Francisco Bay. The pioneer Dr. John Marsh, Washington Bartlett, Governor Henry Haight, Joseph Le Conte, and Francis Marion "Borax" Smith are buried here.

28. In ST. MARY'S CEMETERY, Roman Catholic, head of Howe Street, are the graves of many Spanish pioneers, among them members of the Peralta family.

29. LAKE TEMESCAL REGIONAL PARK, Chabot and New Tunnel Rds., is an abandoned reservoir converted by WPA labor into a recreation center. From the brick boathouse (open May-Sept.; 8:30-7; lockers 10¢; swimming free; canoes and boats 50¢ per hour) juts a long float, equipped with springboards for swimmers. Another float has water targets for casting practice and tournaments.

30. First frame dwelling in Oakland, The MOSES CHASE HOME (private), 404 E. Eighth St., retains only one of the four rooms built in 1850, but several additions have been made. Original ceiling beams, shaped by hand and joined by wooden pegs, are still firm and strong. The Massachusetts Yankee was Oakland's first settler from the "States."

31. The OAKLAND YACHT CLUB, foot of Nineteenth Ave., established in 1913, has berths for about 100 yachts and motorboats. Each year its members contest for three trophies: the Wallace Trophy for sailboats, the Craven Trophy for "star"-type sailboats, and the Tin Cup Derby for motorboats (an engraved tin cup is the winner's award). At one time Jack London was an honorary member. For the club's annual midsummer party, "A Nite in Venice," to which the public is invited, the harbor is strung with colored lights.

32. DIMOND PARK (horseshoe court, picnicking, tennis, swimming), Fruitvale Ave. and Lyman Rd., lies in a canyon shut in at its northern end by precipitous slopes. The 12-acre tract, green with eucalyptus, oak and acacia, extending along Sausal Creek, was named for Hugh and Dennis Dimond, who became owners of this part of Rancho San Antonio. The 105-foot LIONS POOL (bath house; sand beach) is Oakland's principal outdoor plunge. In the park is the DIMOND COTTAGE, built in 1897 of adobe bricks from the original home of Antonio Maria Peralta, which stood at 2501 Thirty-fourth Avenue. The adobe, 16 by 28 feet, built by the Dimond brothers, is now the headquarters of a Boy Scout troop.

33. JOAQUIN MILLER PARK (THE HIGHTS), Joaquin Miller Rd. near Mountain Blvd. (hiking trails; community kitchen;

picnic areas), is a 67-acre highland area purchased by Oakland as a memorial park in 1917. The 75,000 eucalyptus, pine, cypress, and acacia trees were planted by Miller—who resided here from 1886 to 1913—with the aid of friends and visitors. A native of Indiana, Cincinnatus Heine Miller (1839-1913), after a career of Indian-fighting and small-time politics—during which he took the first name of the bandit Joaquin Murietta—became California's white-haired "Poet of the Sierras." Participation in the Alaska gold rush and the Chinese war added more color to his last years. Eccentric in dress and demeanor, Miller was much beloved in England as a poet of the American frontier. He is best-known for his school-text poem, "Columbus," although he wrote prolifically. At "The Hights" (as he spelled the name of his estate), he provided homes for the poets, Yone Noguchi and Takeshi Kanno. George Sterling, Jack London, Harr Wagner, and Edwin Markham were among his frequent guests. Buried in the little cemetery here is Cali-Shasta, his daughter by a Pitt River Indian woman. Later in Oregon he married a young poetess, who bore him three children before she divorced him. A daughter by a still later marriage to Abbie Leland now resides at "The Hights," having reserved a life tenure in it when she sold the property to Oakland.

THE ABBEY, built in 1886, is a small, low gray frame building consisting of three one-room structures interconnected to form a single unit, each room roofed with a shingled peak. Miller said it was inspired by Newstead Abbey in England and spoke of it as a "little Abbey for little Abbie," his wife.

A loop trail beginning at the park's souvenir shop, which is flanked by "Juanita's Sanctuary" and "Juanita's Wigwam," leads past the stone funeral pyre on which Miller wished to be cremated (but was not), the "Pyramid to Moses," the "Tower to Browning," and the "Frémont Monument." Miller was his own mason in building these oddly asymmetrical monuments of native rock. In the center of the park are cypress trees planted in the shape of a cross.

The WOODMINSTER MEMORIAL AMPHITHEATER, constructed by WPA labor under the direction of the Oakland Board of Park Directors, is a memorial to California writers. A cascade beginning near the rear of the amphitheater flows through eight flower-bordered pools to an electric fountain illuminated by constantly changing colors.

34. The 182 acres of SEQUOIA PARK, Joaquin Miller Rd. and Skyline Blvd. (*picnicking, outdoor grills, bridle paths*), are shaded by towering redwoods. Sequoia Point, within the park, a circular landscaped point, provides a panorama of the Bay to the south, bringing into view East Oakland, Alameda, San Leandro, San Leandro Bay, the Oakland Airport, and the Estuary.

35. Best-known women's college west of the Mississippi, MILLS COLLEGE, Seminary Ave. between Camden St. and Calaveras Ave., is also one of the oldest in the United States. The present residential, non-sectarian college began as the Young Ladies Seminary in 1852 in Benicia. In 1865 Dr. and Mrs. Cyrus Taggart Mills purchased the school and six years later removed it to the present beautifully wooded campus of 150 acres at the base of the San Leandro hills.

Mills was patterned after Mount Holyoke Seminary in Massachusetts. As a college of liberal arts, it has schools in fine arts, language and literature, social institutions, natural sciences, mathematics, and education, leading to the A.B. degree, and a school of graduate studies which gives an M.A. or M.Ed. degree. The faculty of 100 members, serving about 600 students, is large enough to permit small classes and individual attention. Visiting faculty members in the graphic arts have included Leon Kroll, Alexander Archipenko, Frederic Taubes, and the Bauhaus group; in music, Henry Cowell, Luther Marchant, and members of the Pro Arte Quartet; in dancing, Martha Graham, Hanya Holm, and Charles Weidman.

The campus buildings are notably successful adaptations in concrete of Spanish Colonial design. Through the Wetmore Gate on Seminary Ave. a winding road leads to EL CAMPANIL, a buttressed tower of tan-colored concrete, the gift of Francis M. "Borax" Smith, in whose pierced belfry is a chime of ten bells cast for the Chicago World's Fair of 1893. A number of residential halls in an informal style are grouped about beautifully landscaped courts and terraces. The MUSIC BUILD-ING, in the style of a Spanish Renaissance church, has a fine doorway with ornate carving and an auditorium with murals by Ray Boynton. Graceful triple arches lead to the foyer of LISSER HALL, whose auditorium seats 600. Before a lofty open arcade leading to the ART GALLERY (*open Wed. and Sun. 2-5*) are two marble Dogs of Fu, Chinese carvings of the Ming dynasty in white marble. In addition to a permanent collection of oils, etchings, bronzes, textiles, and oriental *objets d'art,* the galleries have occasional loan exhibits. The 77,000 volumes in the LIBRARY (*open to visitors*), include the collection of about 5,000 rare books and manuscripts given by Albert M. Bender. The WOODLAND THEATER, a natural amphitheater in a eucalyptus grove, is the scene of outdoor plays. Bordering LAKE ALISO near the northern boundary of the campus is an outdoor stage used for dance programs.

36. CHABOT OBSERVATORY (*open Tues.-Sat. 1-5, 7-9:30*), 4917 Mountain Blvd., named for Anthony Chabot, pioneer, capitalist, and philanthropist, is one of the few California institutions of its kind serving the public schools. Lectures are given to classes from the Oakland schools and from Mills College, which assist jointly in maintenance

of the observatory's large lecture hall, reading room, and astronomical library. Illustrated programs for adult astronomy students and meetings of the East Bay Astronomical Association are held here. The two-story stucco building, on the landscaped hillside, houses a spectroscope and 8- and 20-inch refracting telescopes. Connected with the institution is a meteorological station which collects data for Oakland weather reports.

37. The ALAMEDA COUNTY ZOOLOGICAL GARDENS (*open 9-6; adm. 10¢; picnicking*), Ninety-eighth Ave. and Mountain Blvd., cover 450 well-wooded acres formerly known as Durant Park, now administered by the Alameda County Zoological Society. It contains an arboretum and a small zoo. (In 1940 removal of the Oakland City Zoo from Sequoia Park to a site near the main gate was planned.) Occasional nature-study programs are presented under the direction of Sidney Adelbert Snow, noted big-game hunter and photographer, who lives on the grounds.

38. On the tidal flats of Bay Farm Island in San Leandro Bay is the OAKLAND MUNICIPAL AIRPORT (*lunch room*), comprising 850 acres. Here are located a unit of the United States Naval Reserve, the western terminals of transcontinental air lines, flying schools, and hangars for privately owned planes and local air taxis. Along Earhart Road, which parallels the airport's southeastern edge, are hangars, the administration building housing the Airport Weather Bureau, and a small glass-enclosed exhibition building, displaying an old pusher-type biplane built in 1910 which placed first in a 1912 international competition. The Wiseman plane, first successful heavier-than-air craft built in California, is suspended in the nearby Navy hangar. Five huge corrugated iron hangars, decorated with brightly painted flying directions, house maintenance shops, schools, and operating offices. The island was first used as a port in 1927 when, in three weeks of day and night work, a runway was built to provide a take-off for the Army's mass flight to Hawaii. The present airport and channel are developments made by the city of Oakland largely with WPA labor.

Berkeley

Information Service: Chamber of Commerce, American Trust Bldg., Shattuck Ave. and Center St. Berkeley Travel Bureau, 81 Shattuck Sq. University of California administrative office, California Hall, U. of C. campus. *Railroad Stations:* Southern Pacific, University Ave. and 3rd St. Atchison, Topeka & Santa Fe Ry., University Ave. and West St. *Bus Stations:* Pacific Greyhound Lines and National Trailways, 2001 San Pablo Ave. *Taxis:* Average rate 20¢ first ¼ m., 10¢ each ½ m. thereafter, 1 to 5 passengers. *Streetcars and Buses:* Fare 10¢ or one token (7 for 50¢); to Hayward, El Cerrito, or Richmond, 20¢ or 2 tokens. Transbay electric trains to San Francisco, fare 21¢. *Traffic Regulations:* 25 m.p.h. in residential and business districts, 15 m.p.h. at intersections; 1 and 2 hour parking limit in business districts, all-night parking prohibited in all areas.

Accommodations: Ten hotels.

Concert Halls: Wheeler Hall, U. of C. Greek Theatre, U. of C. Women's City Club, 2315 Durant Ave. *Radio Stations:* KRE (1370 kc.), 601 Ashby Ave. *Motion Picture Theaters (first-run):* Two. *Amateur and Little Theaters:* Wheeler Hall, U. of C., for university productions. International House Auditorium, Piedmont Ave. and Bancroft Way. Women's City Club Little Theater, 2315 Durant Ave.

Archery: Albany Archers, Tilden Park (straw targets). Archery Range, East Shore Highway, Albany (small fee). *Baseball:* Diamonds at Berkeley High School, Grove St. and Bancroft Way, and many public playgrounds.

Boating: Berkeley Aquatic Park. *Football:* U. of C. Stadium, foot of Bancroft Way. Berkeley High School, Grove St. and Bancroft Way. *Golf:* Charles Lee Tilden Regional Park. Berkeley Country Club, E. end Cutting Blvd. *Ice Skating and Hockey:* Iceland, Shattuck Ave. and Ward St.

Bowling: Municipal Bowling Green, Allston Way W. of Acton St. *Riding:* Arlington Hills Riding Academy, Arlington and Brewster Dr. Athens Polo and Riding Stables, 1010 San Pablo Ave. Berkeley Riding Academy, 2731 Hilgard St. Fairmont Riding Academy, Colusa and Fairmount Aves. *Softball:* City playground, 2828 Grove St. City playground, Mabel and Oregon Sts., and many school playgrounds. *Swimming:* Berkeley High School, Grove St. and Bancroft Way (open June 15-Aug. 15). *Tennis:* U. of C. campus. Berkeley Tennis Club (private), Tunnel Rd. and Domingo Ave. Also following recreational areas: City Hall, Allston Way and Grove St.; Grove, 2828 Grove St.; Codornices, 1201 Euclid Ave.; James Kenney, 8th and Delaware Sts.; Live Oak, Shattuck Ave. and Berryman St.; San Pablo, Mabel and Oregon Sts.

Churches (Only centrally located churches are listed): Baptist. First, 2430 Dana St. *Buddhist.* Hegeshi Honganji, 1524 Oregon St. *Christian.* University, 1725 Scenic Ave. *Christian Science.* First Church of Christ, Scientist, Bowditch and Dwight Way. *Mormon.* Church of Jesus Christ of Latter Day Saints, 2150 Vine St. *Congregational.* First, 2345 Channing Way. *Episcopal.* St. Mark's, 2314 Bancroft Way. *Evangelical.* Mission Covenant,

Grove and Parker Sts. *Free Methodist.* Japanese, 1521 Derby St. *Hebrew Orthodox.* Hebrew Center, 1630 Bancroft Way. *Lutheran.* Bethany, 1744 University Ave. *Methodist.* Trinity, Durant and Dana Sts. *Presbyterian.* First, Dana St. and Channing Way. *Roman Catholic.* St. Joseph's, 1600 Addison St. *Russian Orthodox.* St. John's, 2020 Dwight Way. *Seventh Day Adventist.* Berkeley Seventh Day Adventists, Dana and Haste Sts. *Unitarian.* First, 2425 Bancroft Way. *Miscellaneous.* Apostolic Church of the Faith of Jesus, 829 University Ave.; Immanuel Mission to Seamen, 1540 Lincoln St.; Plymouth Brethren Church, 42nd and Rich Sts.; Reihaisho Hershinto, 1707 Ward St.; Unity Center, 2315 Durant St.

BERKELEY (0-1,000 alt., 84,827 pop.) spreads across a great natural amphitheater opposite the Golden Gate, rising from the shore of the Bay eastward to the crest of the Berkeley hills, over which the fogs often drift in late afternoon. To the alumnus, as to the academic world in general, Berkeley means the University of California. But while the university is its outstanding feature, Berkeley is really three or four towns in one. There is the Berkeley of the retired old men and women who trespass on the wooden senior bench near the student union building on the campus and attend lectures where they can "absorb culture in homeopathic doses," as the beloved Charles Mills Gayley used to say. There is the world of those who commute to business in San Francisco; and there is industrial Berkeley, clustered along the Bay west of San Pablo Avenue—a two and one-half mile strip of factories bearing well-known trade names. Around the fringe of this section are massed the homes of the factory workers. This part of Berkeley seems spiritually more akin to industrial Emeryville on the south or to oil-refining Richmond on the north than to the gay bustle of the streets surrounding the campus—streets thronged with men students in corduroys and gaudy sweaters, women students in mock peasant head kerchiefs and jaunty little half-socks.

Among the hills on either side of the campus are the handsome new fraternity and sorority houses, the more modest homes of the faculty, and rambling terraced gardens, almost hiding houses clinging perilously to the side of the hill.

The lower sections of Berkeley adjoining the campus, particularly on the southern side, are given over to student lodgings. Here every other house carries a sign, often "Rooms—Men Only." The men, though harder on the furniture than the girls, are less of a responsibility, because the office of the Dean of Women keeps an eagle eye on the campus homes of undergraduate women. Or the sign may read "Coaching—Mathematics, Russian and Chemistry" or "Typing, Neatly and Cheaply Done."

"Downtown" Berkeley lies along Shattuck Avenue; the main business district, because of the proximity of metropolitan shopping centers, is surprisingly small for a city of Berkeley's size. It changes slowly with the years, although the old steam trains that used to bring students from the city to their eight o'clock classes and the horse-cars that occasionally were derailed by students who wanted an excuse for being late have long since given way to modern electric cars. Even the old red-brick Southern Pacific station, which sat squarely in the middle of Shattuck Avenue, finally gave way to modern stores in 1939.

Berkeley owes its naming to the university. A hundred years ago the site was part of the great Rancho San Antonio of the Peralta family. When it was selected in 1866 as the new location of the College of California, Henry Durant, one of the trustees, gazing out over the Bay, quoted Bishop Berkeley's well-known line: "Westward the course of empire takes its way," and another trustee suggested that they name the new town for the prophetic English philosopher. The village which grew up around the campus was not incorporated until 1878, organization having been delayed by farmers who rejected the idea of imposing the expense of municipal government upon them. By the turn of the century, however, streets had been paved, a reservoir built and pipes laid, residential tracts opened, and the electric trains supplemented the noisy and smoky locomotives of the Southern Pacific.

The San Francisco fire brought so many new residents that the town by 1908 was large enough to make an effort to get the State capital away from Sacramento. At the same time many attractive homes were being built among scattered clumps of oaks on the rising ground north and south of the campus. In the fall of 1923 a grass fire, starting in the hills, destroyed a large part of North Berkeley. New homes and gardens have gradually hidden the scars of the fire.

In the 1930 census the population figures were: 73 per cent native white, 23 per cent foreign white, 2 per cent Negro, and 2 per cent mixed. But the number of foreign students at the university is relatively high. In 1927, when International House was proposed, approximately 10 per cent of all the foreign students in the United States were registered at the University of California. The governments of Australia, New Zealand, and South Africa send many graduate students to Berkeley at government expense, most often to study soil chemistry or some other branch of agriculture. The Egyptian government sends students every year to study citriculture. Berkeley also draws many foreign students of engineering, particularly of petroleum engineering. Occasionally one sees East Indians of the commercial class walking respectfully behind and out of the shadow of the bearded and turbaned Sikhs of the military caste.

Berkeley became, in 1923, one of the first cities of its size in the United States to adopt the city-manager form of government. Its school department claims to have established the first junior high school in the country. Its standing in public health service is indicated by its proud boast that for two decades it has had one of the four lowest infant mortality rates among places of its size in the United States. But it prides itself most on its police department—built up by Police Chief August Vollmer, now retired—whose fame has extended as far away as Scotland Yard.

Vollmer encouraged his staff to experiment: as a member of the Berkeley police department in 1921 Dr. John A. Larson invented the lie-detector, a machine that records the tell-tale changes in heart action and breathing which usually accompany deviations from the truth. In 1921 Vollmer was elected president of the International Association of Chiefs of Police, and in 1929, although not himself a college graduate, he took leave of his command to head a department of research at the University of Chicago with the title of Professor of Police Administration—perhaps the first ever to hold such a title. Vollmer, who now gives regular courses in police administration at the University of California, is a firm believer in a college education for policemen—a fact which caused his men to be called "super-cops." During summer sessions, it is not surprising to see a burly cop saunter out of a classroom, his gun on his hip and a student note book under his arm. As a result, Berkeley police have an unusual standing in the community.

POINTS OF INTEREST

1. The BERKELEY AQUATIC PARK (*boating free with own craft; rowboats, sailboats, electric boats for hire*), East Shore Highway between University and Ashby Aves., is a mile-long, ninety-acre recreational waterfront development built by WPA labor, containing a long, narrow, tide-filled lagoon with a landscaped border. In the southern end of the lagoon, set aside for model-yacht racing, regattas in which the diminutive copies of yachts compete are held occasionally. A small grass-covered island midway along the western shoreline is reserved as a wild fowl sanctuary.

2. The BERKELEY MUNICIPAL FISHING PIER (*fee 5¢*) extends more than three miles over the mud flats to deep water.

3. The BERKELEY YACHT HARBOR, north of the Municipal Fishing Pier, developed in part with WPA funds, will accommodate 500 small craft in waters protected by rock-faced earthen breakwaters.

4. The LAWN BOWLING GREEN, Allston Way west of Acton St., maintained by the city's Recreation Department, has been the scene of world championship tournaments.

5. MORTAR ROCK PARK, Indian Rock Ave. and San Diego Rd., once the site of Indian assemblages, is dominated by a huge irregular mass of rock, which commands a magnificent view of the surrounding territory. Here Indian women ground corn in the mortar-like

rocks, whose smooth cylindrical holes still show the use to which they were put.

6. The seven-acre JOHN HINKEL PARK, Southampton Ave. and San Diego Rd., has an amphitheater seating 400, constructed in 1934 by the CWA, where plays are given by the Berkeley Community Players during the summer months.

7. CRAGMONT ROCK PARK, Regal Rd. at Hilldale Ave., covers four acres surrounding the freak rock formation for which the park was named. From the lookout station 800 feet above sea level is an excellent view of the Bay and its bridges. Easter sunrise services are held here.

8. CODORNICES (Sp., quail) PARK, Euclid Ave. at Bay View Pl., originally a steep, rocky, brush-grown gulch where quail were abundant, has been terraced by WPA workers as a rose garden, with tiers of roses of many varieties. The park has public tennis courts, a playground for children, and a clubhouse for community use.

9. The PACIFIC SCHOOL OF RELIGION (*open to visitors on application*), 1798 Scenic Ave., is a graduate theological seminary, interdenominational and coeducational, established in San Francisco in 1866 as the Pacific Theological Seminary. Moved the next year to Oakland, it was established here in 1925. Its present name was adopted in 1916 on its 50th anniversary. The school prepares students for all kinds of religious work. One department, known as the Palestine Institute, centers its activity in the Holy Land, where it is engaged in Biblical research.

The ADMINISTRATION BUILDING and the HOLBROOK MEMORIAL LIBRARY are of gray cut stone; the men's dormitory is of gray stucco. The library of 30,000 volumes includes a "Breeches" Bible, printed in Geneva in 1560; a group of Babylonian cuneiform tablets; a collection of fourth-century Biblical inscriptions on papyrus; and a rubbing of the inscription on the Nestorian monument in China. An archeological exhibit in the same building consists of relics dating from 3500 B.C.

For the past few years the Pacific Coast School for Workers has taken over the grounds of the Pacific School of Religion for its summer session. A member of the American Affiliated Schools for Workers, it is sponsored jointly by the Extension Division, labor organizations, the State Department of Education, and other interested bodies. Courses are conducted in San Francisco, but in the summer for six weeks union members come here from laundries, hotel kitchens, the water front, and other places of industrial activity to study economics, parliamentary law, and international affairs, in order to go back and better serve their organizations.

10. The HANGAR (*adm. adults 25¢, children 10¢*), 2211 Union St., "Mother" Tusch's aviation museum, is a little white cottage which

has become a familiar spot to aviation fans. During the World War, when a school of military aeronautics was established on the campus, "Mother" Tusch founded the University Mothers' Club to look after the boys away from their homes. Overseas flyers remembered the little white house and its motherly occupant, serving coffee and doughnuts, and sent her souvenirs from the battlefields. Among "Mother" Tusch's treasures is part of the fuselage of an Army plane, on which is carved with a penknife the last message of its pilots, Lieutenant Fred Waterhouse and Cecil H. Connolly, who were forced down on the Mexican border in 1919. One of the most unusual tributes came from a German ace—a pair of silver wings, inscribed: "To the Mother of us all, with love from Capt. Willie Mauss." Recent additions to the collection are the black sealskin cap worn by Admiral Richard Byrd in Little America and the small Bible which Lieutenant Clyde Pangborn carried on his flight around the world. On the walls of The Hangar are the signatures of Captain Eddie Rickenbacker, Colonel Billy Mitchell, Sir Hubert Wilkins, Byrd, Pangborn, and other famous flyers. Only one woman's autograph is there—that of Amelia Earhart.

11. BARRINGTON HALL, 2315 Dwight Way, is the largest of five co-operative dormitories built on the university campus during the depression. The five are organized into the California Students' Cooperative Association, housing 365 men and 82 women. All the work is done by the members themselves, aided by one or two paid employees. Each student puts in about four hours of work each week, enabling him to obtain a room and three meals a day for about $22.50 a month.

12. The CALIFORNIA SCHOOL FOR THE DEAF, Warring and Parker Sts., at the foot of the Berkeley hills, is the only residential school of its kind in California. The course of study embraces a 12-year period, three years of which is preparatory work enabling the child to reach the level of the first grade of the public school system. The entire course is intended not only to give the handicapped child a general education, but also to prepare him for some occupation at which he can earn his living.

13. The CALIFORNIA SCHOOL FOR THE BLIND, 3001 Derby St., sharing the campus of the California School for the Deaf, serves visually handicapped children. Begun in San Francisco in 1860 as a private institution for the deaf, dumb and blind, it was taken over by the State in 1865 and moved to Berkeley two years later. Since 1922 it has been an institution solely for the blind.

14. The rambling, stuccoed CLAREMONT HOTEL, at the head of Russell St., erected in 1904, is surrounded by a large old-fashioned garden.

15. At the BERKELEY TENNIS CLUB (*tournaments May-*

June, Sept.-Oct.), adjoining the Claremont Hotel, "Pop" Fuller developed two champion players, Helen Wills Moody and Helen Jacobs.

THE UNIVERSITY OF CALIFORNIA

Until the turn of the century the University of California occupied a heterogeneous assortment of buildings at the base of the Berkeley Hills on oak-studded slopes traversed by two branches of Strawberry Creek; but in 1896 Phoebe Apperson Hearst awarded a prize of $10,000 for a campus design to Emile Bénard of Paris, and his general layout, with modifications, has since guided the development of the grounds. In 1902 John Galen Howard, an American architect who had studied at the École des Beaux Arts and had worked with Bénard, came to the university, established a School of Architecture, and became supervising architect. The architecture of the campus strongly reflects his influence. He changed many details of the Bénard plan, but French academic influence is apparent everywhere both in the buildings and in their relation to each other.

The beginning of the university dates to the California constitutional convention of 1849, when a clause was adopted providing for the establishment of a university. A subsequent delay of nearly 20 years was due partly to a controversy between those who wished to establish a "complete university" and those who wanted only a college of agriculture and mechanics. Meanwhile Oakland's College of California was chartered in 1855 by two ministers, Henry Durant and Samuel Hopkins Willey. Absorbing the Contra Costa Academy, it had in 1860 a faculty of six and a freshman class of eight. In 1867 the founders and trustees offered to disincorporate and transfer to the State all their assets—the buildings at Oakland, the 160-acre building site at Berkeley, and a 10,000-volume library. The State accepted the offer and on September 23, 1869 the new university opened in Oakland. In September, 1873 the buildings on the Berkeley campus were occupied by 40 students and a faculty of 10.

For many years the combined student enrollment of the University of California's various schools and colleges has made it the largest university in the country. In 1939-40, the enrollment of 16,199 on its Berkeley campus alone surpassed all others. Academically, the university ranks as one of the Nation's best. A survey made under the auspices of the American Council on Education in 1938 gave it a tie with Harvard for first place in a weighted rating of distinguished and adequate departments.

In the value of its "practical" contributions, the University of California has a fine record. Its benefits to agriculture alone are estimated to save California farmers $100,000,000 annually. In addition to experimental work in animal husbandry, horticulture, viticulture, and irrigation, the agricultural departments have developed and introduced to the farmer the spray plant, a device for spraying fruit trees and vegetation through underground pipes; the solar heater to prevent frost injury to orchard trees; the use of humified air for sterilizing dairy utensils; and a milk-cooling system. Boulder Dam, constructed under the direction of Dr. Elwood Mead, formerly of the university faculty, was built with a special low-heat cement developed in the Engineering Materials Testing Laboratory on the Berkeley campus. In the same laboratory test models of the San Francisco-Oakland Bay Bridge and the Golden Gate Bridge were made, while professors of geology were investigating the strata upon which the bridge foundations would rest. Materials used in Boulder Dam, the bridges, and many other public works were first tested by the university's materials testing machine, capable of exerting a pressure of 4,000,000 pounds. The engineering department, cooperating with the United States War Department, compiles data obtained at the university's hydraulic tidal testing basin to aid in the maintenance of ship channels and the preservation of beaches. In its laboratories was developed an improved method of treating leprosy. Vitamin E and the growth- and sex-stimulating hormones of the pituitary glands were discovered by Dr. Herbert M. Evans of the Institute of Experimental Biology. Through experiments conducted in university laboratories, the canning industry overcame botulism, the sugar beet pest was conquered, and the mealy bug eliminated from citrus groves.

Other studies include: consideration of the atmosphere on Mars; a study of living organisms found in a solid rock 225,000,000 years old; translation of a clay tablet from Mesopotamia, which upset accepted theories of how Babylon was governed. Less spectacular are the studies of unemployment, the migrant, and agricultural labor made at the request of State and local authorities by the Bureau of Public Administration, a pioneer in training students for government service.

Perhaps no contemporary piece of abstruse research so captured the imagination of the lay public and the respect of the world's scientists as did the invention of the "atom smasher" or cyclotron by Dr. E. O. Lawrence of the Radiation Laboratory of the Department of Physics. Dr. Lawrence has realized the dream of the alchemist of old, the transmutation of the elements, by bombarding them with his atom smasher. He has already achieved successful production of artificial radioactive elements in sufficient quantities to provide a cheap synthetic substitute for radium. Experiments are still being conducted in the use of the mysterious "neutron ray" in the treatment of cancer. For his work with the cyclotron, Dr. Lawrence was awarded the Nobel Prize for Physics in 1939. In the field of medico-therapy Dr. Lawrence and his staff have also developed a new type of X-ray apparatus capable of producing a continuous supply of X-rays with an energy approaching 1,000,000 volts, for treatment of tumorous growths.

Gifts to the university have been the basis for the establishment of its various schools and colleges—all, with the exception of those at Los Angeles and Berkeley, devoted to specialized fields of study. The Medical School, the Colleges of Pharmacy and Dentistry, the Training School for Nurses, and the Hooper Foundation for Medical Research are located in San Francisco, as are the affiliated College of Fine Arts and Hasting's College of Law. The College of Agriculture has, besides the curricula at Berkeley and Los Angeles, a farm at Davis, the Citrus Experiment Station at Riverside, the Institution of Animal Husbandry at Pomona, and the Forest Station in Tulare County. At Mount Hamilton is the Lick Observatory; at La Jolla, the Institution of Oceanography. Perhaps the most significant evidence of growth was the establishment of the southern branch of the university in Los Angeles in 1919. Beginning with freshmen and sophomore work, it added advanced curricula as the need arose, until in 1927 it received equal rank with the Berkeley institution as the University of California at Los Angeles. Today, in the words of a recent university publication, a California student pursues his studies at whatever campus, school, or research station best suits his needs, because California "has grown from a local school to a state-wide clearing house of knowledge gathered from all corners of the earth."

The Golden Book of the Alumni Association, published in 1936, listed alumni in the four corners of the earth, including a chief engineer for public works in Madras, the manager of a government ranch at Bagdad, a cotton breeder for the Department of Agriculture in Bombay, a chief of the Associated Press for the Balkans, a gold-dredging expert in New Guinea, and a professor in Leningrad College. David Prescott Barrows, Chairman of the Department of Political Science, tells a story which illustrates the way in which alumni bob up in the most unexpected places. In 1917 he was assistant chief of staff in the American Expeditionary Force in Siberia. After an interview with General Semenoff, in charge of White Russian forces at Chita, General Barrows was assigned, as aide-de-camp, a magnificent-looking Cossack dressed in Asiatic splendor. General Barrows was amazed to hear him say mildly, in excellent English, "You don't know me, General, but I have seen you many times on the Berkeley campus. I was a student for two years at your College of Mining."

CAMPUS POINTS OF INTEREST

1. The PRESIDENT'S HOUSE (*private*), Hearst Ave. and Scenic Ave., built in 1911 for use as the official residence of the univer-

sity's executive head, stands on a slight eminence near the north edge of the campus. It is of grey-brown sandstone, with a portico supported by Ionic columns and guarded by marble lions.

2. AGRICULTURE, HILGARD, AND GIANNINI HALLS, built in Italian Renaissance style of white concrete, range around a C-shaped open court near the northwest corner of the campus. They house the College of Agriculture and the Agricultural Extension Division. Nearby are greenhouses (*open to students only*) for experimental work. In the corridors of Giannini Hall is a display of colored hardwoods from many parts of the world.

3. The LIFE SCIENCES BUILDING, Harmon Way between Axis Rd. and Campanile Way, is a massive concrete structure, completed in 1930. On the facade are panels and rosettes in which have been cast conventionalized representations of fish, reptiles, and mammals. Laboratories, classrooms, offices, and libraries of 13 life-science departments occupy the building, which also houses the Institute of Experimental Biology; the Museum of Vertebrate Zoology (*for students only*) with its 160,000 specimens of mammals, birds, and reptiles; and the herbarium of the Department of Botany (*open 8:30-12, 1-5; Sat. 8:30-12*), containing some 500,000 plant specimens from all over the world.

4. The TILDEN FOOTBALL STATUE, Campanile Way west of Life Sciences Bldg., is a bronze statue of two rugby players, by Douglas Tilden, presented by Senator James D. Phelan in recognition of the superiority of the university football teams of 1898-99.

5. The GYMNASIUM FOR MEN, Dana St. between Bancroft and Allston Ways, completed in 1933, has large gymnasium floors and swimming pool, special rooms for wrestling, boxing, and fencing and space for badminton and table tennis. Adjoining it are a baseball diamond and the George C. Edwards Memorial Stadium for track and field sports.

6. SATHER GATE, at the head of Telegraph Ave., most used entrance to the campus, is an ornamental structure of concrete and bronze, erected in 1909 with funds provided by Jane K. Sather as a memorial to her husband, Peder Sather. "To go outside the gate" is an established tradition for student assemblies which do not have the sanction of the university authorities.

7. The ART GALLERY (*open weekdays 10-5*), one block E. of Sather Gate, is a former power house. The two large mosaics on the facade, symbolizing the seven arts, were designed and executed in Byzantine style by Helen Bruton and Florence Swift, assisted by workers of the WPA Federal Art Project. The gallery owns the Albert Bender collection of oriental art and a collection of Russian ikons.

8. BOALT HALL, Sather Gate Dr. between Axis Rd. and South

UNIVERSITY OF CALIFORNIA
BERKELEY, CALIFORNIA

SCALE IN FEET
0 100   500   1000

Dr., housing the School of Jurisprudence, honors the memory of Judge John Henry Boalt.

9. CALIFORNIA HALL, Sather Gate Dr., now the university's administrative headquarters, will become part of the School of Jurisprudence after completion of a new administration building on Telegraph Avenue outside Sather Gate. On the walls of the first floor corridor and auditorium are portraits of notable teachers, regents, and others associated with the history of the university.

10. The UNIVERSITY LIBRARY (*open weekdays 8-10, Sat. 8-6, Sun. 1-10; fee for non-students, $6 a year*), Sather Gate Dr., a large white granite building, has over 1,000,000 volumes. It is the largest college library west of the Mississippi and the seventh in the United States. Besides the main collection there are the Bancroft Library, a world-famous collection of more than 75,000 valuable books and manuscripts on Spanish-American history, the nucleus of which was bought from the historian, Hubert Howe Bancroft, in 1905; the Library of Economic Research; the Library of French Thought, whose basis was the books exhibited by the French government at the Pan-American Exposition in 1915; and the Alexander F. Morrison Memorial Library, reserved for student "browsing." The reference room extends the full north width of the second floor. In the periodical room along the east side of the second floor are 45 copies of famous Velasquez paintings.

11. WHEELER HALL, Sather Gate Dr., main classroom building, contains an auditorium seating 1,050, used for lectures, concerts, and plays. It is named for Benjamin Ide Wheeler, president of the university from 1899-1919.

12. SOUTH HALL, W. Esplanade at South Dr., oldest building on the campus, was constructed in 1873. It houses the offices and some classrooms of the College of Commerce and the departments of political science and of economics.

13. The CAMPANILE (*elevator 9-5, fee 10¢*), as Sather Tower is commonly known, may be called the heart of campus life. It is a shaft of gleaming California granite 302 feet high, with four clock faces and an observation platform. It was built in 1914 as a gift of Jane K. Sather, donor of Sather Gate. Its clock bell orders the university day from morning to night. When the university celebrates its birthday on March 23 and at commencement the chimes ring "Hail to California." On the evening before final examinations begin, the mournful notes of "Danny Deever" give notice of impending tragedies; but during finals the chimes are tactfully silent. Consisting of twelve bells, the chimes were cast in England by John Taylor and Company, who have been casting bells since the days of Chaucer. Charles Weikel, former chimesmaster, wrote and arranged many compositions for them.

In the ground-floor room of the Campanile hangs a plan of the campus, made in 1914 by John Galen Howard, university architect.

14. STEPHENS UNION, Campanile Esplanade on South Dr., a concrete building in Tudor Gothic style, was built in 1921 by popular subscription as a memorial to Henry Morse Stephens, distinguished historian and long a popular faculty member. Here are the offices, "co-op" store, and restaurant of the Associated Students, and the headquarters of the California Alumni Association and its magazine, *The California Monthly*. A display case in the men's club room is the part-time home of the Stanford axe, a huge, broad-bitted lumberman's axe, for whose custodianship the California and Stanford football teams contend in the annual "Big Game." Originally used by Stanford rooters to emphasize the famous "axe" yell, it was captured by California students at a baseball game in 1899. For 31 years it remained in a bank vault, brought out only under heavy guard to taunt the enemy from "the farm," until Stanford students regained it in a tear-gas raid while it was being returned to its resting place. After this melée the two student bodies made a gentleman's agreement, whereby the axe became the "Big Game" trophy.

15. Neighboring ESHLEMAN HALL houses offices of the Little Theater and student publications. This structure, erected in 1930, honors the late John Morton Eshleman, alumnus and one-time lieutenant-governor.

16. The PHOEBE A. HEARST GYMNASIUM FOR WOMEN, Bancroft Way and Bowditch St., provides women students with facilities for badminton, table tennis, and many other activities in its gymnasiums and swimming pools. On the spacious grounds outside, groups of students often engage in tennis, hockey, archery, and interpretive dancing.

17. FACULTY GLADE, between Stephens Union and Men's Faculty Club, is a velvety green sward, shaded by Coast live oaks, along the landscaped banks of Strawberry Creek. For many years the *Partheneia,* an original pageant, was staged here by women students. Max Reinhardt presented *A Midsummer Night's Dream* here in 1935. Alumni luncheons are served in the glade on Commencement Day. The arch over the steps leading into the glade from South Drive was erected in 1910 in memory of Phoebe Apperson Hearst, mother of the publisher and benefactress of the university.

18. Red-brick BACON HALL, E. Esplanade at South Drive, is the second oldest building on the campus. Today it is the headquarters for the Department of Geological Sciences and the Division of Seismology. It also houses the Geological Sciences Exhibit (*open weekdays 8:30-12, 1-5; Sat. 8:30-12*).

19. The HEARST MEMORIAL MINING BUILDING, north of the Mining Circle, was donated by Phoebe Apperson Hearst in 1907 as a memorial to her husband, Senator George Hearst. The plant has unusually fine equipment for the study of mining engineering, including the LAWSON ADIT, a model tunnel which affords mining students practical experience in mine-fire and rescue work. The building contains the Museum of Paleontology (*open weekdays 8-5; Sat. 9-12*), which has the largest collection of vertebrate and invertebrate fossils on the Pacific Coast.

20. FOUNDERS ROCK, near Hearst and La Loma Aves., is the spot where trustees of the College of California met April 16, 1860 and dedicated the site of the campus to learning. It is marked by a bronze plaque, gift of the class of '96.

21. The GREEK THEATER, in a natural amphitheater half hidden in the eucalyptus grove above Gayley Road, seats 8,500. It is an adaptation of the ancient theater at Epidaurus. The enormous stage, 133 feet wide and 28 feet deep, is protected at back and sides by a 42-foot wall (the ancient *skene*), in front of which is a row of Doric columns. Half surrounded by tiers of concrete benches is the pit (the ancient orchestra), before the stage, where huge bonfires are built at student rallies. The theater, a gift of William Randolph Hearst, was first used—although only one-third finished—at commencement in 1903, when Theodore Roosevelt delivered the address. At its dedication in September of that year, students set the tone for its future use by presenting selections from Aristophanes' comedy, *The Birds*. The theater is used for university exercises and student rallies as well as dramatic and concert performances.

22. The BIG C, far up on Charter Hill behind the Greek Theater, is a concrete letter 60 feet high, made and maintained by undergraduates as their university symbol. Painted yellow, it shows up strongly against the background of the hillside. The C was constructed in 1905 by men of the freshman and sophomore classes, who relayed buckets of gravel and cement up the hill in a drenching rain. It was reached only by a steep trail until 1916, when 2,500 students built a zigzag path up the slope in two hours on the day of the quadrennial "Big C Sirkus," February 29. It is now illuminated on pre-game nights, when members of the sophomore class—its official guardians—maintain an all-night vigil to ward off marauders.

23. The MEMORIAL STADIUM, at the mouth of Strawberry Canyon, seats 78,000. Built by popular subscription as a memorial to the university's World War dead, it was first used at the "Big Game" of 1923. On the east side of the field, below the California rooting section, is the ANDREW LATHAM SMITH MEMORIAL BENCH, dedicated in 1927 in honor of the coach of the "wonder teams" of the early

1920's. Unused for the most part except during the football season, the stadium is the scene of commencement exercises each spring.

24. The BOTANICAL GARDENS (*open 9-4*), in Strawberry Canyon east of the stadium, contain more than 50,000 plants of 6,000 species, including special collections of rhododendrons, cacti, and succulents. Plants of rare beauty and value have been brought to the university from such remote places as the Tibetan Himalayas and the South American Andes. An OPEN-AIR THEATER, in a five-acre grove of pine and redwood trees, is a memorial to Stephen Mather, alumnus, who was first director of the National Park Service.

25. INTERNATIONAL HOUSE, on Piedmont Ave. at the head of Bancroft Way, is the second of four such institutions donated by John D. Rockefeller Jr. in the interests of international understanding. Others are located at Columbia University in New York, at the University of Chicago, and at the Cité Universitaire in Paris. The Berkeley building provides living accommodations for 450 students, selected from among the many races and nationalities registered at the university. The number of American students is limited in order to provide room for foreign students.

Alameda

Information Service: Chamber of Commerce, 2546 Santa Clara Ave. City Hall, Oak St. and Santa Clara Ave.

Airports: San Francisco Bay Airdrome, Webster St., one block S. of Posey Tube; Naval Air Station, W. end of island. *Taxis:* Dime Taxi Company, 10¢ per passenger to any point within city limits, 35¢ to Oakland; Alameda Taxi Company, 25¢ 1st m., 20¢ thereafter, 1 to 4 persons. *Streetcars and Buses:* Key system local and intercity buses, fare 10¢ or one token (7 for 50¢); Interurban Electric Ry. transbay service on Encinal and Lincoln Aves., fare to San Francisco, 21¢. *Traffic Regulations:* Speed limit 25 m.p.h. in business and residential districts, 15 m.p.h. at intersections.

Accommodations: One hotel. Beach cottages, monthly rates.

Concert Halls: Adelphian Club, 2167 Central Ave. *Motion Picture Theaters:* Three first-run theaters. *Little Theater:* Alameda Little Theater, Delanoy Hall, 1346½ Park St.

Sports: Boating. Aeolian Yacht Club, Bay Farm Island Bridge. Alameda Boat Club, N. end of Chestnut St. Encinal Yacht Club, S. end Grand St. *Golf.* Municipal Golf Course, Bay Farm Island. *Riding Stables.* Alameda Riding Stables, Bay Farm Island. *Skeet and Trap Shooting.* Golden Gate Gun Club, W. end of island on Southern Pacific Auto Ferry road. *Swimming.* Cottage Beach, 554 Central Ave. Leo Purcell's Beach, 434 Central Ave. Sunny Cove Beach, 456 Central Ave. *Yachting.* Aeolian Yacht Club, Bay Farm Island. Encinal Yacht Club, S. end Grand St.

Churches (Only centrally located churches are listed): Baptist. First, 1519 Santa Clara Ave. *Christian.* First, 2445 San Jose Ave. *Christian Science.* First Church of Christ Scientist, Central Ave. and Walnut St. *Congregational.* First, 1912 Central Ave. *Episcopal.* Christ Church, 1700 Santa Clara Ave. *Hebrew Orthodox.* Temple Israel, 2664 Alameda Ave. *Lutheran.* Immanuel, 1906 Santa Clara Ave. *Methodist.* First, Central Ave. and Oak St. *Presbyterian.* First, Santa Clara Ave. and Chestnut St. *Roman Catholic.* St. Josephs, 1109 Chestnut St. *Seventh Day Adventist.* Alameda Seventh Day Adventists, 1513 Verdi St.

ALAMEDA (sea level-25 alt., 35,133 pop.), is on an island shaped roughly like an elongated violin, lying parallel to East Oakland, with the neck pointing toward the Golden Gate. The island has an average width of about one mile, a total length of six and one-half miles. The two-mile neck and adjoining areas are chiefly occupied by two large airports. The northeast shoreline, along the Estuary, is given over to industry and shipping, while the southwestern shoreline is a popular bathing resort section. Although no State or Federal highway touches Alameda, five vehicular connections link it with the mainland. The five miles of the Estuary and two miles of artificially created tidal canal separating the island from the mainland serve as a deep-water harbor for both Oakland and Alameda. Three bridges cross the canal. Another connects with Bay Farm Island to the south. But the most frequently used entrance is the George A. Posey Tube under the Estuary. Many residents do not know that the city proper was a peninsula until the tidal canal was dredged in 1902. More are unaware that its boundaries include a mainland agricultural district called Bay Farm Island, which now adjoins the filled-in Oakland Municipal Airport. Government Island, once a shoal off the main part of the city, now lies across the main channel of the Estuary, approachable by bridge only from Oakland.

Alameda is one of the oldest East Bay cities, and also one of the most modern. The contrast is found in schools and homes. Modern houses and apartments elbow ornate old buildings set in tranquil gardens on tree-shaded streets. Queer shrubs from foreign ports are common because the city is a well-known "port of retire" for old seamen, who settled here with souvenirs of travel.

All this flat expanse of fertile land, with its numerous sloughs and clumps of big drooping valley oaks, for generations gave shade and food and water to the Costanoan Indians. Included in the Peralta land grant of 1820, it was known as Encinal de San Antonio (the oak grove of St. Anthony) when Americans came here and found, grazing in the lush pasture land, many cattle branded with the Peralta initial. Waterfowl and small game attracted hunters, who found a ready market in San Francisco for their kill, and the thick stands of oaks brought in crews of charcoal burners, who likewise had no difficulty in marketing their product in the growing transbay city and in the Mother Lode's boom towns.

Among the early arrivals were Gideon Aughinbaugh, a Pennsylvania carpenter, and his partner, W. W. Chipman, a lawyer and school teacher from Ohio, who recognized the possibilities of the region. Through the flimsy walls of one of the kindling and cardboard shanties of early San Francisco, Chipman overheard H. S. Fitch, a San Francisco auctioneer, negotiating with Antonio Peralta for the purchase of the Encinal at a price of $7,000. Chipman immediately sought out Peralta and doubled the bid. By this bit of shrewdness the future city of Alameda passed into the hands of the partners, Chipman and Aughinbaugh. They needed money, however, and to obtain it offered Fitch a one-fourteenth interest for $3,000. Fitch accepted, and in partnership with William Sharon took possession of 160 acres.

Chipman and Aughinbaugh began to develop the land and to attract settlers. Grafted fruit trees were brought from the East (there are accounts of peaches in Aughinbaugh's orchard which sold for one dollar each). He secured the use of a small steamer, the *Bonita,* which plied between Alameda and San Francisco. Sunday excursions, watermelon picnics, and gift lots to any one who would erect a $50 building were some of the devices used to further development. With more than 100 settlers by 1853, Chipman and Aughinbaugh took the initiative in founding a town in the vicinity of High Street.

The name, Alameda (poplar-shaded avenue), already in use by the recently organized county, was selected by popular vote. Two other towns also were laid out—one at the Point, named Woodstock, the other at the center of the peninsula, called Encinal.

With the increase of American population in California, the little hamlet, along with its neighbors, Oakland and San Leandro, got its share of new settlers, many of whom, returning unsuccessful from the mines, were looking for homes and land. In 1871 a bridge over the Estuary and a causeway across the marsh were constructed, establishing directed communication with Oakland. Incorporation took place in 1872. The city-manager form of government was adopted in 1917.

In the course of its history Alameda has counted among its residents Mark Twain, Jack London, and Harrison Fisher. The starting point for Robert Louis Stevenson's journeys to the South Seas, it figured prominently in his career. He first came here to visit the Orr family (Scots, like himself), who operated a copra oil mill. Because copra came from the South Sea islands, he grew interested in island lore and outfitted a ship, the *Casco,* to sail there under command of the New England skipper, Captain Albert Otis. Captain Otis, whose own declining years were spent in Alameda, was immortalized as Arty Nares in Stevenson's *The Wreckers.* The novelist later married a sister of Mrs. Orr, in Alameda.

The island's excellent water connections have attracted many large industries, including the shipbuilding yards of the Bethlehem Steel Company and the warehouses of the California Packing Corporation, through which most of the products of the corporation's canneries in the Bay area and central valleys are transshipped to other parts of the country and abroad. Adjoining Cal-Pak's spacious buildings is the Encinal Terminal, which it owns, where more than 1,200 ships dock annually. Close by also are the warehouse and docks of the Alaska Packer's Association, which annually sends an expedition to the fishing waters of Alaska, returning with as many as 1,000,000 cases of canned salmon. Boat yards build yachts and other pleasure craft. Numerous plants turn out such diverse products as pottery, pencils, pickles, preserves, peanut butter, and chocolates.

Alameda was one of the first cities in the country to macadamize its streets. It had the first municipal power plant in California, established in 1890 at a cost of $40,000, which, during 50 years of operation, has earned profits of nearly $3,000,000, used in the construction of many public services and buildings. A health center, a belt line railroad, a public library, a fire-alarm system, a park, and the Municipal Golf Course are some of its contributions to the well-being of Alameda's citizens.

POINTS OF INTEREST

1. The BETHLEHEM STEEL COMPANY SHIPBUILD-ING DIVISION (*no visitors*), 2308 Webster St., was at one time the largest shipbuilding yard on the Pacific Coast, employing 9,000 men. During the World War it built the *Invincible,* a 12,000-ton steamer, in 24 days. Long used as a repair yard, it is being refitted to do its part in the Government's 1940 naval expansion program. From the adjoining steel fabricating plant came all the steel for the Golden Gate Bridge.

2. The SAN FRANCISCO BAY AIRDROME, 2155 Webster St., privately owned, houses several charter, sales, and service companies. Between 80 and 90 ships, passenger and private, are based here, many being available for sightseeing trips around the Bay.

3. The NAVAL AIR STATION (*visitors only on special occasions*), on Southern Pacific Auto Ferry Rd., will be one of the world's largest airports when completed in 1942. Costing more than $15,000,-000 and incorporating both the former Benton Field of the Army and the Municipal Airport, it will have a total area of more than three square miles, of which 881 acres will be land. A 9,000-foot sea wall will protect the shoreline and a 2,400-foot rock-wall jetty will form a large lagoon for seaplanes. Two piers will be able to accommodate the Navy's largest aircraft carriers. The base will contain eight land plane hangars with four main runways, five huge seaplane hangars facing the lagoon, administrative buildings, a small-arms arsenal, storehouses, and quarters for approximately 5,000 officers and enlisted men. Two patrol squadrons numbering 24 seaplanes and three airplane carriers, each with 75 fighting planes, will make this their base of operations. The first China Clipper flight began here November 22, 1935, when the airport was a base for the Pan American Airways System.

4. The GOLDEN GATE GUN CLUB (*targets: 60¢ to members, 70¢ to non-members; picnic grounds; club rooms*), with eight traps and three skeet fields, occupies 160 acres at the extreme west end of Alameda Island on the Southern Pacific Auto Ferry Road.

5. WASHINGTON PARK (*picnic grounds; tennis courts; baseball diamond; cinder track; club house*), Central Ave. and Eighth St., Alameda's largest municipal recreation center, is bounded on the Bay side by a public bathing beach (*lifeguard during summer months; no lockers*). Professional baseball was played here for the first time in California, and from this diamond have come some of the present big

names in baseball: Johnny Vergez, Dick Bartell, Lou Vezelick, and Al Browne. The Alameda Girls Softball Team has twice been crowned United States National champion.

West of Washington Park is the SITE OF NEPTUNE BEACH formerly a popular amusement park, now a residential subdivision. An outgrowth of Neptune Gardens and Croll's Gardens, it was the mecca for boxing and wrestling fans. John L. Sullivan, Bob Fitzsimmons, Jim Corbett, Kid McCoy, Billy Muldoon, Farmer Burns, and Frank Gotch all came here to rest and train.

6. The ENCINAL YACHT CLUB, S. end of Grand St., founded in 1891, sponsors sailing events, and has anchorage for small yachts and other pleasure craft.

7. The 130 members of the AEOLIAN YACHT CLUB, E. end of Calhoun St., take part in frequent class and handicap races and in cruises to Bay, river, and coast points. The Aeolian Juniors, made up of boys under 21, conduct races and regattas with their own fleet, under supervision of junior officers. Many of them have built their own boats.

8. The 18-hole ALAMEDA MUNICIPAL GOLF COURSE (*greens fee: Sat., Sun., holidays, 75¢; weekdays, 50¢*) is on Bay Farm Island directly across the bridge from Alameda.

9. INDIAN MOUND STONE MOUNMENT, in Lincoln Park on High St. at E. end of Santa Clara Ave., commemorates the site of a former Indian shell mound that measured 150 by 400 feet. The mound was leveled in 1908 and the earth and mussel shells used on the roads of Bay Farm Island. The site, now under nearby homes and streets, is indistinguishable. The mound rose 14 feet above the level ground. From it were taken the remains of 450 Indians, all of whom had been buried facing the rising sun with knees drawn up to chins. Near the top was a brass counter bearing the image of George II and dated 1768, which possibly was brought here by Indians in contact with the Hudson's Bay Company.

10. The ALAMEDA PUBLIC LIBRARY, Santa Clara Ave. and Oak St., has a collection of nearly 100,000 volumes, including some valuable Californiana. Relics salvaged from the Indian shell mound, including shell ornaments, cooking implements and a 172-year-old brass counter, are on display.

11. The ALAMEDA BOAT CLUB, foot of Chestnut St., on the Estuary, was established in 1864 as a center for racing shells. Today (1940) the principal activity of its 100 members is participation in motorboat races sponsored by other clubs.

12. The SHIP GRAVEYARDS on the Estuary, N. end of Schiller St. and foot of a rutted, sandy road leading from end of St. Charles St., are the final resting places for many ancient, worn-out vessels. Here is the long-idle *Unimak,* built in 1902 in Alameda, a 124-foot

steam schooner that once pushed her way bravely through the ice of an early Alaska winter, homeward bound and loaded to the beams with the season's salmon pack. Here are the *Kadiak,* a sturdy tug that once worked the Alaska waters, and the unnamed grey hulk called *No. 30,* once a water-carrier in the United States Navy. In contrast to these are rows of steel and wooden ships maintained in a state of idle preparedness, awaiting the command to fire the boilers.

13. The 100-acre GOVERNMENT ISLAND (*visitors welcome Sat. p.m. and Sun.*) in the Estuary, reached by way of the Dennison Street Bridge from Oakland, is the base for a major United States Coast Guard Station, with more than 100 men and seven patrol boats and three Coast Guard cutters on duty. Located here are divisions of the United States Forestry Service and of the United States Public Roads Administration, and a merchant marine school for which the *Northland,* Coast Guard vessel, serves as a training ship. The island was made when the Estuary was dredged in 1916.

In the ADMINISTRATION BUILDING are frescoes by Beckford Young and John Haley depicting the history of road-building and activities of the Coast Guard and the Forestry Service, done under the WPA Art Project.

East Bay Tour 1

Oakland—El Cerrito—Richmond—Crockett—Martinez—Pittsburg—Antioch; 50.5 *m.* US 40, County road, State 4-24.

Paved throughout.
Southern Pacific R. R. and Santa Fe Ry. parallel the route between Oakland and Antioch. Pacific Greyhound Bus Lines serve the area.

From the flat western sections of Oakland and Berkeley, this route follows the contours of San Francisco Bay, San Pablo Bay, Carquinez Strait, and Suisun Bay, passing residential, industrial, and "company" towns in rapid succession—traversing a district whose petroleum-laden atmosphere indicates immense oil storage tanks and great oil refineries—and ends at the gateway to the rich garden region of the San Joaquin delta.

The touring center of OAKLAND, 0 *m.,* is San Pablo Ave., Broadway, and Fourteenth Street.

North from San Pablo Ave., Broadway, and Fourteenth St. on Broadway to Moss Ave.; R. on Moss Ave.; L. on Oakland Ave. to PIEDMONT 1.8 *m.* (800 alt., 9,339 pop.), contoured to glen and upland, a municipal island entirely surrounded by Oakland. Strictly residential, its stately mansions and vine-clad cottages set in terraced gardens border streets that wind in a bewildering maze through canyons, across ridges, and around knolls. Like Oakland, Piedmont was once a part of the 43,472-acre Rancho San Antonio (*see Oakland*). Walter Blair, a New Englander, purchased the site for a ranch in 1852 at $1.25 an acre and in 1870 James Gamble divided it into town lots.

Thirteen-acre PIEDMONT PARK (*community hall, playground, tennis courts*), in the approximate center of the city, is irrigated by a sulphur spring, around which a health resort was built in 1876. Within the park are the largest collection of wild irises in the State and a one-acre sanctuary for Alameda County wild flowers.

North from San Pablo Ave., Broadway, and Fourteenth St. in Oakland, on San Pablo Ave., to EMERYVILLE, 2 *m.* (sea level-60 alt., 2,399 pop.), a highly industrialized municipality dating from the middle 1870's when the Oakland Trotting Track and the picnic grounds at Shellmound Park "in the vicinity of Butchertown" were the chief attractions. In the park, surmounting a large Indian shellmound, stood a dance pavilion. Frequent fairs, circuses and exhibitions; National shooting tournaments; festivals of the Swedish and Caledonian Societies with bagpipe and haggis; and the Butchers' Annual Celebration all brought throngs to Golden Gate Village, as the community was then known. In 1896 it became Emeryville, named for Joseph Stickney Emery, early resident and architect of the San Francisco mint.

In that same year the California Jockey Club purchased the Oakland Trotting Track and changed it to a running track. There was grief in Emeryville when State legislative action abolished horse-racing in 1911; but this blow was a blessing in disguise. The race track properties brought handsome prices as these level acres near two transcontinental railroads attracted industry. Now (1940) there are 120 industries, one for every 21 inhabitants. There is neither church, theater, hospital, nor cemetery. Population is decreasing but every razed residence signalizes the coming of a new industry or the expansion of an old one.

BERKELEY, 3.2 *m.* (sea level-1,300 alt., 84,827 pop.) (*see BERKELEY*).

Right from Berkeley on Ashby Ave.—State 24—which becomes Tunnel Rd., to Broadway; L. on Broadway.

The twin bores of the BROADWAY LOW LEVEL TUNNEL, West Portal at 4.8 *m.* (*see Emporium of a New World: Engineering Enterprise*), serve the opposing lines of traffic. Since completion of this tunnel in 1937, many people employed in the metropolitan area have chosen the sheltered slopes and valleys beyond it for home sites. From the tunnel's East Portal, State 24 descends the canyon of the west branch of San Pablo Creek through low hills.

At 7.5 *m.* is a junction with paved Moraga Road.

Right here, over a low pass into the orchard lands of Moraga Valley, is MORAGA, 4.5 *m.* (475 alt., 61 pop.), a little village whose site was once part of the 13,316-acre Rancho Laguna de los Palos Colorados (Lagoon of the red trees), granted jointly to Joaquin Moraga and Jose Bernal in 1835.

The route continues L. from Moraga on a paved road to ST. MARY'S COLLEGE, 6 *m.*, on a 500-acre campus in an arm of Moraga Valley, through which flows Las Trampas (the frauds) Creek. The $2,000,000 group of buildings designed in California mission style (John J. Donovan, architect) was dedicated in 1928. Springing from the little school opened by Reverend John T. Harrington in 1855 in the basement of old St. Mary's in San Francisco, the present St. Mary's College has grown to include a chain of State-wide preparatory schools and colleges, now administered by the Brothers of the Christian Schools, who assumed control of St. Mary's in 1868. Brother Leo, widely known as a lecturer and an authority on Dante, is a member of the faculty. Of the average student enrollment of five hundred, most major in arts and letters.

In the KEITH MEMORIAL GALLERY are hung thirty-three paintings, eight oil sketches and studies, and several drawings by William Keith, San Francisco artist who died in 1911 (*see Golden Era: Art and Artists*).

The CHAPEL OF OUR LADY OF MORAGA is surmounted by a 120-foot tower and a dome of many-colored tile. In the interior, modeled after a church at Monreale, Sicily, is an elaborately designed marble altar.

MADIGAN GYMNASIUM occupies one corner of a large athletic field, where the "Gaels" of football fame are trained. It is named for Coach "Slip" Madigan, under whose tutelage St. Mary's teams won renown.

Northeast of its junction with Moraga Road, State 24 climbs by an easy grade into the canyon of the Lafayette branch of Walnut Creek.

LAFAYETTE, 11.4 *m.* (200 alt., 750 pop.), is an agricultural trading community and suburban town. In 1848 Elam Brown, immigrant train captain, purchased the 3,500-acre Rancho Acalanes from Candelario Valencia, and sold a tenth of the rancho to Nathaniel Jones. The two erected frame buildings to begin the town.

State 24 cuts through the foothills of Lafayette Ridge across Reesley Valley to Walnut Creek 14.8 *m.* (147 alt., 1,014 pop.), at the southern end of Ygnacio Valley. The business center parallels the creek; the residential section rises into low hills. Because of its location at crossroads the first American settlers gave the town the terse Yankee name of "The Corners." Later the English equivalent of the earlier Spanish name, Arroyo de las Nueces (gully of the nuts), was restored because of the many native hard-shell California walnuts growing along Walnut Creek. Walnut culture, a thriving industry that centers here, began when pioneer growers first grafted the English walnut to hardy young native trees. Many kinds of fruit also are cultivated in the rich valley soil, and there are numerous poultry farms in the region.

South of Walnut Creek, State 21 follows narrow San Ramon Valley between the foothills of Mount Diablo (L) and Las Trampas Ridge (R).

In ALAMO, 18.4 m. (272 alt., 69 pop.), giant maple trees shade the main street, although the village was named by Spaniards for the cottonwoods growing abundantly hereabout. The first adobe built here (about 1848) became in 1853 the only post office between Martinez and Mission San Jose; the mail was delivered by horse and cart twice a week.

Visible at 20.4 m. is TAO HOUSE (private), home of playwright Eugene O'Neill. The white palatial residence stands on a hillside (R) overlooking the road.

DANVILLE, 21 m. (365 alt., 600 pop.), a trading center, was named after Danville, Kentucky.

The side route continues L. from Danville on Mount Diablo Road, climbing out of the orchard lands of San Ramon Valley to the entrance of MOUNT DIABLO STATE PARK (automobile permit, 25¢; motorcycle permit, 15¢; overnight camping permit, 50¢), 25.5 m. The road climbs along a confused mass of DEVIL'S SLIDE (R), 28 m., up Madrone Canyon past the grotesque, animal-like rock formations of the GARDEN OF THE JUNGLE GODS (R), 28.6 m.

Well-defined trails lead northwest from PARK HEADQUARTERS (R), 29.1 m., to the sandstone formation of ELEPHANT ROCK, SENTINEL ROCK, DEVIL'S STAIR-WAY, PIGEON ROCK, and PENGUIN ROCK.

Rising majestically above broad plains, the conical summit of MOUNT DIABLO, 36.2 m. (3,849 alt.), often incorrectly said to be volcanic, is easily recognizable from great distances; it long has been a conspicuous landmark for both Indians and whites. To the east are the great San Joaquin and Sacramento Valleys and the long line of the Sierra from Mount Lassen to Mount Brewer; to the north, Mount St. Helena; to the west, Mount Tamalpais and the Pacific; to the south, Santa Clara Valley between parallel Coast ranges. Eighty thousand square miles of land and sea lie within the extreme limits of vision. All lands in California north of Kern and San Luis Obispo Counties, except the Humboldt region, are surveyed by reference to Mount Diablo (a meridian base).

Pedro Fages and his company in 1772 were the first white men to come near the mountain. Four years later Juan Bautista de Anza followed the trail blazed by Fages. General Mariano G. Vallejo reported that in 1806 a military expedition from San Francisco fought the Bolgone Indians, who were encamped on a foothill seven miles north of Kah Woo Koom (mighty mountain), as the Indians called Mount Diablo. During the battle "an unknown personage, decorated with the most extraordinary plumage and making divers movements, suddenly appeared. The Indians were victorious and the incognito, probably a medicine man impersonating the puy [evil spirit, or devil] . . . departed towards the mount. The defeated soldiers . . . named the mount 'Diablo' . . ."

In 1841 the first emigrant train to enter California by way of the Sierra Nevada, the Bidwell-Bartleson party, used Mount Diablo as a guide. Colonel Leander Ransom established Diablo as a base point for Government surveys in California in 1851. In 1862 the Whitney survey expedition climbed and measured the mountain. Before the days of automobiles it required a full day to ascend the steep and dusty road to the summit. A hotel on the mountainside, which cared for overnight visitors, was burned by settlers who objected to trespassers.

Crowning the summit are the heavily buttressed walls of MOUNT DIABLO MUSEUM, built of native miocene sandstone. The structure (under construction 1940) has a three-story octagonal tower flanked by an L-shaped wing. The main entrance opens into the ground floor of the tower, built around the base meridian marker. Against the walls is a series of dioramas and

Across the Bay

PACIFICA, GODDESS OF TWO EXPOSITIONS   *Sculpture by Ralph Stackpole*

CLIPPER IN FLIGHT OVER TREASURE ISLAND   *Clyde H. Sunderland Photo*

FOUNTAIN OF WESTERN WATERS, GOLDEN GATE EXPOSITION

EVENING STAR, IN THE COURT OF THE MOON

OAKLAND BUSINESS DISTRICT FROM LAKE MERRITT

OAKLAND

IN THE SEVENTIES

UNIVERSITY OF CALIFORNIA

AIRVIEW

OAKLAND LONG WHARF, BUILT IN 1871

OAKLAND WHARF TERMINAL OF CENTRAL PACIFIC (1878)

BIG-WHEELED *NEWARK* (1877-1921)

HOME OF DERELICTS—SHIPS AND HUMAN BEINGS

Howard B. Hoffman Photo

MISSION SAN JOSE DE GUADALUPE

VINEYARD IN LIVERMORE VALLEY

pictures relating to establishment of the mountain as a base meridian point and a triangulation base for the United States Geodetic Survey. In the adjoining wing are the Hall of Science, containing botanical, zoological, paleontological, and geological exhibits, and murals illustrating prehistoric animal life; and the Hall of History, with a series of dioramas and murals depicting Indian life and religious concepts, Spanish exploration and settlement in the Diablo region, early American settlements, and local industries, particularly the Mount Diablo coal mines. The second floor of the tower is an observation room. Above the windows are large photomurals showing the greatest distances in each direction which can be seen with the naked eye. The upper story of the tower is surmounted by a powerful revolving electric beacon.

In Alameda County's extreme northwest corner is ALBANY, 6.2 m. (sea level-300 alt., 11,420 pop.), with its many one-family homes of white stucco. The town site was part of the huge Rancho San Antonio granted to Luis Maria Peralta in 1820. The town was known as Ocean View until 1909, when the electorate renamed it in deference to Mayor Roberts, who came from Albany, New York.

The GOLDEN GATE TURF CLUB (under construction April, 1940), Fleming Point, will when completed share racing dates with Tanforan and Bay Meadows. Also under construction is the WESTERN REGIONAL RESEARCH LABORATORY, Buchanan and Fillmore Sts., a large U-shaped, three-story concrete building which will house a branch of the United States Bureau of Agricultural Chemistry and Engineering. It will be devoted to chemical, physical, and biological experiment in an effort to find new markets and uses for farm crops and commodities.

EL CERRITO, 6.9 m. (sea level-500 alt., 6,154 pop.), occupies the southern portion of the old Rancho San Pablo, granted in 1823 to Francisco Maria Castro. It dates from 1917, when the residents of 2,500 acres, some in Richmond and some in what was known merely as the "Cerrito District," voted for incorporation.

The large white CASTRO ADOBE standing (R) a few yards off San Pablo Ave. on Cerrito Creek, was built in the 1840's by Don Victor Castro, youngest son of the grantee of Rancho San Pablo. It has 34-inch outer walls and includes a private chapel. Bret Harte used the house as the locale of his play, *The Two Men of Sandy Bar*.

In the eastern residential district of RICHMOND, 9.2 m. (sea level-100 alt., 22,707 pop.), an arrow-shaped electric sign above the highway points (L) to the heart of the city. Though less than 40 years old, Richmond is Contra Costa County's largest city and the principal West Coast port for the transshipment of oil. It extends from the Contra Costa hills across three miles of low, level terrain to a steep headland from which two peninsulas—Point Richmond to the southeast and Point San Pablo to the northwest—jut into San Francisco Bay. Between Point San Pablo and San Pedro Point on the opposite Marin County shore is San Pablo Strait, joining San Francisco and San Pablo Bays. A six-mile water front fringed by an industrial belt and a series of modern home districts semicircling the business district comprise the 27 square miles of this scattered town. Although it has fine homes on the hillslopes east of San Pablo Avenue, many schools and other public buildings, parks and playgrounds, Richmond's many vacant blocks, fronted by sign boards and generally unrelieved by trees or shrubs, give the town an unfinished look characteristic of young communities.

Until 1900 this was farming and grazing land. In 1857 the first settler, John Nicholl, bought 200 acres of Rancho San Pablo. The hilly land from Point San Pablo to Point Richmond was early acquired by Jacob M. Tewksbury, surgeon and land-grabber. In 1870 the greater part of the present water front and industrial belt, known as the Potrero (pasture) District, was separated from the mainland by a slough. As an island it would have been declared closed Federal land (as were all the islands in San Francisco Bay by the Act of 1866), but by building a small dam across the southern end of the slough, Dr. Tewksbury caused shoaling and ultimately the closing of the waterway, until then deep enough to accommodate a small sloop. In 1872 the government declared the tract a peninsula, and, as such, a part of old Rancho San Pablo and the property of Tewksbury.

When the Central Pacific Railroad entered the district in 1877, it passed up Richmond's present site and built a station called Stege two miles southeast, but the Santa Fe in 1899 selected the site as its western terminus, thereby starting an industrial development. The Standard Oil Company built the first unit of its great refinery here in 1902. The dredging of the harbor began in 1912. Since 1926 the city has shared ownership and operation of its harbor with private interests.

The four terminals along the Richmond water front handle an annual cargo of more than 9,000,000 tons. Oil is by far the principal cargo, borne here by tankers from the Orient and pumped into the tanks that mushroom the hills. There are more than 60 industries, including fish-reduction plants, chemical works, an asphalt products plant, and tile, brick, enamel, and pottery works.

The STANDARD OIL REFINERY (*adm. by pass*), Standard Ave., occupies a tract of 1,800 acres. It has a daily capacity of 100,000 barrels of crude oil, employs between 2,000 and 3,000 workers, and manufactures more than 500 petroleum products.

The FORD MOTOR COMPANY ASSEMBLY PLANT (*visitors 9-3 weekdays; guides*), 1414 S. Tenth St., covering 58 acres, has about 1,000 employees.

A center for both yachting and motorboating is THE RICHMOND YACHT CLUB, Second St. and Inner Harbor Canal. Principal events are a championship regatta in June and a "beachcomber's ball" in September.

NICHOLL PARK (*tennis, handball, baseball, bowling*), Twentyninth St. and McDonald Ave., is Richmond's largest recreation center. The eight-room JOHN NICHOLL HOUSE, 2800 McDonald Ave., built in 1857 of redwood, is shaded by great eucalyptus trees more than 70 years old.

Left from McDonald Ave. in Richmond on Garrard Blvd. to a junction with Western Dr., 4.6 *m.* (Point Richmond); R. on Western Dr. to a junction with a paved road, 6.2 *m.*; L. here 0.5 *m.* to the Richmond-San Rafael Ferry (*car and driver 70¢; with four passengers, 80¢*), which crosses the northern end of San Francisco Bay to San Quentin Wharf.

Western Drive continues to WINEHAVEN, 8.7 *m.*, sheltered by Molate Point (L), where formerly a large winery occupied the extensive buildings facing San Pablo Bay. It is now a ghost town, its plant and warehouses empty of machinery, its company-owned hotel and rows of cottages, which once housed 150 workers and their families, decaying in peaceful loneliness. So favorable for the aging and blending of wines were climatic conditions in this sheltered Bayside spot that $1,500,000 were invested in this property in 1906. The plant was abandoned in 1921 after a brief attempt at making grape juice for a dry Nation. But to it clings the memory of the fine California wines it processed—wines that competed for world favor with the best of other lands.

SAN PABLO, 11.4 *m.* (28 alt., 489 pop.), was named for Rancho San Pablo, a four-league tract which Francisco Maria Castro, Spanish artillery corporal, acquired in 1823. Castro died a few years later, leaving 12 children, one of whom, Martina, married Juan B. Alvarado, Mexican governor (1836-42) who later came into possession of the greater part of this rancho.

Its rear wall facing the highway, the ALVARADO ADOBE, US 40 and Church Lane, 90 feet long with broad porches and overhanging gables, has served as the storeroom of a grocery. It was built in 1838 by Antonio, eldest son of Francisco Castro. After American occupation of the State, Governor Alvarado made it his home until his death in 1882.

Left from San Pablo on a hard-surfaced road 1.2 *m.* to a junction with a driveway leading (R) to the GUTIERREZ ADOBE (*private*), visible from the road. Two frame wings have been added to the original 24- by 48-foot building whose thick walls, sheathed in wood and resting on a stone foundation, are well preserved. This adobe, built about 1845, was the home of Candido Gutierrez and his wife Jovita. Under one of the wings is the grave of Maria Emma Gutierrez, who died at the age of six. Her tombstone, inscribed with a Spanish verse, almost touches a floor beam.

At 12.4 *m.* on US 40 is a junction with a hard-surfaced road.

Left on this road, at the northern tip of Pinole Point, is the company town of GIANT, 2 *m.* (10 alt., 120 pop.), plant-site of the Atlas Powder Company. Although it has homes for about 30 families, a majority of the workmen live elsewhere. Formerly called Nitro, the place dates from 1867, when the Giant Powder Company, first company in California to manufacture dynamite, built a plant here.

US 40 veers northeast, still following the contour of the Bay. The Contra Costa hills decline into rolling ridges which flatten out as they approach the water. This region was known as the Sobrante district during late Mexican and early American days, the tract being *sobrante* (unclaimed or left-over portion) between Ranchos San Pablo and El Pinole. Sheep and cattle trails wind through occasional groves of eucalyptus and willow.

At the foot of hills commanding views of Bay and mountains, PINOLE, 16.4 *m.* (32 alt., 919 pop.), through which runs Pinole

Creek, is chiefly a residential community for employees of plants along the Contra Costa shore. The town is named for Rancho El Pinole, claimed in 1823 by Lieutenant Ignacio Martinez, who named it in commemoration of the rescue of a party of Spanish soldiers, lost in this district, by a band of friendly Indians, who fed them a coarse gruel made from acorns, which they called *pinole*. The canyon, farther east, where they first lost their bearings, came to be known as the Cañada del Hambre (valley of hunger) later corrupted to Alhambra.

In 1849 a young Englishman, Dr. Samuel J. Tennant, once physician to the King of the Sandwich Islands, stopped here on one of his trips to the gold regions, met Rafaela, daughter of Don Ignacio, and later married her. On that part of the rancho inherited by him and his wife, he founded the town of Pinole.

At 16.6 *m.* is a junction with a hard-surfaced road.

Left on this road is the company town of HERCULES, 0.7 *m.* (8 alt., 343 pop.), where the Hercules Powder Company established its plant in 1869 to provide powder for the mining industry. The residential district borders the road which winds along the tree-covered ridge fronting San Pablo Bay. As a measure of safety, powder and acid houses are built in separate pockets. Underground storage magazines are scattered throughout the flat lands to the east. The plant covers 2,800 acres and has a capacity of 250,000 pounds monthly.

At 17.4 *m.* is a junction with State 4.

Right on State 4 up Franklin Canyon, the fertile valley of Rodeo Creek, still partly covered with live oaks. The cleared land is planted to apricots, walnuts, and tomatoes.

At 9.2 *m.* is a junction with a paved road—the former State 4; L. here 0.1 *m.* to the RANCHO LAS JUNTAS ADOBE (*private*), a well-preserved white house built in the 1840's, facing away from the road under old locust trees.

On former State 4 at 2 *m.* is Martinez.

On State 4 at 9.4 *m.* the large, old-fashioned, cupolaed JOHN STRENTZEL HOUSE (L) overlooks rolling orchard land. Here the great naturalist, John Muir (1838-1914), who originated the first plans for a system of National parks, spent the latter part of his life. The estate was originally part of Rancho Las Juntas.

At 9.7 *m.* is a junction with hard-surfaced Alhambra Road; R. here to the JOHN MUIR HOUSE (L), 1.1 *m.* (*private*), the original part of which was built in 1853 by Dr. John Strentzel, who gave it to his daughter and Muir after their marriage in 1880. The Muirs lived here for ten years (1880-90), moving to the Strentzel House shortly after Dr. Strentzel's death. Many of the books, pieces of furniture, and other possessions used by Muir are here. Near a large eucalyptus tree visible from the road Muir and his wife are buried. An annual pilgrimage to the graves is made on the Sunday nearest April 21, anniversary of his birthday.

Also on Alhambra Road is the JOHN SWETT HOUSE (*private*), 1.6 *m.*, on the banks (R) of a tree-shaded stream on Hill Girt Ranch. John Swett (1830-1913), State Superintendent of Public Instruction from 1863 to 1867, co-founder of the first State normal college and intimate friend of John Muir, lived here. Nearby is a well-preserved adobe, built in the 1850's, when this was part of Rancho Las Juntas.

From its junction with Alhambra Road, State 4 continues east to a junction with State 21, 12.7 *m.*

Right on State 21 to the LOUCKS HOUSE (*private*), 0.4 *m.*, built by G. L. Walwrath in 1853 on a hill (L). The timbers, cut from Moraga redwoods, are covered with sheathing that was brought round Cape Horn. George P. Loucks bought the house in 1856.

PACHECO, 0.8 *m.* (21 alt., 200 pop.), a sleepy inland village, stands beside Walnut Creek, a stream that served as the boundary line for two ranchos —Las Juntas and Monte del Diablo. Grayson Creek, which also flows through Pacheco, joins Walnut Creek north of town to form Pacheco Creek. Within a few months after the town site was laid out in 1860, the village burned to the ground. A devastating flood in 1862, two more fires in 1867 and 1871, and an earthquake in 1868 were no boost to the town's growth.

Left from Pacheco 1.8 *m.* is CONCORD (65 alt., 1,369 pop.), a pleasant tree-shaded town, busy shipping point for the produce of Diablo Valley. The young village laid out in 1876 around the plaza was called Todos Santos (All Saints) by the Spanish and Drunken Indian by the Americans. Early hopes for the district were outlined in the *Contra Costa Gazette* of February 13, 1886: "Contra Costa County is destined to become a paradise of vineyards and orchards, of which Ygnacio and Diablo Valleys will be the central portion." The prediction has in a measure been realized. Strawberries and vegetables are also grown in large quantities.

At Concord and Salvio Aves. stands the PACHECO HOUSE, a sturdy adobe with balconies and shuttered windows, set among pepper trees. Now encased in wood and well preserved, the century-old house was the home of Salvio Pacheco, grantee of Rancho Monte del Diablo, embracing 17,921 acres of the surrounding fertile valley.

State 21 continues south from Pacheco to a junction with State 24, 3.4 *m.*

The main side route follows State 4 from its junction with State 21 to a junction with State 24, 16 *m.*, with which it unites as State 4-24, and continues L. to a junction with former State 4, 19.7 *m.* (*see below*).

US 40 crosses a low range of hills into the valley of Rodeo Creek. At the mouth of the creek on San Pablo Bay is RODEO, 19.3 *m.* (12 alt., 1,288 pop.). During Spanish and early American days great rodeos were held yearly up the canyon. There is still some cattle-raising in the back country. The Bay is in view as US 40 continues across the rolling terrain, with great oil tanks on the hillsides—a portion of the 900 in this district.

The smell of petroleum near OLEUM, 20.2 *m.* (76 alt., 217 pop.), comes from the Union Oil Company Refinery. The plant refines 35,000 barrels of petroleum daily. The "cracking" towers which tower above the highway are gigantic stills in which crude oil is heated to 700° Fahrenheit. The volatility of the component parts of the oil determines at which level of the tower they will be sucked out by the condensers and deposited in other tanks. The high octane aviation gasoline is drawn off at the top of the tower, ordinary gasoline and kerosene at a lower level and the heavier motor and fuel oils near the bottom.

TORMEY, 20.8 *m.*, a station (L) on the Southern Pacific line, was named for John and Patrick Tormey, whose 7,000-acre cattle ranch with a three-mile frontage on San Pablo Bay was before 1861 a part of Rancho El Pinole.

At 21 *m.* is a junction with a paved road.

Left on this road is the company town of SELBY, 0.2 *m.* (0-100 alt., 141 pop.), named for Prentiss Selby, who established the plant in 1884. A recently erected 605-foot-high smokestack, second in size only to one in Japan, marks the location of the American Smelting and Refining Company plant. Ore vessels unload at company docks; chief products are gold, silver, lead, and antimony.

Ascending a hill, US 40 climbs to a wide parking space, 21.5 *m.*, cut in the hillside directly above San Pablo Bay, which affords a view of Carquinez Strait, Carquinez Bridge, and the north Bay hills and valleys. The broad expanse of San Pablo Bay narrows into six-mile-long and one-mile-wide CARQUINEZ STRAIT. The town of Vallejo and the Mare Island Navy Yard lie opposite. A long break-water protects the deep channel to the Navy Yard; towering steel masts mark a powerful Naval radio station.

John Sutter, in command of three small vessels, looked out upon these shores en route to empire and riches in 1839; and this was the water route for men and supplies during the Gold Rush. Today ocean-going vessels buck the swift currents on their way to the deep-water port of Stockton, while flat-bottomed river boats push to and from the great central valleys. In season hundreds of tiny craft bob on the swells, as fishermen pit their skill and patience against the wariness of the gamey striped bass.

At 22.3 *m.* is a junction with a paved road, on which the route branches R. from US 40.

Left here on US 40, across CARQUINEZ BRIDGE (*45¢ per car, 5¢ per passenger*), is VALLEJO, 3.5 *m.* (*see North Bay Tour*).

The route continues R. on the paved road to CROCKETT, 22.7 *m.* (25 alt., 3,885 pop.), which rises from the narrow strip of land fronting Carquinez Strait up the steep adjoining hills. The original owner of the town site, Thomas Edwards, Welsh by birth and a former mate on Mississippi River steamboats, drove his own covered wagon to California in 1849-50. Securing 1,800 acres along the Strait, he went into the cattle business. With the coming of the Central Pacific in 1877, the Edwards ranch became the site of Valona Station. In 1881, when a foundry selected the site as a new home, Edwards laid out the present town. He named it for J. B. Crockett, a former member of the California Supreme Court, whom he had known in St. Louis as a young lawyer.

In 1897 the California Beet Sugar Refining Company erected a small refinery on the shore, the nucleus of the present CALIFORNIA HAWAIIAN SUGAR REFINING CORPORATION PLANT (*visiting hours 10-1*). The corporation has its own ships which bring some half million tons of raw sugar from the Hawaiian Islands to its docks annually. The plant refines 2,600 tons daily, employing 2,000 men at peak, and disbursing up to $2,500,000 in pay rolls each year.

East of Crockett the route parallels Carquinez Strait. Now at sea level, now on the hillsides, the road winds around points and dives into canyons.

In PORT COSTA, 25.2 *m.* (11 alt., 593 pop.), an elm-shaded lane (L) leads down to a cove which was formerly an important harbor. When grain was California's principal crop, sailing vessels of many nations loaded wheat at this port. Until 1930, when the Southern Pacific built a bridge across the strait (*see below*), the main line trains were ferried from here to Benicia. One of the boats, the *Contra Costa*, with a capacity of 36 freight cars and two locomotives, was the largest railroad ferry in the world.

MARTINEZ, 31 *m*. (12 alt., 7,341 pop.), sits snugly on a crescent-shaped cove on Carquinez Strait, where the hills turn south to form the narrow Alhambra Valley into which the town is growing. Martinez was laid out in 1849 by Colonel William M. Smith on lands of Rancho El Pinole (*see above*), to which in 1850 was added, east of Del Hambre Creek, a part of Rancho Las Juntas (the junction points), granted in 1852 to William Welch, a Scot. When Contra Costa County was organized in 1850, Martinez became the county seat. River boats docked here, and a ferry crossed to Benicia. In 1878 the Central Pacific built a branch line from Port Costa to Martinez and later another line south into the San Ramon Valley. Since 1905 the Mountain Copper Company has manufactured fertilizers and various copper derivatives. The town, however, grew slowly until 1914, when the Shell Oil Company with its refinery became the chief industry (now employing more than one thousand). The population has tripled since 1910. Martinez also ships wine, acids, alcohol, furniture, fishoil and meal, spring water, redwood panels, and electric fixtures.

1. Right from Martinez on State 21 to a junction with State 4, 4.3 *m*. (*see above*).
2. Left from Martinez on Ferry St. to the Martinez-Benicia Auto Ferry (*car and driver 55¢, each additional passenger 10¢*), which crosses Suisun Bay to BENICIA, 2 *m*.; this water link is a continuation of State 21.

The main route goes east on Escobar Street (old State 4) through the Shell Oil Refinery property and past the SOUTHERN PACIFIC RAILROAD BRIDGE, which spans the eastern end of Carquinez Strait between Suisun Point and Army Point. The bridge was completed in 1930 at a cost of $12,000,000.

The refinery site of the Associated Oil Company is at ASSO-CIATED, 34.5 *m*. (12 alt., 250 pop.), a company town which until recently was called Avon. The refinery has a capacity of 48,000 barrels daily; it maintains great loading docks and pipe lines.

PORT CHICAGO, 37.8 *m*. (18 alt., 1,032 pop.), formerly called Bay Point, looks out toward the low-lying islands of Suisun Bay. It grew up with the C. A. Smith Lumber Company which came here in 1907 and flourished during the World War when the Pacific Coast Shipbuilding Company maintained yards here, but later declined in population when these companies moved away. Most of the residents, many of them Scandinavians by birth or parentage, are employed in nearby industrial towns. The harbor is much visited by yachtsmen and fishermen.

Another company town is NICHOLS, 39.7 *m*. (20 alt., 300 pop.), home of the General Chemical Company, where up to 200 are employed at peak.

East of Nichols, Suisun Bay narrows to a deep channel into which pour the Sacramento and San Joaquin Rivers after draining the great central valleys.

At SHELL POINT (L), 42.9 m., are a chemical plant and experimental laboratories of the Shell Oil Company, with about 300 employees.

PITTSBURG, 46.2 m. (21 alt., 9,610 pop.), faces the deep waters of New York Slough, near the confluence of the Sacramento and San Joaquin Rivers. Although it is a highly industrialized town, it has clean, well-paved streets, and many of its residents own their own homes.

The founder of the first settlement here was Jonathan B. Stevenson, ex-colonel of New York Militia, who led a regiment of New York Volunteers to California to help restore order in 1847. Stevenson turned to real estate with the idea of founding a "New York of the Pacific." In 1849 he purchased a part of Rancho Los Meganos (sand dunes), including the site of Pittsburg, engaged an obscure young engineer, one William Tecumseh Sherman—destined to become well-known in the State of Georgia—to lay out this Pacific Coast Manhattan, and tried to infuse Californians with his own "big-town" enthusiasm. Those who thought the city would become a "second New York" were doomed to disappointment, for the citizens sat up nights waiting for the boom and fighting off the hordes of mosquitoes infesting adjacent swamps. By 1865 they had become resigned to the waiting and the mosquitoes—and to the town's name of "New York Landing," which had been substituted for the colonel's grandiloquent "New York of the Pacific." When in the 1880's coal was discovered on the slope of Mount Diablo, the town was renamed Black Diamond. In 1910, after the Columbia Steel Company had built a modern mill, it received its present name.

The mills, foundries, and shops of the COLUMBIA STEEL CORPORATION PLANT (visitors admitted by special permission), where rolled steel products are manufactured, cover 387 acres. This plant is the principal subsidiary on the Pacific Coast of the United States Steel Corporation.

ANTIOCH, 50.5 m. (42 alt., 3,563 pop.), lies on the south bank of the San Joaquin River. The town is the gateway to the rich San Joaquin delta, which produces the bulk of the Nation's asparagus. Along its water front pass ships and barges to Stockton, one of the country's leading inland ports. The founders of Antioch, J. H. and W. W. Smith, ministers by profession and carpenters by trade, arrived in San Francisco from Boston on July 6, 1849. The brothers took up jointly two quarter-sections of land where Antioch now stands. On December 24, 1849, they set up tents and broke ground, working the land just enough to hold it, while carrying on their carpenter work. On February 5, 1850 the Reverend W. W. Smith died, but his brother remained at "Smith's Landing." Learning that a shipload of settlers from Maine had arrived in San Francisco planning to found a colony in California, he hurried to the city and offered each a lot for a home. They brought with them the traditions of a sturdy, God-fearing race and selected the Biblical name of Antioch for their new home. Antioch prospered during the Gold Rush, when ships with men and supplies made it a port of call and farmers began to cultivate the surrounding rich agricultural lands.

Today Antioch's largest industry is the Fibreboard Products Company, occupying a 30-acre tract and employing 400 people, which produces boxboard, paper boxes, packing cases, and wallboard. Other industries include a shipbuilding plant and several fruit and vegetable canneries.

The substantial GEORGE W. KIMBALL HOUSE, Third St., erected in 1851, was one of the first structures in the State to be built of Douglas fir—the "Oregon pine" of lumbermen.

East Bay Tour 2

Oakland—San Leandro—Alvarado—Centerville—Irvington—Warm Springs—Milpitas—San Jose; 41.7 m. State 17.

Paved roadbeds throughout.
Southern Pacific R. R. parallels the route; Peerless Stages between Oakland and San Jose; East Bay Transit Motor Coaches between Oakland and San Lorenzo.

This route follows the rich agricultural lands on the east side of San Francisco Bay, country occupied by Franciscan missionaries and Spanish *rancheros* long before the coming of Americans.

South from Fourteenth St. and Broadway in OAKLAND, 0 m., on Broadway; L. on Eighth St. (State 17), which curves into E. Twelfth St.

SAN LEANDRO, 8.7 m. (50 alt., 13,656 pop.), is a commercial and residential center on a narrow strip of exceptionally fertile land between San Francisco Bay (R) and low foothills (L). A green wedgelike plaza and old-fashioned frame buildings soften the business district's otherwise typical Main-Street atmosphere. Both the old frame houses and the new stucco-finished bungalows are fronted by well-kept gardens. The more pretentious old wooden homes have an air of faded grandeur. West of East Fourteenth Street (San Leandro's main business artery) are factories, packing sheds and canneries. When the canning season is at its peak, trucks loaded with fruit and vegetables lumber through the streets, and overalled men and women thread their way past great stacks of lug boxes lining the sidewalks.

The city's site was formerly part of Rancho San Leandro, granted Don Jose Joaquin Estudillo in 1842. Before the United States Government could confirm the title, however, many settlers had staked out claims. In early days San Leandro was an important stagecoach stop between Oakland and San Jose. Of all the stage drivers who made the run, the most hell-roaring was Charley Parkhurst, a swaggering bully with one eye covered by a black patch, lips and chin habitually stained by tobacco juice, who wore a buffalo-skin cap and turned up the cuffs of his blue jeans to show off elegant boots. Not until "his" death was Charley discovered to be a woman, Charlotte Parkhurst, who had come to California at the age of twenty in 1848. Unsuspected, she registered as a voter 50 years before woman's suffrage, her name (in its masculine form) appearing on the Santa Cruz register for 1866.

The State's largest Portuguese settlement, comprising more than 25,000 in Alameda County, centers in San Leandro. Founders of the colony (originally from the Azores and Madeira) came here from Sandwich Island sugar plantations where, because of a labor shortage, they had been held in virtual peonage. In the 1870's many Portuguese sailors, picked up at the Azores by New Bedford whaling vessels, rounded Cape Horn, jumped ship in San Francisco, and came here with little more than the small gold earrings which the majority of them wore. By their industry and thrift these patient, liberty-loving people were able to send passage money to other Azorean countrymen eager to take up life in the New World. The Portuguese, among the first farmers of Alameda County, have remained close to the soil. The dense Portuguese population here celebrates with church services, banners, street parades, and fireworks the Feast of the Holy Ghost.

Lying in a famed garden belt, San Leandro is a great center of floriculture. More than 3,800 workers are employed in the hothouses of this area. The flowers grown, chiefly sweet peas, camellias, gardenias, and orchids have an annual retail value of more than $10,000,-000. The nurseries supply flowers for the Pasadena Tournament of Roses, the Portland Rose Festival, and the New Orleans Mardi Gras. Thousands of acres in this area are devoted to dairying, truck farming, and fruit raising. San Leandro has a large fruit and vegetable cannery; its factories make or assemble calculating machines, automobiles, trucks, tractors, pencil slates, and pencils.

In ROOT PARK, E. Fourteenth St. and San Leandro Creek, a historical marker indicates the boundary between Rancho San Antonio and Rancho San Leandro.

The ESTUDILLO HOUSE (*private*), 1291 Carpentier St., erected 1850 or 1851, is the city's oldest residence. It was badly damaged in the 1868 earthquake. The balcony extending along two sides of the 14-room house, which still has its original clapboard sheathing and window sashes, is supported by wooden-covered brick pillars. On the lower floor were originally the kitchen, dining room, wine cellar, and quarters for Indian servants; on the upper floor were living quarters for the family. Behind the mansion is a fig tree over 90 years old, while nearby stands an almost equally venerable pear tree. Two large gnarled stumps in the front yard are remains of Alameda County's first pepper trees.

A women's social club is housed in the old IGNACIO PERALTA HOME, 563 E. Thirteenth St. Sergeant Luis Maria Peralta, grantee of Rancho San Antonio, divided his holdings among his four sons in 1842, and Ignacio, coming into the southern portion, built this home in 1860. The house, a one-story, rectangular structure, is of brick, the first in the county built of that material. Extensively repaired and remodeled, it is painted a light tan. The front porch, extending the width of the house, is shaded by two large magnolias.

Left from San Leandro on East Fourteenth Street 2 m. to the OAKLAND SPEEDWAY, a privately owned one-mile banked dirt track, claimed to be the fastest of its kind in the United States. A 500-mile event is held here each Labor Day, besides auto, midget car, and motorcycle races during the year. The grandstand seats approximately 11,000.

South of San Leandro, where blue mountains appear across the Bay, orchards, hayfields, and truck gardens checkerboard the flat land. Diminutive Japanese women wearing large sunbonnets and legginged overalls work in berry fields and truck gardens. Tilled field on hillsides (L) create a patchwork quilt.

SAN LORENZO, 12 m. (31 alt., 500 pop.), commercial center for surrounding farms and orchards, was once known as Squatterville. Here on the banks of San Lorenzo Creek Americans began in 1851 to overrun Don Jose Joaquin Estudillo's Rancho San Leandro. Some of the squatters expressed their pioneer disrespect for property rights by shooting Estudillo's horses and cattle and fencing watering places away from his stock. Following a court decision favorable to Estudillo in 1854, they began to take leases and eventually bought the land.

The former SAN LORENZO HOTEL, now a tavern and private dwelling, is a two-story building beneath whose casing of brown shingles is the original siding. Built in 1854 by Charles Crane, it was a stage station on the Mission Road between San Jose and Oakland.

In a fertile agricultural area is MOUNT EDEN, 15.8 m. (25 alt., 500 pop.), consisting of little more than a church, a country store, and the inevitable gas stations. The name is misleading, for the town site is flat. Established in 1850, it was known in the early days both as Eden's Landing and Johnson's Landing. John Johnson, first American to extract salt commercially along San Francisco Bay, shipped his product to pioneer settlements of California from a crude landing near here.

1. Right from Mount Eden on a paved road 1.8 m. to the LESLIE SALT WORKS, extending over flat land, where water from the Bay, confined in square shallow areas enclosed by banked-up earth, is reduced to crude salt by evaporation. Windmills, squat copies of the Dutch type, pump water from one

area to another. Huge piles of white salt stand like cones of snow. Long before the white man came Indians gathered crude salt from natural basins along the nearby shore line.

At 3 m. is the east approach to the seven-mile-long SAN MATEO TOLL BRIDGE (*toll, 65¢ for car, driver, and four passengers*), constructed of cement made from oyster shells dredged in the Bay.

In San Mateo, 13.1 m. (*see Peninsula Tour*), is the junction with US 101 Bypass (*see Peninsula Tour*).

2. Left from Mount Eden on a paved road is HAYWARD, 2 m. (115 alt., 6,547 pop.), at the base of low rolling foothills, surrounded by fertile orchard land and poultry farms. On the west side of the town are packing sheds, canneries, and cannery workers' homes. To the east the streets slope up to a more pretentious residential district with many fine gardens.

The town, which occupies a portion of the Rancho San Lorenzo, granted to Guillermo Castro in 1841, derived its name from William Hayward, who in 1851 mistakenly pitched his tent in Palomares Canyon on Castro's land with the intention of homesteading. Later Hayward purchased a plot on the rancho from Castro. Since roads leading to the gold fields passed through Hayward's property, his rude habitation soon became a trading place for miners. The shrewd Yankee established a combined stagecoach inn and general store. Soon the fame of "Haywards" was such that San Francisco people made the trip by boat and stagecoach to spend vacations there.

The shipping and canning of apricots, peaches, cherries, peas, spinach, and tomatoes is the town's chief industry, occupying 2,500 persons at the height of the season. There are also hatcheries that yearly ship some quarter-million baby chicks. In and around the town are many nurseries, conservatories, and lath houses growing plants and flowers.

The HAYWARD HOTEL ANNEX, 953 A St., a part of William Hayward's inn (*see above*), built in 1853, has some of the original hand-made doors and window sashes.

The MARKHAM SCHOOL, named in honor of Edwin Markham, author of the world-famous "The Man with the Hoe," occupies ground on which stood the old Laurel School where Markham, while a struggling young poet, once taught.

Proprietor in the 1870's of the VILLA HOTEL, on Castro St., was Tony Oakes, ballad singer, who published *Tony Oakes' Songster* in 1878. The hotel, built prior to 1860, was known as the American Exchange and as Oakes' Hotel.

DUBLIN, 11.1 m. (367 alt., 200 pop.), a small crossroads town at the junction with State 21, once called Amador, was a portion of Rancho San Ramon, granted in 1833 to Jose Maria Amador, a hard-boiled soldier, onetime major-domo of Mission San Jose. Centered here was his 16,517-acre rancho, stocked with great herds of cattle, sheep, and horses. In 1846, when Captain John Charles Frémont, ostensibly making "surveys," rode through the property and confiscated 57 of Amador's horses, a quarrel arose; but Frémont, at the head of his column of campaign-toughened fighters, presented a formidable argument to which Amador was forced to yield. The enterprising Amador was perhaps the first industrialist in the region now comprising Alameda County. Using Indian and Mexican labor, he early manufactured soap, leather goods, blankets, wagons, and other commodities. After 1852, when James Witt Dougherty purchased most of the Amador grant, the settlement was known as "Dougherty's Station." Because the area became settled largely by the Irish, the little town ultimately became known as Dublin. Surrounded by very fertile land, it is noted for fine Hereford stock, and dairy and farm products.

Little white frame ST. RAYMOND'S CHURCH, built in 1859 by Tom Donlan, was the first place of worship in the valley. A hawthorne-lined driveway leads behind the church to the cemetery in which have been interred the pioneers of the region. Jig-saw scrolls ornament the overhanging eaves of the two-story AMADOR HOTEL, on the west side of US 50, built in 1860 by James W. Dougherty with redwood lumber brought from Redwood City.

In 1870, John Scarlett, a local bartender, purchased the hotel. A modern front has been added to the first story.

Straight ahead (south) on State 21 from Dublin, along the western edge of Amador Valley and the eastern base of Pleasanton Ridge, 1 m. to the remodeled JEREMIAH FALLON HOUSE (L), built in 1850 of redwood timbers hewn from the San Antonio forest east of Oakland. The house was moved here from a previous location when the highway was rerouted.

A giant oak shades the ALVISO ADOBE (L), 3.4 m., built in 1846. The one-story house, with a storehouse in an abutting wing, overlooks vast green alfalfa fields extending to Pleasanton (see below). The adobe is used as a dining room, kitchen, and club room for men employed on the large dairy ranch that operates the property.

The white-plastered AUGUSTIN BERNAL ADOBE (R), 5.8 m. (private), dates from 1850. The roof extending over the long front porch is supported by heavy square posts. The gable windows are later additions. The present ranch is a small part of the vast 48,000-acre Rancho El Valle de San Jose, which included a large part of the Livermore and Sunol Valleys. It was granted in 1839 jointly to Augustin Bernal, his brother Juan Pablo, Antonio Maria Pico, and Antonio Maria Sunol (see below).

At 6.2 m. on State 21 is the junction with an improved road; R. here 0.3 m. to the former PHOEBE APPERSON HEARST RESIDENCE, a white, Spanish-styled, two-story building topped by two towers and roofed with red tile. Here the wife of Senator George Hearst frequently—and lavishly—entertained students from the University of California. Centered in the patio is a marble well-head of Veronese sculpture from which the estate took its name, Hacienda del Pozo de Verona (estate of the Veronese well). Inside the mansion are 40 rooms. The surrounding 500 acres, lying on the low foothills of Pleasanton Ridge and wooded with many fine varieties of conifers, white oaks, and cork elms, were bought by Senator Hearst in 1890 and converted into a blooded horse-breeding farm. For several years after Mrs. Hearst's death a golf course and country club occupied the estate. In 1940 it was converted once more to a stock-breeding farm.

At 6.3 m. on State 21 is the junction with the Pleasanton-Sunol road (see below).

West from Dublin the main side route follows US 50 across the level stretches of the fertile Livermore Valley to SANTA RITA, 14.8 m. (346 alt., 40 pop.), originally part of Rancho Santa Rita issued in 1839 to Jose Dolores Pacheco.

Right from Santa Rita on a paved road is Pleasanton, 2.8 m. (see below).

The ROBERT LIVERMORE MONUMENT (L), 20.2 m., built of native rock in 1935, commemorates the first English-speaking settler in this region. Livermore, who had served in the British navy, entered the merchant marine service only to jump his ship, the Colonel Young, at Monterey Bay in 1822. Quickly learning Spanish, he became a favorite among the Mexicans. After marrying Señorita Josefa Higuera, whose father owned the Rancho Agua Caliente, encompassing the present site of Warm Springs (see below), Livermore came with his wife and José Noriega into this valley in 1835, settled on the 8,800-acre Rancho Las Positas (the little water holes), and planted the first orchard and vineyard in the valley. Livermore died in 1858 and was buried at Mission San Jose de Guadalupe (see below).

At 20.6 m. is the junction with a paved road, on which the route goes R. LIVERMORE, 21.3 m. (487 alt., 2,744 pop.), located partly on what was once Robert Livermore's Rancho Las Positas, is a cattle and agricultural community where "ten-gallon" hats and jingling spurs mingle with more conservative attire. Near Livermore is a "cow country" little changed since frontier days. During the annual Livermore Rodeo in June, residents don "Western" hats, high-heeled boots and chaps, and proceed to take the town apart.

Alfonso Ladd named the town site Laddsville as early as 1850. In following years many settlers drifted into Livermore Valley where they harvested bumper crops of wheat, barley, and oats. But not until the advent of the Central Pacific Railroad in 1869 did the town burgeon into importance. The introduction of the wine industry assured it of a prosperous development. Livermore Valley has been called the Sauterne capital of America. James Concannon, the Wente Brothers, and others, discovering here chalky soils similar to those of the Sauterne areas in southwestern France, sent to France for cuttings in the early 1880's. The yield of grapes, one and one-quarter tons per acre, is small, but the varieties are of the highest quality. Vintages from the imported cuttings have won gold medals in competition with wines from grapes of the parent stock.

Right (south) from Livermore on L Street, which crosses the Arroyo Mocho and becomes a paved county road, 4.2 m. to the UNITED STATES VETERANS' HOSPITAL (*visiting hours: weekdays 11-1, 3-5, 7-8; Sun. and holidays 10:30-1, 3-6*). In the white stucco buildings with red tile roofs, about 300 tubercular veterans are treated.

The main side route continues from Livermore on West First Street to the junction with a paved road, 27.1 m., and L. here across the Arroyo del Valle.

PLEASANTON, 27.3 m. (361 alt., 1,272 pop.), is the center of an area devoted to agriculture, dairying, grape culture and wine-making. The local wineries sponsor an annual festival called "La Fiesta del Vino." The town's name honors General Pleasanton, a cavalry officer who served under John Charles Frémont in the Missouri campaign of the Civil War. Though sedate and quiet today, Pleasanton was once melodramatically "Western," with fire-spitting guns, swinging saloon doors, and spangled dancehall girls. Pleasanton's old-fashioned houses and white wooden church appeared in the motion picture *Rebecca of Sunnybrook Farm,* which, with Mary Pickford in the title role, was filmed here in 1917-18.

Laid out in the early seventies, the PLEASANTON RACETRACK became famous throughout the country for its harness races and trotting exhibitions. The track west of town is still in use as a trial ground for promising horses; the stables and adjacent grounds are also used as a resting place for racing stock from Tanforan, Santa Anita, and other tracks.

The ROSE HOTEL, 540 Main St., a shabby three-story building built in 1874, formerly was much patronized by owners of thoroughbreds and racetrack followers.

Founded in 1902, the GARRATTI WINERY (*open to visitors*), 124 St. John St., makes both dry and sweet wines and brandy. It has two oaken casks whose heads are examples of fine wood carving.

The JUAN P. BERNAL ADOBE, on the north bank of Arroyo del Valle, was built in 1852. A soldier of the San Francisco and San Jose presidios, Bernal here became a large landowner. His daughter married an Austrian, John W. Kottinger, first storekeeper in Pleasanton, who erected an adobe on the opposite bank of the arroyo.

South of Pleasanton, the valley narrows into the Arroyo de la Laguna. At 29.2 m. is the junction with State 21 (*see above*), on which the route continues through the arroyo to the junction with Niles Canyon Road, 31.5 m.

Straight ahead through a grilled iron gate 0.5 m. to the SUNOL WATER TEMPLE and a shaded picnic ground (*open 7-7*). The Water Temple (Willis Polk, architect), inspired by the ancient Temple of Vesta at Tivoli, consists of a circular arcade of ten Corinthian columns supporting a dome. Immediately below the dome is a deep circular enclosure through which flows a torrent of water from the Sierra Nevada, which having been filtered here, flows on to San Francisco via Crystal Springs Lake (*see PENINSULA TOUR*).

The main side route goes R. on Niles Canyon Road across the Arroyo de la Laguna to SUNOL, 33.1 m. (250 alt., 600 pop.), an agricultural center at the northern end of Sunol Valley, which is drained by Alameda Creek. The town was named after Antonio Sunol, who prior to settling here served in the French navy. Sunol and others were granted the Rancho El Valle de San Jose in 1839. The region's chief products are apricots, tomatoes, walnuts, grapes, grain, and hay.

West of Sunol, Alameda Creek winds through steep, narrow Niles Canyon. The creek is crossed and recrossed as the road winds and twists into the canyon, with it buckeyes and wide-spreading sycamores. In the shade are many spots for picnicking, camping, and swimming.

A stone aqueduct, paralleling the road south from 38 *m.*, once carried water to Vallejo's Mill, whose ruins still stand in Niles (*see below*).

NILES, 39.4 *m.* (77 alt., 1,517 pop.), is the center of an intensive flower-fruit- and vegetable-growing area. The town stands on part of what was Rancho Arroyo de la Alameda, 17,705 acres granted in 1842 to Jose de Jesus Vallejo, an older brother of General Mariano Vallejo. Its name honors Judge Addison C. Niles, who in 1871 was elected to the California Supreme Court. In the "nickelodeon" era, when movies were in their silent but lusty infancy, the now defunct Essanay Studios, in which Charles Chaplin, Ben Turpin, and Wallace Beery began their movie careers, were located here.

The side route goes L. from Niles on a four-lane highway (formerly US 101 E) to the junction with a paved road, 39.7 *m.*, where it turns R.

At 42 *m.* is the junction with State 17 in Centerville (*see below*).

Named to honor Juan B. Alvarado, Mexican governor (1836-42), ALVARADO, 18.8 *m.* (11 alt., 1,800 pop.), is a partly industrialized town with a large Portuguese population. It stands on part of former Rancho Potrero de los Cerritos (pasture of the little hills), granted to Agustin Alviso and Tomas Pacheco in 1844. At the height of the Gold Rush the ranch was purchased by two Americans who planted it to potatoes and received $100,000 for their second crop. So great was a minor "gold" rush to the potential potato diggin's of Alvarado that the next year's crop glutted the market and no one realized a profit.

In the early 1850's three rival towns were laid out here: Union City, New Haven, and finally Alvarado. On March 15, 1853, Henry C. Smith, founder of New Haven, introduced into the State legislature a bill to create Alameda County, "designating New Haven as the county seat and Alvarado as seat of justice." The new county officials met in the upper story of Smith's store in New Haven, but their first minutes are dated "Alvarado, April 11, 1853," indicating that the name Alvarado had been accepted for the entire community as well as the county seat.

Center of a large acreage devoted to sugar beets, the HOLLY SUGAR COMPANY (*open to visitors during operation, approximately Aug. 15 to Christmas*) is a modern, many-windowed factory with a tall white stack.

At 22 *m.* is the junction with a hard-surfaced road.

Right on this road to the DUMBARTON TOLL BRIDGE, 6.9 *m.* (*toll, 40¢ per car, 5¢ each person*). At 10.7 *m.* is the junction with US 101 Bypass (*see Peninsula Tour*).

Commercial center for farmers and orchardists, CENTERVILLE, 23.6 *m.* (50 alt., 1,700 pop.), stretches along the highway, its two rows of glaring modern store fronts broken occasionally by an old-fashioned frame structure. Originally known as Hardscrabble, the town in the early 1850's consisted of a small store on the old Mission Road to San Jose. One of the first schools in the State was organized here in 1852. Centerville grew slowly and uneventfully until the earthquake of 1906

started a fire which all but destroyed the village. Today the town subsists on surrounding farms, a metal-products company, and a cannery.

Right from Centerville on a paved road is NEWARK, 3 *m.* (21 alt., 1,535
pop.), another small industrial town. First known as Mayhew's Landing,
it was founded about 1875 by James G. Fair, one of the Nevada silver millionaires, and A. E. Davis, who later renamed it for his birthplace in New Jersey.
A stove-manufacturing company, established in 1882 and now employing
500 men, is Newark's outstanding industry. In the vicinity are two Nationally
known salt companies which extract salt from Bay water (*see above*) by solar
evaporation. A mile west of the business district is a chemical plant producing ethylene dibromide and other compounds. Shooting preserves located
along the Bay shore accommodate duck hunters.
The NEWARK SUB-STATION OF THE PACIFIC GAS AND ELEC-
TRIC COMPANY is the "largest pool of power in the world." More than a
half-million horsepower of electrical energy flows into it from various power
plants throughout the State, to be stepped down for distribution.
At 7 *m.* is the Dumbarton Bridge (*see above*).

In the midst of open fields and orchards is tree-shaded little IRV-
INGTON, 26.8 *m.* (72 alt., 1,000 pop.). Wooden "arcades," extending from square fronts of old frontier-type general stores, shade the
sidewalk. First known as Washington Corners, this was an important
pioneer trading post. It took the name of Irvington in 1884.

Left from Irvington on a paved road 1.2 *m.* to a cement-walled INDIAN
CEMETERY, where a plain granite monument explains that "here sleep 4,000
of the Olhone Tribe, who helped the padres build this Mission San Jose de
Guadalupe" (*see below*). MISSION PEAK (2,508 alt.), a landmark in the
mission days, rises directly ahead.
The RIEHR WINERY (R), 1.4 *m.,* occupies the site of the former summer
home and experimental grounds of Professor E. W. Hilgard (*see BERKELEY:
UNIVERSITY OF CALIFORNIA*). One of the presses in use dates from
1868. Wines produced here were shipped around Cape Horn in sailing vessels.
The rocking motion of ships was said to enhance their quality.
Oldest settlement in Alameda County, MISSION SAN JOSE, 2.1 *m.* (300
alt., 531 pop.), formerly known as Mission Town, was once the scene of
numerous fiestas. When Mexican *rancheros* assembled here with hundreds of
their retainers for sports and amusements, the town's single thoroughfare was
temporarily enclosed and sufficient seats for the population of the entire
countryside were erected. The festivities included feats of horsemanship,
bull and bear fights, barbecues, and gay dances.
Languishing after the decline of the mission era, the village again awoke
after discovery of gold. Miners on their way to the gold fields, fur traders,
trappers and desperadoes stopped here. The dining room of the Red Hotel
served as a dance hall. The wife of the hotel manager asserted her individuality by adorning herself with five-dollar gold pieces in place of buttons.
As late as 1859 the last bull fight was staged.
Fourteenth of the 21 California missions, MISSION SAN JOSE DE
GUADALUPE (*adm.* 25¢), founded by Padre Fermin Francisco Lasuen on
Trinity Sunday, 1797, originally was known as La Mision del Gloriosisimo
Patriarca Señor San Jose (The Mission of the Most Glorious Patriarch, St.
Joseph). According to legend, disagreement about the selection of a site among
the members of an exploration party was settled by prayer and the law of
gravitation. A huge stone, after being blessed, was rolled down a steep
hillside. Where it came to rest the mission was built.
The mission founders knew privation, struggle, and opposition. To Christianize the Indians, who sometimes fought against preemption of their land,
it was sometimes necessary to use the sword and the whip. The natives often

rebelled against the hard, monotonous work forced upon them. During church services guards equipped with long goads moved among the congregation, prodding natives who assumed other than a kneeling position. For outstanding work, however, the Indians were rewarded with beads and gaudy trinkets. It is recorded that friction developed even between the *padres* and the military when soldiers refused to serve as *vaqueros* or to do other non-military work.

Despite all these obstacles the mission grew to become one of the most prosperous of the mission establishment, being fourth in wealth and second in the number of converts.

Under the guidance of capable padres many converts were taught trades and crafts. Indeed, Padre Duran, beloved mission prefect, developed a stringed orchestra of more than 20 musicians who were in constant demand at social functions. Padre Duran also made good wines and better brandies. The old leather bound "guest book" of the mission, now among the chief treasures of St. Mary's of San Francisco, contains the signatures of men of science, travelers from many countries, as well as trappers, woodsmen, and outlaws who were early mission visitors.

After secularization, Mission San Jose fell into such a state of deterioration that in 1846 it was sold for only a fraction of its former value. After California entered the Union the Land Commission restored the property to the Church. It is now under the custody of the Sisters of St. Dominic. The first mission building, constructed of heavy timber and covered with a grass roof, later was replaced by a more elaborate structure of adobe which was destroyed by earthquake in 1868. All that remains of the original cluster of buildings is a large common room, whose thick walls are weatherworn and cracked. The dark interior is festooned with cobwebs. The present place of worship, built of wood, stands on the foundation of one of the original structures. In 1884 a fire destroyed several nearby buildings; water was scarce, but the chapel was saved by barrels of wine which vintners from the surrounding countryside had stored in an old mission cellar. Among old relics at Mission San Jose are some vestments worn by mission founders, candlesticks, a baptismal font surmounted by a wrought-iron cross, and two old mission bells cast in 1815 and 1826.

On the hillside behind the mission building is the QUEEN OF THE HOLY ROSARY COLLEGE, a training school for sisters of the Dominican order. In the modern concrete building about a hundred nuns prepare for teaching. The old red-brick building adjoining is the convent, established in 1890. The school's site was part of the mission property. Many of the old olive trees along the lane leading to the convent and cemetery were planted by the *padres.*

At 4.5 *m.* on State 21 is the junction with a dirt road; L. here 0.6 *m.* to the SANTA INEZ LODGE (*private*), now the summer home of the Sisters of the Holy Names, a large two-and-a-half-story building with mansard roof which was formerly a resort hotel, near six warm springs, flowing at the rate of 60,000 gallons per day. First white man to see the springs, Juan Bautista de Anza, named them Agua Caliente in 1776. Fulgencia Higuera in 1836 obtained a land grant to this property, which he named Rancho del Agua Caliente. He sold the rancho in 1850 to Clement Columbet, who made it a fashionable spa. After the 1868 earthquake partially destroyed his hotel, A. A. Cohen and William Ralston bought and remodeled it. In 1870 they sold out to Leland Stanford, who set out a fine vineyard and in 1887 built a red-brick winery, still standing west of the hotel. The property passed in 1920 into the hands of Frank Kelly, who tore down some of the old buildings, built new ones, and laid out gardens. Stanford's vineyard was dug up and the winery converted into stables for Kelly's race horses. In 1927 Kelly sold the ranch to the Sisters of the Holy Names.

At 4.8 *m.* on State 21 is a junction with a paved road: L. on this road, which becomes a dirt road, 1.1 *m.* to the ABELARDO HIGUERA ADOBE, once the home of the brother of the grantee of Rancho del Agua Caliente (*see above*). Its crumbling walls have been replaced on two sides with wood. It is now used as a storehouse.

At 5.4 *m.* is the junction with State 17 at Warm Springs (*see below*).

WARM SPRINGS, 30.4 *m.* (65 alt., 59 pop.), an agricultural hamlet, received its name and its past fame from the springs of the nearby SANTA INEZ LODGE (*see above*).

At 32.9 *m.* is the junction with unpaved Jacklin Road.

Left on Jacklin Road 1 *m.* to the HIGUERA ADOBE HOUSES, residence of Jose Higuera, grantee of Rancho les Tularcitos. The two-and-one-half-foot walls of the newer adobe, built about 1831, are protected by a two-story wooden superstructure. This adobe is now used as a home for transient pea-pickers in season. Crumbling ruins are all that remain of the older adobe, built about 1822, which stands a few yards to the right.

MILPITAS (little maize fields), 34.5 *m.* (13 alt., 450 pop.), once part of a vast land grant, is now an agricultural settlement. First called Penitencia, for the creek that runs through it, it was renamed because of the usual mispronunciation by Yankees, for Nicolas Berryessa's Rancho Milpitas. Milpitas is somewhat of a political barometer: "As goes Milpitas so goes the State." The reports of voting here many times have indicated State-wide election results before complete returns were in.

Left from Milpitas on paved Calaveras Road 2 *m.* to the junction with Piedmont Road, where stands (R) the neat, white ALVISO ADOBE (*private*), built here on Arroyo de los Coches about 1841 by Jose Maria Alviso, who succeeded Berryessa as owner of Rancho Milpitas. The second story, of frame, was built some time later.

Calaveras Road continues east and then north through the rugged mountains to CALAVERAS RESERVOIR (R), 12 *m.*, an auxiliary source of water for San Francisco. As far back as 1875 there were plans for municipal development of this site, but the Spring Valley Water Company, which was already supplying the city, purchased these lands and water rights also. After the company was purchased by the city, Calaveras Valley was converted into a 32,000,000,000-gallon reservoir in 1925 when an earth and rock fill dam was completed at the lower end of the valley. A dam on Alameda Creek, about three miles east of the reservoir, diverts water to Calaveras by way of a 9,709-foot tunnel. From the reservoir a 44-inch pipe line carries water to the Hetch Hetchy aqueduct that empties into Crystal Springs Lake by gravity (*see Peninsula Tour*).

At 20 *m.* is the junction with State 21 at Scott Corners (*see East Bay Tour 2*).

On the bluff above the Coyote River, crossed by State 17 at 38.3 *m.*, on the grounds of the Clark Nursery, is the LARGEST EUCALYPTUS IN CALIFORNIA, planted in 1868. Its trunk is nine feet in diameter.

SAN JOSE, 41.7 *m.* (100 alt., 57,651 pop.) (*see San Jose*).

North Bay Tour

The North Bay area is a land of contrasts. Gray fog swirls over its high mountain tops and down steep slopes forested with giant redwoods; highways wind through its flatlands past sleepy towns that doze in the sun; quiet creeks drain its valleys and clear streams rush down its dark canyons to Bay and ocean. Paved highways have replaced dusty roads; tiny vineyards of early winemakers have expanded to cover whole slopes and wide flatlands; orchards and gardens and modern chicken hatcheries spread over the valley floors. The Russian River, the sandy beaches and sheltered coves are popular vacation spots, and the mountain slopes are terraced in rows of modern homes inhabited by men and women who work in San Francisco. The rugged Pacific shore and the Bay's indentations are favored by fishermen, and yachtsmen sail their craft around the headlands and between the islands.

San Francisco—Sausalito—San Rafael—Vallejo—Benicia; 52.7 m. US 101, State 37, County roads.

Paved roadbed throughout.
Pacific Greyhound interurban busses serve Marin County.

This route follows US 101 across the Golden Gate and cuts north through low hills bordering San Francisco and Richardson Bays. It swings east on State 37, following the contour of San Pablo Bay to the mouth of Suisun Bay, where inland waters of the Sacramento and San Joaquin Rivers pour through Carquinez Strait. Its course is through vacation communities, yachting centers, little towns overlooking the Bay, houseboat colonies, wide dairy acres, and flat marshlands.

North from Van Ness Ave. and Fulton St. in SAN FRANCISCO, 0 m., on Van Ness Ave. to Lombard St.; L. on Lombard; R. on Richardson Ave. to the main approach of Golden Gate Bridge.

The bridge approach rises gradually on concrete piers across the northern edge of the Presidio. At 4.7 m. is the toll plaza (*automobiles, 50¢; pedestrians, 10¢*) of GOLDEN GATE BRIDGE. For 1.2 miles the route follows the longest and highest single-span suspension bridge in the world, an integral link in the great highway between Canada and Mexico.

435

At 6.6 *m.* is the junction with a paved road.

Right on this road through a part of FORT BAKER UNITED STATES MILITARY RESERVATION, 0.5 *m.* SAUSALITO, 2.4 *m.* (8-600 alt., 3,506 pop.), faces San Francisco from the steep flanks of the Marin hills. Its one business street is built on a narrow shelf beside the Bay, where pleasure craft, fishing boats, and Coast Guard cutters lie at anchor. All have one thing in common—a view of the Bay.

The first white man to come here was Spanish navigator Captain Juan Manuel de Ayala, who named the cove Ensenada del Carmelito (Bay of Little Mount Carmel). The Spaniards who followed named the spot Saucelito (from *salcedo*—willow) for its many small willow thickets.

The cabin of the young Irishman, John Read, who settled here in 1826, was the first permanent home of a white man in Marin County. When Read died from the excessive bleeding practised by the physicians of the day, his widow married the bandit, "Three-fingered Jack" Garcia, friend of Joaquin Murrieta.

In 1838 an Englishman, Captain William Antonio Richardson, was granted the 19,000-acre Rancho Saucelito. He was a harbor pilot, operated a trans-bay ferry, raised cattle, traded with Yankee ships, and sold water from Sausalito's springs to Yerba Buena.

Sausalito once was known as a town where gambling dens and saloons rid the unwary of his money quickly and efficiently; and its elections were stormy battles. But since 1907 it has been a haven of graceful living. Fishing and the building of small craft are its only important industries.

The DANIEL O'CONNELL MONUMENT, Bulkley and Harrison Aves., a granite bench shaded by pepper trees, is a memorial to the Irish poet and political refugee.

On the slope below the monument the thick, bastion-like WALLS OF SEA POINT, a former home of William Randolph Hearst, face the Bay above Bridgeway Blvd. Hearst razed the palatial home after a quarrel with local residents.

Beside Bridgeway Blvd. at Napa St. the hulks of once-majestic square-riggers, brigantines, and schooners forced out of business by steam slowly decay on the mud bottom. The brigantine *Galilee*, demasted and nosing the shore, is the home of an artist. It was built at the Turner Shipyard at Benicia (*see below*), whose museum cherishes pictures of the trim craft with rakish masts and a smooth white hull. Beside it the stark hull of the S. S. *Phoenix* rests on pilings.

At 4.6 *m.* is the junction with US 101 (*see below*).

On US 101 at 7.1 *m.* is the junction with a private road.

Left on this road 6 *m.* to FORT BARRY UNITED STATES MILITARY RESERVATION, whose fortresses overlook San Francisco Bay. Once part of Fort Baker Reserve, the 893-acre area was set aside in 1904 and named in honor of Civil War veteran General William F. Barry.

Marking the northern entrance to the Golden Gate is POINT BONITA, 7 *m.* Atop the white tower of POINT BONITA LIGHTHOUSE (built in 1855 and reconstructed in 1877), 124 feet above the water, is a 40,000-candlepower light visible for 17 miles. A cannon brought here in 1850 thundered the first fog warnings in the vicinity.

US 101 continues northward into the hills above Sausalito, passes through deep cuts and a long tunnel, and drops down to RICHARD-SON BAY, named for William A. Richardson.

At 10.2 *m.* is the junction with State 1.

Right on State 1, across the Marin Peninsula hills and down Green Gulch to the junction with a gravel road, 6 m.; L. here 0.7 m. across an arm of Big Lagoon to MUIR BEACH (*swimming, fishing*).
State 1 skirts the ocean shore northward to STINSON BEACH, 12.5 m. (*boats, tackle and bait for surf fishing*), a small resort town at the southern end of Bolinas Lagoon.
At 16.8 m. is the junction with a paved road, on which the route turns L. along the western edge of BOLINAS LAGOON, named for Francisco Bolanos, pilot of the Sebastian Vizcaino expedition of 1603.
A few rotting piles at 17.2 m. mark the site of the BOLINAS LIGHTER WHARF (L), where oxen in the 1850's hauled lumber from inland mills in crude wagons whose wheels were solid sections of redwood logs.
At 18.9 m. is the junction with a paved road; R. here 2.6 m. to the RCA STATION (*private*), twin to one on Point Reyes, whose 46 directional antennas transmit short-waves across the Pacific.
At 19.3 m. on the main side road is BOLINAS (10 alt., 125 pop.), a summer resort, with good swimming and fishing.

US 101 continues north over a half-mile-long redwood bridge across the upper reaches of Richardson Bay and on through rolling foothill country bright with wild flowers in spring.
At 12.1 m. is the junction with a paved road.

1. Right on this road 0.7 m. to the JOHN READ RANCH (*private*), where the orchard planted a century ago by Read on his Rancho Corte Madera del Presidio (cut timber for the presidio) still thrives. This was headquarters of the rancho granted Read in 1834, and here he lived with his young Spanish wife, daughter of Yerba Buena's Presidio *comandante,* Jose Antonio Sanchez.
At 3.2 m. is the junction with a paved road; R. here across a causeway to BELVEDERE, 4.3 m. (350 alt., 446 pop.), at the southern end of Belvedere Island in Richardson Bay. A quiet suburban town with fine homes and terraced gardens, it looks out from its steep slopes toward Sausalito and Angel Island.
Belvedere's SAN FRANCISCO YACHT CLUB, on Beach Rd., was organized in 1869, the first yacht club in California.
L. from Belvedere across another causeway to TIBURON, 4.7 m. (10 alt., 327 pop.), on Point Tiburon, southwestern tip of Tiburon Peninsula. Along the shore cluster houseboat colonies. Many homes at the water's edge boast small private piers for swimming and boating. To the southeast, across Racoon Strait, lies the green bulk of Angel Island.
East from Tiburon, then northwest around Tiburon Peninsula to CALIFORNIA CITY, 7.4 m., training base for the CALIFORNIA NAUTICAL SCHOOL (*visitors Sat. and Sun. 1-5*), established in 1929 to train young men for service as officers in the merchant marine. When the training ship *California State* docks after an extended cruise, the 125 cadets live aboard the modern ship and study ashore. The ship is kept in repair by the Navy, by which it is owned; all other expenses are defrayed by the State.
PARADISE COVE, 8.6 m., a sheltered picnicking and camping place, is frequented by the owners of small sailing craft.
At 13.2 m. is the junction with US 101 (*see below*).
2. Left on this road is MILL VALLEY, 2.1 m. (57 alt., 4,799 pop.), a residential town built in the narrow canyons and on the steep wooded slopes along two small streams. Originally part of Rancho Corte Madera del Presidio (*see below*), the town slumbered for two generations, but after the building of an electric railroad from Sausalito it became the home of business men and of artists, musicians, and writers.
OLD MILL PARK, on Throckmorton Ave., is the site of the region's

first sawmill, built by John Read about 1834. Read, an Irish sailor, who had acquired Rancho Corte Madera del Presidio, whipsawed timber here for his house in Sausalito and afterwards supplied lumber for San Francisco. Down the small stream draining Mount Tamalpais' southern slopes he floated the logs to the twin wheels of his water mill, whose frame still stands. Read's adobe, one-half mile northeast, was occupied after his death by the desperado, Bernardino "Three-fingered Jack" Garcia, who married Read's widow.

In Mill Valley the side route turns L. from Throckmorton Avenue on Old Mill Dr.; L. on Cascade Dr.; R. on Molino Ave.; sharply R. on Birch St.; R. on Edgewood Ave.; L. on Sequoia Valley Rd. up a ridge to a junction at the summit with Panoramic Highway, 4.6 m.

Left on Sequoia Valley Road 1.6 m. to MUIR WOODS NATIONAL MONUMENT (picnicking, hiking, riding; no fires permitted), a 424-acre park of virgin redwoods in a mountain ravine. The taller trees are from 200 to 250 feet in height, and from 12 to 17 feet in diameter. The woods, deeply scarred by fire 175 years ago, are noted for their abnormal growths of burls, albino shoots, natural grafts and strange formations. REDWOOD CREEK, where salmon and steelhead spawn, flows through the park at the base of such redwood giants as the Gifford Pinchot Redwood Cathedral Grove, Bridge Tree, William Kent Fir, and Albino Redwood. With the redwoods are dense growths of Douglas fir, oak, and laurel, with azaleas, wild huckleberry, and other plants.

Senator William Kent bought this grove for $45,000 and deeded it to the Nation in 1908 as a monument to John Muir, the naturalist who so loved the California mountains. In the condemnation proceedings necessary to acquire the land, Theodore Roosevelt and Gifford Pinchot gave valuable aid.

The main route follows Panoramic Highway from its junction with Sequoia Valley Road along the northern edge of 960-acre MOUNT TAMALPAIS STATE PARK (camp sites, hiking trails). A wooden trestle, 6.4 m., spans the roadbed of the abandoned Mill Valley and Mount Tamalpais Scenic Railway, laid out with a hand level by the promoters. Built at a cost of $147,000 in 1896, the eight-mile track, known as the "Crookedest Railroad in the World," had 281 curves. At one difficult place a "double bow-knot" paralleled itself five times within 2,000 feet, thereby achieving a rise of 100 feet. Oil-burning logging engines drew trains to the summit.

At 9.4 m. is the junction with a paved road; R. here through Panorama Toll Gate (fee 50¢), which is aptly named, for as the road climbs higher, it affords even wider views of Bay, ocean and mountains.

At Rock Springs, 11.1 m., is the junction with Ridgecrest Boulevard on which the side route turns R. to the MOUNTAIN THEATER (R), 11.3 m. (admission to performances, 50¢), a natural amphitheater on the flank of Mount Tamalpais from which the audience can look beyond the stage across 70 miles of Bay, plain, and mountain. On stone seats rising in circular tiers, from three to seven thousand people gather annually on the third Sunday in May to watch a dramatic production.

Ridgecrest Boulevard curves uphill to MOUNT TAMALPAIS TAVERN, 14.0 m. (parking lot, hotel, restaurant, free camping and picnicking grounds), within a few hundred yards of the summit of MOUNT TAMALPAIS. There are three crests in the Tamalpais Range, West Peak (2,601 alt.), Middle Peak (2,570 alt.), and East Peak (2,586 alt.). From the summit a third of northern California is visible on clear days. The whole of San Francisco Bay spreads out below, spanned by its two bridges, bordered by cities and orchard lands. A white cluster of buildings is San Jose at the southern end. Beyond the Mount Hamilton and Mount Diablo ranges, the flat San Joaquin Valley stretches east to the blue Sierras. Westward, out to sea, the Farallon Islands seem near and ships appear on the horizon. To the north are the multiple Coast Ranges dividing inland valleys.

The first man to climb the peak was Jacob Leese, Marin County pioneer, who made the ascent to refute the Lacatuit Indian legend that evil spirits haunted the mountain. On the summit, Leese set up a cross of tree limbs. Marin, the Indian chief, to prove his valor, climbed up and hung his blanket from the cross, thereby gaining much prestige with his tribe.

On US 101 at 13.8 m. is the junction with a paved road.

Left on this road is CORTE MADERA (Sp., wood-cutting place), 0.5 m. (56 alt., 1,094 pop.), a snug community of homes with outlying model dairy farms. Its name came from logging operations in surrounding hills where Luis Antonio Arguello cut timbers to repair and enlarge San Francisco's Presidio buildings. Corte Madera's BALTIMORE PARK GROVE, on Madrone Avenue, is a small grove of redwoods extending up a narrow canyon. The hilly suburban town of LARKSPUR, 1.6 m. (18 alt., 1,549 pop.), looks out over green marshes and meadows from the base of the hills. Beside the highway (R) is the LARKSPUR BOWL (open Sat., Apr.-Sept.; adm. 50¢), a huge, open-air dance floor accommodating 2,000. Through the platform redwoods thrust their trunks upward, twined with lanterns and electric lights. The pavilion is managed by the Larkspur volunteer fire department, which thus pays for itself without drawing on the town's treasury.

One of the chain of quiet residential towns in Ross Valley is KENTFIELD, 3.1 m. (100 alt., 100 pop.), settled early by men of wealth. In Mexican days the spot where the highway now crosses Corte Madera Creek was known as the Embarcadero and later as Ross Landing for James Ross, who owned the surrounding Rancho Punta de Quentin (Point Quentin). The settlement was next called Tamalpais and finally Kentfield, for Senator William Kent's father, Albert Emmet Kent, who had come here in search of health.

ROSS, 3.6 m. (26 alt., 1,701 pop.), once known as Sunnyside, is a community of homes, many with extensive grounds set in back of tall trees and hedges. It was once part of the vast and much-sought Rancho Punta de Quentin, purchased from Benjamin R. Buckelew by James Ross in 1859. The latter, a Scot, who brought a wife from Tasmania, had become a successful wine merchant in San Francisco. When Ross moved into Buckelew's home, leg-irons used on the convicts who built the house were found in the basement.

Founded in 1875, SAN ANSELMO, 4.6 m. (52 alt., 5,766 pop.), is a town of hillside houses and gardens along winding shaded streets. According to a local tale, it was started by a quarrel between two Irish families who lived at Ross Landing (*see above*). One day, while their husbands were at work on the North Pacific Coast Railroad, the two wives quarreled more seriously than usual; one threw the other into a well and sat on the lid. When rescued by her raging husband, the wife in the well was found clinging to the bucket rope, uninjured and eager for the free-for-all that followed. The railroad company grew alarmed at the ensuing feud for fear it would lose a prized foreman. Hence, one day a section crew heaved one family's shack onto a handcar and pushed it two miles up the tracks. It was unloaded, and there was San Anselmo.

The route goes L. from San Anselmo around the base of RED HILL, where sunrise services are held on Easter.

From the edges of FAIRFAX, 6.6 m. (108 alt., 2,175 pop.), rise brush-covered mountains that have the look of velvet from a distance. The 6,000-acre Rancho Canada de Herrera (valley of the blacksmith's wife), once embracing its site, was granted in 1839 to Pedro V. Sais, a soldier and civil officer in San Francisco. When in 1849 a visitor from Virginia, Dr. A. W. Taliaferro, expressed a wish to buy 40 acres, Sais, with characteristic early California generosity, gave him the land, saying that it was worth that to have a good neighbor. To the large house which Dr. Taliaferro built, came as a visitor in 1856 a direct descendant of the English baron famous in Virginia history, Charles "Lord" Fairfax. Remaining as a permanent guest, he inherited the estate when the doctor died without heirs. After Fairfax's death, the home was for years the restaurant of Madame Adele Pastori,

Italian opera singer, who served meals in the garden under the trees. The property is now occupied by the Marin School for Boys.

Northwest from Fairfax, the route curves over Whites Hill and descends through rolling oak-covered foothill country into San Geronimo Valley.

SAN GERONIMO, 12.1 *m.* (286 alt., 30 pop.), was the home of Lieutenant Warren Revere, grandson of Paul Revere. While hunting elk, Revere, who had been sent by the Government to conduct a survey of timber, found this attractive valley. Buying the two-league Rancho San Geronimo, he settled down to lead the life of a Spanish *ranchero.* The once powerful Nicasio Indians caused him some trouble by running off his horses for food. When he captured an Indian, he forced him to make adobe bricks in payment for the lost horses.

Right from San Geronimo on a paved road over low hills 3.8 *m.* to a junction with a county road; (1) R. here 2 *m.* up Lucas Valley to the LUCAS VALLEY REDWOODS (*picnicking, camping*), named for John Lucas, a nephew of Timoteo Murphy (*see below*), from whom he inherited Rancho Santa Margarita. At 10.6 *m.* is the junction with US 101 (*see below*). (2) Left here is NICASIO, 4.5 *m.* (177 alt., 200 pop.), a tree-shaded hamlet with an old wooden church and school house and a few dwellings in need of paint, dating from the 1850's and 1860's. After disease and drink had decreased the local tribe of Nicasio Indians, Chief Jose Calistro bought 30 acres two miles east of Nicasio and settled his people upon it. The large stand of prime redwood in the region began to fall in 1862 when James Ross built the first mill one and one-half miles east of town. At 13.3 *m.* is the junction with State 1 (*see below*).

The main side route continues west from San Geronimo to the summer resort center of LAGUNITAS, 14.1 *m.* (219 alt., 512 pop.), and plunges into cool Lagunitas Creek canyon between high redwoods and firs, past mountain cabins perched on hillsides and flats along the stream. Fishing is forbidden to protect the salmon that spawn in the shallow, gravelly reaches.

Once known as Taylorville, CAMP TAYLOR (*camping*), 17 *m.* (138 alt.), in a grove of virgin redwoods on a flat next to the stream, is the site where in 1856 Samuel Penfield Taylor built the first paper mill on the Pacific Çoast and employed Chinese to collect rags for raw material. Among old-timers, Lagunitas Creek, whose pure water was particularly adapted to paper making, is still known as Paper Mill Creek.

TOCALOMA, 20.8 *m.* (66 alt., 25 pop.), is a hamlet in a secluded glen on the creek banks.

OLEMA, 22.7 *m.* (68 alt., 150 pop.), with its white-steepled church and tree-shaded houses, has the look of a New England village. Alemaloke was the name of a former Indian village near here. The place was headquarters in 1837 of the great Rancho Tomales y Bolinas. In the 1860's a 12-passenger stage rumbled between here and San Rafael, an old wagon cradled on thick leather straps and covered with tarpaulin. The earthquake of 1906 stirred the old town considerably. According to report, a cow on the nearby Shafter ranch fell head first into a yawning chasm which closed together, trapping the unfortunate animal with rump and tail still visible above ground. When the milkers at Skinner's dairy rushed out of the barn (according to Oscar Lewis and Carroll Hall in *Bonanza Inn*), they saw that "the cypress trees and the rose garden had moved away from the front of the house and now stood in front of the barn. The clump of raspberry bushes had slid down from the north and occupied the space vacated by the roses. The eucalyptus trees had marched to a position opposite the barn and in the process one had shifted from the foot of the line to the head. The piles of manure before the barn had each moved some sixteen feet south of the window to which it belonged."

At Olema is the junction with State 1, which the route follows R. up Olema Creek to the junction with a paved road, 24.4 *m.*, where it turns L.; R. here on State 1 is POINT REYES STATION, 0.3 *m.* (31 alt., 143 pop.), center of a dairy region, surrounded by rolling pastures, which ships butter to San Francisco. State 1 continues north along the eastern shore of TOMALES BAY, a narrow, finger-like inlet first sighted in 1775 by Lieutenant Juan Francisco de Bodega y Cuadra, who believed he had found a passage connecting with San Pablo Bay. Looping inland, State 1 passes through the sleepy farming communities of TOMALES, 18.2 m. (75 alt., 450 pop.), VALLEY FORD, 25 m. (45 alt., 200 pop.), and BODEGA, 31.1 m. (40 alt., 100 pop.). Right from Bodega 1 m. to the SITE OF KUSKOF SETTLEMENT, marked by a flagpole, where Russian colonists raised cattle and grain and converted the Indians to Christianity 130 years ago and (adjoining) the ruins of CAPTAIN STEPHEN SMITH'S ADOBE MANSION, built in 1843, headquarters of the owner of 30,000-acre Rancho Bodega. West of Bodega, State 1 returns to the coast at shallow, marsh-edged BODEGA BAY, named for its discoverer (1775). It skirts the coast northward through thinly settled country, treeless except for occasional clumps of Douglas fir and Bishop pine. At 47.2 m., on the north side of a bridge across the Russian River, is the junction with State 12 (see below).

West from its northern junction with State 1 the main side route goes L. to INVERNESS, 28.2 m. (10 alt., 200 pop.), a summer resort and boating center on Tomales Bay at the foot of wooded hills. The town took its name from the birth place of James Black, a Scottish sailor who arrived in California in 1832 and later took up cattle ranching on a part of Rancho Nicasio facing the east side of Tomales Bay.

The road curves west and south from Inverness over Inverness Ridge.

At 34.2 m. is the RCA RADIO STATION (R), where short-wave antennas, spread over 1,500 acres, catch transpacific signals.

The road continues south along a rocky, windy promontory where many ships have been wrecked.

At 39.9 m. is the junction with a dirt road; R. here 0.7 m. to the UNITED STATES RADIO COMPASS STATION, from which ships at sea take bearings to fix their positions.

At 42.9 m. on the main side road is the junction with a dirt road; L. here 1.3 m. to the UNITED STATES COAST GUARD LIFE-SAVING STATION above the white cliffs facing DRAKE'S BAY. In this sheltered cove Sir Francis Drake beached the Golden Hinde on June 17, 1579 (Julian Calendar) and claimed the region for Queen Elizabeth. He remained for several weeks, revictualing and repairing his ship. In the garden of the life-saving station is a marker commemorating his landing. On the cliffs overlooking the cove stands a white wooden cross, erected by Bishop William Ford Nichols, commemorating the first use of the English language and of the Book of Common Prayer on the California coast. An annual pilgrimage and service on or about St. John Baptist's Day, June 24, is held here.

This coast is the locale of Bret Harte's "The Legend of Devil's Point," according to which Drake chose "this spot to conceal quantities of ill-gotten booty taken from neutral bottoms, and had protected his hiding place by the orthodox means of hellish incantation and diabolical agencies. On moonlight nights a shadowy ship was sometimes seen when fogs encompassed sea and shore . . . the creaking of a windlass, or the monotonous chant of sailors, came faint and far, and full of magic suggestions." Whatever factual basis supports the legend, "a more weird and desolate-looking spot could not have been selected for [its] theatre. High hills . . . enfiladed with dark cañadas, cast their gaunt shadows on the tide . . . sea fog [comes] with soft step in noiseless marches down the hillside, tenderly soothing the wind-buffetted face of the cliff until sea and sky [are] hid together."

At Laguna Ranch, on the east side of Drake's Bay, a chauffeur in 1933 discovered a plate of solid brass which he subsequently discarded near Point San Quentin. Another motorist, halted by a flat tire, rediscovered the plate and offered it to the University of California for inspection. Revealed beneath the blackened surface was this inscription:

"BEE IT KNOWNE VNTO ALL MEN BY THESE PRESENTS
IVNE 17 1579
BY THE GRACE OF GOD AND IN THE NAME OF HERR
MAIESTY QVEEN ELIZABETH OF ENGLAND AND HERR
SVCCESSORS FOREVER I TAKE POSESSON OF THIS
KINGDOME WHOSE KING AND PEOPLE FREELY RESIGNE
THEIR RIGHT AND TITLE IN THE WHOLE LAND VNTO
HERR MAIESTIES KEEPEING NOW NAMED BY ME AN TO
BEE KNOWNE VNTO ALL MEN AS NOVA ALBION
FRANCIS DRAKE"

The main side road continues to the remote tip of the headland, where the white 16-sided pyramidal tower of POINT REYES LIGHTHOUSE, 44.3 *m.*, shines its light 294 feet above the sea. Its 120,000-candlepower light, whose three-ton lens was ground in France and installed at Point Reyes in 1870, is visible in clear weather for 24 miles. But even this beam and the blast of the fog signal have failed to prevent many ships and even one air liner from piling up on the saw-toothed shore.

Across rolling foothill country runs US 101, rising to hilltops and dipping through valleys, with the Bay seldom out of view.

At the tidal mouth of Corte Madera Creek is GREENBRAE, 15.1 *m.* (32 alt., 100 pop.), a colony of house boats, whose occupants live the year around in their compact arks.

Right from Greenbrae on a paved road which winds along the hills that rise above the West Gate (*for official use only*) of San Quentin Prison (*see below*), 1 *m.*, where armed guards are stationed in yellow octagonal towers. The route goes around and above the prison grounds with their neat guard cottages and high wire fences to the junction with a paved road, 2 *m.*, where it turns R. to the SAN QUENTIN WHARF, 2.9 *m.*, now western terminus of the Richmond-San Rafael Ferry (*automobiles and driver, 70¢; automobile and four passengers, 80¢; pedestrians, 10¢*).

At the head of San Quentin Wharf stands the FERRY INN, erected on the piling of the old Buckelew Sawmill by Benjamin R. Buckelew, who sold the site of San Quentin Prison to the State and who was once publisher and editor of *The Californian*. Visible from San Quentin Wharf is RED ROCK, three miles offshore, a two-acre uninhabited island whose color is due to the presence of iron oxides, and where legend has placed buried gold and jewels. Boundary corners of three counties meet on the little island.

In the small village of SAN QUENTIN, 3 *m.* (12 alt., 328 pop.), prison guards and employees live with their families.

The side route ends at 3.1 *m.*, at the main gate of SAN QUENTIN STATE PRISON (*relatives and persons on legitimate business admitted daily 8 and 2; guided tours, 9 and 2 Thurs.*). The snouts of machine guns protrude from nearby towers. Visible beyond the gates are the grey walls and the stocky unornamented cell blocks of the prison, pierced by barred windows. Behind these walls 5,200 men are "doing time." Women, once kept here, now are sent to Tehachapi; recidivists—"two time losers"—are sent to Folsom Prison.

New prisoners usually are put to work in the jute mill making burlap and other rough fabrics; later they are placed in work more suited to their individual abilities. Prison farms and dairies offer some of the men outdoor work. Others are employed in furniture shops, printing plants, machine and plumbing shops, bakeries, and kitchens.

The most famous prisoner here for two decades, labor martyr Thomas J. Mooney, accused of planting a bomb and killing several persons during a parade in San Francisco in 1916, was pardoned in 1939 by Governor

Culbert L. Olson. Also confined here were Matthew Schmidt and J. B. McNamara, defendants in the Los Angeles *Times* explosion case of October, 1910.
Convicts built the first prison cells here in the early 1850's to house other convicts then chained in the black holds of prison boats. The first ten years of the prison's existence were stormy with escapes and uprisings. The most desperate break occurred July 22, 1862, when 400 convicts rushed the front gate, and, using Lieutenant-Governor John F. Chellis as a shield, stormed and carried the gun post near the steamer landing. The convicts released Chellis three miles from the prison and headed for the hills, where they were blocked by a citizens' posse. Thirty-three escaped, three were killed, and the others captured.

North of Greenbrae, US 101 cuts across tidal lands reclaimed from the marshes. In 1866 this road, built three feet above the marsh lands, was a toll road whose surfacing material had been taken from Indian shell mounds. Tolls ranged from two and one-half cents each for sheep and hogs to one dollar, which admitted three yoke of oxen and a loaded wagon. Today's highway is lined by gas stations, "hot dog" stands, and stores. The old ferry boat *Encinal,* moored in the marsh near the road at 16.8 *m.,* is a seafood restaurant.

Seat of Marin County and suburban trading center is SAN RAFAEL, 17.5 *m.* (10 alt., 8,516 pop.). Bisected by San Rafael Creek, the city extends north to steep, round-headed San Rafael Hill. Its business streets are lined with old-fashioned brick buildings; many of its homes are set back of green lawns and tall shade trees.

Father Vicente Sarria founded here, on December 14, 1817, the twentieth of California's missions as an *asisténcia* (auxiliary) to Mission Dolores, whose Indian converts were rapidly dying off from the effects of measles and other diseases contracted from white men. By 1834 the new mission boasted 1,250 converts, but in that year it was secularized and its converts scattered. In 1844 Governor Manuel Micheltorena granted a considerable part of the present town site to Don Timoteo Murphy, administrator of the secularized mission.

In the 1850's the little town became a busy but dirty center for the surrounding ranches. Streets bottomless with dust in summer, with mud in winter, were crowded with dogs, children, and Mexicans, and the few plank sidewalks tripped the unwary. Here the daily Petaluma stage and the thrice-a-week "mud wagon" from Olema and Bolinas connected with the San Quentin stages that met the San Francisco ferries, stopping, "with popping of whips and panting of horses . . . in front of the hotel. Now all is bustle, the men in long dusters, the women swathed in 'veils.' A crowd follows the mail-bag, the women retire to apartments upstairs, and the men line up at the bar . . .'"

Celebration of the founding of San Rafael each October 24 is no longer the gala day it was prior to 1900, when (according to the *Marin Journal*) decent and respectable people took the day off, remained at home behind locked doors, and waited patiently until the last of the celebration had worn off. Three-card monte men, shell game operators, and crooked card-sharpers thronged the town; stabbings, shootings, and fist fights provided work for local doctors; and entertainment centered around horse races, dog and coyote fights, cock fights, and bull fights.

Among the 80 houses of 1866 were "some costly residences with tastefully laid out ground . . ." Some of these still stand in the district north of Fifth Avenue, among them the WILLIAM TELL COLEMAN RESIDENCE, 1130 Mission Ave., a large, rambling, white building incorporating San Rafael's first frame house, put up in 1849. Coleman, a San Francisco merchant and vigilance committee member, established in the valley just north of town a nursery; here among the hills he raised thousands of trees.

The apartment building at 720 Fourth St., a three-story structure with tall, narrow windows, decorated with Georgian pediments, was built by convict labor in 1859 as the CENTRAL HOTEL.

The former HOUSE OF PETER DONOHUE, 1411 Lincoln Ave., now a restaurant, occupies the big, old-fashioned two-story house built by Peter Donohue, Irish blacksmith who founded the Union Iron Works of San Francisco. About 1906 the estate became the property of Leon Douglass of the Victor Phonograph Company, who lived here with his family until 1926.

Of MISSION SAN RAFAEL ARCANGEL little remains but a few fragments of tile. The building was demolished for its timber in 1860; nine years later a new church was built on the site, but this in turn was destroyed by fire in 1917. The present ST. RAPHAEL'S CHURCH, Fifth Ave. and A St., occupies the site of the old mission, which is depicted in a bas-relief above the central door. A statue of Saint Raphael stands in the main tower.

A bank at 1304 Fourth St. marks the SITE OF THE MURPHY ADOBE built in 1844 by Don Timoteo Murphy, who as *alcalde* held here many a *baile* and reception. In 1853, after Timothy Murphy's death, the county court was moved from a leaky room in the old mission to this adobe, which a progressive citizen had bought for $1,000 and sold to the county for $5,000. The old road leading from Murphy's to the freight landing of the 1850's is now C Street.

The first local building of the DOMINICAN COLLEGE, Grand Ave. between Locust and Acacia Sts., was dedicated in 1889 on land given by Don Timoteo Murphy and William Tell Coleman. The dormitories occupy three handsome old residences, but the educational buildings are modern. In addition to grammar and high school departments, the institution offers a full college course. Since its founding in Monterey in 1850 the college has given much attention to music; many distinguished musicians have taught and lectured here. The music library has some valuable illuminated missals and a number of rare books on music. The campus covers 35 acres planted to pine and eucalyptus by Coleman, who tried to reforest the region. Forest Meadows, a part of the campus, is the setting for the WOODLAND THEATER, an outdoor auditorium built in 1934 and used for the annual concerts.

SAN RAFAEL HILL (717 alt.), rising steeply from the north end of B St., is a municipal recreation area, the gift of Captain Robert

Dollar. On the summit, which offers an unusual view, Easter sunrise services are held.

Right from San Rafael on Third St., which becomes a county road running along San Rafael Creek between the hills and marshes. Many fine country homes dot the wooded slopes. The MARIN YACHT CLUB, 1.3 *m.*, participates in all San Francisco Bay regattas. The green marshes end in the Bay waters. Offshore about one mile are the two small MARIN ISLANDS, on one of which the Lacatuit Indian chief Marin sought refuge from the Spanish. Captured, he was baptized at San Rafael. Later his name was given to the county.

At 3.9 *m.* stand the three tall kiln stacks of the McNEAR BRICK WORKS, where haydite, a light concrete aggregate, is manufactured. The road continues east through hilly land owned by the McNear family, pioneer grain and cattle ranchers. The eucalypti that crown the hilltops and the Bay slopes were among 20,000 trees set out in the 1890's.

At 5 *m.* is the junction with an improved road; R. here 0.5 *m.* to McNEAR'S BEACH (*parking fee 50¢; picnic grounds; boats for hire*), once McNear's Landing, which offers good bass and rock cod fishing. The beach is sheltered by the tip of San Pedro Point, westermost of two promontories marking the entrance to San Pablo Bay. An old frame hotel (L), embowered in groves of palms and eucalypti, dates from horse and buggy days.

The main side route continues north across low hills to bluffs above San Pablo Bay. In a small cove is CHINA CAMP, 6 *m.*, where a rickety pier extends over the water (*boats for hire*). Chinese settled here in the 1880's to fish for shrimp. By 1910, twelve hundred Chinese lived here, catching and drying shrimp.

From BUCKEYE POINT (*boats for hire*), 6.7 *m.*, the road continues across the hills that rise abruptly from the Bay. Oak, madrone, bay, buckeye, elderberry, wild lilac, and toyon are abundant.

At 11.4 *m.* is the junction with US 101 (*see below*).

Stretches of US 101 north of San Rafael are lined with rows of eucalyptus trees, planted in the 1880's and 1890's as windbreaks.

ST. VINCENT'S SCHOOL FOR BOYS (*visitors welcome*), 22.4 *m.* (R), occupies a group of Spanish Renaissance buildings. A Catholic orphanage, it was opened in 1855 on land deeded by Don Timoteo Murphy. The 1,800 acres of ground produce all the dairy and farm products used by the school.

The highway winds smoothly up a range of hills and down into a broad valley to the gates (R) of $7,000,000 HAMILTON FIELD (*open only to citizens on official business*), 23.7 *m.*, an Army base for pursuit squadrons named for Lieutenant Lloyd Andrews Hamilton of the Seventeenth Aero Squadron, shot down in France, August, 1918. The airport, begun in 1932, covers 928 acres of drained marshland sloping imperceptibly to the Bay. It was used as a bombing base until 1940.

IGNACIO, 24.7 *m.* (10 alt., 135 pop.), consisting of a few gas stations and lunch counters, was named for Don Ignacio Pacheco, much-married *alcalde* of San Rafael, who owned a large ranch here. His horses were so admired by John C. Frémont that the American explorer is said to have kidnapped him and demanded a ransom in horses.

At 25.3 *m.* is the junction of State 37 with US 101. The route goes R. on State 37.

Left on US 101, in little Novato Valley, where dikes thrown up against the incursion of tides have formed green meadows planted to alfalfa and grain, is NOVATO, 2.5 m. (17 alt., 700 pop.), below the hills bordering San Pablo Bay. The town stands on the former Rancho Novato, granted to Don Fernando Feliz in 1839.

In one of the farm buildings (L) of RANCHO BURDELL (private), 5.7 m., is an adobe wall once part of the home of Camillo Ynitia, last chief of the Olompali Indians. Soon after he sold the Olompali Rancho for $5,200, Ynitia was murdered by his brother, who believed he had hidden the gold in the nearby hills. Jacob Leese, Marin County's first English-speaking settler, once owned the rancho, as did Bezaar Simmons, who built a wooden house here in 1850, and James Black, who gave his daughter the property when she married Dr. Galen Burdell.

The rich earth of PETALUMA VALLEY, 9.6 m., supports cattle ranches, fruit groves, dairies, and chicken farms.

Claiming the title of the "World's Egg Basket," PETALUMA, 13.5 m. (15 alt., 7,983 pop.), which lies at the head of navigation on Petaluma Creek, is the center of a region whose millions of hens lay the utmost modern methods can produce. Poultry-raising here has become an industry in which laboratory experiments blaze the way to more eggs and better hens. From mechanical incubators that turn automatically their trays of eggs, thousands of chicks emerge daily from their shells, immediately to be placed on scientific diets. Along the main street of Petaluma, dominated by the white towers of a grain elevator, cluster grain and poultry equipment stores. Warehouses, factories, and wholesale houses line the creek east of the business section.

In 1834 Petaluma was a sleepy Mexican village within the boundaries of the Rancho Petaluma (see below), which took its name from an early Miwok Indian village. After 1840 the fertile valley experienced a general invasion of settlers. By 1852, Yankees dominated the village. They continued to raise grain, built a flour mill, and shipped their produce down the creek to San Francisco. For nearly a half-century wheat, lumber, wool, bricks, and basalt blocks were carried by a fleet of thirty odd schooners.

The poultry industry, long Petaluma's foremost, began in 1878 when a young Canadian, Lyman C. Byce, coming here in search of health, saw that this region with its even climate, sandy soil, and marketing facilities was admirably suited for chicken-raising. An inventive genius, Byce began manufacturing incubators and brooders, which are today widely used. Connected with poultry-raising are most of the town's industries: feed mills, commercial hatcheries, egg- and poultry-packing plants, box factories, incubator and brooder factories. Since subdivision of the large wheat ranches, dairying has also become an important occupation.

Largest electrically operated hatchery in the world, the SALES AND BOURKE HATCHERY (visitors welcome), 701 Seventh St., occupies a group of red brick buildings. Equipped with thermostatic controls, the incubators rotate their eggs every four hours during the twenty-one day incubation period. In a year approximately two million white Leghorns, a half-million heavy breeds, and a quarter-million turkeys are hatched.

Probably the only drugstore in the world devoted solely to medicines for ailing chickens is the CHICKEN PHARMACY, 176 Main St. The POULTRY PATHO-LOGICAL LABORATORY, 627 F St., is maintained by the University of California under the Division of Animal Husbandry.

Only silk mill west of the Mississippi River is the BELDING THREAD SILK MILL, Wilson and Jefferson Sts., occupying ivy-covered red brick buildings.

Right from Petaluma on Washington Street 2.8 m. to a junction with a paved road; R. here to what was General Mariano Vallejo's CASA GRANDE (caretaker) 4.4 m., built in 1833-34. When Vallejo stood on the broad second-story balcony, his eyes could see no land that was not his own, for the great house was headquarters for his 75,000-acre Rancho Petaluma. The white plaster on the adobe walls is cracked and crumbling in spots, and a shingled roof has replaced the original tiles; but the massive walls are the same that

Vallejo's Kanaka workmen put together, and the original beams of hand-hewn redwood support ceilings and balconies. The rear wing has been destroyed. In the inner courtyard formed by the four great walls, Vallejo's two thousand Indians gathered to hear his orders.

On US 101 at 21.5 *m.* is COTATI (113 alt., 1,000 pop.), founded on land once part of 17,000-acre Rancho Cotati, whose owner, Captain Juan Castaneda, gave up his claim in 1849 to the district's American sheriff, Dr. Thomas S. Page. The sheriff's son, Wilfred Page, laid out the town around a hexagonal plaza, from which the streets radiate in a spider-web pattern. When asked why he had not used simple squares and straight lines in the great expanse of land, Page replied, "Any fool can plant that and come out right, but it takes brains to start on angles and have your plans click."

SANTA ROSA, 29.9 *m.* (160 alt., 12,547 pop.), seat of Sonoma County, is an attractive, prosperous city at the base of the Sonoma Mountain on the eastern edge of a rich alluvial valley. In 1829 Father Juan Amores, on a missionary expedition from San Rafael, named the valley and creek for Saint Rose of Lima but the Indians prevented him from establishing a mission. In 1833, Mariano Vallejo tried to begin a settlement here, but abandoned it in favor of Sonoma. The town was not founded until several years after the discovery of gold, when the Argonauts turned to farming. Almost immediately the enterprising community asked to be made county seat (then Sonoma); they received the honor in 1854.

The earthquake of 1906 wrecked Santa Rosa's entire business district with a loss of forty lives, but the town was rebuilt and has continued to keep pace with the subdivision of the surrounding agricultural lands. Local industries include fruit processing, large-scale manufacturing of ice for refrigerator cars, egg-packing, and the manufacture of shoes.

On the tract which for fifty years was an experimental farm of Luther Burbank (1849-1926), who arrived in Santa Rosa in 1875, are the one-and-one-half-acre BURBANK MEMORIAL GARDENS, Santa Rosa Ave. and Tupper St. Property of the Santa Rosa Junior College botany department, the gardens contain a great variety of plants, including many Burbank discoveries. Under an enormous cedar of Lebanon grown from a seed sent from the Holy Land, Burbank is buried.

While a young man, Burbank accidentally discovered the potato named for him on his Massachusetts truck-farm. With the $150 he received for his discovery and ten of the new Burbank potatoes, he followed his brothers to California. Soon he began the experiments with plants destined to add hundreds of new varieties of vegetables, flowers, and fruits to nursery and seed catalogues. He believed in the inheritance of acquired characteristics, and that these acquired characteristics could be fixed, or be made permanent. Among his best-known hybrids are the spineless cactus; Burbank potato; Gold, Wickson, American, and Climax plums; Splendor and Sugar prunes; and many improved varieties of quinces, berries, and vegetables. His Shasta and Alaska daisies; "crimson flame" and softly colored single and double California poppies; roses; callas; gladioli; dahlias; and many improved flowering shrubs have added color and fragrance to gardens all over the world.

The slim-spired white FIRST BAPTIST CHURCH, B St. between Fifth and Sixth Sts., was built in 1873 of lumber cut from a single redwood tree. Sufficient lumber remained of the same tree to build a five-room residence.

The side route continues L. from Santa Rosa on Sebastopol Avenue (State 12).

In the heart of a countryside which flowers with acres of fruit blossoms in spring is SEBASTOPOL, 37.8 *m.* (68 alt., 1,853 pop.), center of Gravenstein apple and cherry orchards. J. H. P. Morris named the town Pine Grove when he founded it in 1853 on the site of the adobe house of Joaquin Carillo's Rancho Llano de Santa Rosa (Plain of St. Rose). Two years later a local feud ended in a street battle in which one participant barricaded himself in a store. Enthusiastic spectators, recalling the Crimean city of Sebastopol, then in a state of seige, immediately adopted its name, first for the store, then for the town.

Left from Sebastopol on Gravenstein Highway 0.6 *m.* to the SONOMA BUD-
DHIST TEMPLE, ENMAN-JI, which was shipped from Japan for exhibit in the
South Manchurian Railway display at the Chicago World's Fair in 1933 and
afterwards dismantled and erected here. In authentic Kamakura style, the
building has a green pagoda roof, bell-shaped windows, and stucco walls.

North of Sebastopol State 12 runs through orchard lands and vineyards,
skirting the western edge of a rich hop-growing region, to the shores of the
RUSSIAN RIVER, 51.8 *m.* a vacation area for as many as one hundred and
fifty thousand persons annually. Rising in Mendocino County, the stream
cuts directly across the Coast Range. In this part of its course the river's
meanderings have created a string of beaches covered with yellow sand.
The Russians named the river Slavianka (Slavic) when they penetrated the
fertile region in 1812 and began trapping for furs along the stream. The
Americans, who followed, logged the area, built lumber mills, and farmed the
cleared land.

The population of GUERNEVILLE, 52 *m.* (52 alt., 800 pop.), swells in the
summer to seven thousand, filling resort cottages, cabins, and camp-grounds.
The town occupies a wide river meadow encircled by mountains, edged by
firs and redwoods. The business street is lined with one-story, false-front
buildings and old wooden sidewalks. The town took its name from George C.
Guerne, who with Harmon G. Heald erected the region's first sawmill in 1865.

Right from Guerneville on a paved road 2.8 *m.* to 400-acre ARMSTRONG
WOODS STATE PARK (*camping and picnicking*). Here, deep among a fine
stand of redwoods, is the ARMSTRONG FOREST THEATRE, whose redwood log
benches seat 1,800.

State 12 continues to the junction with a paved road 57 *m.;* L. here across
the river is MONTE RIO, 0.2 *m.* (41 alt., 500 pop.), at the foot of steep hills
whose slopes are covered with summer homes and resort hotels. The side
route goes L. from Monte Rio to BOHEMIAN GROVE (*visits by special permission*), 1.1 *m.*, the 2,437-acre redwood grove of San Francisco's Bohemian Club.
Here, in an outdoor theater whose log seats accommodate 1,200, the club since
1878 has held its annual stag Hi Jinks, staging its Grove Play against a natural
background of great trees. During a two-week encampment, some six hundred
men "rough it" in tents or cabins, eat in the open air, tell tall tales around a
campfire, and attend a music-drama written and played by fellow members.

The main side route follows State 12 west from Guerneville along the north
bank of the Russian River to a junction with State 1, 65.6 *m.*

BLACK POINT, 28.4 *m.* (8 alt., 125 pop.), a railroad shipping
point for dairy products, lies in a corner where the hills come down to
the marshes. The dark appearance of the wooded point projecting into
San Pablo Bay suggested the name.

A bascule drawbridge operated by electricity crosses PETALUMA
CREEK, 28.6 *m.* Barges and river boats use this waterway to Petaluma (*see above*), and pleasure craft sail here on week-end excursions.

Hills and meadows are left behind as State 37 enters a region of
strong winds and wide horizons. Tules are the chief growth in these
sloughs, creeks, and tidal lagoons where wild ducks are abundant in
the late autumn.

At 32.9 *m.* is the junction with Sears Point Road, on which the
route goes R.

Left on State 37, which leaves green sloughs where red-winged blackbirds wheel and follows the base of low foothills on which sheep and cattle
graze.

The *embarcadero* (landing place) on Sonoma Creek at the site of SHELL-
VILLE, 7.4 *m.* (10 alt., 84 pop.), once piled high with merchandise bound

to and from Sonoma, was first named Saint Louis by early Missouri settlers. It was renamed for Theodor Schell, one of the promoters of the Sonoma Valley Prismoidal Railway in 1875, who bought 1,400 acres here in 1860. The route goes L. from Shellville on State 12 toward the Sonoma Mountains, past the wide orchards and old ranch houses of Sonoma Valley.

At 9.2 *m.* is a junction with oil-surfaced Petaluma Road; L. here 1.3 *m.* to a junction with a dirt road; R. here to the entrance of the Coblentz Ranch (*private*), 2.2 *m.* About a half-mile from the road, almost hidden by masses of venerable trees (L), are the stone walls and blue-green roof of TEMELEC HALL, built by Bear Flag revolutionist Captain Granville Perry Swift, once the finest private house north of San Francisco. The south wing is said to have been built as early as 1849 by General Persifor Frazer Smith, military governor of California, who sold the 12,000-acre ranch to Swift, a newly rich miner. First and second floors of the 20-room house are surrounded on three sides by colonnaded balconies and the roof is topped by a small gazebo. The massive stone wall in the rear, which once continued around the house and joined the reservoir on the north, was an excellent defense against marauding Indians or bandits. Just south of it were adobe quarters for 40 Indian servants,. At each side of the formal gardens of the front terrace—where cypress, acacia, and lemon verbena, planted by Swift, still flourish—is a tiny ornate stone summer house with high, pointed roof. The two-story stone stable, topped by a tall pigeon cote, once had an inclined driveway for carriages.

Northward from the junction with Petaluma Road through orchards and vineyards State 12 follows the wide road laid out by Mariano Vallejo. On the east side of the valley at the base of low hills is SONOMA, 11 *m.* (97 alt., 1,153 pop.), which has never quite lost its leisurely Mexican air. It owes its existence to Franciscan priest Jose Altimira and soldier Mariano Guadalupe Vallejo. When Governor Arguello urged Altimira in 1823 to consolidate Missions San Francisco de Asis and San Rafael and move them farther north, ostensibly for the health of the Indian neophytes, but also to check Russian colonization, the young priest came into the Sonoma Valley. Here he dedicated the "New San Francisco" before a willow altar.

The Franciscan authorities, annoyed at the young priest's temerity and impulsiveness, insisted that Missions San Rafael and San Francisco de Asis should remain where they were founded. Altimira fought back in long letters until finally he was permitted to have a mission here—the last founded and most northerly of the California missions—which was named San Francisco de Solano. Neophytes from San Jose, San Rafael, and San Francisco built a few mud-plastered wooden buildings below the billowing hills. In a few years permanent buildings of adobe were finished. Stockaded gardens and vineyards surrounded the mission and small herds of cattle, sheep, and horses roamed the valley. When a chief of the local Chocuy-on Indians was baptised "Sonoma," the pleasant name was adopted for the valley and the town that grew up around the mission.

In 1835, the missions having been secularized, Governor Jose Figueroa appointed young Lieutenant Mariano Vallejo as *comisionado* of the Sonoma mission lands and stock and sent him to found a fortified *pueblo* at Sonoma. Without equipment other than his pocket compass, Vallejo laid out the town in large squares about a plaza. He fortified the hills behind the mission with a few small cannons. With the aid of Indians he built barracks surrounded with a loop-holed wall and adjoining them a *palacio* with a two-story castle-like tower which was regarded as one of the most pretentious residences in California. Around the dusty plaza where Vallejo put his perspiring Indian soldiers through their paces were built the homes of relatives and friends to whom were granted the broad reaches of the present valleys of Sonoma, Petaluma, Santa Rosa, and Napa.

After a few sharp skirmishes with neighboring Indians, Vallejo was able to make an alliance with Sem Yeto (the mighty arm), over-lord of many tribes, who persuaded his people to submit to the Spanish. Sem Yeto was baptized at the mission and christened Francisco Solano. (The first con-stitutional convention in Monterey, at Vallejo's suggestion, gave Solano's name to the county east of Napa; a statue has been erected to him in Fair-field.) Under Vallejo's paternal rule the Indians lived in a mild form of peonage.

By the middle 1840's Sonoma already had some American residents. The Spanish eyed uneasily the newer American immigrants—and with good reason, as it appeared in 1846. The *pueblo's* fortifications were no handicap to 33 Yankees led by Ezekiel Merritt, who on the morning of June 14 surprised the garrison's 18 men and "captured" the defenseless commander. Under the crude banner painted with a bear and a star which they hoisted in the plaza, the rebels proclaimed the California Republic. It lasted less than a month, for on July 9, 1846, when Lieutenant Joseph Warren Revere of the U. S. Army took command, the Bear Flag was replaced by the Stars and Stripes. "At last the rag of that dirty rabble had been supplanted by the glorious flag of the United States," wrote Senora Vallejo to the general in the *calaboza* at Sutter's Fort.

When Lilburn W. Boggs, former Governor of Missouri, was appointed *alcalde* of Sonoma by General Stephen W. Kearny, the appointment was contested by John H. Nash, Bear Flag revolutionist who had grabbed for himself the post of *alcalde*. Nash refused to turn over the city records. Only after Governor Richard B. Mason had dispatched Lieutenant William Tecumseh Sherman to seize and carry off Nash did Boggs become head of the community. After a few months Vallejo, who promised not to bear arms against the Americans, returned to Sonoma and settled down to master the difficult language of his new country and act as Indian agent for the district. Garrisoned by the Army, Sonoma quieted down.

Sonoma always has centered around its PLAZA, bounded by Napa and Spain Sts., First St. W. and First St. E. In its northeast corner is the BEAR FLAG MONUMENT, a bronze statue of a pioneer (John MacQuarrie, sculp-tor) holding the new flag, mounted on a 40-ton boulder of volcanic rock. In the center of the Plaza is the buff stone COURTHOUSE AND CITY HALL, which replaced in 1908 an old adobe courthouse that once housed the county seat, although a grand jury had condemned it as "not fit for a cattle shed." When a special election in 1854 decided in favor of the lusty young town of Santa Rosa as county seat, two jubilant new officials drove a team of mules from Santa Rosa one dark night and rifled the courthouse. The county clerk is said to have prodded the mules home with his wooden leg.

The oldest building in Sonoma, the MISSION SAN FRANCISCO DE SOLANO, built in 1824, is an L-shaped adobe roofed with red tile and sur-mounted by a plain Latin cross. Hanging from an ivy-covered framework in front is a bell cast in Peru in 1829. After the secularization of the missions in 1835, the mission church became the parish church, but when a new church was built in 1880, it was sold. The old buildings then served as a hay-barn and a wine cellar; the patio, as a butcher's slaughter yard. A small wooden saloon crowded against the front wall of the church. For years small boys threw rocks through the crumbling walls. After long neglect the mission was purchased in 1903 by public-spirited citizens who presented it to the State. It is now a State landmark and museum.

The MISSION MUSEUM (*open 10-4*) contains early California papers, portraits of pioneers, part of the Sonoma flagstaff, timbers and millstone from Sonoma's first gristmill, Indian baskets shownig beaded and feathered work of the Pomo, long handwrought iron hinges from Fort Ross, and tim-bers from the ship *Ocean Hero*, which was towed to Lakeville and there sunk to serve as an *embarcadero*.

The BLUE WING HOTEL, 217 E. Spain St., is an adobe building 100 feet long whose second-story balcony extending over the sidewalk, similar to one in the rear, is supported by octagonal redwood posts rising to the roof. The original 12-light windows, open beams and wooden ceiling, and hand-made doors with ogee mouldings are well preserved. The museum (*open

2-4, adm. 10¢), formerly the hotel bar, contains a gold scale once used in a store across the street, a music box that tinkles "Linger Longer Lou", a small red altar from the local Chinese joss house, and a long quartermaster's account with John C. Fremont covering the disbursement of $1,242 in small sums. Sonoma's man-power fire engine is flanked by an automobile bought by Luther Burbank in 1915. The collection also includes General Persifor Smith's medicine cabinet and the walnut desk used by Frank Soule while writing *The Annals of San Francisco*.

Its wide verandah facing the Plaza, the old MEXICAN BARRACKS, Spain St. and First St. E., which cost Vallejo $9,000 of his private funds, is a two-story structure built in 1836 of adobe and hand-hewn timbers hauled to the site by oxteam. Used as headquarters for Vallejo's Mexican soldiers and as a munition depot, it was later garrisoned by the Bear Flag rebels and finally by United States officers.

The EL DORADO HOTEL, 145 First St. W., erected in 1846 by General Vallejo's brother, Captain Salvador Vallejo, became a famous California hostelry. The original building is hidden by ugly modern additions except on the north side, where appear the old 42-inch-thick adobe walls. The frame second story has a balcony supported by wooden posts.

The SALVADOR VALLEJO ADOBE (*private*), adjoining the El Dorado Hotel on the south, is a two-story adobe of nice proportions. A row of tall posts rises from the sidewalk to the second-floor roof, which extends over a shallow balcony reached from inside through French doors. Although he had ranchos, vineyards, horses, and cattle, Salvador Vallejo became so financially involved that in 1853 all his personal belongings were attached: even the gold epaulets from his Mexican uniform and such trifles as brandied peaches and feather fans.

Painted in dull red and yellow is the FITCH HOUSE (*private*), 347 First St. W., a two-story adobe with a cantilevered balcony extending over the sidewalk. Built in 1836 by Jacob Leese for Henry D. Fitch, Vallejo's brother-in-law, it boasted the first fireplace in the county. General Persifer Smith made his headquarters here. In the 1850's, St. Mary's Hall, an Episcopalian boarding school for young ladies, occupied the building.

The two-story RAY HOUSE (*private*), E. Spain St. and Second St. E., is a long rectangular adobe and frame structure, the small wooden portion of which was built in 1846 and supplemented four years later with a large adobe addition. The two sides facing the streets are surrounded by rows of redwood posts supporting an open-raftered, low-pitched roof extending eight feet beyond the walls. American Army officers were quartered here in the 1840's and 1850's. Later the building housed the first Masonic organization in the county.

In the northwestern part of town, at the end of a tree-shaded lane opening off W. Spain St., is the VALLEJO HISTORICAL STATE MONUMENT, Vallejo's $150,000 estate, Lachryma Montis (Lat., tear of the mountain), established in 1851. The family home, a two-story yellow house in "American Gothic" style, has a high pitched roof with many gables decorated with elaborate jig-saw tracery. Vallejo's 13th child, Señora Luisa Vallejo Emparan, the last of his immediate family, has a life tenancy of her old home. The whip-sawed house timbers were hauled here by oxteam.

The SWISS CHALET (*open 10-4*), now a museum, is a two-story half-timbered house with the second floor overhanging. The original frame and bracing timbers were shipped around the Horn from Switzerland, numbered for assembly. The enclosing walls are of a soft rose-colored brick. In a recent restoration many of the original oak timbers were replaced with redwood and the whole building set upon a foundation of concrete. The building was used as a store house and as Indian servants' quarters. On the long dining table used by Vallejo and his family of 16 children stand two globes made in 1823, one of the world and one of the skies. In the cases are the sword and uniform the General wore when Mexican *Comandante-General;* his elaborately embroidered christening robe; the silk-lined, enameled jewel case which, with a set of jewelry, was a wedding present to Señora Vallejo; and a charming daguerreotype of the side-whiskered general surrounded by six pretty ringletted, hoop-skirted daughters and granddaughters.

In SONOMA CEMETERY, at the northern end of W. First St., is the grave of General Vallejo (1808-90) and his wife, Francisca Benicia Carrillo de Vallejo (1816-91), marked by a black granite monument.

State 12 goes west from Sonoma on West Napa Street to the junction with a paved road, 12 m., where it turns R.

BOYES SPRINGS, 13.7 m. (150 alt., 400 pop.), long a vacation center, was settled in 1883 by Captain Henry Ernest Boyes, who had come to California from England. Boyes and his wife heard stories of the old hot mineral springs used by the Indians and investigated—the captain digging and Mrs. Boyes hoisting the bucket. Located here are BOYES HOT SPRINGS (mineral water plunge; dancing; lunch counter).

The SONOMA MISSION INN (tennis courts, saddle horses, swimming pool) occupies a large white concrete building with the twin towers, rounded arches, and tiled roofs typical of the California missions.

FETTER'S SPRINGS, 14.1 m., were developed about 1907 on the 100-acre ranch of Mr. and Mrs. George Fetter, who built a hotel there. This resort and AGUA CALIENTE, 14.6 m. (75 alt., 415 pop.), are open throughout the year.

HOOKER'S MONUMENT (L), 15.2 m., a boulder bearing a bronze tablet dedicated to Colonel "Fighting Joe" Hooker of Civil War fame, stands on the edge of the 550 acres which he acquired in 1851, during a two-year leave from the Army, with the thought of becoming a "Southern planter of California." In a clump of oaks 350 yards west is the snug little four-room clapboard HOOKER HOUSE, the timbers of which were cut in Norway and shipped 'round the Horn.

Adjoining is the GEORGE WATRESS HOUSE, a two-story stone and timber building built in 1853 by Hooker's successor on the ranch. Watress, former proprietor of the Astor House in New York, arrived in San Francisco in 1851 and became proprietor of a hotel before moving to Sonoma Valley.

State 12 winds through low, chaparral-covered foothills drained by Calabazas (pumpkin) Creek.

At 18.3 m. is the junction with a paved road, on which the route goes L. to GLEN ELLEN, 19.3 m. (227 alt., 220 pop.), shaded by tall trees that grow along Sonoma Creek, once a railroad terminal and a fashionable summer resort. It has long been famous for its wine grapes. The JACK LONDON MEMORIAL LIBRARY AND COMMUNITY CENTER (L) was built by the Glen Ellen Women's Club and other admirers of the novelist.

The route goes R. from Glen Ellen on a paved road to the entrance to the JACK LONDON RANCH (accommodations; saddle horses), 19.7 m. A private road winds up to the ranch houses—the old Kohler and Frohling winery buildings that London purchased for headquarters and the stone house built by Charmian London after her husband's death. Except for occasional trips, one of which was described in The Cruise of the Snark, Jack London lived here from 1904 until his death in November, 1916.

The ranch, eventually 1,400 acres in extent, did not occupy a great deal of the author's time—cultivation, experimentation and stock breeding being left to employees, many of whom were paroled convicts. London wrote in the mornings, 1,000 words being a day's work. His income, ultimately $40,000 annually, enabled him to be very hospitable.

Some distance from the main buildings, the ruins of WOLF HOUSE stand among charred redwoods. This building, a three-story structure built of rock quarried in the Sonoma hills, had been planned by London as his ideal home, but before he could move in, the place was destroyed by fire of unknown origin. An unmarked boulder not far from the ruins cover London's ashes.

The route goes east on Sears Point Road, a lonely stretch of highway, across marshlands, past sloughs and lagoons to the junction with a paved county road, 42.7 *m.*, on which it goes R.

At 43.7 *m.*, on the outskirts of Vallejo (*see below*), is the junction with Tennessee Street.

Right here over a causeway 0.9 *m.* to MARE ISLAND NAVY YARD (*usually open 9-4:30 daily, subject to special restrictions; cameras checked*), at the southern end of a narrow 3,000-acre peninsula flanked by the Bay on the west and the channel of the Napa River on the east. Here are shipyards, drydocks, machine shops, warehouses, barracks, officers' quarters, a radio station, and a naval hospital. In 1851 President Millard Fillmore set aside Mare Island for a Navy dock; four years later Captain (later Admiral) David G. Farragut became commandant. Before Farragut's arrival a floating drydock built in New York had been shipped around the Horn and reassembled here. First vessel to be repaired was the *Pacific*, in 1853. The first stone drydock, 507 feet long, constructed in the 1870's, is still in use; a second, 740 feet long and able to hold any Navy vessel, was built in 1919. The keel of the first ship built, the wooden tug *Lively*, was laid in 1869. Here during the World War the U. S. S. *Ward* was constructed completely in 17 days, and the U. S. S. *California*, then the Nation's deepest draft battleship, was launched.

The work of more than 7,000 civilian employees and about 1,200 Navy men is directed from the MARE ISLAND ADMINISTRATION BUILDINGS, 1.9 *m.* In the office of the commandant is Farragut's Log, a record of the duties performed here in the 1850's by Farragut.

Across from the Administration Buildings, in Alden Park, is the FIGUREHEAD OF THE U. S. S. *INDEPENDENCE*, all that remains of the famous old wooden battleship, which after more than 100 years' active service was broken up at Mare Island. Among an array of captured guns, is the ANCHOR OF H. M. S. *CENTURIAN*, from the British ship which was lost in 1742 at Robinson Crusoe's Island. The anchor is ten feet long and its irregular lines and flukes show long years of use.

From the *San Carlos*, De Ayala sighted the peninsula in 1775 and called it Isla Plana (flat island). In the 1830's the property was granted by Governor Juan Alvarado to Victor Castro, who sold it about 1850 to Bezar Simmons and John Frisbee (a son-in-law of Mariano Vallejo, who at one time claimed the island). The Government was for many years involved in litigation proceedings with several claimants. It is believed that the island first was called La Isla de la Yegua (the island of the Mare) because General Mariano G. Vallejo found grazing there a prized mare lost when a ferry overturned with a load of livestock in Carquinez Strait.

VALLEJO, 42.5 *m.* (10 alt., 19,747 pop.), a hilly city of treeless residential streets and old-fashioned business blocks, is located at the confluence of the Napa River and San Pablo Bay. The first mention of the town reveals that in 1817 a group of Spanish soldiers led by Lieutenant Jose Sanchez engaged a band of Suisun Indians headed by Chief Malica near Vallejo's site. Sanchez emerged victorious after a short skirmish but the chief retired to his wickiup. When the invaders approached he set fire to it, burning himself to death.

In April, 1850, General Mariano Vallejo donated 166 acres of land for a town site and promised $370,000 for the construction of a State Capitol. Two years later the capital was transferred here from San Jose. The State legislature met in a hastily erected building but, dissatisfied with their accommodations, abandoned it within a week.

Three brothers, Levi, John, and Eleazer Frisbie, played important roles in the history of Vallejo. Levi and John laid out the city in 1851. John, builder of the California Pacific Railroad and manager of Vallejo's great estate, had left the Army in 1848. Levi married Doña Adela Vallejo, said to have been the most beautiful of the General's daughters. Eleazer was appointed first postmaster of Vallejo and later Associate Justice of the California Supreme Court.

Captain Frank Marryat described Vallejo in the 1850's as "a few scrubby-looking hills that bordered on the bay . . ." A store-ship laden with corrugated iron plates for the construction of houses had sunk at her Vallejo moorings. When Marryat raised her and found the cargo unfit for sale in San Francisco, he used the tide to clean the cargo stacked on the beach and soon was able to erect "a very handsome hotel" out of the salvage. When the legislature returned to Vallejo, only to abandon it a·second time, Marryat reported that "the city made to order was then pulled down and sold for old materials . . ."

Having twice lost the capital, the city played for smaller stakes in 1873 when it attempted to take the county seat from Fairfield. Vallejo won in a special election, but Fairfield brought a special suit enjoining the action. After a bill was introduced into the legislature whose passage would divide Solano County so that Vallejo should be separated from it—making her a county seat with no county outside her own confines—Vallejo immediately capitulated and Fairfield retained the county seat.

The industries of Vallejo, located along the water front and on the outskirts of the city, include a brick and tile factory, oil and sugar refineries, a smelter, a die-casting company, and a flour mill. Much of its patronage and not a few of its residents come from Mare Island (see above).

The SITE OF THE SECOND STATE CAPITOL BUILDING, Santa Clara and York Sts., is marked by a bronze plaque.

On Sacramento St. near York St. is the RICHARDS RESIDENCE, a two-story structure built of redwood in the early 1850's by C. B. Richards, first harness maker in Vallejo. Its lower and upper verandahs are supported by columns of redwood, and the original green shutters still hang at the windows.

Facing Mare Island at the foot of Carolina St. is the VALLEJO YACHT CLUB, a two-story structure topped by a square lookout tower. Often docked here is the three-masted schooner, *California,* once representative of the club in the San Francisco-Honolulu race. This clubhouse for more than 35 years has been the goal for yacht races from parts of the Bay region.

Left from Vallejo on State 29, between the Napa River and the Sulphur Springs Mountains, to the entrance (R) to NAPA STATE HOSPITAL for insane persons and alcoholics (*visiting hours: relatives daily, 9-11, 2-4; public Mon., Wed., Fri., 9-11*), 12.1 *m.* At the end of a wide driveway, flanked by dormitories (L) and cottages (R) and bordered by large magnolia trees, is the main building, built in 1873, a four-story structure building in Gothic style. Its red roof, tweaked up into dormers over attic windows, breaks into a square central tower and round conical towers on each corner. The Gothic idea is so omnipresent that the tortoise, a Gothic emblem, is carved on beams within the building. The gray granite entrance portico is adorned with niches in which are white marble statutes symbolic of various virtues. Opened in 1875 with a capacity of 500, the asylum was full by the end of the year. A program of enlargement which has not yet ended was undertaken. By June, 1938 the State had expended more than $4,000,000 here.

In the same year, 3,605 patients, 29.3 per cent in excess of normal capacity, were cared for by 448 officers and employees. In addition to medical care and exercises, occupational therapy and entertainment are provided. A 426-acre farm is stocked with cattle, hogs, and poultry. The truck farms and orchard supply many of the institutions needs.

North on State 29, the well-preserved one-story JUAREZ ADOBE, 13.6 m., built in 1845 (now occupied by a bar and dance floor), was the second of the Juarez adobes on Rancho Tulucay. About 90 feet long, it has walls between two and three feet thick, with deep window embrasures, built of adobe bricks covered with plaster. An earlier adobe in the rear built in 1840 is in ruins. Bricks have tumbled from the walls, revealing the chopped straw used as a binder for the mud. Most of the roof has vanished, but some of the hand-split redwood shakes rest on the huge beams.

NAPA, 14.6 m. (24 alt., 7,718 pop.), seat of Napa County, covers the flat lands around the head of navigation on Napa River and the low hills to the east. Napa River, one of the few naturally navigable streams in California, is joined here by Napa Creek, which flows through the town from the west. The business district extends for several blocks west from the river. Old-fashioned stone, brick, and wood structures give the streets the atmosphere of the 1870's and 1880's but the store fronts are modern and retail shops are busy serving the needs of farmers and town folk.

The Indians called the place Nappo. That they had long lived here was shown when street graders at Franklin and Laurel Streets cut into a burial ground where almost a hundred skeletons, with mortars, pestles, and other artifacts, were found. When settlers came into the valley, the Indians moved their brush shelters to the hills or to the edges of ranches where they could find work. John Bidwell's diary of 1842 says: "Wheat, Corn, and Potatoes are seldom surrounded by a fence, they grow out on the plains and are guarded from the cattle and horses by the Indians, who are stationed in their huts near the fields. You can employ any number of Indians by giving them a lump of Beef every week and paying them about one dollar for same." In 1856, when Napa was a sizeable town, one historian said that the Indians "made the night ring with their revelry . . . and when they could secure the means got dead drunk."

In 1836 Nicolas Higuera, one-time soldier at the San Francisco Presidio, received Rancho Entre Napa to the southwest of the present town. Near the river, he built a house of wicker plastered with mud and thatched with tule grass. Cayento Juarez, who brought in stock the next year, received in 1840 Rancho Tulucay, a two-square-league section east of the river on which he built an adobe (see above). Salvador Vallejo, brother of the General, received Rancho Napa, some 3,000 acres northwest of the town, in 1838 and stocked it with cattle.

First commerce in this country was conducted by "Boston" launches which visited ranchos around the Bay to trade for hides and tallow. In 1841, young John Rose and John C. Davis launched a schooner about the size of a whale boat near the present First Street. John A. Sutter sailed the little Sacramento up the river in 1844, loaded with settlers bound for the fertile valley lands. One of them, Bartlett Vines, later married a daughter of George C. Yount and became the father of Napa County's first American baby. Sutter's return cargo was lime, which he bought from Higuera.

When Higuera gave Nathan Coombs 80 acres in payment for work on the former's new adobe house in 1848, Coombs had a surveyor stake out a town-site. Harrison Pierce bought a load of lumber from Bale and Kilburn's mill on Napa River and began work on a small building, which he intended for a saloon. When Coombs and Higuera came to look it over, they found it right in the middle of the proposed Third Street. Deciding that Mr. Pierce must have been sampling his own wares too generously, they insisted that he move the building out of the street on to his lot. Pierce barely got the roof on his building when gold was discovered. He spent the summer at the mines, but when snow fell in the mountains he came back and opened the Empire Saloon, where he served square meals of beef, hard bread, and coffee for $1.00. A man named Thompson built a store that year, and General Vallejo and General Frisbie opened a second in 1849. After 1850 steamboats churned the water between Napa and San Francisco. First of these was the little "Dolphin," fitted with a locomotive boiler. It was said that she had to be "trimmed" by shifting the passengers and that her tall captain, F. G. Baxter, was always sighted long before the stack. The second steamer was the *Jack Hayes,* brought around the Horn in pieces and assembled at Benicia. Soon boats were carrying not only passengers but the lumber, cattle, and wheat of the surrounding ranches.

The 1850's were roistering days for Napa, for miners found it a good town to winter in. Coin of the realm included gold dust, foreign coins, and the five- to fifty-dollar gold slugs made in San Francisco. By 1854, 400 people lived here. A subscription was taken up in 1855 and the first public school in the valley opened. A small newspaper, the *Napa County Reporter,* appeared on the streets on the Fourth of July, 1856; it was known as a tri-weekly, because after it appeared one week, the publisher spent all of the second week trying to get out the next issue, which would then appear the third week. A new City Hall was built in 1856. A silver boom in the mountains around the valley emptied the town in 1859; one man said, "If they can find silver in Washoe, why not in Napa." Promoters hastily issued and sold stock, but the bubble burst when assays proved the ore to be low in value, and hotel and saloon keepers emptied bulky specimens into the streets "making quite a contribution of paving material to the streets of Napa." These streets were quagmires of muck where bundles of straw were thrown to make paths, and woe "to the unlucky wight who had too much 'tangle-foot' aboard, for a single misstep would send him in mud to his waist." In summer, when the dirt was ground into deep ruts by wagons, they were "canopied with intolerable clouds of dust through which people floundered over a strange mosaic of rubbish, cast-off clothing, empty bottles and sardine cans."

But in the 1860's the first shacks of adobe and split wood were being replaced by more substantial buildings, the citizens trod on wooden plank sidewalks, and bridges spanned the river so that it was not necessary to go to the ford north of town or to take the ferry to get to the other side. In 1865 Napa celebrated the completion of a railroad to Suscol; free rides were given to anyone who "wanted to embrace the opportunity." "Pony," the diminutive, wood-burning engine, was succeeded by the magnificent $9,000 "Napa City," with a four and one-half foot drive wheel. In 1868 the road was continued to Calistoga, where Samuel Brannan feasted the first train load of passengers.

The town's later growth, based on the productiveness of the surrounding country, has been steady though not spectacular. Its products include gloves, athletic equipment, shirts and pants, and basalt paving and building materials.

Surrounded by green lawns and tall elms, the NAPA COUNTY COURT-HOUSE, Second, Third, Coombs, and Brown Sts., was built in 1878, replacing a courthouse erected in 1856. The gray, cement-covered brick building has a tower of the most unexpected contours. George Dyer observes that it "might have been brought from the Kremlin. Moorish windows, turnip top and all."

The NAPA HOTEL, First and Main Sts., oldest building in town, a three-story crenellated structure, has been extensively remodeled since it was built in 1851 by James Harbin.

TULUCAY CEMETERY, on the hills east of Napa on Third St., was opened on land given by Cayetano Juarez in 1858. Many plots are outlined in native stone and names of early families are commemorated in handsome large mausoleums of warm-colored stone. Huge eucalyptus trees shadow the graves and coveys of grey quail mince along the paths.

The route continues east from Vallejo on Georgia Street, which becomes Benicia Road.

SOUTHAMPTON BAY, 50.9 *m.,* on Carquinez Strait, is remembered as the site of the Corbett-Choynski prizefight; here on the grain barge *Excell* the celebrated bloody ring battle was fought June 6, 1889. The fight began at seven in the morning and lasted an hour and forty minutes—until a swig of brandy failed to revive Choynski in the 27th round. Corbett wore three-ounce gloves; Choynski, driving gloves. A sports writer described the opening of the fifth round: "Choynski came up in a rollicking way and did some good work but the professor quickly scored a flush hit with a left on his nose that brought the blood in a deluge."

Where the western end of Suisun Bay narrows to form Carquinez Strait lies BENICIA, 52.7 *m.* (10 alt., 2,913 pop.), a quiet little town whose past is of greater interest than its present. Benicia's founder was Dr. Robert Semple, a lean, hardy Missourian six feet, eight inches tall, who gave the impression of even greater size in his coonskin cap and loosely-fitting buckskin hunting jacket. (According to local legend, he wore his spurs on the calves of his legs when horseback riding and waded Carquinez Strait when the ferry was late.) Semple came to the Bay region from Monterey, where in 1846 he had established California's first newspaper, the *Californian* (*see Social Heritage: Gentlemen of the Press*). He had been a member of the group, who, after the Bear Flag rebellion, had taken General Mariano Vallejo as a prisoner to Sutter's Fort. Quick to note the advantages Benicia's site offered for a thriving metropolis, he had persuaded Vallejo to deed him five square miles of the Suscol Rancho.

Thomas O. Larkin, the American Consul in California, became a partner with Vallejo and Semple when the transfer of the land was concluded in the autumn of 1846. The town laid out the following year was called Francisca, in honor of Vallejo's wife; because of its similarity with the name San Francisco, Señora Vallejo's middle name, Benicia, later was adopted.

The fickle legislature, which had been dividing its attention among San Jose, Sacramento, and Vallejo, made Benicia the State capital in February, 1853. Unfortunately for the town's elaborate civic plans, the legislators abandoned it for Sacramento a year later. A visitor of that forlorn time wrote of Benicia: ". . . instead of raising an imposing front in evidence of man's progress, it hides its diminutive head among the few huts that stand in commemoration of its failure."

Between 1853 and 1868 a steamer ferry, the *Ione,* owned by Semple, operated between Benicia and Martinez, across the strait. Each of her two engines controlled a paddle-wheel, and since the two frequently became asynchronized, the little boat would reel around in drunken circles. At such moments the swift current would add considerably to the skipper's navigating problems.

The largest wooden dry dock ever constructed on the Pacific Coast was built in the shipyard of Captain Matthew Turner in 1895 for a San Francisco company. Today Benicia's chief industry is the canning of meat, fish, and vegetables. Also located here is a large factory that manufactures gold dredges.

The PACIFIC MAIL DOCKS, east of the Benicia-Martinez Ferry Slip, were built when the Pacific Mail Steamship Company established its California headquarters in Benicia. By 1853 they had constructed great wharves, foundries, and machine shops. The company's great early steamers *California, Oregon,* and *Panama* berthed in Benicia between trips for repairs and refueling. After 1881 the company could no longer compete with overland railroad transportation, and the property was sold.

At the lower end of First St. a marker indicates the SITE OF JACK LONDON'S HANGOUT (Jorgenson's Saloon), where the future novelist spent much of his time during the adventurous days of 1892-93 when he was an officer on the fish patrol. London lived on a water-front barge; to his seafaring intimates he was "Curley-headed Jack." His Benicia experiences are recalled in his novel, *John Barleycorn.*

The old STATE CAPITOL BUILDING, on the north side of G St., now the City Hall, library, and museum, a two-story brick building with a Doric portico, was built to house the State legislature, which held its second Benicia session here 1853-54. Later the building became the county courthouse and schoolhouse. The first-floor museum (*open daily 9-5*) houses a collection of pioneer items relating to Benicia: old lithographs of buildings and of the ships that slipped from local ways, ancient guns, a Wells Fargo safe with a secret keyhole; and the inevitable old music box that still plays lively tunes.

In the State's first MASONIC HALL, J St. west of First St., a two-story redwood buiding erected in August, 1851, the legislature met in February, 1853.

ST. PAUL'S EPISCOPAL CHURCH, First and J Sts., a large wooden Gothic structure topped by a slender spire, had cathedral status when Benicia was the see for the Diocese of Northern California. The house of the diocesan, Bishop John H. D. Wingfield, and the entrance gate to the campus are all that remain of the College of St. Augustine, which was the successor to a school founded in 1847.

In 1851 the two-story SOLANO HOUSE, First and E Sts., was built of redwood. Long the leading hotel in the region, it was host to such notable guests as Generals U. S. Grant and William T. Sherman; California Governors Bennett Riley and Frederick F. Low; John Sutter; and Colonel Silas Casey, the famous Indian fighter.

On I St. west of First St. is the marked SITE OF BENICIA SEMINARY. One of the first Protestant girls' schools in California, the seminary was established in 1852 for several denominations by the Reverend Sylvester Woodbridge and others. Its first teachers were sent here by Governor E. Fairbanks of Vermont. The Reverend Cyrus T. Mills, who purchased the school in 1865, was the founder of the present Mills College (*see OAKLAND*).

In BENICIA CITY PARK, First between K and L Sts., is the SITE OF THE FIRST PROTESTANT CHURCH IN CALIFORNIA, established April 15, 1849, by the Reverend Sylvester Woodbridge, a Presbyterian minister. The church declined and was finally closed in 1871 after controversy over adherence to the Union.

A portion of the adobe CALIFORNIA HOUSE still stands on the south side of H St., west of First St. Built by William Tustin in 1847, it became one of California's first hotels. Ex-Governor L. W. Boggs of Missouri performed Benicia's first wedding ceremony here when Frances Cooper became the wife of Dr. Robert Semple. In 1854 the building was sold to John Rueger, who turned it into a brewery.

Doña Maria Concepcion Arguello (Sister Dominica), in the years following her tragic love affair with Count Nikolai Rezanov (later romanticized by Bret Harte and Gertrude Atherton), found religious refuge in ST. CATHERINE'S CONVENT, West L St. between First and Second Sts. The original cream-colored brick building with its old dormer windows still stands. The school has expanded into modern buildings of the mission style.

A private residence on the north side of H St. between Second and Third Sts. was once the PEABODY HOSPITAL, established in 1849. Here returning gold miners were treated by Dr. W. F. Peabody, later Mayor of Benicia.

Brought around the Horn in sections in 1849, the CAPTAIN JOHN WALSH HOUSE, 117 East L St., still stands, well preserved. Walsh settled in Benicia in 1849 and became deputy collector of the then important port.

Still used by the United States Army as an ammunition depot is the BENICIA ARSENAL, north-east edge of town, established in 1851. A large stone building, in its day it was the most pretentious structure in Benicia and a social as well as a military center. The Benicia Barracks was established here in 1849.

1. At Benicia is the Benicia-Martinez Auto Ferry Slip (*Car and driver 55¢, each additional passenger 10¢*), from which ferries cross the strait to MARTINEZ, 2 m. (12 alt., 6,569 pop.) (*see East Bay Tour 1*).

2. North from Benicia on First St. 1 m. to the ROMAN CATHOLIC CEMETERY, where a simple cross marks the grave of Dona Maria Concepcion Arguello.

Down the Peninsula

The wedge-shaped strip of territory known to all San Franciscans as "the Peninsula," broad at its base in the south and pinched to a tip by ocean and Bay at its northern end, is a multicolored land. It embraces tall mountains darkly forested, white sandy beaches enclosed on three sides by steep rocky cliffs, peaceful farms with chaste white buildings, broad walled estates with stately old mansions, and busy towns bright with red and green roofs of modern stucco homes. Spanish explorers and Catholic mission builders, trudging north from established Monterey, were the first white men to look on its hills and water and plain.

Crude ox teams and speeding mounted couriers packed the earth hard on the Peninsula's first trail, a trail that became a road and was named El Camino Real—the King's Highway. As San Francisco grew and spread across the Peninsula's northern tip the city's wealthy built palatial homes on the eastern slopes of the Coast mountains, near to the King's Highway, and drove thundering coachloads of famous guests to the lavish banquets they staged in mansions filled with *objets d'art*.

Today thousands of San Franciscans live on the Peninsula and drive to work or ride the commute trains playing never-ending games of bridge on tables held on knees between coach seats. On Sundays and holidays the many roads and highways that climb along mountain ridges, trace the ocean's shore, and skirt the southern regions of the Bay are black with the cars of picnickers and sightseers who flock to man-made lakes, crowd the barbecue stands, and drink beer in the cafes of tiny towns nestling in the shade against the mountain slopes.

Beyond the base of the Peninsula, sweeping away from the southern end of the Bay, lies the Santa Clara Valley, in springtime a red, pink, and white confusion of blossoms, for its broad rolling acres are an almost endless orchard of apricot and prune trees. And up the slopes that climb gradually toward the forested mountains to the west spread green vineyards. The valley is walled on east and west by mountains. The eastern hills are dotted with live-oak and laurel, and their slopes are green with thick-growing grass as winter changes to spring. Above the foothills rises Mount Hamilton, highest peak of the eastern range, whose crest in winter is sometimes whitened by snow. Redwoods, fir, maple, laurel, and madrone darken the western mountains, where twisting roads emerge at intervals from the thick forest upon sweeping views of deep canyons and distant blue ridges.

At the valley's southern end, some of the richest quicksilver mines in the world once operated, but the buildings are rotting now and the long shafts and tunnels, their length and depth increased by legend, are caving. The valley is rich in legends—and often the legends are substantiated by the crumbling adobe walls of a home built in the days of the ranchos or a weed-grown dirt road, abandoned, leading down into some narrow canyon.

Peninsula Tour

San Francisco—Burlingame—San Mateo—Redwood City—Palo Alto —Santa Clara—San Jose; 101.9 m. US 101.

Paved four-lane road throughout.
Southern Pacific R. R. parallels route; Pacific Greyhound Bus Line follows it.

US 101 follows "down the Peninsula" part of the most famous of all California roads, El Camino Real (The King's Highway), which from the eighteenth century has linked together the long line of missions and *pueblos*. Once little more than a trail, it has seen an ever-growing number of travelers until today, as a four-way arterial, it retains little more of the past than the musical names of its towns and cities.

South from Van Ness Ave. and Fulton St. in SAN FRANCISCO, 0 *m.*, on Van Ness Ave. to Mission St.; R. on Mission (US 101).

DALY CITY, 6.7 *m.* (190 alt., 9,612 pop.), is at the crest of a hill from which the land, given over to vegetable gardens and golf courses, drops to Lake Merced and the ocean. San Bruno Mountain (1,375 alt.) rises steeply in the east. This was originally part of Rancho Laguna de la Merced. The earliest American settlers, homesteaders engaged in growing vegetables, were involved for several years in lawsuits growing out of attempts made by speculators to drive them off their land. Until the 1906 earthquake the northern part of the town site was a dairy ranch owned by John Daly. Many refugees from the great San Francisco fire, given small portable two-room houses, moved here, forming the nucleus of the thriving town. Today many of the residents work in San Francisco. Nurseries here grow violets, gladiolus, dahlias, and heather, all of which thrive on the cool summer fogs.

COLMA, 8 *m.*, formerly a separate town, is now a district of Daly City.

At LAWNDALE, 8.4 *m.* (113 alt., 369 pop.), the quick are greatly outnumbered by the dead. Cemeteries extend into the hills from both sides of the highway. The beautifully landscaped acres, through which streams descend into Colma Creek, provide burial places for members of many nationalities and religious faiths. In GREEK

ORTHODOX MEMORIAL PARK many of the tombstones bear photographs of the deceased developed in enamel and set into the stones. The JAPANESE CEMETERY has many graves marked according to Japanese custom by square wooden posts with pyramidal tops. Some of the vaults in the ITALIAN CEMETERY may be opened and the remains seen behind glass. In the SERBIAN CEMETERY many of the tombstones are in the form of the patriarchal cross common in the iconography of the Greek Orthodox Church. CYPRESS LAWN, largest and oldest of the interdenominational cemeteries, with beautifully kept lawns and clumps of pines and other trees, extends up sloping ground for nearly a mile. In HOLY CROSS, a large Roman Catholic cemetery, is an ornate stone chapel. At the entrance to the CHINESE CEMETERY, occupying a grassy slope overlooking the Bay, stands a shrine with two fireplaces in which the strips of paper carried in funeral processions still are burned.

In the willows along Baden Creek near BADEN, 11.7 m. (33 alt.), now a part of South San Francisco (see below), a tall Alsatian named Charles Lux met in 1857 an ambitious young German, Henry Kreicer. The latter had come to California on a non-transferable ticket belonging to a friend named Miller, whose name he adopted. With Lux he built up a cattle business which soon reached far beyond this part of Rancho Buri Buri. By 1880 Miller and Lux holdings spread over nineteen counties in California (chiefly in the Coast Ranges and the west side of the San Joaquin Valley) and San Francisco's meat business was under their control.

At the BADEN KENNEL CLUB (L), greyhounds once were raced. Since betting on races was illegal in California, the Greyhound Exchange resorted to the ingenious devise of selling "options" on the competing dogs. Before crowds of enthusiastic spectators, the dogs followed a realistic mechanical rabbit around a quarter-mile track. In 1939 the State Attorney General ordered all dog tracks in California closed.

TANFORAN RACE TRACK (gen. adm. 40¢; fall and spring seasons), 13 m., built in the 1880's, attracted San Francisco horse-racing enthusiasts until the Legislature in 1912 made betting on races illegal. When the pari-mutuel system was legalized the track reopened. In 1913 the first flying in California was done here by Jean Poulhan. Crowds gasped in wonder at seeing him go several hundred feet aloft in his little plane.

South of Tanforan the highway is bordered by tall eucalyptus trees set out in the seventies and eighties by large landowners. They once extended in an almost unbroken line from here twenty miles south to Palo Alto.

Much of SAN BRUNO, 14.1 m. (20 alt., 6,496 pop.), lies east of the highway; extensive truck farms extend west to the hills. A small settlement was here before the American occupation, on part of the Sanchez family's Buri Buri Rancho, which extended some nine miles along the Bay shore and between two and three miles into the hills.

When California passed into American hands the Sanchez family were among the few to make a heroic last stand. With a little band of compatriots they captured and held prisoners for several weeks Yerba Buena's *alcalde,* Washington Bartlett, and several other Americans. At the southern outskirts of San Bruno is "UNCLE TOM'S CABIN," a restaurant formerly known as the Fourteen Mile House, whose bar-room occupies one of the earliest hostelries on the "Mission Road," a small cabin erected in 1849, to which later additions have been made.

Left from San Bruno on a paved road 0.8 *m.* to the junction with US 101 Bypass; R. (south) here 0.6 *m.* to the SAN FRANCISCO MUNICIPAL AIR-PORT, one of the largest air terminals in the West. Its 1,376 acres were purchased from the Mills estate in 1927. Four hangars are here, and a large Spanish-styled administration building. Nearing completion is a seaplane base.

The main side route continues north on US 101 Bypass to SOUTH SAN FRANCISCO, 2.8 *m.* (11 alt., 6,517 pop.), at the southern base of San Bruno Mountain. The site of "South City" occupies part of the "home ranch" of Miller and Lux (*see above*). Stockmen and meatpackers, among them Henry S. Crocker, P. D. Armour, G. P. Swift, and Henry Miller, invested here in 1889; later came steel mills, foundries, and manufacturing plants. The town has an attractive residential section with a view of the Bay, but many of the employees of the industrial plants live in San Francisco.

Like San Bruno, MILLBRAE, 15.9 *m.* (8 alt., 1,500 pop.), was until 1849 part of the Buri Buri Rancho. In that year Darius Ogden Mills, a Sacramento merchant and banker, acquired about 3,700 acres, a large part of which still belongs to his descendants. The streets and houses west of the highway are recent developments. The town has several large nurseries.

South of Millbrae US 101 traverses the MILLS ESTATE (*private*) 16.2 *m.,* over which ranged large herds of dairy cattle. This was one of a number of large acreages in San Mateo County where wealthy families in the seventies and eighties made an attempt not altogether unsuccessful to duplicate English country life. With the great increase in the demand for suburban homes after 1906, most of the estates gradually were subdivided, but the fine private park and the dignified Victorian house of Darius Mills have remained unchanged.

BURLINGAME, 17 *m.* (30 alt., 15,897 pop.), lying along both sides of the highway, extending from the Bay shore to Buri Buri Ridge, is almost entirely a suburban residential community. Business is limited to two streets lined with small retail shops. The well-kept residential streets, the modern homes with trim lawns and gardens, a library with 60,000 volumes, the fine school buildings—all reflect a prosperous middle class. The town includes the northern part of Rancho San Mateo, granted to Cayento Arenas by Governor Pio Pico. In 1846 the land was sold for $25,000 to W. D. M. Howard. Emulating the Spanish predecessors, Howard built up a hide and tallow business, but unlike them, he grew wealthy with the growth of San Francisco. Bur-lingame's moderate climate and oak-covered hills early attracted a num-ber of prosperous San Franciscans looking for country home sites, notably A. L. Easton, who in 1860 acquired property and settled in

what is now North Burlingame. Easton and Howard were not the first
to recognize the natural beauty of the land. Captain George Vancouver on his visit in 1792 had observed that ". . . it could only be
compared to a park, which had been originally planted with the true
old English oak . . . The soil was covered with luxuriant herbage and
beautifully diversified with pleasing eminences and valleys; which with
the range of lofty rugged mountains that bounded the prospect, required
only to be adorned with the neat habitations of an industrious
people . . ."

The community bears the name of Anson Burlingame. Son of a
humble Methodist lay preacher, Burlingame had risen rapidly to become
a Congressman from Massachusetts, and in 1861 Lincoln appointed
him minister to China. His Burlingame Treaty made him an international figure, and his unfortunate plan for importation of coolie
labor won him considerable prestige in California. In 1866, while
enroute to China, he purchased 1,043 acres of land adjoining the Easton
property. Though Burlingame died four years later, and had visited
the place only once, when Burlingame Country Club was organized in
1893 it was named for him, as was the Burlingame Post Office a year
later. "Blingum" was for years synonymous with wealth and fashion;
but after the division of the Easton property in 1905, the population
increased and the town took on its present suburban characteristics.

The SOUTHERN PACIFIC RAILWAY STATION, Bur-
lingame Ave. and California Dr., in California mission style, is roofed
with the old hand-made tiles from the mission hospice used by the
Franciscans and early travelers as a stopping place halfway between
Mission Dolores and Santa Clara.

Standing near a wide driveway, with a magnificent view of open
country, semi-forested, rolling hills, and the distant Bay, is the MERCY
HIGH SCHOOL, Adeline Dr. When it was the home of C. Frederick
Kohl it was known as "The Oaks." In Tudor style, it is of dark red
brick trimmed with brown stone (Howard and White, architects).
Little Lord Fauntleroy, starring Mary Pickford, was filmed here.

Between 18.4 *m.* and 18.6 *m.*, El Camino Real is the eastern boundary of HILLSBOROUGH (40-700 alt., 2,745 pop.), which occupies
an irregular, wedge-shaped area between Burlingame and San Mateo.
It was separately incorporated in 1910 to keep out all business establishments. The town has no sidewalks; its homes, most of them set
in grounds a half-acre or more in extent, are surrounded by high hedges.
Along the winding roads are fine old shade trees.

The BURLINGAME COUNTRY CLUB (*private*), Floribunda
Ave. in northern Hillsborough, was organized in 1893, the first country
club in California and one of the first places in the United States where
polo was played. Golf, too, was popular here at a time when but few
Americans played the game.

The WOODLAND THEATRE, El Cerrito Ave., on ground
sloping down toward San Mateo Creek, shaded by oaks, buckeyes, and
bay trees, is used principally for concerts.

The informal Italian gardens of NEW PLACE (*private*), Stone-hedge Rd., residence of the late W. H. Crocker, were laid out by Bruce Porter; the Italian villa was designed by Lewis P. Hobart. In the house are notable nineteenth century paintings by Monet, Millet and Rousseau; some fine work by the Venetians: Bellini, Canaletto, and Guardi; and exquisite bronzes.

Extending from the Bay Shore to wooded hills, the quiet tree-shaded streets of suburban SAN MATEO, 19.8 *m.* (22 alt., 19,367 pop.), surround a bustling shopping district. Here on the banks of San Mateo Creek, where it emerges from a brushy canyon into the oak-covered plain, the Franciscan fathers built of adobe a small chapel and a hospice, for many years the only accommodation for the traveler be-tween Santa Clara and Mission Dolores. As a part of Rancho San Mateo, the land became the property of W. D. M. Howard, who after the earthquake of 1868 saved the roofing tiles of the adobes (later used for the Burlingame railway station). Two pioneer merchants and bankers of San Francisco, Frederick Macondray and John Parrott, built country homes here in the 1850's. In 1863 when the San Fran-cisco-San Jose railroad was completed, streets were laid out to the east of the highway. The town grew slowly; its population in 1890 was only about one thousand. But as the large estates of Howard, Parrott, Alvinza Hayward, William Sharon, and other wealthy early settlers have been divided, large numbers of attractive homes have been built.

Wooded CITY PARK (*ball park, tennis courts*), facing El Camino Real between Fifth and Ninth Aves., was formerly the estate of Cap-tain Kohl, an Alaska fur trader.

Set back of trees and lawns are ST. MATTHEW'S EPISCOPAL CHURCH and BAYLARD HOUSE, El Camino Real and Baldurn Ave. The setting of the buildings resembles that of an English village church. In the church is the tomb of the Howard family.

At the SAN MATEO-BURLINGAME POLO CLUB (*adm. to games, 40¢*), 1900 S. El Camino Real, two seasons of polo are held annually: spring, March and April, and fall, August to Christmas.

The $400,000 BAY MEADOWS RACETRACK (*general adm. 40¢*), on San Mateo's southern outskirts, shares the spring and fall crowds with Tanforan (*see above*). The plant, built in 1934 by a syndicate headed by one-time newsboy, William P. Kyne, accommodates about twenty-five thousand spectators. Standing track records here were set by Alviso, Seabiscuit, and Top Row.

1. Left from San Mateo on East Third Avenue 3.7 *m.* to the San Mateo Toll Bridge (*car, driver, and four passengers, 65¢*). Beyond the eastern end of the bridge is a junction with State 17 at Mount Eden, 13.6 *m.* (*see East Bay Tour 2*).

2. Right from San Mateo on West Third Avenue, which becomes Crystal Springs Road, to a junction with Sawyer Camp Road, 2.8 *m.*; R. here to a junc-tion with State 5 (Skyline Boulevard), 3.7 *m.*, on which the route goes L. over SKYLINE DAM, built across the deep canyon of San Mateo Creek to impound the water of CRYSTAL SPRINGS LAKE, a reservoir for San Francisco's water supply. The lake extends south for five miles, its lower end covering the site of the house of Domingo Feliz, grantee of the Rancho Feliz. Beneath

the water is the site of Crystal Springs, around which grew the vineyards of Colonel Agaston Haraszthy, Hungarian nobleman, who had set out six varieties of wine grapes here by 1852.

At 5.3 m. is the junction with a paved road; L. here to the junction with Cañada Road, 1.2 m.; R. here to the WATER TEMPLE, 3.6 m., a circular structure inscribed: "I give waters in the wilderness and rivers in the desert to my people." This is the west end of the Hetch Hetchy pipe line. Cañada Road continues south through oak-covered hills to Woodside, 9.3 m. (see below).

The main side route goes R. on State 5 onto an earthen causeway across Crystal Springs Lake and climbs wooded slopes to the crest of Cahil Ridge at the junction with the Half Moon Bay Road, 8.3 m., where the main side route goes R. (straight ahead); L. here on State 5 over thickly forested hills to the junction with Kings Mountain Road, 7 m. (see below).

The main side route continues west from the junction with State 5 on the Half Moon Bay Road, twisting down Pilarcitos Creek Canyon to HALF MOON BAY, 13.6 m. (10 alt., 1,000 pop.), a town at the junction with State 1, center of the artichoke-growing Pilarcitos Valley. The original settlement, known as Spanishtown, grew around the adobes of Candelario Miramontes and Tiburcio Vasquez, grantees, respectively, of the local Rancho Miramontes and Rancho Corral de Tierra (enclosure of earth). Half Moon Bay was known during Prohibition for its conflicts between rum-runners and Coast Guard. A submerged reef extending south for two miles from nearby Pillar Point forms a breakwater for the harbor and protects the arc-shaped white sandy beach.

The Nation's commercial production of globe artichokes is confined largely to the coastal strip between Half Moon Bay and Monterey Bay, where the cool foggy summers and mild wet winters make growing conditions ideal. Though widely used in France and Italy, artichokes are not a staple article of food in the United States outside California. They are on the San Francisco market almost all seasons, but the greater part of the crop is cut from January to April. Canning (first done in 1917) provides an outlet for the less marketable small-sized artichokes, the canned product consisting only of hearts.

South of Half Moon Bay the route skirts the coast on State 1 to PURISIMA (immaculate), 18.1 m. (46 alt., 50 pop.), a bleak and decaying old town on a hill above Purisima Creek, which served as the northern boundary of Rancho Cañada de Verde y Arroyo de la Purisima (valley of verdure and creek of the immaculate one), granted to Jose Maria Alviso in 1838.

Once a lumbering town, SAN GREGORIO, 26 m. (100 alt., 75 pop.), lies beside San Gregorio Creek, which drains the vast acreage of the former Rancho San Gregorio, granted to Antonio Buelna. Reaching here on October 24, 1769, Portola camped two days to rest his men, all of them weary and many ill of scurvy. The frame SAN GREGORIO HOUSE, painted a rusty red and half-hidden by tall maples, was once a popular resort.

PESCADERO (fishmonger), 33.4 m. (56 alt., 979 pop.), standing in the flat valley about three miles from the ocean, is within the boundaries of Rancho El Pescadero, granted in 1833 to soldier Juan Jose Gonzales, whose adobe stood on the north bank of Pescadero Creek. Father Crespi, the historian of Portola's party, proposed the founding of a mission near the beach, where an Indian village stood. Pescadero was known as Spotless Town for many years after the ship *Colombia* ran ashore here and was battered to pieces, for the residents—nearly all of whom were New Englanders—salvaged the cargo of white lead and painted their houses gleaming white.

At Pescadero is the junction with Blooms Mill Creek Road (see below).

At LAKE LUCERNE, 38.6 m., sometimes known as Bean Hollow Lagoon, a salt-water lake lying at the mouth of the Arroyo de los Frijoles (Bean Hollow), is the junction with Pebble Beach Road; R. here along the shoreline past Pescadero Point, 2.6 m., to mile-long PEBBLE BEACH (surf fishing). The deposit of pebbles here includes agates and chalcedony, from amygdaloid rocks, made popular by San Francisco jewelers in the eighties. Here stand the ruins of "COBURN'S FOLLY," the large three-story hotel erected by Loren

Coburn in 1892. He spent money lavishly, expecting to have a popular and profitable resort upon the arrival of the proposed Ocean Shore Railroad from San Francisco. The railroad's failure to build this far south left Coburn possessor of a vacant and useless building. He closed the road to the beach, thus bringing on a long series of quarrels with the citizens of nearby Pescadero (*see above*). Barriers which he built across the road were destroyed again and again. Lawsuits followed, and Coburn, who was eventually awarded damages against his fellow citizens for $1,000, became a hated and ostracised old man.

PIGEON POINT, 41.3 *m.*, was named for the clipper ship (*Carrier Pigeon*), wrecked here May 6, 1853. A Portuguese whaling station once was here, and from the pier, lumber and dairy products were shipped. The high cliff is topped by the white conical tower of PIGEON POINT LIGHTHOUSE, 148 feet above water level, built in 1872. Its 900,000-candlepower beam is visible for eighteen miles.

Whitehouse Creek, 10.3 *m.*, is named for ISAAC GRAHAM'S HOUSE (*private*), a lone white, two-story frame dwelling brought around the Horn, for many years a landmark for mariners but now almost hidden by a grove of eucalyptus trees. FRANKLIN POINT, a mile west, commemorates a sea disaster in 1865 when eleven were lost in the wreck of the *Sir John Franklin*.

LA PUNTA DEL AÑO NUEVO (New Year's Point), 49 *m.*, sighted and named by Sebastian Vizcaino on January 3, 1603, is crowned by the white tower of NEW YEAR'S POINT LIGHTHOUSE. Along the shore here the shifting sand frequently reveals evidence of former Indian occupation in the form of arrowheads, skeletons, and shells. The vast and fertile Rancho Punta del Año Nuevo once covered 17,753 acres north from the point. From grantee Simeon Castro the rancho passed into the hands of Loren Coburn, who leased the land to dairy farmers (*see above*).

South of San Mateo the highway climbs the lower slopes of rounded, oak-covered hills—once on Rancho Las Pulgas—which hem in the little valley originally called Cañada del Diablo.

BELMONT, 24.2 *m.* (32 at., 984 pop.) is a town of suburban residences, schools, and sanitariums. In the early fifties, when it was for a short time the county seat, a hotel here was a stopping place for stages.

The former rambling white mansion of William C. Ralston is now one of the buildings of NOTRE DAME COLLEGE, Ralston Ave. In 1854 Count Leonetto Cipriani, an Italian political refugee, acquired the site, Cañada del Diablo (Devil's Valley), and built a small villa, which in 1866 he sold to Ralston. The financier began transforming it into an extravagant show place, adorned with parquetry floors, mirror-panelled walls, and chandeliers. He built greenhouses, a gymnasium with a Turkish bath, stables panelled in carved mahogany, a gas-works to provide gas for illumination and a dam and reservoir to provide water. After Ralston's death in 1875 the big house was successively a private school and a hospital. In 1923 it was occupied by the Sisters of Notre Dame, who removed their convent and college here from San Jose. The mansion is now called Berchman's Hall, honoring one of the founding sisters. Ralston's famous ballroom is the school chapel.

US 101 continues south through country largely devoted to flower growing. Chrysanthemums, the most important crop, have an annual value of about $5,000,000. The growers are usually Chinese, Japanese, or Italians. From here each year on All Saints Day, New Orleans gets thousands of white chrysanthemums for its graves.

Named for the first vessel to enter the Golden Gate, SAN CARLOS, 25.1 *m.* (21 alt., 3,508 pop.), occupies a site within the former boundaries of Rancho Las Pulgas (the fleas), which got its unhappy name from the innumerable fleas infesting the Indian village that stood here. Today it is a pleasant residential town without any remains of the past either in the form of insects or old buildings.

REDWOOD CITY, 27.1 *m.* (10 alt., 12,364 pop.), seat of San Mateo County, was known in Spanish-American days as the Embarcadero because of the slough which was navigable up to what is now the center of the business district. Other names given it were Cachinetac and Mezesville, for S. M. Mezes, who laid out the town in 1854. Shortly after the Gold Rush the fine stands of redwoods nearby attracted lumbermen, who shipped the timber down Redwood Slough. A number of schooners built here carried lumber, hay, and grain to San Francisco. The town has grown rapidly since 1920, but many old frame houses of the fifties and sixties are still standing. A cement works and two tanneries are the largest industrial plants.

Facing Broadway at Hamilton St. is the SAN MATEO COUNTY COURTHOUSE, a resolutely modern building built in 1939, which contrasts incongruously with its neighbor, the former courthouse, an old domed building of Colusa sandstone. The PUBLIC LIBRARY and CITY HALL, Jefferson Ave. and Middlefield Rd., are a well-proportioned group of buildings employing concrete with red-tiled roofs in a severe modern style.

The two-story, square, stuccoed MORGAN HOUSE was moved to Chestnut and Spring Sts. from the tidal lands of the Bay, where it had served as a residence, anchored on piles, for Captain John Stillwell Morgan, promoter of oyster culture in San Francisco Bay.

1. Left from Redwood City on a paved road 3.1 *m.* to the PORT OF REDWOOD CITY, completed in 1937. The channel has been dredged to accommodate ocean-going vessels. Large shipments are made of fresh and canned fruit and vegetables. Lumber, once the chief export, is now the chief import. The PACIFIC PORTLAND CEMENT PLANT (R), 3.2 *m.,* utilizes the oyster shells that bed the bottom of the shallow mud flats; dredged from the Bay, pulverized, and calcined, they are converted into lime.

2. Right from Redwood City on Jefferson Ave. 2.1 *m.* to EMERALD LAKE AND BOWL, in a nine-acre park. A natural bowl seats 12,000 at Christmas and Easter celebrations.

3. Right from the southern end of Redwood City at Five Points on paved Woodside Road is WOODSIDE, 3.9 *m.* (486 alt., 400 pop.), at the southern end of San Raymundo Valley, first settled in the 1830's by William ("Bill the Sawyer") Smith and his partner James Pease, deserter from a British ship, who made carts and farming implements for the *padres* at Santa Clara. Woodside now represents the combined old settlements of Greersburg and Whiskey Hill, where flourished three saloons.

Left from Woodside on Portola Road, past large country houses set well back of hedges and gardens, to the junction with a paved road, 2.1 *m.;* R. here 0.2 *m.* to the junction with a dirt road; R. here to the HOOPER ADOBE (*private*), 0.3 *m.,* built by Charles Brown, an American who deserted a whaling vessel in 1833, acquired part of Rancho Cañada de Raymundo, and settled here. Later Colonel "Jack" Hays used the building as a lodging house for lumbermen. Other owners have been E. W. Burr and John A. Hooper, president of the San Francisco National Bank. Two tall eucalyptus trees and a trim hedge frame the one-story house with its tiled roof extending over the veranda. An enormous Banksia rosebush climbs to the ridge of the roof.

On Portola Road at 2.3 *m.* is SEARSVILLE LAKE (*swimming, boating; adm. week-days 25¢, Sun. and holidays 35¢*). Near here in the fifties was Searsville, with 2,000 inhabitants, a busy center for redwood lumbering and convenient stopping place for mule- and ox-team drivers crossing the ridge. Only reminder of its lusty days are the rows of trees which shaded its main street. In 1890, when the supply of timber was exhausted, the Spring Valley Water Company removed the buildings and built a dam which forms the present lake. It is now a reservoir whose waters irrigate the greenery of the Stanford University campus (*see below*).

The main side route goes west from Woodside on La Honda Road.

At the junction with Kings Mountain Road, 4.7 *m.*, under a large oak, is the JOHN COPPINGER STOREHOUSE, now used as a residence, built in 1854 of hand-hewn timbers by Coppinger, grantee of 12,545-acre Rancho Cañada de Raymundo. The two curious dormer windows of its upper story are slightly awry. Coppinger, who married Maria Luisa Soto, member of an influential Spanish family, built an adobe house here in 1840 which stood until destroyed by the 1906 earthquake.

The route turns R. on Kings Mountain Road to the WOODSIDE STORE, 5.2 *m.*, a two-story shingled structure shaded by a large live oak. Built in 1854 by R. O. Tripp, a dentist, the store (now a library) was the trading center for fifteen sawmills. More than a thousand lumberjacks got their mail, food, and liquor here. Hand-hewn, octagonal posts support the porch roof; the joists also are hand-hewn. "Old Doc" Tripp at ninety-three still presided behind his counter.

At 5.8 *m.* Kings Mountain Road enters wooded HUDDART PARK, a 973-acre undeveloped recreational area bequeathed to San Francisco by James M. Huddart in 1931. The sharply winding road climbs into the wooded canyon to a junction with State 5 (Skyline Boulevard), 9.2 *m.* (*see above*), at the summit of Cahil Ridge, also known as Kings Mountain for a Mrs. Honoria King who formerly kept a tavern accommodating travelers by stage over the toll road from Woodside. The route goes L. on State 5.

At 11 *m.* is OBSERVATION POINT, a stone-buttressed parking lot area offering a superb view of the Peninsula towns, San Francisco Bay, and the East Bay shore. Mount Tamalpais, Mount Hamilton, and Mount Diablo are clearly visible.

Near the summit of Sierra Morena (2,400 alt.) at 11.6 *m.* is the SKYLINE METHUSELAH REDWOOD (L), an ancient lone redwood with storm-shattered top, fifty-five feet in circumference.

State 5 drops by well-engineered grades to a junction, at 14.2 *m.*, with La Honda Road, on which the route goes R.; L. here on State 5 to Saratoga Gap, at the junction with State 9, 13.9 *m.* (*see below*).

The route goes R. on La Honda Road through dense firs and redwoods into the deep canyon of La Honda Creek. LA HONDA (the deep), 20 *m.* (403 alt., 150 pop.) (*hotel, cabins, campgrounds*), was founded in 1861 by John L. Sears of Searsville. The LA HONDA STORE was built for Sears by Jim and Bob Younger, who a little later were arrested as members of the Jesse James gang.

At LA HONDA PARK (*campgrounds, swimming*), 20.5 *m.*, a summer resort, is a junction with a paved road; the route turns L. here on Alpine Creek Road into a densely wooded canyon to the junction with Blooms Mill Road, 22 *m.*; R. on Blooms Mill Road to SAN MATEO COUNTY MEMORIAL PARK (*camping 50¢; special weekly rates*), 26.5 *m.*, a 310-acre grove of redwoods dedicated to the memory of those from San Mateo County who died in the World War.

Blooms Mill Road winds down Pescadero Creek to PESCADERO, 34.5 *m.* (56 alt., 979 pop.), at the junction with State 1 (*see above*).

South of Redwood City the Bay narrows and the level land between the highway and the mountains widens. The country originally had great natural beauty, but the section facing the highway has been so defaced by real estate offices, sandwich stands, and billboards that Bay region drivers have petulantly echoed Ogden Nash's couplet:
"I think that I shall never see a billboard lovely as a tree;
Perhaps, unless the billboard fall, I shall not see a tree at all."
ATHERTON, 29.1 *m.* (52 alt., 1,324 pop.), bears the name of Faxon D. Atherton, a pioneer settler, whose daughter-in-law, Gertrude Atherton, in her autobiography, *Adventures of a Novelist,* recounts much interesting gossip of fashionable life here in the 1880's. Atherton has remained a residential community, its roads winding in and out among tree-lined estates. The MENLO CIRCUS CLUB, Isabella Ave., occupies part of the site of Valparaiso Park, the estate of Faxon Atherton. At the club's annual (August) horse show fine horses from many parts of the country compete for prizes.

MENLO PARK, 30.1 *m.* (63 alt., 2,254 pop.), was named in 1851 for Ireland's Menlo Park by Dennis J. Oliver and D. C. McGlyn, who had purchased 1,700 acres of the Rancho Las Pulgas. The town grew up after the opening of the San Francisco-San Jose railroad in 1863, attracting many people of wealth. More recently families of moderate means have settled here, but except for nurseries and local retail shops Menlo Park has no commercial activities.

1. Left from Menlo Park on Ravenswood Ave. 0.2 *m.* to the PARK MILITARY ACADEMY, occupying a large old-fashioned house surrounded by oak trees. This was formerly the home of Edgar Mills, brother of Darious Ogden Mills.

The square-towered TIMOTHY HOPKINS HOUSE, 0.3 *m.,* stands a quarter-mile south of the road in a grove of fine oaks. In the fifties, this property belonged to E. W. Barron of quicksilver fame. It later passed to Senator Milton S. Latham, but the home built by Barron burned before Latham and his bride could move into it. Latham built the present house, which he named "Sherwood Hall." From him it passed to Mary Hopkins, widow of Mark Hopkins, and from her to Timothy Hopkins, one of the original trustees of Stanford University.

At 0.6 is a junction with Middlefield Road; the route goes R. here.

In 1898 ST. PATRICK'S SEMINARY, 0.9 *m.,* an institution of collegiate rank, was founded by the late Archbishop Thomas Riordan to train men for the Roman Catholic priesthood. The instructors are members of the Order of St. Sulpice; resident seminarians number more than one hundred. The buildings stand well back from the road in a setting of green lawns, great oaks, palms and rose gardens.

At 1.3 *m.* is the junction with Willow Road; L. on Willow Road.

The VETERANS' ADMINISTRATION HOSPITAL, 2.1 *m.,* is a diagnostic center with 900 patients. The buildings stand on attractive wooded grounds.

On Willow Road at 2.4 *m.* is the junction with US 101 Bypass; straight ahead on Willow Rd. to DUMBARTON BRIDGE (*40¢ per car, 5¢ per passenger*), 4.7 *m.*

Visible south of Dumbarton Bridge is the BAY CROSSING OF THE HETCH-HETCHY AQUEDUCTS. Underneath the navigable channel on the east side of the Bay, the steel cylinder and reinforced concrete pipes are entrenched twenty-five feet down in the mud, seventy feet beneath the surface of the water. On the shallower western side of the Bay, the submerged pipes enter a concrete caisson and from there are carried to the San Mateo County shore over a steel bridge resting on concrete piers (*see Emporium of a New World: Engineering Enterprise*).

At 13.4 *m.* is the junction with State 17 (*see East Bay Tour 2*).

2. Right from Menlo Park on Cambridge Avenue 0.7 *m.* to the ALLIED ARTS GUILD (*open weekdays 9-5:30*), an institution organized in 1930 to help finance the Stanford Convalescent Home for Children in Palo Alto. The guild maintains a tea room and a group of studios which display weaving, ceramics, metal- and wood-craft, and block printing. These are housed in a group of buildings admirably designed in seventeenth-century Spanish Colonial style by Gardiner Bailey on land owned originally by John and Margaret Murray, who came here in 1854. The estate's great charm is enhanced by the beautifully appropriate landscaping of the gardens.

Where US 101 crosses San Francisquito Creek, 31.3 *m.*, appears a few hundred feet west, near its bank, the solitary redwood, PALO ALTO (tall tree), a landmark for explorers and travelers since the Gaspar de Portola expedition first saw it in 1769. It was not a tree of remarkable height among redwoods, but standing far removed from any others, it towered above its neighboring oaks, visible for many leagues. It appears in early prints and on the seal of Stanford University as a double-trunked tree; one section has fallen.

US 101 divides Stanford University from the city of PALO ALTO, 31.9 *m.* (63 alt., 16,278 pop.), itself bisected by its chief thoroughfare, University Avenue. When the university came into being in 1891, the greater part of what is now Palo Alto was but a great wheat field dotted with oak trees and a few scattered houses and stores; early students and instructors went to Menlo Park for their mail and food supplies. But by 1894 Palo Alto was large enough to incorporate. Mayfield, now a Palo Alto suburb, once was a separate unregenerate town where Stanford students could drink beer. Industry too has come, in the form of a company making automatic hammers.

The Palo Alto PUBLIC LIBRARY, Hamilton Ave. and Bryant St., has 65,000 volumes and much important material on local history—files of newspapers, old theater and concert programs, and old photographs.

Examples of an intelligent adaptation of the Spanish Colonial style to modern use are the POST OFFICE, Waverly St. and Hamilton Ave.; the CITY HALL, Ramona St. between University and Lytton Aves.; and the PALO ALTO HIGH SCHOOL, El Camino Real and Embarcadero Rd. The same style has been used succesfully on a business block (Ramona St. between University and Hamilton Aves.), where the buildings were designed so they would not destroy a large oak tree.

The COMMUNITY CENTER, Melville Ave. and Middlefield Rd., consists of a group of buildings in Spanish Colonial style admirably placed about three sides of a brick paved court and surrounded by splendid oaks and broad lawns. The buildings were a gift of Mrs. Louis Stern. The Center's activities are supported partly by the city and partly by the organizations using the center. The Palo Alto Community Players give performances in the theater, the central building in the group. Here also are a separate children's theater, a children's museum, Boy Scouts Hall, a ballroom, a reception room, and a dining room and kitchen, all designed to foster Palo Alto community spirit. The junction of US 101 with University Avenue and Palm Drive marks the entrance (R) to the campus of STANFORD UNIVERSITY, founded by Senator and Mrs. Leland Stanford as a memorial to their only child, Leland Stanford, Jr., who died at the age of sixteen. The cornerstone of the first building was laid in 1887; the university was opened in the autumn of 1891. Stanford began not only with a great endowment and a fine group of buildings, but with distinguished faculty members, including Vernon L. Kellogg, Theodore Hoover, Henry R. Fairclough, Robert Eckles Swain, Melville Best Anderson, and Lewis M. Terman. Among its early alumni are Charles K. "Cheerio" Field, Whitelaw Reed, Dane Coolidge, Herbert Hoover, H. L. Davis, Will and Wallace Irwin, Holbrook Blinn, Homer Lea, and Ray Lyman Wilbur. It always has been coeducational. Until 1933 women students were limited to 500; since then the number has been limited to approximately 40 percent of the total enrollment. In 1938-39 there were 4,554 students and 691 faculty members.

The heavy sandstone piers flanking the entrance have taken the place of the low Romanesque towers, pierced by heavy round-headed arches with open pier arcades on each side, which were destroyed in the 1906 earthquake. The great memorial arch, beyond which rose the fine central tower of the Memorial Church—both pivotal features of the unified architectural scheme—also was destroyed.

Right from US 101 on Palm Drive, bordered by shrubs and trees from many parts of the world in a 600-acre arboretum, 0.1 m. to the junction with a paved road; R. here 0.2 m. to PALO ALTO HOSPITAL, a fine modern institution owned by the City of Palo Alto and operated by the university.

On Palm Drive at 0.6 m. is the junction with Pine Avenue.

1. Right here 0.1 m. to the STANFORD MAUSOLEUM, built of white granite in the form of a Greek temple. The entrance is flanked by marble sphinxes; polished Ionic columns support the architrave. Nearby (R) is the TOMB OF HENRY J. LATHROP, Mrs. Stanford's brother, surmounted by a white marble figure called the *Angel of Grief*. The route follows a winding drive (L) from the mausoleum, past the CACTUS GARDEN, which contains a great variety of desert plants. It continues to the TROUTMERE GUERNSEY FARM, 0.7 m. In the large brick barn where Senator Stanford's famous thoroughbreds once were stabled are dairy cattle.

2. Left on Pine Avenue 0.3 m. to the junction with Galvez Street; L. here past the campus tennis courts, football and baseball fields, and track oval 0.3 m. to the STADIUM, seating 89,000, where the Stanford-California football game—northern California's "Big Game"—takes place on alternate years.

Pine Avenue continues past ENCINA GYMNASIUM, men's athletic center, to the junction with Arguello Street, 0.4 m.; R. here past ENCINA HALL (R), 0.6 m., largest of the men's dormitories. Adjoining (L) are two others—TOYON HALL and BRANNER HALL, both in simple Spanish Colonial style. Neither men nor women students may live in fraternity or sorority houses until they have completed the freshman year. About three hundred older students not members of fraternities belong to cooperative eating clubs. One large cooperative organization buys for the entire group. The cost to each student is about $50 a quarter.

The main side route follows Palm Drive south from its junction with Pine

Avenue to the junction with a paved road, 0.7 *m.;* R. here 0.1 *m.* to the LELAND STANFORD JUNIOR MUSEUM (*open daily 10-5; adm. 25¢*), a large neoclassic structure built of yellow sandstone. At the entrance doors are four tall Ionic columns; on each side the facade is ornamented with large mosaics. Nucleus of the museum is the collection made by Leland Stanford, Jr., between 1880 and 1884, including Egyptian bronzes, Tanagra figurines, Greek and Roman glass, armor, mosaics, Sèvres and Dresden ware. In Stanford Memorial Room are collections of personal belongings of the founders of the University, views of its buildings in construction, and details of the mosaics used in the Memorial Church. Another room contains the "Governor Stanford," the first locomotive used on the Central Pacific Railroad (1863), and cases of items related to early California history—among them practically all the implements extant of San Francisco's Mission Dolores.

Also housed in the museum are the Di Cesnola collection of Greek and Roman pottery and glass from the island of Cyprus; Indian mound relics and artifacts; rare art materials from the Orient (the Ikeda Chinese and Japanese Collection); and Chinese and Japanese *objets d'art,* including the well-known De Long Collection of Japanese rarities. Among the rare objects in the Egyptian Room is a collection of Babylonian tablets.

Palm Drive continues south to the junction with a paved road; L. here 0.1 *m.* to the LAURENCE FROST AMPHITHEATRE, a sunken oval seating 8,000, presented by Mr. and Mrs. Howard Frost as a memorial to their son. The approach is through a tree-lined walk. The tiers of seats are placed along terraces of turf, closely cut and beautifully green. Commencement exercises are held here.

Adjoining on the south (R) is the center of Stanford's dramatic activities, MEMORIAL HALL, completed in 1937 at a cost of $600,000. The main theater seats 1,700; the rehearsal theater, 197. Among the University Theater's productions have been Sophocles' *Antigone* (1903), Shakespeare's *Twelfth Night* (1938), and *The Vikings in Helgoland* (1938).

Around a large oval planted to lawn and shrubs, dividing Palm Drive into two roadways, the route curves to the junction with Serra Street, 0.9 *m.,* at the foot of Palm Drive, beyond which extends the Outer Quadrangle (*see below*); R. on Serra Street 0.2 *m.* to SEQUOIA HALL, oldest of the men's dormitories and traditional abode of the Stanford "rough," non-fraternity man of uncurbed spirit.

Heart of the campus is the group of buildings known as the OUTER QUADRANGLE (length 894 feet, width 760 feet). At the northern end of the enclosure, formed by fourteen buildings housing lecture halls and administrative offices with open arcades on the outside, stand the ADMINISTRATION BUILDING (L) and JORDAN HALL (R). Between the two a passage leads to the INNER QUADRANGLE, formed by twelve one-story buildings and the Memorial Church (*see below*)—all connected by a continuous arcade. The red tile roof, the open arches, the long colonnades resembling cloister walks are reminiscent of the California missions, but the work in its essential features is Romanesque, the architect—Charles Allerton Coolidge of Boston—having been a disciple of Richardson. The buff sandstone of rough-faced ashlar used in these, the first buildings to be erected, came from a quarry twelve miles south of San Jose. Both architecturally and academically the two "quads" are the heart of the university. In addition to the original group of buildings there are many newer buildings on streets radiating from here.

The STANFORD MEMORIAL CHURCH (*open daily; services Sun. 11 and 4, also 7:30 p.m. during summer quarter; organ recitals precede services*), faces the cloistered inner quadrangle from the south. Set in the pavement before the entrance are a series of brass tablets, a new one being added for each graduating class. Built by Mrs. Leland Stanford as a memorial to her husband, the church was almost completely ruined by the 1906 earthquake. Rebuilt without its former central tower, the present structure is less graceful than the original. The mosaics of the facade, like those destroyed, were made in Venice; they follow largely the original design. In the spandrils above

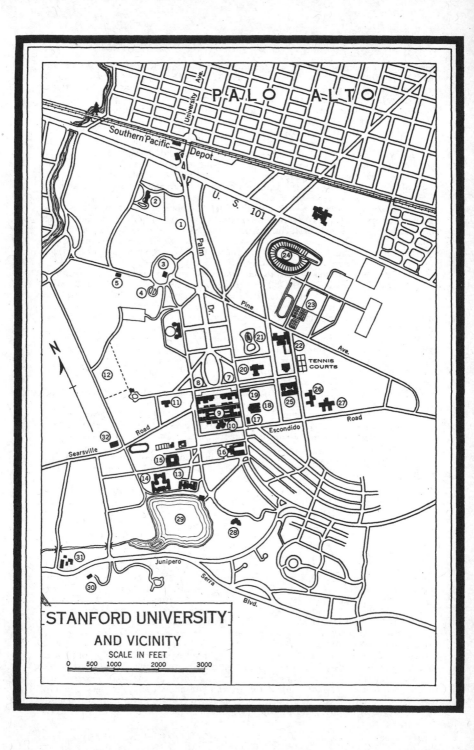

PALO ALTO

University Ave.

Southern Pacific Depot

U. S. 101

Palm

Pine

Dr.

Ave.

TENNIS COURTS

Escondido Road

Road

Searsville Road

Junipero

Serra Blvd.

STANFORD UNIVERSITY
AND VICINITY
SCALE IN FEET
0   500 1000   2000   3000

the triple doorways with their Romanesque piers and carved arches, the mosaics represent figures symbolic of the theological virtues. A large round-headed window fills the central space above the doorways; at each side are three smaller windows. The space above and between this fenestration up to the apex of the roof is filled with a huge mosaic, *The Sermon on the Mount,* against a background of gold.

The mosaic decoration in the vestibule consists of colored medallions in the form of the Chi Rho and the Alpha and Omega against a gold background. The same buff sandstone used for the exterior has been used for the interior walls and piers. The interior is a nave of four bays with narrow aisles, each with a single large round-headed window. The clerestory has two small windows to each bay. The transepts have apsidal endings and balconies, each with a semicircular carved balustrade supported by heavy Romanesque piers. From the crossing, with its four massive arches, seven white marble steps rise the entire width to a shallow choir. The sanctuary rail is of marble. The apse is semicircular with fourteen small recessed arches faced with gold mosaic and three large windows in the upper story. Above the marble altar is a reproduction in mosaic of Cosimo Rosselli's *The Last Supper.* The mosaics which cover the upper walls of the entire interior depict Biblical scenes and individual figures of prophets, patriarchs, and saints. The work lost in the earthquake was replaced from the studios of Antonio Salvati in Venice, where the original designs had fortunately been preserved.

The route goes L. on Serra Street from the foot of Palm Drive to the junction with Lasuen Street, 1 *m.,* and R. on Lasuen Street.

The Romanesque THOMAS WELTON STANFORD ART GALLERY (L), built in 1917, gift of a brother of Senator Stanford, has a small permanent collection of the work of nineteenth-century American artists. Like the buildings adjoining on the south (*see below*), it is a unit in a projected new quadrangle, one of two planned to flank the present Outer Quandrangle (*see above*), on the east and west.

The facade of the LIBRARY (L), 1.1 *m.,* built in 1919, is adorned with

---

STANFORD UNIVERSITY AND VICINITY
"Legend"

1. Arboretum	17. Cubberly Building
2. Palo Alto Hospital	18. Library
3. Stanford Mausoleum	19. Art Gallery
4. Cactus Garden	20. Memorial Hall
5. Troutmere Guernsey Farm	21. Laurence Frost Amphitheater
6. Leland Stanford Junior Museum	22. Encina Gymnasium
7. Administration Building	23. Athletic Field
8. Jordan Hall	24. Stanford Bowl
9. Inner Quadrangle	25. Encina Hall
10. Stanford Memorial Church	26. Toyon Hall
11. Sequoia Hall	27. Branner Hall
12. U. S. Department of Agriculture Experimental Station	28. Residence of the University President
13. Roble Hall	29. Lagunita
14. Lagunita Court	30. Golf Course
15. Women's Gymnasium	31. Stanford Stables
16. Stanford Union	32. Carnegie Institute Laboratory

stone figures carved by Edgar Walter. Its 675,000 volumes include the Hopkins Railway Library presented by Timothy Hopkins in 1892, the 5,000-volume Hildebrand Library of Germanic philology and literature, the Jarboe collection of literature of the French Revolution and Napoleonic era, the Thomas Welton Stanford Australasian Library of early travels and voyages, and the Flugel collection including works of rare fifteenth- sixteenth- and seventeenth-century writers.

Surmounted by a fourteen-floor, 280-foot tower, the adjoining HOOVER LIBRARY FOR WAR, PEACE, AND REVOLUTION, a concrete and steel structure built in 1940 (Bakewell, Weihe, and Brown, architects), houses ex-President Herbert Hoover's collection of 150,000 printed and manuscript items dealing with the World War and its aftermath.

Named for Ellwood P. Cubberley, professor of education, the CUBBERLEY SCHOOL OF EDUCATION BUILDING (L), 1.2 m., is headquarters for students of education.

The STANFORD UNION (R), 1.3 m., is a clubhouse for men built largely through the efforts of Herbert Hoover of the class of 1895. Informal "bull sessions" have for years been held in the "cellar," a small downstairs cafeteria.

At 1.3 m. on Lasuen Street is the junction with Santa Teresa Street; R. here to the junction with Lomita Drive, 1.5 m., where the main side route turns L. on Lomita Drive; straight ahead from this junction on Santa Teresa Street to the two principal women's dormitories: ROBLE HALL (L), 0.1 m., a large vine-covered building, and LAGUNITA COURT (L), 0.2 m., a group of houses set among lawns and trees. Flanked by a swimming pool, tennis courts, and golf and hockey fields, the WOMEN'S GYMNASIUM across the street (R) is a simplified adaptation of the Spanish Colonial style in buff-colored concrete.

The main side route goes L. from the junction with Santa Teresa Street on Lomita Drive.

LAGUNITA (little lake) (R), 1.6 m., a dry lake bed throughout much of the year, is used for water sports after winter rains fill it with a shallow expanse of water.

The RESIDENCE OF THE UNIVERSITY PRESIDENT (R), 1.8 m., is a large Colonial-style house. Stanford has had but three presidents. The first, David Starr Jordan, selected by Senator and Mrs. Stanford in 1891, guided the institution through some difficult early years when, after Senator Stanford's death, the estate became involved in litigation. After Jordan's retirement in 1913, Dr. John C. Branner was president for three years. Branner was succeeded by Dr. Ray Lyman Wilbur.

At 2.2 m. is the junction with Mayfield Avenue, on which the main side route turns R.; L. here on Mayfield Avenue 0.1 m. to the junction with Santa Ynez Street; R. on Santa Ynez Street to the junction with Mirada Street, 0.5 m.; L. on Mirada Street to the RESIDENCE OF HERBERT HOOVER (private) (L), 0.6 m. (623 Mirada St.), overlooking the campus. The ex-President, a graduate of Stanford's first class, was once a faculty member.

The main side route goes R. (west) on Mayfield Avenue, which at 2.3 m. unites with Junipero Serra Boulevard. At 3.3 m. is the junction with a gravelled road, on which the route turns R.

At the STANFORD STABLES (R), 3.4 m., Leland Stanford established his stock farm in 1876. On the base of a monument to a famous trotter are inscribed a list of names and records of Stanford's best horses. A tablet commemorates the pre-Edison motion picture experiment conducted here in 1878 in connection with horse racing. By means of a battery of cameras fitted with electric shutters, men and animals were portrayed in motion.

At 3.8 m. is the junction with Searsville Road, on which the route turns R. The CARNEGIE INSTITUTE LABORATORY (L), 4 m., was organized in 1921 for the purpose of studying the production, distribution, and consumption of food. The Carnegie Corporation endowed the laboratory in 1932.

At 33.2 m. on US 101 is the junction with Stanford Avenue.

Right on Stanford Avenue 0.5 *m.* to the PETER COUTTS COTTAGE (L), standing beside a plain two-story brick library and office building. Both structures were built in the seventies by Paulin Caperon, political fugitive from France who reached America on the passport of Peter Coutts, his cousin. Caperon bought the Matadero Ranch (later purchased by Governor Stanford), and here he developed orchards and vineyards, tunneling the hillside for a water supply. A racetrack for his thoroughbreds was laid out near the present corner of Stanford Avenue and US 101. Caperon and his family returned to Europe in 1880. Young Dr. David Starr Jordan (*see above*) occupied the cottage in 1891. Subsequently the buildings have housed university departments and faculty members.

At 0.8 *m.* is the junction with Stanford Avenue Extension; L. here to the HARRIS J. RYAN HIGH VOLTAGE LABORATORY (L), 1.2 *m.,* where university scientists carry on electrical experiments with equipment which includes transformers of more than 2,000,000-volt capacity.

South of Palo Alto, US 101 enters the great orchard region of the Santa Clara Valley, where more than one hundred and twenty thousand acres are planted to deciduous fruits. Early in the mission period the Franciscans found that both the vine and fruit trees did well in California, but no extensive planting of fruit trees was made until about 1856, when Louis Pellier brought from southwestern France a number of prune scions. To him and to nurserymen goes the credit for the beginning of a great industry. In 1939 there were more than seventy thousand acres in prunes alone. Second in importance of the valley's products is the apricot, to which about twenty thousand acres have been planted in belts relatively free from frost. The variety most grown is the Moor Park. Pears are planted to more than six thousand acres.

Early American settlers in the valley discovered an artesian zone north and west of San Jose which provided ample water for irrigation. Since 1915 the increased pumping draft and the decrease in average rainfall have lowered the ground water level nearly one hundred feet. Some one hundred thousand acres affected by this gradual depletion today are under irrigation.

At 36.7 *m.* is a junction with San Antonio Ave.

Right on San Antonio Avenue is LOS ALTOS, 2.8 *m.* (200 alt., 2,000 pop.), a town of fine houses and gardens on land once a part of Rancho San Antonio.

Surrounded by orchards and truck gardens is MOUNTAIN VIEW, 37.7 *m.* (67 alt., 3,897 pop.). Here are canneries, planing mills, and a plant for pre-cooling berries and fruits before shipment to Eastern markets. Mountain View's Pacific Press Publishing Association, one of the largest presses in the West, is operated by the Seventh-Day Adventist Church.

The site of old Mountain View lies nearly a mile south. Before the building of the railroad, a large hotel here was a stopping place for the daily San Francisco-San Jose stage and a meeting place for settlers from scattered grain and stock ranches. A few old-timers remember with regret the fine quail, pigeon, and duck shooting they enjoyed before the land was planted to orchards.

At 38.5 *m.* is a junction with paved Alviso Road.

Left on Alviso Road 2.3 *m.* to the junction with US 101 Bypass. Stretching northeastward are the 1,000 acres of MOFFETT FIELD (*usually open 9-5; no cameras*), formerly a Navy airbase, today the field of two Army air squadrons. The great hangar, a landmark for miles around, is 1,133 feet long, 308 feet wide, and its height of 193 feet is that of an eighteen-story building. It was the home of the dirigibles *Akron* and *Macon,* both of which met with tragic accidents. Under construction in 1940 was a $10,000,000 AERONAUTICAL RESEARCH LABORATORY which, under the authority of the National Advisory Committee for Aeronautics, will be a sister station to one at Langley Field, Virginia, and will conduct research into unsolved aeronautical problems.

Alviso Road continues east to ALVISO, 7 *m.* (8 alt., 676 pop.), at the head of a navigable slough at the southern end of San Francisco Bay, a small town of treeless streets and weatherbeaten houses. Originally the port for Mission Santa Clara and nearby ranches, it enjoyed a great boom with the Gold Rush. Produce from the valley went from here to San Francisco and up the Sacramento and San Joaquin Rivers in stern-wheelers. Of these old boats the best-known was the *Jenny Lind,* whose energetic captain forced her boilers and caused an explosion that cost thirty-five lives. With the completion in 1864 of the railroad from San Francisco, Alviso's decline began, though freight continued to be shipped by steamer for some years. Prosperity may return to Alviso if the City of San Jose carries out its plans for the creation of a deepwater port on adjoining land.

Left from Alviso 4 *m.* to a junction with State 17 at Milpitas.

The main side route continues south (R) from Alviso. At 9 *m.* is AGNEW (20 alt., 319 pop.). The fine grounds and buildings of AGNEW STATE HOSPITAL border the highway. The mentally deranged, alcoholics, and women narcotic addicts are treated here. With a normal capacity of 2,365, the institution in recent years has been badly crowded. The original buildings, erected when the hospital was established in 1888, were destroyed by the 1906 earthquake.

At 12 *m.* is the junction with US 101 at Santa Clara (*see below*).

On US 101 is SUNNYVALE (95 alt., 3,094 pop.), 41 *m.,* surrounded by orchards and truck gardens, a town of small homes and well-kept streets in a section known for its fine saddle and racing horses. The town site is a part of Rancho Pastoria de la Borregas (the lambs' pasture), which was divided soon after the period of American occupation between Mariano Castro and Martin Murphy, Jr. The latter secured more than four thousand acres southeast of Permanente Creek which included the sites of Mountain View and Sunnyvale. The MARTIN MURPHY HOUSE (*private*), Sunnyvale Ave. near California St., a two-story frame structure built from timber brought around the Horn in 1849, has been occupied continuously by members of the same family.

Right from Sunnyvale on State 9 is CUPERTINO, 3 *m.* (215 alt., 119 pop.), a retail trading center for the surrounding orchard and vineyard country.

Right from Cupertino on Stevens Creek Road to a junction with Permanente Road, 1.5 *m.;* R. on Permanente Road to the $4,000,000 PERMANENTE CORPORATION CEMENT PLANT, 2 *m.* The plant includes a laboratory building, precipitator, mills, 500,000-barrel storage silos, and the tall stack—all built in 1939. The company contracted (1940) to supply 5,800,000 barrels of low-heat cement for the Central Valley's Shasta Dam project. When the two kilns, largest in the world, 12 feet in diameter and 450 feet long, are supplemented with a contemplated third, the Permanente plant will become the world's largest cement manufacturing plant. An important

North and South of the Golden Gate

FROM SKYLINE BOULEVARD THE HILLS UNFOLD TO THE SEA

MONTALVO FOUNDATION OF SAN FRANCISCO
ART ASSOCIATION NEAR SARATOGA

SKYLINE DAM AND BOULEVARD AT CRYSTAL SPRINGS LAKES

PIGEON POINT LIGHTHOUSE

RACCOON STRAITS FROM SAUSALITO, MARIN COUNTY

MUIR WOODS NATIONAL MONUMENT, MARIN COUNTY

IN PETRIFIED FOREST NEAR CALISTOGA

RUSSIAN RIVER PLAYGROUND

STATE CAPITOL (1853), BENICIA

HOME OF LUTHER BURBANK, SANTA ROSA

DIRIGIBLE HANGAR, MOFFETT FIELD, SUNNYVALE

department is that which manufactures fifty tons per hour of sugar rock (carbonate of lime) for beet-sugar refineries.

The main side route continues south from Cupertino on State 9 to SARATOGA, 7.4 m. (500 alt., 1,191 pop.), in the midst of orchards and vineyards on the rolling hills above Campbell Creek. The town was founded by one Martin McCarthy as a convenient starting point for a toll road leading to the fine timber up Campbell Creek. Its early name, McCarthyville, was replaced in 1863 by its present one because, like its New York namesake, it was near several medical springs. Saratoga's later prosperity has come from the surrounding orchards and vineyards. Each spring, when the orchards are at the height of their bloom, the town has its Blossom Festival, a pageant which originated as a service of thanksgiving for the recovery of the orchards from the drought of 1898-99.

1. Left from Saratoga on Saratoga Road to VILLA MONTALVO, 0.5 m., formerly the home of James D. Phelan, at the end of a winding driveway, the entrance gates surmounted by carved griffins. The house of light grey sandstone in the style of an Italian villa is surrounded by broad lawns and formal gardens with rows of tall Italian cypresses leading up to fountains, Etruscan vases, and marble statuary groups. Large Irish yews are a distinctive landscaping feature. A bronze plaque commemorates the fifteenth-century Spanish writer for whom the estate was named, Ordanez de Montalvo, in whose *Las Sergas de Esplandian* (The Exploits of Esplandian), the name "California" first appeared. As a United States Senator, Phelan, who had been mayor of San Francisco, entertained here not only politicans but also writers, painters, and actors. "A Day in the Hills" was an annual event honoring California authors. Phelan bequeathed the estate to the San Francisco Art Association for use as a center where composers, authors, and painters might live while doing creative work. It was opened as such in the summer of 1939.

Saratoga Road continues to LOS GATOS, 4 m. (412 alt., 3,168 pop.), at the junction with State 17 (*see below*).

2. Right from Saratoga on Oak Street, which becomes Bollman Road, 2.8 m. to JOHN BROWN'S LODGE, the home from 1881 to her death in 1884 of Mary Brown, the widow of John Brown of Harper's Ferry. It is said that a substantial part of the $1,850 paid by Mrs. Brown for the ranch was donated by the Negro population in and around San Jose.

The main side route goes R. from Saratoga on State 9 up Campbell Creek.

At 8.7 m. is the junction with Pierce Road; R. here 0.1 m. to the junction with a one-way dirt road; L. here to the PAUL MASSON CHAMPAGNE WINERY (*admission by appointment only*), 1.6 m., a stone structure replacing one destroyed in the 1906 earthquake, where champagne was first produced in California. Coming to California from France in 1852, Charles le Franc found here on the rolling slopes the peculiar combination of soil and climate needed for the aristocratic champagne grapes, Pinot Chardonnay and Pinot Noir. Later Paul Masson married Le Franc's daughter and subsequently inherited the winery.

State 9 continues to CONGRESS SPRINGS, 9.4 m., where D. O. MILLS and Alvinza Hayward in the 1860's financed a fashionable spa with a large, much verandaed hotel. The hotel was burned in 1903, but the springs are still frequented by picnickers (*adm. 10¢*).

West of Congress Springs the route follows State 9 up a wooded canyon to Saratoga Gap at the junction with State 5, 14.8 m. (*see above*).

State 9 descends gradually through a heavy growth of redwood, madrone, live oak, laurel, and buckeye to CALIFORNIA STATE REDWOOD PARK, 26.4 m., occupying a bowl-shaped depression on East Waddell Creek, called Big Basin by early lumbermen. This is part of a dense redwood forest which before lumbering operations began extended a hundred miles from the Pajaro River north almost to San Francisco. About 1885 Ralph S. Smith of Redwood City first attempted to save some of the Coast redwoods from lumbermen. Others, including the Sempervirens Club of San Jose, at length were successful in getting an appropriation from the State Legislature sufficient to purchase the 3,800 acres of Big Basin. By subsequent gifts and purchases, the park was increased to 10,000 acres. Principal tree here is the *Sequoia sempervirens*. At 29.7 *m*. is GOVERNORS' CAMP (*accommodations May 1-Oct. 1; post office, store, inn, cottages; campsites 50¢ per car, picnicking 25¢ per car*). The camp's name commemorates the visits of three governors in 1901 and 1902. The sound of a trumpet brings herds of tame deer here at feeding time. A trail beginning at the camp circles through the giant trees of the park.

On US 101 at 43 *m*. is THE SITE OF THE BATTLE OF SANTA CLARA, the "Battle of the Mustard Stalks," fought January 2, 1847 (on a field covered with tall mustard stalks), when Californians under Francisco Sanchez revolting against plundering Americans were defeated by a small force led by Captain Ward Marston.

Neither the old-fashioned houses on the tree-shaded streets of SANTA CLARA, 47.6 *m*. (72 alt., 6,571 pop.), nor the typically American business blocks dating from the seventies and eighties suggest the town's origin as a settlement surrounding the mission dedicated in 1777 to St. Clare, superior of the first Franciscan nunnery.

The first buildings put up by Father Tomas de la Pena and his colleagues were flooded. The Franciscans rebuilt in 1781, but their second structures, damaged by a severe earthquake in 1812, were destroyed completely by another earthquake six years later. A third adobe church and its surrounding secular buildings were dedicated in 1822 on the site of the University of Santa Clara (*see below*).

So many Americans settled here early in the 1850's that the Spanish-speaking population became a small minority. The town's recent growth has been slow but substantial. Fruit-packing houses, a tannery, a pottery, and a cement works are its principal industrial establishments.

The SANTA CLARA WOMEN'S CLUB, 1067 Grant St., occupies an adobe built in 1782 as one òf the buildings of Mission Santa Clara, the oldest structure in the Santa Clara Valley.

Behind a high rose-colored wall in a park with fine old trees is the CARMELITE MONASTERY, Lincoln St. opposite Franklin St., one of the few houses in the United States of this cloistered order whose members, giving all their time to prayer and contemplation, never leave the monastery.

CITY PARK, Lexington and Main Sts., was the plaza when Santa Clara was a Mexican *pueblo*.

The SECOND SITE OF SANTA CLARA MISSION is marked by a cross and monument at Campbell and Franklin Sts. In the rear of the Bray House (*private*), Scott Lane, an old-fashioned frame dwelling, stands a low one-story adobe with a tiled roof, a lonely relic marking the SITE OF THE SANTA CLARA MISSION INDIAN VILLAGE.

The FERNANDEZ ADOBE (*private*), 401 Jefferson St., a grey-white plastered adobe dating from the 1840's, is shaded by an olive tree and a grapevine of unusual age and size.

The UNIVERSITY OF SANTA CLARA, Franklin and Grant Sts., occupying a fifteen-acre campus, owes its creation to Archbishop Joseph Sadoc Alemany of San Francisco. Hoping to save Santa Clara

Mission from complete deterioration after its secularization, he invited the Jesuit Order to Santa Clara to build a college. In 1851 the Reverend John Nobili adapted what was left of the old adobe buildings to the needs of a school. Although chartered as a university in 1855, it was actually a college of arts and sciences until the establishment of colleges of law and engineering in 1912 (a school of business administration was added in 1924). The enrollment totals about seven hundred and fifty. Santa Clara was the first institution in California to bestow an academic degree; first alumnus was Thomas I. Bergin, A.B., who became a successful attorney.

Among widely known faculty members have been John J. Montgomery, who made a successful flight in a glider as early as 1883; the late Father Jerome Ricard, the "Padre of the Rains," who by a system of co-ordinating the Government forecasts with his own observations based on the sun spots and their relation to atmospheric conditions, hoped to make accurate long-time weather forecasts; and Father Bernard Hubbard, Alaskan explorer and present head of the geology department.

The university buildings in Spanish Colonial style are all comparatively new with the exception of the theater, which dates from 1870. The *Mission Play of Santa Clara* has been produced here several times.

The MISSION SANTA CLARA, reconstructed in 1927 from old drawings of the adobe mission church of 1822, is the university chapel. An earlier restoration was destroyed by fire in 1926. Students and faculty were able to save some articles dating from the Spanish period which have been incorporated in the new building; among these are a large crucifix, the holy-water fonts, the wooden statues of saints at the side altars, and the reredos over the high alter. Three bells dating from the late eighteenth century and destroyed in the fire were replaced by a gift from King Alphonso XIII. The large redwood cross in front of the mission is the one which Spanish soldiers and Indians put up in 1777 on the first site of the mission, and was moved each time the mission was moved.

VARSI LIBRARY, named for the Reverend Aloysius Varsi, S.J., president of Santa Clara from 1868 to 1876, contains 100,000 volumes, among them some rare Spanish works on general science, medicine, and agriculture of the seventeenth and eighteenth centuries.

US 101 south of Santa Clara follows The Alameda, a tree-lined avenue following the old road that linked Mission Santa Clara with the *pueblo* of San Jose de Guadalupe. In 1799 Father Magin Catala planted a double lane of willows on each side of El Camino Real, and in the years that followed they gave a grateful shade to all those traveling between mission and *pueblo:* the bride and groom in lumbering *carreta,* the mounted fast-riding *vaquero* and *ranchero,* and the solemn marchers to the cemetery.

SAN JOSE, 50.8 *m.* (92 alt., 62,298 pop.) (*see San Jose*).

1. Right from San Jose on First Street to San Carlos Street; R. on San Carlos Street, which becomes Stevens Creek Road, to the junction with Bascom

Avenue, 2.9 *m.* on which the main side route turns L.; R. (straight ahead) on Stevens Creek Road 1 *m.* to the junction with paved Los Gatos Road; L. here to the WINCHESTER MYSTERY HOUSE (*adm. 50¢*), 1.3 *m.* This fantastic structure with its strange assortments of roofs, spires, and cupolas contains 143 rooms extending over six acres. It was the creation of Sarah Winchester, widow of Oliver F. Winchester, millionaire manufacturer of firearms, who purchased upon her arrival here in the 1880's the seventeen-room house, then under construction on the site, from which all the rest has evolved. Obsessed with the idea that if building were to stop, she would die, Mrs. Winchester kept a crew of workmen constantly busy for thirty-six years until her death in 1922. The result was a structural nightmare; stairways leading to blank walls, bathrooms with gold-plated fixtures and glass doors, fireplaces without flues, small rooms built inside larger rooms like Chinese puzzle boxes, and her private chamber, in which walls, ceiling, and even the floors were covered with white satin.

The route follows State 17 L. from the junction with Stevens Creek Road on Bascom Avenue to the junction with paved Campbell Avenue, 5.4 *m.;* R. here is CAMPBELL, 0.7 *m.* (195 alt., 1,800 pop.), known as "The Orchard City." Here along Los Gatos Creek, Benjamin Campbell, a Kentuckian, sold lots for the town in 1887, with the proviso that the land should be forfeit to him or his heirs if liquor were sold upon it. The town's three fruit-canning plants produce annually about 7,500,000 cans; its packing plants ship about 150 carloads of dried fruit.

State 17 continues to LOS GATOS, 11.2 *m.* (412 alt., 3,571 pop.), which lies at the point where Los Gatos Creek flows out of its narrow canyon into the broad fertile valley. Extending along both sides of the creek, it merges imperceptibly into surrounding orchards and vineyards. Curving about the town are two mountain ridges, El Sereno (the night watchman) and El Sombroso (the shadowing one). San Thomas Aquinas Creek, a mile to the east was the boundary of Rancho Rinconada de los Gatos (little corner of the cats), which Jose Hernandez got by grant from the Mexican government in 1840 and named for two wildcats that he saw battling in the neighborhood. The first building on the townsite was a flour mill built in 1850 by James Alexander Forbes, a Scot who had been in California since 1832, and who had served as British vice-consul at Monterey since 1843. For lack of water, the mill prospered little. The village that grew up around it was slow to develop until the extension of the railroad from San Jose in 1877. Its later growth has been steady if not spectacular. Today Los Gatos subsists on packing plants which ship apricots, prunes and grapes and two wineries which produce both sweet and dry wines. Its pleasant situation and climate have attracted a number of writers, among them Charles Erskine Scott Wood, Ruth Comfort Mitchell, Sara Bard Field and John Steinbeck.

The FORBES FLOUR MILL, now a sub-station of the Pacific Gas and Electric Company, on the bottom land of Los Gatos Creek, is most easily reached by crossing a foot bridge in the rear of the Los Gatos Grammar School, University Ave. between Main St. and Mullen Ave. The walls, of a hard sandstone, are heavily buttressed, and the lintels are braced with redwood timbers. The mill-wheel was turned by water brought through a wooden flume from a dam further upstream. Only a portion of the original four-story building survived a fire in 1872.

Bordering Los Gatos Creek, MEMORIAL PARK, Main and Park Sts., has a swimming pool, horseshoe courts, and picnic grounds shaded by large plane trees.

The mission-style buildings of the NOVITIATE OF THE SACRED HEART, Prospect Ave. above College Ave., overlook the town from a hill. Founded in 1868, the novitiate is a training school for the Jesuit Order. After four years of training here the novices go to St. Michael's, Spokane, for three years, spend two or three years more in teaching, and finally four years at the theologate branch at Alma in the near-by mountains. The garden has a replica of the famous well of Lourdes. The novitiate owns a vineyard of 485 acres, from whose grapes it makes sweet and dry wines.

2. Right from San Jose on First Street to Alma Avenue, R. on Alma Avenue to the junction with paved Almaden Road, 2.1 *m.;* L. on Almaden Road across the Guadalupe River and up Alamitos Valley.

ALMADEN, 13.8 *m.* (473 alt., 20 pop.), drowses in a pocket in the hills. Its two streets, following the line of Alamitos Creek, are lined with trees, chiefly the smooth-barked sycamore *(Platanus racemosa)*. Behind the narrow brick sidewalks and trim hedges are rows of small adobe and frame houses set in old-fashioned gardens.

The quicksilver mines, for which this region is famous, have (with the exception of the mines of Spain) produced more quicksilver than any other field in the world. They were known to the Indians, who used the cinnabar for coloring their faces and bodies. In 1824 Antonia Maria Suñol, a Spaniard who had been in the French navy and who was then a shop keeper in San Jose, with Luis Chabolla developed the mine in a small way, thinking it contained silver.

Not until 1845 did a Mexican officer, Andres Castillero, discover quicksilver. He realized that if there were extensive deposits his fortune was made, for quicksilver was scarce in Mexico. He filed his claim and, forming a partnership with *Padre* Real of Mission Santa Clara and with some members of the Robles family who had earlier explored the region, he engaged an American named Chard to begin reducing the ore. Chard's equipment was primitive: six whaler's try-pots, three inverted over the other three, to form a furnace.

Two years later Castillero sold some shares to Barron, Forbes and Company of Tepic, Mexico, whose agent, James Alexander Forbes, introduced improved methods. By 1850 the mines had an annual yield worth $750,000. The California gold mines kept up a steady demand for the metal, which was put in iron flasks and taken by oxcart to tidewater at Alviso. The Comstock boom added to the demand. In 1865, the year of greatest output, the mine produced 47,000 flasks of mercury with a value of $2,160,000. That such production had its effect on the world market was shown when Lionel, Baron de Rothschild, lessee of the great Spanish mines, came here as a visitor in the sixties.

Throughout the 1870's the mine continued to be highly profitable. As many as 1,000 men were employed, and the population rose to 6,000. As it became necessary to go deeper for deposits of cinnabar, however, the cost of operation rose. Moreover, quicksilver dropped in price. During the World War, the need for mercury in making fulminate caps created a new boom, and in 1940 the mines again were active.

CLUB ALMADEN, the former Casa Grande, at the northern end of the town, is a large two-story white house built of bricks brought around the Horn from Glasgow. It was erected in 1850 as a hotel. When J. E. Randol became mine owner in 1870, he made it his private residence, in which he entertained lavishly. The drawing room fireplace has an ornately carved ebony mantel with small medallions of mother-of-pearl and painted glass. Back of the house is a swimming pool *(fee: Mon.-Sat., swimmers 35¢, spectators 10¢; Sun. and holidays, 45¢ and 15¢: barbecue pits and tables)*.

The OLD STORE at the southern end of the town, an adobe structure with brick corbie-steps at the gable ends, has been used continuously since its erection about 1850. The main roof, supported by hand-hewn posts, extends over the narrow sidewalk.

South of the old store is the half-ruined MINE OFFICE, an adobe and brick building with a wooden porte-cochere. It contains a brick vault where flasks of mercury were stored.

A trail leads south 300 yards to the smelters and furnaces, from which rise brick towers 150 feet high built against the steep slope of the canyon. The cinnabar, after being pounded into pieces about the size of an egg, was placed in the ore bed. When the fuel was fired, mercury, highly volatile, rose with the smoke into the towers and passed through a series of apertures to be cooled in a condensing chamber. By the time the smoke reached the chimney, the greater part of the mercury had been released and collected.

3. Left from San Jose on Santa Clara Street, which becomes paved, tree-lined Alum Rock Road, to the junction with Mount Hamilton Road, 6 *m.*, on which the main side route turns R.

Left on Alum Rock Road into the wooded, rocky gorge of Penitencia Creek, named for the "house of penance," a small adobe which once stood on the banks, where priests came to hear confessions.

The 643-acre ALUM ROCK PARK, 2.1 *m.* (520 alt.), owned by the city of San Jose, was named for a 200-foot cliff (L) with a surface residuum of alum dust, standing in the lower part of the canyon. Once part of the pueblo lands of San Jose, the park has become a playground landscaped so as to enhance the natural beauty of the surroundings. Before the arrival of the Spaniards, the Indians held their rituals here twice a year, bathed in and drank the health-giving waters. At the lower picnic grounds, in addition to a dancing pavilion, are an indoor swimming plunge (*open Mar.-Nov.; Sun., 25¢-35¢; weekdays, 15¢-25¢*) and individual hot sulphur baths (*50¢*). Six beautifully arched, native rock bridges lead to the various points of interest above the auto parking area. The park's twenty-two mineral springs are housed in rock grottos, reached by trails extending up the canyon from the end of the road. Here also are a deer paddock, a song-bird aviary, and a serpentorium.

From the lower picnic grounds Penitencia Creek Trail ascends the canyon 0.2 *m.* to the junction with a trail; L. here 0.3 *m.* to the JOAQUIN MURRIETA HIDEOUT, a natural cavern thirty feet long and four feet wide, another of the countless places in California where the bandit who has become the subject of a thousand tales is said to have concealed himself. The Penitencia Creek Trail follows up the wooded canyon to the junction with the North Fork Trail, 1 *m.*; L. here 0.6 *m.* to EAST WATER FALLS (1,200 alt.), where the waters of the creek drop sixty feet over a rocky ledge. The North Fork Trail continues to INSPIRATION POINT, 0.9 *m.* (1,500 alt), which affords a wide view of the park and Santa Clara Valley. The main trail goes R. up South Falls Trail to SOUTH FALLS, 2.3 *m.*

The main side route turns R. on Mount Hamilton Road from the junction with Alum Rock Road and climbs rugged oak-dotted slopes to the crest of MOUNT HAMILTON (*no accommodations*), 26.4 *m.*, crowned by silver-domed LICK OBSERVATORY (*open Mon.-Fri. 9-5, Sat. 9-9; Apr. 15-Sept. 15, Sat. 9-10; Sat. evenings, weather permitting, visitors arriving before 9 p.m. may look through telescopes*). The observatory was a gift to the people of California from James Lick, a Pennsylvania piano maker who had followed his trade successfully in South America. Arriving in San Francisco in 1847 with a stake of $30,000, Lick became a millionaire through land investments and miserly practices. Though he was unkempt in appearance and his clothes were often ragged, he was capable, occasionally, of lavish spending, as when he built near Alviso a flour mill finished in mahogany and other expensive woods. At his death in 1876 he left an estate of $3,000,000. With the exception of a small gift to an illegitimate son, all this fortune was devoted to public benefactions.

Lick's deed of trust charged the trustees to expend the sum of $700,000 "for the purpose of purchasing land . . . and putting up on such land . . . a powerful telescope, superior to and more powerful than any telescope yet made . . . and also a suitable observatory connected therewith . . . The said telescope and observatory are to be known as the Lick Astronomical Department of the University of California." On June 1, 1888, the telescope and buildings were completed and a scientific staff from the University of California began its work. Lick's body was removed from Lone Mountain Cemetery in San Francisco and buried in a crypt beneath the great 36-inch equatorial refractor.

Mount Hamilton, named in honor of the Reverend Laurentine Hamilton, pioneer missionary preacher of San Jose and first white man to climb the mountain, is a ridge running east and west and rising to three peaks. Before December, 1876, when the county completed the road to the summit, as specified in Lick's deed of trust, it took five days to get supplies and materials from San Jose. (Even the completed road, climbing 2,000 feet, makes 365 turns in the last five miles of its ascent.)

On the western peak is the silver-domed main building of the observatory, housing a 36-inch and a 12-inch equatorial refractor. The 36-inch instrument has a magnifying power which can be varied from 270 to 3,000 times that of the naked eye. The main building contains also the offices and computing rooms and a technical library of 20,000 items. The movable floor, permitting a rise and fall of 16½ feet, was the first of the kind to be constructed. Detached buildings house a 36½-inch reflecting telescope, a 6½-inch meridian circle instrument, a 6½-inch comet-seeker, a photographic telescope and a three-prism spectrograph. To enable the staff at Mount Hamilton to extend observations in the Southern Hemisphere, an observatory with a 37¼-inch Cassegrain reflector is maintained in Chile.

To most of the 10,000 visitors who each year go through the observatory, the scientists who use the mighty telescopes to penetrate the mysteries of distant space, recording minute and seemingly unrelated flares of ancient light in their effort to plot the courses of remote stars, are a crew who work with facts that are but fantasies. Often graphs and calculi which have taken years to work out are required to account for a single flash of light. During the Australian eclipse in 1922, the Lick Observatory, with fifteen-foot twin cameras, photographed images of the stars. When the photographs were compared with plates made of these stars by the same cameras four months previously, a measured deflection of 1.72″ was shown: the gravitational attraction of the sun had bent the light. Thus a startling theory in physics had been proved in part. In September, 1892, the big 36-inch refractor found the fifth satellite of Jupiter, the first discovered since Galileo turned his glass to that planet. In 1904, 1905, and 1914, three more were discovered and photographed with the Crossley Reflector. The observatory has discovered thirty-three comets, 4,800 double stars, several score spectroscopic binary stars, and many hundred new nebulae. The first great success in photographing comets and the Milky Way was achieved here.

San Jose

Information Service: Chamber of Commerce, Civic Auditorium, W. San Carlos and S. Market Sts. American Automobile Assn. and California State Auto Assn., 1024 The Alameda. Convention and Tourist Bureau, Civic Auditorium. *Railroad Station:* Southern Pacific, 56 Cahill St. *Bus Stations:* Union Bus Station, 25 S. Market St., for Pacific Greyhound and Peerless Stages. San Jose Travel Bureau, 44 W. San Carlos St., for Airline Bus Co. and Dollar Line. *Sightseeing and Charter Service:* California State Auto Assn., 1024 The Alameda. *Taxis:* Rates 15¢ first ½ m., 10¢ each additional ½ m. *Busses:* Pacific City Lines (local and to Santa Clara), 7¢. *Traffic Regulations:* Speed limit 25 m.p.h. Parking limit 1 hr. No all-night parking in downtown area.

Accommodations: Better-class hotels; many tourist camps.

Art Collections: Oriental Museum, Planetarium, Naglee and Park Aves. *Concert Halls:* Montgomery Theater, Civic Auditorium. *Dance Halls:* The Balconades, 181 W. Santa Clara St. Majestic Ballroom, 55 N. 3rd St. Trianon Ballroom, 43 W. San Antonio St. *Radio Stations:* KQW (1010 kc.), 87 E. San Antonia St. *Motion Picture Theaters (first-run):* Three. *Amateur and Little Theaters:* Montgomery Theater, Civic Auditorium. *Road Shows:* Civic Auditorium.

Auto Racing: San Jose Speedway, Alum Rock Ave. *Baseball:* "Semi-pro" teams, Santa Clara Ball Park. *Basketball:* Civic Auditorium. *Bowling:* Boitano,, F. J., 57 S. Market St. Forman's Arena, 409 San Augustine St. Osborne, C. H., 32 W. San Fernando St. San Jose Bowling Palace, 172 W. Santa Clara St. Santone and Howell, 77 N. 1st St. Wagner, Harry, 55 W. San Carlos St. *Boxing and Wrestling:* Civic Auditorium. *Bicycle Racing:* Garden City Velodrome (occasional races May-Sept.), Wabash Ave. and Olive Sts. *Football:* Spartan Field Stadium, S. 7th and E. Humboldt Sts. *Golf:* Hillview Public Golf Course, Tully Rd. and Swift Lane. San Jose Country Club, Alum Rock Ave. La Rinconada Golf Club, Los Gatos. Los Altos Country Club, Los Altos. *Hiking:* Alum Rock Park, Alum Rock Ave. *Riding:* 25 miles of bridle paths in Alum Rock Park. *Stables:* Western Riding Academy, San Jose Riding Academy, Braine Riding Academy, Alum Rock Ave. *Roller Skating:* Auditorium Roller Rink, 1066 The Alameda. *Swimming:* Roosevelt Junior High School pool (*open to the public summer evenings; adm. 35¢, includes suit and towel*), 19th St. and Santa Clara Ave. Woodrow Wilson Junior High School pool (*open during summer*), Grant and Vine Sts. Alum Rock Park, Alum Rock Ave. *Tennis:* San Jose Tennis Courts (*lighted*), S. 7th St. and E. Humboldt St. Backesto Park (12 courts), N. 13th and Jackson Sts.

At the heart of the rich Santa Clara Valley lies SAN JOSE (92 alt., 62,298 pop.), ten miles below the southern end of San Francisco Bay. Center of a rich agricultural region, San Jose's busy downtown district is dominated by tall modern office buildings; but the greater number of its business blocks date from the last quarter of the nineteenth century. Along the shaded residential streets are hundreds of well-kept, old frame houses dating from the seventies and eighties, set among trim lawns and pleasant gardens.

Despite its having been for 70 years a town where only Spanish was spoken, San Jose has retained surprisingly little of this heritage. For three generations it has been predominantly American. The Latin languages heard most frequently today are Italian and Portuguese.

In 1777 Lieutenant Jose Moraga, acting under orders from Don Felipe de Neve, selected nine soldiers "of known agricultural skill" from the presidios of San Francisco and Monterey and five *pobladores* (settlers); these men and their families—66 persons—he took to the site chosen for the *pueblo* San Jose de Guadalupe—about a mile and a quarter north of the present center of San Jose. To each man were given a homesite and a small piece of ground to till. Although the soil was excellent, it was flooded each winter by the Guadalupe River. In 1797 the *pobladores* moved to a new location centering at the corner of what is now South Market and West San Fernando Streets. There is little recorded of the happenings in the *pueblo* during the occupancy of its original site, although in 1784 "some of the settlers were imprisoned and put in irons for refusing to work on a house for the town council," and "two boys drowned an Indian to amuse themselves, but in consideration of their tender years were dismissed with twenty-five lashes administered in the presence of the natives."

In the 1820's the *pobladores* received their first English-speaking settler, Robert Livermore, who moved north after a few years into the valley which now bears his name. Other Englishmen and Americans had arrived before 1835, but by marrying into the Higuera, Galindo, Saiz, and other influential families they became identified with the native Californians. Within another ten years, however, the Americans had so increased that with the reorganization of the *pueblo* after the American occupation of California in 1846, six out of twelve committee men were Americans, as was the new *alcalde*.

With an eye to the *pueblo's* future, the citizens met in September, 1849 and offered to the Constitutional Convention assembled in Monterey some 21 acres "for the sole purpose of erecting State buildings thereon." The offer was accepted. In December of that year the Legislature met in an adobe building at San Antonio and Market Streets. Among the official acts at that first session was the incorporation, March 27, 1850, of the capital city, which thus became the first incorporated community in California (San Francisco's charter was granted three weeks later).

The capital was moved to Vallejo in 1852, thence to Benicia, and finally to Sacramento. The citizens of San Jose strove earnestly but unsuccessfully for its repossession. Victory hove in sight when the Supreme Court decided on an appeal in 1854 that San Jose was the legal capital, but soon afterward it reversed its decision.

As early as 1851 there had been talk of a railroad to San Francisco, for the fare by stage was $16 and the cost of shipping lumber from Alviso, $15 per thousand. The railroad finally came in 1864—"a proof," in the opinion of the San Jose *Mercury,* "of American enterprise, foresight and determination." Cattle and grain were still the chief products, the country south of Gilroy being an almost unbroken wheat field, but the number of orchards was increasing, and some vineyards were already known, particularly that of Colonel Naglee, who had set out (in what is now the northwestern part of town) more than 100 varieties of grapes. Within the city, which by 1870 had a population of about 13,000, were carriage and wagon shops, foundries, breweries, tanneries, and woolen and flour mills run by water from the abundant artesian wells. In this same year the State Normal School was established. With the building of many new homes, San Jose began to call itself the "Garden City."

The subdivision of the great wheat ranches and the planting of orchards continued. San Jose was shipping more and more dried prunes to the Eastern markets. The nascent art of advertising was being used to attract people with money to Santa Clara County. In a ten-acre park the big wooden Hotel Vendome with its fat bay windows was ready in 1889, "with electric lights and hot water."

In 1894 San Jose's Dr. Charles D. Herrold transmitted a distance of 60 feet California's first wireless message. By 1909 he had perfected the first successful "radio telephone station" in America, and by 1913 he was communicating with the Fairmont Hotel in San Francisco. (Except during the World War this station, now KQW, has broadcast without interruption.) Continuing San Jose's reputation for "firsts," Dr. August Greth in 1903 built America's first dirigible, the 85-foot *Spirit of California,* which Captain Thomas S. Baldwin flew over San Francisco. In the same year an ambitious young producer named Sid Grauman (who was later to build Hollywood's Egyptian and Chinese Theaters) opened on Santa Clara Street a vaudeville house which, in deference to the gentility of San Jose, displayed the sign, "No liquor or cigars will be allowed, and no tickets sold to persons not fit to be with women and children." Here Al Jolson made his debut and Roscoe "Fatty" Arbuckle was chore boy and ticket seller.

San Jose's foremost industry, the shipping of fresh, dried, and canned fruit, meanwhile was growing enormously. A little woodshed in 1871 housed Santa Clara County's first commercial cannery when J. M. Dawson and his wife packed 300 cases of peaches, pears, cherries, and apricots. To protect a shipment of fresh fruit sent to Chicago in 1876, John Z. Anderson, former operator of a line of freight teams between California and Nevada, converted a railroad freight car into the industry's first "reefer," or refrigerator car, by packing ice around boxes of cherries. Now green-fruit-packing houses make annually large shipments of such highly perishable fruits as pears, cherries, grapes, apricots, and prunes. Of the County's 43 canneries—the 1939 output of which was 72,000,000 cans, or 4,000 carloads—23 are in San Jose; of its 30 dried-fruit-packing plants, half are in the city. At the season's peak between 15,000 and 20,000 persons are at work in the orchards, canneries, packing houses, and drying yards.

POINTS OF INTEREST

ST. JOSEPH'S CHURCH, 90 S. Market St., occupies the site of the original adobe church built in 1803 and dedicated to San Jose de Guadalupe. The larger adobe which replaced this in 1835 was so badly damaged in 1868 that it was torn down and the present church—an attempt at the neoclassic in wood, brick, and plaster—erected in its place.

On the site around which grew the original *pueblo* is CITY HALL PARK, an oval plaza dividing S. Market St. between W. San Fernando and W. San Carlos Sts. into two wide parkways. It contains the CITY HALL, built in 1889, a three-story building of red brick and cast iron with an ornate cornice and a wooden tower over the central doorway. In the park a plaque marks the SITE OF THE FIRST STATE CAPITOL, NE. cor. W. San Antonio and S. Market Sts. The adobe capitol building was 60 feet long and 40 feet wide, "protected by a veranda all round."

A well-preserved relic of Spanish days, though much out of plumb, the FILIPELLI ADOBE, 243 S. Market St., built about 1840, stands in the rear of a large old-fashioned frame house and has been incorporated with an old one-story clapboard house.

SAN JOSE STATE COLLEGE, occupying the 26 acres of WASHINGTON PARK, S. Fourth, S. Seventh, E. San Fernando, and E. San Carlos Sts., is the successor to the State Normal School established in San Francisco in 1862, first in California. Moved to the present site in 1870, it was burned in 1880, rebuilt and again demolished, this time by the earthquake of 1906. The present group of buildings is built about a courtyard surrounded by elms, pepper trees, and palms. The college since 1921 has offered a four-year course with degrees of A.B. or B.Ed. In 1940, 3,800 students enrolled.

Now used as the infirmary of the San Jose State College, the EDWIN MARKHAM HOUSE, 430 S. Eighth St., is an old-fashioned residence faced with clapboard. Here the poet lived in the early 1870's when a student at the normal school, and here his mother continued to live in later years.

The distinguishing feature of ST. JAMES PARK, N. First, N. Third, St. John, and E. St. James Sts., is a bronze MONUMENT OF WILLIAM McKINLEY erected in 1902. In this park in 1933 occurred the lynching of two men accused of the kidnaping and murder of a wealthy merchant's son. An infuriated mob broke into the jail across the street and brought their victims to the park. The Nation rang with reverberations over the incident, heightened when Governor James Rolph, Jr., announced his approval of the mob's action.

The FOOD MACHINERY CORPORATION, 331 W. Julian St., occupies a long, russet-colored, stuccoed building. The corporation had a modest beginning in Los Gatos in 1883 when a retired inventor, John Bean, perfected a spraying pump, which he began manufacturing there and later in San Jose. Allied manufacturers amalgamated with Bean's Company until by 1940 it had become a $12,000,000 corporation, the largest manufacturer of equipment for canneries and orchards. Nailing machines, turbine pumps, milk-evaporating equipment, and maraschino-pitting machinery are among its many important developments. More than 1,600 persons are employed.

The GARCIA ADOBE, in the rear of 184 San Augustin St., was built about 1840. Formerly a residence, later a barn and hay loft, it is now filled with rubbish. The adobe walls are partly faced with boards.

ROSICRUCIAN HEADQUARTERS, Naglee Ave. from Chapman St. to Park Ave., is the center for North and South America of the "Ancient and Mystical Order of the Rosy Cross" (AMORC). Claiming great antiquity, the order gives the names of Pythagoras, St. Francis, Dante, and Professor Albert Einstein as members. The buildings, which include an auditorium, a lecture hall and laboratories, and an oriental museum, are of concrete in a bewildering variety of oriental styles.

The Moorish arches and buff-colored concrete walls of the EGYP-TIAN TEMPLE AND ORIENTAL MUSEUM (*open Mon.-Fri. 9-5; Sat. 9-1; Sun. 12-5; Mon. eve. 7-9*) are finished to simulate stuccoed walls in the process of peeling. Here the Rosicrucian order has a miscellaneous collection of old books and tapestries; Egyptian pottery, tomb images, and scarabs; and reproductions of an Assyrian gateway and an Egyptian temple. Visitors are given free pamphlets soliciting membership, one of which has an introduction signed, "Profundis XIII."

The PLANETARIUM BUILDING (*open Sun. 2-5, 7:30-9; demonstrations 3:30 and 6; adm. 25¢, children 15¢*), called "The Theater of the Skies," is devoted to the Rosicrucian explanation of the roles of the planets and stars. The planetarium is one of five in the United States.

In the MUNICIPAL ROSE GARDEN, Naglee and Dana Aves., whose five and one-half acres of formal planting are intersected by long aisles of grass, flourish many varieties once popular but now seldom grown. The garden is pervaded by the old-time perfume of the Centifolia, the dusky sweetness of the Damask (Rose of Lancaster), the acid freshness of China roses, the pungency of the moss rose, the scent of winter apples in the foliage of the sweet briar. Standard and hybrid teas much grown 50 years ago, Safrano, Duchess de Brabant, La France, and Captain Christy, are well represented, as are the many newer and more striking hybrids. Against the brick walls grow many varieties of climbing roses.

The well-preserved, grayish-white, two-story SPIVALO ADOBE (*private*), 770 Lincoln Ave., has walls two feet thick. From a crumbling veranda a double door between two seven-foot shuttered windows leads inside, where a polished mahogany stairway climbs to the second floor. The marble fireplace and the lumber used in the structure were brought around the Horn. A fig tree, 8 feet in circumference and 80 feet tall, planted when the adobe was new, stands at the southeast corner.

The CALIFORNIA CANNING AND PACKING COMPANY, W. end of W. San Carlos St., is the largest canning-packing plant in San Jose. The huge canning and packing units each occupy a modern red-brick building roofed with dark tin. Salad fruits and vegetables are canned the year round; asparagus from April to June; string beans, from June to November; spinach from January to April. The peak season for apricots, peaches, plums, pears, and tomatoes comes in July, August, and September.

The two-story STOCKTON HOUSE, Spring and Newhall Sts., built in 1850, is one of a number of houses cut to size and brought around the Horn by Commodore Robert F. Stockton. It has a wide veranda and, rising from the central gable, a square balustraded turret.

PART V
Appendices

A Chronology of the San Francisco Bay Region

1542   Nov. 16 (O. S.)   Portuguese explorer Juan Rodrigues Cabrillo enters gulf outside Golden Gate and discovers Farallon Islands.

1579   June 17. (Julian Calendar). English navigator Francis Drake lands in present Marin County (Drake's Bay), and claims land as New Albion for Queen Elizabeth.

1595   Nov. 6. Sebastian Rodrigues Cermeno enters Drake's Bay and names it La Bahia de San Francisco for Saint Francis of Assisi.

1603   Jan. 5. Sebastian Vizcaino sights extreme southwest point of present San Mateo County and names it Punta del Año Nuevo (New Year's Point).

1769   Oct. 18. Gaspar de Portola expedition arrives in sight of Santa Cruz.

Nov. 1-3. Portola's chief scout, Sergt. Jose Ortega, discovers present San Francisco Bay.

Nov. 7-10. Exploring party sent out by Portola expedition traverses country east of Bay, probably through Moraga Valley as far as San Pablo Bay.

1772   Mar. 27-28. Golden Gate first sighted from present sites of Oakland and Berkeley by Capt. Pedro Fages expedition on way north from Mission San Carlos Borromeo by way of Santa Clara Valley.

1775   Aug. 5. The *San Carlos,* first ship to enter Bay, is piloted through Golden Gate under command of Lt. Juan Manuel de Ayala.

1776   Mar. 28. Juan Bautista de Anza, arriving at site of San Francisco with colonists from Mexico, selects site for presidio.

Mar. 29. Anza selects site for Mission San Francisco de Asis (Mission Dolores).

Sept. 17. Presidio founded by Lt. Jose Joaquin Moraga.

Oct. 8. Padre Francisco Palou dedicates Mission San Francisco de Asis.

1777   Jan. 12. Mission Santa Clara founded.

Nov. 29. *Pueblo* of San Jose de Guadalupe (San Jose), first in California, is founded.

1791   Aug. 28. Mission Santa Cruz founded.

1792   Nov. 14. Capt. George Vancouver arrives in *H.M.S. Discovery,* first foreign vessel to enter Bay.

1797   June 11. Mission San Jose de Guadalupe is dedicated.

1803   Aug. 12. First American vessel, *Eliza,* Capt. James Rowan, enters harbor.

1806   Apr. 8. Count Nikolai Rezanov arrives to buy supplies for starving Russian colony at Sitka.

1812   Sept. 10. Fort Ross, Russian trading post, is dedicated.

1816   Oct. 2.   Russian commander Otto Von Kotzebue and crew arrive in *Rurik* to gather information on Spanish settlements.

1817   Dec. 14.   Mission San Rafael Arcangel, "hospital mission" for sick converts of Mission San Francisco de Asis, is founded.

1820   June 20.   Luis Maria Peralta receives grant (Rancho San Antonio) to vast East Bay area.

1821   Feb. 21.   Spanish rule overthrown in Mexico City by Agustin Iturbide.

1823   July 4.   Mission San Francisco Solano (Sonoma) dedicated.

1825   Mar. 26.   California formally declared province of Republic of Mexico.
Apr. 24.   Oath of allegiance to Republic of Mexico administered at San Francisco presidio.

1826   Nov. 6.   Capt. Frederick William Beechey, of *H.M.S. Blossom,* arrives to make survey of Bay.

1827   Jan. 27.   French trading ship *Le Heros,* Capt. Auguste Duhaut-Cilly, arrives in Bay.

1829   May 5.   Spaniards subdue rebellious Cosumnes Indians in battle near San Jose.

1833   Aug. 17.   Mexican Congress decrees secularization of California missions.

1834   Aug. 24.   Mission Santa Cruz secularized.
Sept.   Missions San Francisco de Asis and San Rafael secularized.
Dec. 7.   First *ayuntamiento* (council) organized in San Francisco district and Francisco de Haro chosen first *alcalde* (mayor) of *pueblo* Yerba Buena.

1835   June 24.   *Pueblo* of Sonoma founded.
June 25.   William A. Richardson, first harbormaster, erects first dwelling in Yerba Buena.

1836   July 1.   Jacob Primer Leese arrives at Yerba Buena and establishes first retail firm.

1837   Dec.   Los Meganos Rancho near Mount Diablo granted to Dr. John Marsh.
Mission San Jose secularized.

1838   Feb. 11.   Rancho Saucelito (Marin County) granted to William A. Richardson.

1839   Apr. 15.   Russian government orders Fort Ross abandoned.

1841   Dec. 30.   Hudson's Bay Company establishes agency at Yerba Buena.
Oct. 19.   Lt. Charles Wilkes, U. S. N., visits Bay on hydrographic survey of Pacific Coast.
Nov. 4.   First overland immigrant party reaches ranch of Dr. John Marsh.

1844   Mar. 8.   Capt. John Charles Frémont and survey party arrive from overland journey at Sutter's Fort.

1845   July 10.   Mexican decree forbids further American immigration.

1846   June 14.   American settlers seize Sonoma and raise Bear Flag of California Republic.

June 24. First battle of Bear Flag Revolt fought near Petaluma.
July 7. Commodore John D. Sloat raises American flag at Monterey and proclaims California annexed to United States.
July 9. American flag hoisted at Yerba Buena and Sonoma.

1847 Jan. 2. Battle of Santa Clara concludes Yankee conquest of northern California.
Jan. 9. First issue of San Francisco's first (and California's second) newspaper, *The California Star,* appears.
Jan. 30. Yerba Buena renamed "San Francisco."

1848 Jan. 24. Gold discovered by James Marshall at John A. Sutter's sawmill on American River.
Feb. 2. Treaty of Guadalupe Hidalgo ends war with Mexico and cedes California to United States.
Apr. 3. First American public school opened in San Francisco.

1849 Jan. 9. First commercial bank established in San Francisco.
Feb. 28. *California,* first Gold Rush steamer, arrives.
Apr. 1. Steamship *Oregon* inaugurates regular mail service to East.
Apr. 30. U. S. Army post established at Benicia.
June 22. Stephen Massett gives first public entertainment in San Francisco.
Oct. 25. Democratic Party of California organized.
Nov. Moses Chase, Oakland's first settler, arrives in East Bay.
Nov. 13. San Jose becomes capital of California.
Dec. 15. First American territorial legislature convenes at San Jose.
Dec. 24. First of six great fires causes $1,250,000 loss in San Francisco.

1850 Population: San Francisco, 34,776.
Jan. 16. First dramatic performance, *The Wife,* is held in San Francisco.
Feb. 18. Legislature creates Bay region counties: San Francisco, Contra Costa, Marin, Santa Clara, Sonoma, Solano, and Napa.
Mar. 27. City of San Jose incorporated.
Apr. 1. San Francisco County government established.
Apr. 15. City of San Francisco incorporated.
June 24. San Francisco Typographical Society, city's first trade union, is organized.
Sept. 9. California admitted to Union.
Kangaroo ferry inaugurates San Francisco-East Bay service.

1851 Mar. 19. Santa Clara College established (chartered 1855).
May 3. San Francisco's fifth and most disastrous fire destroys twenty-two blocks, causing $12,000,000 loss.
June 9. First Committee of Vigilance organized.
Aug. 31. Clipper ship *Flying Cloud* slashes time from New York from 159 days to 89 days, 21½ hours.

1852 Jan. 5. State Legislature opens its third session in Vallejo.
May 4. City of Oakland incorporated.

1853   Mar. 25.   County of Alameda created.
1854   Feb. 25.   State capital established permanently at Sacramento.
       Sept. 16.   Admiral David Farragut establishes Mare Island Navy Yard.
1855   College of California (University of California) incorporated.
       Feb. 23.   "Black Friday," financial disaster, initiates California's first panic.
       Apr. 19.   San Mateo County created.
1856   May 15.   Second Vigilance Committee organized.
1857   Sept. 7.   First Mechanics Fair is held by Mechanics Institute, in San Francisco.
1859   Apr. 30.   College of St. Ignatius (University of San Francisco) incorporated.
       Sept. 13.   Broderick-Terry duel helps crystallize anti-slavery sentiment in San Francisco.
1860   Population: San Francisco, 56,802; San Jose, 4,579; Oakland, 1,543; Alameda, 460.
       Apr. 14.   First Pony Express rider arrives from St. Joseph, Missouri, in San Francisco.
       Oct. 8.   Telegraph line opened between San Francisco and Los Angeles.
1861   Feb. 15.   Fort Point, San Francisco Presidio, occupied by U. S. troops.
       June 28.   Central Pacific Railway Company incorporated.
       Oct. 24.   Overland Telegraph Company establishes communication between San Francisco and New York.
1863   Mar. 15.   Schooner *J. M. Chapman,* Confederate privateer, is seized in Bay.
1864   Jan. 16.   San Francisco-San Jose Railroad completed.
       July 5.   William C. Ralston and associates found Bank of California.
1868   Mar. 23.   Legislature charters University of California.
1869   May 10.   Tracks of Central Pacific and Union Pacific joined.
       Sept. 6.   First transcontinental train arrives in Alameda.
1870   Population: San Francisco, 149,473; Oakland, 10,500; San Jose, 9,089; Alameda, 1,557.
       Mar. 11.   San Jose Teachers' College, California's first normal school, permanently established at San Jose.
       Mar. 18.   Golden Gate Park established.
1871   Mills Seminary (now Mills College) established in Oakland.
1872   Mar. 7.   City of Alameda incorporated.
1873   June 2.   Ground is broken for world's first cable street railway in San Francisco.
1875   Aug. 26.   Bank of California failure causes local panic, followed next day by drowning in Bay of president W. C. Ralston.
1876   July 4.   San Francisco's first public exhibition of electric light.
       Sept. 5.   Rail connection with Los Angeles established.

1877 July 23. Anti-Chinese sentiment results in first of San Francisco's "Sand-lot riots," prompting organization of Committee of Safety under William T. Coleman.

Oct. 5. Workingmen's Party of California organized.

1878 Apr. 1. City of Berkeley incorporated.

1880 Population: San Francisco 233,959; Oakland, 34,555; San Jose, 12,567; Alameda, 5,708.

July 23. Construction of Lick Observatory begins.

1882 May 6. President Chester Arthur signs Chinese Exclusion Act.

1883 Oct. 29. Merchants' and Manufacturers' Association, pioneer employers' council in San Francisco, established.

1885 Dec. 5. Luther Burbank founds experimental farm near Sebastopol.

1890 Population: San Francisco, 298,997; Oakland, 48,682; San Jose, 18,060; Alameda, 11,165; Berkeley, 5,101.

1891 Oct. 1. Stanford University opens to students.

1892 Mar. 19. First "Big Game" between University of California and Stanford.

Jan. 1. California Midwinter International Exposition opens.

1894 Dec. 25. First "East-West" football game (Stanford vs. University of Chicago) is played in San Francisco.

1898 May 26. San Francisco electorate accepts new city charter, authorizing municipal acquisition and ownership of public utilities (put into effect Jan. 1, 1900).

1900 Population: San Francisco, 342,782; Oakland, 66,960; San Jose, 21,500; Alameda, 16,464; Berkeley, 13,214.

1901 Jan. 7-9. Initial step taken to organize State Federation of Labor.

July 30. Teamsters' Union strike starts widespread sympathy walkout.

Dec. 16. State Building Trades Council formed.

1902 Dec. 14. S.S. Silvertown begins laying cable to Honolulu.

1904 Oct. 17. Bank of Italy (Bank of America) established by A. P. Giannini with capital of $150,000.

1906 Apr. 18. Earthquake starts great fire destroying most of San Francisco with loss of $300,000,000.

1907 July 8. Mayor Eugene Schmitz sentenced to five years in San Quentin Prison for corruption in office.

1908 Dec. 7. Abe Ruef, political boss, sentenced to fourteen years in San Quentin.

July 9. Muir Woods, Marin County, becomes Muir Woods National Monument.

1909 Oct. 18. Portola Festival celebrates San Francisco's recovery from earthquake and fire.

1910 Population: San Francisco, 416,912; Oakland, 150,174; Berkeley, 40,434; San Jose, 28,946; Alameda, 23,383.

1913 Dec. 19. Ratification of Raker Act permits development of Hetch-Hetchy power system by San Francisco.

1914 Feb. 16. Silas Christofferson makes first airplane flight from San Francisco to San Diego.

1915   Feb. 20.   Panama-Pacific International Exposition opens.

1916   July 22.   Preparedness Day bomb explosion occurs in San Francisco, resulting in life prison terms for Thomas Mooney and Warren K. Billings (Mooney pardoned Jan. 7, 1939; Billing's sentence commuted to time served Oct. 16, 1939).

1917   July 14.   Twin Peaks Tunnel dedicated in San Francisco.

1919   Nov. 3.   Crissey Field, San Francisco airport, dedicated.

1920   Population: San Francisco, 506,676; Oakland, 216,261; Berkeley, 56,036; San Jose, 39,642; Alameda, 28,806.

1920   July 29.   First transcontinental airmail flight from New York completed at San Francisco.

Sept. 8.   Regular airmail service established between Mineola, N. Y., and San Francisco.

1922   Oct. 1.   Philo T. Farnsworth establishes laboratory in San Francisco where principles of television were first perfected in 1927.

1927   Jan. 17.   Dumbarton Bridge is completed.

May 7.   San Francisco Municipal Airport (Mills Field) dedicated.

May 21.   Carquinez Bridge opens.

1928   Oct. 27.   Posey Tube, under Estuary, connects Alameda and Oakland.

1929   Mar. 3.   San Mateo Bay Bridge opens.

1930   Population: San Francisco, 634,394; Oakland, 284,063; Berkeley, 82,109; San Jose; 57,651; Alameda, 35,033.

1931   Apr. 3.   Mount Diablo is made part of State park system.

June 9.   Construction of U. S. Naval Air Station at Moffett Field (Sunnyvale) begins (transferred to Army Air Corps, 1935).

1932   Jan. 8.   San Francisco's present charter is ratified.

1933   Oct. 12.   U. S. Department of Justice takes over Alcatraz Island as Federal penitentiary.

1934   May 9.   Walkout of maritime workers leads to general strike, first in Bay region's history.

1935   Jan. 12.   Amelia Earhart Putnam lands at Oakland Airport on first solo flight from Hawaii.

Nov. 22.   *China Clipper* leaves Alameda on first airmail flight to Manila.

1936   Nov. 12.   San Francisco-Oakland Bay Bridge opens (work begun July 9, 1933).

1937   May 27.   Golden Gate Bridge opened (work begun Jan. 5, 1933).

Dec. 5.   Broadway Low Level Tunnel in Alameda County opens.

1939   Jan. 14.   Commuters to East Bay say goodbye to the ferry boats; Bay Bridge train service opens following day.

Feb. 18.   Golden Gate International Exposition opens on Treasure Island.

1940   Apr. 21.   Funston Avenue approach to Golden Gate Bridge opens.

May 25.   Golden Gate International Exposition re-opens.

June 14.   Holly Courts, San Francisco's first low-cost housing project, opens.

A Selected Reading List

Aitken, Frank W. *A History of the Earthquake and Fire in San Francisco.* San Francisco, 1906.
Alley, Bowen and Co. *History of Marin County.* San Francisco, 1880.
Armsby, Leonora Wood. *Musicians Talk.* New York, 1933.
Asbury, Herbert. *The Barbary Coast.* New York, 1933.
Atherton, Gertrude. *Adventures of a Novelist.* New York, 1932.
———— *California, an Intimate History.* New York, 1914 (rev. ed. 1927).
Baker, Joseph Eugene. *Past and Present of Alameda County.* 2 vols. Chicago, 1914.
Bancroft, Hubert Howe. *History of California.* 7 vols. San Francisco, 1884–90.
———— *Popular Tribunals.* San Francisco, 1890.
Barry, T. A., and B. A. Patten. *Men and Memories of San Francisco.* San Francisco, 1873.
Beckman, R. G. *The Romance of Oakland.* Oakland, 1932.
Bolton, Herbert Eugene. *Anza's California Expeditions.* 5 vols. Berkeley, 1930.
———— *Fray Juan Crespi, Missionary Explorer of the Pacific Coast.* Berkeley, 1927.
———— *Outpost of Empire.* New York, 1931.
Brown, John Henry. *Reminiscences and Incidents of Early Days of San Francisco (1845-50).* San Francisco, 1886 (later ed. 1933).
Burbank, Luther, with Wilbur Hall. *The Harvest of the Years.* Boston, 1927.
California Historical Society. *Drake's Plate of Brass, Evidence of His Visit to California in 1579.* San Francisco, 1937.
Chapman, Charles E. *A History of California: The Spanish Period.* New York, 1921 (rev. ed. 1928).
Chevigny, Hector. *Lost Empire: the Life and Adventures of Nikolai Petrovich Rezanov.* New York, 1937.
Cleland, Robert Glass. *A History of California; the American Period.* New York, 1922.
Cleland, Robert Glass, and Osgood Hardy. *The March of Industry.* Los Angeles, 1929.
Coblentz, Stanton A. *Villains and Vigilantes.* New York, 1936.
Cowan, Robert E. *Forgotten Characters of Old San Francisco.* Los Angeles, 1938.
Cowan, Robert E., and Robert G. Cowan. *A Bibliography of the History of California.* 3 vols. San Francisco, 1933.
Crocker, Florence B. *Who Made Oakland?* Oakland, 1925.
Cross, Ira B. *Financing an Empire.* 5 vols. Chicago, 1927.
———— *History of the Labor Movement in California.* Berkeley, 1935.

Cummins, Ella Sterling. *The Story of the Files.* San Francisco, 1893.

Dana, Julian. *The Man Who Built San Francisco.* New York, 1936.

Dana, Richard Henry. *Two Years Before the Mast.* Boston, 1840 (later ed. 1936).

Davis, William Heath. *Seventy-five Years in California.* San Francisco, 1929.

Dawson, William Leon. *The Birds of California.* Los Angeles, 1921 (later ed. in 4 vols. 1923).

De Veer, Daisy Williamson. *The Story of Rancho San Antonio.* Oakland, 1924.

Dobie, Charles Caldwell. *San Francisco, a Pageant.* New York, 1933.

——— *San Francisco's Chinatown.* New York, 1936.

Eaves, Lucilla M. *History of California Labor Legislation.* Berkeley, 1910.

Eldredge, Zoeth Skinner. *History of California.* 5 vols. New York, 1915.

——— *The Beginnings of San Francisco.* 2 vols. New York, 1912.

Englehardt, Fr. Zephyrin. *The Missions and Missionaries of California.* 4 vols. and index. San Francisco, 1908–16 (2d ed. in 2 vols. 1929–30).

——— *Mission Dolores.* Chicago, 1924.

Fages, Pedro. *Expedition to San Francisco Bay in 1770.* Berkeley, 1911.

Federal Writers' Project. *California: a Guide to the Golden State.* New York, 1939.

Ferrier, William Warren. *Ninety Years of Education in California. 1846-1936.* Berkeley, 1937.

——— *Berkeley, California.* Berkeley, 1933.

Font, Fr. Pedro. *Font's Complete Diary.* A chronicle of the foundation of San Francisco. Translated and edited by Herbert Eugene Bolton. Berkeley, 1933.

Frémont, John Charles. *Memoirs of My Life.* Chicago, 1887.

Genthe, Arnold. *As I Remember.* New York, 1936.

Glasscock, C. B. *Lucky Baldwin.* Indianapolis, 1933.

Halley, William. *The Centennial Year Book of Alameda County, California.* Oakland, 1876.

Harrison, Edward Sanford. *History of Santa Cruz County.* San Francisco, 1892.

Hart, Jerome. *In Our Second Century.* San Francisco, 1931.

Hittell, John S. *A History of the City of San Francisco.* San Francisco, 1878.

Hittell, Theodore H. *History of California.* 4 vols. San Francisco, 1885–97.

Hoover, Mildred Brooke. Historic Spots in California. Vol. III: *Counties of the Coast Range.* Stanford University, 1937.

Hulaniski, Frederick. *History of Contra Costa County.* Berkeley, 1917.

Hunt, Margaret, and others. *History of Solano and Napa Counties.* Chicago, 1926.

Hunt, Rockwell, and W. S. Ament. *Oxcart to Airplane.* Chicago, 1929.

Hunt, Rockwell, and Nellie Van de Grift Sanchez. *A Short History of California.* New York, 1929.
Irwin, William Henry. *Pictures of Old Chinatown.* New York, 1908.
—— *The City That Was.* New York, 1906.
Issler, Anna Roller. *Stevenson at Silverado.* Caldwell, Idaho, 1939.
James, George Wharton. *In and Out of the Old Missions of California.* Boston, 1905 (rev. ed. 1927).
James, William F. *History of San Jose.* San Jose, 1933.
Jepson, Willis Linn. *A Manual of the Flowering Plants of California.* Berkeley, 1925.
—— *The Trees of California.* San Francisco, 1909 (2d ed. 1923).
Jordan, David Starr, ed. *The California Earthquake of 1906.* San Francisco, 1907.
Kroeber, Alfred L. *Handbook of the Indians of California.* Bureau of American Ethnology, Bulletin No. 78, Washington, D. C., 1925.
Lewis, Oscar. *The Big Four.* New York, 1938.
Lewis, Oscar, and Carroll D. Hall. *Bonanza Inn.* New York, 1939.
Lloyd, Benjamin E. *Lights and Shades in San Francisco.* San Francisco, 1876.
London, Joan. *Jack London and His Times.* New York, 1939.
Lyman, George D. *John Marsh, Pioneer.* New York, 1934.
—— *Ralston's Ring.* New York, 1937.
Merrit, Frank Clinton. *History of Alameda, California.* Chicago, 1928.
Morphy, Edward. *The Port of San Francisco.* Sacramento, 1923.
Murphy, Celeste C. *The People of the Pueblo, or, the Story of Sonoma.* Sonoma, Calif., 1935.
Nelson, Nels Christian. *Shellmounds of the San Francisco Bay Region.* Berkeley, 1909.
Neuhaus, Eugen. *The Art of Treasure Island.* Berkeley, 1939.
Neville, Amelia Ransome. *The Fantastic City.* Boston, 1932.
Nevins, Allan. *Frémont, Pathmaker of the West.* New York, 1939.
Northern California Writers' Project. *Festivals in San Francisco.* San Francisco, 1939.
Older, Fremont. *My Own Story.* San Francisco, 1919 (later ed. New York, 1926).
Palou, Fr. Francisco. *Historical Memoirs of New California.* 4 vols. Translated and edited by Herbert Eugene Bolton. Berkeley, 1926.
Parsons, Mary Elizabeth. *The Wild Flowers of California.* San Francisco, 1902 (later ed. 1914).
Pennell, Joseph. *San Francisco, the City of the Golden Gate.* Boston, 1913.
Phillips, Catherine C. *Portsmouth Plaza.* San Francisco, 1932.
Potter, Elizabeth Gray. *The San Francisco Skyline.* New York, 1939.
Prieto, Guillermo. *San Francisco in the Seventies.* San Francisco, 1938.
Richman, Irving B. *California under Spain and Mexico, 1535-1847.* Boston, 1911.
Rider, Fremont, ed. *Rider's California: a Guidebook for Travelers.* New York, 1925.

Rosskam, Edwin. *San Francisco, West Coast Metropolis.* New York, 1939.

Rourke, Constance M. *Troopers of the Gold Coast.* New York, 1928.

Royce, Josiah. *California from the Conquest in 1846 to the Second Vigilance Committee in San Francisco (1856).* Boston, 1886 (later ed. 1892).

Sawyer, Eugene Taylor. *History of Santa Clara County.* Los Angeles, 1929.

Scherer, James A. B. *The Lion of the Vigilantes.* Indianapolis, 1939.

Shuck, Oscar Tully. *Bench and Bar in California.* San Francisco, 1889.

Soulé, Frank, John H. Gihon, and James Nisbet. *The Annals of San Francisco.* New York, 1855.

Stanger, Frank M. *History of San Mateo County.* San Mateo, 1938.

Stevenson, Robert Louis. *The Silverado Squatters.* London, 1883.

Stewart, George Rippey. *Bret Harte, Argonaut and Exile.* Boston, 1931.

Stoddard, Charles Warren. *In the Footprints of the Padres.* San Francisco, 1902 (rev. ed. 1912).

Taylor, Bayard. *Eldorado: or Adventures in the Path of Empire.* New York, 1850 (rev. ed. 1882).

Thompson, Ruth, and Chef Louis Hanges. *Eating Around San Francisco.* San Francisco, 1937.

Todd, Frank Morton. *The Story of the Exposition* (Panama-Pacific International). 5 vols. New York, 1921.

Tuomey, Honoria. *History of Sonoma County.* Chicago, 1926.

Walker, Franklin. *San Francisco's Literary Frontier.* New York, 1939.

Wallace, W. *History of Napa County.* Oakland, 1901.

Wells, Evelyn. *Champagne Days in San Francisco.* New York, 1939.

White, Stewart Edward. *Old California.* New York, 1937.

Williams, Mary Floyd. *History of the San Francisco Committee of Vigilance of 1851.* Berkeley, 1921.

Woon, Basil. *San Francisco and the Golden Empire.* New York, 1935.

Wright, Benjamin C. *Banking in California 1849-1910.* San Francisco, 1910.

———— *San Francisco's Ocean Trade, Past and Future.* San Francisco, 1911.

Young, John P. *San Francisco: A History of the Pacific Coast Metropolis.* 2 vols. Chicago, 1912.

———— *History of Journalism in California.* San Francisco, 1915.

Index

505

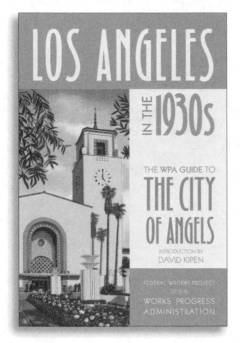

THE FEDERAL WRITERS PROJECT (FWP) of the Works Progress Administration (WPA) not only provided jobs and income to writers during the Depression, it created for America an astounding series of detailed and richly evocative guides, recounting the stories and histories of the 48 states (plus Alaska Territory and Puerto Rico) and many of the country's major cities.

LOS ANGELES IN THE 1930S

The WPA Guide to the City of Angels

Introduction by David Kipen

Los Angeles in the 1930s returns to print an invaluable document of Depression-era Los Angeles, illuminating a pivotal moment in L.A.'s history, when writers like Raymond Chandler, Nathanael West, and F. Scott Fitzgerald were creating the images and associations—and the mystique—for which the City of Angels is still known. Many books in one, *Los Angeles in the 1930s* is both a genial guide and an addictively readable history, revisiting the Spanish colonial period, the Mexican period, the brief California Republic, and finally American sovereignty. It is also a compact coffee table book of dazzling monochrome photography, whose haunting visions suggest the city we know today and illuminate the booms and busts that marked L.A.'s past and continue to shape its future.

DAVID KIPEN, former *San Francisco Chronicle* book editor, was for five years Director of Literature at the National Endowment for the Arts.

$24.95 paper   978-0-520-26883-8 (W)

www.ucpress.edu